UNEASY PARTNERSHIP

UNEASY PARTNERSHIP

The Politics of Business and Government in Canada

Geoffrey Hale

We welcome comments and suggestions regarding any aspect of our publications – please feel free to contact us at news@utphighereducation.com or visit our Internet site at www.utphighereducation.com.

Library and Archives Canada Cataloguing in Publication

Hale, Geoffrey, 1955–
Uneasy partnership: the politics of business and government in Canada / Geoffrey E. Hale.
Includes bibliographical references and index.

ISBN-13: 978-1-55111-504-7
ISBN-10: 1-55111-504-2

1. Industrial policy—Canada—Textbooks. 2. Canada—Economic policy—Textbooks.
3. Business and politics—Canada—Textbooks.
I. Title.

HD3616.C33H34 2006   338.971   C2006-904322-1

North America
5201 Dufferin Street
North York, Ontario, Canada, M3H 5T8

2250 Military Road
Tonawanda, New York, USA, 14150

ORDERS PHONE: 1-800-565-9523
ORDERS FAX: 1-800-221-9985
ORDERS E-MAIL: utpbooks@utpress.utoronto.ca

UK, Ireland, and continental Europe
NBN International
Estover Road, Plymouth, PL6 7PY, UK
TEL: 44 (0) 1752 202301
FAX ORDER LINE: 44 (0) 1752 202333
enquiries@nbninternational.com

The University of Toronto Press acknowledges the financial support for its publishing activities of the Government of Canada through the Book Publishing Industry Development Program (BPIDP).

Printed in Canada

RECYCLED
Paper made from
recycled material
FSC® C021757

This book is the product of more than a decade of teaching and research on the politics of business and government as well as their interaction with the policy processes of both federal and provincial governments in a variety of policy fields. Many people in government, industry associations, and different businesses have been generous with their time and useful insights that have contributed to the author's ongoing research.

The author is greatly indebted to students and colleagues at the University of Lethbridge, as well as anonymous reviewers for Broadview Press, for their feedback on earlier drafts of this book. I would particularly like to thank Alan Siaroff, Richard Mueller, Harold Jansen, and Chris Kukucha for their insightful comments and suggestions. Brad McKenzie and Julia Mitton provided timely and effective research support. The university administration provided much welcome course relief on two occasions to facilitate the book's writing and completion.

Michael Harrison, Greg Yantz, editor Betsy Struthers, and the staff of Broadview Press have been patient, encouraging, and supportive in seeing the book through to completion—but none more so than the author's wife Susan.

This book is dedicated to the memory of my former colleague Dan Horigan, whose deep ethical commitment and passion to see the "little guy" get a fair shake from government helped to inspire much of my engagement in government relations in a previous career, along with the belief that committed and persistent individuals can still make a difference in influencing government policies for the greater good.

Geoffrey Hale

PART 1

The Context for Business-Government Relations in Canada: Ideas, Ideologies, and Historical Development

Introduction

Few areas in the study of politics engage as many dimensions of political, economic, and social life as the multiple, overlapping, and sometimes conflicting relations between government and business. The frequent dependence of politicians and governments on businesses, large and small, for economic development, job creation, and political support has made the mobilization of this support a major element of democratic political life since the late-eighteenth and early-nineteenth centuries. The resulting networks of mutual obligation have prompted countermeasures by competing economic and social interests, often including significant business elements, to limit the power of economic elites and to redistribute political and economic power.

The growth of governments and their increasingly pervasive involvement in social and economic activity in the mid- and late-twentieth centuries have politicized many areas of economic and social activity that were previously considered private matters. At the same time, they have encouraged the multiplication of interest groups to project and protect their members' interests in the design and delivery of government policies and programs and in the creation of more effective constraints on government actions that may threaten the well-being of different elements of society.

At one level, some observers have described the result of this process as "the embedded state" in which the decisions of citizens and businesses are increasingly constrained by the institutions and policies of government bureaucracies. At another level, it is seen to have resulted in the "marketization of politics" in which the expanded role of government has contributed to the fragmentation of its structures and purposes, exposing many of them to capture by "special interests" inside and outside government. Not so long ago, these trends were widely thought to have eroded the capacity of governments to provide coherent leadership in dealing with pressing social or economic problems or to respond effectively to public opinion (Cairns 1986; Offe 1984; Lowi 1985). Although the success of Canadian governments in regaining control of their finances during the 1990s has restored their public credibility to some degree, many citizens often feel that their opinions and interests have little influence or value compared with those of political and economic elites (Ekos 2000b; Howe and Northrup 2000: 4-10, 29-36).

Some of these challenges emerge from organized social movements. Organized labour's support of anti-capitalist and anti-globalization movements is one example of this kind of protest. The network of environmental groups favouring international regulatory regimes intended to subordinate economic activity to environmental concerns, such as that of the Kyoto Protocol, is another.

Other challenges reflect the reaction of some business and related interest groups to what they perceive as excessive government favouritism in the distribution of grants, contracts, subsidies, and other poorly coordinated policies that reduce Canadians' economic well-being in return for limited social benefits. Still others involve calls by interest and advocacy groups for reforms in the financing of political campaigns, tighter regulations of lobbying and other interest group activities, and other measures to limit the role of "special interests" within government.

This book seeks to put these and related debates into the broader context of governments' role in overseeing economic and social relationships, and of the ways that governments, business, and other social and economic interests interact through the political process.

Organization and Outline of *Uneasy Partnership*

This book addresses three major elements in the study of business-government relations. Part I considers the influence of political, economic, and social ideas on government's place in the economy and the history of Canada's economic development. Chapter 1 provides a general introduction to the political context for the study of business-government relations in Canada. Chapter 2 examines major concepts of economic well-being that have come to shape the objectives, design, and evaluation of economic policies. It also explains their implications for governments in designing policies to balance these objectives and their relevance for business-government relations. Chapter 3 examines a number of competing and overlapping approaches to the study of power relationships, and their analyses of the sources and limits of "corporate power" in Canadian society. Chapters 4 and 5 examine the historical evolution of business-government relations in Canada, initially as a search for strategies to promote the development of an emerging Canadian economy, subsequently in the search for a political and economic consensus capable of generating broad prosperity and a reasonably fair distribution of economic opportunities.

Part II examines the effects of political and economic structures and institutions both on the workings of the economy and on relations between businesses and governments. Chapter 6 examines the legal and sectoral organization of Canada's economic structure, its relative economic openness, and the resulting implications for market competition. Chapter 7 assesses the impact of federal political institutions on the emergence of Canada's regional economic structures, along with the differing economic bases and levels of development of its provincial economies. Chapter 8 reviews the effects of international economic trends and events on Canada's economic structure and their implications for business-government relations. Chapter 9 considers the historical uses of government business enterprises as political and economic policy tools, as well as their evolving role within the Canadian economy.

Part III discusses the organization of the policy process and the groups that attempt to influence it from inside and outside government. Chapter 10 examines the political organization of business and its relationship to various policy communities and networks through which government decision-makers, interest group stakeholders, and other elements of state and society engage one another on related policies and issues. Chapter 11 assesses the internal policy processes of government and their implications for the ways in which policy-makers and interest groups, including those representing business, interact with one another, along with the factors that contribute to or undermine the success of business lobbying activity. Chapter 12 details the external policy process and the competitive processes of engaging, influencing, and managing the marketplace of media and public opinion. Chapter 13 considers the role of litigation, along with the organization and processes of administrative law in shaping relationships among businesses, governments, and other social actors. Finally, Chapter 14 outlines the historic and evolving relationship between businesses and political parties as organized appetites for the brokerage of competing interests and the pursuit of political power.

Throughout the text, key terms appear in bold; these are defined in the Glossary at the end of the book. Questions for discussion and review appear at the end of each chapter, along with suggestions for further readings.

CHAPTER 1

Business and Government: The Politics of Mutual Dependence

The Reality of Mutual Dependence

North American ideas of the business marketplace often exalt an ethos of rugged individualism in the building of private businesses and their survival in a world of intense competition and unforeseen changes in the business environment. While this vision may have an element of reality, particularly in more entrepreneurial sectors of the economy, it is only one part of the bigger picture.

Businesses—large, small, and in-between—depend on governments for more or less stable sets of rules that are necessary for them to carry on successfully. They frequently look to governments for protection against threats to their well-being or for a hand up (or a hand-out) in competing with others. They may also seek changes to or compensation for the effects of other government policies that, while attempting to promote the public good, create unintended or counterproductive barriers to economic activity. From the earliest days of Canadian history, these activities have been as likely to promote political competition among different businesses and the people who run them as they have been to provoke competition with other social and economic interests.

Governments—federal, provincial, and municipal—depend on business investment for the economic activity and growth that is vital to the prosperity and employment of their citizens, the generation of tax revenues to pay for public services, and enough public satisfaction to win them periodic re-election. Politicians also consistently look to businesses for the financial support necessary to win and hold public office, while they attempt to win votes from other groups of Canadians with other interests they expect governments to serve.[1]

Since the colonial era, government cooperation with business has been a major factor in the ability of politicians to promote the settlement and development of Canada's huge underpopulated land-mass, particularly when it comes to helping its relatively underdeveloped regions catch up with more populous and prosperous areas of the country. At the same time, other social and economic interests have organized to challenge the ability of the strongest business groups to define the public interest in ways that serve their own interests.

Governments also have their own interests—not least, the capacity to perpetuate themselves and to define their policy goals independently of any particular group

---

1 As noted in Chapter 14, federal legislation passed in 2003 gives federal political parties much greater access to public funds to compensate for strict limits on business and union contributions. However, campaign finance laws in most provinces are more flexible.

of citizens—that can result in conflicts with business. The study of business-government relations and the ways in which governments attempt to balance competing business interests with those of other social and economic groups is vital to understanding many different elements of the political system and how these different parts fit together.

The reality of our political and economic systems—and of the relationships between businesses and governments—is one of mutual interdependence. The relationship between business and government consistently and inevitably blends elements of politics and economics for both sets of parties, for neither "business" nor "government" can credibly be considered as unitary actors given the regional, sectoral, and organizational diversity of both clusters of organizations and interests. In a Canadian context, that diversity is reinforced by the realities of federalism and regionalism and by the often-competing interests of different economic and societal sectors. It is also reflected in the organizational and economic fragmentation of business interests and that of the numerous departments and agencies in various levels of government.

Political and bureaucratic influence over economic activity is pervasive. It may be exercised directly through specific policy decisions and government actions, indirectly through framework policies that shape the context for both public and private economic decision-making, or by allowing broad discretion for personal and private choices in the marketplace.

The diversity of business and social interests creates fertile ground for political conflict as different groups attempt to influence government policies in their favour and as Canada's federal and provincial governments often take very different views of the public interest. At the same time, Canada's openness to international economic forces makes the political system increasingly dependent on the effective operation of the market economy to create new wealth, sustain and expand economic opportunities and employment, and generate the tax revenues needed to pay for public services. Without a growing economy, government decisions that redistribute income, opportunities, or market share, directly or indirectly, through taxes, transfers, regulations, or some other **policy instrument** can easily become a **zero-sum game** in which one group's economic gain is offset by another's loss.

This chapter examines the major political goals of governments in defining the terms for their intervention in and regulation of the Canadian economy and how these objectives have evolved since the colonial era and Confederation. It also considers the implications of these strategies for relations among governments, businesses, and other groups in society, and the emergence of political ideologies as means of shaping, justifying, and challenging the exercise of political power in the workings of the economy.

Political Ideas and the Role of Government in the Economy

Public expectations of governments' role in the economy may be shaped by **normative** factors: societal concepts of the public good to be fostered or social evils to be corrected. They also reflect pragmatic issues such as citizens' relative economic well-being, their need for political support or protection against hostile economic circumstances, and the perceived ability of political leaders to deal with these issues through government action. The political process functions as a parallel market-place in which different interests inside and outside government collaborate and compete to influence and control policy decisions affecting their vital interests.

Governments exist not only to promote the public good but also to define it in ways that link the perceived interests of a majority or sizeable plurality of citizens with their policies and priorities. Competing ideas (and ideologies) define, justify, and challenge the relationship of governments with different aspects of the economy. These ideas are often historically determined, reflecting past conflicts, compromises, and decisions that shape existing institutions and public expectations.

Canadians have usually expected their governments to play an active role in pro-moting their economic well-being whether in the distribution of public works and government contracts in the patronage-driven politics of the nineteenth and early twentieth centuries or by attempting to combine a dynamic market economy with a growing welfare state and increased social opportunities through the Keynesian policies pursued after World War II. Since adult suffrage replaced property qualifi-cations as the basis for voting rights in most Western states, economic prosperity and its equitable distribution within society have become major factors in voters' evaluation of governments. Governments that preside over relatively high levels of economic growth and increasing prosperity for most of their citizens tend to be re-elected. Governments that fail to address these issues effectively tend not to get re-elected unless the alternatives are seen as even less promising.

However, citizens also look to government to protect their interests from what economists call the **negative externalities** of economic decision-making: the direct or indirect effects of economic activities that harm other people. These problems may emerge from abuses of economic or political power by businesses, unions, or other economic associations; through negligence that affects the health, safety, natural environment, or property rights of others; or from the domestic impact of economic forces originating beyond Canada's borders. Political parties, social move-ments, and even business groups have championed various forms of government regulation to soften the rough edges of the marketplace; to promote greater social equity, fairness, and cohesion; or simply to exploit the political process to promote their members' interests.

Political systems that fail to take steps to deal with massive economic disloca-tions, such as rising inflation or mass unemployment, may be challenged by political parties and organized interests that champion alternative policies (or structures) to address these issues. Similarly, governments or political systems that tolerate widespread inequalities of income or opportunity without providing the means for citizens or groups to improve their social and economic well-being are likely to be challenged by political movements calling for a fundamental restructuring of social and economic relationships.

Government policies are also heavily influenced by existing economic structures. Even when governments seek to introduce significant changes in the workings of the economy, these usually require the cooperation of major economic actors to make them work and to avoid serious political conflict (Doern and Phidd 1983).

Policy decisions also reflect the evolution of Canada's federal system in its efforts to reconcile and balance both regional interests within a broader system of national policies and the influence of international trading and financial systems that have constrained the choices of Canadian businesses and governments for hundreds of years before globalization became a household word. These decisions may also result from legal precedents set by courts or administrative tribunals called to adjudicate disputes between governments, citizens, or both.

In a liberal capitalist democracy such as Canada or the United States (US), there are two basic approaches to the distribution of social and economic opportunities among citizens. The first allocates opportunities and resources through the political system at the discretion of elected politicians, bureaucrats, or quasi-autonomous regulatory structures. The second is a more or less competitive market economy functioning on the basis of known rules that are generally applicable to all participants as producers, workers, or consumers. Canada's economic system reflects significant elements of both approaches.

In practice, the two approaches overlap significantly. The principles and processes of rule-making are informed, to varying degrees, by political factors as much as by legal or technical policy considerations. At the same time, the relative openness of Canada's market economy and its interdependence with those of other countries both influences policy choices in Canada and imposes practical constraints on its political processes.

Political Objectives of Economic Regulation: An Historical Overview

The history of Canada's economic development and that of other Western industrial nations demonstrates that there are a number of different ways to politicize economic decision-making. Indeed, the concept of an economic marketplace functioning more or less independently of direct political direction and control only entered the mainstream of political and economic thought during the eighteenth century in response to the misuse and abuse of power by the ruling oligarchies of Britain, the American colonies, and Western Europe (Landes 1998; McDonald 1985; Muller 1993).

However, as rulers' efforts to exercise political and economic power at the expense of their citizens have rarely resulted in lasting prosperity or growing national wealth, many governments have sought to encourage economic development, prosperity, and the loyalty and support of their citizens by using their power to foster mutually beneficial alliances with major economic and social interests. In response, groups disadvantaged or left behind by these policies have often tried to capture political power to promote the redistribution of income, wealth, and economic opportunities to less favoured segments of society.

The spread of democracy in the nineteenth and twentieth centuries has reinforced the role of politics in legitimizing the structures and outcomes of economic activity. These debates may be the result of more or less consistent political ideologies championed by political parties or social movements, the adaptation of governing elites to political challenges, or the evolution of new political and economic ideas intended to balance the goals of promoting economic growth with varying degrees of social cohesion.[2]

The emergence during the twentieth century of large professional bureaucracies to design and administer the policies and programs of a growing public sector has increased the capacity of government elites to play a central role in the workings of the economy. At the same time, the principles of democratic government require some means in addition to periodic elections to give legitimacy to the policy preferences of these elites. At a political level, this challenge is often resolved by the use of government policies to build alliances between those wielding political power and major economic interests. The power of the state may also be used to redistribute economic opportunities and benefits to particular groups in society, either in the name of equity and justice or as a means of appealing to the self-interest of particular social and economic groups in return for their political support or acquiescence in government policies.

Expanding State Power and Autonomy

Government involvement in the economy has always expressed some concept of national interest or public good. The national interest may be conceived in the relatively narrow terms of *raison d'état*: the preoccupation of governing elites with the protection and expansion of their power to serve the interests of the state. Other approaches emphasize the promotion of their citizens' greater economic and social well-being or, in times of turmoil and rapid change, the protection of citizens from political and economic shocks beyond their control (see, for example, Nordlinger 1981; Iacobucci, Trebilcock, and Haider 2001; Laidler 1985; Banting, Sharpe, and St. Hilaire 2001).

Mercantilist approaches to economic policy are based on open or tacit state partnerships with private capitalist enterprises and other major economic interests with sufficient political clout to secure government support "in the national interest." The high-tariff National Policy of the late nineteenth and early twentieth centuries may have been the most prominent example of a mercantilist economic strategy in Canada, but neither was it the first or the last of its kind.

Historically, the economic policies of governments have reflected their rulers' efforts to finance their activities and to preserve and expand their political and military power (Kennedy 1989; Hughes 1991; Landes 1998). The **mercantilist** economic policies of the seventeenth and eighteenth centuries carried out by Britain, France,

---

2 The balancing of economic growth, social cohesion and good governance has been described as the "triangular paradigm of social progress" (Johnston 1999).

Spain, and other colonial powers were intended to expand the economic power and independence of these monarchies. The creation and sale of monopolies by royal edict, the development of colonies as sources of gold and other scarce commodities, and the regulation of international trade were all part of a broader system of policies intended to make royal governments more economically self-sufficient. The creation of a positive balance of trade was intended to generate a large enough surplus (or to reduce the deficits of extravagant courts) to finance a standing army capable of reinforcing royal power and reducing royal dependence on assemblies of nobles and prosperous commoners for voting tax revenues. If successful, such policies made it financially possible to impose a strong central government independent of these interests. They also enabled rulers to expand and defend their kingdoms and colonial possessions amid the dynastic wars of the era. While mercantilism may be a relic of the colonial era, it has left a political and intellectual legacy of economic nationalism and dependence on government action or sponsorship to promote economic development that will be discussed later in this chapter.

Another effect of mercantilism and its successors was the economic dependence of colonial economies on the imperial power for defence or internal security, capital to finance economic development, and external markets for their products. This pattern of dependence, which often came to be perceived as exploitation, was often reproduced as colonies gained their political independence and sought to become more economically self-sufficient through the settlement and exploitation of their own frontier lands. The pursuit of relative autonomy has often been linked to the development of domestic commercial and financial networks capable of financing new economic activity and establishing more equal business relationships with "outside" interests. It has also spurred the growth of competing political identities, including those provided by various forms of Canadian economic nationalism, Quebec nationalism, and regionalism as political elites attempt to mobilize public support behind their "nation-building" or "province-building" strategies of becoming "masters in their own homes."[3]

This approach has heavily influenced scholars and writers working from a socialist or social democratic perspective who argue that business, as a class, has enjoyed a privileged position in its dealings with governments (Coleman 1988; Atkinson and Coleman 1989). However, while selective political favouritism may be successful for a time in fostering economic development, it inevitably provokes resentment and political competition from other social and economic interests (including other business interests) that demand a leveling of the playing field, usually in the form of equal access to government subsidies, transfers, and protective regulations.

These policies are in direct conflict with ideologies of the market system. Rooted in classical liberal or contemporary **neo-conservative** political economy, **market liberalism** stresses the importance of individual liberty, the private ownership of

---

3 "Maîtres chez nous"—masters in our own home—was the slogan of nationalist governments during Quebec's Quiet Revolution of the 1960s and 1970s.

Box 1.1: Nationalism and the Politics of Identity

Dominant political/ economic power	Pursuit of autonomy/greater range of political and economic choices
Imperial Power Britain (before 1945); US (since 1945) Multinational corporations, linked to but independent of international economic system	Canadian Economic Nationalism • business + government (liberal nationalism) • government vs. business (interventionist nationalism)
Central Canadian Domination	Regionalism/Province-building • make federal government more responsive to regional interests marginalized in national decision-making, usually through political and economic decentralization. • build strong provincial/regional political and economic institutions to serve needs of citizens, major regional economic interests.
English-Canadian Domination	Quebec Nationalism • strengthen autonomous decision-making power of Quebec governments in all areas of social, economic, and cultural policy—inside or outside Canada. • build internationally competitive French-speaking business class, corporations.

property, the rule of law, and the diffusion of both political and economic power to maximize the social and economic well-being of individuals and the collective well-being of the community. Market liberalism seeks to achieve the maximum freedom of economic activity from political control, along with the preservation of competition, the maintenance of social order (or "social cohesion") and the promotion of economic opportunity and well-being (Novak 1982; D'Aquino and Stewart-Patterson 2001; Mintz 2001). These qualifications are important because they recognize the role of government in providing a stable and transparent legal framework to promote the common good. However, as noted by Adam Smith, many businesses tend to voice support for the ideology of the marketplace to the extent that it serves their interests, while seeking protection or support from governments to "level the playing field" when it works to their disadvantage.

The dominant political ideas that have shaped Canadian government policies towards business and the economy since World War II have adapted elements of market liberalism to public expectations of an active role for government in enabling citizens to achieve greater economic security and in promoting a more "equitable" distribution of opportunities and, sometimes, outcomes in society. However, the specific ways in which governments and competing political interests define these goals change over time. So do the specific policies introduced by governments to pursue these goals in response to changing circumstances, resources, and perspectives.

Building Political Alliances with Major Economic and Social Interests

Political alliance-building may reflect the strategic interests of governments (or a "ruling class"), or the efforts of political entrepreneurs to build a viable electoral coalition in order to promote political or societal change. Governments may champion particular social and economic interests as a matter of ideological conviction, political calculation, economic necessity, or in response to changing perceptions of economic opportunity and risk. Economic policies that offer potential benefits to a broad cross-section of citizens and interests are particularly attractive to governments in a democracy.

Neo-mercantilism emerged as a strategy for political and economic development in the late eighteenth and early nineteenth centuries in the US and subsequently in other countries, including Canada. The state sought to use protective tariffs (taxes on imports) and regulations to promote the development of infant industries, create a shared economic interest between the new national government and emerging commercial and industrial classes, finance public works, and support domestic economic expansion, often by developing the sparsely settled hinterlands of the new nations.

This "Hamiltonian system" of protective tariffs and state subsidies for "internal improvements" became the basis for the National Policy used by Canadian governments to promote economic development, east-west trading links, and the gradual settlement of northern and western Canada after the 1870s (Bliss 1985; Forster 1986). Neo-mercantilist strategies of state-sponsored economic development were also central to the programs of industrialization and modernization pursued by Germany and Japan during the nineteenth century. The writings of Friedrich List extended this concept of "industrial strategy," which has so heavily influenced the development of many emerging industrial nations during the twentieth century (Fallows 1993).

The effect of these ideas on Canadian public policies during the last century can be seen in government initiatives designed to foster Canadian control over economically strategic industries such as banking, wheat marketing, interprovincial rail and air transportation, and broadcasting and other cultural industries. Most provinces also developed, to varying degrees, their own "province-building strategies" in order to foster the development and diversification of their economies by extending incentives to outside investors, providing preferential treatment to local businesses, supporting the growth of regionally strategic industries, or using Crown corporations as instruments to promote development and growth (Bliss 1987). Elements of this approach can still be seen in the continued reservation of certain industries, such as banking, railroads, broadcasting, book publishing and book retailing, for Canadian ownership and control.

These policies helped to create an environment of mutual dependence between governments and the commercial, financial, and industrial interests so favoured. However, while this process did not involve "drawing a firm line between the economy and the polity," as suggested by some observers, it did imply a clear distinction of roles between business and government in which business managers enjoyed a high degree of independence in "making decisions on investment and workplace organization" (Bliss 1987; Marchildon 1996; Atkinson and Coleman 1989).

"Alliance-building" strategies may also reflect the demands of social and economic interests for governments to reduce perceived barriers to their economic advancement, to dismantle special privileges seen to benefit a relative few at the expense of many others, or to bring greater coherence to a wide range of government policies.

Canada's history has many examples of alliance-building by particular social groups in their efforts to offset economic disadvantages by political action. Farmers' groups organized political movements in Ontario and Western Canada in the late nineteenth and early twentieth centuries in efforts to reverse or offset the effects of protectionism on their livelihoods. Trade unions have consistently traded political support for favourable labour legislation and improvements to social policies. Small businesses have often pursued favourable tax and regulatory environments to help them compete with large corporations or to reduce the arbitrary power of governments over their day-to-day business operations.

However, social and economic changes may result in economic and regulatory benefits conferred by governments in the name of fairness during one era becoming examples of special privilege or **rent-seeking** in another.

During several eras of Canadian history, a reaction has set in against excessive government economic controls and favouritism in the distribution of economic benefits and in favour of a greater liberalization of the rules governing economic activity, including reduced trade barriers; lower taxes; and more generalized, less intrusive rules governing economic activity. Support for economic liberalization has largely depended on the degree to which its benefits are shared—or are seen as likely to be shared—throughout the community. Agrarian interests in late nineteenth-century Canada championed commercial union with the US as an alternative—if one ultimately rejected by the electorate—to federal policies widely seen to favour Central Canadian manufacturing interests at their expense. Both business and popular support for Keynesian macro-economic policies after World War II were a reaction to the unpopularity of extensive wartime rationing, price controls, and federal micro-management of the economy. Reactions to the growth of government during the 1970s and early 1980s reflected widespread perceptions not only that it was harmful to business and economic development, but that it was reducing the living standards and opportunities available to many ordinary middle-class Canadians.

Distributive Politics

Governments also seek public support for their policies by using their power to redistribute economic opportunities and benefits to particular groups, whether to serve different concepts of equity and justice, as a means of appealing to their economic self-interest, or both. At the micro-economic level—that of individual business and consumer decisions—political decision-making may be used to direct benefits and opportunities towards particular industries, regions, or other economic players whose support is enjoyed or sought by political or bureaucratic elites. It may also be used to impose penalties and restrictions on other groups or activities in order to serve the interests of the government and its political allies and constituents.

Distributive politics may be practiced in the name of the "public interest," "fairness," "equal opportunity," or the "correction of market failures"—often meaning the failure of private businesses or consumers to produce economic outcomes desired by political leaders, bureaucrats, or related groups of voters. The effective result of such policies can be the use of political power to pursue political and economic self-interest by businesses and other producer groups, politicians, civil servants, or other social and economic interests.

There are numerous examples of this kind of economic intervention. Business subsidies, tax preferences, protective regulations, economic regulations (or labour laws) limiting competition, and various forms of price regulation are only a few. In a democratic political system, economic regulations favouring one group tend to promote the emergence of organized **interest groups** seeking comparable benefits from the state.

For much of the twentieth century, such intervention was justified by economists who contended that rational economic planning by governments would lead to a more equitable, just, and efficient distribution of resources in society than the unregulated workings of the "free market." Many social scientists have come to recognize the limitations of government intervention in an open society and the challenges of translating well-meaning policy intentions into desired outcomes. The fragmentation of government decision-making in a complex, diverse society often results in commitments to competing, even contradictory, policy goals. Governments must also balance rival concepts of equity and justice based on different views of the public interest to define these goals in the first place.

Political ideas of equity and justice are contested concepts whose articulation and application are heavily influenced by ideological factors. Social democratic egalitarianism is rooted in the concept of **vertical equity**: the redistribution of income, wealth, and opportunities by governments from more economically favoured to less favoured segments of society. Critics of the capitalist system, in both its liberal or mercantilist forms, have often faulted it for contributing to an unequal distribution of wealth, income, power, and opportunity. These outcomes, in turn, are seen to lead to (or result from) an excessive concentration of political and economic power in the hands of a few wealthy owners of property and their client groups. Socialist critics called on government to take ownership and control of the means of production by democratic or revolutionary means. Today, social democrats and many liberals are more likely to advocate the expanded use of state power to regulate economic activity in the interests of the majority of wage-earning workers, to provide extensive social benefits through the use of redistributive taxation, and, on occasion, to break up large concentrations of wealth.

However, vertical equity is only one dimension of distributive equity. **Horizontal equity** emphasizes the importance of comparable treatment of persons or businesses in comparable circumstances. The many different forms of government intervention often result in individuals or businesses being placed at a competitive economic or social disadvantage because of subsidies, taxes, or regulatory preferences given to particular groups. Apart from economic arguments, many Canadians have strongly embraced arguments of legal and political equality against government policies that artificially privilege particular individuals or businesses at the expense of others. This normative preference may be reinforced by utilitarian arguments that the public interest is best served by policies that promote the greatest good of the greatest number by "maximizing net gains and minimizing net losses," not merely an interest in redistribution for its own sake (Iacobucci, Trebilcock, and Haider 2001: 43-44).[4] However, such an approach implies a shift from primarily political criteria for decision-making to largely economic ones.

Many forms of government regulation have been introduced in response to social and economic inequities and abuses in efforts to anticipate and prevent (or mitigate) future problems. Regulatory measures may address both **market failure**—negative externalities created as a result of the undisciplined workings of the marketplace— and **government failure**—the unintended or destructive effects of otherwise well-intentioned government policies.

Equality need not imply uniformity. Government intervention is often justified on the basis of "compensatory" or "corrective justice." The first approach, which is visible in some welfare state, economic subsidy, and "equal opportunity" programs, is intended to compensate for the absence of social or economic advantages that enable individuals to compete in or contribute to society on a comparable basis to that of "average" citizens or businesses. The targeting of job creation and training subsidies to areas of high unemployment or to assist unemployed workers are two examples of this approach.

Policies to enforce corrective justice are intended to compensate citizens for specific injuries committed by other individuals, businesses, or governments, including breach of contract, negligence towards others' health or well-being, or abuses of economic or political power (Iacobucci, Trebilcock, and Haider 2001: 51-58). These approaches may require direct payments to individuals or businesses, as with legal awards for breach of contract or unjust dismissal and legislative provisions for severance pay, or punitive damages for unfair competitive practices such as misleading advertising.

---

4 The political reaction against the effects of rent-seeking and special privilege in government policies has been fuelled by a broad literature rooted in *public choice* theory. For a few examples, see Laidler 1985: 29-38; Hartle 1988; Hartle 1994; Richards 1997.

Rising populations and prosperity during the twentieth century typically led governments to invest in expanded public services that contributed to higher living standards and increased opportunities for successive generations of citizens. However, the effects of chronic budget deficits, rising government debt, and demographic changes, especially population aging, on public finances between the 1970s and 1990s raised significant concerns over **generational equity**: the relative status or economic well-being of individuals in different generations, usually assessed in terms of the impact of decisions made by members of one generation on the living standards and opportunities of succeeding generations (Corak 1998). These concerns have reinforced political efforts to maintain the sustainability of public services by balancing budgets, reducing public debt relative to the size of the economy, and prefunding projected increases in public pensions and other forms of social insurance through the creation of sizeable investment funds (Association of Canadian Pension Management 2000; Hale 2001b; Robson 2001).

Finally, no discussion of distributive politics in Canada would be complete without acknowledging the regional aspects of Canadian economic and social policies. Politicians are elected to represent particular geographic areas, not just political parties or ideologies, and to ensure that their constituents receive their "fair share" of benefits from governments in return for taxes paid. Regional pressures for "equitable" access to improved transportation and communications, public and private investment, government projects, income transfers, and social services are reflected in the regional orientations of political parties, the regional policies of federal and provincial governments, and the complex web of federal-provincial relationships which are embedded in the structures of Canadian politics.

Politics, Ideology, and the Economic Role of Governments

Political legitimacy does not rest simply on a foundation of raw power, political will, or unvarnished appeals to self-interest, significant as these factors may be in the real world of politics. Popular appeals to justify or challenge particular policies or the broader social and political order often reflect political ideologies: simplified systems of ideas that enable politicians or interest groups to mobilize voters around shared values, interests, and political goals. Ideology is a means of shaping the content and limits of political discourse, together with public expectations of the roles and limits of "acceptable" government action.

Political theorists and ideologues often attempt to define ideologies as systematic, internally coherent bodies of theory or political vision that describe the world as they perceive it and as they believe it should be and that provide the steps necessary to close the gap between current realities and an idealized social or political order.

In practice, however, political ideologies tend to evolve as composite political and philosophical agendas that reflect untidy coalitions of interests, values, and overlapping social and political goals rather than systematically organized efforts to promote "group think." These agendas often emerge from the efforts of social and political interests to challenge a political system that has been relatively ineffective in responding to their interests and concerns. Interests threatened by such challenges may develop ideological responses that systematize values and beliefs previously taken for granted to justify existing social practices or attempt to discredit ideological challenges to major political ideas and institutions (Christian and Campbell 1990: 4-20. Hall 1989; Bradford 1998).

Canada's regional and cultural diversity has not precluded the use of ideological appeals by either political parties or organized interests. To become politically effective, ideological frameworks for policy development and political coalition-building must be flexible enough to engage a broad cross-section of social and economic interests across the country. They must also be able to adapt to the ongoing economic and social changes that have turned Canada into one of the world's most open economies and multicultural societies.

In practice, ideological competition to shape governmental and economic institutions and public policies since the 1940s has taken place within a context of an **embedded liberalism** that seeks to integrate and reconcile within itself the central elements of Canadian nationhood and economic and social progress (Ruggie 1995; Courchene 2001a). Ideological debates are as likely to feature disagreements between different elements of the business community as they are to become a contest between business groups and other social and economic interests, including public sector elites. For relatively small open economies such as Canada's, the politics of embedded liberalism must take into account not just domestic political and economic issues but international factors as well. These realities are examined at greater length in Chapter 8.

The principal ideologies that have helped to shape Canadian political debates and business government relations have evolved in response to a mix of political and economic shocks and policy failures. **Political shocks**—threats to the political status quo that force governments to rethink established policies or political values—may result from the rise of new political movements or ideas that challenge the reigning political consensus and compel some level of accommodation to their demands. Major political shocks that changed the focus of Canadian politics during the twentieth century include the emergence of a politically competitive socialist party in several provinces in the 1940s; Quebec's Quiet Revolution of the 1960s and 1970s, culminating in the election of a sovereigntist government; the influence of Thatcherism and Reaganism on conservative thought in Canada; and the adaptation of Canadian liberalism to the Canada-US Free Trade Agreement (FTA) and Canada's growing economic integration in North America.

External policy shocks—major changes to the political or economic context for government policies that threaten to destabilize major elements of the political or economic system—have frequently triggered shifts in Canadian government policies. During the twentieth century, these shocks included the **Great Depression**; the shift of global economic leadership from Britain to the US after World War II; global energy price shocks during the 1970s and 1980s; and the persistent, if episodic impact of US unilateralism and protectionism on Canadian foreign economic policies.

Internal policy failures—the inability of existing ideas or institutions to respond effectively to changing political, economic, and social conditions—may discredit both individual governments and their approaches to the role of government. For example, the federal government's embrace of a free trade agreement with the US in the 1980s would have been politically inconceivable except for the political and economic failures of the Trudeau government and its embrace of state-centred economic nationalism in the early 1980s.

Political ideologies also evolve in response to ongoing competition and dialogue among political ideas and interests, which come about either in response to political and policy challenges or as part of a broader process of intellectual adaptation to changing circumstances. We will now examine evolving interpretations of liberalism and their relationship with Canadian nationalism, socialism (and social democracy), and conservatism as major ideologies that have influenced political debates over the role of government in the economy and relations between businesses and governments.

Liberalism

Liberalism has been the dominant political ideology in Canada at least since the 1940s. However, Canadian liberalism is very much a composite ideology that has evolved significantly during this period. Different scholars identify different elements in the intellectual collage of Canadian liberalism. Christian and Campbell note that the policies of the federal Liberal Party have reflected a shifting balance between the expectations of business Liberals and social or "welfare" Liberals (Christian and Campbell 1990: 41-96; Johnson 2002). However, just as the influence of liberalism as an ideology has often transcended the boundaries of the Liberal Party, the partisan agendas of "big-L" Liberalism have often reflected current political conditions and challenges as much as any coherent ideological program.

Some scholars associate the concept of **business liberalism** with classical liberalism's idealization of the minimal state as applying generalized rules of public benefit to protect individual liberty from force, fraud, or governmental favouritism while leaving as much room as possible for citizens to act cooperatively for their own good and that of the communities to which they belong.[5]

This approach may be useful as an intellectual cliché that serves the interests of some advocates of a "market economy" and their ideological opponents. However, it fails to describe the real-world behaviour of organized business interests in attempting to use or secure government policies favourable to their economic and political interests, including a stable social and political climate, while accommodating agendas of other social groups that do not conflict fundamentally with these objectives.[6]

---

5 This summary of classical liberalism is derived from Hayek 1944: 13. Christian and Campbell (1990: 6-7, 78-81) tend to identify what they describe as "business liberalism" with classical liberalism of varying degrees of "purity."

6 Business liberals' selective and pragmatic application of market liberal principles and state intervention to foster economic development is a common theme of businessmen in politics from C.D. Howe to Paul Martin. See Bothwell and Kilbourn 1979; Mitchell 1983; Bercuson, Granatstein, and Young 1986).

Nor does it describe the typical behaviour of politicians and governments in attempting to foster economic development within a largely capitalist economy, balance competing interests, and pursue election or re-election.

The culture of business liberalism has accommodated itself comfortably in successive eras to many policies that are incompatible with the limits on government intervention prescribed by classical liberalism as long as they accommodated the interests of established businesses while pursuing other government objectives. The common thread linking Keynesian economic policies, the multiplication of selective tax preferences for particular industries and forms of economic activity, and major increases in government regulation—none of which are particularly associated with classical liberalism, free markets, or the minimal state—is a pragmatic commitment to the fostering of private enterprise and a favourable business climate (Atkinson and Coleman 1989a; Taylor 1991; Taylor, Warrack, and Baetz 2000: 16-24, 61-68).

Canadian **social** or **welfare liberalism** has tended to emphasize the regulatory and redistributive role of the state in securing the common good. Rather than equality of outcomes, its advocates have tended to support the incremental extension of the welfare state and public services as a means to economic security and greater equality of opportunity for all Canadians. Social liberals have also tended to see governments as a political counterweight to the concentrated power of particular social and economic interests by using the fiscal and regulatory powers of the state to foster small business development, the viability of the family farm, safe and equitable workplace conditions, or various forms of social and environmental regulation. The growth of redistribution and regulation may be encouraged as a matter of principle or in response to concrete problems; for instance, consider the "Red Toryism" that has constituted one strand of historical Canadian conservatism. However, the expansion of the state has usually been constrained by the need to encourage economic growth so that the costs of redistribution or public services do not result in a "zero-sum society" (Thurow 1981) that can undermine the political consensus sustaining Canadian liberalism. The search for "balance" between its economic and social agendas led socialists like former New Democratic Party (NDP) leader T.C. Douglas to satirize centrist Canadian liberalism as "getting money from the rich and votes from the poor by promising to protect each from the other" (Mitchell 1983: 391).

While maintaining a broad sphere of economic and social freedom, Liberal assumptions of selective state intervention to promote economic growth, redress social concerns, expand public services, and alleviate poverty have been shared by supporters of most non-social democratic parties in the late twentieth century. Political debates have generally emphasized particular issues of distributive politics or the relative balance between private and state initiatives, not the underlying assumptions of the political and economic system. The realities of brokerage politics between the 1950s and 1980s prevented either the predominant Liberal or Progressive Conservative (PC) parties from ignoring either business or welfare liberals without risking their capacity to win elections or remain in office.

The development of **Keynesian economic policies** between the 1940s and 1970s contributed to rising public expectations that governments would shield Canadians' living standards from rising inflation and other economic shocks, expectations that ultimately proved to be politically and economically unsustainable. Social or welfare liberals and other groups dependent on expanded government spending for their economic well-being resisted reductions in public spending, while business liberals and related interests resisted the tax increases necessary to pay for them. As a result, chronic budget deficits, chronic inflation, and rising levels of unemployment forced governments to rethink the assumptions of Keynesian liberalism during the late 1970s and early 1980s (see Bradford 1998: 135-76; Lewis 2003: Chapters 4, 6).

Another level of conflict within liberalism reflected the debate over the degree to which governments should intervene to provide Canadian ownership and control over the economy. Bradford identifies two major strands of business liberalism—**liberal nationalism** and **liberal continentalism**—which have co-existed for many years (Bradford 1998: 6-8; these issues are discussed at greater length in Chapter 5). Business support for nationalist policies has often reflected competing expectations of (or dependence on) the state to provide a favourable regulatory environment for business activities, including restrictions on foreign investments. Different business interests have often supported government ownership of specific industries, especially public utilities, to the extent this stabilized markets or reduced business costs, or they opposed it if it was seen to impose excessive costs or regulatory constraints on their interests.

However, the liberal consensus came unraveled when the Trudeau government of 1980-84 opted for a strategy of **interventionist nationalism** involving higher taxes and expanded federal regulation and control over the private sector (Milne 1986; Smiley 1987; Simeon and Robinson 1990; Hale 2001b: 170-76). The political backlash against these policies made it possible for the Mulroney government (1984-93) to negotiate a free trade agreement with the US that virtually precluded a return to state-centred economic nationalism on a large scale, except at a prohibitive risk of economic disruption.

The evolution of Canadian liberalism has reflected a series of ideological challenges. Keynesianism was a reformist response to the challenge of democratic socialism in the 1940s. During the 1970s and 1980s, liberalism faced competing challenges from social democratic and corporatist critics on the left and from the emergence of neo-conservatism on the right. The **neo-liberalism** of the 1990s responded to neo-conservative critiques of an "overextended" state while engaging in selective activism to facilitate structural economic change and maintain the sustainability of valued public services (Canada, Department of Finance 1994; Hale 2000; Hale 2001c; Hale 2002).

Socialism and Social Democracy

Democratic socialism and its reformist "cousin," social democracy, provided the most politically significant challenges to various forms of liberalism and the capitalist economic system between the 1930s and the mid-1980s. Traditional social democratic concepts of social justice and democracy are closely linked to the promotion of egalitarianism: the promotion of equality, not only of social or legal status, but of political and economic outcomes as well (Broadbent 1999).

Social democratic approaches to economic policy, including state capitalism and the extensive use of economic and social regulations to manage various forms of economic activity, tend to take a more adversarial approach to the market economy and private business. They challenge what they view as the relatively privileged position of business and the owners of capital in shaping economic policies in competition with other interests. Social democratic policies attempt to achieve political dominance over the economic system so that the distribution of economic and social opportunities and resources can be determined by political means, usually in the name of achieving a more equal distribution of opportunity, income, and power.

Early socialist ideas were driven by a combination of moral fervour, outrage at economic and social conditions, and the belief that capitalism as a system was doomed to disappear either as a result of evolutionary policies of social reform and government regulation or wholesale changes to be imposed by governments in response to popular demands (Wiseman 2001).[7]

The Regina Manifesto of 1933, the founding platform of the Cooperative Commonwealth Federation (CCF), predecessor of the NDP, outlined a thoroughgoing program for nationalizing large swaths of the economy, systematic regulation of the rest, and a comprehensive welfare state financed by heavily redistributive taxation on income and wealth. While the CCF attempted to implement much of this platform when it governed Saskatchewan between 1944 and 1964, its main effect was to spur liberal and conservative parties to support the extension of welfare state programs and Keynesian economic policies during that era.

Unlike most European countries, Canada has never possessed a broadly based national workers' party committed to the systematic reorganization of society along socialist lines. The NDP, formed in 1961 from a merger between CCF remnants and the leadership of Canada's trade union movement, has remained internally divided over electoral strategies and the relationship between Canadian social democracy and the capitalist market economy.

More recently, the capacity of liberal capitalist systems to reinvent themselves in response to social and economic change has altered the character of the debate. Reformist social democrats tend to emphasize the role of politics and the state in providing citizens by political means what the market cannot provide, either through improvements to social security or the removal of barriers to full participation in society by members of marginalized groups, while at the same time they recognize the limits of politics (Eppler 1999; Rae 1998: 165-94).

---

7 Consistent with the British Labour tradition of parliamentarism, most of the CCF's social democratic leadership took a consistently anti-Communist position during the Stalinist era and the early years of the Cold War.

Social democrats tend to favour a much stronger role for the state in economic management and regulation, as well as a stronger commitment to redistributive taxation and to state delivery and control over public services. This tendency is reinforced by the emergence of close political links between social democratic political parties, notably the NDP and the Parti Québécois (PQ), and public sector unions that now account for the majority of unionized workers in most provinces. While unsuccessful in rising beyond third-party status in federal politics, the NDP generated many of the ideas, policies, and programs that, under the sponsorship of other parties, fuelled the expansion of Canadian governments between the 1940s and 1980s.

An alternative social democratic approach to the economic role of government, borrowed from European social democratic governments, has heavily influenced political and economic developments in Quebec. Rooted in the state-centred nationalism of the 1960s and early 1970s, successive Liberal and PQ governments have created strongly **corporatist** structures to shape the cooperation of business, labour, and other organized economic interests under the guidance of the provincial government.[8] Unlike social democratic governments in other parts of Canada, PQ governments in particular have been able to secure both business and union cooperation based on a shared nationalist ideology and the use of strategic public investments to foster the growth of private Quebec-based businesses. However, similar efforts to foster corporatist economic and social policies in other provinces have generally failed to win lasting support from either unions or business except on a limited sectoral basis.

Significant differences remain between social democrats who believe in the capacity of the state to harness private corporations to serve the needs of society in a mixed economy and socialists committed to confrontation with and the transformation of the capitalist system under different expressions of government and worker control.[9] A socialist minority inside and outside the NDP has championed greater confrontation with business and an overtly anti-capitalist agenda promoting more comprehensive structural economic reform under government control. Since the negotiation of the FTA in 1987-88, these groups have sought alliances with nationalist, feminist, environmentalist, and anti-capitalist social movements to provide a more extensive ideological alternative to liberal market capitalism.

Political scientists have noted three major factors in the relative influence of socialism or social democracy on political discourse and the role of governments in Canada: the structure of the party system, the relative capacity of trade unions to mobilize their members in support of social democratic parties, and the effect of

---

8 The corporatist tradition can be traced to Catholic social teachings in the 1930s, which resulted in industrial standards legislation intended to improve working conditions and create a political barrier against the spread of (secular) industrial unions from the United States.

9 The corporatist impulse finds different expressions, from the tripartite industry and environmental councils introduced by NDP and PQ provincial governments to recent proposals to mandate "corporate social responsibility" through international agreements. For example, see Ontario, Premier's Council 1988; Khoury, Rostami, and Turnbull 1999.

social democratic competition in strengthening the relative influence of social or distributive liberals within Liberal and PC governments.

Canada's parliamentary and electoral systems have usually encouraged the development of two principal parties capable of forming a government. Third parties typically function at the margins, providing ideas to the two major parties but rarely gaining enough strength to replace one or the other as voters' primary alternatives. Social democratic parties, replacing either Liberal or conservative parties, have consistently formed either the governments or official oppositions in BC, Saskatchewan, Manitoba, and Quebec for extended periods, while periodically holding the balance of power in federal and Ontario politics. Becoming major elements in their provinces' two-party systems has enabled them to shape the political agenda for extended periods.

Social democratic competition has often strengthened the relative position of social or welfare liberals within Liberal and Conservative (or PC) governments. Many inner-city and resource industry-dominated constituencies have been characterized for many years by two-party competition between NDP (or PQ or Bloc Québécois) and either Liberal or Conservative (or PC) party candidates. This process contributes to what economist Anthony Downs has described as the "median voter effect" in which two-party competition tends to dilute parties' ideological rigour as they pursue relatively non-ideological swing voters in the political centre (Downs 1957). As with socialist movements in previous eras, the current anti-globalization movement has encouraged neo-liberals to place greater emphasis on the distributive aspects of their policies.

The relative influence of organized labour in generating financial, organizational, and electoral support for social democratic political parties has been another significant element in the relative political success of social democracy in Canada. This influence can create a strong reciprocal relationship. Provinces with effective social democratic parties are more likely to have labour legislation favourable to the formation and growth of unions that, in turn, help to shape their political culture and expectations of government policies.

The shift of politically successful social democratic governments in many European and most English-speaking countries to accommodation with the international market economy during the 1990s has prompted politically competitive social democratic parties in some provinces—notably Saskatchewan, Manitoba, and Quebec—to follow suit (Rae 1998; Giddens 2000). This approach has triggered intense resistance by elements of organized labour and anti-capitalist social movements, leaving Canadian social democracy deeply divided over the most effective approach to balancing the promotion of economic growth and higher living standards with greater economic and social equality.

Competing Concepts of Conservatism

Conservatism has often been described as an anti-ideology: historically contingent, heavily influenced by particular local or national traditions, and usually articulated in response to specific social, economic, or ideological challenges (Kirk 1993; Oake-shott 1991: 407-37). This relationship is particularly visible in Canadian conservatism during the late nineteenth and early twentieth centuries. Ontario-based conserva-tism, which dominated national conservative politics for many years, was informed by neo-mercantilist theories that emphasized an active role for the state, allied with business, in economic development. Other major elements included traditions of British Empire Loyalism and the Tory commitment to social order and cohesion embodied in the phrase "peace, order and good government." Quebec conservatism, whatever its formal political expression, reflected both that province's dominant Catholic culture and the dependence of French-Canadian political elites on the capi-tal provided by the English-speaking business interests of Montreal and Quebec City. During the 1940s and 1950s, a populist form of conservatism supportive of small producers and local entrepreneurs began to emerge in Western Canada, particularly in Alberta and British Columbia (BC). Provincial conservative parties incorporat-ing different combinations of these traditions governed for extended periods during the twentieth century in BC, Alberta, Ontario, and Quebec. However, intellectual and political fragmentation has meant that occasional federal conservative gov-ernments usually have been little more than disparate, relatively short-lived "throw them out" coalitions assembled to displace worn-out Liberal governments (Flana-gan and Harper 1998: 174).

The adjustment of most business interests to postwar Keynesian business liber-alism and the efforts of so-called Red Tories to compete for the support of social liberals by promising to expand public services and the welfare state resulted in the domination of federal politics during the 1960s and 1970s by two broadly cen-trist political parties differing more in personalities and cultural issues than in the proper role for governments in the economy. One result of this consensus, in sharp contrast to the US, was the absence of any distinct or coherent expression of politi-cal conservatism in Canada beyond a sporadic resistance to increased state control over private economic activity (Newman 1968; Simpson 1980).

The emergence of sharp ideological debates over the role of government resulted from the progressive alienation of many business liberals, particularly small business owners and opponents of economic nationalism, from the relatively interventionist policies of the Trudeau governments of the 1970s and early 1980s. These criticisms were reinforced by the growing influence of neo-classical economists and by the anti-statist rhetoric of Margaret Thatcher in Britain and Reagan Republicans in the US. However, their application in practice has been limited by internal divisions among business liberals, traditional "Red Tories," libertarian individualists, and populist anti-statist conservatives suspicious of big government and cultural liberalism.

The neo-conservative critique of liberal and social democratic governments emerged from the perceived overextension of governments during the 1970s. Cana-dian governments, along with those in other countries, were accused of pursuing policy goals beyond their capacity or competence. Many conservatives criticized the growth of public sector deficits and debts, arguing that the spiraling costs of government were absorbing resources that could be used more productively and responsibly by private citizens and businesses (Simon 1978; Wilson 1984). Their analysis drew heavily on the ideas of neo-classical economists who distinguished between the role of governments in providing a general policy framework for economic activity, investment, and growth and the inherent limitations of politicians and regulators attempting to substitute their "judgments ... for the judgments of those in the marketplace" (Economic Council of Canada 1981; Wilson 1984: 2).

The neo-conservative advocacy of capitalism and the limited state is based not only on its claim to greater economic efficiency, but also on its linkage between economic freedom and human freedom in general (Bottomore 1985: 84; see also Friedman and Friedman 1980; Gilder 1981). It emphasized the necessity of governments, like citizens, "to live within their means." To do this, many conservatives argued for a reduction in social entitlements so that previously universal social benefits would be targeted more towards "those in need" and a greater emphasis on the application of business methods and market incentives to the operation of government policies and programs. Social responsibility would take the form of assisting and enabling individuals who could do so to take greater responsibility for their lives and actions, either by making benefits conditional or by introducing more user pay elements to the delivery of public services (Wilson 1984: 19). These ideas were developed progressively by a series of policy institutes and think tanks that emerged between the 1970s and 1990s (for two sharply contrasting views of think tank influence in Canada, see Abelson and Carberry 1998; and Carroll and Shaw 2001).

The reaction of regional and business interests to the policies of the Trudeau government resulted in strong scepticism among conservatives towards economic nationalism (and the centralization of political and economic power in general) as a cloak for the expansion of state power at the expense of individual and private interests (Milne 1986). The growth of decentralist and anti-statist attitudes among conservatives and business liberals reinforced purely economic arguments in leading the federal PC Party to champion the negotiation of the FTA in 1987-88.

However, the actions of PC governments during the 1980s rarely lived up to their rhetoric, particularly in the areas of promoting smaller government and spending and deficit reduction. Public expectations for the maintenance of public services generally defied efforts at budget cutting, although most conservative governments had committed themselves to lowering income tax rates even if this meant expanding definitions of income subject to taxation (Bercuson, Granatstein, and Young 1986; Hale 2001b: 181-222).

The cumulative impact of chronic deficits, the corrosive effect of rising interest costs on other public services, the tax increases imposed by federal and provincial governments of all political stripes to limit the growth of deficits, and the recession of the early 1990s resulted in declining living standards for most Canadians and growing frustration with the inability of traditional policies to correct these problems. The failure of moderately conservative (or traditional business liberal) policies to live up to the expectations created by conservative rhetoric led to the emergence of populist conservative movements in several provinces and in federal politics which called for an end to tax increases, far deeper reductions in government spending, and a significantly reduced role for governments in the economy (Manning 1992; Ibbitson 1997; Bruce, Kneebone, and McKenzie 1997; Lewis 2003: 143-63). While these demands did not involve the return to the "night watchman state advocated by some libertarian groups and feared by many on the left, they promoted a far more selective, disciplined approach to government intervention in the economy. They also resulted in the fragmentation of the federal Tory coalition into its constituent parts—Western populists and small-c conservatives in the Reform Party (later the Canadian Alliance), Quebec nationalists in the Bloc Québécois, and a Red Tory remnant of PCs (for the political tensions between populism and neo-conservative anti-statism, see Flanagan 1995).

For purposes of this study, neo-conservatism is defined as a range of views broadly committed to limiting the size and scope of government on both normative and empirical grounds. Neo-liberalism, on the other hand, describes a pragmatic, technocratic use of market forces to discipline the operations of government in achieving public policy goals and to integrate economic and social policy objectives through the selective use of state intervention.

To the extent it is meaningful to discuss neo-conservatism as an ideology in the early twenty-first century—and 73 per cent of business owners and executives responding to a recent survey describe themselves as "small-c conservatives" (Ekos 2000b)—it involves a commitment to the ideas of personal responsibility, limited government, a market-oriented capitalist economy based on widespread private ownership of property, internationally competitive tax levels, and a utilitarian approach to government regulation and social policies based on the provision of measurable net benefits to society.

The cumulative effect of these challenges was to force a rethinking of traditional liberal approaches to the policies of government and the adaptation by governments of all ideological stripes to the reality of fiscal limits and the disciplines of international economic competition. It has also contributed to the emergence of a neo-liberal policy consensus that, while preserving a significant role for government intervention in the economy, places far greater emphasis on fiscal discipline, the accommodation of market forces within government policies, and a more consistent coordination of economic and social policies to serve complementary goals (Courchene 1990; Canada, Department of Finance 1994; Greenspon and Wilson-Smith 1996; Canada, Standing Committee on Finance 1999a).

Politics, Ideology, and the Economic Role of Government in the Twenty-First Century

The political and economic environment for Canadian liberalism has changed significantly between the 1980s and the early twenty-first century. Federal and provincial governments must accommodate a range of political and economic forces, including North American and global economic integration, rapid technological change, and an aging population which they may be able to influence at the margins but which are largely beyond their effective control.

Neo-liberalism (in the North American, rather than European sense) has evolved into a view of government that attempts to promote economic competitiveness in an increasingly open economy with broader participation by citizens who will benefit from economic growth through access to high levels of education, employment, and the provision of sustainable public services.

Its advocates, in both Canada and the US, have tended to emphasize the creation of government industrial policies in support of entrepreneurship in a sort of sectorally targeted neo-mercantilism (Rothenberg 1984; Ontario, Premier's Council 1987; Reich 1992; Canada, Industry Canada 2002). It views fiscal discipline, balanced budgets, and the systematic application of business methods to delivering public services as the means for restoring public trust in government and sustaining valued public services rather than as part of a broader critique of the role of governments in society (Kernaghan, Marson, and Borins 2000; Canada 2001a; Hale 2001b).

The promotion of market-based economic growth, higher standards of living, and greater social and economic equality are still seen as the objectives of government. However, the ability of the state to achieve these goals in an open, diverse, and pluralistic society appears to be largely dependent on the willing cooperation and participation of private businesses and individual citizens rather than on increased state planning and regulation. The new liberalism of the twenty-first century reflects a conscious adaptation to four prevailing realities of political and economic life in North America and much of the English-speaking world. First, the process of globalization has forced all governments to consider not only the domestic implications of their policy decisions, but the ways in which they relate to networks of economic, social, and political activity that cross national borders. Second, the effects of ongoing technological change have significantly affected the organization and regulation of economic activity from framework economic legislation to industry structures and greater transparency in regulatory systems. Third, increased international competition imposes pressures on both private businesses and governments to increase their efficiency, thus keeping costs competitive and enhancing productivity and competitiveness in comparison with other jurisdictions. Finally, an aging population has forced governments to reconsider their social and labour market policies and to look for new ways to make them fiscally and economically sustainable (Hale 2001e; Hale 2002; Burleton and Drummond 2001).

These changes have not eliminated tensions between business and government. Nor have they precluded the continuing competition for control over government priorities between the technocratic, managerial liberalism of business and some bureaucratic elites and the traditional patterns of distributive (or interest group) liberalism noted earlier in this chapter (Hale 2001b; Hale 2002). Government continues to play a significant role in the Canadian economy through a wide range of fiscal, social, and regulatory policies. The economic principles that shape this role will be examined in Chapter 2.

Key Terms and Concepts for Review (see Glossary)

business liberalism
corporatist
embedded liberalism
external policy shocks
generational equity
government failure
Great Depression
horizontal equity
interest groups
internal policy failures
interventionist nationalism
Keynesian economic policies
liberal continentalism
liberal nationalism
market failure

market liberalism
mercantilist
negative externalities
neo-conservative
neo-liberalism
neo-mercantilism
normative
policy instrument
political shocks
rent-seeking
social or welfare liberalism
vertical equity
zero-sum game

Questions for Discussion and Review

1. What is meant by the "interdependence" of political and economic systems? What are some examples of this interdependence in contemporary Canadian life?

2. How does growing state involvement in economic life contribute to growing efforts by social and economic interests to influence the decision-making processes of governments? What are some approaches intended to link these activities to a broader concept of the public interest?

3. Compare and contrast mercantilism and neo-mercantilism as strategies for economic development. Discuss similarities and differences in relations between governments and businesses under the two systems. What is rent-seeking, and to what extent is it a normal outcome of (neo-)mercantilistic government policies?

4. What are the four major concepts of equity that governments attempt to serve through the exercise of "distributive politics"? How do different concepts of equity create cross-cutting pressures on governments or on relations between businesses, governments, and other social interests?

5. What are the three kinds of shocks that can undermine political consensus and create opportunities for ideological and policy changes in government? What are some recent examples of these shocks in Canadian federal and provincial politics and in business-government relations?

6. What are the major factors that contributed to the evolution of Canadian ideological outlooks in the late twentieth century? What implications have these changes had for relations between governments and business?

Suggestions for Further Readings

Cairns, Alan. 1986. *The embedded state: state-society relations in Canada*. In *State and society: Canada in comparative perspective*. Vol. 31, Background Papers, Royal Commission on the Economic Union and Development Prospects for Canada. Coord. Keith Banting. Toronto: University of Toronto Press. 53-86.

Coleman, William D. 1988. *Business and politics: a study of collective action*. Kingston and Montreal and Kingston: McGill-Queens University Press.

Corak, Miles (Ed.). 1998. *Government finances and generational equity*. Ottawa: Industry Canada (February).

Hall, Peter. 1989. *The political power of economic ideas*. Princeton, NJ: Princeton University Press.

Hartle, Douglas. 1988. *The expenditure budget process of the government of Canada: a public choice-rent seeking approach*. Toronto: Canadian Tax Foundation.

Hughes, Jonathan R.T. 1991. *The governmental habit redux: economic controls from colonial times to the present*. Princeton, NJ: Princeton University Press.

Iacobucci, Edward M., Michael J. Trebilcock, and Huma Haider. 2001. *Economic shocks: defining a role for government*. Policy Study #35. Toronto: C.D. Howe Institute.

Laidler, David (Ed.). 1985. *Approaches to economic well-being*. Toronto: University of Toronto Press.

Lasswell, Harold. 1950. *Politics: who gets what ... when ... how*. New York: P. Smith.

Lewis, Timothy. 2003. *In the long run we're all dead: the Canadian turn to fiscal restraint*. Vancouver: University of British Columbia Press.

Rae, Bob. 1998. *The three questions: prosperity and the public good*. Toronto: Penguin Books.

Richards, John. 1997. *Retooling the welfare state*. Toronto: C.D. Howe Institute.

Russell, Peter (Ed.). 1999. *The future of social democracy*. Toronto: University of Toronto Press.

CHAPTER 2

The Role of Government in the Economy: Economic Perspectives

The purpose of economic policies—and of government intervention in the economic decisions of individuals, businesses, and other organizations in society—is to foster conditions that enhance the economic well-being of individual citizens and the broader society. Most economists agree that public policies are most effective in promoting increased prosperity by providing a stable but adaptable framework of rules that enable individuals, businesses, and other organizations (including those in the public sector) to pursue their economic well-being in ways that contribute, directly or indirectly, to the collective well-being of a particular society.

Economic policies that are successful in increasing overall levels of national income, thereby improving living standards for individuals and families and generating a more widespread distribution of prosperity, involve a multi-dimensional balancing act. They seek to promote overall economic growth while ensuring that the vast majority of citizens have at least the opportunity to share, directly or indirectly, in the benefits of that growth. However, the functional organization of governments and the geographic concentration of many industries often shift the focus of economic policy-making to emphasize its sectoral and regional effects.

The past generation has also demonstrated the importance of **sustainability** in economic policies. In macro-economic policy—government decisions related to the overall levels and distribution of economic activity—sustainability refers to the capacity to balance the current consumption of goods and services with investments that will increase future economic opportunities. It has also come to refer to the ability of governments to combine improvements in citizens' material living standards with environmental preservation and related quality-of-life issues.

This chapter examines major concepts of economic well-being that have come to shape the objectives, design, and evaluation of economic policies in Canada. It will explain their implications for governments in designing policies to balance these objectives and their relevance for business-government relations. Finally, it examines the growing use of **performance benchmarks** both to assess economic progress and competitiveness and to focus government policy initiatives on enhancing particular aspects of economic well-being.

These ideas do not exist in isolation from politics. Indeed, they may have considerable influence on political discussions of the ways in which individuals, communities, and governments can and should relate to one another through the policy process and in the economic marketplace.

Major Concepts and Objectives of Economic Well-Being

The concept of economic well-being is debated by economists on both normative and empirical grounds that reflect both philosophical differences and disputes over economic analysis. So do the policy choices that would contribute most effectively to the promotion of economic growth and the widespread sharing of its benefits among Canadians through improved standards of living. The debate over living standards, and the best ways to define and improve them, is also a debate between competing economic and political orthodoxies and the efforts of governments to straddle these competing outlooks (see, for example, Laidler 1985; Fortin 1999; Banting, Sharpe, and St. Hilaire 2001; Conference Board of Canada 2001).

Government economic policies have traditionally addressed four major goals:

- the promotion of sustainable economic growth and improved living standards;
- the promotion of economic efficiency, including measures to offset the effects of market or government behaviour that undermine the efficient operation of the economy (**market failure** and **government failure**, respectively);
- the provision of public goods; and
- promoting "fairness" and "equity."

More recently, large-scale technological change, changes in forms of business organization, and trends towards continental and global economic integration have encouraged governments to facilitate and, in some cases, encourage adaptation to structural changes in the economic environment.

Most economists would agree that governments do not "create" economic growth as much as create the conditions in which individuals, businesses, and other organizations can grow through their individual and collective efforts. Economists influenced by the neo-classical economic tradition tend to emphasize the conditions necessary to achieve economic efficiency and growth as a precondition of generally improved living standards (Mintz 2001; Martin and Porter 2000; Sachs and Warner 2000).

Aggregate economic growth reflected in national income or Gross Domestic Product (GDP) statistics may result from any combination of growing populations, rising participation rates in the paid labour force, increased levels of capital investment, or increased efficiency in the use of labour, capital, and technology. Economist Pierre Fortin writes that "there are only four ways private households and corporations can get richer: by putting more people to work, by producing more output per worker, by retaining a larger fraction of domestic income after tax, transfer and net foreign payments, and by cashing in on higher relative export prices" (Fortin 1999: 12).

Table 2.1 notes changes in Canada's GDP, per capita GDP, and real (after inflation) disposable income between 1961 and 2001. A recent Industry Canada study indicates that the biggest contributors to the growth of real (after inflation) output between 1962 and 1998 were growth in the quantities of labour and capital investment (Diewert 2002: 37-38). Demographic projections of a shrinking labour force within the next decade suggest that Canada will need to generate and attract higher levels of investment than its major competitors and faster growth in labour productivity for continued growth in general living standards (Bruce and Dulipovici 2001; Burleton and Drummond 2001).

Table 2.1: Measurements of Economic Activity and Well-Being

	GDP (Millions of Current Dollars)	GDP Per Capita (Current dollars)	Real disposable income per capita (2001 dollars)
1961	$ 41,253	$ 2,258	$ 9,424
1971	$ 98,630	$ 4,491	$ 13,042
1981	$ 360,471	$ 11,716	$ 18,998
1991	$ 685,367	$ 24,450	$ 19,920
2001	$ 1,092,246	$ 35,141	$ 21,425

Source: Statistics Canada 2002b: Cat. #11-210-XPB, 3,24,43; author's calculations.

Social democratic economists tend to emphasize the distributive effects of economic policies, including their impact on employment levels and the degree to which lower and middle income earners share in the general prosperity (Osberg 1985; Osberg 2001). Economic changes usually involve a mix of gains and losses with some people being better off and others worse off. Noting that economic losses tend to weigh more heavily on those with less to lose, many economists support philosopher John Rawls's insistence that economic policies give priority to improving the well-being of the least well-off members of society (Osberg 1985).

Since World War II, the promotion of greater economic equality has generally taken four main forms:

- the provision of direct financial assistance through a variety of income transfer programs,
- a redistributive tax system with varying degrees of "leakage,"
- improved public services designed to provide basic social needs and improved opportunities,
- and promotion of high levels of employment and job creation.

Redistribution may contribute to both economic and social benefits. However, emphasizing redistribution over the promotion of economic growth may reduce overall economic efficiency and output as a result of high marginal tax rates, thereby imposing losses on society greater than the benefits—a phenomenon known as **deadweight loss**. Therefore, economists tend to argue in favour of designing tax systems in ways that generate the maximum benefits to recipients in return for the least costs to society in terms of related administrative costs and tax-induced distortions in decision-making (Laidler 1985: 22-25; Boadway and Kitchen 1999).

Recent efforts to build an economic policy consensus have tended to focus on integrating economic and social policy goals so that they can be made to complement and reinforce one another, rather than being mutually contradictory. This emphasis addresses the challenge of **Pareto efficiency** (or allocational efficiency): achieving an allocation of resources so that it is impossible to make anyone better off without making someone else worse off. As a result, government policies intended to enhance both efficiency and fairness should provide for "winners" from policy changes to compensate "losers" to enhance the overall economic well-being of society (Brander 1995: 20-23; Courchene 1991).

Increased management efficiency or **productivity**—the capacity to increase overall economic output relative to additional units of input, including labour, capital, and technology—is central to improvements in living standards as it increases the range of choices available to participants in the marketplace. The spread of industrialization and growing competition in international markets forces both businesses and governments to increase productivity in order to be able to improve citizens' living standards while maintaining current levels of profits and government revenues for the provision of public services (Brander 1995: 8; Sharpe 1998; Garelli 2001).

The influence of neo-classical economics and the concept of market forces, even in a context of extensive government spending and regulation, reflect the understanding of economists that prosperity cannot be taken for granted and that rational decision-making requires the recognition of trade-offs in choices among competing goods in order to make the most of available economic resources and expand the overall size of the economic pie.

Firms and Profits, Supply and Demand

Translating these objectives into some semblance of reality requires an understanding of the economics of supply and demand along with the theory of the firm. Economic markets involve not only individuals but companies or firms: legal entities of different sizes through which individuals and groups carry on business. Most firms employing more than a few people are corporations: organizations incorporated under the terms of relevant federal or provincial laws. Incorporation limits the liability of the firm's owners or shareholders to the amount of capital invested in the firm rather than making them personally liable for the company's debts. Private business corporations exist to produce goods and services for profit; thus, the revenues resulting from business activity should be greater than the costs of carrying on business. Shareholders seek levels of profit sufficient to provide them with returns comparable to or greater than other potential investments with similar levels of risk. These returns may be obtained through the payment of dividends to shareholders or through the accumulation of **capital gains** that may be realized when they sell all or part of their shares in the corporation.

Economic markets involve a complex mixture of economic actors who perform a variety of roles: workers (or producers) and consumers, sellers and buyers, borrowers and lenders (or investors). The risk-reward trade-off is one of many ways in which individuals and businesses carry out economic activity subject to the principles of supply and demand. Market participants balance relative risks and benefits in light of available information and their own priorities in making choices in the production, distribution, and allocation of goods, services, labour, and capital. Increasing prices for a product—or a unit of labour or the return of a dollar of capital—create incentives for increased production (or supply) until there are more products, or workers, or investment capital than the market can absorb, after which prices tend to fall. Similarly, scarcities in the supply of a product or service, including labour, are likely to force up its price as consumer demand exceeds the available supply.

Governments may influence the activity of markets in many ways:

- by making rules that increase or decrease the costs of transactions or shift them from one economic actor to another;
- by providing or requiring the provision of information that enables market participants to make more informed decisions on the supply, quality, and value of products and services;
- by providing incentives, such as subsidies or tax breaks, for certain economic activities and disincentives for others;
- by direct government participation in the supply of goods and services in ways that can either encourage or discourage innovation and competition from other suppliers;
- by rationing the supply of particular services traditionally under government control or financed from public funds; and
- by redistribution of income between individuals or groups or to balance current spending or consumption with both voluntary and "forced" savings, such as social insurance programs, to provide for future income needs.

The capacity of a broadly capitalist economy coexisting with high levels of public services to generate widespread and increased prosperity is central to the political legitimacy of private enterprise and the market system. The central role of businesses in generating increased employment, higher standards of living, and a stable stream of government revenues to finance public services and the income transfers of the welfare state is critical to the influence of business groups over economic and related social policies. The diverse and dynamic nature of the market economy and of competing business interests, linked to those of other groups in society, influences the policy tools available to governments in pursuing their objectives. It also increases the importance of balancing competing interests and goals through the political process so that governments can enjoy both broad public support and the support of stakeholder groups whose interests are most likely to be affected by specific policies.

The following sections examine each of the major objectives of government policies in greater detail, along with some of their implications for relations among governments, businesses, and other interests.

Economic Growth and Stabilization

Economic growth provides the solvent by which governments may redistribute income through taxes, transfers, and improvements to public services so that such policies do not become a zero-sum game in which the benefits received by some social and economic groups come primarily at the expense of others.

The conditions necessary for growth also reflect the complex interaction of individuals, businesses, other organizations, and governments in pursuing a wide variety of personal preferences and organizational and policy goals in both the economic marketplace and the overlapping markets for political ideas and political influence or power. These include **macroeconomic policies** (or stabilization policies) intended to stabilize overall levels of economic activity through the use of fiscal and monetary policies; **structural adjustment policies** intended to address sources of economic rigidity and facilitate the adaptability of businesses, governments, and individuals to changing economic circumstances; and **microeconomic policies** that affect the decisions and choices available to individuals as investors, workers, savers, consumers, and managers.

Fiscal and Monetary Policies

Fiscal policy includes the major policy instruments that shape the overall levels and distribution of government revenues and spending, as well as the budget balances (surpluses or deficits) that result. Discretionary fiscal policies affect several areas, including:

- changes to the levels and distribution of government spending resulting from deliberate policy changes or new legislation (as opposed to **automatic stabilizers**; see below, pages 40-41);
- changes to particular tax rates or to the tax mix: a government's relative reliance on certain revenue sources compared to others;
- decisions to stimulate the economy through a mix of tax reductions and spending increases, resulting either in larger deficits or smaller surpluses; and
- decisions to constrain the economy's overall growth rate in order to restrain inflationary pressures, frequently by pursuing the opposite mix of policies.

Fiscal policies are usually presented to the public in the context of a government's annual budget, although the budget process and the political marketing associated with it have become year-round processes in recent years. Fiscal policies do not function in isolation either from political decisions of "who gets what ... when ... how" (Lasswell 1950) or from the wider economic environment. The budget process usually triggers a scramble among interest groups, including competing groups representing different business sectors, to maximize benefits from governments in the form of lower taxes or increased spending and to minimize or shift the costs of those benefits to other groups. Similar competition takes place inside and between different levels of governments as politicians seek to maximize the political benefits of spending increases or tax reductions and to disguise or shift the costs (and political risks) of paying for these benefits (Hartle 1988; Hale 2001b).

Governments that attempt to manage these trade-offs by incurring chronic deficits to finance current spending will usually face a day of reckoning when taxes must be increased significantly to pay for rising interest costs on past borrowing or when foreign creditors demand changes in national economic policies. Economic policies that fail to account for the effects of careless environmental, occupational, or public health practices may also contain hidden price tags that generate long-term social and economic costs.[1]

Governments use **monetary policy** to manage the money supply (affecting levels of credit and inflation), interest rates (affecting the cost of borrowing), and exchange rates (the relative value of national currencies). However, in open economies such as Canada's that are characterized by high volumes of trade and capital flows, central banks cannot manage all these policy targets at the same time (Freedman 2002). In recent years, Canada's monetary policies have been focused on maintaining low and relatively stable rates of inflation, within a range of 1 to 3 per cent, and, secondarily, on constraining or stimulating the rate of economic activity by raising or lowering interest rates.[2] Although the Bank of Canada has some flexibility in setting interest rate and other monetary policy targets, it takes into account the actions of other major central banks, especially the US Federal Reserve Board and the multiple effects of Canada's growing integration within the North American economy.

Along with most other major industrial countries, Canada maintains a floating exchange rate policy, in which the value of its currency fluctuates against other currencies based on several factors including relative volumes of trade, relative prices of imports and exports, cross-border capital flows, and relative inflation and interest rates. During the 1990s, the Canadian dollar's declining value, especially against the US dollar, contributed to a growing trade surplus. Some critics argue that it also contributed to a relative decline in Canadian living standards by depreciating the value of wages and salaries paid to Canadian workers.

The "loonie's" recovery to the range of 85 to 90 US cents in 2005-06 has changed the nature of some of these trade-offs while forcing businesses in several export-dependent industry sectors to become more competitive (Caranci 2004; Stinson 2004). However, it has also diffused many of the criticisms of economists who have suggested that Canada abandon its discretion in monetary policy either by setting

---

1 For a discussion of the use of economic incentives and disincentives to encourage better environmental stewardship, see OECD 2001: 187-207.
2 For an overview of policy discussions in this area, see Laidler 1997 and Dodge 2002.

a fixed exchange rate relative to the US dollar or by moving to a common currency, most probably the US dollar.[3]

Stabilization Policies

Stabilization policies are intended to promote the general economic welfare and a degree of social and economic order by using fiscal and monetary policies to stimulate or constrain the growth of **aggregate demand**—a country's total consumption of goods and services—in order to even out the peaks and troughs of the business cycle. During the Great Depression of the 1930s, consumer purchasing power was inadequate to purchase the potential industrial output of most national economies, leading to high levels of unemployment. As a result, most English-speaking countries, including Canada, Britain, and the US, introduced various forms of **Keynesian stabilization policies** during the 1940s and 1950s. In most cases, these policies were also intended to reduce the direct government regulation of day-to-day economic activity experienced during World War II while giving governments the power to stimulate or constrain overall levels of economic activity to promote economic growth, reduce unemployment, and maintain relative price stability (low inflation). They also were intended to redistribute the benefits of economic growth to larger numbers of citizens through expanded public services and income support programs, providing a social safety net that would mitigate the hardships resulting from periodic unemployment and thus stabilize economic activity.

Some elements of government budgets are designed to respond to overall levels of economic activity by serving as "automatic stabilizers." For example, an economic slowdown or **recession** (two quarters of negative GDP growth) results in lower profits, a decline in taxes collected, and a corresponding increase in social benefits paid through programs such as Employment Insurance and social assistance without any changes in government policies. Conversely, periods of rapid economic growth usually result in sharp increases in taxable profits, investment, and employment income. If governments run deficits during periods of recession or slow economic growth, prudent fiscal policies suggest that "windfall" revenues from rapid growth should be used to pay down debt incurred earlier in the business cycle or the growing costs of interest charges on public debt will reduce the capacity of governments to stimulate the economy through discretionary fiscal and/or monetary policies during the next downturn (OECD 1999: 137-49).

Government policies may also seek to reallocate economic activity over time to manage various kinds of social and economic risk. These measures include provisions for employment pensions, retirement savings plans and social insurance programs, public debt repayment, or incentives for private savings and investment. High savings and investment rates provide capital for new business investment, job

---

3 To date, the consensus of senior policy-makers and monetary economists is that such policies would incur significant costs that would probably outweigh their benefit to Canadians. For a taste of this debate, see Grubel 1999; Courchene 2001a; Laidler and Poschmann 2000; Drummond 2001.

creation, and the financing of public infrastructure. They also enable citizens to set aside current income to meet foreseeable future expenses and generate a stream of investment income to provide higher living standards and increased security in retirement or in case of disability.

The relative success of Keynesian policies in promoting increased prosperity and general increases in living standards during the 1950s and 1960s led many voters and interest groups to expect governments to serve as the guarantors of economic growth and increased prosperity. However, these expectations contributed to chronic budget deficits during the 1970s and 1980s when governments sought to protect their citizens against a series of economic shocks. Rising inflation and unemployment rates that defied the efforts of governments to control them through conventional economic policies led to the collapse of the Keynesian consensus in most Western industrial countries (see O'Connor 1973; Crozier et al. 1975; Skidelsky 1977).

The inability of fiscal policies to deal with both rising inflation and chronic unemployment (**stagflation**) led to an increased emphasis on monetary policies, particularly high interest rates, to reduce inflation even at the cost of a severe recession in 1981-82. However, public expectations of government action to stimulate job creation and growth resulted in high structural budget deficits, which occurred despite relatively strong economic growth and rising employment levels. The result was a vicious cycle of deficits, rising debts, high interest rates, and slower growth (Hartle 1993; Dodge 1998). These events prompted a rethinking of the policy tools used by governments to promote consistent levels of economic growth.

Several factors have reduced the ability of governments to "manage" the economy through short-term stabilization policies. Structural changes, particularly the growing integration of smaller national economies into larger continental and global economic systems, have made it significantly more difficult for national governments to control overall levels of short-term economic activity as opposed to trying to "steer" its evolution over a number of years. The growth of provincial spending and taxation to levels roughly equal to that of the federal government has reduced the latter's capacity to design effective economic policies without a significant degree of provincial cooperation.[4] The prospect of an aging population and shrinking workforce relative to the size of Canada's population limits the degree to which governments can finance current services with deficit spending without reducing the living standards of the next generation (Dodge 1998; CSIS Commission on Global Aging 2001).

Although public opinion is still influenced by Keynesian assumptions that budgetary policies can have a significant effect on short-term economic conditions, support for structuralist policies such as improving access to education, balancing the budget, and selective tax reduction has become reflexive after years of government

---

4 Provincial revenues in 2002-03 totalled $242 billion, including $35 billion in federal cash transfers, compared with $177 billion in federal revenues. Federal and provincial governments share most major sources of revenue (Canada, Department of Finance 2003).

advocacy (Earnscliffe Research and Communications 2001a; Earnscliffe Research and Communications 2001b; Earnscliffe Research and Communications 2001c).

Macroeconomic Policies and Structural Economic Change

These factors have led macroeconomic policies to balance medium-term stabilization goals with the promotion of structural economic change. Federal and provincial fiscal policies, including the levels and distribution of taxes and spending and overall budget balances, tend to emphasize the promotion of increased economic competitiveness and the sustainability of core public services, although the specific mix of policies to further these goals can vary significantly from one government or jurisdiction to another (Canada, Standing Committee on Finance 1999; Hale 2001b: 262-79; Hale 2006).

The replacement in 1990 of the old Federal Sales Tax on manufactured goods by the Goods and Services Tax (GST)—a value-added tax on all goods and services purchased in Canada—recognized the vital importance of export industries to Canada's competitiveness and growth, especially as Canada had recently signed a free trade agreement with the US. Similarly, the government has since systematically reduced tariffs on most imports as a result of trade agreements with other countries. These changes are addressed in greater detail in Chapter 8.

Both the federal and some provincial governments have begun the process of making corporate tax rates competitive with those of Canada's major industrial competitors while shifting more of the business tax burden to "benefit-related taxes" and user-fees, though not without some criticism of the latter from the business community (Hale 2001b: 293-316). These policies reflect a neo-liberal emphasis on wealth creation by establishing a positive investment climate that includes but is not limited to competitive tax rates. As individual taxpayers tend to lack the mobility of corporations, redistributive elements of taxation tend to place greater emphasis on personal income taxes. However, the realities of the political marketplace—especially politicians' need to compete for votes—have ensured that the size of personal income tax reductions in recent years has substantially outweighed those of corporate tax cuts (Hale 2001a: 74-84).

The government has also shifted a significant share of its spending from passive income transfers to individuals to active labour market measures that assist workers in expanding their skills and earning opportunities. It has combined this with significantly increased transfers and tax breaks to offset the costs of post-secondary education to help citizens adapt to the needs of a changing economy (Hale 2002).

Governments may still engage in economic stabilization by running large budget surpluses during years of exceptional economic growth in order to pay down debt, for example, or by reducing interest rates in anticipation of (or response to) a significant economic slowdown. However, mainstream economic theory has shifted from encouraging short-term economic stimulus or constraint to medium-term policies that provide a greater degree of continuity, predictability, and stability (Dodge 1998: 284-88; McCallum 1999; Mintz 2001).

Since the mid-1980s, economic policies in major English-speaking democracies have shifted to a greater emphasis on structural or *framework policies* intended to create a predictable and supportive environment for increased investment and economic activity in an economic system increasingly influenced by global and continental economic forces. These framework policies, which include the broad principles, rules, and structures governing competition, trade, tax, labour market policies, and major regulatory systems, are part of a broader system of **microeconomic policies** that attempt to shape or regulate the economic activity of individuals and businesses within a competitive marketplace.

Promoting Economic Efficiency

Neo-classical economic theory is based on the assumption that economic activity resulting from the voluntary exchange of private property—including labour, goods, services, or financial assets (including cash)—will prompt behaviour by individuals that not only increases their own welfare, but also the welfare of others. The reality of **economic scarcity**—the principle that human needs and wants are usually greater than the resources available to fulfill them—lends itself to the pursuit of **economic efficiency**: the attempt to increase the value of outputs (e.g., goods, services, or capital) that can be obtained in exchange for a particular value of inputs (e.g., labour, capital, or technology).

At the same time, economists recognize the importance of government policies in promoting conditions conducive to the efficient operation of the market economy. These conditions involve predictable transparent rules that allow producers, consumers, and investors to make rational informed decisions in the midst of uncertainty, on the assumption that competitive markets tend to allocate resources more efficiently than politicians or government regulators. They also include the definition of property rights, including the right of contract, and the ability to enforce those rights in civil or criminal law. They may also involve steps to mitigate or correct market failures caused by imperfect competition, abuses of market power, or perverse economic incentives.

Economic theory also recognizes the importance of consistent legal rules to protect citizens from force or fraud in economic activities and from the ability of powerful or dishonest economic actors to abuse their powers to the disadvantage of others. Such rules are necessary for the fulfillment and enforcement of contracts and for the stability that facilitates the growth of economic relationships based on mutual benefit. They are also necessary to limit the tendency of governments to display favouritism to particular individuals or groups in ways that may detract from the overall well-being of society. The principle of **economic neutrality** emphasizes the desirability of avoiding government-induced distortions in allocating economic resources, so that workers, managers, investors, and consumers will make the most of the resources available to them. In practice, however, governments regularly "second-guess" markets by providing incentives and disincentives for many kinds of activities through taxation and regulatory, subsidy, and other policies, regardless of their impact on economic efficiency.

Information asymmetries—disparities in the availability of information about a product or service to buyers and sellers—may distort prices or result in transactions unfairly weighted to the advantage of one or the other. For example, consumer and financial services legislation may require full disclosure of product risks or available financial information to protect consumers against abuses of market power, such as insider trading.

Certain business practices may create **negative externalities**: intended or unintended outcomes that interfere with the rights of others or that impose avoidable social costs, such as risks to the health and safety of others or significant levels of social distress (such as large-scale layoffs in a single-industry community). Government policies may seek to regulate such activities through consumer and product safety legislation and social regulations of various kinds. They may force particular businesses to bear a greater burden of the negative externalities resulting from their operations, as with programs such as Workers' Compensation or pollution control and emissions-trading rules. Alternately, they may choose either to "socialize" these risks through various social insurance programs or direct government provision or to employ a combination of these and other policy measures.

Other structural problems that may invite different kinds of government intervention include labour market rigidities that create barriers to entry in certain occupations or hinder the adaptation of markets to changing demand for particular occupations or skills, significant amounts of seasonal employment, and long-term unemployment (Conference Board of Canada 2001: 36). Governments also regulate anti-competitive practices through competition and consumer protection laws. However, there is little consensus on the degree or conditions under which mergers and corporate concentration contribute to economic efficiency, as opposed to restricting competition, consumer choice, and innovation (Canada, Standing Committee on Industry 2000; Trebilcock et al. 2000; Canada, Standing Committee on Industry, Science and Technology 2002; also see Chapter 6).

However, government policies intended to anticipate, regulate, or correct problems resulting from business activities or other individual actions may themselves result in unintended consequences that impose serious costs on the economy, society, or the workings of the political system. For example, a poorly designed system of regulation may significantly increase costs to consumers, limit desirable innovations, or create incentives for individuals or groups to beat the system in different ways. It may also expand incentives for individuals and groups to invest scarce resources in manipulating the political process to their advantage (rent-seeking) rather than finding better or more creative ways of generating profits by increasing their efficiency or providing greater value to their customers. Poorly designed government transfers may simply increase economic dependence and stagnation, rather than enabling underdeveloped regions to compete more effectively for investment and employment (McMahon 2000a). Economists have come to describe such outcomes as examples of **government failure** (as opposed to market failure).

Productivity, Efficiency, and Microeconomic Policies

A major preoccupation of government in recent years has been the search for ways to improve the economic efficiency both of markets and government policies to foster greater levels of innovation, productivity, and value for consumers' and taxpayers' dollars alike. The pursuit of greater efficiency has become synonymous with increasing productivity, both in private sector markets and in the provision and financing of public services. There is broad agreement among economists that encouraging improvements to productivity is a central element in the improvement of Canadians' living standards over the long term. Canada's aging population, the reality and prospect of declining savings rates (Fougère and Merette 1999; Bérubé and Côté 2000; Statistics Canada 2004a: 14 April), and the steady decline in the proportion of working Canadians to pensioners all underline the importance of increasing the productivity of labour and capital if standards of living are not to decline substantially in coming years (Dodge 1998; Sharpe 1998; Canada, Standing Committee on Finance 1999b; Canada, Standing Committee on Finance 1999b; Finlayson 2001).

Major elements of the productivity agenda have included:

- enhancing competition among providers of goods and services and consumer/citizen choice, both in domestic markets and by reducing barriers to the movement of goods, services, and (to a lesser extent) people across national borders;
- searching for more flexible, efficient approaches to organizing the activities of businesses, governments, workers, and consumers;
- changing approaches to government regulation to make greater use of incentives to complement or replace traditional "command and control" styles of regulation;
- fostering innovation through research, invention, and the commercialization of new technologies;
- investing in education and marketable skills (human capital) that increase the flexibility and productivity of citizens in the marketplace; and
- reducing rates of taxation on broader bases of income and consumption, while reducing the economic inefficiencies (or deadweight loss) resulting from high marginal tax rates and tax design (Canada, Standing Committee on Finance 1999a; Mintz 2001; Courchene 2001c; Canada, Industry Canada 2002; Canada 2002).

The effects of pressures for increased efficiency have been quite visible in recent years. Business productivity has increased, although not as fast as in some other countries. Governments have re-evaluated their core functions, streamlining many public services and contracting out others. Although the exchange rate of the Canadian dollar against the US dollar has dropped by almost 30 per cent between 1990 and 2002, before rebounding in value in 2003-06, technological innovation and increased competition have held down price increases on most imports to a much lower level.

The realities of growing international competition for goods, services, and capital mean that economic observers do not just compare a country's current economic performance against its past performance, but they compare it also against the performance of its major competitors and the "extent to which national economies have the structures, institutions and policies in place for economic growth over the medium-term" (McArthur and Sachs 2001: 28). The mobility of capital, goods, and services across national borders means that national or regional standards of living depend on the capacity to attract and retain capital, skilled managers, and workers, and to match or exceed the productivity improvements resulting from innovation, new technologies, and greater efficiency.

Since the delivery of goods, services, and income transfers by governments accounts for between 30 and 50 per cent of national incomes in most industrial countries, the competitiveness of businesses and workers in the private sector is also linked to public sector productivity, particularly in the provision of public goods and in balancing the claims of equity and efficiency. Regulations and social policies that provide incentives for more efficient resource allocation, greater work effort, and economic self-reliance are more likely to result in economic growth and increased prosperity than policies that ignore or discount these objectives. There is a growing literature in public administration and public policy that emphasizes the role of internal markets in the organization and delivery of public services to increase both the efficiency and effectiveness of public services (e.g., see Kernaghan, Marsen, and Borins 2000; Dunn 2002; Canada, Standing Senate Committee on Social Affairs, Science and Technology 2002). These ideas have also influenced changes in the provision of many public goods by governments.

The Provision of Public Goods

Public goods are those services which society considers necessary for its well-being but which the market may not be able to produce or distribute efficiently or in desired amounts. Society may benefit from the provision of many goods or services that it may not be efficient for individuals or small communities to provide for themselves or which may be subject to the problem of free riding: unintended use by individuals who have not paid for the service.

Economists distinguish between pure and quasi-public goods. **Pure public goods** are goods or services that all or most individuals in a particular market can obtain without having to pay for them directly (non-excludable) and without diminishing the supply available to other persons (non-rival) (Strick 1999: 24). Functioning currency systems and national defence are examples of pure public goods. Clean air and water were once considered pure public goods, until large-scale population growth, pollution and related health and environmental concerns created sufficient pressures on the sustainability of these resources to require some forms of government regulation.

Other goods and services, labeled **quasi-public goods**, may provide significant public benefits (**positive externalities**) above and beyond the returns that may be captured by their producers and consumers under normal market conditions. Current forms of economic organization may or may not permit suppliers to charge consumers directly for the costs of quasi-public goods consumed, as in the case of fire protection, public utilities, a public highway, or certain kinds of scientific research. Limited private savings, high costs of capital, and other factors may preclude private investors from providing these goods and services in the quantities desired by the community. As a result, there may be a significant public benefit from direct or government-sponsored provision of these services. However, the inherent limits on funds available to provide public services suggest that, as long as they can choose how much of a service to consume, a significant part of the costs of providing such services should be passed on to individual citizens through benefit-related taxes or user fees.

Depending on the availability of capital and technology and the markets to be served, quasi-public goods may include products such as the large-scale generation and distribution of electricity and telecommunications (especially to remote or underdeveloped areas) and infrastructure development for major roads, bridges, airports, water, sewage, and environmental management services, although regulated markets have emerged in recent years for private provision of most of these services.

Governments may or may not produce such products or services directly. In many cases, they may have the option of providing public goods directly, through "arm's-length agencies," under contract with private or cooperative producers, or through the regulation of private economic activity. In some cases, the definition of public goods may be a function of social (or political) choice and cultural tradition. Nations with well-developed civil societies, capital markets, and entrepreneurial cultures may provide a wide range of goods and services considered public goods in other countries through cooperative or private channels, with the option of filling market gaps through social insurance or direct state provision.[5] Changes in technology, business organization, and the capacity of capital markets to finance infrastructure development and other public services has led to an unparalleled degree of innovation in the provision of public goods in recent years.

Fairness and Equity

Governments may decide that access to social and economic benefits may be achieved more effectively through regulatory or legislative action than through pri-

---

5 For example, health services may be provided as a public service through a mix of public and non-profit organizations financed through various forms of social insurance, as in several European countries, or through a mix of private insurance, social security, and social assistance, as in the US.

vate or cooperative provision through the marketplace. Individuals and communities are not equally endowed with skills, resources, and opportunities or the ability or willingness to take advantage of them.

Governments may respond to public demands for certain opportunities or outcomes to become a right or entitlement of citizenship. These rights may or may not be subject to corresponding obligations or responsibilities, such as the legal obligation of persons receiving Employment Insurance benefits to be available for employment. Contingent rights may be subject to certain qualifications; for instance, employment laws that attempt to balance the rights and responsibilities of employers and employees. Inherent rights shift the burden of economic and social adjustment to other economic actors or to society as a whole.

The idea of fairness or equity is used to justify many forms of government intervention in the economy. Some of these arguments have already been addressed in the discussion of distributive politics including the use of redistributive taxation (**vertical equity**); social insurance and income transfer programs; and taxpayer-financed health, education, and child care services. Other examples include human rights (or anti-discrimination) legislation, systems of regulation that attempt to balance the overlapping or competing interests of various stakeholders, and programs intended to offset or reduce economic disparities between Canada's diverse regions.

The concept of equity is quite elastic and can be applied to a variety of social and economic disparities depending on the capacity of various interests to secure public sympathy or support from governing elites. The disparities in population, wealth, and political power among Canada's regions and provinces have made the pursuit of greater interregional equity a major preoccupation of Canadian politics since Confederation. These concerns are not unique to Canada. Other federal states and multinational associations such as the European Union have institutionalized regional policies as a way of dealing with issues of economic disparity and population mobility.

Similarly, in recent years, there have been significant political debates on the application of equity principles in the marketplace and public policies to the role of women, visible minorities and Aboriginal peoples, the disabled, the elderly, and other groups. These debates often contrast the presuppositions of neo-classical economists, who argue that individuals, not groups, are the principal focus of economic analysis, and welfare economists who place a greater emphasis on the distributive impact of institutions and policies on social groups.

Assisting Adaptation to Structural Economic Changes

The past generation has witnessed a period of almost continuous transformation of the global economy, involving major innovations in business organization and capital markets, the restructuring of existing industries, and the invention of new ones as a result of widespread technological changes and changes in regulatory systems. Such changes have promoted the emergence of new systems of national rules and international agreements to facilitate and manage these trends. Canada's relatively small open economy has been directly affected by these waves of change.

Many government policies during the 1970s and 1980s concentrated on shielding Canadians from the effects of economic adjustment—often in the name of equity or fairness—in the hope than many of these changes would prove temporary. Indexing of tax systems and public benefits were intended to shield the public from many of the effects of inflation. Subsidies to reduce the price of imported oil were financed by taxes on Canadian energy exports, with the difference being financed by higher federal deficits. Generous unemployment insurance benefits helped to subsidize employment in seasonal industries while reducing incentives for the unemployed to move to areas or industries with more stable employment patterns. Ongoing economic stimulus was financed by chronic federal deficits, with current tax revenues barely financing the cost of current services, let alone the rising interest charges on the debt (Hale 2001b: 150-62, 181-90; Green et al. 1994; McMahon 2000a).

The Macdonald Royal Commission appointed by Prime Minister Trudeau to examine these problems recommended a significantly different approach in its 1985 report. It recognized that Canada's economy was caught up in an irreversible process of structural change resulting from growing international economic integration, technological change, and Third World competition for Canada's traditional manufacturing and resource industries. It proposed a series of economic and social policy reforms intended to encourage "adaptation" to economic change, "the efficient allocation of resources," high levels of stable employment, and rising living standards (Canada, Royal Commission on the Economic Union and Development Prospects for Canada, Royal Commission on the Economic Union 1985: Vol. 1: 113-71). Its emphasis on adjustment measures that "facilitate rather than resist" change has become central to the evolution of Canadian economic policies since the late 1980s and has assisted citizens to adapt to these changes through a variety of policy measures (Canada, Royal Commission on the Economic Union 1985: Vol. 1: 242; Canada, Department of Finance 1994a; Canada, Standing Committee on Finance 1999; Hale 2001d). To spur both governments and businesses to accelerate the adjustment process, the commission recommended that Canada negotiate a comprehensive free trade agreement with the US.

Key aspects of structural change during this period included:
- reducing tax and regulatory barriers to international trade and investment through a number of international agreements;
- the balancing of federal and provincial budgets during the 1990s, usually through a mix of higher taxes and spending reductions;
- a reduced emphasis on universal social programs in favour of targeted benefits and benefit-related taxation intended to link economic and social policy goals; and
- the spreading effects of technological change in both Canadian and international economies.

Many of the changes that have taken place since the early 1980s have led more and more economists and other policy-makers to speak of the New Economy—sometimes called the **knowledge-based economy**—as something very different from what has gone before. Canada's trade with the rest of the world is larger than that of any other major industrial country relative to the size of its economy. Exports of goods and services totaled 38.1 per cent of GDP in 2003 (International Trade Canada 2005: 4). The fastest growing sectors during the 1990s were those benefiting from the reduction or elimination of tariffs and other trade barriers under Canada's trade agreements with the US and Mexico (Schwanen 1997; Canada 2001b).

Canada's prosperity, and that of most other major industrial economies, is seen to depend increasingly on the innovation, new technologies, and new ways of doing business in the New Economy driven by evolving information technologies and in more traditional industries; in both areas they are vital to increasing the productivity of labour and capital. These changes are increasing the challenge of international competitiveness and of balancing the demands for economic competitiveness with the needs of governments to maintain political support for their policies.

Facilitating adjustment takes a number of different forms, depending on circumstances and the political and economic outlooks of particular governments. It may involve the reduction or removal of economic or regulatory barriers to market forces, thereby allowing businesses and investors to reallocate resources in the marketplace. Examples include the removal of economic regulations and subsidies on freight rates, reducing ownership restrictions in Canada's financial sector, and opening telecommunications industries to increased competition. Adjustment policies may also involve support for the retraining or relocation of workers whose jobs are affected by industry restructuring or technological change, often in cooperation with industry and union representatives.

Some governments have moved away from relatively hands-on engagement with economic development to a more indirect role in the creation of **framework legislation** that shapes the efficient operations of markets, provides the physical and technological infrastructures necessary for economic expansion, and enables individuals to acquire and apply the skills (human capital) required by the new economy. The arguments used to support increased spending on and incentives for education and skills acquisition link the pursuit of increased economic efficiency with efforts to ensure that more Canadians will share in the benefits of the New Economy (Lipsey 1996; Canada, Standing Committee on Finance 1999; Thomas J. Courchene 2001c).

Others governments have used public policies to promote the development of strategic industries intended to serve as engines of economic growth for regional or national economies. The innovation and technology policies of the federal government and several provinces have reflected a mix of the two approaches in recent years.

Governments, policy-makers, and experts typically attempt to balance these competing demands and objectives by developing, formally or informally, an overall framework for understanding the nature of social and economic activity and government's role in it. These paradigms provide a shared understanding of how the world works and of the realistic policy goals for decision-makers, opinion-shapers, major "stakeholder" groups in the political and economic systems, and citizens as a whole, albeit at very different levels of complexity and understanding. These policies, while varying widely in matters of timing and detail depending on the specific policy preferences of individual governments, reflect the emergence of a new neo-liberal paradigm of government that will be discussed in greater detail in Chapter 5.

Measuring Economic Performance Standards and Benchmarks

In the 1984 US presidential election, incumbent Ronald Reagan asked, "Are you better off than you were four years ago?" So many voters answered with an enthusiastic "yes" that he won a landslide victory. When Reagan was first elected in 1980, the "misery index"—the sum of inflation and unemployment rates—was 20.7 per cent. By the fall of 1984, it had dropped to 11.8 per cent. The degree to which Reagan's policies contributed to the change was long the subject of controversy among economists and partisan commentators. However, the "Great Communicator's" capacity to present voters with relatively complicated economic ideas in simple, easy-to-understand terms did as much for his political prospects as did the US economy's recovery from the recession of 1981-82.

Table 2.2: "Misery Index": Canada and the United States, 1976-2004

	1976	1979	1980	1984	1988	1992	1993	1996	1997	2000	2004	2006*
Inflation (CPI)												
Canada	7.5	9.2	10.2	4.3	4.0	1.5	1.8	1.6	1.6	2.7	1.9	2.2
US	5.8	5.8	11.3	13.5	4.3	4.1	3.0	2.9	2.3	3.4	3.4	2.7
Unemployment												
Canada	7.0	7.5	7.5	11.3	7.3	11.3	11.2	9.7	9.1	6.8	7.2	6.7
US	7.7	5.8	7.2	7.5	5.5	7.5	6.9	5.4	4.9	4.0	5.5	
Total												
Canada	14.5	**16.7**	**17.7**	**15.6**	*11.3*	12.8	**13.0**	11.3	*10.7*	*9.5*	*9.1*	**8.9**
US	**13.5**	17.1	**20.7**	*11.8*	9.6	**10.5**	9.9	8.3	7.2	*7.4*	*8.1*	

* Election in January; data for 2005.
Note: Bold type indicates incumbent government or president defeated in election. Italic type indicates that incumbent government or president was re-elected.
Source: *OECD Economic Observer*, Statistics Canada, US Bureau of Labor Statistics.

Table 2.2 demonstrates that both Canadian governments and US presidents whose terms of office coincided with a rising misery index were turned out of office in six of six elections held under these circumstances between 1976 and 2000. (In this context, President George W. Bush's re-election in 2004 was a significant anomaly.) Those presiding over more positive economic statistics were re-elected in five of six elections during this period. The misery index has long since been replaced by other, more sophisticated measurements of economic performance. However, as noted in the Business Council of British Columbia's devastating comparison of BC's economic performance during the 1990s with that of other provinces, (see Box 2.1) benchmarking has become a widely used and often effective means of promoting increased political accountability for economic performance.

Box 2.1: Highlights of BC's Dismal Decade

BC's ranking within Canada on several key economic performance measures, 1991-2000

- 10th in the growth of real per capita GDP
- 10th in the growth of real fixed business investment
- 10th in export growth
- 10th in economy-wide productivity improvements
- 9th in the growth of real fixed business non-residential investment
- 9th in the growth of pre-tax corporate profits
- 9th in the growth of manufacturing shipments
- 2nd in net job creation
- 1st in population growth

Source: Business Council of British Columbia 2001.

Why Benchmarking?

Several factors have helped to make economic performance standards, or benchmarks, a major factor in the communication of economic policy performance and objectives during the past generation. As noted earlier, voters tend to look to governments to promote economic prosperity and, with it, their own well-being. Benchmarking helps politicians and the media communicate complex economic and social issues in simple terms that can be packaged easily in a newspaper headline or 30-second news clip.

The spread and increasing power of computer technologies has made it easier to process a wide array of economic statistics and to communicate them to a wide audience through the Internet and other electronic media. Both academic economists and policy advocacy groups, or **think tanks**, use economic statistics and indices to communicate their research, policy analyses, and proposals to policy-makers, the media, and the public, sometimes in competition with one another. Some of these analyses are quite sophisticated, drawing on extensive research to establish linkages between particular benchmarks and aspects of economic performance of concern to government.

The use of benchmarks and performance standards serves both political and economic purposes. Governments are making increased use of performance benchmarks to clarify the objectives of their economic policies and to persuade citizens that these policies either have made or will make them better off, both in absolute terms or in comparison with other jurisdictions. Several Canadian governments, following the example of other industrial states, have entrenched fiscal rules and benchmarks, including laws requiring balanced budgets under most circumstances, to discipline their fiscal policies and preserve the sustainability of public services over the medium and longer term (Kennedy and Robbins 2001; OECD 2002).

Growing international economic linkages have increased the visibility and public awareness of comparative economic performance and the factors that contribute to it. For example, federal and provincial governments in Canada regularly publish comparative statistics that seek to demonstrate their economic performance or relative cost structures in comparison with other jurisdictions in Canada, across North America, and around the world. The World Economic Forum, a business-financed think tank, has built a partnership with prominent economists at Harvard University to develop an annual index of international competitiveness using a mixture of hard data and surveys of senior economic decision-makers (Schwab, Porter, and Sachs 2001; see also KPMG 2002). Such alliances between think tanks and prominent academics can often gain considerable credibility with government policy-makers and media commentators, particularly when their analyses are based on solid research and when they avoid overt political or ideological partisanship.

Benchmarking is also used in public administration, both in attempting to set standards against which performance improvements can be measured and as a tangible basis for awarding performance bonuses to senior public servants (Kernaghan, Marson, and Borins 2000: 218-19). Interest groups and think tanks may also use the benchmarking of social and economic statistics as a way of mobilizing public opinion and pressuring governments to take actions on their concerns.

Box 2.2: Why Use Performance Standards?

Governments
- define goals/targets for government/societal action
- mobilize public or bureaucratic support for government policy
- simplify complex issues for public consumption
- obtain (or challenge) performance legitimacy

Interest Groups/Think Tanks
- define goals, demonstrate gaps between actual/potential policy
- mobilize public opinion, prompt government action
- simplify complex issues for public and media consumption
- challenge (or obtain) performance legitimacy of government and/or competing interest group

Conclusion

The role of economic theory is to identify the causes of positive or substandard economic performance and to suggest more effective ways of achieving desired policy objectives. The successful application of economic theories to increase prosperity and mitigate a variety of other economic problems tends to increase political consensus and to create a relatively stable environment for relations among governments, business groups, and other major social interests. Government revenues generated by increased prosperity can be used to address social and economic problems and to limit the degree of political conflict among competing groups in society.

The failure of economic theories, or the policies derived from them, to meet public expectations normally contributes to greater degrees of social and political conflict which, if not adequately resolved, can call into question the foundations of the economic system, the role of government in the economy, and its relations with business. The next chapter examines debates over the power and influence of business in both politics and society.

Key Terms and Concepts for Review (see Glossary)

aggregate demand
automatic stabilizers
capital gains
deadweight loss
economic efficiency
economic neutrality
economic scarcity
fiscal policy
framework legislation
government failure
information asymmetries
Keynesian stabilization policies
knowledge-based economy
macroeconomic policies
market failure
microeconomic policies
monetary policy

negative externalities
Pareto efficiency
performance benchmarks
positive externalities
productivity
public goods
  • pure public goods
  • quasi-public goods
recession
stagflation
structural adjustment policies
sustainability
think tanks
vertical equity

Questions for Discussion and Review

1. What are five major objectives of economic policies in Canada? What are some of the principles used in balancing these objectives? How have these trade-offs contributed to the integration of economic and social policies in recent years?

2. How have changes in economic theory influenced the balance between the use of macroeconomic and microeconomic policies to promote economic growth and stabilization in recent years? How do you think these changes in emphasis might affect relations between business and government?

3. What are three general functions of microeconomic policies? How has the emphasis of Canadian microeconomic policies shifted in response to structural changes in the Canadian and global economies?

4. What is the difference between pure public goods and quasi-public goods? What practical implications for the delivery of public services result from this distinction? Do these distinctions have potential implications for relations between businesses and governments?

5. What is the role of performance benchmarks in economic policy-making? Suggest some reasons that governments—or interest groups—might use benchmarks in their efforts to promote chosen policy preferences.

Suggestions for Further Readings

Banting, Keith, Andrew Sharpe, and France St. Hilaire. 2001. *The review of economic performance and social progress.* Montreal: IRPP.

CSIS Commission on Global Aging. 2001. *Global aging: the challenge of the new millennium.* Washington, DC: Center for Strategic and International Studies (August).

Courchene, Thomas J. 2001. *State of minds: towards a human capital strategy for Canada.* Montreal: IRPP.

Dodge, David. 1998. Reflections on the role of fiscal policy. *Canadian Public Policy* 24(3): 275-89.

Dodge, David. 2002. The interaction between monetary and fiscal policies. *Canadian Public Policy* 28(2): 187-201.

Fortin, Pierre. 1999. *The Canadian standard of living: is there a way up?* Toronto: C.D. Howe Institute (19 October).

Hale, Geoffrey. 2001. *The politics of taxation in Canada.* Peterborough, ON: Broadview Press.

Laidler, David (Ed.). 1985. *Approaches to economic well-being.* Background Paper 26, Royal Commission on the Economic Union and Development Prospects for Canada. Toronto: University of Toronto Press.

Lipsey, Richard. 1996. *Economic growth, technological change, and Canadian economic policy.* Toronto: C.D. Howe Institute (November).

Mintz, Jack M. 2001. *Most favored nation: building a framework for smart economic policy.* Toronto: C.D. Howe Institute.

Rao, Someshwar, and Andrew Sharpe (Eds.). 2002. *Productivity issues in Canada.* Industry Canada Research Series. Calgary: University of Calgary Press.

Strick, John C. 1994. *The economics of government regulation: theory and Canadian practice.* Toronto: Thompson Educational Publishing.

Strick, John C. 1999. *The public sector in Canada: programs, finance and policy.* Toronto: Thompson Educational Publishing.

World Economic Forum. Annual. *Global competitiveness report.* New York: Oxford University Press.

CHAPTER 3

Sources and Limits of Business Influence:
Theories of Business-Government Relations

One of the major controversies in the study of political economy in general, and that of business-government relations in particular, is the role of corporate power in shaping both specific government decisions and the broader context of public policy. The concept of corporate power is a disputed one that reflects competing ideas of democracy, the nature and role of class solidarity, and power in the process. These disputes are echoed in debates over the degree to which governments should exercise control over economic decision-making. Differing assessments of the capacity of governments, businesses, or citizens to exercise political or economic power also depend significantly on the level of analysis used to measure and interpret the application of these concepts.

The intensity of this debate may have declined somewhat in recent years as Canada's political and economic systems have adapted to the tumultuous changes occasioned by the effects of economic globalization, along with the negotiation and extension of North American and international trade agreements. These changes include the dismantling of the nationalist and protectionist policies of the Trudeau years; large-scale changes to corporate structures, capital, and labour markets; the systematic efforts by governments of all political stripes to balance their budgets; the parallel restructuring of social policies; and Canada's growing integration within the North American economy.

The broad direction of these changes has enjoyed the general and often enthusiastic support of Canada's business community, both large and small, whatever their criticisms of specific policy decisions or priorities may be. However, these trends have also prompted some groups to charge that they are part of a broader corporate agenda intended to transform the nature of Canadian society, dismantle or severely restrict the welfare state, and limit the role of political decision-making in the economy (McQuaig 1996; Rice and Prince 2000). The cumulative effect has been to reinforce certain elements of what Atkinson and Coleman have described as Canada's "firm-centred industry culture" and its emphasis on:

- the "self-sufficiency" of individual businesses and the capacity of most business sectors to function without direct state interference or support in the economic marketplace;
- the "independence of management in making decisions on investment and workplace organization" as opposed to legislated provisions for union participation as in some European countries;

- limits on the intrusion of politics into economic decision-making, even though the legal framework for economic activity is frequently a by-product of political decisions and trade-offs (Atkinson and Coleman 1989: 32-33).

As noted in Chapters 1 and 2, Canadian governments frequently seek public approval and re-election based on their ability to promote economic prosperity, much of which is dependent on private businesses for job creation, investment, and economic growth. Some scholars argue that this process results in an "autonomous," "privileged," or "dominant" position for business within the political system. They assume that the politicization of economic decision-making based on an authoritative state is or should be normative; that is, it should be the ideal standard on which real world behaviour is based (Clement 1975; Coleman 1988: 261-65; Carroll 1986; Atkinson and Coleman 1989: 32-52).

This attitude of presumptive hostility to business and most forms of capitalism is challenged by neo-liberal and neo-conservative political writers whose concept of democracy is based on the idea of limited government, authoritative within its own sphere, but leaving a wide range of freedom and discretion to individual economic and social behaviour (Hayek 1973; Nisbet 1975; Ellul 1979). It distinguishes between the concepts of governance, which provides for a decentralization of political and economic decision-making based on loosely shared and reciprocal norms of behaviour and a wide range of relative autonomy, and government, which is a formal framework for authoritative legal action (Rosenau 1992: 4).

An empirical analysis of government involvement in the economy suggests that while the influence of neo-liberal ideas over government policy and public opinion has grown demonstrably in Canada since the 1980s, the Canadian state has scarcely withered into a shadow of its former self. The proportion of Canada's national income assigned to government revenues at all levels actually increased from 39.5 per cent in 1985, the first full year after the Mulroney government took office, to 42.9 per cent in 1990 and 43.7 per cent in 2000 before subsiding to 40.4 per cent in 2004. During the same period, total government spending declined somewhat from 45.9 per cent in 1985 to 40.5 per cent in 2000 and 38.9 per cent in 2004, although at the peak of the 1990-92 recession, it did reach the unprecedented peacetime level of 52.1 per cent (Statistics Canada 2002b: Cat. #11-010, 3, 12, 13; 2004 data based on Statistics Canada 2005c; author's calculations). These changes reflect a more strategic role for the federal government and the steady growth of provincial spending relative to overall public spending as well as a renewed commitment to balanced budgets by most governments, regardless of nominal political ideology.

These figures—along with the sizeable expansion of social regulations limiting the autonomy of businesses (and others) during the 1980s and 1990s[1]—suggest that

---

1 Studies by the Fraser Institute suggest that while the rate of new regulatory initiatives has declined during the 1990s, the number and costs of administering government regulations remains significantly above the levels of the 1980s (Jones and Graf 2001: Table 15).

the Canadian state is alive, well, and very much involved in the lives, social opportunities, and economic decisions of its citizens, whatever the undeniable reality of business influence within the political system. However, the role of corporate influence within Canada's political system and the effects of ongoing changes in Canada's economic system on the choices available to governments and citizens remain a matter of widespread public debate and, for some, bitter alienation from the entire political system.

This chapter addresses the nature of power and the factors that contribute to and limit the exercise of business power within Canada's political system. It examines several prominent theories used to describe or predict the exercise of power within society and their application within Canada. Finally, it considers the role of small business in Canada's political and economic system and its role in both reinforcing and diffusing the power of business groups.

The Problem of Power

A central question in democratic political theory addresses the capacity of citizens to translate their goals and policy preferences into the decisions and priorities of governments and other decision-making elites and to manage conflicting norms, interests, and preferences in ways that serve the public good. This capacity is directly related to the problem of power—the ability of some groups, either within society or the state, to enforce their policy preferences at the expense of others, even in the face of strong public opposition.

This section outlines four broad concepts used to define and assess the effectiveness of power inside and outside government. First are **outcome manifestations**: the capacity of a political actor to affect or change political outcomes and to impose one's policy preferences on an otherwise unwilling political system or to prevent policy outcomes that conflict with one's own interests, even when such outcomes may enjoy broad political support. The second—**process manifestations**—examines a number of ways in which groups can use the policy process to serve their own interests, both in cooperation and competition with other social or governmental interests (Stanbury 1988). The terms **structural power** and **intellectual power** are used to describe the ways in which different social groups, including businesses, can make their own interests, values, and ideas central factors in defining or redefining the public interest.

The level of analysis used to measure and assess the exercise of power or the capacity of different individuals and groups to make autonomous decisions may have a significant effect on the findings of research into the exercise of political or economic power. Scholars of public policy have identified at least four different levels at which power may be exercised through institutions and regimes, although there is significant disagreement on the use of terminology and boundaries. The organization and regulation of political and economic activity may be analyzed in the context of international systems, national or regional structures (with the latter having somewhat greater significance in Canada), framework or society-wide systems of rules governing particular forms of social or economic organization, and sectoral regimes in which the scope for exercising power may be relatively narrow but deep (Doern et al. 1999: 8-12).

The interrelationship of different regimes may increase or decrease the scope for independent action or the exercise of autonomous powers by governments, businesses, and other societal actors. Although political, legal, economic, and social systems may be designed to provide greater or lesser degrees of freedom to individuals and organizations, the complexity of social and economic organization often leads to very different outcomes than those initially anticipated by policy-makers.

Outcome Manifestations

A key expression of power is the relative degree of autonomy possessed by individuals or groups in obtaining desired political outcomes. Nordlinger has noted that government officials frequently possess a considerable degree of autonomy (or independence) from the policy preferences of societal actors, including the owners and managers of businesses.

Autonomy may take the form of shaping policy outcomes through direct political action in ways that are effectively beyond the control of other political actors. These outcomes may coincide with or differ significantly from those desired by other political actors (Nordlinger 1981). Major expressions of policy autonomy outlined by Stanbury include:

- the ability to initiate and have implemented on a regular basis policy actions that are strongly opposed by other major policy players;
- the ability to obstruct or veto policy actions that otherwise have wide support;
- the ability of a group to alter (or reverse) a well-established policy that is seen to work to its disadvantage—even if it is satisfactory to most others—often by changing the terms of debate;
- the ability to determine the outcome of elections by shifting one's support for one party to another (Stanbury 1988).

Successfully Ignoring Public/Societal Opinion

The most visible form of political power is the ability of political actors to force governments and/or other parts of society to accommodate or accept their policy agendas or to successfully defy a political consensus adverse to their interests or political preferences.

Government officials can be said to wield this kind of political power by refusing to translate societal preferences—the consensus of public opinion or politically active citizens—into public policy or by taking action in clear defiance of public opinion (Nordlinger 1981: 29). Business groups may be said to exercise effective power when they force governments to change their agendas to conform to those reflecting a consensus of the business community.

In Canada, examples of this kind of state autonomy are not hard to find. The Mulroney government's decision to force through the introduction of the Goods and Services Tax (GST), despite the opposition of as many as 88 per cent of Canadians in published opinion polls, may have been a contributing factor to its electoral defeat three years later. But this did not prevent government officials from keeping the GST in place, despite the election of a Liberal government pledged to replace it (see Hale 2001b: Chapter 8). During the 1990s, large segments of public opinion were strongly resistant to many specific spending cuts introduced by governments, even while accepting the general need for overall spending budgetary constraints.

Successful business challenges to governmental authority occur periodically when governments retreat from proposed policy changes in the face of concerted business lobbying, which usually concentrates on issues of substantially greater interest to business groups than to the general public. Examples of such retreats include proposed tax reforms in 1969-71 and 1981-83; the failure of proposed reforms to competition policies in 1971-75; and, to some extent, the National Energy Program of 1980-85, although the latter also prompted strong opposition from provincial governments (Hale 2001b: Chapters 6, 8; Stanbury 1977; Doern and Toner 1985). However, governments' dependence on private economic actors to finance ongoing investment and job creation limits the degree to which governments in largely capitalist societies can challenge the fundamental interests—as opposed to particular policy preferences—of business without running the risks of major economic disruptions and the possible loss of political power.

The mere existence of converging or compatible political agendas between business and government may or may not reflect an exercise of power. Senior government decision-makers may have come to similar conclusions either through being predisposed to the recommendations of business groups, rational policy analysis of their own, or calculations of mutual advantage to be gained through cooperation with business groups. Such decisions may suggest that business groups possess extensive influence but do not necessarily point to the exercise of business power in the sense of autonomous and irresponsible political decision-making. The capacity of governments to resist many of the political preferences of organized business groups and large corporations while accommodating others suggests a more complex pattern of political and economic relationships.

The capacity to impose or obstruct policy change depends on several factors. These include the degree of consensus among policy elites or the degree to which one group of political actors can exploit divisions among the others to achieve their objectives. When elites are divided, the effective exercise of power often depends on the relative capacity of competing groups to mobilize public opinion, to exploit the policy process to achieve an effective stalemate, or to persist in the incremental adaptation of policy objectives until their internal logic becomes persuasive to other groups. The relative capacity of governments, businesses, and other political and social actors to exercise this form of power may also depend on the relative complexity of issues at stake, the number and cohesion of stakeholders, and the relative abilities of stakeholders to use the policy process to their advantage.

Controlling the Fine Print

Another more subtle form of autonomy or power suggested by Nordlinger is the capacity of state actors to pursue their own preferences in detail at times when there is a convergence on general policy objectives between governments and societal interests (Nordlinger 1981: 74-98). Public opinion and many societal interests are often blissfully ignorant of the details of policy implementation. As a result, governments, sometimes working with other interests, are able to implement policies in ways that further their own interests or preferences. In so doing, they may also create precedents or conditions conducive to favourable policy decisions in the future. The capacity to influence or control the fine print of policy implementation is usually the privilege of policy professionals inside government and of institutionalized interest groups that have preferred access to the policy process as recognized and often respected stakeholders in those decisions.

Particular business interest groups may or may not enjoy preferred access to government policy-makers when specific policies are under discussion. However, over time, business groups may often develop relationships of mutual respect and trust with government officials that enable them to influence the fine print to accommodate their interests in ways consistent with the government's broad policy goals. This process is particularly evident in the design of technical tax legislation of particular interest to certain industry sectors and in the drafting and modification of regulations in many areas (Hale 2001b: 120-23; Atkinson and Coleman 1989). Thus, the network of professional relationships established by members of business groups inside and outside government can play a significant role in the technical aspects of economic policy-making. This process-oriented approach to government policy-making will be discussed in greater detail in Chapter 11.

Changing the Terms of Debate: Intellectual Power

Another form of independent power or autonomy is the capacity to shift the terms of public debate over time so that adverse public opinion—or that of organized social groups—gradually conforms to the policy preferences of major state or other political actors. This result can be accomplished by persuasion or through the co-opting of societal actors in various ways so that the grounds for their opposition are either removed or conciliated. Governments may also use their control over the policy process to introduce a series of incremental changes that, over time, create their own rationality, momentum, or sense of inevitability while marginalizing other policy options. Several scholars have documented these trends in analyzing broader shifts in fiscal and economic policies during the 1980s and 1990s (Hale 2001b; Lewis 2003).

The ability to shape public policy debate is closely related to the capacity to shape or use underlying assumptions and values related to particular policies. These may involve the broad social or political environment for a particular policy, structural issues related to the appropriate organization of a particular activity or economic sector, the goals and objectives of specific policies, or the particular practices that should translate these goals into actions and outcomes.

There is little doubt that business groups have the capacity to influence public and/or governmental opinion and the policy process in order to help shift a policy consensus in ways favourable to themselves. In some cases, the policy changes of the past 20 years have followed shifts of governmental opinion that have preceded or led public opinion. This influence may be exercised directly, through the actions and networking activities of business groups, or indirectly, either through the actions of policy advocacy groups, or think tanks, whose intellectual or ideological outlooks reflect or complement those of organized business interests, or by affecting changes to the agendas of political parties.[2]

However, the political effectiveness of think tanks (and indirectly of business and other interest groups) in exercising intellectual power is usually subject to two major conditions. First, government policy-makers must be willing to engage and endorse their ideas both in the ways in which they may define policy problems and opportunities and the measures they suggest as solutions to those problems (Hall 1989; Abelson 2002).

Secondly, they must pass the test of public opinion. Politicians, journalists, and other opinion shapers should be able to popularize proposed policy ideas so that they are not only plausible to the average voter but also able to withstand the scrutiny and challenges of competing interests which may also have the ability to influence public opinion (Hall 1989: 370-86). After all, other political and bureaucratic actors may seek to exercise **countervailing power** by appealing for public support for alternative policies that offer potential benefits to a broader cross-section of society or by undermining the credibility of proposed changes through appeals to strongly held values and interests.

The negotiation of free trade with the US and the decision of federal and provincial governments to confront their budget deficits aggressively during the early 1990s, rather than just complaining about them, are two examples of major policy changes in which governments actively sought to persuade public opinion to accept positions consistent with the policy preferences of business. However, serious students of public policy have questioned whether these policy shifts may not have owed as much to internal policy shifts or turf battles within governments as to the influence of business (Doern and Tomlin 1991; Greenspon and Wilson-Smith 1996; Savoie 1999; Lewis 2003). In other cases, public opinion has forced governments to reverse their policies, sometimes in conjunction with business preferences, sometimes in ways sharply at variance with them.

The challenge of demonstrating the role and extent of business power in such situations is to isolate cause and effect in situations when government policy-mak-

---

2 For two contrasting approaches to the role of policy advocacy groups or think tanks, see Abelson and Carberry 1998 and Carroll and Shaw 2001.

ers (or public opinion) may respond to a number of different factors, including business influence but not limited to it.

Process Manifestations of Power

All citizens and societal interests enjoy the right to participate in the decision-making processes of government to some extent. However, the ability to influence the policy process depends on several factors:

- the willingness of governments to provide access to different parts of that process;
- the ability of particular groups to make their voices heard;
- the resources available to different groups to participate effectively;
- the willingness of government policy-makers to take their positions or suggestions actively into consideration; and
- the timing (and extent) of their participation.

Effective Access to Resources

All sorts of groups, including business groups, are formed regularly to influence governments directly or indirectly. Businesses possess a number of advantages when attempting to influence government policy, particularly when compared to ordinary citizens, who usually lack the time, knowledge, and other resources to engage the policy process except on a limited range of issues within their own communities.

Many businesses are already members of existing associations, thus reducing the start-up costs of identifying and mobilizing supporters in large numbers. As they frequently have a significant financial interest in the effects of government decisions, they are more likely to invest in the process of monitoring and influencing these decisions than are most private citizens. Their financial resources, while limited and subject to numerous demands, are often more extensive than those of many other groups. Networking, timely cooperation, and the pooling of resources among different groups can expand the resources available to smaller groups at the cost of having to negotiate common ground with others whose interests may vary in detail from their own. In some policy areas, leading members of business groups may also have personal and professional connections with senior government decision-makers that enable them to voice their concerns directly, rather than through intermediaries.

The complexity of the policy process and the difficulties faced by most outsiders in dealing with it have created a growing range of business opportunities for specialized government relations consultants and professional lobbyists to market their services as intermediaries between businesses, interest groups, and governments. The perceived need that many businesses and business associations feel to retain such advisors in their dealings with government—whether for offensive or defensive purposes—is as much a comment on the relative power of business groups within the political system as the fact that they may possess the resources to invest in professional lobbying services.

Consultation: Real or Symbolic?

Most governments have greatly extended their formal consultation processes in recent years as part of the broader process of managing and legitimizing changes to policies and programs.

Consultations may occur as part of a serious discussion with interest group stakeholders and citizens about the options facing governments in a particular policy area. Alternately, they may be little more than a pro-forma or symbolic exercise intended to demonstrate that a public sector organization has asked for public input on something it intends to do anyway or, perhaps, as a trial balloon to test the waters for possible action. These issues are addressed at length in Chapter 12.

The professionalism, priorities, and relative commitment of interest groups to influencing particular policy decisions are important factors in determining whether their interaction with parliamentarians and government officials is mainly a formality or whether it succeeds in engaging the attention of policy-makers.

Status within the Policy Community

The influence of business and other interest groups in the policy process often depends on whether they are recognized by policy-makers as important stakeholders in the outcomes of existing or proposed policies whose interests and concerns must be addressed, as problems or obstacles to be overcome to achieve government objectives, or as marginal (or even irrelevant) actors whose views can be safely ignored.

Certain business groups may be natural stakeholders in economic policy decisions that affect them directly or on issues of social regulation where their cooperation is useful in enabling government officials to reach their objectives without causing unnecessary disruption or political conflict. However, in many cases, achieving this status requires extended effort along with the capacity to build relationships and to offer something of value to decision-makers who may need to balance a variety of interests inside and outside government to reach their goals.

The number of organized business associations, their capacity to specialize in particular areas, and their collective capacity to pool resources in order to adapt to changing government structures and political circumstances give business groups the collective capacity to access governments at many different points. While this does not guarantee a hearing, let alone desired outcomes, it does demonstrate the potential to exercise influence and power when these resources are used effectively.

Timing of Access to the Policy Process

Networking and institutional resources can also enable business and other interest groups to exercise greater influence over a policy decision by virtue of the timing of their intervention. However, the capacity to obtain access to the policy process does not necessarily imply the capacity to control it or to consistently achieve desired policy outcomes.

Government officials can use a number of techniques to control the degree of access enjoyed by business and other interest groups to the policy process. These include the management of information, the timing of decisions of when to go public with intended policy changes or actual decisions, and the capacity to shape consultation processes, as well as the evaluation of feedback received from stakeholders and citizens. As a result, the influence of business groups varies with the structure and relative openness of decision-making processes, the number of competing interests with effective access to the process, and the ability of interest groups to build effective coalitions with potential allies inside and outside government. These processes will be addressed in greater detail in Chapter 11.

The minority of business groups whose interests are institutionalized within the policy process use this advantage to get a head start on potential competitors in influencing policy choices. However, relatively few business groups have the capacity to challenge other institutionalized interests on their own turf unless they are prepared to invest the time, money, effort, and professional resources to assemble a coalition capable of exercising countervailing power.

Ability to Control Process

Groups whose interests are institutionalized within the policy process may be able to influence or control it to the extent that their views, values, and priorities are shared by those responsible for particular policy decisions. The greater the degree of technical specialization and the greater the degree to which governments depend on societal interests (including but not limited to business) to design and/or implement specialized policies and programs the greater the degree to which those groups may be able to control the policy process.

Outsider groups, including many representing selected business interests, usually lack the awareness of process necessary to contest policy insiders or the professional resources needed to meet them on their own terms. However, this does not prevent them from attempting to publicize and politicize an issue in order to persuade politicians and the general public that the so-called experts have lost sight of some important part of the public interest. The cultivation of the news media may enable groups without institutional resources to offset their lack of process expertise, although it is not a guarantee of favourable outcomes in any policy conflict.

Structural Power

A fourth form of power, which may be reflected in the other three, is structural power: the capacity, over time, of a group to make its interests and values part of the normal environment guiding the political, economic, and social systems, thereby implicitly reinforcing or marginalizing certain ideas of the public interest. A group may be said to enjoy structural power when its underlying interests, values, participation, and support are significant elements in the consideration and evaluation of a policy structure or policy changes.

In any economic system characterized by private ownership and control of the means of production, business groups will enjoy a significant measure of structural power, particularly if governments lack the means or the popular support to foster alternative approaches to creating employment, generating investment, and promoting economic growth (Gellner 1986: 301). Whether this power constitutes unfair privilege, as suggested by Coleman (1988) and others, will depend largely on whether it is conferred by government favour on a select few or whether it reflects a widespread societal consensus that those citizens most directly affected by government decisions should have a right to participate, directly or indirectly, in the process of making them.

There is little question that businesses, as a whole, enjoy considerable structural power within a political and economic system in which economic growth and widespread material affluence play a vital role in the election and re-election of governments and in the policy decisions that contribute to the governments' ability to secure and maintain public support.

The existence of business structural power within the political system is quite compatible with a democratic political system if it can be shown to serve the interests and policy preferences of a majority of citizens or if governments can also accommodate the legitimate claims of competing social interests through the policy process. However, when that power is translated into policy decisions that align governments against a majority of public opinion or that actively disregard the interests of large segments of society, such actions strike at the heart of democratic government as an exercise of power by the consent of the governed.

Theories of Political Influence and Competition

Political theory is important to the analysis of business-government relations at several levels. At an *empirical* level, it attempts to describe how the political system, the interactions between political and economic decision-making, and the ways in which the preferences of particular interests and social groups are (or are not) reflected in political decision-making actually work. At a *normative* level, it addresses the relationship between the actual functioning of political and economic systems and broader concepts or ideals of the public good which reflect the observer's moral, intellectual, or ideological commitments. Such theories may attempt to justify or challenge existing institutions, practices, and priorities. At a *prescriptive* level, political theories may suggest ways of narrowing the gap between the actual and potential performance of political and economic systems in serving both interests and values of society as a whole and those of particular social and economic interests. Different approaches to the study of political theory tend to emphasize the role of economic factors, societal and elite influences, and state preferences as decisive factors in shaping the options available to political actors and the decisions they take.

Competing analyses of political systems and power relations also reflect different contexts and methodologies of analysis ranging from grand political theories (or meta-analysis), which attempt to provide a coherent, unified analysis of political, economic, and social relations, to theoretical analyses applied to the operation of particular policy systems at a national, regional, specialized sectoral, or local level. Some theories that may be persuasive at one level fail the test of empirical (fact-based) analysis at another.

A number of political and social theories have emerged in response to these questions. The following section will address the implications of six broad schools of thought. Elite, class-based, and pluralist theories tend to emphasize the role of social forces and structures and their influence on the state. These approaches have been challenged in recent years by statist, corporatist, and public choice analyses that consider ways of balancing or reconciling group interests with a broader vision of the public interest.

Elite Theories

Elite theories tend to emphasize the dominance of society by a ruling class minority, which exercises effective power over a large majority of citizens who have little or no influence over major political decisions. Elites are defined as those capable of exercising substantial power and influence over the public and over political outcomes (Etzioni-Halevy 1997: xxv) through the exercise of economic power, control over organizations, or the ability to mobilize public support. The leadership of elites is normal in any form of social organization, even those purporting to represent and serve the interests of the masses (Michel: 243-50).

Classical elite theory contrasts the formally competitive world of democratic elections with what it portrays as the *oligarchic* rule of a relatively closed, relatively cohesive political class. It emphasizes the distinctive character of the ruling class as an identifiable group within society, its capacity for self-preservation in the face of social and political change, and the distinctiveness of its interests from those of the vast majority of politically disengaged citizens. Meisel summarizes this approach in his "three C's" formula: "group consciousness, coherence and conspiracy" (Meisel 1962: 16; Mosca 1939; Mills 1956).

Alternately, elite pluralists emphasize the diversity of political elites as representatives of different social and economic interests among the population. They view political competition as a contest among elites for a share in government or an increased capacity to influence the terms of public debate. Political competition is seen as the "contest for control ... not between the many and the few but between one elite and another" (Meisel 1965: 2; Porter 1965; Sartori 1987; Etzioni-Halevy 1993; Abelson and Carberry 1998). The evidence for these competing outlooks may vary from one country and historical era to another.

Traditional elite theory emphasizes the capacity of a relatively narrow segment of society, characterized by shared ties of kinship, class, education, and economic interest, to dominate the senior ranks of a society's major power centres, including the leadership of the state, the military, an established church, and major economic institutions. Porter notes that "a system of privilege exists where higher occupational levels are preserved, or tend to be preserved, for certain social groups" (Porter 1965: xi). The idea of an oligarchic ruling class initially derived from analyses of European societies dominated by aristocratic and plutocratic elites in the late nineteenth and early twentieth century by European sociologists, including Gaetano Mosca, Vilfredo Pareto and Robert Michels, and by later American followers such as C. Wright Mills and William Domhoff.

Mosca identified two strata within the ruling class: one comprising the official rulers; the other, much larger, composed of the executive class which transmits, communicates, and mediates their orders to the ruled masses. Pareto shared this concept of upper classes as an elite subdivided into "governing and non-governing elites" (Meisel 1965: 6; Bottomore 1964: 2). In this view, elite cohesion tends to take priority over competition among its factions, particularly when it faces significant challenges to its authority or dominance. Evidence of this phenomenon in contemporary Canada may be adduced from the usually hostile reaction of much of Canada's upper middle classes to various expressions of populism, as reflected in the columns of major media outlets such as the *Globe and Mail* or the CBC, even as they disagree on particular policies or priorities in other areas.

Mosca acknowledged that counter-elites may emerge from ruled classes, especially when the communication gap between rulers and ruled becomes too wide. The dominant elite may preserve its position and adapt to changing circumstances by co-opting talented members of dissident movements or by using the tools of democratic competition and the provision of improved social benefits to appeal for mass support without changing the basic composition of social and economic relations. Under such circumstances, elections are often seen as contests among factions of the ruling class—pluralistic on the surface, but involving few real divisions on fundamental issues (Mosca 1939: 154; Schumpeter 1942: 269-83).

Pareto conceptualized the idea of the "circulation of elites"—the concept that social elites either renew themselves by co-opting or sharing power with the most capable and distinguished members of the lower classes or that they are likely to lose power to competing elites who are more effective in representing or competing for the support of other social groups. This outlook perceives elections as competitions between in and out group elites for popular support (Meisel 1965: 11-13; Pareto, cited in Meisel 1965: 35-36).

Elite theorists often emphasize the distinction between the attitudes and interests of the ruling classes and those who are subject to their rule and are sceptical of the capacity of elites to represent the interests of ordinary citizens. Critiques of political inequality can lead to the development of class-based systems of political or social analysis. They may also contribute to pluralist efforts to divide power among competing social and economic groups or to populist arguments targeted at any concentration of power exercised at the expense of the average citizen (Clement and Myles 1994: 91-115).

Socialist and populist writers tend to point to the concentration of economic power and the close relationships between political and economic elites to suggest that a high degree of elite cohesion exists in Canadian political and economic life. This suggests the conclusion that politicians, civil servants, and the knowledge elites of academia and the mass media are either instruments or conscious agents of a corporate agenda intended to extend its own power at the expense of the majority of ordinary citizens (Parker 1972; Lewis 1972; Clement 1975; Clement 1983; McQuaig 1987).[3] Populist writers of a more individualist orientation may challenge the perceived exploitation of ordinary citizens by statist or state-dependent elites, corporate elites, or both.

The concept of a ruling elite capable of monopolizing decision-making power to the exclusion of other social groups is a direct challenge to democratic political theory. Effective democracy depends on the willingness of a significant cross-section of citizens "to participate freely in supervising and controlling the temporary rulers and to bring them to account" (Friedrich, cited in Meisel 1965: 179). It may also depend on the willingness of decision-making elites to trust the public's capacity for informed judgement enough to accept checks on the autonomous use of their power (Bell 1992: 3-37). However, alternative analyses have emerged which present different perspectives on elite behaviour in contemporary society.

Elite Pluralism

Theories of **elite pluralism** differ from traditional theories of elite cohesion in emphasizing the diversity and relative decentralization of elites, based on their different functions in society and their respective spheres of competence. They assert that social institutions such as governments, major corporations, the judiciary, organized labour, the mass media, academia, and large voluntary organizations exercise a considerable degree of autonomy in their operations. As a result, institutional elites both compete and cooperate with one another for influence, access to resources, and decision-making autonomy. Efforts of one group to encroach upon the prerogatives of another are likely to prompt resistance and the search for allies to check or reverse this encroachment (Bottomore 1964: 9-13; Porter 1965: 201-15; Etzioni-Halevy 1993: 60-61).

Theorists of elite pluralism—or democratic elite theory, as it is also known—typically contend that government *by* the people is impossible in practice and that the principles of democracy are satisfied when positions of power are open in principle to everyone. Other conditions for effective democratic participation include electoral competition for political power and effective means for making those holding political power answerable for their actions. Political competition, the separation of power among political, bureaucratic, and judicial elites, and the countervailing power of other political groups may effectively limit the centralization of power, even if they do not result in popular sovereignty in most political decisions. While political elites

---

3 For a conservative populist perspective, see Bell 1992.

may limit the unaccountable power of economic elites, limits on the role of political decision-making in economic or social life are seen as necessary to ensure the freedom and autonomy of individual citizens and other social groups (Schumpeter 1942: 289-96; Bottomore 1964: 10-12; Sartori 1987: 145-56; Etzioni-Halevy 1993: 55-60).

Porter (1965) noted at least six distinct sets of institutional elites in Canadian society in the late 1950s, before the rapid growth of the modern Canadian state. These included economic, political, bureaucratic, labour, media, and ideological elites. The latter two groups are sometimes described as information and cultural elites (see Box 3.1).

Arguably, the diversity of most elite networks has grown significantly during the past 40 years, offsetting the centralization of political power within senior levels of government and the effects of economic liberalization on relations between business and government (Ornstein 1998). Canada's relatively decentralized system of federalism has also provided opportunities for policy innovation and the exercise of countervailing powers between federal and provincial governments (Breton 1985). New centres of autonomous institutional power that have emerged in the judiciary and in competing networks of policy advocacy provide checks on the arbitrary exercise of power by other groups and outlets for competing and dissenting policy ideas.

Box 3.1: Mapping Canadian Elites

Institutional Power
- Prime ministers; provincial premiers; former prime ministers and premiers; senior political advisors to prime ministers, premiers, and former premiers in major provinces.
- Senior cabinet ministers and former cabinet ministers in the federal government and larger provinces.
- Supreme Court justices, chief justices of provincial courts of appeal, and long-serving heads of major quasi-judicial agencies and tribunals.
- Senior public servants with extended experience at upper levels of federal and provincial civil services.
- Current and former chief executive officers (CEOs) of major Crown corporations and public sector agencies.
- Long-serving executives of major public sector institutions, such as Crown corporations, major educational institutions, hospitals, etc.

Economic Power
- Long-serving CEOs of Canada's 100-200 largest corporations.
- Senior investment managers of major financial institutions, especially those capable of mobilizing shifts in market power or international currency values.
- Heads of major unions, especially those representing the majority of workers in major industries.
- Leaders of major economic interest groups, especially those representing industries critical to major national or regional economic interests.

Information Elites

Mass Media

- Senior executives of major national or regional newspaper chains, such as Can-West, Torstar, Quebecor/Sun Media, Power Corporation.
- Major urban newspaper editors and producers of national radio and television networks capable of agenda-setting through selection (or suppression) of leading stories and who are responsible for hiring and firing commentators who interpret news to the broader public.

Think Tanks

- Specialized bodies that commission, finance, publish, and publicize research that influence national and regional policy agendas over time, for example, C.D. Howe Institute, Caledon Institute on Social Policy, Institute for Research on Public Policy, Conference Board of Canada.

Academic

- University presidents and senior members of university faculties through their capacity to set agendas for academic funding, research, and promotion (including distribution of funds through granting councils).
- University presidents and senior members of university faculties through their influence on institutional leaders, think-tanks, and the media.

Cultural Elites

- Publishers and public and private funding bodies which finance and distribute books, movies, music, art, and other cultural products.
- Best-selling authors on serious subjects.
- Cultural celebrities or icons who succeed in using their status to promote or oppose particular values and objectives.

A central critique of elite theories, whether these emphasize elite cohesion or competition, is that they tend to downplay the role of class differences and distinctions in the exercise of political and economic power.

Class-Based Theories

Class-based theories of politics stress the role of economic and class interests in shaping political and economic institutions and choices and of class conflict based on inequality of income, wealth, and power as a defining element of political debate. Some of these theories, particularly those derived from various aspects of **Marxism**, provide a radical critique of capitalist societies aimed at discrediting both the theory and practice of capitalism and suggesting various approaches to the creation of worker or state control of the means of production. Social democratic variants of Marxist analyses tend to emphasize the creation of countervailing systems of power to balance and constrain the power of capital through a mixture of state ownership, government regulation, and worker participation in management and policy-making. Non-Marxist approaches, such as those of the early twentieth-century German sociologist Max Weber, distinguish between class, with its economic basis, and status—distinctions in social honour which both influence the life choices available to members of social and occupational groups and which are often the "basis of political and economic power" (Gerth and Mills 1958: 184-94).

According to Marx and his disciples, the economic structure of production and the relationship of individuals and groups to the means of production are fundamental to social relationships and the exercise of political and economic power. For such theorists, politics in early capitalist societies, including Canada's, reflect the efforts of capitalists—the owners of business enterprises—to secure direct or indirect control over the state in order to serve their economic interests (such critiques are not limited to Marxists; see Myers 1968). The capitalist pursuit of profits comes at the expense of other social interests—employees or wage earners, who are exploited for the surplus value of their labour; and small, independent producers, such as farmers or tradesman, whose capacity to earn an independent living is constrained by the capitalist accumulation of capital. This is exacerbated by the tactics used to expand market share and profits. Large-scale production facilities alienate workers from the value of their labour, force small-scale producers out of business and into a status of economic dependence as employees, and centralize control over a disproportionate share of national wealth and economic power in the hands of a relatively small clique of monopoly capitalists whose interests are fundamentally in conflict with those of the working class.

This analysis anticipated the emergence of large industrial corporations during the Second Industrial Revolution in Europe and North America between 1870 and 1930. A wave of industrial consolidation resulted in the emergence of a handful of dominant corporations in many major industries and an unprecedented centralization of economic power in the hands of big business and its political representatives (for a discussion of this process in Canada, see Carroll 1986 and Marchildon 1996). This concentration of corporate ownership has led to charges of monopoly capitalism, despite the steady turnover in the ranks of major corporations due to technological change, the breakup or bankruptcy of some companies, the emergence of others through the capitalist process of creative destruction, and the gradual opening of most of the Canadian economy to increased foreign competition (Clement 1986; for a very different interpretation, see Newman 1999).

The pursuit of increased business efficiency increases the exploitation of subordinate classes. These groups, in turn, organize to protect and promote their interests through collective action, both through the creation of strong industrial unions and by seeking to exercise democratic control over business activities through the political process.

Lenin contended that the process of domestic business consolidation would lead to increased levels of foreign investment and the emergence of global corporations that would extend patterns of domestic exploitation into international markets. Both Marxist and non-Marxist theorists have emphasized the role of international capitalism in creating an environment of dependence in underdeveloped economies. Frontier societies tend to depend on outside capital for the development of the staple agricultural and resource industries that provide the initial basis for economic development and for the construction of transportation links necessary to carry their production to distant markets. Dependence on staple exports makes small producers vulnerable to the vagaries of prices set in international markets and to the political influence of capitalists and their local business partners on their own governments (Carroll 1986: 1-13; Howlett, Netherton, and Ramesh 1999: 58-63).

This dependency thesis provided a significant basis for the growth of Canadian economic nationalism between the 1960s and 1980s and for continuing opposition to what has become known as globalization. It has provided the intellectual underpinning for state-led economic development strategies, the expansion of public ownership and economic regulation, restrictions on foreign ownership, and the fostering of cultural nationalism as part of a broader strategy that Neil Bradford has described as "interventionist nationalism" (Bradford 1998; Innis 1930; Watkins 1963; Levitt 1970; Williams 1994; Howlett, Netherton, and Ramesh 1999: 89-99).

Marxist theorists view Canadian business elites as a "dominant class (which) typically plays a hegemonic role in shaping the economic and political structures through which it rules" (Carroll 1986: xiii). "Business"—typically defined as the executives of a few hundred large corporations controlling the "commanding heights" of the economy—holds a "privileged position" which enables it to act independently from the power of the state and to obtain recognition of its interests as a central element in public policy (Atkinson and Coleman 1989: 32; Carroll 1986; Coleman 1988: 278-81). Class linkages, based initially on shared family and educational connections and later on shared organizational networks, shape shared attitudes towards the role of the state in providing a politically secure environment for the accumulation of capital and the relative autonomy of corporations in a market economy (Porter 1965).

However, while some class-based analyses view the state as a direct instrument of capitalist domination of society (Etzioni-Halevy 1997: xxv), which is itself "dominated and staffed by representatives" of capitalist interests (Howlett, Netherton, and Ramesh 1999: 67), most recognize that the state possesses a degree of decision-making autonomy to mediate among competing interests and manage social conflict (Carroll 1986: xiii). Keynesian political economy, the extension of the welfare state, legal protections for unions and collective bargaining, and various forms of social and economic regulation by government all reflect the efforts of government to balance capitalist accumulation with its legitimation by disciplining markets and sharing the benefits of economic growth with other elements of society (O'Connor 1973). This structural view of the state is consistent with the concept of mutual dependence—the political and economic interests of the state in providing public services and encouraging social cohesion are closely linked to the prosperity of the capitalist system.

The influence of class-based theories of politics on business-government relations in Canada can be seen in several ways. They have given advocates of increased government control over the economy a practical and theoretical rationale for their agendas, challenging the political and economic legitimacy of market economics and relative business autonomy in the process. They have been used to justify both reformist policies of government regulation and anti-capitalist strategies intended to justify and guide increased state ownership and control of the economy.

At the same time, these theories have forced advocates of liberal and neo-mercantilist economic policies to give greater consideration to the distributive effects of their policies by posing a political and ideological challenge to the legitimacy of the economic system, as discussed in Chapter 1.

However, a number of observers have contended that, as much or more than competing class interests, it is the existence of divisions or fractions among business elites and the capitalist class competing among themselves for political and economic advantage, often in combination with other social groups, that permits capitalism to coexist peacefully with a more or less democratic political system (for example, see Therborn 1977).

Pluralist Theories

Pluralist theories are based on the assumption that government decision-making reflects, or should reflect, competition among divergent social and economic interests that have the capacity to exercise effective political influence through a variety of organizational forms (Dahl 1982; Pross 1992). Pluralist theory identifies democracy with the diffusion of both political and economic power either through formal political institutions to entrench the separation of powers or the creation of institutional counterweights against the potential abuse of economic power. As such, pluralism is a reaction against both elite and state-centred theories of power and the Marxist view of liberal democratic societies as subject to the domination of a capitalist ruling class (Lowi 1985: 31-34). Pluralist theories are frequently present in analyses of interest group politics: the effort of organized groups to secure policies favourable to their interests through the political process.

Interest group organization often mirrors the organizational structures of governments, as particular groups focus their political activities on influencing government bodies that have the greatest capacity to advance or threaten their interests (Olson 1965; Coleman 1988; Coleman and Skogstad 1990). Neo-pluralist analysts have expressed concern that the growth of government and the resulting decentralization of bureaucratic decision-making have contributed to the tendency of public policies to reflect the inordinate influence of special interest lobbies, including those of many business groups, at the expense of a broader or more coherent vision of the public interest.

Pluralist theories originated in the attempts by eighteenth-century political writers to strike a balance between the pursuit of order strong enough to exercise effective governmental authority and the preservation of citizens' liberty and property from the arbitrary exercise of political or governmental power. Institutional checks and balances were considered essential in ensuring that different social and economic groups would be able to seek and obtain effective representation within government. Moreover, governments and social groups were expected to respect a diversity of values and allegiances among citizens, even though these might lead to conflicts within governmental institutions or independently of them among social groups with competing values, identities, and interests.

Liberal pluralism provides a rationale not only for limiting governmental power by dividing it, but also for governmental activism as a counterweight to the power of other groups within society and for greater equality of opportunity for different individuals and groups within society. Each of these approaches to pluralism may be found, in varying degrees, in modern liberal democratic societies. Some liberal scholars state that "pluralism within and without are weakening the coherence and competence of the nation state, forcing it to come to terms with competing interests and values" (Bellamy 1999: ix). Others suggest that this is precisely the objective of pluralist approaches to the organization of political and economic systems.

At an empirical level, political scientist Nelson Polsby identifies at least three levels on which a society can demonstrate pluralistic characteristics. At one level, there should be a functional division of decision-making power within both government and society allowing for the autonomous operation of different social and political organizations with different and overlapping roles. These multiple cleavages reflect differences in identity and interest both within and among different groups in society.

Second is the existence of a reasonable degree of freedom for citizens to form or participate in different groups whose variety of interests, values, and loyalties is based on overlapping political, cultural, geographic, economic, occupational, social, and religious identities, to name only a few. This idea is rooted in the principle that no one group, including the state, should be able to claim a citizen's exclusive and undivided loyalty.

On a third level, citizens should enjoy a significant range of choices in the options available for communicating their interests, concerns, and values to leaders or elites and for enforcing some degree of accountability for their actions (Polsby 1985). The capacity of citizens to exercise a number of choices in defining and asserting their interests enforces a greater degree of accountability on elites by providing alternative means for the mobilization of public opinion or the expression of public policy goals.

These choices may be expressed through political parties, especially if these are decentralized to permit greater membership involvement in selecting candidates or shaping policy commitments; through a wide range of interest groups; through having a choice among news media outlets; and through participation in a vigorous and diverse civil society of autonomous voluntary associations (Sartori 1987).[4] The proliferation since the 1960s of interest and advocacy groups representing large numbers of Canadians is a significant expression of pluralism.

However, the responsiveness of government on broad issues of policy may also be eroded through the proliferation of special interests and their capacity to develop privileged relationships with different segments of government on specialized issues of policy. Real power in governments is often concentrated in the hands of a rela-

---

4 The term "polyarchy" was coined by the American political scientist Robert Dahl. See also Berger and Neuhaus 1977; Putnam 2000.

tively small number of politicians and advisors with limited accountability to their parties or voters between elections (Savoie 1999; Simpson 2001). Interest groups may collude with senior policy-makers to exclude from power and influence other groups that might threaten their power and status. Many groups may exercise influence in dealing with narrowly focused issues but have little effect on broader policy issues.

Neo-pluralist theory, sometimes called interest group liberalism, emphasizes the fragmentation of government decision-making in response to the logic of bureaucratic organization and the creation of specialized public organizations to address particular policy issues or the concerns of specific social groups or economic interests. The logic of collective action suggests that different interests will invest their time, money, and effort to influence government policies that disproportionately affect them. It also suggests that small, cohesive groups are often able to focus their lobbying efforts more effectively to extract benefits from the public policy process than are larger groups with more diverse memberships. Over time, these efforts may lead to **clientelist** relationships, as policy-makers increasingly come to identify the public interest with the interests of those groups with which they deal most frequently (Olson 1965; Lowi 1985: 50-63). The growth of government intervention, whether in the forms of extensive regulation, subsidies, or the mobilization of private interests, including non-governmental organizations (NGOs), as explicit instruments of government policy, erodes the functional distinctions between state and society and the relative autonomy of both. This process may result not only in the phenomenon of the embedded state, but also the marketization of government in which groups deemed essential to the implementation of government policies obtain privileged access to the policy process (Cairns 1986: 70-83; Offe 1984).

Special interest government may respond in detail to the policy preferences of particular groups on issues that affect them most directly. However, it may also frustrate the effective coordination or implementation of broader policies in the public interest or in response to shifts in public opinion, leading to what critics have described as "interest group capture" of government agencies and the "tyranny of the status quo" (Friedman and Friedman 1983). Studies of government operations and business-government relations in Canada have recognized the existence of neo-pluralist relationships in a number of areas, including aspects of industrial policy, agricultural policy, and the operations of some regulatory agencies (Economic Council of Canada 1981; Coleman 1988; Atkinson and Coleman 1989; Coleman and Skogstad 1990; Savoie 1990: 290-315).

A number of conditions can contribute to the growth of neo-pluralist or clientelist relationships between interest groups and governments. A weakening of central government agencies or budgetary controls may lead to the decentralization of power within government bureaucracies, reduced accountability to citizens by their elected representatives, and the latter's diminished capacity to coordinate policies for the greater good. Governments may contribute to this process by creating new departments or agencies when old ones seem unable to deal with pressing political or policy problems. The growth of specialized government agencies prompts groups of businesses or other social interests to organize or to shift the focus of their lobbying in order to ensure that their interests are considered and accommodated in the actions and decisions of these bodies. The requirement for specialized technical knowledge may limit the number of groups with the resources to deal effectively with a particular agency or may exclude non-experts from effective influence over the policy process. The cooperation of policy-makers and social organizations, including those representing business, may result in a harmonization of interests or values that effectively leaves out those whose interests or policy objectives conflict with those of policy insiders, resulting in the creation of what VanWaarden has described as "robber coalitions" (VanWaarden 1992: 44; Lowi 1985; Peters 1984: 157-60). These groups may also work together to fend off potential threats from other parts of government.

Box 3.2

	Statism	**Corporatism**	**Public Choice**
Role of State	Embodies, defines national interest.	Guides national interest by mobilizing major support from major social and economic actors.	Political leaders, parties, government bureaucracies are organized, self-interested, and have appetite for power.
Relations between state/ societal actors	Define public good independently of societal actors. Use state power to guide, direct, control societal interests to serve state objectives. State organizations largely autonomous from societal control.	Attempts to incorporate "peak organizations" representing business, labour, and other key social interests within broader decision-making processes of government. Capacity for consensus-building depends on capacity of group leaders to control members, and maintain a degree of autonomy from them.	Multi-level exchange process among politicians, bureaucrats, interest groups, businesses, etc. in pursuit of shared advantage. Pursuit of self/group interest dominant principle of political action. No group possesses enough resources to gain, maintain power or competitive advantage without cooperation/ assistance of others.

Senior government decision-makers have a number of options in responding to these criticisms. Centralizing control over budgets and policy-making enables **central agencies** to enforce their priorities on line departments and special agencies. Budgetary constraints provide opportunities to consolidate and reorganize government agencies in order to break up communities of interest between civil servants and interest groups, while encouraging the development of new approaches to policy-making. Governments may seek to ensure more equitable and balanced representation of major social interests at different levels of government to facilitate policy coordination and social cohesion. Alternately, commissioning an external review of the policies or performance of government agencies may to subject them to independent scrutiny and generate a new policy consensus (Aucoin 1995b; Bradford 1998; Kernaghan, Marson, and Borins 2000). Some of these strategies are discussed in greater detail in Chapter 13.

These approaches consider the state to be an autonomous actor capable of mobilizing ideas, resources, and public opinion in support of policy change and understand institutional structures as vehicles for the deliberate organization of actions by governments, markets, and society.

Statism

Statism describes a school of political thought that emphasizes the central role that is or should be played by state institutions and decision-makers within society. Statist theories may be normative to the extent that they view state institutions as the embodiment of the national interest, transcending the claims of political parties, social classes, or collections of interest groups to represent the public good. In such cases, they identify the well-being of the nation with strong state institutions that have the capacity to define the national interest and to mobilize their own resources and those of the broader society in support of policies intended to achieve their goals. These theories may also be empirical in describing the attitudes or methods for enforcing the preferences of state decision-makers, with or without the cooperation of business and other societal interests, when they conflict with those of major societal interests or the general public (Galbraith 1973; Nordlinger 1981; VanWaarden 1992). A statist approach to policy-making may coexist with democratic political institutions; however, it requires elected officials either to set clear priorities and policy goals for a professional public service or for the two groups to cooperate closely in policy development.

The legitimacy of the state also derives from a claim to disinterested expertise and the ability of state decision-makers to identify and enforce ideas of the public interest that transcend the interests of any political, economic, or social faction. As a result, decision-makers in authoritative state institutions often form a separate class with its own interests, closely linked to the structures and interests of state institutions, and distinct from those of other social interests. These ideas are consistent with Weberian traditions of bureaucracy, although their application varies widely from one country and time period to another (Gerth and Mills 1958: 196-244). However, they can also prompt alternative interpretations that attempt to evaluate assertions of serving a public interest by assessing the extent to which proposed policies or actions serve the interests of particular governmental organizations and the officials who manage or work for them as much as the interests of particular social groups or a broader public. More recent theories of institutionalism are a somewhat watered down form of statism capable of projecting the interests and priorities of state decision-makers amid the global interdependence of the early twenty-first century or of accommodating and steering market forces in channels consistent with a variety of government policy objectives (Atkinson 1993; Campbell and Pederson 2001).

Statist theories stress the necessity of bureaucratic decision-making in modern states to mobilize public and private resources in the service of the common good, to ensure the consistent and relatively impartial administration of the laws, and to encourage greater efficiency and professionalism in the operations of government. The statist tradition of public policy-making is unabashedly elitist. As the "inarticulate mass" of the people is seen to lack the expertise, capacity, or wisdom to govern effectively, senior officials of the state exercise power in the name of "the people," "the nation," "the working classes," or whatever body is the nominal source of their power (Gerth and Mills 1958: 224-25).

The exercise of state power may involve alliances with major private economic interests—as in the mercantilist and neo-mercantilist economic policies discussed in Chapter 1—or with other social and economic interests. The capacity (or promise) of the developmental state to promote and stabilize greater levels of economic development has been a key factor in legitimizing growing state control over the economy. The use of state power to counteract excessive concentrations of political or economic power, to redistribute income and opportunity among citizens through the institutions of the welfare state, and to manage the complexities of a changing world have all been used as explanations or justifications for state decision-makers to pursue and exercise greater degrees of autonomy from societal influence or control.

As a result, theories of state autonomy have provoked ideological rancour and partisan critiques from across the political spectrum. These critiques challenge the legitimacy, responsiveness, or effectiveness of statist approaches to decision-making, often by appealing to normative principles of democratic accountability. They may also call into question the capacity of governments to fulfil the myriad of conflicting social and economic expectations that they have created without undermining the entrenched social and economic rights and privileges of many groups within society.

Expressions of statist power relations within Canada's political system include forms of intergovernmental bargaining, particularly when these take place without procedures for the involvement of or consultation with societal groups whose interests may be directly affected by their outcome. Certain areas of government decision-making may be effectively insulated from public input, reflecting the extreme complexity of issues at stake or the relative weakness of interest group organizations' monitoring of specific areas of government policy. Divisions among societal stakeholders on major policy issues—for example, periodic changes to Canada's Employment Insurance system—enable state actors to enforce their own policy choices, even those that vary significantly from stakeholder preferences (Nordlinger 1981; for an examination of statist approaches to policy-making in social and tax policies, see Hale 1998b; Hale 2001b: Chapters 4, 5, 10; Montpetit 2003).

Another reflection of statist assumptions is the capacity of state decision-makers to obtain a lower standard of legal, regulatory, or political accountability for their own behaviour than may be applied to citizens or businesses under their authority. Examples of this phenomenon include the provision of preferential regulatory status to government agencies in competition with private businesses or the capacity of a government agency to exercise policing powers that are not subject to effective judicial oversight.

An alternative approach to the projection of political power independent of societal interests involves the use of government resources to build up the political and financial resources of the governing party through the exercise of patronage in staffing government agencies, the allocation of contracts, and the creation of programs primarily of benefit to supporters of the party in power. The cumulative effect of these initiatives blurs the distinction between the governing party and the state and expands the independence of the governing party from other societal forces. Stewart has noted that the use of public resources by the executive to perpetuate its hold on power was a fundamental characteristic of colonial governments that expanded with the growth of federal and provincial governments in the first 50 years after Confederation. Recent observers of Canadian politics have observed similar tendencies in the contracting policies of the federal government (Stewart 1986; Office of the Auditor General 2002; Travers 2002; Spector 2002: A23). These issues are addressed further in Chapter 13.

In recent years, public concerns over the integrity and political accountability of governments for their actions have resulted in the growth of legal and political constraints on statist approaches to policy-making. Since 1985, the Charter of Rights and Freedoms has enabled the courts to impose much stronger due process requirements to limit the arbitrary exercise of governmental power at the expense of citizens' or businesses' legal rights. Increased public pressures have led to the greater transparency in government policy-making that is embodied in Access to Information laws, legal requirements for pre-notification of legislative and regulatory changes, political expectations of public consultation processes, and the expanded use of the Internet for access to government information. Perceived abuses of government power have led to an extensive mobilization of voluntary organizations and advocacy groups (civil society) to influence government policies. As economic activity and intergovernmental negotiations increasingly cut across national boundaries, societal groups have sought either to build cross-border coalitions of interests or to escape what they perceive as arbitrary government control by shifting economic activity to jurisdictions more responsive to their interests.

These cross-cutting pressures force governments to increase their efforts to legitimize both the processes and outcomes for making policies in areas in which public scrutiny has been relatively limited (Stairs, 2002: 161-76). They have also led policy-makers and researchers to examine different models of institutional design intended to create frameworks of laws, rules, and incentives linking the behaviour of private citizens, businesses, interest groups, and even other governments with various policy objectives while limiting their direct recourse to coercive (or command-and-control) approaches to the use of state power.

One approach to this process has been for governments to formalize the participation of major classes of economic stakeholders in the policy process in a variety of social decision-making partnerships.

Corporatism

The corporatist tradition emerged from the efforts of several European nations to overcome high levels of political and class conflict during the early years of the twentieth century. It seeks to formalize the participation of major social interests in the policy process and to institutionalize a process of consensus-building that will enable the vital interests of business, labour, and other major social interests to be represented in government decisions. This process, when expressed in the form of state corporatism, may marginalize or replace traditional democratic forms of legislative representation, as it did in Mexico under the authoritarian rule of the PRI between the 1920s and the 1990s, in Fascist Italy, and in Salazar's Portugal.

Corporatism may also coexist with and complement democratic elections and buffer transitions of power from one party to another. A number of European countries, including Germany, Austria, the Netherlands, and Sweden, have evolved different forms of centralized corporatist participation and consensus-building since the 1940s. Other countries, including Canada, have experimented with sectoral corporatism—delegating the administration of major policy areas to institutionalized representatives of major interest groups.

Corporatist decision-making structures have the advantage of stability and the ability to reduce social and class conflict by institutionalizing habits of cooperation among social groups. They also force participants in the policy process to negotiate the burdens of adjustment to changing economic circumstances.

A major condition for the survival of societal corporatism is the ability of governments to enforce and maintain a structure of hierarchical peak organizations capable of representing the collective interests of organized business, labour, agriculture, and other major societal groups. These groups must be able to make authoritative decisions on behalf of their components, which then shape the decision-making environment for similar decision-making partnerships at the regional, local, and/ or individual firm level. However, such arrangements, with their strong emphasis on collective consensus-building, may also create rigid institutional structures that leave little room for individual opting out, accommodating to changing economic circumstances, or for incorporating new or divergent interests or new trends in public opinion that may emerge as a result of social and economic change (Coleman and Skogstad 1990; VanWaarden 1992).

The development of corporatist decision-making structures in Quebec, in which business, labour, farm, and other groups cooperate closely with government officials in a wide range of consultative processes, reflects the collectivist traditions of Quebec society, as discussed in Chapter 1. This process has paralleled the emergence of the Quebec state as a vehicle for the empowerment of organized labour, strong public sector unions, and the new French-speaking business and professional classes that emerged from the Quiet Revolution.

However, while other governments have attempted to introduce corporatist strategies to build a political consensus between business and labour interests, especially Liberal and NDP governments of Ontario between 1985 and 1995, corporatist approaches to the development and administration of public policy have generally failed to take root in English-speaking Canada despite the strong support of many academics. This failure can be traced to a number of structural and cultural causes and to the availability of policy alternatives far more attractive to much of Canada's business community (Gunderson and Sharpe 1998).

The successful introduction of corporatism depends on the strong exercise of central authority by a government that is deeply committed to the consensus-building process and capable of forcing the cooperation of business, labour, and other interests as unified, organized groups in the policy process. It also depends on a government's capacity to enforce its policy preferences over two or more electoral cycles so that all parties—including the opposition party most likely to replace it in government—come to see the new social partnership either as a positive good or a lesser evil than the disruption of such arrangements.

The fragmentation of Canadian political and economic life has made it difficult, if not impossible, to implement societal corporatist policies at a national level. Traditions of individual rights, political decentralization, and interest group competition have made it relatively easy for dissatisfied groups to opt out of corporatist decision-making structures and have frustrated the emergence of peak organizations able to enforce their decisions on their members.

The Trudeau government of the 1970s flirted with corporatism for a time, but it was never able to win the trust of either major business or labour groups, or to overcome countervailing pressures to decentralize power over economic and social policies to the provinces in response to regional alienation and pressures for Quebec separation.

The fragmentation of business groups by region, size, and industry sector also means that no authoritative group capable of bridging these differences has been able to form. Business cooperation has been more likely to take the form of both systematic opposition to social democratic governments viewed as hostile to business interests and efforts to elect a more business-friendly government at the next election. This fragmentation contrasts sharply with Australia, a federal state with a parliamentary system of government in which the central government effectively controls most of the main levers of fiscal and economic policy, thus enabling it to incorporate relatively centralized business and labour federations into their policy-making structures should its leaders wish to do so (Castles, Gerritsen, and Vowles 1996; Brown 2002).

Although Canada's political culture has a strong tradition of informal bargaining among competing elites, its parliamentary traditions and populist elements, whether of the right or left, have also hindered the development of corporatism as a parallel decision-making system dominated by a partnership of big business and big labour. Civil servants have also looked with scepticism at the prospect of sharing their control over policy development with organized interest groups. The majority cabinet governments that have usually emerged from patterns of two and three party competition within Canada encourage the losers in corporatist bargaining to seek political alliances to replace the government. As a result, political competition in Canada continues to centre on the winner-take-all process of electing majority governments based on shifting coalitions of interests and voters.

Public Choice Theories

Public choice theory involves the application of theories of economic behaviour to the political process. It views the political arena as a marketplace in which politicians, bureaucrats, interest groups, and other actors both cooperate and compete for power, status, and tangible benefits, including the ability to shift the costs of government on to other groups.

Public choice theory is based on three broad assumptions, beginning with **methodological individualism**: the concept that societies, classes, governments, and organizations do not make choices or decisions, individuals do. As such, it discounts approaches to politics that treat elites or classes, including business, as largely undifferentiated groups that act in similar ways from common motives. In contrast to statist outlooks, it also rejects the assumption that government policies and state actions are routinely based on rational assessments of the public interest by disinterested public servants. Secondly, methodological individualism assumes that individuals tend to participate in the political process to the extent that they perceive their interests to be at stake. The greater the opportunity or risks involved, both political and economic, the more likely that individuals and groups will invest their time, money, and effort in influencing the political process.

Those engaged in the political process act in ways that maximize their utility or well-being, whether this is defined in economic or other terms, based on the information available to them. As McMahon notes, "politicians and bureaucrats, like the rest of us, act in accordance with their own preferences and to their own advantage" (McMahon 2000a: 26). Shared values, interests, or perceptions of the public interest may influence these decisions, but individuals retain the capacity for rational choice.

Citizens or businesses invest in additional information, or in obtaining political influence, to the extent that they can reasonably expect to obtain a return on their investment. The relative disengagement of citizens from the political process can be explained as a product of **rational ignorance**, in which the costs of obtaining sufficient knowledge and expertise to become politically effective typically outweigh the benefits to be derived from political involvement or lobbying compared with similar investments in other activities. Similarly, the types and levels of investment by individuals and organizations in the political process are frequently characterized by **bounded rationality** and **satisficing**: a rough balancing of costs of benefits by focusing on areas of political involvement perceived to yield the highest rate of return relative to the investment necessary to obtain it. As a result, low voter turn-outs, especially during periods of limited political conflict, and the highly fragmented decision-making processes of governments already discussed, can reduce govern-ments' accountability to citizens while creating conditions conducive to the growth of clientelism, interest group capture of decision-making processes, or both.

Public choice theory asserts that a central motivation of both politicians and civil servants is direct or indirect access to power and control over resources. Members of both groups exercise procedural power through their capacity to set or influence the political agenda, their access to or control over information, and the legal power to assert a government monopoly over rule-making or the provision of particular services. However, as particular governmental actors often compete with one another for available resources, this reality often leads them to cooperate with other social interests, including business groups, to build or maintain politi-cal support for their policies.

Thirdly, public choice theory views politics as an exchange process. Individuals exchange votes or services in return for current or future benefits, not merely in the abstract pursuit of the common good. Individuals or groups cooperate in various aspects of the political process to the extent they expect to obtain benefits from doing so (Buchanan 1999a: 455-68; Hartle 1988; Stanbury 1994). The process of politi-cal exchange may result in policies that increase the overall well-being of society, for example, by providing better information to guide the decisions of governments, pooling the resources of citizens for the efficient provision of public goods, or lim-iting behaviour that causes harm to others. However, political activity may also enable individuals or groups to exploit the power of government in ways that actu-ally reduce the overall well-being of society (Mueller 1989: 247-73).

Between the 1970s and 1990s, public choice theory spawned a growing literature, in Canada as elsewhere, which questioned the effectiveness of government policies in serving a discernable public interest and evaluated decision-making processes for their capacity to contribute to or undermine the development of policy processes conducive to enhancing the economic and social well-being of citizens in measur-able ways (Buchanan 1999b; Buchanan, Tollison, and Tullock 1980; Tulloch 1989: vii). This literature emphasized the role of conflicting interests and priorities among pub-lic sector decision-makers for Canada's chronic fiscal difficulties, the ability of inter-est group coalitions to block reforms intended to increase the sustainability and effectiveness of public services, and the need for institutional changes that would enable governments to deliver more consistently on their policy commitments and to enhance the quality and cost-effectiveness of public services (for example, see Hartle 1988; Savoie 1990; Hartle 1994; Richards 1997; Savoie 1998 provides an out-standing analysis of the Chrétien government's response to these critiques).

Public choice theory does not have an inherent normative bias towards promot-ing greater or lesser government involvement in society, although it does empha-size the need for expanding the capacity of citizens to hold the state accountable for its actions and the practical challenges to accomplishing this goal. However, by demonstrating the capacity of policy-makers to act in as self-interested a fashion as any other social group, it has effectively challenged the conventional wisdom of the mid-twentieth century that government policies are generally the product of a benevolent state with a clear, well-informed view of the public interest.

By underlining the potential for self-interested political competition in economic and social policies, public choice theory has sparked a renewed interest in the role of neo-classical economic theory and the design of market systems capable of enhancing economic efficiency and overall economic well-being while considering other policy objectives. It has also generated increased concern from voters and advocacy groups for increased transparency and accountability in government.

Sources and Limits of Business Power: An Evaluation

The theoretical models summarized above outline a wide range of possible interpretations of relations among business, government, and other social interests in Canada, some of which may be more persuasive—or supported by more consistent evidence—during some periods of Canadian history than others. These interpretations also draw on a range of different methodologies that lend themselves to different conclusions depending on the context in which business and the workings of institutional and power relations are examined.

We will now consider evidence about the extent and limitation of business power within the Canadian political system, including the exercise of structural and intellectual power, the capacity of business groups to influence the political process, and the role played by small business in both reinforcing and qualifying the effects of business power within the Canadian political system.

Structural Power

There is little doubt that private business decisions have a pervasive influence over economic activity that limits the capacity of governments to impose comprehensive political control over private decision-making. The notion that democratic government exists by consent of the governed applies as much to economic decision-making as to most other areas. The capacity of business groups to withdraw consent from the economic decisions of governments that affect their collective well-being, either by shifting their activities to other jurisdictions, mobilizing public support in favour of alternative policies, or shifting their collective political support in ways that contribute significantly to election results are all considerations that shape the decision-making climate of Canadian governments.

However, the possession of political and economic resources does not automatically translate into the capacity to make effective use of them. The collective power of business groups is limited by the capacity and willingness of governments to subordinate business preferences to those of state actors or public opinion and to accommodate and balance the expression of competing interests through the political process. Business interests must persuade opinion-makers and public opinion that their policy preferences serve the broader public interest and can accommodate and facilitate the goals and values of other economic and social interests more effectively than competing ideas or policy agendas (see Box 3.3).

The fragmentation of business interests by region, industry sector, size, and the effects of market forces on particular businesses or sectors creates political opportunities for competing social and economic interests, while expanding opportunities for governments to assert their autonomy. Business associations must often compete with one another and with other organized interests to influence the decisions of elected officials and senior policy-makers. This competition gives governments considerable discretion when setting policy priorities or implementing particular policies. Governments also have substantial autonomy in determining how the policy process will be structured, which departments or agencies have jurisdiction over particular policy fields, which groups will be consulted (at what stage of the process and under what circumstances), and how decisions will be explained to the public and then implemented.

Box 3.3

Structural Power	Countervailing Power
Sources of Business Power Structural power—dependence of governments on large-scale business investment, domestic and international capital flows, job creation for economic growth, diffusion of prosperity.	*Limits on Business Power* • Government policies balance competing business interests, along with other social and economic policy objectives. • Fragmentation of business interests needed for them to secure re-election. • Government exercise of political and legal power subject to re-election, maintenance of public support in competitive political system. • Government control over most aspects of policy process.

Public attitudes towards the role of government, and the latter's periodic need to maintain public support and to secure re-election give other elements of society the opportunity to press their claims on the public interest, often in opposition to business priorities on particular issues. This reality allows both governments and other social and economic interests to exercise countervailing power in ways that not only may accommodate business interests, but which also either subordinate them to a broader view of the public interest or encourage business accommodation of competing interests within the political process.

Intellectual Power: Influence over Political and Economic Ideas

The growth of government and its power over the economic system for most of the 40 years after World War II, despite frequent concerns expressed by business groups over specific policy initiatives, suggests that Canadian governments were able to expand their political autonomy from business during much of this period.

However, while both the Liberal and PC parties adopted policies heavily influenced by social democratic ideas during this era, this process did not prevent most Canadian governments from working with business groups to secure common objectives. In most jurisdictions, business groups were able to prevent or reverse the introduction of what they perceived to be radical changes to the economic structure. However, these victories rarely enabled them either to reverse the growth of government or to persuade governments to impose lasting changes on economic or political structures.

A major condition for business groups to influence the political culture and the climate of ideas influencing public policy has been the building of coalitions with other social and economic interests that validate their claims to serve the public interest and that result in a general shift in public opinion. Arguably, this cooperation has taken place to some extent since the mid-1980s, often with government encouragement. There has been a general decline in public support for active government intervention in business decision-making, as witnessed by declining public support for business subsidies and increased public acceptance of balanced budgets and the economic changes resulting from globalization and free trade. However, these changes have not affected public attitudes towards government's role in the provision of public services, the redistribution of income to those in greatest need, and improved access to government-run education and health care services (Earncliffe Research and Communications (1995-2000), public opinion surveys conducted for the Department of Finance).

Pollster Frank Graves of Ekos Research suggests that Canadian public opinion is primarily pragmatic rather than ideological in its outlook—that business and governments are evaluated on their ability to serve the needs and goals of ordinary citizens (Ekos Research Associates 2000a). Government awareness of public expectations, combined with the need to balance competing interests and outlooks among public sector elites, enforces a similar pragmatism on all but the most ideologically oriented of governments. Business views, while often given particular weight in shaping economic policies, are thus only one component—and often a marginal one—in shaping public policies (see Tables 3.1 and 3.2).

The capacity of business associations to act as a unified group in shaping public debate is reinforced by the relative cohesion of business elites in support of broad policy positions favourable to a market economy, smaller government, and greater individual and corporate self-reliance (see Table 3.2.) However, their ability to translate this relative cohesion into specific policies is limited by the need to secure the support of authoritative decision-makers within government and by governments' need to secure public support in managing change.

Ekos Research suggests another source of countervailing power in debates over public policy ideas: the commitment of senior government decision-makers, leaders of major NGOs, and academic opinion-leaders to different views of the role of government or the public good.

Table 3.1: Public Views on Group Influence over the Policy Process

Which of the following two groups (have/should have) the
most influence in defining public policies in Canada?

	Have more power	Should have more power	Difference
Media	63%	31%	+ 32
Senior business leaders	54%	44%	+ 10
Lobbyists/interest groups	51%	33%	+ 18
Senior public servants	47%	42%	+ 5
Parliamentarians	47%	56%	- 9
Average citizens	25%	77%	- 52

Source: Ekos Research Associates 2000a; author's calculations.

Table 3.2: Comparing Public and Elite Ideological Outlooks

Thinking about your overall political persuasion, would you say that you are more of a
small "l" liberal or a small "c" conservative?

	All Canadians	Public Elite	Private Elite	NGO Elites	IPAC Delegates*
Responses	[n=2493]	[n=288]	[n=161]	[n=106]	[n=318]
liberal	30%	43%	8%	42%	64%
neither	43%	25%	17%	22%	14%
conservative	25%	29%	73%	34%	20%

*IPAC delegates: delegates to Institute of Public Administration in Canada conference, mainly
academics and public servants.
Survey dates: General public, July 2000; Elite, July 1999; IPAC, August 2000.
Source: Ekos Research Associates 2000c.

Ability to Swing Electoral Outcomes

Technical studies of electoral outcomes reveal the fragmented nature of public opinion and the numerous and often overlapping factors that can contribute to shifts in voter loyalties (Clarke et al. 1991; Clarke et al. 2000; Nevitte et al. 2000). The ability of business groups—or any other societal interest—to play a decisive role in the conduct of elections depends on their ability to influence the behaviour of sufficient numbers of soft or floating voters to swing enough close constituency races to affect the outcome of an election.

Expressions of successful business partisanship include a visible and significant shift in the level or distribution of corporate contributions among parties to provide one party with a sizeable campaign advantage over its competitors or the success of business groups in polarizing public debate on a decisive issue capable of determining the outcome of an election. Historians suggest that decisive partisanship by business interests has occasionally played a significant factor in electoral outcomes, as in the debate over free trade with the US in the elections of 1891 and 1911[5] or periodically in provincial elections in which parties have been polarized along pro- and anti-business lines.

However, detailed studies of voter behaviour by pollsters and political scientists suggest that overt business influence is only one factor, and far from the most influential one, in determining the outcomes of contemporary election campaigns. Moreover, recent changes to federal legislation impose strict limits on business contributions to political parties and restrict non-party advertising during election campaigns. These changes promise to curtail this element of business influence, along with that of other well-organized and well-funded interest groups, in the political process.

Influencing the Political Process

The collective capacity of businesses to support business organizations and hire government relations professionals to represent their interests within governments gives them a substantial capacity to influence the policy process, particularly on issues on which they are seen to be major stakeholders by politicians and senior public servants.

However, the large number and specialized nature of business associations may also undermine their effectiveness by generating competing voices that can be balanced or marginalized by governments in pursuit of other policy objectives. Other stakeholder groups—for example, organized labour on issues of labour law, health and safety, and other workplace issues, or groups of public sector professionals in areas of government administration—may hold institutionalized positions in certain policy communities which limit the capacity of business interests to lobby effectively in those areas.

One way of assessing the balance of interests on particular issues may be to determine the number of different interest organizations that make representations during government consultations. (Lists of briefs or presentations to parliamentary committees or government consultation papers are frequently attached to the resulting public reports.) While the number of presentations is not a proxy for quality, timeliness, or the ability to catch the attention of policy-makers, they may suggest the balance of organized stakeholders who have sufficient interest in or awareness of the issues to participate in the debate.

5 For a discussion of the role of business in the 1911 federal election, see Marchildon 1996.

The resources of governments are usually significantly greater than those of any single business group, particularly given the significant number of demands for public input that business associations and other interest groups may face during an average year. This reality—and the fact that few groups possess broad enough expertise to participate effectively in more than a relative handful of policy communities—forces most interest groups to specialize in their dealings with government. For these reasons, while business may possess more resources collectively than any other group in society, this advantage is at least partly dissipated by the large number of policy changes and other government interventions affecting business activity that may engage the attention of businesses, business associations, and their professional advisors.

The Politics of Small Business

The concept of elite pluralism and the challenges of translating concepts of class power into the study of business-government relations in Canada come into focus more clearly when we consider the political role of small business in Canada. The persistence and growth of small businesses is one dimension of the constant regeneration of capitalism, even in an era of economic globalization and transnational corporations. The spread of mass production techniques and the emergence of corporate giants and transnational corporations capable of dominating national and global markets for various products and services during the twentieth century led many observers to believe that small-scale enterprises would become a dying vestige of nineteenth-century capitalism. The conventional wisdom suggested that small firms could not possibly compete with big corporations except as marginal niche players of limited relevance to overall economic activity.

However, small businesses have continued to play a significant role in Canadian economic and political life during the past 30 years. Small businesses and self-employment represent a growing share of private sector employment in Canada, constituting as much as half of all Canadians working in the private sector in 2002, with regional figures ranging between 62 per cent in Saskatchewan and 47 per cent in Ontario.[6]

The small business sector is extremely heterogeneous. It includes self-employed contractors, tradespeople, and service firms of all kinds, along with prosperous firms with dozens of employees and millions of dollars in sales whose owners often play a significant role in the leadership of their communities. Successful governments of all political parties, including moderate social democratic ones, compete for the support of this large pool of voters by providing preferred business tax rates and by attempting to reduce the effects of regulation and red tape on small business owners.

The political influence of small business groups has often been used to support policies of smaller government, deficit reduction, and trade liberalization. The eco-

---

6 A 2003 BC government study estimated small business and self-employment in firms with fewer than 50 employees at 51 per cent of private sector employment across Canada in 2002 (BC Stats 2003).

nomic contributions and social influence of small business owners within their communities reinforce public support for overall business views of the economy and the social values of individual responsibility and hard work which underpin them. At the same time, they also reinforce tendencies towards populism and suspicion of large concentrations of economic power that may challenge the claims of big government, big business, or organized labour to speak for the public interest. As a result, the political role of small business both complements and balances that of large corporations within Canada's economic and political systems.

The Political and Social Roles of Small Business

Small businesses in Canada play a political role on several levels. The large numbers of small businesses and their active involvement in community life are an important factor in shaping public attitudes towards the economy, the role of governments, and relations between citizens and the state.

Business associations play an active role in attempting to influence government policies at all levels of government. National organizations, particularly the 100,000-member Canadian Federation of Independent Business, have lobbied for more than 30 years to promote a more favourable political, fiscal, and regulatory environment for small businesses. Other broadly based business associations, such as the Canadian and provincial Chambers of Commerce, also lobby for small business interests, while representing larger corporate interests as well. Many sector and trade associations also have as members large numbers of small companies, although they are often dominated by a few large companies that contribute a significant share of their budgets.

Canada's system of constituency-based representation in Parliament and its relatively decentralized system of federalism enable small businesses to play a significant role in local party organizations and elections. Small businesses are a major source of candidates and financial and organizational support for local constituency associations. These personal and political relationships between small business owners and members of Parliament (MPs) often count for as much or more than the formal lobbying resources of corporate interests.

Small business owners are a strong source of support for a culture of self-reliance, individual responsibility, and community involvement in many parts of Canada. This culture helps to shape public attitudes towards business and government, despite the existence of other, competing influences. As the local face of "people's capitalism" (Canadian Federation of Independent Business 1999), small businesses enjoy higher levels of social approval and support than almost any economic institution except operators of family farms. They help to legitimate the capitalist system through their role in job creation, their visible service to their communities, and by placing the prospect of economic independence within the reach of the average citizen through successful self-employment. These factors also draw organized small business interests into conflict with statist or collectivist interests that champion a larger public sector, more redistributive tax and spending policies, or the intensive bureaucratic regulation of economic activity.

Although regional variations exist, small business owners appear to support not only government restrictions on abuses of power by the corporate sector, but also restraints on the size and power of governments and unions to control the lives of individual citizens. The size and diversity of the small business electorate tends to attract the attention of conservative, liberal, and moderate social democratic political parties as they attempt to build viable political coalitions. In provincial political cultures characterized by polarization between political parties supported by business and organized labour, they have contributed a populist touch. This is particularly true of provinces such as Quebec, BC, and Newfoundland, where the economic elites of Montreal, Vancouver, or St. John's may be viewed with almost as much suspicion by people outside these centres as the corporate elites of Bay Street.

However, while small companies may reinforce the collective social and political power of business in many ways, they also contribute to a diffusion of business power in others. Small businesses, working with and through local and regional business elites, have built alliances with provincial governments in support of province-building strategies that have contributed to the decentralization of economic power in Canada. The efforts of provincial governments to assert their jurisdiction over economic development since the early years of Confederation have reflected widespread concerns that federal policies have provided excessive benefits to national commercial, industrial, and governmental elites at the expense of regional interests. Regional economic interests have also used provincial governments as a source of countervailing power to balance the influence of large national corporations, especially in areas such as transportation services, financial services and capital markets, and public utilities.

The interests of large and small businesses may conflict in detail, particularly in areas such as taxation, the effects of regulation—which can be used to restrict competition and market access as much as to promote it—and the regulation of anti-competitive practices in the marketplace. Small businesses have long sought to mobilize the regulatory powers of government to limit the market power of chain stores and other **oligopolies** and its use at their expense. In 1998 small business interests vocally challenged the proposed mergers of four large chartered banks into two and provided much of the political impetus for the intense resistance of Liberal government backbenchers to further corporate concentration in this area (Whittington 1999). While big business generally supported the introduction of the GST in 1990, it was bitterly opposed by most small businesses (and most Canadians) who forced the Canadian Chamber of Commerce to withdraw its support for the measure.

The individualistic culture of small business and the challenges of harmonizing the competing interests of big and small business have undermined the abilities of governments to create corporatist decision-making structures that bring together representatives of business, labour, and other major economic interests in an effort to build policy consensus. Small firms also are apt to reject the concept of collectivist economic decision-making as something totally foreign to their motivations for being in business. Moreover, small business workforces tend to be non-union and dependent on the ability to use a wide variety of flexible work practices in adapting to unpredictable circumstances.

The relationship between small and large businesses, as between business and government, is one of mutual dependence but also mutual wariness. The effects of the technological revolution and the growing individualism of Canadian society have created conditions for the adaptation of small businesses to the economic challenges of the twenty-first century. Given the need for politicians to respond to the expectations of their constituents and the high visibility of small business owners and their associations within the political system, governments are likely to accommodate the interests of small businesses in designing economic policies and delivering public services for quite some time to come.

Conclusion

Assessments of business power within the political system are heavily influenced by the ideological assumptions of those studying the issue and the level of analysis at which these studies take place. The strong emphasis placed on citizens' economic well-being in Canadian politics and the Canadian economy's heavy dependence on private business investment and job creation for economic well-being link the political legitimacy of governments with the capacity to maintain a relatively positive business climate and high levels of economic activity. This dependence places advocates of anti-capitalist ideologies, who are among the sharpest critics of business power, at a significant political disadvantage in proposing alternative approaches to public policy.

Business interests also exercise considerable intellectual power through widespread public acceptance of the capitalist system as the normal mode of economic production, although the actual forms of business organization and activity are challenged periodically to justify their activity or correct real and perceived abuses. This influence is tempered by the populist strain in Canadian political culture, by fragmentation and political competition among business interests, and by the widespread public acceptance of government action to limit actual and potential abuses of power by businesses and other social groups.

The extent of business influence varies widely within the political process, depending on the relative influence of other stakeholders and the capacity of political or bureaucratic decision-makers to control the policy process and to mobilize public opinion in favour of their initiatives. Other key factors are the political skill of business groups in identifying their interests with a broader vision of the public good and in accommodating the interests of other social groups within their own agendas.

Discussions of the collective power of business—or the power of business as a class—are relevant to contemporary Canadian politics primarily when issues of structural economic change pit the interests of the state or a major part of Canadian society against the collective interests of the business community. The diversity of these interests, the fragmented structure of the Canadian state, and the frequent overlap between business interests and the economic interests of individual citizens and many social groups mean that policy conflicts usually involve internal debates and shifting alliances within and among these groups. When elite conflict becomes too intense or consistent, citizens may be called in to referee either as voters or through other expressions of public opinion.

As a result, a central challenge of business-government relations in Canada is to manage the process and effects of economic change to limit the degree of political conflict and to accommodate a variety of competing interests.

Key Terms and Concepts for Review (see Glossary)

bounded rationality
central agencies
class-based theories
clientelism
countervailing power
developmental state
elite pluralism
elite theory
intellectual power
Marxism
methodological individualism
neo-pluralism
oligopoly

outcome manifestations (of power)
pluralist theory
process manifestations
rational ignorance
satisficing
sectoral corporatism
societal corporatism
state corporatism
statism
structural power
trade associations
welfare state

Questions for Discussion and Review

1. What is power? Compare and contrast outcome manifestations and process manifestations of power in political and economic life. Give three examples of each.

2. What is structural power? What factors contribute to the ability of business groups to exercise structural power within the political and economic systems? In what ways is this power subject to limits or to countervailing power?

3. Compare and contrast the major ideas of elite, elite pluralist, class-based, and pluralist theories in addressing power relationships within society and between societal interests and the state. What evidence exists for elements of each theory in contemporary Canadian politics and society? How does evidence for competing theories suggest possible limits on the application of each one?

4. Compare and contrast the roles of state actors and major interest groups in statist corporatist polities. What conditions do you think are necessary to reconcile statist, corporatist political systems with democratic principles? To what extent do these conditions exist in Canada today?

5. Compare and contrast statist and public choice theories of the political process. What assumptions does public choice theory make about political actors that complement or conflict with those of other theories discussed in this chapter? Can you see evidence to support these assumptions in media coverage of government operations or the political process?

6. How do the political and economic activities of small business both reinforce and diffuse the power and influence of business within the political system? Give examples of each after reviewing the websites of major small business and big business organizations.

Suggestions for Further Readings

Abelson, Donald E. 2002. *Do think tanks matter?* Montreal and Kingston: McGill-Queen's University Press.

Cairns, Alan. 1986. The embedded state: state-society relations in Canada. In *State and society: Canada in comparative perspective*. Vol. 31, Background Papers, Royal Commission on the Economic Union and Development Prospects for Canada. Coord. Keith Banting. Toronto: University of Toronto Press. 53-86.

Clement, Wallace. 1975. *The Canadian corporate elite*. Toronto: McClelland and Stewart.

Clement, Wallace, and John Myles. 1994. *Relations of ruling: class and gender in postindustrial societies*. Montreal and Kingston: McGill-Queen's University Press.

Coleman, William D. 1988. *Business and politics: a study in collective action*. Montreal and Kingston: McGill-Queen's University Press.

Etzioni-Halevy, Eva (Ed.). 1997. *Classes and elites in democracy and democratization*. New York: Garland.

Hall, Peter A. 1989. *The political power of economic ideas*. Princeton, NJ: Princeton University Press.

Hartle, Douglas. 1988. *The expenditure budget process of the government of Canada: a public choice-rent seeking perspective*. Toronto: Canadian Tax Foundation.

Hayes, R. Helmes, and J. Curtis (Eds.). 1998. *The vertical mosaic revisited*. Toronto: University of Toronto Press.

Nordlinger, Eric A. 1981. *On the autonomy of the democratic state*. Cambridge, MA: Harvard University Press.

Pross, A. Paul. 1992. *Group politics and public policy*. 2nd ed. Toronto: Oxford University Press.

Stanbury, W.T. 1988. Corporate power and political influence. In *Mergers, corporate concentration, and power in Canada,* ed. R.S. Khemani, D.M. Shapiro and W.T. Stanbury. Halifax: Institute for Research in Public Policy. 417-31.

Stanbury, W.T. 1994. *Business-government relations in Canada.* 2nd ed. Toronto: Nelson.

Tulloch, Gordon. 1989. *The economics of special privilege and rent seeking.* Boston, MA: Kluwer Academic Publishers.

VanWaarden, Frans. 1992. Dimensions and types of policy networks. *European Journal of Political Research* 21.

CHAPTER 4

Business, Government, and the Politics of Development: 1760-1970

The development of economic policies and the practice of business-government relations do not take place in a vacuum. They are shaped by political, economic, and social institutions that are the results of historical events and forces produced not only by the competition and interaction of interests through the political process but also by different ideas about the role of government, the nature of Canadian society, and the ways of identifying local, regional, sectoral, and class interests with a broader vision of the public interest.

The study of economic history can be useful in three ways. First, such study places the problems and opportunities of the present in the context of past decisions that have emerged from political conflicts and compromises. Second, it helps people in the present identify recurring issues and problems, learn from past successes or failures in resolving those problems, and recognize changes in the social or economic environment that may require the adaptation of past policies to new circumstances. And third, it provides reasons for fighting the ideological battles of the present through a selective scrutiny of the past. History provides a fertile source for the documentation of an imagined national identity, regional and class grievances, historical roles for the state, or a grand historical narrative that justifies the policy positions of the present by appealing to a partial vision of the past.

Recurring Issues and Problems in Canada's Economic History

This chapter examines four recurrent issues and problems in Canada's economic history, their implications for relations between governments and businesses, and the role of government in the economy. These are:

- the central role of government policies in promoting economic development and diversification;
- the challenges of responding to changing international economic conditions;
- the role of economic policies in promoting social harmony or cohesion; and
- economic policies as tools of nation-building.

Promoting Economic Development and Diversification

Canada's small population, large land mass, and economic potential have made the promotion of economic development and diversification a central priority of governments and business leaders since the colonial era. For most of its history, Canada has been a land of underdeveloped economic potential. The agricultural and resource riches of its enormous frontier have provided opportunities to thousands and then millions of ordinary Canadians and to a more select group of empire-building entrepreneurs and nation- (or province-) building political leaders. However, the dependence of most regional economies on one or two dominant staple industries, particularly at the earlier stages of their development, has encouraged the pursuit of economic diversification as a major priority of economic policy.

Resource dependence has often made Canada particularly vulnerable to unilateral policy shifts by its major trading partners: Britain and the US. As a result, the staples theory of economic development emerged as a major historical interpretation of the economics and politics of economic dependence and its implications for Canadian politics and business-government relations. The continuing efforts of governments to intensify economic development and the growing roles of managerial and technological innovation in this process are also discussed below.

Responding to Changing International Conditions

Canadian economic policies have often been shaped by international economic forces beyond the control of colonial, national, or provincial governments. Major shifts in the commercial, trade, and investment policies of its central trading partners have repeatedly triggered adaptive responses by Canadian governments.

In particular, four great turning points in Canadian political and economic history have resulted from the failure of the economic system—or of governments—to meet the basic expectations of its citizens.

The economic panic of 1837 was the spark that led to armed rebellions against the colonial government, and ultimately, the introduction of governments responsible directly to Canadians (Creighton 1937). Combined with Britain's unilateral introduction of free trade in the 1840s, these events contributed to the emergence of Canada as a separate transcontinental political and economic unit.

Post-Civil War protectionism in the US and the global depression of the 1870s were vital in shaping the economic policies of post-Confederation governments. Canada's **National Policy** imitated US economic nationalism, fostering domestic industries and markets through high tariffs and large-scale investments in railroads and other infrastructure to create a national Canadian market. While the National Policy's promised economic benefits took effect only slowly, high levels of net immigration and the rapid industrialization of the so-called "Laurier boom" enabled Canada to boast the fastest growing economy in the industrial world between 1896 and 1913 (Urquhart 1988).

The **Great Depression** of the 1930s discredited both mercantilism and the laissez-faire business ideology that had been preached rather more than practiced before that time. Combined with the emergence of Keynesian economic policies and the extension of the welfare state in the years after World War II, it legitimated the idea of government as a guarantor of citizens' economic opportunities and greater economic equality while opening Canadian markets to increasing levels of international trade and investment (Simeon and Robinson 1990: 107-33; Bradford 1998: 23-52). These policies also facilitated Canada's adaptation to international economic changes, through greater cooperation with the US and active participation in the growing network of international economic institutions (Canada, Royal Commission on the Economic Union 1985: Vol. 1, 131-61, 225-29). They reinforced Canada's transition from being a component of the British imperial system towards growing economic integration with the US. This provoked a strong sense of Canadian nationalism between the late 1950s and 1970s, a nationalism which reflected growing differences between business and governmental elites.

The collapse of the postwar economic order and a series of global energy price shocks during the 1970s and early 1980s destabilized the postwar Keynesian consensus and led to a systematic rethinking of the role and scope of governments in both Canada's economy and society. These debates, which are examined further in Chapter 5, gradually focused on the search for an effective role for governments in response to trends towards economic globalization.

Promoting Social Cohesion

The success of any economic system, particularly in a democracy, depends on its capacity to secure and maintain the support of the majority of citizens and organized social groups. Social cohesion—or social harmony as it was called during the nineteenth century (Forster 1986: 202-03)—is a basic condition both for the security of property and economic relationships and for increased social and economic opportunity. Many historians view this political and economic balancing act as a central role of governments either by distributing economic patronage and opportunities in the pursuit of electoral success or by balancing pressures for economic growth and social or regional redistribution in more recent times.

The same logic that has consistently prompted government initiatives to promote economic development, support the building of transportation infrastructure, and use government control of key industries to support economic diversification has also led Canadians to secure their political and economic interests through the pursuit of government intervention. From the earliest days of responsible government, patronage and pork-barreling were the political glue that held Canada's political parties together (Siegfried 1992; Stewart 1980: 1; Noel 1971). As a result, social cohesion (or conflict) has been closely linked to the balancing of social and economic interests or to governments' failure to achieve such balance to the satisfaction of major groups in Canadian society. Competition for economic or regulatory benefits from government has also been a driving force for federal-provincial competition in Canadian politics (Innis 1956: 78-96; Bliss 1985; Stewart 1986).

Nation-Building

Historian H.G.A. Aitken has described the response of Canadian governments to these forces as a policy of "defensive economic nationalism" in which they portray their policies as nation-building initiatives that will enable Canadians to exercise greater control over their national economic destiny (Aitken 1967; Aitken 1990). The persistent reality of competing regional interests has prompted similar responses from provincial governments. As a result, Canadian governments have often pursued strategic alliances with business elites as instruments of national or provincial economic development, paralleling the neo-mercantilist practices of other industrial countries. The boom and bust cycles of the staples-based economies, the traditional vulnerability of Canada's business community to economic forces beyond its control, and the challenges of pursuing large-scale or long-term economic projects in an often unstable economic environment consistently have led Canadian businesses to seek government support in creating a positive business environment.

The emergence of new national economic strategies has often followed periods of social and economic turmoil prompted at least in part by external economic shocks beyond the control of Canadian governments. Federal governments have sought to increase their control over these uncertainties either by pursuing greater Canadian economic sovereignty, by negotiating reciprocal agreements with other countries to establish consistent rules for the conduct of economic activity, or by a combination of both strategies. However, Aitken notes that while the "tactics of economic development" have usually been driven by the logic of private economic interests, governments have consistently provided strategic political direction or guidance for the development and locational decisions of key industries (Aitken 1990: 112-21).

These issues have arisen during each era in Canadian history. The ways in which they were resolved—or left unresolved to fester until a subsequent round of political conflict—have played significant roles in shaping relations not only between business and government but also among other competing economic and social interests. We will begin by looking at three major eras in Canadian political and economic history between the early nineteenth century and the 1970s: British colonial rule, Canada's growth between Confederation and World War II, and the Keynesian political economy of the postwar decades. We will examine the major factors shaping the development of the Canadian economy, the responses of its governments to them, and their implications for the shifting relations between governments and major economic interests.

Colonial Canada and the Staples Economy

Canada emerged as an independent nation between the early nineteenth and mid-twentieth centuries through several phases during which the political basis of government shifted from the rule of British governors, assisted and supported by colonial oligarchies dominated by local commercial elites, to an increasingly professional governmental apparatus supported by parliamentary and legislative majorities.

At the beginning of the nineteenth century, British North America was a geographical abstraction fragmented into a number of separate colonial administrations and discrete economic units. Except for that of the Hudson's Bay Company and its Montreal-based competitor, the NorthWest Company, economic activity during the early colonial period (1760-1840) was primarily localized. The economic structures of the colonies—Nova Scotia, Newfoundland, Prince Edward Island (after 1769), New Brunswick (after 1784), and Lower and Upper Canada (after 1791)—were separate and distinct, sharing little except the dominant influence of British imperial and colonial policies.

Historian Gordon Stewart argues that "the key to understanding the main features of Canadian national political culture after 1867 lies in the political world of Upper and Lower Canada between the 1790s and 1840s" (Stewart 1986: 5). Five major themes emerge from the historical literature on this period:

- the dependence of the scattered economies of British North America on their colonial relationship with Britain, initially as part of the imperial trading system and subsequently as part of the international financial system based in the City of London;
- the dependence of most Canadian colonies on staple exports of natural resources and agricultural products to finance their economic growth and the costs of borrowed foreign capital;
- the development of a largely statist and clientelist approach to relations between governing elites, the business and professional classes that provided the colony's economic leadership, and the local communities generally composed of primary producers and small merchants;
- government provision of strategic guidance in economic development, often in partnership with regional economic elites, contributing to periodic fiscal and economic overextension, particularly during the wide swings of the business cycle which were a regular feature of the period's economic life in much of the industrial world; and
- the effects of economic shocks in destabilizing the political system, often leading to major changes in the environment for business-government relations and government responses to economic concerns.

These patterns were frequently translated into the political and economic life of Canada during the first 80 years after Confederation and in modified forms thereafter.

Canada's Economies as Colonial Dependencies

European colonies in North America were treated as dependencies, and often marginal ones, of royal or imperial government policies. Prior to 1760, French and British colonies in the northern half of North America were thinly settled military outposts, heavily dependent on a few staple exports. These exports, primarily fish in Newfoundland and Nova Scotia and furs in New France, usually failed to pay for the upkeep of the colonies. The development of the *Canadien* fur trade was often subordinated to French imperial policies intended to subsidize alliances with local First Nations in order to create a *cordon sanitaire* around Britain's American colonies (Norrie and Owram 1996: 53-57). In the treaty negotiations following the British conquest of New France in the Seven Years War (1756-63), France followed the logic of mercantilist economics by surrendering its Canadian colonies to regain control over a few rich sugar-producing islands in the Caribbean.

After the US War of Independence, the influx of loyalist settlers into Canada and the Maritime colonies, along with others hunting for cheap frontier land, prompted the emergence of separate political settlements in Upper and Lower Canada and the Maritime colonies. Settlement was scattered and based primarily on subsistence agriculture or fishing. Montreal thrived as the terminus of the continental fur trade, financed by partnerships of Scottish merchants which evolved into the North West Company. An export-oriented lumber industry grew up in the Maritimes and Lower Canada during the Napoleonic Wars to meet the strategic needs of the Royal Navy (Innis 1956: 114-15).

Following the War of 1812, British imperial policies significantly influenced the political economy of British North America. The imperial government encouraged the settlement of British veterans in North America, particularly in Upper Canada, as a way of reducing population pressures in the home country and expanding the socially reliable population of the colonies. While the consolidation of the bankrupt Hudson's Bay and North West Companies resulted in the decline of the Canadian fur trade after 1821, high preferential imperial tariffs gave British colonies a competitive advantage that encouraged the growth of timber and, later, wheat and flour exports (Innis 1956: 108-22; Norrie and Owram 1996: 116-26; Forster 1986: 3).

British settlement policies, which combined military settlements with large-scale grants to private land companies, also shaped the development of the Canadian colonies. British garrisons provided relatively stable markets and a cash economy for local farmers and merchants as well as an official class that dominated local political life. Land companies, financed by joint-stock investments of British investors, were intended to facilitate settlement, construct roads, and provide other services. The result was a decentralized pattern of development, dominated by local patrons and their agents, in both Upper and Lower Canada (Norrie and Owram 1996: 116-26; Skelton 1966: 4-15; Noel 1990: 40-78). British requirements for military defence and communications prompted the construction of the Rideau and Welland Canals during the 1820s and the location of railway networks after the 1840s. A secondary effect of these construction projects was the frequent overextension of colonial government finances.

The politically and economically dependent status of Britain's North American colonies prompted growing political conflict between the 1820s and 1840s that contributed to the Rebellions of 1837 in Lower and Upper Canada and a general agitation for responsible government in all the colonies. Ironically, the shift of power to elected colonial governments during the 1840s, at least in local matters, coincided with the unilateral British adoption of free trade and the phasing out or removal of the preferential tariffs that had benefited Canadian exports.

Colonial politicians used their power to promote aggressive railroad-building policies during the late 1840s and 1850s as a stimulus to economic expansion. They relied heavily on the ability of local entrepreneurs and railway promoters to borrow in British capital markets, often supported by loan guarantees. The result was the overextension of colonial finances and a series of fiscal crises (Piva 1992; Skelton

1966: 20-48, 107-26). In retrospect, these policies revealed the excessive dependence of the Canadian economy on a handful of agricultural or resource staples to finance economic expansion. This process, later described as part of the **staples theory** of economic development, encouraged governments to foster the growth of an independent Canadian business class.

The Staples Theory and Economic Dependence

The study of Canadian economic history has been heavily influenced by the staples theory of economic development pioneered by Harold Innis, W.A. Macintosh, Donald Creighton, and other economists and historians of the early and mid-twentieth century. Innis noted that the development of Canada's regions was dependent on the export of a single dominant resource product: New France of furs, Newfoundland of fish, New Brunswick and Lower Canada (Quebec) of timber. Wheat became the dominant export product of Canada West (formerly Upper Canada and now Ontario) after 1840 and of the prairie provinces between the 1890s and the mid-twentieth century. Colonial government on the west coast emerged in response to the gold rush of the late 1850s, which was followed by intermittent booms in BC's emerging mining, fish canning, and forestry sectors following its entry into Confederation.

Table 4.1: Trade of British North American Colonies by Product, 1853

Product	Nova Scotia		New Brunswick		Prince Edward Island		Province of Canada	
	Imports	Exports	Imports	Exports	Imports	Exports	Imports	Exports
	(% of total)		(% of total)		(% of total)		(% of total)	
Agricultural	35.9	21.9	34.2	2.9	17.8	65.0	13.9	48.1
Fishery	8.0	35.9	2.3	5.3	3.0	10.1	1.2	1.8
Forest	0.7	16.2	2.8	82.1	0.2	18.1	0.3	48.2
Manufacturers and Miscellaneous	44.5	10.9	53.6	6.7	70.9	6.8	80.2	1.2
Mineral	1.7	9.4	2.6	2.0	1.2	–	1.9	0.6
Wines/liquors	9.2	5.7	4.5	1.0	6.9	–	2.5	0.1

Source: Saunders 1984: 103; Norrie and Owram 1996: 91.

Colonial and early national Canada typically lacked the domestic sources of capital necessary to pay for economic development or to recoup the costs of settlement, defence, and transportation infrastructure. As a result, most regions initially depended on the export of a staple resource to finance these activities and to pay for imports of manufactured goods. Table 4.1 provides a snapshot of colonial dependence on agricultural and resource exports in the early 1850s. While local manufactures, often linked to these sectors, accounted for a growing share of economic activity in most provinces except PEI, most colonies depended heavily on staple exports of farm, fish, or forest products and imported manufactured goods, primarily from Britain.

The initial development of Canadian resource industries, especially timber, during the early nineteenth century was fostered by Britain's need for a secure source of supply during the Napoleonic Wars. British tariff policies gave colonial industries preferred access to British markets and those of other British possessions until the mid-1840s, when Britain unilaterally opened its markets to the world. Reform governments in Nova Scotia, New Brunswick, and the colony of Canada followed suit, retaining only a low revenue tariff. By the 1850s, growing trade with other British colonies and the US left only New Brunswick primarily dependent on British markets for its exports, as the beginnings of urbanization resulted in growing domestic markets (Forster 1986: 23; Norrie and Owram 1996: 90, 182-83).

Some historians have emphasized the role of staple dependence in contributing to economic underdevelopment and dependence. For example, Aitken argues that

> the persistence of this simple structure and the economic characteristics of the staples themselves retarded capital accumulation and made it difficult to get sustained economic growth under way. Unlike the situation in the United States, where export earnings from cotton played a decisive role in the financing of early industrialization, Canada's staples, until the establishment of the western wheat economy in the early twentieth century, contributed little to diversification. (Aitken 1990: 111)

However, others note that, over time, the production of staples generated forward linkages: economic activity based on processing and adding value to resources to obtain a higher return from initial investments. These activities, often linked to improvements in transportation systems and lower freight costs, generated sufficient savings to promote greater economic development and greater diversification. As large enough markets emerged to support local industries, staple production could also result in backward linkages to domestic suppliers of the goods and services necessary for their efficient operation, as noted in Box 4.1, although the degree of development depended largely on the size and stability of regional markets (Innis 1956; Watkins 1963; Bertram 1967).

While the staples theory is persuasive in some ways, neo-classical economists suggest that it tends to oversimplify the complexities of Canada's economic history while ignoring aspects of that history that do not fit into the model, such as the diversification of agricultural activity that accompanied gradual urbanization in most provinces. Dependency theorists have argued that the patterns of economic (and, sometimes, political) exploitation associated with this dependence were later translated into economic and political relations between central Canadian elites and residents of other regions of Canada. However, the staples theory remains useful as an analysis of the initial stages of economic development, although it has limited contemporary application (Norrie and Owram 1996: 3-4, 177, 205; Bertram 1967: 98).

Box 4.1: The Staples Theory and Economic Development

FISH → Fish processing	**GRAIN**→ flour milling
⇑	⇑ → brewing/distilling
⇑	⇑ → intensive livestock feeding
⇑	⇑ → meat packing
⇑	⇑ → value-added meat production
Shipbuilding and repair	Railway (or truck) transport ← related
Ships' supplies	Transportation equipment ← manufacturing
Marine biology	Farm supplies & equipment ← activities at certain
	Construction materials ← points in market
	← growth

TIMBER   → Sawmills
→ Pulp and Paper (after 1890)

⇑

Equipment manufacturing
Chemicals (after 1900)
Hydroelectric power (after 1900)

The political implications of dependence on a handful of primary industries to finance Canada's requirements for economic expansion are undeniable. European settlement of Canada was closely linked to the development of agriculture and natural resources. The settlement of the frontier required heavy investments in canals, railways, and roads to promote economic development and diversification. Indeed, the central role played by railway construction in Canadian economic life during the 1840s and 1850s prompted Allan MacNab, the Conservative premier of Canada West, to comment that "railways became our politics" (Skelton 1966: 16-17). MacNab, who combined the chair of the legislature's standing committee on railways and telegraphs with the presidency of the Great Western Railway for some years, was the first of several major Canadian politicians over the next 70 years whose political and business interests were deeply intermingled (Bliss 1987: 185). The financing, building, and politics of railways played a central role in Canadian political life well into the twentieth century.

Canada's small population lacked the money income or savings to develop colonial (and later continental) expansion by financing the growth of railways and industrial and other large enterprises. Colonial governments attempted to fill this gap with as extensive a range of public works projects as their limited resources would allow. They also provided extensive subsidies for the private construction of canals and, later, railways that frequently blurred the distinction between public and private enterprise. However, the development of public works on a large scale required financial resources beyond the capacity of either local government or business to secure through tax revenues or foreign borrowing (Bliss 1987: 161-90; Piva 1992: 257-83).

Prices for resource products fluctuated with market conditions while the costs of financing government debt increased steadily; both contributed to periodic economic crises. Most economic interests sought to build alliances with governments or, after the onset of responsible government in the 1840s, to create coalitions capable of delivering economic benefits to local communities, regions, and industries. Legislators traded votes for railway projects—the regional development projects of the era—and, sometimes, shares in railway companies. Several members of Canada West Premier Francis Hincks's cabinet sat on the Board of Directors of the Grand Trunk Railway, prompting accusations of corruption when the railroad ran into financial difficulties between 1856 and 1862. These factors reinforced the early tendency of colonial governments towards state-centred approaches to economic development and the use of political power and patronage to bind the interests of local leaders and their clients to those of governing elites (Skelton 1966: 20-28, 45-46; Bliss 1985; Bliss 1987: 185).

Statism and Clientelism

The most persistent legacy of colonial Canada was the politicization of economic activity, particularly if pursued on a substantial scale. Following the debacle of the US War of Independence, colonial governors and administrations actively used patronage and influence to promote and protect their interests, support economic growth, and limit the capacity of elected legislatures to control their activities. The result was a series of governing oligarchies who manipulated the power of the state to serve their interests and create networks of political and economic clients to help them maintain their power (Innis 1956: 179; Stewart 1986: 1-6; Noel 1990: 40-78).

Noel describes political and economic relations in colonial Canada, particularly Canada West, as a system of **developmental clientelism** that evolved and adapted to changing circumstances throughout the nineteenth century. This clientelism took the form of a series of regional and local patronage networks characterized by mutual obligation between clients and patrons, who often combined control over land and other economic resources with administrative and political office-holding. Politics were highly localized. Elected members were closely linked to the social and economic interests of client networks (Noel 1990: 15, 40ff; see also Noel 1971: 17-22).

The direct involvement of colonial governments in economic policies—from the distribution of government contracts, to the location and financing of public works and railroad building, to the tariffs or subsidies enjoyed by particular industries—created public expectations that the exercise of political power would be linked to the enjoyment of economic benefits. Major cities at the hubs of railway networks could extend their economic and political influence over surrounding regions not only by their control over distribution networks, but by the growing influence of major urban newspapers. This metropolis-hinterland relationship increased the political power of urban political, financial, and industrial elites in late colonial and early national Canada (Norrie and Owram 1996: 190).

Box 4.2: Overview of Canada's Economic History, Early Colonial Era (to 1840s)

Centre of Political Power	Major Sources of Political and Economic Conflict	Catalysts for Major Changes
British governor, supported by colonial oligarchy of office-holders and commercial elites.	• Use of political influence to distribute benefits to friends, supporters of colonial oligarchy. • Conflict between governors and representative assemblies over priorities of colonial governments.	• Large-scale immigration → English-French, class tensions. • Economic crash, rebellions of 1837. • Unilateral changes in British commercial, trade policies (1840s).

As a result, success in Canadian politics required both economic and political management, a capacity to broker competing regional interests, a willingness to cultivate regional and local elites, and a commitment to an "active" style of government capable of "facilitating provincial and regional economic development through government guarantees of private and local initiatives" (Noel 1990: 310-14). Noel's description of colonial politics in Ontario applies to varying degrees to other parts of Canada both before and after Confederation. Aitken notes that colonial "governments mobilized private capital to serve political ends when it suited their priorities, but also substituted strategic political considerations for economic or commercial ones when they chose to do so" (Aitken 1990: 113). As a result, conditions of economic development were usually subject to continuing political favour.

Political conflicts during the colonial era sometimes took the form of resistance to oligarchic leadership. The frequently arbitrary use of power by colonial governors to favour friends and supporters sparked frequent conflicts before 1837. These took a number of forms: competition for power and economic opportunities between French- and English-speaking communities in Quebec; the resistance of rural communities to domination by the commercial and financial interests of Montreal, Toronto and Halifax; and the pursuit of responsible government (control over executive power by elected majorities in colonial assemblies).

After the introduction of responsible government in the 1840s, colonial policies centred on the conflicts of factions—most of them linked to shifting coalitions of local economic interests—for control over the levers of power. Politics became less oligarchic and more democratic. Colonial governments began to be more responsive to local rather than imperial interests, and the projection of economic interests usually took the form of party politics (Stewart 1986: 6).[1] After Confederation, these pressures

---

1 BC, in which a stable party system did not emerge until the 1903 provincial election, is a notable exception (Barman 1991: 99-103).

often evolved into provincial rights movements committed to championing local or regional interests against those associated with the federal government of the day.

Responding to Economic Shocks

The development of Canada's economy during the nineteenth century is closely related to the attempts by colonial and Canadian governments to promote settlement, improve transportation networks, expand markets for staple products, and, with the progress of time, to diversify their economies. Rapid population growth stretched the colonies' resources to their limits on several occasions. Political change frequently followed economic crises, notably in 1837-39, 1847-49, and 1857-59. These crises exposed the colonies' economic weaknesses and forced governments to broaden their political base or to seek wider markets for their products (Piva 1992: 257-58).

Creighton has pointed to the Panic of 1837 as a critical factor in destabilizing the economies of Lower and Upper Canada, deepening existing political discontent, and triggering armed rebellions against colonial governments (Creighton 1937). The British government's unilateral decisions during the 1840s to remove or phase out tariff duties on most imported goods and other regulatory barriers to trade—and with them, the **imperial preference** enjoyed by Canadian timber producers, flour mills, and other export industries—also deeply disrupted Canadian economic life.

Box 4.3: Overview of Canada's Economic History, Late Colonial Era, 1840s-1867

Centre of Political Power	Major Sources of Political and Economic Conflict	Catalysts for Major Changes
Imperial: Canada marginal actor in emerging international economic system (first era of globalization). Domestic: Colonial governments become accountable to majority in elected assemblies, subject to governor's influence in smaller colonies.	• Competition among shifting political factions to control patronage and commercial policies that favour client groups. • Competition for access to railroad networks leading to overextension of public finances. • Responses to economic, political shocks resulting from actions of imperial and US governments. English-French conflicts, mutual insecurity.	• Unilateral British declaration of free trade, elimination of colonial tariff preferences (1846). • Negotiation, later abrogation of Reciprocity Treaty with US (1854-66). • British desire to reduce costs of maintaining North American colonies (1860s). • Canadian pursuit of transcontinental commercial empire.

These economic shocks prompted some Montreal business interests to champion Canada's annexation by the US. Colonial governments responded by pursuing alternative markets for Canadian exports, leading to the signing in 1854 of the **Reci-**

procity Treaty with its southern neighbour. The treaty provided tariff-free access to more than 90 per cent of the existing trade between the two countries. It also provided each country with reciprocal access to the other's coastal fisheries, a US priority strongly resented by Nova Scotia. Canadian exports to the US increased four-fold in the decade after 1854. Rapid growth in both British and US export markets and cheaper, more efficient transportation systems offset the effects of increased competition while spurring the rapid expansion of Canada's railroad network (Skelton 1966: 63ff; Norrie and Owram 1996: 181-200).

However, the depression of 1857-58, which spread from the US, created a financial crisis in Canada. Interest charges on direct and government-guaranteed debt, much of it incurred to finance railroad construction, exceeded 60 per cent of government revenues. The Canadian government, heavily dependent on customs tariffs for its revenues, responded by increasing tariff rates. Although these were reduced when prosperity returned during the early 1860s, they triggered resentment both from pro-tectionist interests in the US and from British commercial interests, who wondered why Britain should be subsidizing colonies committed to increasing tariff barriers on British exports. As a result, the British were receptive to the interest of Canadian political leaders in greater self-government and encouraged the idea of the confed-eration of all Britain's North American colonies (Skelton 1966: 107-12; 141-42). When the Americans repudiated the Reciprocity Treaty in 1866, this reinforced the nation-building efforts of the Macdonald-Cartier government.

Building a National Economy: The National Policy, Canada's Industrial Revolution, and the Political Economy of Regionalism

The 60 years following Confederation marked the emergence of Canada both as a nation-state and as a largely integrated national economy. For one thing, its popula-tion doubled between 1871 and 1921. The absorption of the Hudson's Bay Company's territories and treaty settlements with their mainly Aboriginal population, combined with the building of three transcontinental railroads and the opening of Western Canada to European settlement, turned Canada from a scattered series of British colonies into a continental nation.

Political debate over economic policy during this period reflected the persistent challenge of balancing the interests of farmers and the growing urban populations of Canada's major cities. Both farming and industrial interests had championed higher tariffs during the 1830s and 1840s in response to depressed market conditions and in retaliation to US protectionism. The widespread depression of the mid-1870s prompted the federal Conservatives to answer the calls both of manufacturers for increased tariff protection to strengthen Canadian industries and of a significant minority of farmers for protection against rising US grain imports (Forster 1986: 10).

While a majority of Canadians remained dependent on agriculture, directly or indirectly, until World War I, the growth of urban centres prompted growing gov-ernment attention to the development of manufacturing industries. These policies often prompted conflicts between agrarian interests, conscious of their declining influence within Canada after 1880, and the manufacturing and financial interests which came to be concentrated increasingly in southern Ontario and Quebec. An industrial working class also emerged as a politically significant interest by the 1870s. However, large-scale class conflict between employers and workers did not become a major issue in Canadian politics until the industrial consolidations of the Laurier era resulted in the emergence of big business interests distinct from smaller producers.

There were three distinct eras of economic development and evolution of government-business relations between 1867 and the Great Depression. The Macdonald era (1867-91) was marked by Canada's adoption of the neo-mercantilist National Policy, whose protective tariff, railway-building, and frontier settlement strategies sought to integrate Canada's scattered regions within a transcontinental national economy. The Laurier era (1896-1919) witnessed the unprecedented expansion of the Canadian economy, large-scale European immigration and settlement of the Canadian West, rising political conflict between corporate and agrarian interests, and growing pressures for more intensive government intervention in the marketplace. These pressures grew with the economic and social disruptions of the 1920s, culminating in the Great Depression of the 1930s.

Government, Business, and the Economy during the Macdonald Era (1867-91)

The generation following Confederation was marked by the growth of Canada into a transcontinental nation, the gradual consolidation of political and economic institutions balancing national and regional interests, and the adoption of neo-mercantilist policies of economic development in response to US protectionism and relative economic stagnation.

These policies reflected incremental changes to and adaptations of policies initiated by colonial governments during the 1850s and 1860s rather than a sharp departure from the policies of the late colonial era (Fowke 1952). Ambitious politicians and entrepreneurs championed the idea of nation-building, which resulted in the construction of Canada's first transcontinental railway in the early 1880s. Federal-provincial relations during the era reflected a mix of partisan competition and the efforts of regional economic interests to develop effective political counterweights to federal policies that often worked to their disadvantage (Stevenson 1994). However, the general economic stagnation of the 1870s enabled Sir John A. Macdonald's Conservatives to cultivate the support of manufacturing and urban interests on a platform of protectionism and economic nationalism that became the central elements of what became known as the National Policy.

Several major factors that contributed to Confederation also lent themselves to what historian Hugh Aitken has described as federal policies of **defensive economic nationalism** during most of the half-century after 1867.

The government (was) compelled to accept responsibility for creating and conserving a national economy. This ... presented its political leaders with the task of defining and continually redefining a strategy of national economic survival sufficiently feasible and attractive to offset the ever-present alternative of absorption by the larger and more powerful economy to the south. The implementation of such strategies has led to very large public investments and has brought the political leadership into intimate alliance with influential business groups. (Aitken 1990: 111)

Confederation responded to the political deadlock of the 1860s by delegating control over a number of divisive regional issues to the provinces while leaving most of the major levers of economic development in federal hands. For example, the *Bank Act* of 1871 contributed to the growth of a national banking system centred in Montreal, Toronto, and Halifax. Federal laws regulating the insurance industry that required foreign-based companies to locate sufficient assets in Canada to cover their liabilities prompted the growth of a Canadian-based insurance sector. These measures contributed to the growth of the finance capitalism that would organize Canada's second industrial revolution. However, while alliances between bankers and entrepreneurs were vital to the growth of large-scale corporate enterprises in Canada, British-style regulations required the separation of investments in deposit-taking institutions (banks), mortgage loan firms, and insurance companies. These rules limited the kinds of financial buccaneering notorious in contemporary capitalism in the US, although debates over the practices of finance capitalism at the time left plenty of room for their extension (Bliss 1987: 255-80).

Table 4.2: Canadian Population and Rates of Growth by Decade

	Population* (thousands)	Rate of population increase by decade (per cent)	Net immigration (per cent)
1871-81	3,689	17.2	- 1.5
1881-91	4,325	11.7	- 3.4
1891-1901	4,833	11.1	- 2.7
1901-11	5,371	34.2	15.1
1911-21	7,207	21.9	4.3
1921-31	8,788	18.1	2.6
1931-41	10,377	10.9	- 0.9

* census population at beginning of period
Source: Urquhart 1988: 6.

Confederation also expanded the financial and population base of the new Dominion, potentially providing the resources to exploit its northwestern frontier after Macdonald's government acquired control over the sprawling territories of the Hudson's Bay Company in 1869. The settlement of new territories as potential markets for Canadian products became increasingly important after the US Congress cancelled the Reciprocity Treaty in 1866 and erected high tariff barriers to Canadian and other imports. As most of Ontario's best agricultural land had been settled by the time of Confederation, steady population growth demanded more land, together with outlets for the production of its growing manufacturing sector. The lure of cheap land on the US frontier and greater opportunities in US cities produced a steady stream of southward emigration which consistently exceeded the flow of new immigrants to Canada until the beginning of the twentieth century (see Table 4.2.) These factors, combined with the fear that US settlers and commercial interests would flood into and ultimately annex Canada's new North-West Territories, prompted government-led expansion into the Canadian West.

Box 4.4: Overview of Canadian Economic History, Early National Era (1867-1890s)

Centre of Political Power	Major Sources of Political and Economic Conflict	Catalysts for Major Changes
Domestic: Federal political dominance, offset by growing provincial resistance. Close linkage between federal Conservative government (1867-73, 1878-96) and the commercial elites of Montreal, Toronto, Halifax. Imperial: International economic system, British control over Canada's international relations.	• Competition to control patronage, public works, commercial policies for benefit of client groups. • Responses to international economic forces—free trade vs. protectionism; recessions of mid-1870s, 1890s. • Growing urbanization, balancing manufacturing and agricultural interests. • Federal-provincial, centre-periphery competition to control economic development policies to protect provincial autonomy and economic interests.	• Recession and continuing US protectionism (1870s) as stimulus to National Policy. • Building of CPR, opening western Canada to European settlement. • Provincial rights movements in Ontario, Quebec, Nova Scotia, and Manitoba seeking control over provincial economic development. • Judicial Committee of Privy Council rulings supporting provincial powers in economic policy.

Railroads and Nation-Building

The politics of railroads during this era reflected several major aspects of business-government relations: political and financial interdependence of government and business, the use of railroads as instruments of national development, and the politics of economic nationalism. The Dominion lacked a direct transportation link to the newly acquired provinces of Manitoba (1870) and BC (1871), forcing travelers and shippers to go through the US. The federal government committed itself to build a transcontinental rail link to BC as one of the conditions of that province's accession to Confederation.

The first syndicate established to build a Canadian Pacific Railway (CPR) fell apart amid political scandal, vicious infighting between Montreal and Toronto business interests, and widespread business scepticism that an all-Canadian project across more than 2,000 miles of wilderness populated almost entirely by First Nations could be economically viable. Macdonald chose Montreal shipping magnate Sir Hugh Allan over Toronto railroad and construction interests to head the first CPR syndicate. Forcing Allan to sever his business links with US railroad investors, the government insisted that the line be built from Lake Nipissing in northern Ontario to a point on the Pacific coast in return for a $30 million subsidy and a sizeable land grant.[2] Macdonald's Conservatives won a closely contested election in 1872 with an enormous injection of Allan's cash, subsequently estimated at $350,000. When details of these transactions surfaced in 1873 during the so-called **Pacific Scandal**, Macdonald was forced to resign (Creighton 1955: 210-12).

The subsequent Panic of 1873 destroyed the market for financing new North American railroads and pushed Canada into a prolonged economic slump. The Liberal government of Alexander Mackenzie took a cautious, pay-as-you-go approach to railroad building. It completed the Intercolonial Railway to the Maritimes begun in 1867 as a condition of Confederation, although the cost overruns and political interference associated with the line's construction and operations assured that it would continue to be a financial albatross for many years.

After Macdonald's return to office on a protectionist platform in 1878, the federal government aligned itself with a new railroad syndicate headed by George Stephen, President of the Bank of Montreal; Donald Smith, formerly Canadian head of the Hudson's Bay Company; and railroader James J. Hill, a Canadian expatriate with extensive US experience. In return for the group's commitment to an all-Canadian route, the government provided a $25 million subsidy, 25 million acres of free land along the railway's right-of-way, and government construction of the most technically difficult sections of the route west of the Lakehead and inland from the Pacific coast.[3] The government also provided the CPR with a 20-year monopoly on railway construction between its main line and the US border, as well as emergency loans when bankruptcy loomed before the end of construction in 1884 and 1885. To secure political support for these loans in an era of relatively loose party discipline, Macdonald was forced to subsidize extensive railway construction to serve other parts of the country.

The building of the CPR profoundly influenced patterns of settlement and economic development in western Canada. As initial settlement was greatest in Mani-

---

2 Historians of this period suggest multiplying currency values by 100 to provide a rough comparison with current purchasing power and economic impact.

3 The value of this construction was estimated at $38 million (Bliss 1987: 214-16). Norrie and Owram (1996: 233) suggest that, in the absence of an existing market to provide traffic for the railroad, these subsidies were necessary to ensure construction, although they more likely represented the difference between the CPR's early profits and average market rates of return.

toba, the location of the only north-south transportation link west of Detroit, Winnipeg became the region's dominant manufacturing and financial centre. The railway determined the sites of such major cities as Regina, Calgary, Vancouver, and other communities, influencing land values and economic opportunities for many years. Large federal land grants gave the railway a vested interest in promoting western settlement. Although settlement beyond Manitoba proceeded slowly until 1900, the CPR provided a major outlet for the manufactured goods of central Canada as well as BC's emerging forest industries. Until the completion of competing transcontinental railroads almost 30 years later, it dominated the market for shipments to and from most of the region, contributing to enduring tensions between western agricultural and central Canadian financial and manufacturing interests in competing for government protection and support (Barman 1991: 107-14).[4]

The Laurier government elected in 1896 responded to these pressures from its western constituents by capping and subsidizing freight rates in return for the construction of a new CPR line to serve the mining sites of BC's Kootenay region and launching a massive program of new railroad construction. The resulting Crowsnest Pass subsidy became a mainstay of western agricultural production until the 1980s. These policies reflected an evolving combination of brokerage politics with the neo-mercantilist economic policies known as the National Policy.

The National Policy

The US government's embrace of protectionist policies following the Civil War reinforced the efforts of Canadian political leaders, most of whom had close links to the colony's economic elites, to look for new avenues for domestic economic expansion. The depression of the 1870s and the Canadian government's failure to negotiate tariff reductions with the Americans contributed to Macdonald's return to office as champion of the new National Policy. While the Liberal government had increased tariffs in 1874 to raise revenues during the depression, the federal Conservatives used the mobilization of protectionist interests, especially among manufacturers, as part of a calculated effort to undermine Liberal support among Canadian manufacturing interests.

The National Policy that set the pattern for the federal government's economic policies between the late 1870s and the 1920s was a mixture of protective tariff policies, selective government subsidies, railroad policies to create a national market and open new lands for settlement, and other measures to promote strategic and regional industries as part of a broader program of economic development and diversification. It was also intended to protect and create employment for a rapidly urbanizing population, improve the linkage of regional markets within an integrated national economy, and promote mutually reinforcing patterns of development and

4 For a discussion of federal-provincial tensions over railroad policy and the repeated use of the federal power of disallowance to cancel provincial railway charters, see Stevenson 1994: 150-53. These tensions were reinforced by federal control over public lands in Manitoba and the western territories.

growth across Canada, although some historians and economists suggest that this conclusion may owe as much to *ex post facto* analysis as strategic intent (Bliss 1987: 285-86). Fowke notes that Macdonald's National Policy was the culmination of a series of initiatives to create a transcontinental Canadian nation with the capacity to exploit the economic potential of British North America as a single market, with common economic policies and transportation links as a response to nationalist and protectionist US policies (Fowke 1952: 271-75).

Advocates of protection argued that it would encourage economic diversification, the growth of manufacturing industries and of wages paid to their workers, and increased domestic markets for the producers of other commodities. They urged protection as a means of dealing with boom and bust economic cycles that encouraged rapid business expansions during good times, only to be followed by oversupply, falling prices, intensified competition, tighter credit, business failures, and rising unemployment. According to this outlook, protection would offset the advantages of US and other foreign competitors in terms of market size, economies of scale, and easier access to credit (Forster 1986: 117).

The Ontario Manufacturers Association, which played a leading role in the protectionist lobby, was successful in organizing parallel campaigns by merchants and industrial workers in Ontario despite limited cooperation from protectionist groups in other provinces. Politicians, not interest groups, performed the vital political task of balancing competing interests. Federal Finance Minister Samuel Tilley's tariff revisions of 1879 were based on widespread consultations with a fragmented business community and an effort to balance the interests of different groups of manufacturers. Most of these favoured low tariffs on raw material imports and higher tariffs on finished goods, many of which were raw materials for other manufacturers. The result was a highly complex tariff schedule which reflected **brokerage politics**: the effort to balance a variety of local and economic interests to sustain the government in office (Forster 1986: 204; Forster 1990). Tariff rates were selectively increased upwards during the 1880s, rising from an average duty of 23 per cent in 1879 to 32 per cent in 1891 and 30 per cent in 1896 before declining slightly under the Laurier government. Even so, a majority of imported goods entered Canada duty-free, even at the peak of the National Policy.[5]

The political significance of the National Policy may have been greater than its economic impact, at least during Macdonald's lifetime. It enabled the prime minister to appeal to both English-Canadian and French-Canadian nationalism by creating an external economic enemy to unite their differences in defence of Canada's national interest. Macdonald was able to mobilize the nationalist (and anti-US) sentiments fostered by these policies, along with significant bonds of economic self-interest, to frustrate the demands of farmers and other economic actors who championed free trade with the US in the elections of 1891.

---

5 Seventy per cent of items entered Canada duty-free in 1879, 61 per cent in 1896 (Norrie and Owram 1996: 249).

Reactions against the centralization of powers in Ottawa—sometimes prompted by the partisan use of federal powers of disallowance and reservation to override provincial statutes—were largely limited to provincial politics until the 1890s. Provincial rights movements in Ontario, Quebec, Nova Scotia, and Manitoba gained strength during the 1880s, both challenging the federal government's colonial attitude to the provinces and demanding greater provincial autonomy and increased recognition of regional interests in federal policies. These demands laid the foundation for a substantial decentralization of economic power to the provinces after Macdonald's death in 1891 (Stevenson 1994; Russell 1993: 39-45).

The vested interests created by the National Policy were left largely undisturbed when the Liberals swept to power in 1896, although Laurier's conversion to free trade split his party in the 1911 election and confirmed the Conservatives as the champion of protectionism and Ontario interests for the next generation. High tariffs remained a central feature of Canadian economic policies until the 1940s. Perhaps most significantly, the National Policy entered into the mythology of Canadian economic history as a successful model for government leadership of economic policy and promoting economic nationalism.

More recent economic historians have suggested that the National Policy's legacy is more ambiguous. It did contribute to moderate rates of economic growth during the 1880s and early 1890s,[6] while laying the foundations for the large-scale settlement of the Canadian prairies during the Laurier years. Responding to chronic US protectionism, it laid the foundations for Canada's second industrial revolution and, with it, the concentration of political and economic power that became a staple of controversy for much of the next century. Other concerns, such as the effects of tariff protection on business efficiency and competitiveness or the incentives provided for foreign investment and control over Canadian industries, became issues for future generations to debate.

The Laurier Era and the Second Industrial Revolution

The Laurier government (1896-1911) continued to implement the broad outlines of the National Policy while adapting it in a number of ways to meet the concerns of social, economic, and regional interests that felt they had been short-changed by the Macdonald government.

A series of court actions by Ontario Premier Oliver Mowat established the legal basis for equality between the two levels of government that was effectively conceded by Macdonald's successors during the 1890s. Several major rulings by the Judicial Committee of the Privy Council (JCPC)—Canada's final court of appeal before 1949—affirmed the rights of provincial governments to regulate economic activity within their own borders, enabling business and other economic interests allied with provincial governments to challenge federal policies within certain limits.

---

6 Real GNP growth in Canada averaged a healthy, if not spectacular 2.8 per cent between 1877 and 1896, 1.5 per cent on a per capita basis (Marchildon 1996: 9).

The opening of the prairies to large-scale European settlement beginning in the 1890s and the continuing flood of immigration into other parts of the country contributed to rapid population growth. Between 1901 and 1914, Canada's population grew by 44 per cent from 5,300,000 to 7,630,000 (Bliss 1987: 340). Real economic growth during the Laurier boom (1896-1911) averaged 6.6 per cent, which was higher than in any other industrial or emerging economy, even the US (Marchildon 1996: 7-8).

Box 4.5: Overview of Canadian Economic History, Canada's Second Industrial Revolution (1890s-1920s)

Centre of Political Power	Major Sources of Political and Economic Conflict	Catalysts for Major Changes
Federal restraint in exercise of economic power (except World War I); ad hoc responses to specific challenges. Active provincial leadership in regional development.	Industrial vs. agricultural interests: • free trade election of 1911; growing industrial consolidation. • conflicts over tariffs, freight rates, exercise of market power by corporate interests. Growing regional conflict.	Major population growth; railroad, resource, and agricultural booms (to 1913). Huge capital influx contributes to structural changes in Canadian industry: • corporate consolidation—major industrial mergers. • growth of finance capitalism. • centralization of economic power in Montreal, Toronto.

Part of this growth resulted from high levels of immigration, the rapid settlement of the Canadian prairies after 1900, and the unprecedented increase in wheat production. However, an even larger share of growth resulted from a wave of foreign investment in Canadian industries, the introduction and restructuring of new technologies and manufacturing processes, and the emergence of corporate enterprises capable of mobilizing and managing economic activity on a large scale (Marchildon 1996; Norrie and Owram 1996: 223-24, 240-41).

The wheat boom of the Laurier era is often cited as a major illustration of the staples theory. Urbanization and population growth in Europe, combined with falling domestic and transatlantic shipping costs, vastly increased the demand for Canadian wheat and flour in European markets. Western settlement, rising populations, and railway building also created significant new markets for Canadian manufactured products, especially its iron and steel industry (Norrie and Owram 1996: 233-39).

While allowing provincial governments to pursue their own economic development projects, Laurier also continued Macdonald's national railroad-building Program. To foster western settlement and growth, while appeasing farmers' anger at the CPR monopoly, the Liberals subsidized the development of two national competitors to the CPR—the Grand Trunk Pacific and the Canadian Northern. It also built its own National Transcontinental Railway across the forests of northern Ontario and Quebec, providing Quebec and the Maritimes with expanded access to the transcontinental railway system. Provincial governments contributed their own railway-building subsidies to ensure as many communities as possible would be linked to the national system. Federal, provincial, and private railroads also opened up the northern districts of Ontario and Quebec and the interior of BC to mineral and forestry development (Bliss 1987: 313-29; Barman 1991: 178-82, 194-96). This process has been traditionally described as pure staples theory:

> Federal railway policy ensured that grain would move east, through Canadian handling and distribution facilities, and on Canadian rail lines, rather than south, to join American supplies. Tariffs ensured that Canadian manufactured goods could compete with imported ones, providing not just revenue for central Canadian businesses, but also return traffic for the railways. (Norrie and Owram 1996: 239)

A secondary effect of both federal and provincial railway policies was the expansion of opportunities for patronage, clientelism, and fundraising for governing parties. Not only did governments heavily subsidize railway entrepreneurs and contractors, they also milked them for political contributions, often skimmed from padded payrolls, and actively used related employment opportunities to generate a flexible reserve of votes. Such practices became a main component of partisan political controversy (Norrie and Owram 1996: 239). Outrage at the systemic corruption of the party system helped to fuel populist movements for reform after World War I.

An alternative view of economic development during the Laurier era points to the interaction of population growth, technological changes, and large-scale infrastructure developments with the emergence of large, professionally managed corporate structures, requiring unprecedented levels of capital investment, in a **Second Industrial Revolution**. Beginning in the late 1880s, a series of technological and managerial changes contributed to the transformation of economic activity across much of the industrial world. These included technological changes in manufacturing; the shift from iron to steel in many sectors; the gradual introduction of electricity and hydroelectric power generation; and the development of the internal combustion engine and new industrial products and processes including chemicals, plastics, and synthetic fibres (Norrie and Owram 1996: 223-24).

These capital-intensive industrial activities lent themselves to large-scale enterprises rather than small-scale family businesses. Sizeable manufacturing, financial, utility, and industrial combines emerged with the capital to pursue major economic ventures and the economic power to dominate or eliminate smaller competitors.

As early as 1891, the Massey and Harris companies had combined to form Canada's largest farm implement manufacturer. A wave of corporate consolidation came after the turn of the century: 275 individual firms were combined into 58 industrial enterprises between 1909 and 1912 (Bliss 1987: 338); for instance, financier Max Aitken (later Lord Beaverbrook) organized the mergers of several competitors into Canada Cement in 1909 and the Steel Company of Canada in 1910. Similar growth was seen in the resource industries, particularly in mining in BC and northern Ontario and the pulp and paper industry in Quebec, Ontario, and BC.

Some of these mergers were defensive in character: they were intended to enable Canadian firms to compete against huge US corporations. Others were the product of financial entrepreneurs such as Aitken, James Dunn, and George Cox, whose capacity to organize large stock offerings in British and US markets transformed large segments of the Canadian economy.

Governments often cooperated with such financial and industrial barons, who could help finance and manage the processes of economic development that would bring the benefits of large-scale economic growth to all parts of Canada, not just the already developed communities of southern Ontario and Quebec. In some cases, these businesses proved to be highly efficient competitors who increased production and reduced prices to consumers. In others, they became financially overextended or abused their market power at the expense of suppliers and consumers. Concern over the growth of corporate **cartels** to limit competition prompted the Laurier government to pass changes to the *Tariff Act* in 1897 to remove protection for any industry engaging in such activity (Marchildon 1996: 209). The federal government also passed anti-combines legislation in 1889 and 1910, but these measures proved relatively ineffective in controlling abuses of market power.

Marchildon suggests that the purpose of this anti-combines legislation was to distinguish between good monopolies, whose increased returns to shareholders reflected greater managerial and economic efficiency, and bad monopolies that were primarily the result of financial manipulation and abuses of economic power (Marchildon 1996: 209-14). Similar debates took place in the US between advocates of government action to break up dominant or monopolistic firms (called "trusts") and supporters of government regulation committed to monitoring and regulating business activities in the public interest. As Canadian laws required high standards of proof to establish criminal intent by corporate executives engaged in collusive activities, governments gradually introduced other forms of economic regulation intended to balance the competing interests of different producer groups and consumers.

The development of large corporate enterprises in which senior managers functioned at a considerable distance from employees also contributed to increasing labour militancy. International craft unions spread from the US into Canada, taking control of the Canadian Trades and Labour Congress during the 1890s. In reaction to low pay, economic insecurity, and poor working conditions, industrial unionism emerged later in the mining towns and other resource industries of northern and western Canada. However, while unions had been extended recognition in federal law as early as 1872, both federal and provincial laws still tended to treat employment contracts as private matters to be resolved between employers and employees during this era. Union membership declined from 17 per cent to 7 per cent during the prosperity of the Laurier boom, only to recover sharply during the economic turmoil during and after the World War I (Bliss 1987: 356; Barman 1991: 206-24).

Both public opinion and significant elements of the business community demanded government intervention to limit or offset the power of the industrial combines. Conservative business interests in Ontario, spearheaded by Adam Beck, the first chairman of the public utility that became Ontario Hydro, championed public power at cost as an alternative to the exactions of private power monopolies (Freeman 1996: 10-58). Provincial governments in Alberta and Manitoba set up their own publicly owned telephone systems as an alternative to eastern monopolies. The federal government set up the Board of Railroad Commissioners to regulate freight rates and limit the profits that large railroad interests could extract from shippers, large and small. In some cases, these measures echoed the initiatives of progressive governments in the US; in others, they reflected regional or national responses to the problems as well as the benefits of economic concentration. Ontario also introduced Workmen's Compensation legislation in 1915 to protect workers against the economic risks of industrial accidents.

However, the willingness of Canadian businesses and governments to copy US innovations in corporate organization, financial markets, and government regulations did not extend to the creation of a single North American market by removing the protectionist tariffs enshrined under the National Policy. When Laurier bowed to pressure from his supporters in rural Ontario and western Canada to negotiate another Reciprocity Treaty with the US in 1910, many of his business and financial supporters abandoned his Liberal Party, along with much of the urban working-class vote. The forces of English-Canadian nationalism combined with corporate interests to defeat Laurier in the federal election of 1911 (Marchildon 1996: 215-27).[7]

The economic disruptions of World War I led to additional demands for government intervention, particularly by farmers who were hard hit by rising prices and federal regulation of grain prices for the war effort. Federal controls on freight rates meant that the railroads fostered during the pre-war boom years could no longer finance their debts. The Grand Trunk Pacific and Mackenzie and Mann's Canadian Northern systems went bankrupt and were nationalized by the federal government in 1917.

This example of government economic development strategies—dubbed mega-project-based development by a later generation—creating top-heavy corporate empires that were too big to fail, yet too indebted to succeed, became a recurring effect of federal and provincial policies over the years. Nationalization of the rail-

---

7 The rhetorical excesses of the anti-free trade forces in the 1911 election bring to mind more recent events. Marchildon notes that the poet Rudyard Kipling "submitted an open letter to the Montreal Star suggesting that reciprocity for Canada really meant reciprocity with the much higher murder rate in the United States" (Marchildon 1996: 227).

ways, while the least disruptive option available to the Conservative government of
Sir Robert Borden, imposed huge costs and debts on the federal government which
sharply limited its capacity for new economic initiatives during most of the 1920s
and 1930s (Bliss 1985).[8]

Disruption, Depression, and War: 1919-1945

The economic, social, and political pressures unleashed by World War I seriously
disrupted both the Canadian economy and traditional elite-dominated patterns
of clientelism in economic policy and business-government relations. Canada's
economy experienced a series of economic shocks after the war, culminating in the
social and economic catastrophe of the Great Depression, which undermined public confidence in existing forms of capitalist organization and created a receptive
environment for social reform and significantly greater government intervention in
economic life.

These factors, combined with growing corporate concentration, created a persistent political backlash that changed the face of Canadian political life. Postwar
agrarian populism challenged both the traditional party system and its patronage-
centred approach to politics and business. The Great Depression spawned both
organized populist and socialist challenges to existing forms of capitalist organization, prompting the established national parties to endorse a larger government role
in the economy and to lay the foundations of the welfare state.

World War II resulted in the unprecedented centralization of economic power in
the hands of the federal government in its relations with both the provinces and the
private sector. However, while Ottawa retained extensive control over macroeconomic policies after the war, its adoption of Keynesian economic theories struck a
new balance between overall government guidance of the economy and extensive
private sector discretion in day-to-day business activities.

Two Decades of Economic Turmoil

The interwar years were marked by persistent economic turmoil that disrupted previous patterns of economic activity and political and social relations. The monetary
expansion triggered by World War I resulted in several years of high inflation. The
average cost of living increased by 71 per cent between 1916 and 1920.[9] The end of
war-related exports and belated efforts to restrain credit provoked a sharp recession in 1919-21 as exports dropped by more than 25 per cent. Farm prices dropped
by half between 1920 and 1923. Record numbers of businesses failed (Bliss 1987: 383-
86; Norrie and Owram 1986: 317-20). Some of these shocks were by-products of the

---

8 Federal and provincial loan guarantees to the Canadian Northern alone totalled more than $170 million
in 1916, a staggering sum given the limited size of governments during the era. Nationalization was viewed
as a lesser evil than the effects of bankruptcy on the Canadian financial system and public finance, particularly in the middle of a war (Norrie and Owram 1996: 320-21).

9 Industrial wage rates also grew sharply—in sharp contrast with farm incomes (Statistics Canada, 1999,
Tables K1-7, E198-208).

international economic instability of the era. Others were the result of both business and policy failures in Canada.

Prosperity returned to some parts of Canada during the 1920s, but patterns of growth varied widely between regions and industry sectors (Norrie and Owram 1986: 293). Driven by growing export demand and rising levels of foreign, especially US, investment, Ontario experienced rapid expansion in its mining, forestry, and automotive sectors. BC grew rapidly during the decade, as the opening of the Panama Canal and pre-war improvements in its railroad system encouraged rapid growth of its resource industries. Vancouver became the country's third largest city. Quebec's economy, especially its resource industries, also experienced steady, if unspectacular growth. However, the agricultural economies of the prairies were forced to make painful adjustments.

The Maritimes also began a period of steady economic decline during this period, as their leading coal and steel industries suffered from oversupply, falling global prices, and bitter industrial turmoil. High freight rates and distance from central Canada markets inhibited the growth of new industries. Manufacturing employment dropped by 44 per cent in urban areas of Nova Scotia and New Brunswick between 1920 and 1926, while the Maritimes' share of Canada's manufacturing value added dropped from 9 per cent in 1911 to 5 per cent in 1939 (Savoie 2001: 19-23). The Maritime Rights Movement of the early 1920s succeeded in winning additional federal freight rate subsidies for the region, but these measures had little effect on longer term economic trends.

Urbanization continued in most parts of Canada. High tariff policies spurred a significant increase in American investment in Canadian resource and manufacturing industries, and the US replaced Britain as the largest source of foreign investment in Canada and its largest export market (Savoie 2001: 317-38).

Federal policies during the 1920s were relatively cautious, reflecting the huge burden of war debt and the continuing drain of subsidies to the Canadian National Railway, formed from the wreckage of the Grand Trunk, Canadian Northern, and National Transcontinental systems in 1923. William Lyon Mackenzie King's Liberals required the support of agrarian and labour MPs elected under the Progressive Party banner to remain in office for much of the decade. In an effort to maintain his support in central Canada, King accepted sharp tariff reductions on farm implements while maintaining high tariffs on most other manufactured goods (Gillespie 1991: 145-67; Oliver 1977: 170-71). Inheriting the decentralist policies of the Laurier era, along with a fragile party characterized by deep regional divisions, he was reluctant to interfere in areas of provincial jurisdiction. His economic policies sought to balance cautious financial management with the selective accommodation of populist pressures and regional demands.

However, while Canada shared in the worldwide boom of the late 1920s, the patchwork quilt of national and regional subsidies within an overall framework of protectionism could not protect its economy from the shattering effects of the Great Depression which devastated most of the industrial world between 1929 and

1939. Canada was more seriously affected than any other industrial country, with the exception of the US. Average price levels dropped 22 per cent, and the real GDP dropped by 26 per cent between 1929 and 1933—43 per cent in nominal dollar terms. Regional effects were even greater. For example, average per capita income in Saskatchewan dropped a staggering 72 per cent during the first four years of the crisis (Bliss 1987: 418-19; Smith 1975: 204).

The effects of the Depression fell most heavily on the farm sector, especially on the prairies. Total farm incomes, already in decline, collapsed after 1929, falling 83 per cent between 1929 and 1933, as persistent drought and crop failures reinforced the trials of international markets. Table 4.3 summarizes the extent of the economic collapse and slow recovery of the 1930s.

Table 4.3: Measuring the Crash

1926 = 100	1926	1929	1932	1933	1937	1939
GDP (nominal)	100	119	74	68	102	109
Exports	100	91	39	42	79	73
Total farm income	100	64	17	11	46	59
Corporation profits (nominal)	100	122	- 30	23	86	111
Unemployment (per cent of labour force)	3.0%	2.8%	17.6%	19.3%	9.1%	11.4%

Source: Statistics Canada 2002b; Bliss 1987: 418-19; author's calculations.

Governments whose resources were stretched to the limit by the rising costs of unemployment relief lacked the financial or theoretical resources to deal with the crisis. One provincial government after another was thrown out of office by voters desperate for a political remedy. Conservative Prime Minister R.B. Bennett, elected in 1930, belatedly introduced a series of initiatives borrowed in part from Roosevelt's New Deal in the US. However, his government was routed in the 1935 election as the Liberals campaigned on the slogan "King or Chaos."

Canada limped through the rest of the Depression while King continued his cautious political and financial balancing act, until the outbreak of World War II provided the impetus needed for industrial mobilization and full employment. However, the pressures of social and political conflict during these years were not so easily contained at the provincial level. The decentralization of economic responsibility to the provinces increasingly channelled pressures for economic and social reform into provincial politics.

Decentralizing Economic Power to the Provinces

The 1920s marked the ongoing shift from a business environment dominated by the federal government to one in which the provinces played significant, but very different roles that directly affected the environment for economic development and business-government relations.

The federal Liberal Party, led by Laurier and Mackenzie King between 1887 and 1948, was broadly committed to the compact theory of Confederation, which acknowledged the sovereignty and equality of federal and provincial governments within their respective areas of jurisdiction. While this position did not preclude federal-provincial conflicts during lengthy periods of federal Liberal rule during the first half of the twentieth century (1896-1911, 1921-30, 1935-57), it permitted the emergence of a number of strong provincial governments committed to controlling the terms of economic development within their own jurisdictions. The longer these governments were entrenched, as illustrated in Table 4.4, the more likely they were to be protective of their own jurisdictions and political power, and confident that they were at least as capable of promoting the economic well-being of their citizens as an often remote federal government. When jurisdictional issues were contested in the courts, the JCPC continued to favour a decentralist interpretation of the constitution, as in *Toronto Electric Commissioners vs. Snider* (1925), which confirmed provincial jurisdiction over labour relations as an extension of provincial regulation of property and civil rights.

Table 4.4: Provincial Ruling "Dynasties" in the Late Nineteenth and Early Twentieth Centuries

	Party	Years in Office	Number of Premiers
Nova Scotia	Liberal	64—1884-1925, 1933-56	5
Quebec	Liberal	39—1897-1936	4
Alberta	United Farmers	16—1919-35	3
	Social Credit	36—1935-71	3
Saskatchewan	Liberal	33—1905-29, 1934-43	5
Ontario	Conservative	25—1905-19, 1923-34	4
Manitoba	United Farmers	21—1922-43	1

With the settlement of the prairies, frontier development shifted to the resource-rich regions of the Canadian Shield and the BC interior—areas in which economic development was largely shaped by provincial policies (Canada, Royal Commission on Dominion-Provincial Relations 1940: 112-37; Oliver 1977: 170). Ontario, Quebec, and BC all emphasized an open-for-business policy of encouraging large-scale investments in their provinces' timber, pulp-and-paper, mining, and hydroelectric resources. Regulations were usually designed (and sometimes circumvented) to provide ready business access to resources and to encourage—and sometimes mandate—further processing within their provinces. Large amounts of US capital flooded into all three provinces to take advantage of low resource royalties and mining taxes and large amounts of cheap power; ultimately, however, this contributed to overcapacity, wasteful production policies, and depressed prices, particularly in the forestry sector (Oliver 1977: 343-52; Saywell 1991: 241-44).

The growth of provincial functions that affected business created many opportunities for political patronage and clientelism. Increased liquor regulation and government-controlled distribution as an alternative to the failed experiment of Prohibition made many businesses dependent on political favours for their livelihoods. The spreading use of automobiles and the political benefits of reducing rural isolation encouraged increased road-building by governments, especially in election years. Private power producers, whose ownership and operations were closely intertwined with major industrial interests on both sides of the border, maintained close relations with provincial governments in Quebec and BC, although government-owned Ontario Hydro remained a major element in the development of that province's chief industries and in rural development. The linkages between government policies and services and economic development provided a fertile climate for patronage and machine politics in most provinces and for populist appeals to "throw out the rascals"—although, as often as not, one set of rascals was likely to replace another (Saywell 1991: 241-44; Black 1977; Saywell 1991: 223-26; Whitaker 1977; Noel 1971).

Although most provinces were overextended financially by the costs of financing unemployment relief during the Great Depression, it was the provinces, rather than the federal government, that took much of the lead in providing public works projects to provide employment and encourage economic recovery.[10] When the Rowell-Sirois Commission (formally the Royal Commission on Dominion-Provincial Relations) recommended a sizeable transfer of powers from the provinces to the federal government in 1940, Ontario, BC, and Alberta vetoed the proposal, except for the transfer of jurisdiction over Unemployment Insurance to the federal government.

Social Turmoil, Political Conflict, and Change
The interwar years were characterized by recurring waves of populist backlash against the economic and social disruptions of the industrial era and postwar economic life. The rapid inflation of 1916-20 resulted in increased labour militancy as workers organized unions to assist them in keeping up with the rising cost of living. The Winnipeg General Strike of 1919 was the most spectacular, but certainly not the only expression of labour grievances (Bliss 1987: 383-89; Barman 1991: 206-24).

Agrarian discontent overflowed into a militant farmers' movement seeking federal and provincial policies more responsive to rural interests and greater government control over concentrations of private economic power.[11] Despairing of consis-

---

10 Federal transfers during this period were provided grudgingly, reflecting a mix of short-term political fixes, economic conservatism, competition for political advantage, and conflicting personalities (see Hutchinson 1953: 174-79; Saywell 1991: 247-53; Kendle 1979: 110-16, 127-33, 147-71).

11 Some farmers' organizations also created economic cooperatives as a way of balancing the economic power of large corporations, reducing costs for primary producers, and providing them with a larger share of the economic return from the processing of agricultural products. However, the influence and survival of these groups often depended on the separation of their activities from partisan politics (Oliver 1977: 90-91). For contrasts with agrarian politics in Saskatchewan, see Smith 1975: 55-56; 66-107.

tent support for farmer interests from traditional political parties dependent on the financial support of business (Oliver 1977: 91), agrarian parties ran separate slates of candidates in federal and provincial elections. The Progressive Party sent the second largest bloc of MPs to Ottawa in 1921. Farmers' parties also elected governments in Ontario (1919-23), Alberta (1919-35), and Manitoba (1922-43). Agrarian activists supported public ownership of utilities and government regulation of railroads and other examples of concentrated economic power. However, they tended to be sceptical of government interference in their day-to-day business activities and supportive of measures to decentralize political and economic power. The farmers' movement was linked to the contemporary social gospel movements for the social and moral reform of society that challenged many of the established political and economic conditions of the era (Allen 1992).

The reform movements of the 1920s, dependent on different coalitions of regional, class, and ethnic support in each region of the country, accelerated the fragmentation of Canadian party politics. While united in opposition to the corruption and cynicism of the major parties, populist Progressives became increasingly divided over the direction of both economic and social reform. Some sought to reform the capitalist system, using the power of governments to make it more responsive to the needs of small producers and emphasizing the social values of individual responsibility and self-reliance, assisted where necessary by cooperative activity and government regulation. Others pressed for more radical social and economic change; social partnerships between farmers and organized labour; the expansion of social welfare programs; more redistributive taxation; and greater government control over banks, railroads, power utilities, and other major corporations. Both groups used the rhetoric of class warfare, challenges to special privilege, and demands for greater government intervention, especially since the Great Depression had caused mass unemployment, hundreds of thousands on relief, and the devastation of the farm economy (Oliver 1977: 94, 116, 130-32; Smith, 1975: 225ff; Barr 1974: 13-34).

The populist search for economic and social reform spawned several new political movements during the 1930s. The Cooperative Commonwealth Federation (CCF) was created in 1933 by the fusion of labour parties with the left wing of the farmers' movement to champion the socialization of economic activity, a planned economy, and a major expansion of social welfare programs. By 1934, the CCF had formed the official opposition in BC and Saskatchewan and was making significant inroads in the politics of Ontario.

Social Credit, which also emerged on the prairies as an inflationist response to the Depression, combined revivalist religion, direct democracy, demands for provincial control of the banks, debt refinancing, and the large-scale printing and distribution of money to increase consumer purchasing power. Swept to power in Alberta in 1935, much of its program was ruled unconstitutional by the Supreme Court or disallowed by the federal government before the end of the decade (Barr 1974: 107-12). However, while its influence in neighbouring Saskatchewan was short-lived, it re-emerged in BC during the 1950s as the party of populist individualism and business development.

Traditional brokerage political parties sought to co-opt the leaders of reform movements into their organizations to demonstrate their responsiveness to changing social and economic circumstances and diffuse demands for more radical reforms. Similar tactics kept the Saskatchewan Liberals in power for most of the period between 1905 and 1944 and enabled Ontario Liberal populist Mitch Hepburn to build a coalition between rural Liberals, Progressives, and urban labour interests in the 1930s. At the same time, BC's Duff Pattullo embarked on a grand program of what he called socialized capitalism: public works and government economic regulation. The federal Conservatives sought to broaden their political base by recruiting veteran Manitoba Farmers' Premier John Bracken to become their leader in 1943, in the process changing the party name to Progressive Conservative. Their Ontario counterparts adopted an extensive program of social legislation within the framework of a somewhat more regulated market economy that enabled them to regain and retain power between 1943 and 1985.

In Quebec, voters ended almost 40 years of conservative, business-oriented government in 1936 by electing the populist Union Nationale, an opportunistic coalition of Conservatives, liberal reformers, and nationalists. While its leader Maurice Duplessis introduced a number of policies favourable to small producers and unorganized workers, he abandoned most of his promises of social reform before losing power in 1939. Returned to office in 1944 as part of an anti-conscription backlash, he perfected the amalgam of paternalistic government, patronage-driven machine politics, and support for business-led economic development that may have been typical of provincial politics in the 1920s but which was increasingly out of fashion in most provinces by the 1950s.

However, while most of these developments were responses to the economic and social emergency of the Great Depression, the renewed prosperity and optimism arising from World War II opened the door to a new economic policy consensus that shaped business-government relations for most of the next generation.

Wartime Economic Policy and the Politics of Industrial Change

The federal government took a much more active role in economic leadership during World War II. As in 1914-18, it introduced price controls, established extensive bureaucratic controls over all forms of war-related production, and conscripted large numbers of business leaders into the management of the war economy. Ottawa used its emergency war powers to facilitate collective bargaining by unions and laid the foundations for government tax and spending policies to become the balance wheel of the economy, partly through promising the extension of the welfare state.

These measures were necessitated in part by the need to coordinate economic activity to support the war effort and to maintain social cohesion to ensure the efficient operation of war industries. However, they also responded to growing public and business expectations of social and economic reforms to avoid a repetition of the boom and bust economic cycles of the 1920s and 1930s. Canada's political, business, and other opinion leaders agreed that a different approach to economic policy would be necessary if the second postwar era were not to relive the uncertainties and conflicts of the pre-war era. The transition process, along with substantial reductions in the remaining wartime economic controls, was facilitated by the trust developed between business leaders and the federal government, particularly its leading economic minister, **C.D. Howe** (Bliss 1987: 445-47).

Historian Donald Creighton suggests that the public's experience of the inconveniences of "wartime scarcities, controls and bureaucratic regimentation" made many voters more responsive to proposed reforms that would provide overall government guidance to the economy and greater social equity without the need for detailed government intervention in the day-to-day economic choices and activities of individuals and businesses (Creighton 1976: 103-04). These trade-offs formed the basis for the Keynesian political economy of the postwar era and what some have called the **Second National Policy**.

Keynesian Political Economy and the Second National Policy

Canadian economic policies went through major changes during and after World War II. These changes were heavily influenced by the conventional goals of economic policy described earlier: economic development and diversification, responses to (and attempts to anticipate) international economic shocks, the pursuit of social cohesion, and the processes of nation-building. However, they involved a major rethinking of the major policy instruments that had characterized the first National Policy of the 1870s to 1920s.

After 1935, the federal government set in motion several major policy reviews to examine the causes of the Great Depression and to recommend changes in the policies and structures of Canadian governments that would enable them to prevent or mitigate the effects of future economic upheavals. Although it took a number of years for these initiatives, including the Rowell-Sirois Commission of 1937-40 and the Marsh Committee on Reconstruction of 1943-45, to work their way into government policy, they were the basis of what became known as the federal government's Second National Policy (Bradford 1998: 35-51).

The Second National Policy was intended to prevent a recurrence of the Great Depression and to address a number of the structural factors that had contributed to economic instability between the wars. It had five major components:

- Rather than emphasizing protectionist policies to develop domestic Canadian industries, the federal government entered into a series of international agreements that gradually opened Canadian markets to foreign competition while fostering large-scale foreign investment in Canada.
- Rather than allowing the business cycle to take its own course, the federal government actively adopted Keynesian demand management policies to

stabilize economic activity and stimulate private sector investment and job
creation.

- The expansion of the welfare state, while promoting social cohesion and
  sharing the benefits of economic growth, was also intended to serve as
  an instrument of economic stabilization, maintaining consumer demand
  during economic downturns.
- Federal and provincial governments also made it easier for unions to
  organize and use collective bargaining to enable their members to share in
  the benefits of economic growth and negotiate the process of adjustments to
  future economic shocks.
- Finally, rather than introducing central government planning, as advocated
  by socialist academics and advocates of greater state control of the economy,
  government intervention in the day-to-day workings of the economy was
  rather more selective, focusing on strategic sectors and creating a positive
  environment for business and employment growth. (Simeon and Robinson
  1990: 113-15)

As a result, the postwar emphasis on macroeconomic policies and a phasing-out
of wartime controls meant that, in most industries, government policies would
exert indirect guidance rather than direct control over the investment decisions and
operations of business.

From Economic Nationalism to Limited Internationalism

By the 1940s, protectionism was no longer seen as a viable strategy for economic
development. Canada had failed to blast its way into foreign markets through the
use of high tariff policies during the 1930s. In fact, such tariffs were widely perceived
to have been a contributing factor to the economic dislocation of the Great Depression. Imperial free trade, which had been a fall-back policy for the Bennett Government of 1930-35, was not a viable option in the aftermath of World War II as Britain
lacked the hard currency to resume its role as Canada's principal trading partner
and most other Commonwealth nations were too distant from Canada to be major
markets for its products.

Liberal Prime Minister Mackenzie King, who had lost his parliamentary seat in
the 1911 election over free trade, rejected the political risks of a free trade agreement
with the US in 1947. However, Canada became a party to a series of multilateral trade
agreements through the newly formed General Agreement on Trade and Tariffs
(GATT) and other organizations throughout the 1940s and 1950s, which were committed to phased tariff reductions on a wide range of manufactured imports and
other forms of international cooperation to restore prosperity and reduce international conflict. These organizations provided a means of balancing as well as projecting the influence of the US as the world's dominant economic power. They also
enabled Canada to play an active role in the international economic system of the
era while engaging the US in a "special relationship," reflected in several bilateral

agreements that gave Canada preferred access to US capital and markets (Canada, Royal Commission on the Economic Union 1985: Vol. 1, 226-27; Hart 1985).

As foreign exchange restrictions were gradually eliminated between 1945 and 1951, the federal and most provincial governments welcomed a flood of foreign investment into Canada, mainly for the development of Canada's manufacturing and resource industries. The buildup of war-related industries, especially in Ontario and southern Quebec, had contributed to the renewal of Canada's industrial base. The demand for Canada's raw materials, and the expansion of its manufacturing capacity in response to pent-up consumer demand across North America, contributed to a prolonged economic expansion that was only briefly interrupted by the pressures of the Korean War. The forestry and mining industries of BC, northern Ontario, and northern and eastern Quebec grew rapidly during this period, providing welcome employment and rising standards of living. Alberta, which had been virtually bankrupted by the Depression, benefited from the discovery and development of sizeable oil and gas reserves, although the rest of the prairie provinces trailed other parts of Canada in population and economic growth through much of the postwar era. Atlantic Canada, including Newfoundland which joined Confederation in 1949, began to reverse its huge income gap with the rest of Canada during the 1950s and 1960s, although industrial development there progressed slowly (Savoie 2001: 26; Brodie 1990: 156-57).

While regional economic disparities declined somewhat during the 1950s and 1960s, as noted in Table 4.5, their persistence helps to explain the enduring appeal of John Diefenbaker's economic populism in outer Canada during the late 1950s and 1960s and the rise of the populist Créditiste movement in rural Quebec during the early 1960s.

Table 4.5: Personal Income per Capita by Province

(per cent of Canadian average)

	1946	1951	1961	1966	1971
BC	114.9	119.0	115.0	110.7	107.4
Alberta	107.8	111.2	99.8	98.6	96.8
Saskatchewan	96.1	107.9	72.2	90.0	78.5
Manitoba	103.0	100.8	94.1	91.3	92.1
Ontario	115.7	118.2	118.4	117.0	117.4
Quebec	81.5	83.9	90.0	89.7	90.3
New Brunswick	75.2	66.9	67.1	69.3	71.6
Nova Scotia	85.9	69.2	76.7	73.5	75.7
PEI	58.2	54.8	59.7	63.7	61.9
Newfoundland	–	48.3	59.8	60.3	63.5

Source: Canada, Department of Finance 1992: adapted from Table 16.2.

The 1950s also marked a significant opening of Canada's economy and its rapid integration in the larger North American economy, although some industries retained significant tariff protection. Canadian industries had benefited from full involvement in and integration with the Anglo-American war effort during World War II and were bolstered by Canada's participation in the North Atlantic Treaty Organization (NATO), the Korean War, and the North American Air Defense (NORAD) agreement. The result was the negotiation of formal defence production sharing agreements with the US that led to a rationalization of manufacturing between the two countries. Although the federal government took active steps to foster the development of a national aircraft industry during and after World War II as one element of a larger industrial strategy (Bliss 1987: 460-62, 470-77), the viability of such industries depended on consistent access to US and other foreign markets and the increased productivity resulting from longer production runs, access to new technologies, and the rationalization of production facilities.

Similar reasoning resulted in the negotiation of the **Auto Pact** in 1965, which permitted the full integration of the automobile manufacturing industries on both sides of the border. As the federal government included safeguards requiring the production of one vehicle in Canada for every one sold here, the agreement led to rapid industrial growth and the emergence of a large Canadian auto parts manufacturing industry.

Canadian nationalists, particularly Toronto businessman **Walter Gordon**, who chaired the Royal Commission on Canada's Economic Prospects in 1955-56, began to express concerns about increasing US control over Canada's economy (Bradford 1998: 61-66). However, although Gordon became finance minister in the Liberal Government of 1963-65, his views were met with strong resistance not just from Canada's business community but also from the federal bureaucracy (Bradford 1998; Newman 1968).

Some observers, particularly on the left, have suggested that the Second National Policy gave new life to business dominance over Canadian economic policies between the 1940s and 1960s. Certainly, business elites enjoyed close personal and professional linkages with federal ministers responsible for economic policy during this period. Provincial governments in the four largest provinces—Ontario, Quebec, BC, and Alberta—were also strongly pro-business, although growing government bureaucracies began to change the nature of business-government relationships at the provincial as well as federal level.

The growth and increasing confidence of the federal public service has led a number of critics to suggest that the greatest impetus for Canadian economic policy during this era came from technocratic liberals within the federal bureaucracy, who were reinforced by the driving political leadership of Trade and Commerce Minister C.D. Howe and his successors within the federal government (Bradford 1998; Bliss 1987). Their most significant policy innovation was the introduction of Keynesian macroeconomic policies to regulate the business cycle as an alternative to both laissez-faire economic policies and state planning and control of economic activity.

Keynesian Macroeconomic Management

The federal government's endorsement of Keynesian macroeconomic demand management policies was a direct response to the economic shocks of the 1930s and to the need for policies that would encourage both business investment and social cohesion. As long as the Department of Finance maintained relatively centralized control over the levers of Canadian macroeconomic policy until the early 1970s, Keynesian policies provided both the political and economic balance to sustain economic growth and mitigate the effects of periodic downturns in the business cycle. Despite rapid population growth of 75 per cent between 1946 and 1971, real per capita GDP increased by 90 per cent during this period. As noted in Table 4.6, per capita GDP grew steadily during the 1950s and 1960s, except for the period between 1957 and 1961.

Some economists have suggested that Keynesianism provided a means to enable the accumulation of capital necessary to promote continued private investment and economic growth, while it also legitimized the economic system by redistributing the benefits of growth through the expansion of public services and income transfers (for example, see O'Connor 1973). For this reason, it satisfied both the expectations of business groups that desired the benefits of government leadership without the restrictions of government interference in day-to-day business activities and the concerns of organized labour and other economic interests for government action to promote high levels of employment and rising standards of living. Bradford (1998) has suggested that the highly decentralized nature of business organization and the disagreements among different business groups on new approaches to economic policy left the federal government with considerable policy discretion. (For a contrary view, contrasting Canadian policies with the left-Keynesian policies of postwar social democratic governments in Europe, see Campbell 1987 and McDougall 1993).

Table 4.6: Growth of Population, Per Capita GDP after World War II

	Average annual population growth %	Annual per capita real GDP growth %
1967-71	1.6	3.1
1962-66	1.9	4.7
1957-61	2.7	- 0.4
1952-56	3.0	2.7
1947-51	2.8	2.2

Source: Statistics Canada 1999: Tables A1, F225, author's calculations.

The federal government's ability to implement these policies was greatly increased by its centralization of economic power during World War II. Ottawa took control over all major sources of government revenue, making such transfers to the provinces as necessary to maintain basic public services. These tax rental agreements, which gave Ottawa command of the major levers of fiscal policy and enabled it to establish conditions on many of its transfers to the provinces, resulted in a greater peacetime economic centralization than at any time since the nineteenth century. Constitutional amendments also enabled Ottawa to take control over Unemployment Insurance in 1940 and to implement a national Old Age Pension system in 1951.

However by the 1960s provincial governments were becoming increasingly resentful of federal paternalism, contending that they were capable of making their own fiscal policy decisions and setting their own priorities without direction or control from Ottawa. While Liberal governments of the 1940s and 1950s had enjoyed strong representation from most parts of Canada, those of the 1960s and 1970s had to deal with a rising wave of Quebec nationalism and a lack of strong western representation in federal cabinets. These trends gradually undermined the legitimacy of federal leadership in economic policy and reinforced the slide towards distinct provincial economic strategies as business groups, especially in Quebec and western Canada, increasingly looked to provincial capitals rather than Ottawa as their economic champions. The result was a gradual decentralization of policy control during the 1960s and 1970s, less effective federal control over fiscal policies, and a growing tendency towards federal-provincial competition in regional development policies.

Expansion of Welfare State Policies and Collective Bargaining

As noted earlier, a number of regional and class-based protest movements had emerged during the 1930s to challenge federal economic policies and the role of large corporations in national and regional economies. These challenges, particularly the rising popularity of the socialist CCF, prompted the federal government to initiate a series of social policy reforms during the 1940s which laid the foundations for the modern welfare state.

National programs such as family allowances and old age pensions, along with national standards for provincial social programs financed through federal transfers, helped to mitigate demands for large-scale economic changes and reduce the kinds of social conflicts that had accompanied economic disruptions after World War I. As already noted, they also served as vital elements of Ottawa's Keynesian stabilization policies after World War II.

The influx of US capital also brought with it the rapid growth of US industrial unions belonging to the Congress of Industrial Organizations (CIO). Although provincial governments in Ontario and Quebec had resisted the efforts of CIO unions such as the United Auto Workers to organize major Canadian industries, the federal government encouraged collective bargaining as a way of maintaining industrial peace during the war. With the peacetime restoration of provincial control over labour relations, most provinces adopted the Rand Formula, which enabled unions to collect membership dues from non-members as an alternative to unionized closed shops.

US-style business unionism emphasized improvements in worker rights and living standards through collective bargaining rather than direct state control of industrial relations. Although most unions supported the expansion of the welfare state, they firmly rejected the expansion of state ownership and planning, which they suspected as a way of substituting state exploitation of workers for capitalist exploitation. In return, most Canadian governments tacitly encouraged international unions in their efforts to replace the handful of local communist-influenced unions which had gained substantial influence during the 1930s, especially in single industry resource communities. These policies enabled governments to reduce tariff levels gradually for many Canadian industries without triggering greater industrial conflict, while providing workers with the means to secure a larger share of the benefits of prosperity.

Strategic Federal Intervention in Key Industries

Both business and labour mythologies have sometimes celebrated the 1950s as a golden (or benighted) era of laissez-faire capitalism, largely due to the close personal relationship between C.D. Howe, who served as Minister of Trade and Commerce between 1945 and 1957, and leading members of the corporate community. Howe certainly sought to foster a positive business environment. However, he also exercised extensive power over national economic development policies, fostering selected strategic industries through a combination of state ownership, preferential regulations, and government procurement projects (Bothwell and Kilbourn 1979: 104-15, 212-17, 230-38, 283-98).

Howe used government-owned Trans-Canada Airlines as an instrument of national development and exercised extensive influence in the defence and aircraft industries, which he viewed as a means of strengthening Canada's technological and industrial capacity. During the 1950s, he sought to make the building of the Trans-Canada Pipeline to bring western natural gas to central Canadian markets on an all-Canadian route a national project comparable to the building of the CPR. However, Howe's often arbitrary methods and the active role played by US expertise and investors in the project both disturbed Canadian nationalists and gave opposition parties a tool to portray the St. Laurent government as an arrogant instrument of corporate interests (Bothwell and Kilbourn 1979: 299-320; Bliss 1987: 457-77). These factors contributed to the Liberals' defeat in the 1957 election after 22 years in power and a resurgence of Canadian nationalism that would challenge the assumptions and the policies of the Second National Policy.

The success of federal economic policies during most of the 1950s and 1960s—interrupted by the slow growth that characterized most of the Diefenbaker years between 1957 and 1963—left many government policy-makers believing that they had solved the riddle of stable economic growth. The sometimes erratic populism and nationalism of the Diefenbaker era confirmed the support of much of Canada's business and public sector establishments for the federal Liberals as Canada's "natural governing party" (Newman 1968). However, this consensus was undermined by the rapid expansion of government spending during the 1960s and the resurgence of economic nationalism as a means of asserting greater government control over the economy.

These forces, combined with the international economic shocks of the 1970s, also undermined the effectiveness of Keynesian economic policies in promoting economic growth, high employment, and price stability. As a result, the political and economic consensus that had generally sustained **business liberalism** as Canada's dominant political ideology and that enabled Canadian governments to maintain an uneasy balance between nationalist and continentalist policies came unraveled, leading to unprecedented conflict between business and the federal government and the search for a new national policy for Canada.

The End of an Era

Canada's economic history has consistently reinforced both public expectations of an active role for government in the economy and efforts by Canadians to protect themselves against the arbitrary or partisan use of political power in the economy. The interaction of these forces has contributed to the evolution of institutional structures that have both channeled and constrained the political and economic options available to Canadians.

Federal politics have been characterized at different times by an emphasis on economic nationalism and nation-building. However, the realities of partisan politics have always dictated that the regional distribution of economic benefits are often as important, if not more so, than contemporary ideas of economic rationality. Competition among regional economic interests has also strengthened the role of provincial governments in economic development and in building regional networks of economic influence. Periods of rapid economic growth such as the Laurier era and the 1950s have made it easier for politicians to balance competing economic, social, and governmental interests despite pressures from groups that felt themselves to have been left behind amid the rising tides of prosperity. Periodic recessions tended to reinforce these conflicts, particularly when international economic shocks threatened the economic security of many Canadians and forced major industries to adapt to a changing business environment.

The general prosperity resulting from the post-World War II boom enabled governments to grow rapidly and to expand a wide range of services and income transfer programs that promoted greater economic security and social harmony without undermining the competitive position of Canadian businesses. They also resulted in large bureaucracies that changed the context for how government dealt with the economy, so encouraging the founding of numerous interest groups, many of them representing business, to manage relations with different levels of government. The relative success of Keynesian economic policies in promoting economic growth and rising living standards increased both public confidence in government policy-makers and the latter's confidence in their own ability to manage a wide range of economic and social conditions through government action. However, while postwar optimism peaked about the time of Canada's centennial celebrations in 1967, a series of domestic and international conditions combined to disrupt the comfortable certainties of postwar Keynesian political economy.

Beginning in the early 1970s, the Canadian economy entered an extended period of structural economic and technological change comparable to the period between the 1870s and the 1890s which saw the emergence of the National Policy and the massive social and economic changes that accompanied the Second Industrial Revolution. These changes disrupted the postwar balance between the interests of businesses, governments, and other social groups. These conflicts—and the effects of political and economic change on business-government relations and the economic role of the state—will be examined further in Chapter 5.

Key Terms and Concepts for Review (see Glossary)

Auto Pact	imperial preference
brokerage politics	National Policy
business liberalism	Pacific Scandal
cartel	Reciprocity Treaty of 1854
C.D. Howe	Second Industrial Revolution
defensive economic nationalism	Second National Policy
developmental clientelism	staples theory
Great Depression	Walter Gordon

Questions for Discussion and Review

1. What are four overarching issues that have shaped Canadian economic history since the early nineteenth century? How are they reflected in government policies and business-government relations during the different periods discussed in this chapter?

2. Some economic historians describe the economy of nineteenth-century Canada as a "staples economy" characterized by "dependence." What do they mean by these terms? Provide examples. What are some of the limitations of the staples theory?

3. Some economic historians suggest that the relationship between Central Canada and its outlying regions has paralleled that between Canada in its early economic relations with France and Britain. What evidence is there to support or challenge this outlook?

4. What impact did the National Policy of the late nineteenth and early twentieth centuries have on Canadian economic development? To what extent did it foster or reinforce public expectations of the role of government in the economy? What

mercantilist practices have persisted in Canada into the late twentieth and early twenty-first centuries?

5. Compare and contrast the statist perspectives of "defensive economic national-ism" as an explanation for federal economic policies with neo-Marxist theories of Canadian governments as "clients of the business community." What evidence is there for these competing outlooks on "patron-client" relations between business and government?

6. To what extent did the business liberalism of the Second National Policy reflect continuity and/or change from previous federal approaches to economic devel-opment and the promotion of social cohesion?

Suggestions for Further Readings

Aitken, H.G.A. 1967. Defensive economic expansion: the state and economic growth in Canada. In *Approaches to Canadian economic history*, ed. W.T. Easterbrook and M.H. Watkins. Toronto: McClelland and Stewart. 183-221.

Bliss, Michael. 1985. "Forcing the pace: a reappraisal of business-government rela-tions in Canadian history. In *Theories of business-government relations*, ed. V.V. Murray. Toronto: Trans-Canada Press. 106-17.

Bliss, Michael. 1987. *Northern enterprise: five Centuries of Canadian business*. Toronto: McClelland and Stewart.

Bothwell, Robert, and William Kilbourn. 1979. *C.D. Howe: a biography*. Toronto: McClelland and Stewart.

Bradford, Neil. 1998. *Commissioning ideas: Canadian National Policy innovation in comparative perspective*. Toronto: Oxford University Press.

Easterbrook, W.T., and M.H. Watkins (Eds.). 1967. *Approaches to Canadian economic history*. Toronto: McClelland and Stewart.

Forster, Ben. 1986. *A conjunction of interests: business, politics and the tariff*. Toronto: University of Toronto Press.

Hart, Michael. 2002. *A trading nation: Canadian trade policy from colonialism to glo-balization*. Vancouver: University of British Columbia Press.

Innis, Harold A. 1956. *Essays in Canadian economic history*, ed. Mary Q. Innis. Toronto: University of Toronto Press.

Marchildon, Gregory F. 1996. *Profits and politics: Beaverbrook and the gilded age of Canadian finance*. Toronto: University of Toronto Press.

Noel, S.J.R. 1990. *Patrons, clients, brokers: Ontario society and politics 1791-1896*. Toronto: University of Toronto Press.

Norrie, Kenneth and Douglas Owram. 1996. *A history of the Canadian economy*. 2nd ed. Toronto: Harcourt, Brace and Co.

Simeon, Richard, and Ian Robinson. 1990. *State, society and the development of Cana-dian federalism*. Toronto: University of Toronto Press.

Stewart, Gordon T. 1986. *The origins of Canadian politics: a comparative approach.* Vancouver: University of British Columbia Press.

Whitaker, Reg. 1977. *The government party: organizing and financing the Liberal Party of Canada 1930-58.* Toronto: University of Toronto Press.

CHAPTER 5

Business, Government, and the Politics of Economic Upheaval: 1970 to Present

The political environment for economic policy-making and business-government relations has been transformed since the early 1970s as both domestic events and international trends have challenged many of the basic assumptions of government policies. During the 1970s and early 1980s, a series of political and economic shocks combined to destabilize the postwar Keynesian consensus and to undermine **business liberalism** as the dominant ideology of the state in fiscal and economic policies. These shocks contributed to intense competition and conflict among social and economic interests seeking to protect themselves against the potentially adverse effects of change. They also contributed to ideological debates as governments were unable to meet all the expectations created by increased state activism without a serious redistribution of political and economic power.

These circumstances forced both federal and provincial governments to seek alternative policies capable of combining the traditional objectives of economic development, nation-building, and social cohesion. The result was an extended period of political and economic instability, which subsided during the late-1990s as governments evolved a new consensus with business and other social interests on the broad lines of fiscal, economic, and social policies.

This chapter examines the factors that contributed to the rise of Canadian economic nationalism and the breakdown of the Keynesian consensus during the 1970s and the resulting contest for power among alternative concepts of state-society relations capable of providing a strategic vision for economic policies. It explains the evolution of Canadian neo-liberalism during the late 1980s and 1990s in response to changing domestic and international conditions and examines the parallel shifts in relations between businesses and governments at both federal and provincial levels. Freer trade, balanced public sector budgets, and structural economic changes were all results of Canada's growing integration with the North American and global economies.

Politics and Business since 1970: A World in Constant Flux

The evolution of Canadian economic policies and, with them, the environment for business-government relations since the 1960s can be summarized by assessing the challenges facing the federal government through four more-or-less distinct periods. At the risk of oversimplification, these are the first and second Trudeau eras (1968-79 and 1980-84), the Mulroney period (1984-93), and the Chrétien years (1993-2003).

The efforts of the first Trudeau government to balance regional, social, and economic interests fell apart due to regional conflicts and the economic effects of international oil shocks and rising deficits. The failure of the short-lived Clark government to confront these challenges effectively opened the door to Trudeau's return to power in 1980 and his efforts to introduce a new National Policy that would assert federal leadership in the fields of fiscal and energy policies, a new national industrial strategy, and constitutional reform. The state-centred nationalism which characterized the beginning of the Trudeau Restoration attempted to reverse the decentralization of power to the provinces and the private sector. However, it succeeded only in antagonizing both groups deeply, and in giving greater economic and political leverage to business and other interests committed to smaller, less interventionist government and more market-oriented economic policies.

The PC government of Brian Mulroney elected in 1984 lacked a coherent platform capable of balancing its promises of fiscal discipline and more business-oriented economic policies with its commitments to maintaining the social policies and programs of the Trudeau-era welfare state (Bercuson, Granatstein, and Young 1986). Ironically, it was a royal commission chaired by former Trudeau minister Donald Macdonald that provided the impulse for a series of policy changes initially introduced by Mulroney and later extended by the Liberal governments of Jean Chrétien and Paul Martin.

These changes transformed the environment for business-government relations and forced both federal and provincial governments to look for new ways of sustaining and coordinating their economic and social policies to adapt to economic and demographic trends beyond their immediate control. A series of negotiations resulted in a broad free trade agreement between Canada and the US in 1988, its extension to include Mexico and a new global trade agreement concluded in 1994. These treaties reinforced Canada's continuing economic integration with the US and compelled governments to modify the policy instruments traditionally used to promote economic growth and job creation. Both provincial and federal governments finally mobilized the public support necessary to overcome chronic budget deficits and to achieve fiscal balance or modest surpluses by the late 1990s. Policy consolidation, rather than a continuation of rapid change, has been the order of the day in most jurisdictions since 2000.

During the late 1980s and early 1990s, federal policies of free trade, deficit reduction, and social policy reform were widely attacked as part of a so-called corporate agenda. Critics suggested that Canadian governments were being manipulated by corporate interests seeking to "dismantle the state" and roll back the achievements of the Keynesian welfare state (Pierson 1994; McQuaig 1993; McBride and Shields 1998). An alternative, and more persuasive, explanation is that governments came to recognize the limits of existing policies and sought alternatives that would reconcile the role of the state in promoting economic growth and social cohesion with measures to encourage the competitiveness of Canadian business.

The Crisis of the Keynesian State: Government, Economic Policy, and Business in the 1970s

The principles of business liberalism that had enabled postwar Canadian governments to balance public expectations of economic growth, policy stability, social

cohesion, and nation-building faced a series of significant challenges during the
1970s: rising Canadian economic nationalism, increased competition among interest
groups to influence the policies of a rapidly growing public sector, and the centrifugal forces of Canadian politics that confronted the political and economic leadership of the federal state.

Combined with the international economic shocks of the 1970s, these forces
undermined the effectiveness of Keynesian economic policies in promoting economic growth, high employment, and price stability. Economic instability undermined the consensus that had sustained the Second National Policy during much
of the 1950s and 1960s. Rapid increases in global energy prices, rising inflation, and
unemployment disrupted most major industrial economies, including Canada's.
These factors, and the relatively ineffective policy improvisations introduced to deal
with them, undercut the credibility of federal economic leadership (Hale 2001b: 135-
202). As a result, the 1970s and 1980s were characterized by unprecedented conflict
between business and the federal government and the search for a new national
policy for Canada.

The following sections examine the pursuit of a coherent political and economic
approach to the design and implementation of economic policies during the 1970s
and 1980s. Three broad schools of thought that informed debates over the relationship between economic policy, nation-building, and Canadian nationalism during
the Trudeau years will be considered and the political and economic factors that
undermined both the Keynesian consensus on economic policy and the capacity
of Canadian governments during the era to formulate and implement a coherent
alternative to that strategic consensus will be examined.

Competing Views of Economic Liberalism and the Role of the State

A central theme in past discussions of Canadian economic policies has been the
efforts of federal (and sometimes provincial) governments to create frameworks of
ideas, institutions, and policies intended to provide political and economic coherence to their strategies of economic and social development.

Political scientist Neil Bradford describes national policies as "overarching federal
development strategies for achieving economic growth and social cohesion within
the Canadian political community." The underlying concepts of Macdonald's National
Policy and the Second National Policy of the post-World War II era have already been
discussed in Chapter 4. Since the mid-twentieth century, these nation-building ideas
have often been presented as "programmatic action plans" that were meant to translate their goals into action through specific policy programs (Bradford 1998).

Peter Hall (1989) and others have suggested that governments or political parties tend to work within existing frameworks of policies and ideas until existing
theoretical or ideological systems for organizing public policy are no longer sufficiently adaptable to contemporary challenges of governing to allow governments
to fulfill the main political, economic, or social expectations of their fellow citizens.
The 1970s and 1980s were an outstanding example of such an era in Canadian eco-

nomic history. Since at least the mid-1950s there had been challenges to the Second National Policy and its efforts to balance a certain vision of Canadian nation-building with Canada's growing economic integration with the US. The 1957 report of the Royal Commission on Canada's Economic Prospects, chaired by Walter Gordon, challenged many of the assumptions of these postwar federal policies (Bradford 1998: 60-62). Gordon's critiques had relatively little impact for more than a decade, despite his rise to prominence as finance minister in the Pearson Liberal government between 1963 and 1965. However, his ideas provided much of the rationale and impetus for the resurgence of Canadian nationalism in politics and economics between the 1960s and the 1980s.

Economic development policies pursued by federal and provincial governments during the 1950s and 1960s generally reflected a mix of **liberal nationalism** and what Bradford describes as **liberal continentalism**. The nationalist critiques of Gordon, economists of a more socialist or social democratic persuasion such as Abraham Rotstein and Melville Watkins (Bradford 1998: 86-95; Rotstein 1966; Canada, Task Force on the Structure of Canadian Industry 1968; Canada 1972), and the Gray Report of 1970, provided much of the intellectual framework for the emergence of **interventionist nationalism** as a means of projecting active state leadership in nation-building and economic policies.

Liberal nationalism emphasized the promotion of national and regional economic development and Canadian nationhood through active government economic leadership, often in partnership with Canadian (or regional) business interests, and through using state capitalism as a tool for economic development. Examples of the first approach included Ottawa's promotion of a Canadian aircraft industry with protective regulations and government contracts following World War II and its regulatory restrictions on foreign ownership of financial institutions (Bliss 1987; Norrie and Owram 1996). However, governments of all political persuasions also used Crown corporations and other government business enterprises as leading instruments of national or provincial industrial strategies. BC Premier W.A.C. Bennett's nationalization of BC Hydro and its ferry industry, the developmental role of Hydro Quebec in fostering that province's engineering and construction industries, Nova Scotia's efforts to rebuild the province's antiquated coal and steel industries under government ownership all reflect elements of this approach. The different functions of government business enterprises and their impact on business-government relations will be examined further in Chapter 9.

The second vision has been characterized as liberal continentalism (Bradford 1998: 7). This outlook emphasized the central role of market economics, private investment, and innovation as the main sources of wealth creation, economic growth, and higher living standards. It emphasized that the role of governments in the economy was to create a policy framework suited to private investment and job creation, the efficient workings of the marketplace, and the correction of specific problems or abuses through legislation or regulation. Supporters of this outlook generally encouraged foreign investment as a means of accelerating economic development, particularly in underdeveloped regions of the country, and of facilitating technology transfers to increase the competitiveness of Canadian industries. The continentalist perspective also welcomed the gradual liberalization of trade through multilateral agreements, growing penetration of US markets by Canadian businesses, and greater access to US capital markets to finance business expansion. One of the more significant examples of this approach, as we saw in Chapter 4, was the negotiation of the Canada-US Auto Pact in 1965, which prompted the consolidation of Canadian and US production facilities for cars, trucks, and related components.

Market-oriented economists became increasingly critical of government subsidies to business, the preferential regulatory treatment often given to Crown corporations or favoured Canadian businesses, and other policies they criticized as unsustainable or destructive of Canada's competitiveness and living standards. Although these challenges to neo-mercantilist policies began to gain influence during the 1960s, they coalesced during the late 1970s as a much stronger neo-conservative critique of the methods and directions of state intervention in the economy (Bradford 1998: 7-8, 83-85, 107-08).

However, in the short term, the growing influence of foreign investment and control over Canada's economy spurred the growth of the third major economic vision of the period, which Bradford characterizes as interventionist nationalism (Bradford 1998). Canadian nationalists in all political parties expressed concerns over the growing influence of US corporations in the Canadian economy and the potential impact on Canada's ability to manage its own economy. Many worried that future investment decisions would reflect the narrow economic interests of foreign shareholders rather than shared interests in the growth of Canada's national and regional economies.

Advocates of interventionist nationalism emphasized the necessity of government leadership to assert greater Canadian control over the economy and to correct its structural weaknesses. Many of these weaknesses were attributed to excessive foreign ownership of Canada's resource and manufacturing industries and the inefficiencies of branch plants organized primarily to serve the Canadian market. Nationalists were also highly critical of Canada's excessive dependence on foreign capital and technology for its economic development and of the tendency of Canadian resource industries to export much of their production rather than processing and manufacturing higher value-added products capable of generating higher incomes for Canadians.

By the 1960s, foreign companies dominated major sectors including automobile manufacturing, electrical products, aircraft, rubber and chemical production, oil refining and distribution, and a number of other major industrial sectors (Levitt 1970). Table 5.1 notes that, by 1963, foreign firms controlled more than one-third of the assets of Canadian non-financial industries, 60 per cent of assets in manufacturing, and 74 per cent of its oil and gas industry. These trends were in sharp contrast to nationalist and mercantilist sectoral policies that continued to protect the market shares of established Canadian firms in banking, broadcasting, publishing, transportation, telecommunications, and other industries, thus limiting competition and often resulting in higher prices for Canadian consumers.

Table 5.1: Non-Resident Control as a Percentage of Selected Canadian Industries, 1926-63

Industry	1926	1948	1963
Manufacturing	35	43	60
Petroleum and natural gas	—	—	74
Mining and smelting	38	40	59
Railways	3	3	2
Other utilities	20	24	4
Total	17	25	34

Source: Levitt 1970: 61.

These ideas evolved gradually during the 1960s until they became the dominant policy discourse for the NDP and a significant influence within the federal Liberal Party. During the 1970s and early 1980s, advocates of interventionist nationalism encouraged governments to take a larger share of resource rents, by both tax and regulatory means, to finance an ambitious industrial strategy to increase domestic economic capacity and reduce dependence on foreign capital (Bradford 1998: 7, 85-90).

Provincial governments were at the forefront of interventionist nationalist policies during the 1960s and 1970s. Successive Quebec governments established a number of Crown corporations to direct economic development into various strategic economic sectors and set up provincial investment corporations that would in turn invest in regionally owned businesses and make cooperation with the provincial government a necessary element in the business strategies of most large companies in the province. The governments of Saskatchewan and Manitoba took similar steps during the 1970s, creating Crown corporations in strategic sectors in order to exercise greater control over their provinces' industrial development (Chandler 1983b).

During the 1970s, the Science Council of Canada advocated the development of a comprehensive industrial strategy using government contracts, Crown corporations such as the Canada Development Corporation and Petro-Canada, and support for strategic private industries to take control of the commanding heights of the Canadian economy. These policies were also intended to foster the development of high technology industries that could provide the impetus for the next generation of Canadian economic growth (Science Council of Canada 1978; Bradford 1998: 77, 107; Bell 1990).

However, several factors limited the spread of nationalist policies. Both the federal cabinet and senior bureaucrats were deeply divided between advocates of nationalist policies and opponents who viewed them as economically disruptive (Bradford 1998: 91-95). Both the Pearson government of the 1960s and the early Trudeau governments sought to link nationalist measures with the self-interest of major segments of the Canadian business community, generally constraining policy choices to those that were adaptable to existing patterns of economic activity.

Canada's dependence on US capital markets to finance large development projects imposed practical limits on Canadian governments' ability to implement discriminatory nationalist policies without adverse consequences. Contemporary monetary policies depended on the continued influx of foreign capital to offset current account deficits deepened by the repatriation of dividends by foreign-controlled firms in Canada. On several occasions during the 1960s and early 1970s, the federal government had to appeal to Canada's special relationship with the US to avoid being side-swiped by US policies that could have had serious effects on the access of Canadian businesses and governments to that country's capital markets by either limiting their ability to pursue new projects or increasing overall costs of capital to Canadian borrowers. The progressive decentralization of political and economic power during the 1970s also constrained the ability of the federal government to pursue interventionist nationalist policies contrary to major regional interests without threatening its own political legitimacy.

If interventionist nationalism stressed the failure of markets to meet desired policy goals without government intervention and direction, neo-conservative (and, later, neo-liberal) critiques of interventionist nationalism rejected the arguments of market failure underlying these policies. Instead, they accused the growing politicization of economic activity of contributing to economic inefficiencies and fostering excessive public expectations that governments would prop up uncompetitive businesses (Simons 1978: 7-8; Economic Council of Canada 1979; Economic Council of Canada 1981).

A series of international economic shocks during the 1970s brought these debates to the political forefront and increased the political pressures upon the federal government to exercise economic leadership. However, they also contributed to the strength of decentralist forces that challenged the legitimacy of Ottawa's claim to be the ultimate arbiter of the national interest.

Centrifugal Forces in Canadian Politics and Economic Policy

By the 1960s, a number of centrifugal political and economic forces combined to force a steady decentralization of political and economic power. These factors included the spread of Quebec nationalism and the subsequent demands of the larger provinces for greater fiscal and policy autonomy.

Political parties became increasingly regionalized during this period, with Liberal strength concentrated in Quebec, PC support on the prairies, and effective competition limited to Ontario, Atlantic Canada, and BC. This encouraged regional economic interests to look increasingly to provincial governments rather than Ottawa as their main sources of economic opportunity and political influence. Province-building strategies reflected a state-centred approach, as in Quebec or in provinces with NDP governments; cooperative partnerships with various business interests; or some combination of the two (Chandler 1983b).

The government of Quebec had always strongly dissented the postwar centralization of power, whether in fiscal and economic policies or the use of the federal spending power to establish national social programs in areas of provincial jurisdiction (Simeon and Robinson 1990: 176-86; Arbour 1994). The election of a modernizing Liberal government in Quebec in 1960 prompted the **Quiet Revolution**: voters gave a series of moderately nationalist provincial governments clear mandates to take control over the main levers of power to give French-speaking Quebecers the same kinds of economic and social opportunities enjoyed by other Canadians. These policies involved the assertion of Quebec's place as an equal partner and founding nation within Canada and an end to the perceived subordination of Quebecers in a political system dominated by English Canada and an economic system dominated by Montreal's English-speaking business elites.

Federal governments sought to accommodate these aspirations by transferring increased powers over taxation and increased social transfers to the provinces, so that provincial revenues (including transfers) increased from 36.2 per cent to 54.7 per cent of total government revenues between 1961 and 1978. Provincial spending increased from 33.4 per cent to 48.6 per cent of total government spending during the same period (Canada, Department of Finance 2000: 39-43). The maturing of provincial bureaucracies resulted in greater self-confidence and a decline in deference to the policy judgements of Big Brother in Ottawa. As a result, provincial governments repeatedly and effectively challenged federal policy initiatives during the 1970s when they were seen to be detrimental to regional economic interests (Simeon and Robinson 1990: 224-30).

These disputes were reinforced by conflicts over control of energy prices and revenues after 1973. During the Trudeau years, while the Liberals dominated federal politics in Quebec and recovered some strength in Atlantic Canada, several provincial Liberal parties began to distance themselves politically and organizationally from their federal cousins in the interests of political survival.

Paradoxically, the growing decentralization of political and economic power also provided a rationale for more assertively nationalist federal policies. In some cases, Ottawa used federal power and money to encourage support from business and other economic interests, although the politics of clientelism was mediated by federal bureaucrats as much as by politicians. In others, it meant asserting the power of the federal state against both the provinces and the private sector as the sole legitimate arbiter of the national interest. The culmination of these policies came in Trudeau's efforts to introduce a **Third National Policy** following the 1980 election (Milne 1986; Smiley 1987).

Economic Instability, Growing Deficits, and the Breakdown of Keynesian Consensus

The postwar Keynesian consensus was founded on several premises that won broad acceptance from private economic interests and Canada's major political parties. The federal government's macroeconomic policies stabilized the working of the economy, increasing economic demand to mitigate the effects of unemployment and preventing rapid economic growth from fuelling the rise of inflation. They resulted in a steady increase in the standard of living without the need for major conflicts in the allocation of resources between private savings and investment on the one hand and government spending and income redistribution on the other. Governments controlled or mitigated the effects of external economic shocks on the economy and, indeed, took action to protect living standards and business competitiveness. These actions led governments to intervene as required in the day-to-day activities of business and the marketplace in order to resolve specific policy problems.

In 1971, the US government cancelled the Bretton Woods' monetary agreements, which had made the US dollar the world's unofficial reserve currency. It also imposed a 15 per cent across-the-board tariff on imports in response to a looming balance of payments crisis. These actions disrupted Canada's special relationship with the US and caused the Trudeau government to look for ways to reduce Canada's economic dependence on US markets.

Initially, nationalist measures such as the creation of the **Foreign Investment Review Agency** in 1973 and Petro-Canada in 1975, remained firmly within the limits of liberal nationalist traditions. Foreign investments might be screened to ensure that they provided net benefits to Canada, and some businesses complained about higher royalties on production of provincially owned resources. However, these policies did not cause major conflicts between Canadian businesses and governments as long as they were within international norms and allowed well-managed businesses to make a reasonable rate of return.[1]

Table 5.2: Stagflation: Rising Inflation, Unemployment, and Slow Growth

	1974	1975	1976	1977	1978	1979	1980	1981
Inflation rate (CPI)	10.7	10.9	7.5	7.8	9.0	9.2	10.1	12.4
Growth in real per capita GDP	6.4	0.2	5.9	0.9	0.7	3.6	0.6	0.9
Unemployment rate	5.3	6.9	7.1	8.1	8.3	7.4	7.5	7.5

Source: Canada, Department of Finance 1992-96; author's calculations.

A series of other economic shocks, particularly the Organization of Petroleum Exporting Countries (OPEC) oil price crisis of 1973 and 1978-81, undermined the uneasy balance between liberal nationalism and continentalism. The federal government responded with policies intended to protect citizens and energy-consuming businesses from the effects of rising oil prices and the persistent inflation that

---

1 Trudeau biographers Christina McCall and Stephen Clarkson (1996: 111) suggest that Trudeau "was inclined to dismiss both nationalist and business views (during this era) as irrelevant whining." For different approaches to this debate, see Grant 1983; Beckman 1984; Science Council of Canada 1984.

resulted. As noted in Table 5.2, inflation was consistently over 7 per cent after 1974, while economic growth barely kept pace with inflation and population growth, and unemployment edged upwards. This **stagflation** led Ottawa to improvise a series of economic policy shifts whose limited effectiveness gradually eroded public confidence in government economic leadership (Hale 2001b: 136-38, 150-54).

Following a series of bitter battles with business interests over proposed tax reforms in 1969-71 (Bird 1970; Brooks 1988), the Trudeau government indexed personal income tax rates and exemptions, along with many social benefits, to inflation in 1973. It also provided businesses with selective tax reductions in an effort to stimulate job-creating investment and to limit friction between business and welfare Liberals. Federal spending grew significantly faster than inflation or Canada's population after the introduction of indexing, despite efforts to restrain its growth during the late 1970s. At the same time, federal revenues failed to keep pace either with the growth of spending or that of the economy, resulting in what was later described as "the scissors crisis of public finance" (Hale 2001b: 153; Tarchys 1983).

The federal government also held Canadian oil and gas prices significantly below world levels to protect individual and business consumers. It used its regulatory powers to limit energy exports, levying an oil export tax and applying its proceeds to subsidize foreign oil imports. These policies deepened regional divisions between the oil and gas producing provinces of western Canada and the energy consumers in other parts of the country.

Rising inflation also contributed to record levels of strike activity as unionized workers sought to protect themselves against inflation, only to see further price increases pass on to consumers. The Trudeau government responded by imposing wage and price controls in 1975, reversing the position that had helped it to win the 1974 election. With inflation and unemployment rising together in defiance of conventional Keynesian wisdom, the federal government began to search for alternative economic policies that would enable it to meet voter expectations while strengthening its ability to deal with economic forces increasingly beyond its control.

Nevertheless, conflict continued to grow between government and business, both large and small. The steady expansion in the size of governments and their regulatory intervention in business activities clashed with business preferences for internationally (and sectorally) competitive tax rates and greater freedom to carry out their activities without what many viewed as undue or ill-informed government interference. Government involvement in the economy and society led to an increasing bureaucratization of economic activity and created a cultural gulf between the political and economic expectations of business and those of a new class of policy-makers with a very different view of governments' role in promoting the public interest (Campbell and Szablowski 1979).

The result was a retreat from business liberalism, as business interests viewed big government as an actual or potential enemy whose size and influence needed to be reduced. At the same time, labour and other social groups dependent on governments for their incomes, status, and power sought to expand the power of the

federal state to exercise greater control over the economy, subordinating both provincial governments and private businesses to a new vision of the national interest.

Explaining the Growth of Business-Government Conflict during the 1970s

The steady decline in relations between organized business groups and the federal
government during the first decade of the Trudeau era (1968-78) had few, if any,
precedents in the history of Canadian business-government relations. By the end
of the 1970s, significant elements of government viewed the business community
with a mixture of mistrust and contempt, a view intensely reciprocated by many of
the latter. Believing they had made considerable efforts to protect large and small
firms, along with other Canadians, from the economic disruptions of the era and
to accommodate business concerns over the size and scope of government, many
public officials viewed business concerns as increasingly out-of-touch with the
demands placed on governments by other elements of Canadian society (Clarkson
and McCall 1996: 118-33; Johnston 1986: 62-66). In their turn, business leaders viewed
their counterparts in the federal government as ill-informed about the realities and
competitive pressures they faced in the marketplace, overly assured of their own
competence in managing other peoples' business, and overly intrusive in attempting
to regulate many areas of day-to-day business activity in ways that appeared to serve
no discernable public interest.

McMillan and Murray summarized five competing and overlapping interpretations of conflicts among governments, organized business interests, and other
societal interests during the period (McMillan and Murray 1985: 297-302). The Inter-
pretive School emphasized the growing "differences in motives, attitudes and ideologies" of major politicians, senior civil servants, and business leaders. Contrasting
the shared background of government and business leaders of an earlier generation, it pointed to the growing career specialization and social isolation of leaders in
government and business as a significant factor in what often appeared to be their
mutual incomprehension and mistrust (for example, see Foster 1982).

The Failure of Business School attributed the relative ineffectiveness of business
lobby groups to their failures in coordinating their efforts, reconciling internal differences in their dealings with governments, understanding the policy processes
and imperatives of government, and developing realistic strategies for managing
government relations (for example, see Gillies 1981; Foster 1982: 28-35). This interpretation found its mirror image in the Failure of Government School, which blamed
the breakdown in business-government relations on changes in government policy
processes that reduced the historic role of strong ministers in strong ministries in
favour of efforts at government-wide (or centrally driven) policy coordination, thus
reducing opportunities for constructive interaction between business and government in diffusing or resolving problems. Some of these critics also noted the decline
of political party organizations as effective instruments for reconciling competing
interests and influencing government policy decisions directly or through the par-

liamentary process (McCall-Newman 1980; Meisel 1991). Ironically, many of these arguments were reversed during the deficit-cutting years of the 1990s.

The Mechanisms of Interaction School emphasized the weaknesses of the government consultation process in helping governments to build shared understandings of policy problems and potential responses and their prospective impacts on major stakeholders. McMillan and Murray summarized this perspective by suggesting that "the wrong people are involved too late in the decision-making process and with too little information" (McMillan and Murray 1985: 301-02; see also, Canadian Tax Foundation 1982; MacEachen 1982).

All of these interpretations, each of which has a degree of validity, stress the competition and conflict among competing social and governmental interests that has been the primary emphasis of this narrative (the Social Context School). These conflicts came to a head during the 1980s.

The Politics of Polarization: The National Energy Program and the Crisis of Canadian Nationalism

The 1980s marked a watershed in Canadian economic policies and their effects on business-government relations comparable to previous paradigm shifts such as the entrenchment of protectionism in the 1870s and the Keynesian Revolution of the 1940s. The Trudeau government returned to office after the 1980 election seeking to transform Canadian political and economic life through the active exercise of federal power. Its major initiatives, including the **National Energy Program** (NEP), unilateral efforts at constitutional and tax reform, and its stumbling efforts to introduce a national industrial strategy directly challenged many of the central interests of provincial governments and large segments of the private sector.

However, while Trudeau's politics of polarization proved temporarily successful, his ambitious agenda ran aground during the deep recession of 1981-82. The federal PCs succeeded in riding the resulting political backlash into power in 1984 by appealing to a wide range of social and economic interests antagonized by the previous government. Facing many of the same structural economic changes which had frustrated his predecessors' best efforts, Brian Mulroney gradually adopted a neo-liberal economic agenda of free trade with the US, modest tax and social policy reforms, and constitutional changes aimed at bridging growing regional differences. Mulroney's party broke up in the 1993 election as its component factions of Quebec nationalists and western populists spun off new political parties. However, most of his economic and social policies were adapted and extended by the Liberal governments of Jean Chrétien and Paul Martin.

Trudeau's Third National Policy: The Limits of State-Centred Nationalism

The federal Liberals were deeply divided in the 1970s by efforts to balance the competing expectations of their supporters and to conciliate both business and social Liberals through selective tax reductions and spending increases. These events made it increasingly difficult to achieve the trade-offs required to exert effective government leadership in the midst of a looming economic crisis while abiding by the restraints business liberalism had traditionally imposed on the exercise of government powers.

Federal and provincial governments of all parties competed for public support by fostering widespread expectations of entitlement to higher living standards, competitive taxes and rates of return, improved public services and income transfers, and protection from the effects of rising inflation, oil prices, and other economic shocks as expressions of their benevolence and presumed competence in delivering desired social and economic outcomes. Assorted business interests were as active, if not more so, in pursuing their piece of the action as were other social interests. By the late 1970s, these competing objectives could be achieved only by shifting the costs of adjusting to social and economic changes to groups that lacked the political clout to stand up for their own interests; by piling up debts to be paid by a future generation; or by confronting the logic of a zero-sum society in which the benefits for members of winning coalitions would be paid for by members of losing coalitions, based on a very different definition of the public interest.[2]

These conditions contributed to the polarization of Canadian political debates during the 1980s, first under the Trudeau government's proposals for fiscal, economic, and constitutional reforms and subsequently with the Mulroney government's partial reversal of Trudeau-era policies and its pursuit and implementation of trade liberalization with the US and other industrial economies.

The perception that Canada's economic problems resulted largely from market failures or the failure of the market system to serve national political goals—policy effects that were often held to be more or less synonymous—gave rise to the ascendance of interventionist nationalism over business liberalism (Bradford 1998: 7-8). Increasing world oil prices, rampant inflation, higher US interest rates, and the growing mobility of capital in global markets tested the capacity of governments, in Canada and elsewhere, to live up to public expectations of a benevolent, competent government capable of protecting its citizens from economic upheaval.

If governments' legitimacy depended on their capacity to protect large numbers of citizens and businesses from domestic and external economic forces, then they needed to increase their political and fiscal capacity to pursue these objectives. Although nationalist policies appealed to the latent undercurrent of anti-Americanism in Canadian politics, straining Ottawa's relations with the US for a time, their introduction, dilution, and ultimate reversal were primarily shaped by domestic political and economic conditions and conflicts. (For different perspectives on Canada-US relations during this period, see McCall and Clarkson 1996: 187-205; Bothwell 1998: 209-21).

Following their loss of the 1979 federal election to a minority PC government led by Joe Clark, the Liberals re-evaluated their policies and made a calculated decision

---

2 Some observers might suggest that these conditions are endemic under most conditions of political competition among social interests or classes. However, their expression became significantly more explicit in Canada during the 1980s (see Thurow 1980; Olson 1982). For a more recent discussion, see Lewis 2003.

to build a social democratic coalition of interests favourable to strong federal leadership in Canada's economy and society (Milne 1986; Axworthy and Trudeau 1990; Johnston 1986: 61-62). The Clark government's failure to reconcile its supporters in Alberta and Ontario over a new energy pricing agreement in response to fast rising world oil prices created a political opening for the Liberals to serve as champions and protectors of the country's energy consumers. Indeed, Clark's unexpected electoral defeat in February 1980 returned Trudeau to power with the most ambitious political agenda of any government in more than a century.

The Trudeau strategy included at least five major proposals for changes to Canada's constitutional, economic, and social policy structures: massive federal intervention in Canada's burgeoning energy sector under what became the NEP; the restructuring of Canada's tax system to increase revenues, redistribute income, and give the federal government increased control over key sectors of business activity; the creation of a National Industrial Strategy; a major expansion of the welfare state; and the patriation of Canada's Constitution with a Charter of Rights and Freedoms. Smiley has described this strategy as a Third National Policy, paralleling the nation-building efforts of Sir John A. Macdonald in the nineteenth century and the efforts of post-World War II Liberal governments to lay the foundations of the welfare state. Doern called the 1980 Liberal program "the most coherent exercise of political belief and principle by the Liberals since the early years of the Pearson government (Smiley 1987; Doern 1982: 1).

Trudeau and his advisors viewed the separatist movement in Quebec, the province-building economic strategies of other provincial governments, and the resistance of business groups to increased government control of the economy in much the same light: as the encroachment of narrow interests on Ottawa's ability to pursue policies in the interests of the nation as a whole. Smiley described Trudeau's policies, which confronted a large number of entrenched political and economic interests in rapid succession, as the "political equivalent of a five-front war" (Smiley 1987: 183; Milne 1986).

The National Energy Program and Business-Government Conflict

The NEP was the most comprehensive expression of interventionist nationalism during the Trudeau era. Large-scale foreign control of Canada's major integrated oil companies and the hostility of the energy-producing provinces towards federal efforts to take a larger share of energy revenues made the negotiation of new federal-provincial agreements exceptionally difficult even under the short-lived Clark government of 1979 (Simpson 1980). As a result, the NEP was conceived in secrecy before its release in November 1980 as a pre-emptive strike on provincial energy revenues and jurisdiction that would give the federal government the political and fiscal leverage it needed to respond effectively to the global energy crisis while continuing to protect energy consumers in central and eastern Canada from the costs of rising world oil prices.

The NEP attempted to Canadianize the oil industry through a mix of expanded state ownership and preferential tax and regulatory treatment of Canadian-controlled firms. Petro-Canada had been created in the mid-1970s as an instrument of national policy in the energy sector; however, the NEP's proposal to allow the company to pre-empt ownership of 25 per cent of any new oil or gas discovery on federal Crown lands struck many business people as an undesirable precedent for confiscation of their property without adequate compensation (Johnston 1986: 77).[3]

The NEP also attempted to guarantee security of energy supply by limiting oil and gas exports and by shifting the balance of federal tax and subsidy policies to promote energy exploration and development on federal Crown lands in the Arctic and off the Atlantic Coast. By holding Canadian oil and gas prices below world levels, the federal government sought to champion individual and business consumers against arbitrary price increases by foreign or domestic oil sheiks. It also tried to align the self-interest of Canadian energy companies with federal policy goals by substituting a number of targeted grants for previous tax concessions and by creating incentives for foreign firms to sell majority control of their Canadian operations to Canadian investors. It also made general proposals to recycle surplus government revenues to finance major industrial projects intended to generate increased employment and business activity to reinforce other federal objectives.

Given sufficient time and the cooperation of the OPEC cartel in continuing to increase global oil prices, these policies might have succeeded in achieving their objectives. Ottawa and Alberta, the two main antagonists, succeeded in coming to an uneasy truce in ways that accommodated the interests of both parties at the expense of producers and consumers. However, the bursting of the OPEC bubble after 1982 undermined the economic basis of federal energy policies and ended the energy crisis which had made the NEP politically possible. Even so, the NEP left many western Canadian political and business interests bitterly alienated from the federal government and deeply committed to the election of a new government committed to reversing Trudeau's policies.

The NEP was only one of several policy initiatives that provoked business conflict with the federal government. Finance Minister Allan MacEachen's budget of November 1981 proposed tax reforms to reduce the federal deficit, finance promised improvements to federal social policies, and reduce the record interest rates (above 20 per cent) that had spilled over the border as US and Canadian central banks sought to curb rising inflation. A secondary objective was to substitute targeted government grants for many tax breaks, thus giving federal officials greater control over the use of these funds at the expense of business discretion.

However, technical flaws and the lack of traditional pre-budget consultations magnified business perceptions of federal hostility and ineptitude, triggering a mas-

---

3 Bliss notes that the NEP also encouraged foreign oil interests to sell out to Canadian interests at the top of the market, leaving Canadian firms heavily indebted and at serious risk when oil and gas prices plummeted after 1983 (Bliss 1987: 541-45, 556-50).

sive political backlash that prompted several revisions of the federal plan (McCall and Clarkson 1996: 234-40; Hale 1996: 204-82; Hale 2001b: 162-69). Just as important politically, these events coincided with the onset of a sharp recession, reinforcing internal Liberal divisions and making it relatively easy for the government's critics to blame it for economic problems.

Recession, Retreat, and the Trudeau Legacy

The NEP and MacEachen's tax reform budget so poisoned the political relationship between business groups and the federal government that most other elements of the Liberal agenda were quietly shelved in response to the subsequent recession of 1982. The federal government sought to recover business trust and support to create jobs, stimulate economic recovery, and regain its public reputation for competent economic management. As a result, Trudeau's final 18 months in office marked yet another return to the politics of business liberalism, reinforced by all-out Keynesian pump-priming of the economy (Hale 1996; Clarkson and McCall 1996: 249-72, 385-88; Hale 2001b: 170-74).

The Trudeau Restoration of 1980 has entered into the mythology of Canadian nationalism as a "heroic delusion" (McCall and Clarkson 1996) that challenged the combined forces of business power, free market ideology, and US hegemony in the interests of an independent, social democratic Canadian nation, but failed to overcome political and economic forces stronger than any Canadian government. Although this description may contain elements of truth, Trudeau's Third National Policy was as much an improvised response to a series of political and economic crises as it was a coherent statement of political principle.

Under normal economic circumstances, Trudeau's proposals for sweeping policy changes might have succeeded had the government mobilized the beneficiaries of its proposed reforms into a new political coalition. However, its confrontational tactics fostered bitter and sustained opposition from organized business interests and provincial governments threatened by the centralization of fiscal and economic power at their expense. Combined with the effects of the worst recession since World War II, these conflicts isolated the government from the core of its middle- and working-class political support. As a result, it was forced to seek accommodation with its critics in the ultimately vain hope of re-election.

The short-lived Third National Policy discredited interventionist nationalism in the eyes of many voters, giving credibility to its opponents' claims that government failure, not market failure, was the principal cause of Canada's economic woes. It also gave economic nationalism an anti-business tinge that made many Canadian businesses, large and small, increasingly receptive to economic integration and, ultimately, a free trade treaty with the US that would make federal economic policies more responsive to market forces.

Trudeau's appointment of his former minister, Donald Macdonald, to head a Royal Commission on "the Economic Union and the Development Prospects for Canada" in 1982 was a belated effort to seek consensus on a new set of economic policies that could promote economic development, national unity, and social cohesion and would also assist Canadian governments in adjusting to or overcoming international economic shocks. Perhaps the supreme irony of Trudeau's economic legacy was that the **Macdonald Commission** was to provide the blueprint for the dismantling of his policies and the entrenchment of neo-liberal and continentalist policies that were anathema to his senior officials and supporters.

Changing Directions: The Macdonald Commission, Neo-Liberalism, and Free Trade: Government and Business during the Mulroney and Chrétien Eras

Neo-liberalism emerged as the dominant paradigm for Canadian fiscal and economic policies over four electoral cycles between the election of the Mulroney government in 1984 and the end of the Chrétien government's second term of office in 2000 (see p. 28 for discussion on distinctions between neo-liberalism and neo-conservatism in Canada during the 1980s and 1990s). The Mulroney government that swept to power in September 1984 initially championed a return to the traditional politics of business liberalism—promoting private investment, job creation, and business expansion while declaring existing social programs to be a sacred trust that would be secured by the fruits of economic growth. When this business-as-usual approach to politics proved to be unsustainable, Mulroney adopted many of the recommendations of the Macdonald Commission that had been appointed by his predecessor.

We will now examine the historical evolution of the neo-liberal agenda between the mid-1980s and the first decade of the twenty-first century as an overlapping set of structural policy reforms, fiscal strategies, and efforts to promote social cohesion during a period of almost constant economic and social change. We will also look at the reasons for the relative political success and durability of the neo-liberal experiment, despite the wrenching effects of political and economic change, compared with the political and economic failure of the Trudeau government's efforts to introduce a more or less systematic policy of interventionist nationalism during the early 1980s.

Rethinking the Role of Government: Pressures for Change

The structures, policies, and operations of Canadian governments of all political affiliations have been transformed since the late 1980s. Four major economic and social factors have forced them to rethink their relationships with the operations of the economy and the purposes and methods they use to redistribute income and opportunities to Canadians.

First, the efforts of national and provincial governments to manage the effects of **globalization** through a series of international agreements and domestic policy changes have forced all governments to consider the ways in which their policy decisions affect networks of economic, social, and political activity that cross national borders. Canada's traditional east-west economic relationships have been transformed into a patchwork of interprovincial and international relationships that greatly complicate the process of managing national economic policies (see Chapter 8). Canada's free trade agreement of 1988 with the US, expanded to include Mexico in 1994, was a major catalyst for this process. However, multilateral trade negotiations leading to the formation of the World Trade Organization (WTO) in 1995 may ultimately have an even greater impact on federal and provincial regulatory policies.

Second, the attempts by federal and provincial governments to protect their citizens and businesses from international economic shocks during the 1970s and 1980s proved to be unsustainable as chronic deficits contributed to higher taxes, declining public services, and interest rate levels that discouraged investment and economic growth. The resulting fiscal crisis, which became apparent as combined federal and provincial budget deficits totaled $66 billion or 9.5 per cent of GDP in 1992-93 (Canada, Department of Finance 2000a: 9, 10, 36), prompted governments of all political descriptions to make deficit reduction and the restoration of sustainable government finance the top priority of the 1990s. The specific mix of policies used to reach these goals varied widely between governments, even those of similar political affiliations. However, the pressures of international competition and an aging population have made sustainable public finance a necessary component of coherent economic policies and consistent levels of public services for Canadians.

Third, technological change and international competition have had a significant effect on the ways in which governments regulate economic activity. These changes have not led to the consistent harmonization of Canadian economic and social policies with those of neighbouring countries, especially the US, as feared by critics in the 1980s. Typically, however, they have led to regulatory reforms that have fostered increased competition, reduced government regulation of prices and production levels, encouraged the commercialization and/or privatization of government enterprises, and prompted innovations in social and environmental regulations to accommodate economic adjustments while attempting to control their negative side effects (or externalities) on citizens, communities, and the environment.

Fourth, these processes have significantly altered governments' approach to social policies. Public spending on income transfers and the delivery of major public services such as health care and education have remained the single largest component of federal and provincial expenditure during the 1990s. However, the pressures of economic adjustment and fiscal sustainability have prompted a significant rethinking of social policy objectives (Canada, Department of Finance 1994; Courchene 1994; Courchene 2001c).

Neo-liberalism has maintained an active role for the state in income redistribution and the provision of public services. However, it has also insisted on a far greater coordination of economic and social policy goals to make them complementary and mutually reinforcing, both enabling citizens to take advantage of social and economic opportunities and requiring a degree of mutual obligation as part of this process.

Mulroney's First Term: Managing by Trial and Error

The Mulroney government of 1984-88 was elected with sizeable and often contradictory public expectations. Mulroney had promised that he would bring government's finances under control, preserve Canada's social programs as a sacred trust, create a favourable climate for business and entrepreneurship, and reconcile the regional and middle-class grievances that had derailed the Trudeau government's ambitious reform agenda of the early 1980s (Bercuson, Granatstein, and Young 1986; Hale 2001b: Chapter 7). His initial commitment to managing change with a minimum of social disruption boomeranged as entrenched social and economic interests resisted the major adjustments necessary for a government spending $150 for every $100 collected in revenues. As a result, his agenda evolved as a mix of incremental responses to policy problems too large or complex to lend themselves to quick fixes and a limited number of structural policy initiatives—free trade, tax reform, competition policy reform, sectoral deregulation—that laid the foundations for future direction.

Many of the ideas for the reforms initiated during the Mulroney years and carried out by his Liberal successor Jean Chrétien, were inspired by the Macdonald Commission. It called for a rethinking of business liberalism to achieve better coordination of economic and social policies to assist Canadians in adjusting to changing international economic conditions and regaining public trust for politicians and governments (Canada, Royal Commission on the Economic Union 1985; Courchene 1990; Hale 2001d).

Macdonald's vision of liberalism emphasized a reduced but more effective role for the state both in promoting economic opportunity and enabling all citizens to take advantage of it. Rather than seeking to "dismantle the state" as charged by its social democratic critics (for example, McBride and Shields 1997), the governments that followed Macdonald's precepts sought to restore public trust and credibility in the political process. To help them do this, most tried to end chronic deficits, balance their budgets, and distinguish more carefully between services that lent themselves to direct government provisions and those that could be provided either by the private sector or on a more business-like basis by public agencies (Canada, Department of Finance 1994; Kernaghan, Marson, and Borins 2000; also see Chapter 9).

Macdonald's 1985 report outlined proposals for large-scale policy change that were too sweeping to be fully developed, let alone implemented by the Mulroney government during its two terms in office. While many business interests favoured a more rapid and intellectually consistent process of change, the government placed a higher priority on building a broader constituency for its re-election.[4] By the midpoint of its first mandate, it chose the path of least political resistance by loosening fiscal policy, soft-pedaling efforts at deficit reduction, and seeking accommodation with the provinces. It avoided undue political risks on several fronts, shelving pro-

---

4 A senior federal official interviewed as part of the author's research into federal budgetary and tax policies during the period strongly suggested that Mulroney was deeply aware of the fragility of his 1984 election mandate and of the government's support, which declined steadily during his first two years in office.

posals for major sales tax reform in favour of modest income tax reforms in 1987-88. The latter financed broadly based tax reductions from the proceeds of higher business taxes (Hale 2001b: Chapter 7).

The biggest exception to this general pattern of incremental reform was Mulroney's decision to initiate negotiations for a broad **Canada-US Free Trade Agreement** (FTA) in the hope of obtaining more secure access to Canada's most important export market and of protecting Canadian businesses and workers from the effects of protectionist US trade rules. The shift of the traditionally protectionist Canadian Manufacturers Association to support for free trade in 1983 removed a major political barrier to a more ambitious approach to trade liberalization (Doern and Tomlin 1991: 20).

Mulroney's success in mobilizing a political coalition supportive of free trade also reflected domestic political conditions. Most provincial governments perceived free trade as an opportunity to diversify or protect markets for their industries' principal goods and services. The government of Quebec, in particular, identified free trade as an opportunity to strengthen the competitiveness of its economy and to reduce its dependence on markets in English Canada. The governments of Alberta, BC, and Saskatchewan, facing competition for their products in international commodity markets, perceived free trade as both an opportunity to secure export markets and a means of preventing a recurrence of federal economic policies that could limit their ability to control their own development. Many business interests, while recognizing the economic opportunities in free trade, also viewed the FTA negotiations as a form of insurance against a recurrence of the interventionist nationalist policies of the Trudeau era. By mid-1986, this was a significant possibility as the Mulroney PCs trailed both the Liberals and the NDP at 22 per cent in the polls.

The federal government carefully organized the negotiations to secure the support of major interest groups and provincial governments for its strategy, identifying both opportunities and areas of potential concern through a system of industry sector councils and a number of policy coordinating committees. In one of the most systematic consultation processes it had ever undertaken, the federal government secured broad business confidence, while identifying domestic interests whose exemption from the agreement would be necessary to diffuse political opposition. While Mulroney staked his government's future on the free trade deal, the 1988 agreement was sold to the Canadian public in traditional terms by the promise of more jobs, higher incomes, greater job security, and increased economic opportunity (Doern and Tomlin 1991: 108-25).

FTA-imposed limits on preferential regulations and subsidies challenged many traditional policy tools that had been used to promote or protect Canadian industries, thus limiting the capacity of future governments to return to the nationalist and neo-mercantilist development policies of the past and repudiating Trudeau-era economic nationalism. These features of the FTA were compelling to its supporters, particularly business and provincial governments, and repellent to its opponents.

Business interests generally supported the Mulroney government's agenda, while questioning the depth of its commitment to its rhetorical goals of deficit reduction

and reduced economic regulation. However, the government's systematic consultation with business groups and the ideologically charged environment of the 1988
election ensured it strong support from corporate Canada and most organized small
business groups in that watershed election campaign as the best deal likely to be
obtained in the foreseeable future.

Nationalist groups, organized labour, and other interest groups dependent on
extensive government intervention generally opposed the negotiations. However,
they lacked a clear focus for their attacks until the deal had been signed. The Liberal-
dominated Senate refused passage of the FTA's enabling legislation until an election
could be held on the issue. Liberal leader John Turner, a long-time Liberal nationalist, led the campaign against the FTA, strongly supported by labour and social policy
groups and a minority of business interests. Although public opinion was evenly
divided on the FTA, the Mulroney government won a narrow victory in the bitterly
contested 1988 election (Doern and Tomlin 1991: 205-42).

The Consequences of Free Trade

The implementation and extension of the FTA, and the rapid adaptation of Canadian
industries in the broader North American economy made it practically impossible
to reverse these policies without massive economic disruption. The further integration of Canadian firms in North American markets has made free trade central to
the calculations of Canadian businesses, investors, and many of those who work
for them. Both Canadian exports and investment abroad grew rapidly during the
1990s. Canadian manufacturers exported more than half their production by the
mid-1990s, while in 1997 foreign investment and takeover activity by Canadian firms
resulted in the total value of Canadian direct investment abroad exceeding that of
foreign investment in Canada for the first time (Nadeau and Rao 2002: 140; Statistics
Canada 2005a). In fact, in the early twenty-first century, the international exports
of every Canadian province except Manitoba consistently exceed their exports to
other provinces. A series of regional and international agreements extending the
principles established in the FTA—most notably the NAFTA with the US and Mexico
(1994) and the completion of the Uruguay Round trade negotiations, which resulted
in the reorganization of the WTO in 1994-95—have expanded the interdependence
of Canada's economy with the international trading and investment system. These
issues will be explored further in Chapter 8.

The Mulroney government was also able to consolidate other major, if less visible,
policy changes that complemented its trade-driven industrial policy of economic liberalization and restructuring the regulatory environment for Canadian businesses.
The logical consequences of free trade negotiations contributed to a process of **path
dependence** in which one set of policy changes were closely linked to another in
an increasingly dense network of interrelated policies and institutions. These initiatives—including major changes to Canada's *Competition Act* (1986), financial sector
regulation (1987, 1992), corporate income and commodity tax systems (1988, 1990),
regulatory regimes governing transportation (1987) and telecommunications sec-

tors, and the commercialization or selective privatization of Crown corporations—contributed significantly to the restructuring of the Canadian economy in response to continuing trends towards global economic integration and competition.

Most of these changes were introduced following extensive consultations with major stakeholders and other interests, following the pattern introduced by the Trudeau government after 1982. As a result, the technical details of proposed policy changes were often exposed to detailed review and amendment before their approval by Parliament, thus making it harder to unravel the policy trade-offs built into structural policy reforms. Most of these measures enjoyed greater or lesser degrees of business support, often based on balances between different business (and other) interests. However, several resulted in higher taxation and other costs of fiscal and economic adjustment that were deeply unpopular with business groups and other social interests.

Sales tax reform was the most controversial of these changes. The introduction of the GST after the 1988 election was intended to spread the cost of existing consumption taxes across a broader economic base. Retaining the existing 13.5 per cent federal sales tax on manufactured goods was logically inconsistent with a free trade environment, especially in the absence of a comparable tax in the US. However, Finance Minister Michael Wilson's tax reform proposals prompted a bitter public debate that evoked many of the passions of the 1988 election. Business groups were deeply divided over the GST, with manufacturing, capital-intensive, and export interests supportive and most small businesses and service industries strongly opposed.

By 1993, the structural policy changes associated with free trade and fiscal retrenchment were too far advanced to reverse. However, they had not yet generated enough direct economic benefits for the average voter to offset the dislocation resulting from economic adjustment and to prevent the PC's electoral destruction (Hale 2001b: 187–90). Even though some observers view these policies as a reflection of the exercise of corporate power at the expense of the state or with the ideological complicity of governments (McQuaig 1987; McQuaig 1993; Myles and Pierson 1997), much of the intellectual leadership for these changes came largely from the ranks of the federal public service, rather than from politicians or even business leaders (Doern and Tomlin 1991; Savoie 1999; Greenspon and Wilson-Smith 1996). Many of these initiatives, and the details of their implementation, were largely driven by political and bureaucratic rationality, accommodating the input of both business groups and other social interests whose support the government hoped to secure. Had there been strong bureaucratic resistance or scepticism about the general direction or major details of most of these policy changes, it would have been clearly communicated to the Chrétien Liberals after their election in 1993 along with suggestions on how to modify or reverse them. Instead, most major Mulroney-era initiatives were extended and consolidated by his Liberal successors.

The fragmentation of groups calling for more sweeping (and contradictory) political changes led the Liberals to campaign as the party of cautious, reasonable change rather than seeking to reverse most of Mulroney's major policy initiatives.

Organized labour and its traditional allies in the federal NDP failed to secure public support for alternative economic policies, which were based on more interventionist approaches to government at a time when provincial governments and social democratic governments in most other English-speaking countries were adjusting to the pressures of globalization.[5]

The rise of new parties, such as the Reform Party in western Canada and the Bloc Québécois in Quebec, provided an alternative outlet for populist discontent with rapid political and economic change during the early 1990s and undermined the NDP's post-Depression role as a major source of new policy ideas for both Liberal and PC governments. Steep drops in living standards during the early 1990s made voters receptive to politicians who would work with business to create jobs and promote economic recovery, while softening the sharp edges of economic restructuring (Lewis 2003).

The decision of the Clinton administration in the US to endorse NAFTA, subject to safeguards on labour and environment issues, reflected the prudent accommodation of liberals in both countries to new economic realities and the limits they imposed on government activism, despite the persistent misgivings of many of their supporters (Hufbauer and Schott 1993; Blanchard 1998: 73-102; Cameron and Tomlin 2000). Clinton's proposals provided a political bridge that enabled the federal Liberals under their new leader, Jean Chrétien, to square their commitments to make free trade more responsive to Canadian interests with larger economic and political realities after their election in 1993. More importantly, however, they created the basis for the emergence of a new, centrist ideological consensus that emphasized managerial pragmatism in the balancing and integration of fiscal discipline, economic development, and the redistributive activities of the welfare state (Greenspon and Wilson-Smith 1996; Savoie 1999).

Chrétien-Martin Liberalism: Adapting to Political and Economic Change

The Chrétien government was elected in 1993 with a mandate to modify the policies of the Mulroney government to the extent necessary to reconcile fiscal responsibility with economic recovery and the protection of social programs. At the same time, tax increases introduced since 1988, combined with the recession of 1990-92 and slow economic recovery, had sufficiently reduced Canadians' living standards that voters had little appetite for a return to governmental activism, especially if it conflicted with economic recovery. The result was a continuation and extension of the Mulroney government's main fiscal, social, and trade policies, but these were packaged in ways that stressed the continued role of government in promoting economic growth and job creation, reducing economic inequality, and enhancing social cohesion.

---

5 The NDP's problems were accentuated by deep divisions among its supporters in Ontario, where NDP Premier Bob Rae's social contract to reduce huge provincial deficits by rolling back public sector contract settlements was bitterly resisted by most of his supporters in organized labour and related activist groups (Walkom 1994).

International and domestic political considerations provide the explanation for the persistence and extension of the neo-liberal policies of the federal government after 1993, slightly repackaged in rhetoric but applied in a far more systematic and disciplined fashion during Chrétien's first two terms of office (1993-2000). The economic costs of reversing progressive North American economic integration were seen to be significantly greater than the consolidation of these policies with minor adjustments. Most businesses had made the often challenging economic adjustments to free trade, including significant investments in plant and equipment and changes in their business strategies to adapt to changing competitive conditions (see note 4 above; Kwan 2000; Cross 2002a). Business liberals such as Finance Minister Paul Martin, Industry Minister John Manley, and Trade Minister Roy MacLaren had recognized this shift as early as 1991 and led a serious reappraisal of Liberal economic policies. Remaining debates were about issues of detail, not the core principles of trade and economic liberalization. This policy was strongly supported by senior federal officials, particularly in key economic policy departments, who advised the new government.

Canada's economic recovery during the mid-1990s was driven by exports to a rapidly growing US economy. Canadian trade policies might champion a diversification of Canadian export markets but not at any significant cost to close Canada-US economic relations. The absence of a credible economic alternative to free trade or deficit reduction was made more obvious by the need for exceptional levels of foreign borrowing by federal and especially provincial governments to finance record deficits during the early 1990s. Finally, the decimation of the NDP opposition in the 1993 election meant that the separatist Bloc Québécois, as the strongest voice for interventionist nationalism in Parliament, was politically isolated and lacked the credibility or will to mobilize widespread public opposition to the government's policies outside Quebec.

The Chrétien government inherited a federal deficit which had ballooned to $42 billion, or 36 per cent of federal revenues, by 1993-94. Although it had won the 1993 election on a policy of gradual deficit reduction, continuing fiscal pressures led it to rethink its fiscal and economic strategies shortly after taking office. The Department of Finance's October 1994 discussion paper, "A New Framework for Economic Policy" (Canada, Department of Finance 1994), outlined a comprehensive strategic framework intended to promote economic and employment growth, reduce the deficit, and address structural obstacles to improvements in living standards. It set out four main structural objectives that have been pursued with relative consistency:

- achieving fiscal sustainability;
- assisting individual Canadians, particularly those whose jobs or ability to find work were threatened by ongoing economic changes, to adapt to the changing economic environment;
- redesigning social programs to encourage and assist lower income Canadians to seek and find available work; and

- assisting the adjustment of Canadian businesses and workers to the new or **knowledge-based economy** (KBE).

Most provincial governments have adopted variations of this mix of policies, depending on the specific challenges and opportunities facing regional economies and the political commitments of their own governments. They recognized that their ability to translate their rhetoric into action would depend on a return to fiscal discipline and balanced budgets. While not all governments balanced their budgets before initiating significant tax cuts or spending increases, most recognized that achieving fiscal balance would give governments greater freedom in balancing demands from competing social interests for lower taxes and higher spending.

Restoring Fiscal Balance

The government's initial emphasis was on a disciplined approach to deficit reduction that involved a systematic review and prioritization of government activities and spending commitments. The rapid growth of foreign-held debt from 21.0 to 40.7 per cent of GDP between 1984 and 1994 made the Canadian economy increasingly vulnerable to international financial markets. Finance Minister Paul Martin came under significant pressure from business and financial markets to take more aggressive measures to reduce the deficit (Greenspon and Wilson-Smith 1996: 153-70, 195-227).

A combination of fiscal discipline, reductions in transfers to provinces, and very cautious budget projections enabled Martin to balance the federal books by 1997-98 and to post rising surpluses in subsequent years (Hale 2001b: 226-39; Hale 2001c). Most provinces embarked on similar deficit reduction efforts between 1992 and 1996, although, as noted above, the timing and specific mix of tax increases and spending reductions reflected regional conditions and political commitments (Hale 2000; Richards 2000).

The focus of federal and provincial governments on balancing and subsequently maintaining balanced budgets forced business groups to modify their own political agendas. Proposals for tax reductions had to be justified against competing priorities within a fiscal framework of balanced budgets and gradual debt reduction or by corresponding reductions in subsidies or other benefits to business (for example, see Goar 2003). Governments became increasingly successful in challenging interest groups to put their demands for higher spending or lower taxes towards an overall budgetary strategy, rather than a continual demand for more (Hale 2001b: 117). However, as in previous years, most governments tended to pursue looser fiscal policies, involving different mixes of tax cuts and higher spending, as they approached the time to seek re-election (Kneebone and McKenzie 1999). In some provinces, notably Ontario, these trends have resulted in renewed deficits.

Sustained prosperity since 2000 has resulted in less fiscal discipline and sharp increases in public spending by the federal government and most provinces (Hale, 2006b).

Investing in Skills, Education, and the New Economy

Cost containment was not the only objective of neo-liberal social policies. A series of initiatives at both federal and provincial levels has emphasized the need to refocus social and educational spending on measures to assist individual Canadians in their adjustment to the new economy and changing demands for skilled labour. Federal and provincial politicians of all parties have pointed to the close connection between education and employment levels during the 1990s, with Canadians with university and community college degrees enjoying far higher employment rates than those without.[6] As noted by a senior Martin advisor, "most Canadians realize that education may not guarantee a secure, well-paying job, but its absence more or less guarantees the lack of economic security and employment" (Interview, Department of Finance, 1998).

The approach taken by the Chrétien government, and imitated by most provincial governments with slightly different rhetoric, was to emphasize a balance in policies aimed at encouraging economic growth and increased employment on the one hand and promoting greater economic equality, opportunity, and security on the other (Hale 2001c). Changes in the Employment Insurance system introduced in 1995-96 signaled the government's commitment to shift funds from passive income support programs to so-called active labour market policies intended to encourage and equip Canadians to acquire the education, skills, and training needed to adapt to a changing economy. Part of this process involved shifting EI premium surpluses averaging $6.5 billion annually to other government uses between 1996 and 2001 (Hale 1998; Human Resources Development Canada 2001; Hale 2002). Although these practices were criticized, for different reasons, by both business groups and organized labour, they made it possible for Ottawa to finance both increased social transfers and tax reductions after balancing its budget in 1998.

A more enduring effect of growing budget surpluses was increasing federal and provincial investments in post-secondary education and skills development as part of its broader productivity agenda. The reinvestment (or new spending) policies of the federal government were focused primarily on three major objectives that sought to integrate the government's social and economic objectives while promoting greater social cohesion and promoting a wider distribution of the benefits of technological change to Canadians:

- increasing access to education and skills training needed to provide trained workers and secure employment, particularly in the KBE;
- promoting increased research and innovation through a combination of increased funding for basic research and tax incentives for commercial research and development; and

---

6 See below, Table 6.5.

- gradually restoring federal transfers to the provinces to finance health care and other social services affected by the transfer cuts implemented as part of Ottawa's deficit reduction program of the mid-1990s. (Hale 2002: 20-42; Canada 2002).

The federal government has also taken a number of steps reminiscent of traditional industrial policies to foster the development of high technology industries that are at the heart of the new economy or KBE. These include a combination of programs and tax subsidies for research and innovation, more broadly based tax measures to foster venture capital investment in such industries, and investments in technological infrastructure to expand Canadians' access to the Internet and related services.

The KBE has also contributed to the increased mobility of capital and highly skilled labour, in the process increasing the costs of political friction between business and government. High technology industries are often characterized by high degrees of integration and mobility across international borders. The integration of capital markets in Canada and the US has made it more difficult to apply traditional ownership tests in promoting the development of national champions, although this has not stopped some politicians and governments from trying to do so. Even so, changes in Canada's economic structure limit governments' capacity for the coercive application of national regulatory policies and industrial policies (Canadian Manufacturers and Exporters 2001a; Canadian Manufacturers and Exporters 2001b).

Explaining Political Shifts, Anticipating the Future

The shifts that have taken place during the last generation in Canadian politics, economic policies, and business-government relations are the subject of profound disagreement. These disputes often reflect different analytical approaches to the study of political and economic life: normative vs. empirical and individualist vs. collectivist in orientation.[7] They are also a reflection of observers' competing ideological outlooks.

Neo-conservative critics of governments emphasize that activist governments continue to engage in excessive taxation, spending, and regulation that undermine both business competitiveness and the opportunities and living standards of individual Canadians. Examples of this outlook may be found in conservative newspapers such as the *National Post*, think tanks and advocacy groups such as the Fraser Institute and the Canadian Taxpayers' Federation.

Anti-capitalist critics of federal and provincial policies during the 1990s have argued that they represent the pervasive influence of a corporate agenda that has dominated political discourse and marginalized competing political viewpoints. This outlook is most prominent among the leadership of organized labour; think tanks

---

7 Methodological individualism views groups as collections of individuals with the capacity to exercise a degree of choice in their actions; methodological holism has a more collectivist orientation that views the actions of both individuals and groups as conditioned by the exercise of power in a political or societal context. See, for example, Toboso 1995.

and advocacy groups such as the Canadian Centre for Policy Alternatives, the Parkland Institute, and the Council of Canadians; the federal NDP; and assorted social movements and activist groups that make up the anti-globalization movement.

A large body of opinion gravitates between these two tendencies, sharing parts of their outlooks on selected issues but attempting to balance the mixture of individualist and collectivist (or communitarian) outlooks that accommodate elements of both. Traditional reform liberals had fought the trend towards globalization, arguing that it undermined the capacity of the state to protect national sovereignty, protect workers in industries vulnerable to global competition, and manage economic and social policies according to priorities defined by governments. Neo-liberal and neo-conservative governments during the 1990s argued that globalization and high government deficits were largely frustrating the ability of governments to pursue these policies anyway. Accordingly, they believed it was more realistic to work with other countries to define a more consistent set of rules governing economic behaviour, rules that left room for national economic differences rather than attempting to restrict flows of trade in investment in the hope of controlling economic forces larger than any single government.

There is little doubt that the changes in the overall direction of fiscal and economic policy have enjoyed broad support from Canada's business community, both as a welcome change from the political deadlock that prevented effective responses to continuing changes in the Canadian and global economies and as evidence that business and government are pursuing comparable, if not always identical, policy objectives.

Governments view the general cooperation of businesses and organized business interests as an important component of economic policy, but economic policy is about more than government policy towards business. The objectification of business as the 1,200-pound gorilla pounding the government table, dominating debate, and foreclosing policy options may dominate the perspective of ideologues embittered at their own marginalization within the political process. However, in today's economic environment, few politicians would deliberately set out to antagonize business interests in the systematic and comprehensive fashion probably needed to conjure up such a political nuisance.[8]

A more measured assessment of changing political attitudes during the 1990s suggests that these changes reflect a return to a greater specialization of roles between government and business. Although most governments acknowledge their dependence on business investment and job creation to meet their economic and social policy goals, policy choices and priorities often subordinate business priorities to the broader objectives of specific governments.

---

8 Arguably, even most social democratic governments of the 1990s have attempted to limit the degree of political conflict with business interests most critical to their own constituencies, while attempting to accommodate or address business concerns on policies in which central government priorities are not at stake. This is not to say that they have been consistently successful or that business interests have not sought to promote the election of more politically congenial governments.

The capacity of governments to maintain this equilibrium will hinge on several factors. Ottawa's ability to generate regular annual budget surpluses, last seen in the early 1950s,[9] creates substantial political pressures to relax the fiscal discipline that has enabled recent finance ministers to set a consistent fiscal and economic agenda rather than being pushed and pulled in all directions by interest groups seeking policy favours. These pressures tend to be reinforced during periods of minority government, such as that following the 2004 federal election.

As in the 1960s and early 1970s, a generation accustomed to taking economic growth for granted may demand a more activist role for governments that replaces the mutual accommodation of recent years between government and business with more substantive conflicts of political philosophy and economic interest. Alternately, the aging of Canada's population may increase pressures to promote economic growth to limit conflicts between a growing number of retired Canadians dependent on public services and transfers and a stagnant or shrinking labour force whose taxes will have to cover the rising costs of such services (Robson 2001; CSIS Commission on Global Aging 2001; England 2001).

However, the changes in Canada's economic structure since the 1980s—the major forms and systems of economic activity which define and shape economic activity at both national and regional levels—suggest that these challenges and conflicts may be dealt with in ways that reflect a very different business environment. These issues will be examined in greater detail in the next part of this book.

Key Terms and Concepts for Review (see Glossary)

business liberalism
Canada-US Free Trade Agreement
  (FTA)
Foreign Investment Review Agency
globalization
interventionist nationalism
knowledge-based economy
liberal continentalism
liberal nationalism

Macdonald Commission
Mechanisms of Interaction School
NAFTA
National Energy Program
path dependence
Quiet Revolution
stagflation
Third National Policy

---

9 The federal government reported eight annual budget surpluses between 1946-47 and 1953-54. The fiscal and economic statement of November 2005 projected the ninth consecutive federal surplus since 1997-98 (Gillespie 1991: Table B-1; Canada, Department of Finance 2005).

Questions for Discussion and Review

1. What factors contributed to the re-emergence of Canadian economic national-ism as a growing political force in the late 1960s and early 1970s? Why was the Trudeau government reluctant to embrace interventionist nationalism during the 1970s?

2. What major political and economic factors contributed to the breakdown of the Keynesian consensus on the role of government in the economy during the 1970s? Why?

3. What are four explanations for the deterioration of relations between business and government during the 1970s? What weight does each place a) on the politi-cal judgement of individual business or government decision-makers and b) on a breakdown of political processes for policy evaluation and political consultation?

4. What were the major elements of Trudeau's Third National Policy? Why did Trudeau attempt to polarize economic policy disputes in 1980-81? Why did these policies fail to achieve their objectives a) politically and b) economically?

5. Discuss the Macdonald Royal Commission and free trade as elements of Trudeau's economic legacy. Why did Mulroney succeed in implementing many of his pro-posals for major policy change when Trudeau failed?

6. What major political and economic factors led the Chrétien government to extend and consolidate Mulroney's economic policies during the 1990s? What implications have these policies had a) for the role of the Canadian state and b) for business-government relations?

7. Evaluate arguments for and against the idea of a corporate agenda as the expla-nation for the consolidation of neo-liberal policies in the 1990s. How do political and economic incentives other than business pressure help to explain the actions of senior politicians and civil servants?

Suggestions for Further Readings

Axworthy, Thomas A., and Pierre E. Trudeau (Eds.). 1990. *Towards a Just Society: The Trudeau years*. Toronto: Penguin.

Bradford, Neil. 1998. *Commissioning ideas: Canadian National Policy innovation in comparative perspective*. Toronto: Oxford University Press.

Canada, Royal Commission on the Economic Union and Development Prospects for Canada. 1985. *Report*. 3 vols. Ottawa: Supply and Services Canada.

Canada, Department of Finance. 1994. *Agenda: jobs and growth—a new framework for economic policy*. Ottawa: Department of Finance (October).

Courchene, Thomas J. 2001. *A state of minds: towards a human capital future for Canadians*. Montreal: IRPP.

Doern, G. Bruce, and Brian Tomlin. 1991. *Faith and fear: the free trade story*. Toronto: Stoddart.

Greenspon, Edward, and Anthony Wilson-Smith. 1996. *Double vision: the inside story of the Liberals in power*. Toronto: Doubleday.

Hale, Geoffrey. 2001. *The politics of taxation in Canada*. Peterborough, ON: Broadview Press.

Levitt, Kari. 1970. *Silent surrender: the multinational corporation in Canada*. Toronto: Macmillan of Canada.

McCall, Christina, and Stephen Clarkson. 1996. *Trudeau and our times, Volume 2: the heroic delusion*. Toronto: McClelland and Stewart.

Milne, David. 1986. *Tug of war: Trudeau, Mulroney and the provinces*. Toronto: Lorimer.

Simeon, Richard, and Ian Robinson. 1990. *State, society and the development of Canadian federalism*. Toronto: University of Toronto Press.

PART 2

Canada's Economic Structure and the Environment for Business-Government Relations

Introduction

Political ideas and theories may attempt to explain, justify, or challenge existing economic and social relationships. However, these relationships are heavily influenced by the political and legal institutions that provide the durable organizational structures and rules that organize and shape the political process and the workings of the economy. The study of institutional arrangements within both political science and political economy is increasingly important to policy-makers and governments attempting to increase the effectiveness of their policies, particularly when they are seeking to combine or balance particular economic and social objectives with the efficient and equitable workings of the market economy.

Achieving these objectives requires an understanding of the country's **economic structure**—the basic characteristics and divisions of economic activity within a particular geographic area or within an overall economic system or network. It also requires some understanding of the ways in which the structures and processes of government policies interact with those of economic markets and how they affect a broad range of market participants, including different kinds of businesses, consumers, investors, and workers.

The nature of a country's economic structure can be influenced over time by the economic policies of its government and by the activities of both economic and policy entrepreneurs, as discussed in previous chapters. The different aspects of a country's economic structure—and the organized economic and political interests associated with them—influence the policy choices available to governments, the resources available to implement them, and the political environment in which these decisions are made.

Canada's contemporary economic structure is characterized by three major features that cut across the institutional and structural elements discussed in the next four chapters and which speak directly to the challenges of effective policy-making within a democratic capitalist system: complexity, varying degrees of openness, and dynamism.

The first challenge of economic policy structures and processes—and of groups attempting to influence them from inside or outside government—is their variety and complexity. This complexity is symptomatic of the scope and diversity of economic activity, corporate forms, and government policies across Canada. It is magnified by the need to balance and reconcile competing objectives of government policies that directly or indirectly affect market functions and business operations.

There is an inherent paradox in the politics of complex bureaucratic systems: the greater their complexity, the greater becomes the desire of societal interests, including business, to make those segments of the bureaucracy most directly affecting their activities (and politicians associated with them) more responsive to their interests and policy goals. The more responsive governments become to the particular interests of businesses and other social groups, the greater the problems of policy coordination, as discussed in Chapter 3.

The response of Canada's political systems to this paradox, as in several other industrial countries, has been to pursue greater openness in the workings of market forces within general policy frameworks. These frameworks may be national in scope, incorporating both senior levels of government, or international, involving cross-border flows of goods, services, people, and/or capital. **Economic openness** is the degree to which citizens, businesses, and other organizations are free to enter, adapt, or withdraw from particular forms of economic activity—both within particular political jurisdictions and across political boundaries—without extensive and intrusive government regulation and control. It also involves the contestability of markets: the degree to which new or different economic actors can compete with existing market participants in particular areas of economic activity and their relative openness to technological and managerial innovation.

Innovation is central to the concept of **economic dynamism**: the openness, susceptibility, and adaptability of economic actors and structures to changes both in major aspects of the particular markets in which they function and in the broader economic environment. The increased openness of large elements of the Canadian economy to international competition and technological, organizational, and policy changes during the past generation has created an environment of considerable economic dynamism, both in the sense of creative destruction suggested by economist Joseph Schumpeter (1950: 82-84) and in challenging governments to adjust both many of the ways in which *they* carry out their functions and many of the assumptions which guide their regulation of economic activity.

Organization of Part II

The following four chapters examine the underlying concept and key elements of Canada's economic structure as it enters the twenty-first century and their implications for the economic role of government and for relations between businesses and governments.

Chapter 6 reviews major elements of the legal and economic organization of Canada's economic marketplace, such as ownership, competitive structures, the sources and scale of economic activity, and the role of capital markets. It also addresses the significant ways in which these structures have changed in recent years and the implications of these changes for government policies and relations among governments, businesses and other societal actors.

Canada's huge geography, including its **economic geography**—"the spatial and sectoral distribution of economic activity" (Wallace 2002: 3)—further increases the complexity of managing Canada's diversity: the major differences in the size and distribution of populations between and within regions and the significant variations in resource endowments and industrial structures. It is also the product of past political decisions that have shaped historic patterns of economic development and political culture in Canada's provinces and regions, creating the political diversity that has resulted in Canada's relatively decentralized federal system. Federalism and regionalism have contributed to enduring regional differences in the political and policy environments governing economic activity and business-government relations in Canada's provinces and regions, particularly the ways in which regionally varied economic and social interests have competed to influence the exercise of political power. Chapter 7 assesses the impact of federal political institutions on the emergence of Canada's regional economic structures, along with the differing economic bases and levels of development of its provincial economies and their effect on relationships among regional, national, and international economic interests.

The political economy of Canada's regional diversity is complicated further by its growing economic integration within North America, so that north-south (and other international) economic linkages become as important as traditional east-west linkages as a means of promoting economic diversification, growth, and higher living standards. Chapter 8 assesses the ongoing effects of globalization and North American integration on federal and provincial economic policies, business strategies, and relations among business groups, governments, and other societal actors.

Canadian governments have frequently used state ownership as an instrument of economic policy and national or regional economic integration, particularly by using the ownership of transportation infrastructure and public utilities to promote economic utilities, compensate for shortages of private capital, and cushion particular regions or sectors from economic shocks resulting from the overextension of private businesses. Chapter 9 examines the evolving role of government business enterprises in Canada and the factors that are influencing the commercialization and privatization of public enterprises. It also considers the emergence of new hybrid forms of economic activity in the delivery of public services that cross the traditional boundaries of public, private, and non-profit sectors and the implications of these changes for relations between the broader public sector and private businesses.

Key Terms and Concepts for Review (see Glossary)

economic dynamism

economic geography

economic openness

economic structure

Canada's Economic Structure: Diversity, Dynamism, and the Political Economy of Business-Government Relations

Economic structure is a term that describes the basic characteristics and divisions of economic activity within either a particular geographic area or an overall economic system or network. It is important to distinguish between the two because, while the authority of a government is typically exercised over a particular territory and its residents, very few economic systems that have developed beyond the primitive stages of barter are economically self-sufficient.

The structures and networks of business ownership and activity play a vital role both in the nature and levels of economic activity and in how these factors interact with the institutions and policies of governments. This chapter addresses these matters on two broad levels: the structures of business activity enabled or mandated by laws and public institutions and the ways in which these structures interact with two kinds of markets. First are markets for the production and distribution of goods and services, including the nature and extent of competition within those markets, and second are markets for control of corporate structures and the economic activities in which they engage.

The interdependence of economic actors makes all policy decisions subject to the risk of unintended consequences so that decisions intended to benefit or control one group may spill over into the economic lives of others. The openness of economic life implies that citizens and businesses have the right or opportunity to exercise choices that may affect the choice of policy instruments by governments—or their relative effectiveness. These choices may be reflected in the mobility of workers or capital, the criteria used by individual or institutional investors in evaluating the relative risks and returns of investments in particular businesses or financial markets, and the decisions of businesses to locate their operations in particular areas rather than others or to organize their supply chains and distribution networks in different ways.

The dynamics of structural economic change resulting from the responses of businesses and governments to technological change and economic globalization since the 1970s have dramatically altered the ways in which Canada's economy is organized and the environments within which it functions. Continuous change has increased the importance of fostering Canada's international economic competitiveness and of enabling citizens, businesses, and governments to adapt to circumstances often beyond their immediate control (Porter 1991; Wallace 2002: 59-68).

These factors help to make Canada a challenging country to govern—one that continually defies the application of "one-size-fits-all" remedies to any problem or challenge. Failure to understand this diversity, or to take it into account in making political or policy decisions, is likely to trigger political conflicts as those groups whose interests are disregarded or ignored seek to protect them through the political process.

Complexity, Openness, and Dynamism in Economic Structures

Economic structures evolve both in the context of shifting economic relationships and in the overarching reach and more specialized concerns of political and regulatory institutions. The institutional structures of government tend to be organized in ways that reflect past and present forms of economic organization, either facilitating or hindering emerging ones. They represent past political decisions to recognize the political and economic importance of particular interests and policy fields through cabinet representation, the organization of government departments, and regulatory systems. They also help to shape the interaction of interest groups with governments. Most business and other interest groups tend to focus their lobbying activities on a relative handful of departments—or particular components of those departments—that affect their activities most directly.

This chapter examines four major dimensions of Canada's economic structure—the ownership and control of economic activity, the competitive environment facing Canadian businesses in different economic sectors, the sources and scale of economic activity, and the role played by financial and **capital markets** in Canada's economic system—in the context of the three overarching qualities, noted in the Introduction to Part II, that help to shape these processes: complexity, relative openness, and dynamism. It also considers the effects of structural and technological change—often described as the new economy or the knowledge-based economy—on the role of governments in the economy, their implications for government policies, and the relations between business and government.

Complexity

Economic structures in developed industrial countries such as Canada are complex and highly diverse, incorporating different functional economic sectors and types of business activity, which typically involve overlapping networks of economic, political, and social relationships with varying degrees of specialization and interdependence. Both the patterns of business competition and the nature, extent, and jurisdictional boundaries of government regulation that help to shape them can vary widely even *within* different segments of particular economic sectors. In Canada, for example, different elements of sectors such as transportation (air, rail, trucking), financial services (banks, insurance, securities), energy production and distribution (oil/gas, coal, electricity, nuclear), and construction (institutional, residential, commercial) are subject to widely varying competitive conditions and approaches to government regulation, sometimes between federal and provincial (or territorial) governments and sometimes within the same government or order of government (for detailed discussions, see Doern and Gattinger 2003; Clancy 2004).

Economist and philosopher Friedrich Hayek has suggested that the greatest challenge facing any effort at central state planning of the economy is the difficulty that government policy-makers have in measuring, let alone understanding, the innumerable economic interactions of producers and consumers in a complex industrial economy.[1] Ironically, as noted in Chapters 4 and 5, the growth of government between the 1940s and the 1980s expanded the complexity of this process both for policy-makers and for citizens and interest groups attempting to influence government decision-makers and hold them accountable for their actions. The emergence of multiple centres of bureaucratic activity often paralleling the multiple centres of economic activity in the modern economy creates huge challenges of political and administrative coordination. The greater the extent of government intervention, the greater becomes the challenge of managing conflicting objectives and balancing competing societal expectations and demands through the political process.

The effects of complexity on policy-making and business-government relations in Canada can be seen on at least four different levels: the structure of business operations, the institutional structures and processes of government, regional variations in economic activity and the organized interests related to it, and in the accumulation of overlapping and often competing policy objectives.

Openness

The concept of openness affects the characteristics of economic organization and regulatory systems both within a particular political space or geographic area and across political and geographic boundaries. It reveals the degree of freedom enjoyed by citizens and business to enter (or exit) particular areas of economic activity, either individually or as part of broader business networks. It also speaks to the degree of competition existing within particular industry sectors and the competitive factors—such as access to capital, freedom of voluntary exchange, or the arbitrary exercise of market power—that may either facilitate or hinder competition to the benefit of consumers.

Open economic systems, particularly those which enable their citizens to engage in foreign trade or business ventures with foreigners with relatively few restrictions, become part of more complex networks of economic activity that may be strengthened or otherwise influenced by the actions of their governments. The relative openness of markets to external economic factors may be measured according to the relative volume and distribution of international—and, in Canada, interregional—trade and capital flows, including the levels and types of foreign investment. These factors are heavily influenced by the legal systems governing both international and domestic economic transactions. However, even relatively closed economic systems (characterized by high levels of trade regulation or government control over

---

1 Hayek's objections are both pragmatic and ethical, as they are based on the tendency of unchecked regulatory authority to result in the arbitrary exercise of power (Hayek 1944: 24-39; Hayek 1960).

the movement of goods, services, labour, and capital) may engage in extensive economic relations with neighbouring (and sometimes far-off) countries.

Openness also applies to traditional boundaries between different kinds of business activity—such as industry subsectors in which different businesses provide similar but slightly differentiated products to very different groups of customers—between public and private enterprise, and between both of these forms of economic organization and non-profit organizations for the pursuit of shared social and community objectives. The restructuring of Canada's public sector during the 1980s and 1990s has led to new forms of public-private partnerships both in the delivery of public services and in managing the overlapping functions of each sector. These issues are addressed further in Chapter 9.

Dynamism

Dynamism is the adaptability of economic actors and structures to changes in the broader economic environment. These may result from political or economic shocks as discussed in Chapters 4 and 5, technological innovations, domestic or international competitive pressures arising from the normal workings of the market economy, or changes in the structures and workings of both businesses and governments in response to these pressures.

The concept of **economic dynamism**, described as "creative destruction" by economist Joseph Schumpeter (1950: 82-84), is inherent to the functioning of a competitive capitalist market economy. Competition breeds innovation both in meeting existing consumer demand and in creating new products, processes, and services that alter the choices and opportunities available to consumers. This process frequently results in the displacement of existing forms of economic activity, particularly in those businesses and other organizations that are less able to adapt their operations.

In recent years, these changes can be seen in Canadian financial and capital markets, including the emergence of the mutual fund industry and the widespread use of income trusts as vehicles for savings and investment, respectively; the emergence of several dynamic sectors of high technology industries; and the consolidation and dynamic restructuring of Canada's energy production and distribution sectors, among numerous others. For example, only 20 of Canada's 40 largest corporations in 1964, including five of Canada's 12 largest publicly traded energy sector firms, were still in business or functioning as independent entities in 2004 (*National Post Business* 2004: 36; for further discussion of organizational and regulatory dynamism in Canada's energy sector, see Hale 2005a), as noted in Table 6.1. During the past 25 years, many of Canada's major corporate empires such as Argus Corporation, Consolidated Bathurst, Dome Petroleum, Eatons, Macmillan Bloedel, Molson, Seagram, Southam, and Woodwards have gone out of business or have been absorbed by other firms, while others have evolved into very different kinds of businesses. These trends, which reflect the growing openness and dynamism of both domestic and international markets for corporate control, have helped to transform the ownership structures of Canada's largest corporations.

Table 6.1: Canada's 40 Largest Corporations, Then and Now (1964-2004)

	Total	Canadian-Controlled	Foreign-Controlled	Still Top 40	Still Top 41-100
Substantially same business structure and ownership profile.	13	8	5	7	4
Substantially different business structure and profile, including merger with major competitor.	7	7	–	2	3
Company acquired by another business or no longer in operation.	20	14	6	–	1*

* Successor firm, not otherwise included in first two categories.
Source: *National Post Business* 2004: 36; author's calculations.

Since government policies often represent the institutionalization of responses to the problems of the past, open economic systems tend to prompt the organization of coalitions of interests to promote economic and policy change that will accommodate different approaches to defining the public interest.

Ownership and Control of Economic Activity

Canada's economic structure in the early twenty-first century is a system of advanced capitalism increasingly integrated with the North American and global economies. It is characterized by high degrees of private ownership of business organizations and a growing diffusion of share ownership through capital markets, although selected industries have significant levels of government ownership.

Although ownership and control are typically associated in smaller enterprises, modern corporate structures typically separate ownership—the right of shareholders to share in a corporation's profits or increased market value—from strategic or operational control. Strategic control—the ability to direct a firm's priorities and business strategies—may be exercised by senior management or a board of directors, particularly in widely held companies with no single controlling shareholder. Operational control is usually in the hands of professional managers with relatively small ownership stakes.

The predominance of capitalist forms and structures is largely taken for granted in the realm of Canadian public policy, although debates continue on ways to improve balancing the rights and interests of various stakeholders and the general public in both law and policy.

The maturing of Canadian capital markets in recent years and the increasingly active role played by **institutional investors**—investment banks, mutual funds, and pension funds with significant equity holdings in many firms—have greatly increased the importance and visibility of **corporate governance** issues, particularly after a series of highly publicized corporate scandals in the US, Europe, and

Canada resulted in major losses to shareholders. As institutional shareholders manage the savings of millions of ordinary Canadians (and citizens of other countries), directly affecting their economic well-being and security in retirement, these issues have assumed much greater political and economic importance than in the past.

The principal form of business organization is the corporation: a distinct legal entity that allows individuals to engage in economic activity while separating personal from business liabilities and that enables groups of unrelated individuals or businesses to pool economic resources in return for a claim on current and future profits. Large private sector corporations account for the largest share of business assets, profits, and revenues. However, smaller firms account for the majority of private sector employment. **Government business enterprises** (GBEs), non-profit institutions, and cooperatives also play significant roles in particular economic sectors.

The economic behaviour of corporations, both large and small, reflects the strategies of firm owners and managers for expanding or maintaining profitability, the relationships of businesses to one another within a particular industry or economic network, and the economic and legal environments shaped by historical and contemporary economic factors. Economic historians suggest that cultural factors—notably attitudes towards risk-taking and entrepreneurship, levels of social trust, and popular and governmental respect for contracts and property ownership—also play a significant role (Gerlach 1992; Landes 1996; Fukuyama 1995; DeSoto 2000).

Federal and provincial governments help shape the environment for business organization and property ownership. The *Constitution Act, 1867* (formerly the *British North America Act*) divides responsibility for economic regulation between the two senior orders of government. In some cases, one level possesses the authority to codify the legal framework for the operations of particular business sectors. In others, there is significant overlap, as many businesses have the option of incorporating federally or provincially depending on the scope of their operations. This has often provoked conflicts between federal and provincial governments as organized interests try to persuade one level of government to intervene on their behalf to limit or counter the power of the other.

Corporation law is part of a broader system of property rights that provides legal security for the ownership of property and the resolution of disputes related to property ownership and the enforcement of contracts. These assumptions are deeply rooted in Canada's system of common law, the independence of its courts, and the practices of a number of specialized quasi-judicial tribunals that have emerged to apply and enforce the law at arm's length from federal and provincial governments. Box 6.1 notes the major federal laws that provide a legal framework for the operations of businesses and other economic interests.

Box 6.1: Legislation Governing Economic Organization and Business Ownership at the Federal Level

- *Canada Corporations Act*: governs the structure and responsibilities of federally registered non-profit organizations.

- *Canada Business Corporations Act*: governs the structure and responsibilities of federally registered business (for profit) corporations.

- *Canada Cooperative Associations Act* and

- *Canada Cooperatives Act*: provide legal frameworks for cooperatives and associated groups of cooperatives.

- *Bankruptcy and Insolvency Act,*

- *Companies' Creditors Arrangement Act*, and

- *Winding-up and Restructuring Act*: framework laws governing bankruptcy and insolvency, including procedures for dividing the assets of bankrupt individuals and firms.

- *Boards of Trade Act*

- *Pension Fund Societies Act*

- *Trade Unions Act:* governs the structure and responsibilities of federally regulated unions.

Note: Other federal laws, e.g., the *Bank Act*, may provide a legal framework for businesses in specific industries.
Source: Corporate Law Policy Directorate, Corporate Governance Branch, Industry Canada.

The growing integration of North American capital markets raises significant questions about policy leadership in this area. The regulation of investment dealers and stock markets is primarily a provincial responsibility. A series of corporate accounting scandals in the US has prompted Congress and US regulators to impose a series of new regulatory standards for corporate governance and market disclosure that affect Canadian corporations which do business in both countries. Many major corporations and some provincial regulators have lobbied for a single regulatory framework in Canada, either through the transfer of regulatory jurisdiction to the federal government or enhanced interprovincial coordination. Although these issues have not yet been resolved, they reveal the growing complexities of maintaining both national and regional policy autonomy and discretion at a time of increased North American economic integration.

Patterns of Ownership and the Market for Corporate Control

The effects of business ownership on economic activity are evident in a number of ways. The control over individual corporations or business empires by a small cohesive group of shareholders may concentrate wealth and economic power in relatively few hands in the economy as a whole. Alternately, business and property ownership may be widely diffused, with millions of ordinary citizens benefiting to some degree by sharing in business ownership and the distribution of profits as well as having well-paid employment. It may also be apparent in the level of competition in particular industries, something that will be addressed in the next section of this chapter.

Corporations may be privately owned by a single individual or family, **closely held** by a small group of dominant shareholders, or **widely held** by a large group of shareholders with no single owner holding a majority or controlling block of the company's voting shares. Such corporations are usually professionally managed by executives who may or may not own any significant number of the company's shares. Large, professionally managed corporations, whether closely or widely held, are the dominant form of business structure in Canada. Companies that are closely held—and industries that are dominated by such firms—may be said to have a limited market for corporate control as are industries, such as banking, in which individual shareholdings are subject to legislated limits. As a result, corporate management tends to have much greater autonomy in running and setting the strategic direction of such firms.

The extent and contestability of the market for corporate control is a major factor that distinguishes Anglo-American models of capitalism from their European and Japanese counterparts. The relative openness of a marketplace to external challenges to management control of particular firms—the hostile takeover—or major shareholders' ability and willingness to hold senior executives accountable for their performance depend on several factors including the prevailing cultural norms of corporate and financial elites, the degree to which governments or financial markets allow corporate executives to insulate themselves from external challenges, and the presence of government-imposed restrictions on corporate mergers or takeovers by foreign (and sometimes domestic) investors, which may have the same practical effect. Greater managerial autonomy may facilitate the pursuit of long-term corporate strategies that strengthen firms' profitability and competitiveness, contributing to a country's overall prosperity and increased living standards for its citizens. However, it can also induce complacency and declining adaptability to changing markets, particularly in historically successful firms enjoying substantial market share and some degree of state-conferred protection against domestic innovation or international competition.

Historically, economic activity in Canada has been typified by a number of large, family-controlled corporations such as Eatons, Woodwards, Sobeys, Steinbergs, and Billes in retailing; Molsons and Bronfmans in brewing and distilling; Bombardier in transportation equipment; and Westons, Desmarais, and Irvings in multi-sector conglomerates. However, the entrepreneurial character, discipline, and sometimes ruthlessness that built these empires have rarely persisted beyond one or two generations, leading to the break-up of corporate empires or the gradual shift of control to professional managers and investors. In recent years, the Canadian market for corporate control has become significantly more open and dynamic, reflecting the growth and innovations of Canadian capital markets; the increased openness of

Canadian, North American, and global markets to international investment; and the willingness of major corporations to divest themselves of significant business assets to pursue more focused business strategies.

Widely held companies, in which no one shareholder or cohesive group of shareholders holds more than 10 per cent of a company's voting shares, accounted for more than 30 per cent of Canada's largest 100 corporations in 2004, a significant increase from earlier years; 34 per cent were privately owned or closely held by Canadians, and another 23 per cent were subsidiaries of foreign firms or closely held in partnership between Canadian and foreign investors (*National Post Business* 2005). Table 6.2 notes the evolution of the ownership structures of Canada's 100 largest companies between 1998 and 2004.

Table 6.2: Ownership Structures of Canada's 100 Largest Corporations (by Revenue)

	1998	2004
Widely held, Canadian	18%	31%
Privately or closely held, Canadian		
• dominant partner with 50% + of voting shares	24%	19%
• with significant shareholder 10-49% of voting shares	18%	15%
Subsidiary of foreign-owned corporation	25%	20%
Narrowly held, major foreign partner (10% + of shares)	7%	3%
Government business enterprise	9%	10%
Cooperatives	4%	2%

Source: *Financial Post* 500 (July 1999, June 2005).

Corporate Concentration: Sources and Limits

Canada's economic structure and the market for corporate control have often been affected by the extent of and government attitudes towards **corporate concentration**: the degree to which economic activity in many sectors is controlled by a relatively small number of corporations. Major industries in which a majority of sales or corporate assets are dominated by five or fewer domestic producers include airlines, auto manufacturing, banking, breweries, daily newspapers, grocery retailing, railways, steel manufacturing, and telephone services.

Canada has a relatively high degree of intercorporate ownership, in which ultimate control, as opposed to nominal ownership, is determined through the use of holding companies and the effects of options, insider holdings, convertible shares, and interlocking directorships (Statistics Canada 2002c). The form of corporate activity in particular industries is determined by several factors, including the scale of economic activity and capital investments required to compete effectively in regional, domestic and international markets; access to investment capital; and relative openness to international investment and competition. Regulatory structures may also create barriers to entry or create cost structures that discourage new market entry. Factors contributing to increased market openness and competition include technological diffusion and innovation that create opportunities for new entrants and entrepreneurial ventures.

Past government policies have both accommodated and contributed to a high degree of corporate concentration in Canada. Periods of industrial innovation and entrepreneurship during which large numbers of new businesses emerged have often been followed by waves of mergers and consolidation, as the strongest players attempt to take over less efficient competitors, rationalize production, achieve economies of scale, and, sometimes, eliminate or structure the terms of competition. The industrial boom of the Laurier era was characterized by one such merger wave. Others occurred after World War II and during the 1970s. A number of economic observers suggest that the economic restructuring resulting from North American free trade and large-scale technical change contributed to an even larger wave of mergers during the 1990s (Marchildon 1996; Canada, Royal Commission on the Economic Union 1985: Vol. 2, 216-17; Bliss 1987).

The maturing of Canadian capital markets in recent years has contributed to a far more dynamic environment for the emergence, ownership, and restructuring of major corporations, thus offsetting the trend towards corporate concentration. The emergence of large pools of capital—particularly pension funds and mutual funds—managed by independent investment professionals has significantly increased the number of independent actors in Canada's capital markets, along with those of most other industrial countries. This has resulted in greater pressure for the accountability of corporate executives to shareholders who now include, directly or indirectly, a significant proportion of the Canadian public.[2] The willingness of these institutional investors to play a more active role in corporate governance is challenging the traditional autonomy of corporate executives from shareowners. It has also contributed significantly to the financing of record numbers of corporate mergers, acquisitions, and related reorganizations during the 1990s. The US *Sarbanes-Oxley Act* and other measures to promote improved corporate governance have resulted in some regulatory changes in Canada, as well as increasing the responsibility of boards of directors to oversee the activities of corporate management.

Government policies have been ambivalent in dealing with the growth of corporate concentration. The *Combines Investigation Act* of 1910 was intended to prevent the emergence of monopolies and other forms of anti-competitive behaviour that prevented the efficient functioning of the marketplace. However, despite periodic amendments, the federal government never succeeded in obtaining a criminal con-

---

2 Almost half (49 per cent) of adult Canadians owned shares or mutual fund units in 2000, compared with 37 per cent in 1996. This figure does not include indirect ownership through pension funds (Blackwell 2000). Assets of trusteed pension funds totaled $712.8 billion in March 2005 (Statistics Canada 2005f: 22 September); those of mutual funds totaled $570.0 billion in December 2005 <http://www.ific.ca>.

viction under the anti-monopoly provisions of the act.[3] Its replacement, the *Competition Act* of 1986, sought to balance the protection of domestic competition with the encouragement of economic efficiency that may result from mergers—again with mixed results. The 1977 report of the Royal Commission on Corporate Concentration, chaired by a former federal deputy minister of finance, voiced the conventional wisdom of contemporary governments that while corporate concentration has the potential for abuse, it also contributes to greater economies of scale, competitiveness, and stability for Canadian firms (Canada, Royal Commission on Corporate Concentration 1977: 407; Canada, Royal Commission on the Economic Union 1985: Vol. 2, 217-18). In practice, governments have often substituted increased regulation of corporate activity for the promotion of competition in order to obtain a politically acceptable sharing of these benefits between businesses, their shareholders, other stakeholders (including unions), and a broader public.

Canadian economic nationalism and legal restrictions on foreign ownership have significantly contributed to corporate concentration by encouraging the emergence of national (or provincial) champions in selected industries—particularly in the transportation, financial services, and communications media industries—and by limiting the number of potential buyers for both publicly traded and closely held firms. A 2002 study indicated that seven of the ten largest companies on the Toronto Stock Exchange (TSX), together with 45 companies representing 39.6 per cent of the TSX index's market capitalization, are still in sectors protected from foreign takeovers or competition (Mandell-Campbell 2002: FP1; see Table 6.3).

Table 6.3: "Seven of the Top 10 S&P/TSX composite index members have foreign ownership restrictions."

1. **Royal Bank of Canada**	**5.28%**	2. **Bank of Nova Scotia**	**3.85%**
3. **Toronto-Dominion Bank**	**3.53%**	4. EnCana Corp.	3.20%
5. **Manulife Financial**	**3.09%**	6. **BCE Inc.**	**3.06%**
7. Alcan Inc.	2.80%	8. **CIBC**	**2.63%**
9. **Bank of Montreal**	**2.56%**	10. Barrick Gold Corp.	2.54%

Ranked by Market Capitalization.
Bold type: industry with foreign ownership restrictions
Source: Mandell-Campbell 2002.

Such a situation was made possible by the emergence of new entrepreneurs and forms of business organization, the effects of technological change and international competition in altering the nature of many industries, regulatory amendments to foster increased competition, the expansion of Canadian capital markets to provide alternative sources of funding for corporate takeovers and acquisitions, and the fail-

---

3 Ross notes that the Crown won 124 of 176 cases launched under combines legislation between 1889 and 1976 but that successful prosecutions occurred mainly in the areas of restraint of trade and illegal retail price maintenance practices (Ross 1998: 1-2, 3-8).

ure of many family business empires to manage succession issues effectively (Newman 1998; Kwan 2000).

Policy debates over corporate governance, concentration, and competition vary widely, depending on the number of interests engaged in particular sectors, their relative willingness to contest market entry by political means rather than by adjusting their business strategies to changing competitive conditions, the prevailing outlooks of government policy-makers, and the degree to which issues are debated in largely political rather than economic or technical terms.

Foreign Ownership

About 22 per cent of all business assets and 25 per cent of the assets of Canadian non-financial industries are owned by subsidiaries of foreign-controlled corporations with greater or lesser degrees of management autonomy from their parent corporations. Foreign ownership is highest—over 40 percent—in sectors such as oil and gas extraction, coal mining, manufacturing, and insurance carriers (Wesson 1998: 73-81; Statistics Canada 2002b: 19 June).[4]

In recent years, governments have shifted the focus of their policies from the promotion and protection of a distinctly Canadian business class to encouraging greater efficiency and competitiveness in international markets. The risk of takeovers encourages managers to increase shareholder value in a competitive marketplace or face the possibility of losing operational (or ownership) control of their companies. However, it has also created the prospect of the further migration of head offices and, with them, senior decision-making positions in major businesses from Canada, causing significant concerns for many business executives and policymakers. These issues will be addressed further in Chapter 8.

Small Businesses

The political and economic role of small business has already been discussed in Chapter 3. Companies with fewer than 100 employees accounted for at least 49 per cent of private sector employment in 2004. More than 95 per cent of these were Canadian-owned. The economic activity of small firms is often interrelated with those of larger ones as suppliers, customers, or as parts of marketing and distribution systems associated formally or informally with large corporations. While medium-sized firms with 100 to 499 employees employed about 16 per cent of the Canadian labour force in 2001, many of these firms are part of larger corporate structures (Industry Canada 2005, 11).

Relatively few medium-sized Canadian companies succeed in maintaining themselves as independent firms beyond a single generation. Some observers have described Canada's private business sector as a two-tier economy, with a relatively small number of very large corporations and a very large number of small firms. As

---

4 For a more skeptical view of the relation between exchange rates and foreign takeovers, see Schembri 2002.

growth-oriented medium-sized firms are the most likely source of new big businesses to replace the ones absorbed through corporate mergers and acquisitions, both federal and provincial governments have sought to create incentives for their growth. Such measures include reducing regulatory barriers for medium-sized firms to go public by offering their shares for sale on Canadian stock markets, lowering the gap in marginal income tax rates between small Canadian-controlled corporations and larger firms, and permitting investors in small firms to roll over capital gains from sales of one small business investment into others without taxation. Provincial efforts to build up local business classes, which include lower tax rates for small businesses in nine provinces and greater regulatory flexibility in many areas, are intended to promote increased local ownership and leadership in regional economies.

Government Business Enterprises

The structure of Canada's economy has also been heavily influenced by a large number of government-owned corporations, often known as Crown corporations. Some of these compete in the provision of goods and services with privately owned corporations in the marketplace. Others, particularly the government-run public utilities, liquor, and gambling operations which generate the largest share of government business profits,[5] are monopolies or enjoy preferred market position conferred by regulation. Many—including government-owned financial institutions, recreational facilities, or managers of public infrastructure—serve specific public policy functions defined by law or government policy in support of various kinds of private economic activity. While Canadian governments have retreated from direct participation in a number of industries since the 1980s, twelve Crown corporations still numbered among Canada's 100 largest companies by revenue in 2003 (see Table 9.2). The trends towards commercialization—the consistent application of market disciplines and management methods to GBEs, including the need to compete with private profit-making businesses—and privatization—the transfer of ownership from government to private investors—have significantly changed the operating environment for many Crown corporations. These issues will be discussed in greater detail in Chapter 9.

Non-Profit Corporations

Non-profit corporations are another major form of economic activity in Canada. Non-profits are formed to carry out a wide range of public purposes either as extensions of governments or as voluntary private activities. A 1999 federal report estimated that there are 175,000 non-profit organizations that employ over 1.3 million Canadians (Canada, Voluntary Sector Task Force 1999: 16). Government-funded organizations in the broader public sector and non-profit organizations account for

---

5 Lottery, liquor, and gambling enterprises generated $8.1 billion of the $10.1 billion in after-tax profits earned by provincial government enterprises in 1999 (Statistics Canada 2002c: 21 January).

more than 17 per cent of employment in Canada, mainly in the health, educational, social service, and related fields.

Many non-profits enjoy the benefits of charitable status, including the capacity to give receipts eligible for tax credits in return for contributions. Many compete, to some extent, with private businesses in specific sectors of the economy, particularly those providing a range of personal services from child care and nursing homes to training institutions and retail businesses used as means of financing the public service activities of related non-profit organizations.

A number of non-profit institutions, particularly hospitals and universities, have developed ongoing working relationships with private sector corporations. Some of these relationships, which reflect efforts to diversify sources of capital funding through charitable fund-raising initiatives, are consistent with the activities of other non-profit organizations. Others, which involve joint ventures, partnerships, and other cooperative activities relating to research and the commercialization of intellectual property, have blurred these distinctions, creating challenges for both businesses and organizations within the broader public sector.

Cooperatives

A smaller but regionally significant area of the Canadian economy is made up of cooperatives. Cooperatives may be organized by producers, consumers, or workers for mutual assistance and economic benefit. Members share in surpluses from operations as well as sharing to some degree in their governance, especially in smaller ones. However, unlike shares in private or publicly traded corporations, shareholders in cooperatives can only be reimbursed by the organization for the value of their shares.

Major elements of this sector are financial cooperatives and credit unions, which are significant participants in the financial services industries of several provinces, especially Quebec, Saskatchewan, and BC; there are also cooperatives in the agricultural sector and other primary producers. In some provinces, cooperative federations have developed competitive food and general retailing operations. In 1999, the assets of non-financial cooperatives totaled about 2 per cent of GDP (Canada, Agriculture Canada 2001).

Developments in the corporate world have forced many cooperative organizations to rethink their approach to the production and delivery of goods and services. While this trend has caused some cooperatives—particularly in the grain marketing sector—to abandon cooperative ownership structures in favour of publicly traded share ownership (Howes 2001: C3), others have sought to expand and merge with other cooperatives to achieve greater economies of scale in the marketplace.

Degrees and Types of Competition

A second major aspect of the economic structure is the degree of competition that occurs or is allowed in particular industry sectors. Neo-classical economic theory suggests that optimal economic outcomes result from efficient markets characterized by fair and informed transactions between willing buyers and sellers. The presence of competition expands consumer choice and disciplines sellers, forcing them to offer goods and services at prices and levels of quality acceptable to consumers and limiting their ability to engage in unfair business practices without the risk of losing customers and market share to other firms. However, while competition may be an "indispensable spur to economic efficiency and growth" (*The Economist*: 70), there is far less agreement over the types and extent of public policies necessary to achieve these objectives.

The competitive marketplace often fails to live up to the expectations of economic theory. Buyers and sellers may not enjoy equal advantages in the marketplace. Some may be able to exercise **market power** to enforce their preferences at the expense of producers or customers. Others may lack sufficient information to make informed judgements about the appropriate price or quality of a product or service due to **information asymmetries** between buyers and sellers. Some may be able to translate political power into economic power through **rent-seeking** activities that use the political system to redistribute income and economic opportunities through preferential or discriminatory government action. Individuals and businesses competing in the marketplace may engage in irrational or self-destructive behaviour in ways that affect not only their own well-being but that create economic chain reactions that disrupt entire industries or economies. These outcomes may often result from the bankruptcy of a single firm, the disruption of an industry central to a community or region's economic vitality, or from prolonged government subsidies of industries that prevent them from taking the steps necessary to becoming economically self-sustaining. However, despite their failings, competitive market systems based on private economic ownership and initiative have proven to be the most effective mechanisms ever devised for providing human needs and wants and increasing overall economic prosperity.[6]

Government policies may reflect the competitive nature of an industry by adapting to changing market circumstances. Alternately, governments may attempt to shape the structure of an industry, either by intervening in its formative stages or by changing the rules that govern its activities to achieve specific economic, social, or political goals.

Competitive structures exist along a continuum of potential options, as noted in Box 6.2. However, for the purposes of relative simplicity, these will be summarized in four categories: perfect competition, monopoly, monopolistic competition, and oligopoly.

Perfect Competition

Perfect competition can be said to exist in theory when a market is characterized by large numbers of willing buyers and sellers of similar products or services,

---

6 This analysis recognizes that there are multiple models of capitalism, informed by different economic, political, social, and cultural systems around the world, and that the interaction of these systems in international markets has prompted many of their participants to learn from one another and adopt aspects of one another's systems over time.

relatively easy entry and exit for market participants, and an absence of sufficient market power enabling either individual producers or consumers to consistently dictate prices or the terms of competition. In such markets, consumers typically have access to sufficient information to permit informed decisions on the value of products and services. Moreover, individual employers and employees are likely to have little influence on relative wage and salary levels within the industry (Sawyer 1979: 18; Brander 1995: 133; Reid and Meltz 2001: 149-51).

Personal and business service industries are often examples of market structures tending towards perfect competition, particularly in large urban areas or industries for which geographic location is a relatively unimportant factor. These industries require entrepreneurs to provide relatively little capital in order to go into business. There is also relatively easy substitution of one product or service for another, as in the case of restaurant meals or other tourism and hospitality industries. Large organizations may exist but do not exercise sufficient market power to preclude smaller, more specialized competitors from entering the market or engaging profitably in business. Other examples of industries tending towards perfect competition include personal grooming services, business service centres, and retail sectors that market specialty products rather than depend on price sensitivity and volume buying.

Box 6.2: The Competition Continuum

Monopoly (Single seller)	Dominant	Oligopoly	Monopolistic	Perfect
←				→
Monopsony (Single buyer)	Firm		Competition	Competition

Monopoly and Monopsony

The conceptual opposite of perfect competition is a **monopoly**: an industry in which there is only one seller of a particular product or service in a particular market. Monopoly industries are characterized by major differences in economic power between the seller and buyers, who rarely have the option of substituting other products or services for those provided by the monopoly. Monopolies traditionally have little incentive to provide consumers with minimum prices or greater levels of innovation in the absence of competition. For this reason, they are usually regulated by government agencies.

Monopoly sectors typically have very high barriers to entry. Businesses seeking to enter these markets may not be readily able to mobilize the capital, expertise, and economies of scale necessary for profitable production, particularly as the monopolist may be able to lower prices long enough to drive potential competitors out of business in a practice known as predatory pricing. For example, few entrepreneurs—or even large corporations—possess the capital necessary to replicate the existing electricity distribution networks of public utilities or the telephone and cable distribution networks of established firms in those industries. Other sectors, such as Canada's sugar industry, have exploited protective government regulations to create an effective duopoly (two dominant producers), although other kinds of sweeteners do compete effectively for market share. As a result, monopoly sectors are usually characterized by high levels of government regulation.

Monopolies may also be created as a direct or indirect result of government intervention. Governments may choose give a legislated monopoly to a particular producer (including a government-run corporation) as a matter of public policy. In the past, governments have opted to establish public monopolies over certain industries such as public utilities, including telephone and electric power; for the protection of the public, as with liquor distribution and gambling; or for the promotion of a national identity, as with airlines and television in their early years.

Natural monopolies are businesses in which increasing returns to scale are significant enough that any feasible level of demand can be met at lower average cost by a single firm than by two or more firms (Brander 1995: 138). However, technological change and the implementation of different market structures in other countries have eroded the claims of a number of natural monopolies, including the telephone industry and public utilities.

Monopsony is a competitive structure that has a single buyer instead of a single seller. While there are relatively few examples of monopsony in the private sector (De Beers's historic control over international diamond markets is an imperfect example), governments frequently attempt to use their regulatory powers to impose order on otherwise volatile markets or to guarantee public access to certain services. Supply management through agricultural marketing boards, the control of the Canadian Wheat Board over grain exports, and the mandatory public administration of insured health services are three examples of such policies.

A numbers of industries are not monopolies but are characterized by a dominant firm that controls at least 50 per cent and often much more of the market for a particular good. Dominant firms may impose price levels, marketing practices, or technical standards that force smaller competitors, suppliers, or customers to conform to their preferences. As such, they have many of the characteristics of monopolies and are often subject to government regulation. Air Canada, Microsoft Corporation (through its dominance of markets for operating system software for personal computers), book retailer Chapters-Indigo, and Interac (the consortium linking bank-owned automated tellers) are four examples of dominant firms in their respective industries.

Monopolies are politically controversial as they often exploit consumers in the absence of clear and transparent regulation in the public interest. This is equally true of public monopolies, which may extend the power or revenues of governments in ways that enable them to ignore or marginalize the concerns of citizens and consumers. Monopolies, monopsonies, and dominant firms experience high degrees of unionization, both to protect workers from the exercise of market power by corporations and to extract a share of **monopoly rents** in the form of higher wages, staffing levels, and other benefits than would likely prevail in competitive market settings.

Regulation is not the only option available to governments in controlling or limiting abuses of monopoly power. Competition (or antitrust) legislation enables governments to restrict the emergence of monopolies through mergers or takeovers, or to break up monopolies into clusters of smaller independent businesses that may be lesser deterrents to new competitors. For example, the federal Competition Bureau has used its powers under the *Competition Act* to force major integrated oil firms to sell off many of their gas stations to smaller competitors as a condition of approving large-scale mergers and to limit the emergence of dominant firms in regional markets. Similar measures have been suggested as a way of accommodating possible mergers between major chartered banks.

Changes in regulatory structures, particularly those affecting business control, foreign ownership, and market access, may also facilitate increased market competition by reducing barriers to market entry and allowing innovative firms to exploit new technologies and market opportunities identified in other countries. Governments may choose to open their markets to foreign competitors on a reciprocal or unilateral basis, thus forcing domestic monopolies, dominant firms, and oligopolies to compete for market share with foreign producers. One major objective of Canada's negotiation of bilateral and multilateral free trade agreements during the 1980s and 1990s was to expose Canadian firms to increased competition in order to achieve increased consumer choice, lower prices, and greater economic efficiency—a strategy that has been largely successful in most sectors. While many domestic Canadian industries still have highly concentrated levels of corporate ownership, these policies have generated the benefits of increased competition in a number of industries.

Oligopoly

An **oligopoly** is an industry dominated by a few firms, each of which has a significant market share. Typically, three or four firms may supply 50 per cent or more of the relevant market. These firms are interdependent, responding to changes in competitors' products, prices, and marketing practices in order to maintain market share. They often attempt to acquire additional market share either by purchasing smaller competitors or by pursuing strategies of **horizontal** or **vertical integration** (see Box 6.3). Major oligopolistic industries in Canada include banking, railways, automobile manufacturing, brewing, integrated meat packing, gasoline refining and marketing, daily newspapers, and television broadcasting.

Oligopolies have high barriers to entry. These may include the need for large amounts of capital, extensive economies of scale or scope that make it difficult for new or small firms to compete effectively, or high regulatory or technological barriers to entry. Smaller firms may succeed in establishing a market niche in competition with the principal members of the industry—for example, independent gas stations or microbreweries—but major firms may use their market power to marginalize such businesses through price-cutting and other strategies, acquire them, or drive them out of the market if permitted to do so by government competition watchdogs.

Box 6.3: Horizontal and Vertical Integration

Horizontal integration: The acquisition or consolidation of firms with complementary lines of products and/or services within a single company or corporate group.

Vertical integration: The mobilization, through acquisition or expansion, of the different parts of a supply chain including different elements of production and distribution within a single corporation or corporate group.

Oligopolies may engage in tacit cooperation to limit the effects of competition in markets, although such behaviour may be subject to regulatory challenges. Oligopolies that engage in price-fixing to maximize revenues or that cooperate to divide markets among themselves, thus minimizing effective competition within an industry, are said to have formed a **cartel**. This practice is illegal in Canada, unless specifically sanctioned by governments, as in the cases of agricultural marketing boards (supply management).

Oligopolistic industries frequently have high degrees of unionization, often by a single industrial union which attempts to engage in pattern bargaining with the industry's major employers as a means of removing employee compensation from competition and sharing in the benefit of employers' market power through relatively high wages (Chaykowski 2001: 240-41; for a more detailed case study, see MacLachlin 2001: 214-44). For these reasons, major unions often oppose government policies that expose such industries to increased competition, whether domestic or international.

Canada's competition laws, while intended to protect both other businesses and consumers from abuses of market position by large corporations—particularly in industries characterized by high degrees of corporate concentration—were historically ineffective in limiting anti-competitive practices by Canadian businesses. Changes introduced in 1986 gave officials of the Competition Bureau expanded powers to regulate corporate mergers and takeovers and provided for the disallowance by the independent, quasi-judicial Competition Tribunal of mergers that would unduly restrict competition. However, the law also provided for mergers to be approved if, in the tribunal's judgement, the resulting benefits of increased economic efficiency outweigh the costs to consumers of reduced competition. This provision has limited the government's effectiveness in limiting the continued concentration of business ownership in many industries (Ross 1998).

In practice, opening oligopolistic industries to increased international competition has been the most effective strategy used by governments against them in recent years. For example, in the steel industry, foreign firms such as British-based transnational Mittal Steel and Brazil-based Gerdau Ameristeel have bought and integrated smaller Canadian firms within their global networks, while Canadian-based

Ipsco has expanded its production facilities across North America. Major Canadian pipeline firms such as Trans-Canada and Enbridge have also expanded their corporate networks across North America, while diversifying into power generation, while US-based Duke Energy has acquired major regional pipelines in Canada. Such corporate strategies have the advantage of expanding cross-border networks of shared interests that can create effective counterweights to protectionist interests at home and abroad, although possible limits have been suggested by the ability of US shippers and railroads to block the expansion of Canadian National's proposed merger with the giant Burlington Northern Santa Fe network in 2000 (Dib 2002; Clancy 2004; Hale 2005a).

The increased openness of oligopolistic mass production industries to international competition and the international distribution of protection as well as the reorganization of many mass-production industries into more specialized competitive forms of business organization are two major reasons for the relative decline of unionization and union density, at least in the private sector during the past 20 years. However, this trend has not progressed nearly as far in Canada as in the US, where private sector union density in 2004 was 8 per cent, compared to about 18 per cent in Canada (Commission for Labour Cooperation 2003; Reich 2005: B04; United States, Bureau of Labour Statistics 2005).

Monopolistic Competition

In practice, many business sectors thrive on competition. However, the key to generating higher than average rates of return often comes from the development of specialized market niches that enable businesses to secure monopoly rents—or higher than average rates of return—on certain goods or services for a period of time. The concept of **monopolistic competition** is based on product differentiation: the "idea that firms in an industry are producing products which are similar but not identical to each other" (Sawyer 1979: 29). This may be achieved as a result of innovation (combined with the ability to secure and enforce intellectual property rights), specialized expertise that can command higher prices in the marketplace, or locational advantages. Examples of monopolistic competition include patent-protected innovation in the development of new products (e.g., pharmaceuticals), technical processes or specialized software; specialized professional expertise; and geographical advantage (OECD 2003: 116). As an example of the latter, Canadian travelers beyond major cities will often see signs on certain establishments announcing the "last services (e.g., gas, groceries) for 100 kilometers" as an incentive to stop and top up before continuing their journey.

Such advantages are no guarantee of continuing profitability or competitive edge, which must often be maintained by consistent innovation and the development of new products and skills in response to changing markets. However, the capacity of consumers to obtain substitute products or services limits the capacity of individual suppliers to fix prices unilaterally without risking the loss of market share. Entry and exit costs in such industries are fairly low. Small and medium-sized firms can often compete efficiently due to high degrees of specialization (Brander 1995: 140).

However, the competitive environment for many Canadian industries has increasingly been shaped as much by North American and international economic forces as by domestic market conditions in recent years. This process can be seen from the evolution of Canada's industrial structure in the late twentieth century.

Sources and Scale of Economic Activity

Economists have traditionally segmented economic activity into three broad categories: primary industries, involving the production or extraction of raw materials and natural resources; secondary industries that transform these resources into "semi-finished" or finished products; and tertiary or service industries that provide a wide range of personal, business, and government services. However, changes in business organization and the diffusion of specialized computer (and other) technologies have increasingly blurred traditional distinctions between goods-producing and service industries in recent years, particularly in the burgeoning business services sector (Wallace 2002: 68). The promotion and commercialization of research and the introduction of new technologies and management methods have also blunted past distinctions between public and private sector activities, as well as those of research-based organizations in the health and education sectors.

Primary Industries

Canada has evolved from a largely agricultural and resource-based economy in the late nineteenth century to an industrial and service-based economy with improvements in productivity and transportation, the growth of major metropolitan areas (city-regions) and related industrial activity, and the emergence of a large enough economic surplus to finance the provision of a wide range of government and personal services.

The effects of these changes are most visible in the shifting distribution of employment between economic sectors as noted in Table 6.4. Employment levels in agriculture and other primary industries have declined in absolute terms since the 1970s. Although not growing as fast as overall levels of employment, manufacturing and construction employment have trended upwards in absolute terms, while fluctuating with levels of economic activity. Employment in most service sectors has grown steadily, even in the broader public sector, despite cutbacks resulting from budget reductions during the 1990s.

Primary industries, such as agriculture, forestry, fishing, mining, and energy industries, are primarily engaged in the production and extraction of raw materials and natural resources. In recent decades, most primary industries have shifted from being relatively labour intensive to capital intensive, using large amounts of investment in machinery and technology to increase the value produced by each worker.

The influence of primary industries is strongest in the resource-based communities of small-town and rural Canada, many of which depend on a single dominant employer or industry for their prosperity and economic opportunities. Some communities may be able to diversify their economies, particularly through investments in seasonal or year-round tourist and other service industries. However, many other resource-dependent communities, particularly those isolated from major population centres or transportation routes, face an uncertain future.

Table 6.4: Employment by Industry

	1970	1980	1989	2001
Total goods	37.4%	**32.8%**	**30.6%**	26.2%
Agriculture	6.5%	4.5%	3.6%	2.2%
Other primary	2.7%	**2.8%**	2.5%	2.0%
Manufacturing	22.3%	**19.7%**	**17.0%**	**15.4%**
Construction	5.9%	**5.8%**	**6.5%**	**5.7%**
Total services	62.6%	67.2%	73.0%	76.0%
Transportation	8.8%	**8.5%**	5.3%	**5.2%**
Trade	16.8%	**17.2%**	16.4%	**16.2%**
FIRE*	4.8%	**5.7%**	**6.5%**	**5.9%**
Business services		6.9%	**10.5%**	
Personal and other services		15.1%	**16.0%**	
Health, education and public services		19.4%	**22.2%**	

* FIRE – Finance, Insurance, and Real Estate
Bold Type: increase in overall employment from previous decade.
Sources: Statistics Canada 2002b: 31; Canada, Department of Finance 1992: 59.

Most commodities produced by such industries are traded on international markets. This is a major example of "economic openness" but one that increases pressures on Canadian producers to increase their efficiency and productivity—the amount and value of production relative to related costs of labour and capital—in order to remain competitive with producers in the developing world.

Secondary Industries

Secondary industries, including manufacturing and processing, construction, and public utilities, transform raw materials into semi-processed and finished goods for individual, business, and other consumers. The development of manufacturing industries was a key priority of governments during Canada's earlier stages of development in order to escape the staples trap: the excessive dependence on exports of raw or semi-processed resources that left many regions dependent on global prices and demand for Canadian resources. The emergence of Alberta's petrochemical industry, the cultivation of large-scale meat processing industries in western Canada, the development of large-scale construction and engineering sectors associated with provincially owned utilities, and, more recently, the linkage between the location of nickel processing facilities in Newfoundland and provincial licensing for the development of the huge Voisey's Bay nickel mine in northern Labrador all speak to the relationships between resource industries, government policies, and economic diversification (Freeman 1996: 119-20; McLachlin 2001: 75-79; Macdonald 2002).

Manufacturing industries provided 17.3 per cent of Canada's GDP in 2004, compared with 12.1 percent in the US (Statistics Canada 2005g); United States, Bureau of Economic Analysis 2005). Canadian manufacturing industries have been centred historically in Ontario, which accounted for more than 52.3 per cent of manufacturing output in 2004, and to a lesser extent in Quebec (Statistics Canada 2006a). Manufacturing's relative share of economic activity and employment has declined in Canada, as it has in the US and other Western industrial economies. Increased competition, industrial restructuring, and the spread of new technologies have contributed to a relative decline in manufacturing employment from 24 per cent of overall employment in 1961 to 13.7 per cent in 2005, although with far higher levels of production for each worker. However, some industries that have been at the forefront of new technological developments, such as motor vehicles and parts, telecommunications equipment, and machinery industries, have grown significantly since the 1960s.

The spread of regional and global trade networks and globally integrated production processes have created similar pressures for manufacturing industries as for Canada's resource industries. The gradual liberalization of Canadian tariff policies since the 1960s has led to the rationalization of production facilities and the development of complex supplier networks across national borders. It has also seen the emergence of Canadian as well as foreign multinationals with networks of foreign affiliates, which are conduits for a majority of Canadian imports and exports (Cardillo 2002). Competitive pressures have forced export-oriented companies, both domestic and foreign-controlled, to become significantly more efficient. As a result, their productivity tends to be higher than comparable firms producing primarily for the domestic Canadian market (Baldwin and Dhaliwal 2001).[7]

The integration of manufacturing and related service operations, especially systems management and transportation services, across wide geographic areas has put an increased emphasis on the study and development of global supply chains as a major element in both corporate strategies and Canadian trade and border management policies. The adaptability of corporate supply chains is also a major factor in Canadian manufacturers' ability to adjust to major currency fluctuations—particularly the rapid appreciation of the Canadian dollar against its US counterpart in 2002-05—without having to engage in large-scale layoffs or plant closings.

---

7 Productivity growth tends to be reflected in overall average wage levels in manufacturing industries, rather than in those of particular industries characterized by higher productivity. Industry-specific effects of higher productivity tend to benefit consumers directly through lower relative prices (Baldwin, Durand, and Hosein 2001: 30-32).

Tertiary or Service Industries

The tertiary or service sector has been the fastest growing source of economic activity and employment in Canada in recent years, accounting for 76 per cent of employment and 68.7 per cent of GDP in 2001. Canada's economic growth has always depended on the capacity of its service industries, ranging from transportation (including trucking, rail, and air transport), communications (telecommunications, communications media, and related industries), and financial services (banking, insurance, investment, and related services) to link producers with markets and to provide the capital and credit facilities necessary for business investment and expansion.

However, the services sector also includes a wide range of other industries such as government, educational, health and social services; business and commercial services; the tourism and hospitality sector; and a wide range of personal services. In addition to traditional service sector employment, which is often characterized by low skill levels and wages, service industries are at the heart of the knowledge-based economy responsible for the development of new technologies and processes for the transformation of ideas into increased economic activity and a higher quality of life.

Brander (1995) suggests a number of reasons for the steady growth of service sector economies during the late twentieth century: higher per capita incomes, which give citizens the ability to substitute the purchase of services for informal economic activity; increased leisure time and the demand for related services; the spread of labour-intensive services associated with increased personal consumption; and the growth of distribution and retailing networks to meet this demand. Service sector growth also results from increased public demands for sanitation, public health, and other public services and the growing range of regulatory functions carried out by governments either in response to public demand or policy-makers' perceptions of public benefit.

The sectoral distribution of economic activity has always varied widely between regions. Although there are still significant differences in the composition of regional economies—an issue whose political implications are addressed in Chapter 7—the spread of the service economy means that these differences are most significant in the goods-producing economy of provinces and regions.

Innovation and the Knowledge-Based Economy

As we have seen, rapid technological changes during the past generation and the growing integration of Canada's economy with that of North America and the wider world have led many observers to discuss the emergence of the "new" or "knowledge-based" economy (KBE) as a key factor in economic development and higher living standards (Castells 1996; Lipsey 1996; Thurow 1999; Courchene 2001c). New technologies and production processes are transforming the nature of economic activity, prompting governments to shift much of their policy emphasis from promoting resource-based development (along with related manufacturing industries) to the development of human capital: skilled, adaptable, creative workers, managers, and entrepreneurs capable of functioning in an environment of continuous technological and economic change (Canada, Standing Committee on Finance 1999a: 135-37).

However, while the rapid growth of innovation-driven sectors, notably information technology and telecommunications, has been a central preoccupation of business journalists and economic policy-makers (for example, see Drucker 1994; Courchene 1997; Warner 2000; Canada, Standing Committee on Finance 1999: 80-107, 135-57), the application of these processes has affected the ways in which many other sectors of the economy function and relate to one another (Mendelsohn and Smith 1999; Garelli and Rauch 2001). At a structural level, governments have come to identify major investments in innovation, research, and related education with the capacity for long-term economic competitiveness and rising living standards (Lynch 2000; Canada, Industry Canada 2002; Canada 2002b). At the level of day-to-day economic activity, the effects of computerized inventory control systems in reducing the accumulation of inventories by Canadian businesses during the economic boom of the late 1990s is partially credited with Canada's prompt recovery from the economic downturn of 2001.

Table 6.5: Employment Growth by Highest Level of Education Attained, 1990-99

	Number	Percent
Post secondary diploma or degree	2,255,000	155.8%
High school diploma	139,000	9.6%
Less than high school	- 947,000	- 65.4%

Source: Lynch 2000.

The ongoing reality of structural economic change has a number of effects both on government economic policies and on business-government relations. Sectors in relative economic decline are more likely to lobby governments for subsidies and protectionist legislation, although with export industries now accounting for about 40 per cent of Canada's national income, governments are less likely to respond to these demands than they once were. While turnover in employment due to the creation and closure of businesses and plants has not increased significantly in recent years, virtually all new jobs created during the 1990s required some form of post-secondary education (see Table 6.5). Rather than shielding individuals and businesses from the effects of economic change, governments are more likely to use resources to help them adapt to changing economic circumstances, although the means of doing this can vary widely depending on the circumstances (Canada, Department of Finance 1994; Canada, Standing Committee on Finance 1999). Tax rules are less likely to discriminate in favour of particular sectors, such as manufacturing or resource industries, in favour of a more economically neutral approach that shies away from governments picking winners and losers (Technical Committee on Business Taxation 1997; Alberta, Alberta Business Tax Review 2000); Quebec and, to a lesser extent Ontario, are exceptions to this trend.

The Broader Public and Non-Profit Sectors

Structural economic changes, particularly those related to the growth of the KBE, are also affecting the operations of the broader public and non-profit sectors and their interaction with private sector firms. Governments are engaging in a wide range of **public-private partnerships**, drawing on the specialized expertise of private companies for the development and delivery of public services, a subject addressed further in Chapter 9.

Educational and health care institutions, which make up a large share of the broader public sector, are increasingly engaged in research partnerships with private companies, raising complex issues of intellectual property ownership and blurring traditional boundaries between the public and private sectors. Since the 1960s, most of these institutions have functioned as independent non-profit bodies largely dependent on government transfers and subsidies. The spread of the KBE and the inherent difficulties of bureaucratic organizations in fostering innovation and commercializing research have led to the promotion by governments of a culture of innovation through growing collaboration among governments, businesses, and research institutions.

This interaction of business, government, and universities has been described as the **triple helix**, suggesting a complex amalgam of interpenetration and interdependence that recognizes both the distinct interests and objectives of each group and a shared interest in the development of knowledge and its application to specific scientific, engineering, medical, and other challenges (Etzkowitz and Leydesdorff 1997; Etzkowitz 2002).

Governments play an active role in the financing, and sometimes promotion, of basic research that advances the frontiers of knowledge, both through universities and specialized research institutions. The commercialization of research requires a different set of skills, linking academics and businesses in a variety of processes that involve a balancing of economic and ethical factors that reflect the different roles and priorities of each group (Doern and Sharaput 2000; Doern and Reed 2000).

The capacity of both governments and corporations to purchase research as a commodity enables both groups to mobilize specialized resources to serve their political, policy, and commercial objectives. However, it also underlines the potential conflicts in missions, priorities, and values. Unless managed with a clear view to the different interests and values of all stakeholders, conflicts may erupt over the ownership and control of the economic activities that result from these partnerships. The definition of these relationships is increasingly important to the functioning of the market economy and its relations with governments and diverse research communities of scientists, academics, clinical specialists, and other elements of society.

Capital Markets: Sources and Processes
for Financing Economic Activity

One dimension of capitalism is the private ownership and organization of property and economic activity in a market system structured with greater or lesser degrees of government involvement. Another dimension, that of capital or financial markets, addresses the processes for financing economic activity and the creation of wealth.

Financial and capital markets are the processes for organizing, mobilizing, and converting the savings of individuals and organizations to meet the financial needs of other individuals, businesses, governments, and economic actors. These concepts are remote to many people, even though they have become deeply embedded in the assumptions of day-to-day life. People participate in financial markets every time they use a savings or chequing account; swipe a credit card; take out a mortgage, lease or bank loan; or save for future needs through an education savings plan, employer pension plan, or registered retirement savings plan. On a larger scale, markets for stocks, bonds, mutual fund units, and other financial instruments allow larger organizations, including governments, to finance large-scale operations by creating a resale market for their financial obligations. These processes of **financial intermediation** function within a broader system of private contracts and government regulations intended to manage financial risk and facilitate accountability among participants in the financial marketplace.

Governments both regulate and are active participants in capital markets. Public policies attempt to promote stability in the marketplace, shape the legal framework for the organization of the financial services sector, and support or promote various forms of economic activity, from private home ownership to massive business investments. Governments also depend on capital markets to finance their own operations and those of many government enterprises.

Access to capital is important to individuals, businesses, and communities seeking to grow faster than their own incomes or cash flow permit. It helps to create **liquidity**, the ability of businesses or investors to obtain sufficient cash or equivalents in a timely manner to meet their commitments and obtain greater flexibility in the use of their assets through access to credit (Canada, Office of the Superintendent of Financial Institutions 1995; Brander 1995: 434-35). Capital markets also allow for a diversification of risks in specific investments by enabling investors and intermediaries to bundle investments for purchase by other investors through such vehicles as mutual funds, income trusts, and other asset-backed securities. Efficient capital markets are vital for the expansion and growth of modern capitalist economies, enabling higher standards of living both in Canada and around the world.

However, the ability of markets to function largely depends on a legal system that can define and secure property rights, both within individual countries and across international borders, not only for the benefit of large-scale participants but also for individuals and small-scale enterprises as well. It is also influenced by tax laws that may promote or constrain higher levels of private savings, investments in risk capital, and entrepreneurship or encourage their reallocation from one type of economic activity to another.

Capital markets policies involve several different dimensions, including the availability and cost of capital to Canadian corporations, investment decisions involving both the market for corporate ownership and control and the location of capital investment by major corporations, and the regulatory frameworks governing the activity of different kinds of financial institutions. Canada's emergence as a net lender in international capital markets has changed many of the political and economic assumptions surrounding the issue of foreign investment. These will be addressed in greater detail in Chapter 8.

Box 6.4: Financial and Capital Markets: Linking Borrowers and Lenders

Lenders Sources of Savings	Financial Intermediaries	Borrowers Uses of Savings
Personal Savings • chequing/savings accounts • GICs (guaranteed investment certificates) • RRSPs/Employment pensions Contingent Savings • insurance policies (individual/group) • life/health/auto/house/dental, etc. Investment Vehicles • RRSPs/Employment pensions • Stock market investments • Bonds (government, other) • Mortgages and other asset-backed securities, etc. Corporate Profits • reinvested or distributed to owners Government "Savings" • budget surpluses used to repay debt or create public investment funds • public pension funds: invested to finance future benefits	Banks Trust companies Credit unions Investment dealers Insurance Companies (life/general) Mutual fund dealers Pension funds Income trusts Other specialized actors	Consumer credit • credit cards • asset financing (home/auto/other) • education loans Business credit • short-term • asset financing • long-term debt Equity • share ownership in companies Government credit • short/long term bonds • unconventional financing

Governments have promoted the Canadian ownership of financial institutions as a major element of national policy that has enabled them to mobilize capital, both directly and in partnership with private sector corporations, for national and regional economic development. At the same time, Canadian financial institutions, particularly banks and investment dealers, have been vital intermediaries between Canadian capitalists and sources of foreign capital (for example, see Skelton 1920; Marchildon 1996).

Framework legislation regulating the financial services sector gives governments a vital role in mediating differences between borrowers and lenders and in both defining and limiting jurisdictions for financial institutions. For many years, governments encouraged the diffusion of power within the financial services sector by creating separate regulatory regimes for banks, trust companies, insurance companies, and investment dealers—the so-called four pillars—with limits on intersectoral competition and cross-ownership.

Canadian regulation of the financial sector before 1985 was based on the idea of national government regulation of a largely closed or domestically oriented economy.[8] Federal policies promoted the national ownership and regulation of banks, although limited foreign investment was permitted in some financial industries. Government policies also encouraged the development of capital markets by providing tax incentives for Canadians to save for their retirement through pension funds and registered retirement savings. Canadian savings were primarily directed to investment in Canada through government regulations or financial institutions regulated by governments; for example, the former 10 per cent rule limiting foreign investment by pension funds or registered retirement savings plans. In recent years, these restrictions have been phased out in the interests of encouraging greater liquidity and competitiveness in capital markets and obtaining higher rates of return on Canadians' savings and investments.

However, structural changes that have affected the economy for goods and services have been followed by the increasing globalization of financial services and business consolidation within the financial services sector. Since the mid-1980s, Canada has followed other major industrial countries in dismantling most of the regulatory barriers between the four pillars of the financial services sector while encouraging a limited opening of the sector to foreign competition. As a result, Canada's banking sector has one of the highest levels of corporate concentration of any major industrial country. Canada's five largest banks controlled 81 per cent of domestic banking assets in 1996, compared to 40 per cent in Britain and 19 per cent in the US (Canada, Task Force on the Future of the Canadian Financial Services Sector 1998a: 114). While Canada's major chartered banks, which have gained control of most major national investment dealers since the 1980s, are relatively small players in the industry by international standards, this high degree of consolidation has made federal politicians reluctant to authorize further large-scale mergers in the industry.

At the same time, specialized financial services companies, both Canadian and foreign-controlled, have expanded their operations in pursuit of profitable market niches such as credit cards, mutual funds, and asset financing, thus reducing the dependence of large corporations on traditional forms of bank credit. However,

---

8 Canadian financial entrepreneurs have been active in tapping the capital markets of Britain and the US as well as financing Canadian corporate expansion into the markets of the Caribbean and Latin America since the nineteenth century (Bliss 1987; Marchildon 1996). However, the primary focus of Canadian financial regulation in the twentieth century has been the stability of the Canadian financial services sector.

smaller businesses remain heavily dependent on banks and other traditional lenders (Canada, Task Force on the Future of the Canadian Financial Services Sector 1998b: 36-37). The proposed mergers of four major chartered banks into two superbanks in 1998 provoked a strong political backlash from other business, consumer, and political interests, who feared the effects of reduced competition on access to financing and the provision of basic banking services in smaller communities (Whittington 1999). The federal government vetoed the merger proposals and, to date, has been reluctant to consider the merger of two large banks.

The internationalization of Canadian business has been paralleled by the rapid growth of financial investments by middle-class Canadians seeking profitable opportunities for their mutual fund and pension fund investments. Declining inflation and interest rates drove Canadians to shift billions of dollars in savings from passive investments into stock markets, contributing to the stock market boom of the 1990s and the rapid growth of mutual fund companies within the financial services sector. By 2000, 49 per cent of Canadian adults owned shares or mutual fund units (Blackwell 2000). As noted earlier, the institutional investors who manage most of these funds are playing an increasingly active role in the market for control of Canadian corporations.

Another example of innovations in Canadian capital markets is the rapid growth of **income trusts** as investment vehicles for financing the reorganization of mature businesses, taking advantage of anomalies in the tax system and low rates of return in other financial markets since 2000. By 2004, the formation of income trusts had replaced issues of new equity shares as the main vehicle for financing business expansions and reorganizations—usually through the conversion of companies from corporate status to income trusts or by spinning off existing assets into income trusts to generate capital for other business ventures—especially in the real estate, oil and gas, utilities, and mining sectors (Berman 2005: FP15; Hale 2005d).

Some critics have argued that income trusts are all too effective as vehicles for deferring income tax and that they encourage a misallocation of resources by shifting investment to less innovative and productive forms of economic activity (Edgar 2004; for a contrary view, see Jog and Wang 2004). However, proposed tax changes in the 2004 budget which would have limited access to income trusts by institutional investors ran into sharp criticisms from both the financial sector and other industry sectors in which their use had become increasingly widespread and were finally withdrawn (Torys LLP 2004). Following extensive controversy, Finance Minister Ralph Goodale announced in November 2005 that the federal government would reduce taxes on certain corporate dividends to reduce the tax advantages of holding income trusts[9] (Canada, Department of Finance 2005; Hale 2006b).

---

9 Ironically, Goodale's announcement resolved one political controversy while creating another. The sharp spike in market trading prompted by apparent leaks of his intended announcement resulted in an RCMP investigation that, when announced during the middle of the 2005-06 federal election campaign, resulted in a sharply negative public reaction that contributed to the Liberal defeat in January 2006.

The huge sums of money and related opportunities to acquire and exercise economic power have helped to make the regulatory environment for capital markets one of the most heavily politicized of any area of economic policy in the early twenty-first century. With private savings rates in decline, Canadians are dependent on high returns on their financial investments to cushion the impact of an aging population on the sustainability of public services in Canada. The continuing trend towards the consolidation of businesses in the financial service sector raises ongoing questions of how the regulatory environment should balance the industry's domestic and international competitiveness. A parallel question is how to balance national and regional policy priorities in the regulation of Canada's securities industry, an area of jealously guarded provincial jurisdiction.

Conclusion

Canada's economic structure has always helped to shape the environment for economic policies and business-government relations. Neither the public nor private sector is organized according to the tidy, symmetrical stacked boxes of organizational theory. The organization of modern corporations frequently cuts across industry sector boundaries. These corporations coexist with and often participate in other forms of economic cooperation and competition, including strategic alliances and business networks, which tend to evolve over time. This complexity creates challenges for policy-makers attempting to establish and enforce equitable market rules which are likely to affect different businesses and consumers in comparable ways and to adapt those rules to changes in the nature and composition of the marketplace, particularly during periods of rapid innovation.

The growth of government and its pursuit of multiple policy objectives contribute to a high degree of complexity in the proliferation of government organizations and legal structures with overlapping and sometimes conflicting mandates, even before the added complexities of international economic agreements and federalism are added to the mix. This complexity can be seen in the creation of multiple sectoral regulators dealing with issues of labour relations, occupational safety and health, municipal planning and land use, natural resource management, compliance with environmental regulations, at least four different segments of the financial services sector (including pensions), and other specialized forms of regulation—all of which function at varying arm's length degrees from the ministers and government departments to which they are ultimately (or nominally) accountable.

This complexity privileges organizations and groups with specialized expertise, both inside and outside government. It is amenable to incremental or step-by-step changes in specific rules to deal with specific problems of coordination or market or government failures. It can also create major challenges for regulatory coordination, as in the overlapping and sometimes conflicting mandates of environmental regulators and those responsible for land-use or natural resource management.

Both market failures and government failures may create rigidities in the workings of particular economic sectors or regulatory systems. The embedded character of many of these rules in political and economic life makes large-scale change difficult unless governments can reach political consensus with key stakeholders or unless it can mobilize and engage public opinion sufficiently to overcome the opposition of vested interests to large-scale change. For this reason, the major systems of rules governing an economic structure have been likened to elements of an economic constitution, which may evolve over time, but which require either a systemic crisis or the support of political super-majorities to bring about comprehensive change.[10] The effects of an open economic system tend to expose these rigidities, both by exposing major economic groups to competitive disadvantages and demonstrating the availability of policy alternatives that may provide more effective ways of pursuing desired policy objectives.

These factors have contributed to the decisions of most governments to adapt to structural economic changes originating beyond Canada's borders, to foster greater openness to market forces and international competition in Canadian economic life, and to assist individual Canadians to adapt to these changes. Rather than acting aggressively to break up large concentrations of economic power within Canada, Canadian governments have been more inclined to introduce policy and regulatory changes that subject historic monopolies and oligopolistic industries to varying degrees of international competition.

These decisions have contributed to the institutional and economic dynamism that have characterized Canada's economic structure and facilitated its ability to adjust to the structural economic changes of the past generation. They can be seen in the renewed encouragement of foreign investment, the reduction of regulatory barriers to foreign firms' entry into Canada, and the accommodation of technological and regulatory changes conducive to increased domestic competition and the evolution of new forms of business activity. They are also evident in the maturing of capital markets and the growing activism of institutional shareholders, both in the market for corporate control and in promoting corporate governance measures that encourage greater accountability of corporate managers to shareholders and regulators.

However, despite these changes, two substantial realities remain largely unchanged: Canada's regional economic diversity and the complexities of federal-provincial relations in balancing regional interests and policy goals within Canada. These issues are the major focus of the next chapter.

---

10 Brennan and Buchanan describe the basic institutions of a liberal democratic society as part of its economic constitution in the sense that "a constitution is conceived as a set of rules, or social institutions within which people operate and interact with one another ... rules (which) set boundaries on what activities are legitimate" (Brennan and Buchanan 1980: 3; see also Hale 2001b: 63-85.)

Key Terms and Concepts for Review (see Glossary)

capital markets	liquidity
cartel	market power
closely held companies	monopolistic competition
corporate concentration	monopoly
corporate governance	monopoly rent
economic dynamism	monopsony
economic structure	oligopoly
financial intermediation	perfect competition
framework legislation	public-private partnerships
government business enterprise	rent-seeking
horizontal integration	triple helix
information asymmetries	vertical integration
institutional investors	widely held companies

Questions for Discussion and Review

1. The features of capitalist economies often vary widely between countries. What are four major characteristics of the ownership of Canadian businesses? How have some of these features changed in recent years?

2. What are four major types of market organization discussed in this chapter that can contribute to greater or lesser degrees of competition? Give examples of each. What implications does each one have for the workings of Canada's economy? For government economic and regulatory policies?

3. What factors have contributed to the growing openness of Canada's economy? What implications do these changes have for the operations of Canadian businesses? For government policies?

4. Canada's economy has traditionally been dependent on the development and processing of natural resources and other primary products. To what extent does this traditional image still apply?

5. What is the knowledge-based economy? What are some of its implications for traditional business operations? For patterns of employment? For relationships among business, government, and traditionally non-profit knowledge-based sectors?

6. What is the role of capital markets in financing economic activity? In shaping the competitive environment for business operations? How have changes in capital markets helped to transform the operations of the Canadian economy since the 1980s?

Suggestions for Further Readings

Canada, Task Force on the Future of the Canadian Financial Services Sector. 1998. *Report of the task force.* Ottawa: The Task Force (September).

DeSoto, Hernando. 2000. *The mystery of capital.* New York: Free Press.

Doern, G. Bruce, and Ted Reed (Eds.). 2000. *Risky business: Canada's changing science-based policy and regulatory regime.* Toronto: University of Toronto Press.

Hoberg, George (Ed.). 2002. *Capacity for choice: Canada in North America.* Toronto: University of Toronto Press.

Lipsey, Richard G. 1996. *Economic growth, technological change and Canadian economic policy.* Toronto: C.D. Howe Institute (November 6).

Sarra, Janis (Ed.). 2004. *Corporate governance in global capital markets.* Vancouver: University of British Columbia Press.

Thurow, Lester C. 1999. *Building wealth: the new rules for individuals, companies and nations.* New York: Harper.

Wallace, Iain. 2002. *A geography of the Canadian economy.* Toronto: Oxford University Press.

CHAPTER 7

Federalism, Regionalism, and the Context for Business-Government Relations

Federalism and regionalism are dominant realities of Canadian political life. They have shaped the country's development by structuring its governments and representative institutions to serve distinct geographic interests through the election of members of Parliament and provincial legislatures on the basis of local constituency boundaries. Canadian federalism divides political and legal responsibility for major elements of economic and social life between two senior orders of government, both of which have a significant effect on business operations and the social interests shaped by them.

Political debate in Canada revolves around regional issues and economic structures, which vary widely across the country. For much of our history, major political parties have been coalitions of regional and provincial interests. **Regionalism**—the shared identification of citizens with a region as a distinct political or social community based on conscious differences in political, economic, and social interests and structures (Schwartz 1974: 309-10; Matthews 1983: 14-16)—has long influenced the political environment for economic policies and business-government relations. Simeon and Robinson (1990) have described this effect as **societal federalism**: the interaction of federalism with underlying economic and societal differences to create different political cultures and social and economic environments for the conduct of politics in Canada's provinces and regions. The result has been the emergence of provincial governments that are not only constitutionally equal with the federal government within their respective areas of jurisdiction, but which are seen by citizens as the principal representatives of regional interests within Confederation. This political legitimacy, combined with the periodic political weakness of federal governments, has helped to make Canada one of the world's most politically and economically decentralized federations (Watts 1999).

The roles assumed by both federal and provincial governments in the promotion of regional economic development, and the policy instruments used to carry out these roles. play a significant part in shaping the economic structures of provinces and regions. These policy choices help to structure the environment not only for relations between governments and business but with other economic interests as well. Regional economic structures and the policies of provincial governments have adapted themselves, to varying degrees, to the growing openness and dynamism of Canada's economy discussed in Chapter 6. However, the *political* institutions of Canadian federalism have adapted rather more slowly to these trends, reflecting the considerable differences in the economic circumstances and internal political trade-offs associated with these processes in different provinces (for example, see Simeon 2003).

This chapter examines the federal-provincial balance of powers and its effects on Canada's economic structure and the environment for business-government relations. It outlines major economic differences among regions and provinces and how these affect regional political cultures, the size and role of governments and the environment for business-government relations. It considers the role of provincial governments in province-building and the federal government's efforts to promote regional economic development—and its own political legitimacy—in response. Finally, it considers the effects of increasing North American integration on relationships among governments, businesses, and other economic interests.

Federalism and Regionalism

Federalism is a system that divides power between national and subnational levels of government. In Canada, neither order of government is subject to the other within its constitutionally defined fields of jurisdiction, as interpreted by the courts in responding to legal disputes arising from political conflicts.

Canada's federal division of powers, established in the *Constitution Act, 1867* (formerly the *British North America Act*) originally provided for a relatively centralized federation. In the late nineteenth century, federal powers were used repeatedly to override provincial laws, enforce federal primacy in economic policies, and promote a centralized view of Canadian federalism (Stevenson 1993: 177-252). However, as discussed in Chapter 4, a combination of judicial decisions and the mobilization of a strong provincial-rights coalition capable of exercising power in Ottawa for most of the period between the 1890s and the 1940s contributed to a significant decentralization of power to the provinces. The pendulum of centralization and decentralization has continued ever since. The assertion of provincial and regional interests within national politics—either within the federal government and party system or through the agency of provincial governments—is a central aspect of regionalism in Canada.

The federal government affects the environment for economic development through its regulatory oversight over major sectors of the economy—including banking, currency, and interprovincial transportation and communications—and its control over customs, international trade, diplomatic relations, and major aspects of tax policy. These factors are major elements in Canada's **economic union**: the legal framework that enables goods, services, and people to move freely between provinces (see Box 7.1). Ottawa's renewed capacity to generate budget surpluses in the early twenty-first century has enabled it to play a more active role in shaping provincial economic and social policy priorities through its use of the **federal spending power**: the policy-making authority derived from its discretionary power to allocate funds to areas of provincial jurisdiction.

Box 7.1: Canada as an Economic Union

Section 121 of the *Constitution Act, 1867*, provides that "all Articles of the Growth, Produce, or Manufacture of any one of the Provinces shall, from and after the Union, be admitted free (i.e., without customs duties) into each of the other Provinces."

Section 6(2) of the *Constitution Act, 1982* affirms the right of all citizens and permanent residents of Canada to "take up residence ... and pursue the gaining of a livelihood in any province."

Provincial governments enjoy broad powers of taxation and economic and social regulation that enable them to play an active and sometimes primary role in shaping economic and related social policies that affect the political, economic, and cultural environments for business operations and business-government relations. This role is reinforced by provincial ownership of natural resources on vast tracts of Crown land and related regulatory powers and jurisdiction over municipalities and related issues of land use. In addition, the provinces have important responsibilities for labour and environmental policies and in the construction and maintenance of public infrastructure. Box 7.2 outlines major areas of federal and provincial responsibility relating to economic policies.

Box 7.2: The Federal-Provincial Division of Powers
(partial list relating to economic policy)

Federal	Provincial
(Section 91, *Constitution Act, 1867*)	(Sections 92 and 93, *Constitution Act, 1867*)
All forms of taxation	Direct taxation only
"Regulation of Trade and Commerce"	"Property and Civil Rights"
Interprovincial and international trade	Economic development within a province
Bankruptcy and insolvency	Education (and training), social services
Interprovincial transport (including communications)	Highways, public works within provinces
Intellectual property rights (patents, copyright)	Municipal government
Banking, currency	Provincially chartered non-bank financial institutions
Labour (industries under exclusive federal jurisdiction)	Labour (all other industries)

Shared Jurisdictions
Agriculture
Immigration
Law enforcement
Pensions (after 1950)
Consumer affairs
Environment

The emergence of regionalism as a political force is due to several factors. Differences in population and political and economic power between regions during the late nineteenth and early twentieth centuries nourished demands for greater provincial autonomy and self-government in a political culture characterized by a far stronger commitment to the representative role of parliamentary institutions than in today's Canada (Vipond 1991; Moore 1997; Romney 1999). Economic and cultural differences reinforced demands for greater provincial control over economic development policies in order to provide greater responsiveness to local and regional interests. The provinces, particularly Ontario, were successful in persuading the courts that their constitutional power over property and civil rights should be interpreted broadly. Moreover, provincial political parties played a leading role within the federal party system.

The politics of regionalism have been rooted in a shared sense of grievance over the unfulfilled promises of equal citizenship within Confederation. As such, they reflect pressures from regional interests—including different combinations of business, agrarian, and labour interests—seeking to expand their economic opportunities and to reduce their dependence on (or to escape subordination to) external economic interests, particularly those based in other parts of the country. This has contributed to competition over the exercise of political jurisdiction in many areas, sometimes leading to constitutional litigation. More often in recent years, it has led to the practical necessity of cooperation, the shared recognition of distinct interests, and mutual accommodation.

Impact of Federalism on Canada's Economic Structure

The evolution of Canada's federal system and the politics of regionalism have contributed to the emergence of significantly different regional political and economic cultures resulting from the progressive decentralization of provincial fiscal and taxation policies, economic development strategies, natural resource management policies, and labour relations policies (Atkinson and Chandler 1983b; Hale 2000).

Provincial governments project provincial and regional interests in national politics both as representatives of social and economic interests within their political communities and as independent agents in dealings with other governments and outside economic interests. Control over natural resources, including energy resources, has been central to the economic development policies of most provinces at one time or another. Provincial resource policies have been critical in fostering the development of regional transportation and infrastructure networks and related patterns of settlement and in defining the relationships between individual governments and key industry sectors. These arrangements have reinforced trends towards societal federalism—and sometimes clientelist relationships—in these sectors. The ability and willingness of provincial governments to project this role has been increased in recent years by regional divisions within Canada's federal party system and growing regional variations in north-south trade.

The problem of overlapping jurisdictions provides not only fertile ground for federal-provincial conflict but also for the active participation of business and other interest groups in these disputes in pursuit of their own agendas and priorities. Recent surveys indicate that small and medium-sized businesses in particular view provincial governments as having a greater impact on their operations than other levels of government, as indicated in Table 7.1, although responses to such questions may well reflect the geographic scope of respondents' operations.

Table 7.1: Levels of Government with the Greatest Impact on Respondents' Business Operations: 2001

	BC	AB	SK	MB	ON	QC	NB	NS	PE	NF	Canada
Provincial	62	32	56	41	30	34	43	38	60	41	39
Local/municipal	16	25	14	26	32	29	20	21	7	25	26
Federal	15	32	21	21	23	9	22	25	22	18	20
Don't know	6	12	9	12	15	29	15	16	12	15	15

Source: Canadian Federation of Independent Business 2001.

The tendency towards societal federalism is strongest in Quebec, where several generations of academics, policy analysts, and commentators on federalism have evolved a strong philosophical commitment to federalism as a means of defending the distinct social, cultural, and political identity of that province's French-speaking majority (for example, see Rocher and Rouillard 2002).

The political realities of federalism have been far more fluid than suggested in formal debates over the division of powers. The effective powers of federal and provincial governments over economic development have shifted almost from decade to decade. They have also reflected the growing financial and bureaucratic resources available to provincial governments in designing and administering public policies and public services, as well as the shifting balance of centralizing and decentralizing forces within both orders of government. Table 7.2 demonstrates that even before federal transfers, provincial governments generate an even larger share of overall government revenues within their own jurisdictions than does the federal government.

Pressures for strong national leadership created by world wars or national crises have usually contributed to greater centralization of powers. The perceived need to accommodate regional alienation in the interests of national unity and the relative capacity of provincial governments to exercise their responsibilities without direct federal assistance have reversed the pendulum periodically. Although conflicts over the degree of centralization or decentralization in Canada's federal system sometimes have the appearance of a zero-sum game, federalism also provides a framework for the coordination and balancing of different political priorities.

Table 7.2: Distribution of Government Revenues, excluding Transfers

	Federal	Provincial	Local	CPP/QPP
1950	65.2%	20.8%	14.0%	
1960	60.8%	21.8%	17.3%	
1970*	44.8%	36.2%	15.1%	3.9%
1980	40.0%	41.9%	13.4%	4.6%
1990	40.1%	41.8%	13.0%	5.2%
2000	41.1%	41.7%	11.1%	6.2%
2003	39.1%	41.7%	11.6%	7.6%

* Change in methodology in 1970.
Source: Treff and Perry 2002, 2005: Table B-3, author's calculations.

The paradox of federalism—particularly **executive federalism** (the brokering of intergovernmental differences between and among federal and provincial first ministers and cabinet ministers) and administrative federalism (parallel processes involving civil service decision-makers engaged in related policy fields)—is that the more closely governments work together to address common policy problems, the greater the likelihood that significant economic and social interests outside government may be neglected or sidelined in policy outcomes. As a general rule, horizontal policy fields that engage broad swaths of economic or social policy, particularly those related to fiscal federalism or the environment, are more likely to lend themselves to the balancing of *governmental* interests, sometimes at the expense of related societal interests. Primarily sectoral policy fields such as natural resources, labour market development, or regionally specialized industries are shaped frequently by decentralized decision-making processes capable of accommodating varied and often competing regional interests.

The two approaches intersect in the field of trade policy. Federal-provincial cooperation is a vital factor in the management of major trade negotiations, which require the balancing of different regional interests, sometimes involving the same industry, as in the example of Canada's protracted softwood lumber dispute with the US (Skogstad 2001; De Boer 2002; Kukucha 2005). During the 1990s, Canada's integration in the North American and global economies also prompted federal and provincial governments to negotiate the **Agreement on Internal Trade** in an effort to reduce provincial barriers to the movement of goods, services, and people across the country. While some provinces have been slow to implement the agreement, a series of interprovincial negotiations have successfully harmonized provincial legislation affecting the mobility of skilled workers and professionals. North American integration has also strengthened the role of the federal government in balancing and coordinating regional economic interests when managing disputes over trade policy and regulation (Doern and MacDonald 1999; Forum of Labour Market Ministers 2001; Hale 2004).

Regional Economic Differences and Disparities
and the Politics of Regionalism

The politics of regionalism can be seen in the competition between federal and pro-vincial governments and between regional interests and in political competition within provinces—urban versus rural, more developed versus less developed regions, major commercial centres and their economic elites versus the smaller communi-ties. The same dynamics of regional disparities and the challenge of accommodating regional interests in the priorities of governments are often central issues of provin-cial politics and interest group competition.

The term regional disparities is often used to emphasize the inequalities in political and economic power among Canada's provinces and regions. These differ-ences are evident in the distribution of population, economic activity, and employ-ment and income levels between and within provinces. Contemporary discussions, prompted by the steady growth of Canada's major cities, are as likely to emphasize the relative wealth and power of major urban regions compared with smaller towns and rural areas in each province as traditional east-west divisions (Canada West Foundation 2001: 17-19; Whitson and Epp 2001). We will now look at the major dif-ferences in levels and types of regional economic activity that both reflect and con-tribute to disparities in income, wealth, and economic power.

Population

Population differences between regions indicate their relative economic influence, if not always their political influence. Population growth can be seen as "an important barometer of a province's and, indeed, a region's prosperity" (Roach and Berdahl 2001: 5). Larger provinces tend to exert greater influence and power within the fed-eral government as Canada's majoritarian political system, influenced by regional voting blocs, marginalizes regional and other minorities unless (and sometimes, even if) they can find a secure place within the governing party.

Table 7.3: Regional Growth/Decline as Share of Canada's Population

	1921-51	1951-81	1981-2001
Ontario	- 1.7%	+ 8.0%	+ 7.3%
Quebec	+ 7.8%	- 8.7%	- 8.8%
Atlantic*	+ 1.4%	- 20.5%	- 17.0%
West	- 6.1%	+ 8.1%	+ 4.5%
• Manitoba/ Saskatchewan	- 26.2%	- 28.7%	- 14.6%
• Alberta/BC	+ 18.6%	+ 36.2%	+ 12.1%

* Including Newfoundland since 1949.
Source: Statistics Canada 2002e.

Over time, demographic shifts influence overall levels of economic activity as well as relative political influence. McMahon (2000a) and Savoie (2001) have pointed out the relationships between the relative decline of Atlantic Canada's population, its political and economic influence within Canada, and regional alienation. Quebec's persistent defence of provincial rights and, subsequently, provincial autonomy since the 1880s is closely linked to its people's desire to preserve their identity, status, and interests both as a minority within Canada and a majority in Quebec. Table 7.3 notes the distribution of population by region and province and the population shifts that have taken place during the twentieth century.

Population growth since the 1960s, driven significantly by immigration, has centred on the urban regions of Ontario, BC, Alberta, and, to a much lesser extent, Quebec. Manitoba, Saskatchewan, and much of Atlantic Canada have experienced population stagnation and, in some cases, decline. In an effort to reduce the political effects of these changes, federal representation of smaller provinces has been frozen at the levels of the mid-1970s, resulting in the under-representation of Ontario, BC, and Alberta in the federal Parliament.

Table 7.4: Major Urban Centres as Proportion of Provincial Populations, 2001

	Cities over 500,000	Cities of 100,000-500,000	Cities over 100,000 (cumulative)
Canada	48.3	14.2	62.5
Ontario	52.3	17.8	70.2
Quebec	56.3	9.1	65.3
BC	50.0	13.0	63.0
Alberta	61.9	0.0	61.9
Manitoba	59.2	0.0	59.2
SK	0.0	42.6	42.6
NS	0.0	37.8	37.8
NF	0.0	32.8	32.8
NB	0.0	16.9	16.9
PEI	0.0	0.0	0.0
Territories	0.0	0.0	0.0

Source: Statistics Canada 2002e.

An analysis of demographic and economic trends suggests that western Canada is a much less cohesive region than in the past, with steady in-migration and population growth in Alberta and BC and relative population decline in Manitoba and Saskatchewan (Roach and Berdahl 2001). Since the 1960s provincial governments in the two larger provinces have asserted their desire to exercise political and economic influence consistent with their growing populations and economic strength. Conversely, it is not surprising that, except for Quebec, provinces whose populations have grown more slowly than the country as a whole have been most supportive of increased federal power and the extensive transfer payments to people and provinces that go with it, except when federal policies have conflicted with their core interests, such as rights over resource management.

Another major difference between regions is the degree of urbanization. Income levels, employment rates, and economic diversification—and with them, the revenue-generating capacities of governments—tend to be higher in major cities than in the small town and rural areas of most provinces. Population, incomes, and economic opportunities in rural areas surrounding major cities are also proportionately higher (Bollman 2000: slide 36; Burleton 2004: 7; Statistics Canada 2005e). Table 7.4 notes the different shares of population in major metropolitan areas by province.

Income, Employment, and Regional Development

Wide differences in levels of economic development and activity by region and, frequently, within regions can be attributed to the timing of settlement; levels of natural resource endowments; and the physical and financial infrastructures necessary to transport goods to market profitably, take advantage of economic opportunities, and generate the capital necessary for economic diversification and higher standards of living. Levels of economic development can be measured in several ways including the GDP (the total value of goods and services produced annually in an economy, either economy-wide or per capita), employment and unemployment rates, average personal income, and average *disposable* income (the income available to individuals or families after taxes are paid and government transfers received). Business support for more activist government policies of economic development is much more likely in regions facing relative economic stagnation or decline (Canadian Federation of Independent Business 2001; Clancy 2004).

Regional differences in GDP per capita can be distorted by a number of factors, not least the effects of volatile commodity prices on economic activity. Table 7.5 notes that regional disparities in personal and disposable income (or take-home pay) are significantly less than those in the GDP per capita. A significant part of this difference is accounted for by sizeable interregional transfer payments, financed largely by taxpayers in Ontario and Alberta. However, sustainable economic development and higher living standards ultimately depend on the capacity of a regional economy to generate increased levels of employment and investment to generate higher levels of productivity (Fortin 1999: 13-32).

Contemporary theories of regional development suggest that the normal workings of the economy should reduce regional differences in employment and income levels as long as microeconomic policies support private investment, increased productivity, and improvements in marketable skills and human capital. Equally important is the provision of infrastructure necessary for public health and economic development, particularly the efficient marketing of goods and services (McMahon 2000b; Porter, et al. 2001).

Governments and the interest groups that support them frequently attempt to speed up this process by offering incentives and inducements for outside investment or by setting regulatory requirements for additional investments in return for securing access to provincial resources. However, provincial and regional development policies have often reflected competing visions of federalism and different approaches to the promotion of economic growth and diversification.

Table 7.5: Personal Income and Disposable Income per capita, 2003

(Canada = 100)	Per Capita GDP	Personal Income	Disposable Income
NWT	206.6	146.7	153.4
Alberta	140.9	114.7	115.3
Yukon	110.0	121.2	129.9
Ontario	105.0	106.1	105.7
Saskatchewan	96.3	84.7	87.2
NF	90.2	81.5	83.7
BC	89.4	94.1	94.7
Quebec	88.4	94.6	93.6
Manitoba	85.3	90.1	91.9
Nunavut	82.3	114.2	126.7
NS	80.2	89.2	91.0
NB	77.5	84.3	86.6
PEI	73.3	81.1	82.5

Source: Statistics Canada 2004c: 393-94, 397.

Economic Disparities: Political and Regulatory Responses

Political responses to economic disparities both before and after World War II took three main forms. Economic interests that perceived themselves to be disadvantaged by federal policies mobilized to promote their interests in federal policies, either by getting involved with political parties seeking major social and economic change or by allying themselves with one of the mainstream parties in order to hold the balance of power within the federal Parliament. In some cases, such as the restoration of regional employment insurance entitlements to Atlantic Canada and rural Quebec before the 2000 election, the electoral arithmetic of brokerage politics has prompted federal governments to offer policy concessions to specific regional interests in order to preserve or regain their electoral majority. On rarer occasions, such as the Diefenbaker PCs' upset victory in 1957, the election of the Mulroney government in 1984, and Stephen Harper's rise to power in 2006, a coalition of the 'outs' capable of appealing to enough disadvantaged interests across the country challenged the political status quo.

Alternately, groups that perceive themselves to be permanent minorities within Canada have promoted strong provincial governments to champion regional interests and priorities. Regional elites often debate whether to look to Ottawa for policies and resources necessary to assist the development of their economies or to expand provincial powers to make social and economic policies more consistent with their priorities. Interests centred in larger provinces often pursue both strategies to keep either level of government from taking its citizens for granted.

Federal governments have often attempted to accommodate regional interests in national decision-making by appointing **regional ministers** with political and policy responsibilities for a particular province or region (Bakvis 1991). Regional interests may also be institutionalized within the federal bureaucracy by setting up special federal departments or agencies responsible for regional development. The Department of Regional Economic Expansion (DREE), set up during the late 1960s, was later replaced by an alphabet soup of successors in the late 1980s and 1990s: the Atlantic Canada Opportunities Agency (ACOA), Western Economic Diversification (WED), FEDNOR, a federal regional development program for northern Ontario, and FED(Q), a similar program for Quebec. Their value has often been questioned, both on grounds of economic effectiveness and their potential for excessive political favouritism (Savoie 2001: 45-56; McMahon 1997; McMahon 2000a; Murrell 2001). However, whatever their efforts to achieve regional balance, postwar federal economic policies have tended to reflect the continued political and economic dominance of the political and commercial elites of central Canada.

After World War II, provincial governments have become increasingly involved in fostering economic development and diversification by encouraging the increased processing of natural resources within their boundaries. This process of province-building matured during the 1960s and 1970s. Initial successes led a number of provincial governments to pursue a more independent approach to their economic development policies, which often clashed with modest federal efforts to limit the expansion of foreign economic interests within Canada, although the federal government did allow the progressive decentralization of fiscal and economic powers to provinces with sufficient political and economic capacity.

These policies, while initially intended to accommodate the demands of Quebec's moderate nationalists, became vital elements in the development of strong provincial governments in western Canada and, periodically, in Newfoundland and Labrador. They often took the form of expanding provincially owned utilities and, often, transportation systems as part of a mega-projects approach to large-scale resource and industrial development or by buying control of strategic firms in industries central to their economies. The specific strategies used by social democratic governments in Quebec, Manitoba, and Saskatchewan differed significantly from those of more business-oriented governments in neighbouring provinces (Atkinson and Chandler 1983; Arbour 1994). The pursuit of economic diversification was a major emphasis of most provincial governments, but one that enjoyed differing levels of success.

While generous regional subsidies and unemployment benefits reduced overall income disparities somewhat during the 1970s and 1980s, McMahon has demonstrated that they contributed to a new form of "transfer dependence" that hindered the adjustment of regional economies in Atlantic Canada and eastern Quebec to changing economic circumstances and subsidized employment without promoting sustainable economic development outside these regions' major cities (McMahon 2000a; May and Hollett 1994).

Regional Economic Structures and the Context for Business-Government Relations

The legal and political structures of federalism have contributed to the regional differentiation of Canada's economy by giving provincial governments control over economic development policies and transportation systems within their provinces, the ownership of national resources, and the political incentive to use those powers to promote the economic well-being of people and businesses within their territory.

Table 7.6: Regional Sectoral Mix
Average share of output* from 1995 to 1999, per cent

	Canada	BC	Prairies	Ontario	Quebec	Atlantic
Primary	6.3	6.6	**18.5**	2.1	2.9	5.9
• mining, quarrying, and oil-well-drilling industries	3.8	2.7	**14.2**	0.8	0.8	2.8
• logging, forestry	0.6	**2.6**	0.3	0.2	1.0	0.6
Manufacturing	17.5	9.6	9.5	**23.4**	**20.2**	10.5
• transportation equipment	3.1	na	0.6	**5.7**	2.3	na
• electrical and electronic products	1.5	na	0.6	**2.2**	1.6	na
Goods-producing industries (total)	32.8	25.8	**38.7**	33.0	33.0	26.2
Services-producing industries (total)	67.2	**74.2**	61.3	67.0	67.0	**73.8**

*Output measured by real GDP at factor cost.
Bold Type: regional share significantly above national average.
Source: Brady and Navin 2001: 22 (reproduced with permission of Bank of Canada).

Canada's provinces are characterized by very different endowments of natural resources, geographical proximity to major markets, access to investment capital, degrees of urbanization, and migration levels that have influenced their growth. Table 7.6 notes the average output of key industry sectors by region during the late 1990s. Primary industries, especially Alberta and Saskatchewan's oil and gas sectors, have generated a much higher share of GDP in western Canada than in the rest of the country, even before the continuing energy boom of recent years. Manufacturing remains significantly more important to the economies of Ontario and Quebec than

other regions, although manufacturing output has increased significantly in both
Alberta and New Brunswick.

Competition among economic interests, often organized along geographic lines,
has shaped the political culture of each province as well as encouraging the province-building initiatives noted above to promote a more balanced geographic and
social distribution of the benefits of economic development—or, at least, one sufficient to secure their governments' periodic re-election. As discussed in Chapter 4,
province-building policies evolved typically from an early emphasis on the politics
of clientelism, through periods of developmental capitalism, to varying mixtures
of state capitalism and bureaucratic clientelism, in which provincial governments
actively promoted provincial champions as central elements in the process of economic development and government patronage continued to play a major role in
both entrepreneurship and the distribution of economic benefits.

This section examines the evolution of provincial and regional economic structures across Canada, the internal characteristics that determine their economies
and demography, the role of provincial governments and political competition in
shaping the evolution of those structures, and the major factors affecting the development of contemporary regional economies.

British Columbia

BC's economy was built initially on the development of its resource industries, particularly the forest and mining sectors. The completion of the CPR and the building
of its Crowsnest Pass line opened the province both for settlement and resource
exploitation in the 1880s and 1890s. Resource development policies, particularly
under the long Social Credit government of W.A.C. Bennett (1952-72) were focused
on "stimulating economic development by encouraging and assisting private producers" (Chandler 1983b: 54). Manufacturing industries, ranging from sawmills and
pulp and paper to food processing industries, emerged from the processing of the
province's natural resources and agricultural staples. Since the 1980s, a post-staples
economy based primarily on business services, tourism, community services, and
related public sector services has become increasingly significant (Caves and Hobson 1980; Barman 1991).

Its size, mountainous geography, and widely dispersed population are principal
causes of BC's economic and political divisions. Vancouver's coastal and mountain
hinterlands yielded the foundations of the province's enormous resource wealth.
However, tapping this wealth required large investments from corporations based
outside the province and, later, from the provincial government. Either way, economic decision-making has been highly politicized, with competing interests scram-
bling to mobilize political power in the pursuit of wealth and public benefits.

The processes of large-scale resource exploitation contributed to the growth of
industrial unionism and the emergence of a political climate conspicuously polarized between conservative and socialist political parties. At the same time, its large
small business sector gave the province's politics a distinctly populist tinge. The Lib-

eral, Coalition, and Social Credit governments that ruled the province for most of the period between 1933 and 1991 were heavily engaged in the processes of province-building: building highways, opening up the resource-rich interior, and using provincially owned utilities and transportation systems as instruments of economic development (Mitchell 1983; Barman 1991). The NDP governments of the 1990s presided over a period of general economic decline, followed by a radical restructuring of the province's public sector by a market-oriented Liberal government elected in 2001.

Historically, the province has been divided into four main regions—the Lower Mainland, Vancouver Island, the Northern Interior, and the Southern Interior, centered on Kamloops, Kelowna, and smaller communities in the Kootenays. About half of the province's population lives in the Lower Mainland—the Greater Vancouver Regional District and the lower Fraser Valley—a rich agricultural district that has become heavily suburbanized in recent years. Vancouver and the Lower Mainland are a magnet for immigrants from China, the Indian subcontinent, and much of Asia. Skilled immigrants helped to fuel an investment and real estate boom during the 1980s and to build numerous commercial links with other nations around the Pacific Rim. More recently, a thriving high technology industry has grown up in the Lower Mainland.

Vancouver Island and the Northern Interior are heavily dependent on the province's forest and mining industries. The economies of the Southern Interior, including the Okanagan and Kootenay Districts, are more diversified but still largely resource-based. Forest products accounted for more than half of BC's exports during the late 1990s, despite continuing trade disputes with the US. Resource and related industries accounted for almost 80 per cent of provincial exports. Since 1990, the province's investment climate has been undermined by gradual declines in the prices of many commodities; US regulatory harassment of the softwood lumber industry; political and legal uncertainties over Aboriginal land claims; and competing agendas among resource producers, environmental activists, Aboriginal communities, and governments. China's rapid economic growth and demand for natural resources have partly offset these trends in recent years.

Unlike most provinces, colonial and early Canadian governments did not negotiate treaties with BC's Aboriginal population as a precondition to organized settlement. A series of Supreme Court rulings, most notably the 1997 *Delgamuukw* case, implicitly recognize Aboriginal land claims to Crown lands on which much of the province's resource industry takes place (*Delgamuukw v. British Columbia* 1010 [1997] 3 S.C.R). To date, negotiations involving federal and provincial governments with Aboriginal communities have made only limited progress in resolving competing claims or establishing clear rules for land ownership and resource and tourism development. As a practical matter, corporations wishing to carry on business must build relationships and come to agreement with Aboriginal communities as well as provincial authorities over employment, land, and resource management practices or run the risk of losing their investments. Resolution of these disputes has become a key priority for business interests in the province.

Alberta

Alberta's economy is the most heavily urbanized in western Canada. Calgary, its financial centre, and the more heavily industrial Edmonton region account for about 63 per cent of the province's population. The rest is divided about evenly between the parkland and agricultural regions of northern, central and southern Alberta surrounding smaller regional centres including Red Deer, Lethbridge, Medicine Hat, Grande Prairie, and Fort McMurray, the heart of large-scale oil-sands development. The Calgary-Edmonton corridor has been one of the fastest growing regions in Canada in recent years.

Unlike polarized BC, Alberta has one of the most stable political climates in Canada, experiencing only two dominant majority governments and six premiers since 1935. After an initial experiment with Depression-era radicalism, the long Social Credit administration (1935-71) settled into a period of careful conservative government, balancing the interests of farmers, small businesses, and the province's oil industry. Its PC successors (1971 to present), enthusiastically endorsed the province-building techniques of larger provinces, championing the province's business classes and urban areas and ensuring a generous distribution of oil revenues to support smaller communities. Provincial governments have usually been able to shift the political blame for occasional economic downturns either to the vagaries of global energy prices or to federal interference in the provincial economy, while adapting their policies to changing economic circumstances. As a result, political competition tends to be externalized in competition between provincial and federal governments, rather than internalized as in the far more polarized politics of BC and Saskatchewan.

Alberta's political stability has given it one of the most favourable environments for business and entrepreneurship in Canada. Its government has invested heavily in economic diversification to escape the traditional boom and bust cycles of its resource industries. Resource royalties, primarily from the oil and gas industry, accounted for almost 40 per cent of provincial revenues during the mid-1980s, before the bottom fell out of the energy market, triggering record provincial deficits. Radical budget-cutting measures and the province's emphasis on debt reduction during the 1990s enabled it to balance its budgets, cut both personal and corporate taxes to attract investment, and give Alberta one of the most competitive personal and business tax rate systems in North America, despite the roller-coaster effect of fluctuating energy prices on provincial budgets.[1]

While still heavily dependent on energy exports, Alberta's economy has become significantly more diversified in recent years, spawning a number of high technology sectors linked to both traditional and emerging economies. Its manufacturing sec-

---

1 Alberta's energy revenues have ranged from 14-15 per cent of total provincial revenues in 1991-93 and 1998-99 to temporary peaks of 37 per cent in 1985-86, 24 per cent in 1996-97, 41 per cent in 2000-01, and 40 per cent in 2005-06. Declines in world oil and gas prices have contributed to annual reductions of 20 per cent or more in provincial energy revenues in five of the past 20 years (Alberta Finance, historical budget figures 1985-86 and 2005-06; Alberta Finance 2005).

tor passed BC in 1999 as the third largest in Canada, measured by output. Machinery and electronic products industries have emerged in recent years, adding to the established manufacturing and transportation sectors that are linked to the province's primary and resource industries: food processing, energy resources (including chemicals) and forest products (Scotton 2001; Alberta, Ministry of Economic Development 2002: 4; Alberta, Ministry of Economic Development 2002: 3).

As a result, Alberta enjoyed rapid population growth and a business investment boom even before the rebound of oil and natural gas prices after 2000. Reinforcing a strongly conservative, pro-business political environment, per capita business fixed investment is almost double the Canadian average in recent years, and Calgary has become the second largest centre for head offices in Canada.

Saskatchewan and Manitoba

Before the energy boom of the 1970s, economic geographers typically lumped Alberta, Saskatchewan, and Manitoba together as "the prairies": largely rural agricultural and resource-based economies with somewhat different political cultures but broadly similar economic structures. These similarities have long been offset by significant differences in the political cultures of the three provinces, which some political scientists attribute to the diverse cultural influences and patterns of settlement during the late nineteenth and early twentieth centuries and different responses to the social and economic trauma of the Great Depression (Wiseman 1991).

Rapid growth of the wheat economy during the early twentieth century spurred the growth of farmers' movements in both federal and provincial politics. However, these movements expressed themselves in very different ways: in Alberta, they evolved into the conservative populism of Social Credit; in Saskatchewan, they embraced a series of socialist and later social democratic governments; and in Manitoba, they elected a series of cautious, stable, centrist governments under a variety of labels. The progressive alienation of the west from federal Liberal governments during and after the Diefenbaker era (1957-68) may have resulted in an increased emphasis on regionalism in federal politics; however, it also strengthened the position of provincial governments with distinct approaches to economic and social development (Smith 1996).

The legacy of agrarian politics can be seen in strong cooperative systems in Saskatchewan and Manitoba; an extensive system of federal and provincial Crown corporations used as instruments of economic development and stabilization; and, more recently, in a commitment to cautious financial management and balanced budgets. Both provinces have experienced relative population stagnation since the 1960s, with rural population decline, gradual agricultural diversification from the dominant wheat economy, and steady urbanization. Agriculture in Saskatchewan and Manitoba accounts for a much higher share of overall employment than in other regions of the country (in 2003 10.1 per cent in the former and 5.6 per cent in the latter). Gradual trends towards urbanization are reflected in the politics of both provinces.

The economic evolution of both provinces has reflected the dynamics of their political systems: Saskatchewan tends to be polarized between socialist or social democratic and free enterprise parties, with Manitoba favouring centrist broker-age politics, with occasional exceptions, and alternating between moderate conser-vative and social democratic governments since the late 1950s. The NDP's gradual accommodation to the market economy has reduced the degree of political polar-ization that traditionally characterized both provinces, although Manitoba politics have rarely been as ideologically driven as those of its western neighbour.

In Saskatchewan, agriculture has gradually been replaced by the production of minerals, oil, and gas as the province's largest industries (Saskatchewan 2002: 13). Eco-nomic activity and income levels tend to ebb and flow with international commodity prices. Saskatchewan's oil and gas resources briefly made it a "have" province during the energy boom of the late 1970s. However, the collapse of both grain and energy prices during the late 1980s plunged the province deeply into debt, and forced the NDP government elected in 1991 to follow the same path of deficit reduction, spend-ing discipline and fiscal prudence as most other provinces during the 1990s—balanc-ing its budget on average since 1994-95 and reducing its debt (Hale 2006a).

Saskatchewan's populist social democratic culture has contributed to high lev-els of public spending and services relative to the size of its population and, until recently, among the highest tax rates on individuals and businesses of any province. In 1999, a provincial tax reform commission found that these factors were contribut-ing to the migration of significant numbers of farmers and business people to Alberta, thus substantially eroding the province's tax base (Hale 2000; Saskatchewan 1999).

Manitoba's economic structure reflects the major demographic and geographic divisions of the province. Its largest city, Winnipeg, accounts for about 60 percent of the province's population and much of its manufacturing sector. Winnipeg's demo-graphic composition and its political orientations are closer to those of other large cities across the country, Calgary excepted, than to the rest of the Manitoba or the prairies. Its agricultural regions in the province's southwest, centered on Brandon, have diversified significantly in recent years into value-added processing activities, so that agriculture now generates about 5 per cent of the province's GDP. The prov-ince's north is a major producer of mineral and renewable energy resources.

A diversified manufacturing sector, producing a wide range of consumer and industrial goods, accounted for about 13 per cent of Manitoba's GDP in 2001. Food processing has grown rapidly to become the province's largest manufacturing indus-try, accounting for about one-quarter of its manufacturing shipments in recent years (Manitoba 2002: A4, A6). Manitoba's exports are the most diversified of any western province, cushioning it against the volatile commodity prices of recent years (Roach 2002: 17).

Ontario

Ontario is Canada's largest, most diversified economic region. It is the centre of Canada's manufacturing, financial, and emerging technology industries, as well as an important producer of agricultural and resource industries. Since Confederation, federal economic policies have been focused, in large measure, on the development of Ontario's economy as the lynchpin of Canada's east-west trading system, and its manufacturing and financial industries were the principal beneficiaries of the National Policy. It early developed a diversified and widely distributed manufacturing sector which accounted for 52 per cent of Canada's manufacturing output in 2004 (Statistics Canada 2005c: Tables 304-0014 and 304-0015; author's calculations).

Although Ontario was the cradle of Canada's provincial rights movement in the nineteenth century and well into the twentieth century, its governments since World War II have worked closely with their federal counterparts as guardians of Canada's industrial heartland (Courchene with Telmer 1998). As a result, regionalism in the province involves the competition of regions within the province—particularly eastern and northern Ontario—for a fair share of economic opportunities and the benefits of government spending or favourable regulation, rather than an assertion of provincial self-interest against a remote or insensitive federal government.

More Ontarians—74 per cent in 2001—live in large cities than citizens of any other province. The province counts at least 22 cities and 6 metropolitan areas with populations over 100,000. The Greater Toronto Area (GTA)—Toronto and the sprawling metropolitan regions around it that were home to 45 per cent of Ontarians in 2001—attracts almost half of Canada's immigrants every year (Statistics Canada 2005h, author's calculations; Hou 2005: 9).

The Auto Pact of 1965, which eliminated cross-border tariffs, helped Ontario's automotive industry to become its largest manufacturing sector, generating almost half its exports in the late 1990s. The province has become the largest car and truck producing jurisdiction in North America, surpassing Michigan in 2004. While most major car and truck assembly plants are US- or Japanese-owned, the industry has a strong, internationally competitive auto parts sector with significant Canadian ownership. It is a major factor in the economies in such medium-sized cities as Windsor, London, Cambridge, Kitchener, Brampton, St. Catharines, Oakville, and Oshawa, as well as a major customer of its steel industry, clustered in the Hamilton-Niagara and Durham regions. These industries have been heavily unionized since the 1930s, contributing to three-way political competition among PCs, Liberals, and the NDP in many communities around the province, although in several industrial cities, the principal competition has been between Liberal and NDP candidates (Hale 1997).

Ontario has also evolved as the centre for many of Canada's information technology and communications equipment technology industries, particularly in the Ottawa and Kitchener-Waterloo regions. Toronto has become the centre for much of Canada's financial services sector, including three of its five largest banks, its two largest insurance companies, and much of its securities industry. As a result, Ontario plays a leading role in financial services regulation. Business and financial services are now the two largest employers in the province's export-oriented business clusters (Ontario, Institute for Competitiveness and Prosperity 2002: 27).

Supportive federal and provincial policies for cultural industries, including protective regulations, subsidies, and preferential tax treatment, have resulted in the growth of sizeable publishing and entertainment industries. Employment in Ontario's (and Toronto's) entertainment sectors is now the third largest in North America after those of Los Angeles and New York City, suggesting that developmental clientelism is still alive and well as a significant feature of the province's political climate, whatever the ideological rhetoric of individual governments (Noel 1990, 310; Ontario, Institute for Competitiveness and Prosperity 2002: 37). Along with Quebec and Alberta, Ontario is one of three provinces with its own corporate income tax (CIT) system, which enables it to offer tax incentives (or expenditures) to support selected industries.[2]

Eastern and northern Ontario are more typically dependent on small-scale manufacturing, resource industries, small-scale agriculture, and government operations. The decentralization of both federal and provincial public services in the 1980s and 1990s resulted in the broader public sector becoming the largest employer in smaller cities such as Kingston, Sudbury, Sault Ste. Marie, and Thunder Bay. This has reinforced the tendency towards bureaucratic clientelism in the distribution of economic opportunities and created a sizeable constituency for high levels of public spending in many of the province's smaller communities. Both regions, while sparsely populated, also have significant tourist industries, which make the balancing of employment and environmental concerns a major factor in their politics.

Ontario's economic interests continue to play a disproportionate role in shaping Canada's economic policies (Courchene 1998; Savoie 2001). Exports, 90 percent of them to the US, accounted for 46 per cent of Ontario's GDP between 1995 and 1999, more than any other province. In 2001, Ontario's two-way export trade was more than three times its two-way trade with all other provinces combined, a ratio far higher than that of any other province.

Until recent years, Ontario's political culture has been largely consensual and managerial in character, focusing on the development of the economy and the efficient management of its public institutions in relative harmony with a wide range of economic interests (Noel 1990: 310-14). The province's size and diversity has encouraged an emphasis on brokerage rather than ideological politics—the balancing of economic and political interests by a strong provincial government committed to facilitating provincial and regional economic development through the active support of private economic interests, efficient public services, and strategic state intervention in key sectors. As a result, until the mid-1980s, changes of government were few and far between.

The breakdown of the post-World War II political consensus and the economic restructuring that followed affected Ontario more than any other province, resulting in three changes of government between 1985 and 1995. The emergence of huge, sustained budget deficits after 1990 led to a sharp political reaction and the election of a PC government, under Mike Harris, which was committed to lower taxes, market-oriented economic policies, and a more narrowly focused role for government

---

2 Prior to the 2006 federal election, Ontario was negotiating with the federal government over the possible harmonization of provincial and federal CIT systems.

in the economy and society. Harris's successors have largely reverted to Ontario's traditional centrist political culture.

As the main beneficiary of Canada's economic union, Ontario was generally supportive of the extensive system of federal-provincial transfers financed primarily by its taxpayers (and those of Alberta) as long as the economic policies of other provinces did not discriminate against Ontario-based businesses. These concerns were a major factor behind the negotiation of the 1995 Agreement on Internal Trade, which committed the federal government and all provinces to identify and reduce barriers to the movement of people, goods, services, and capital among Canada's regions. However, continued structural budget deficits have led recent Ontario governments into a more confrontational relationship with the federal government.

Quebec

Nowhere in Canada have provincial politics and the politics of federal-provincial relations played a more significant role in economic development and business-government relations than in Quebec. Rather than regionalism, this process has reflected the competition between the Quebec and federal governments to be seen as the principal political representatives of Quebecers and the protectors of the linguistic, cultural, and economic interests of its population, particularly its French-speaking majority.

The mainstream approach to federalism in Quebec provincial politics since the 1940s has emphasized provincial autonomy and control over all major areas of jurisdiction established in Canada's 1867 Constitution, including the province's powers over taxation, economic development, natural resources, social spending, language, culture, and education. This compact theory of Confederation is based on the constitutional doctrine of the sovereign equality of federal and provincial governments within their areas of jurisdiction as affirmed by the courts in the 1880s and 1890s and repeatedly reaffirmed by Quebec's political and intellectual elites. As a result, Quebec collects *both* its own personal and corporate income taxes independently of Ottawa and manages many of its own social programs rather than engaging in shared-cost agreements with the federal government.

Persistent demographic realities have shaped the internal and external environments for business-government relations in Quebec. While more than 80 per cent of the province's population is French-speaking, 95 per cent of Quebecers outside the Montreal area are francophones. Almost half of Quebec's population—and virtually all of its English-speaking and immigrant population—live in the Montreal area. Quebec City, major cities such as Saguenay (formerly Chicoutimi and Jonquière), Gatineau, Sherbrooke, and Trois Rivières, and most smaller regional centres are overwhelmingly French-speaking. This concentration of linguistic and ethnic communities in recent years has polarized the political choices between nationalist (or separatist) and federalist parties, with electoral outcomes often determined by the choices of soft nationalist voters. As result, the political and economic interests of these voters have been vital to both federal and provincial politics in Quebec and their impact on economic development policies.

Federal and provincial policies have encouraged the distribution of strong, relatively competitive manufacturing sectors in small-town Quebec, particularly in the Bois-Francs and Estrie regions east of Montreal and the Beauce region south of Quebec City. A diversified manufacturing sector accounts for almost as large a share of employment in Quebec as in Ontario.

Much of Canada's supply-managed agriculture, particularly its dairy and poultry sectors, is located in rural Quebec, particularly in areas between Montreal and Quebec City. Counties with large numbers of dairy farmers were among the relatively few areas of rural Quebec to vote "no" in the 1995 provincial sovereignty referendum. These factors play a significant role in Canada's agricultural trade policies.

The province's northern and far eastern regions, like their counterparts in northern Ontario, Manitoba, and BC, rely heavily on their forest and mining industries and on provincial investments in hydroelectric power development. These regions have higher than average rates of seasonal employment, resulting in chronically high unemployment similar to resource-dependent regions of Atlantic Canada. In recent years, Quebec has negotiated a series of agreements with the James Bay Cree and Inuit peoples to recognize land claims and their role in resource management.

Quebec's political culture since the colonial era has emphasized the central role of distributive politics: the use of political connections to secure favourable economic treatment, particularly the preferential distribution of public works. Before the 1960s, Quebec's economy was dominated by the English-speaking business class of Montreal. French-speaking Quebecers may have been actively engaged in politics, the professions, small-scale commerce, and agriculture, but *les anglais* dominated the commanding heights of industry, banking, and finance. Although Quebec became Canada's second most industrialized province, keeping pace with rapidly growing Ontario (Migué 1998: D5), French-speaking Quebecers were usually relegated to subordinate positions, with average income levels well below those of other Canadians until the 1970s.

The **Quiet Revolution** of the 1960s and 1970s replaced one form of elite accommodation with another. A series of governments greatly expanded the economic role of the state, invested heavily in education and social services, and used their regulatory powers to make French the primary language of business and society. Government spending in Quebec, and the taxes necessary to finance it, became among the highest in Canada. As a result, Quebec has had a strongly corporatist and social democratic political culture under both Liberal and Parti Québécois (PQ) governments. The province's politics have been central to the political and economic calculations of virtually every federal government since the 1960s, most of which have been led by Quebecers or have depended on a large contingent of Quebec MPs for their ability to govern.

The restructuring of Quebec's economy under state guidance has gone through three stages. During the 1960s and 1970s, provincial governments systematically pursued the constitutional and political resources necessary for Quebecers to break off the shackles of what their leaders regarded as political and economic colonialism. They took full control of both its personal and corporate tax systems and insisted on being compensated for opting-out of a series of federal social programs. A rising nationalist politician named René Lévesque nationalized the province's electric power companies in the early 1960s and turned Hydro Québec into an engine for the development of its vast energy resources, fostering large-scale domestic engineering and construction sectors and cultivating a strong public sector managerial elite. Successive Quebec governments set up numerous Crown corporations as instruments of economic development. They encouraged the growth of the *Caisses Populaires* movement as a decentralized alternative to the major chartered banks, particularly in small town and rural Quebec. Perhaps most significantly, by taking control of the newly created Quebec Pension Plan, they enabled the plan's investment managers at the **Caisse de dépot et placement** to become the lynchpin of Quebec's emerging venture capital sector, investing heavily in an emerging Quebec entrepreneurial class (Arbour 1994).

The challenge of Quebec nationalism—sometimes described as profitable federalism—and the election in 1976 of a PQ government committed to Quebec sovereignty, drew Ottawa into a contest of competitive subsidies to persuade ordinary Quebecers that their well-being was linked to Quebec's continued participation in Canada and a strong federal government. The PQ government of 1976-85 substantially expanded the rights of labour unions, mandated that French become the working language of business and employment throughout the province, and continued to expand the province's welfare state.

Both moderate federalists and sovereigntists, including many trade unionists, supported Canada's entry into the FTA in the late 1980s. They saw the agreement as a means of further modernizing and diversifying Quebec's economy and reducing its dependence on Canadian markets and English-Canadian capital. The consolidation of Quebec, Inc. during the 1990s was characterized by the continued growth of provincial business subsidies and tax incentives (Murrell 2001)[3] to promote the development of the province's high technology sector and investments in its more remote areas and a concerted effort by the Caisse de dépot to support Quebec's national champions amid the 1990s wave of mergers and takeovers.

These policies have had a pervasive impact on Quebec's economic structure and on relations among governments, business, and other societal actors. The provincial government dominates the province's capital markets through its regulatory control of Quebec's securities industry and its close political ties to Quebec's French-speaking financial elites. Although the Caisse has shifted towards a more market-driven investment strategy in recent years, the Liberal government of Jean Charest, elected in 2003, has found it difficult to sustain proposals for mildly neo-liberal policy

---

3 Quebec's provincial business subsidies exceeded direct taxes on business in seven of eight years between 1992 and 1999 (Statistics Canada 2002f).

changes in several other fields (Arbour 1994; Yakabuski 1998: B1; Migué 1998; McNish, et al. 2002: B1). **Complementary federalism** has encouraged the concentration of much of Canada's aerospace and pharmaceutical industries around Montreal, as well as the systematic use of federal investment agencies to promote economic development in many areas of the province. In some cases, this activity has been accompanied by revelations of extensive political corruption arising from the efforts of the Liberal federal government to maintain its political standing.

Despite heavy government intervention—or because of it, as some economists suggest (Migué 1998; Crowley and Kelly-Gagnon 2001)—business fixed investment in Quebec averaged 23 per cent below the national average between 1963 and 1999 (Quebec, Ministère des Finances 1999: 21). Some of this investment shortfall is undoubtedly due to political uncertainties resulting from the continued sovereignty debate and to the province's relatively high personal tax rates. However, huge provincial subsidies and targeted tax preferences have given key provincial industries a cost structure that is competitive with other provinces and that is relatively favourable compared with major US cities (KPMG 2002: 37).

Atlantic Canada

The economies of Atlantic Canada have struggled with economic disadvantage and dependency for many years. Although the region's major cities, especially Halifax, are pockets of relative prosperity, overall levels of income, employment, and business investment have lagged behind those in the rest of the country for many years, while regional levels of unemployment and transfer dependence have been consistently well above national averages. Small business formation—a major factor in job creation in the rest of Canada—is significantly below the national average.[4]

These figures reflect, in part, the region's relatively low level of urbanization and its heavy dependence on resource commodities and seasonal industries, particularly outside its major cities (Wallace 2002: 179-96). Atlantic Canada is the least urbanized region of Canada and has the smallest proportion of its economy devoted to manufacturing and goods production, although there are significant differences among individual provinces. Employment in primary sectors is almost double their national share of employment.

Rural New Brunswick has always depended significantly on its forest industries—both lumber and pulp and paper—for employment opportunities. Rural Nova Scotia and Newfoundland and Labrador (hereafter referred to simply as Newfoundland) have significant forest and mining industries, although the latter's fishing and fish processing industry has declined to the point that it generated only 3.5 per cent of the province's employment and GDP in 2000 (Newfoundland and Labrador 2002). An internationally competitive food processing industry, based on the McCain and Irving industrial empires, has been created in New Brunswick, while Newfoundland

---

4 Statistics Canada reports that the distribution of small businesses per 10,000 population is 16 to 25 per cent below the national average in the Atlantic provinces (*Globe and Mail* 1998: B12).

has benefited from rising investments in offshore oil and gas exploration and development in recent years.

Social programs, especially employment insurance, have been designed to support seasonal employment in industries requiring less skilled employees (May and Hollett 1994). However, these programs have often worked to perpetuate the region's economic dependence, maintaining the economic status quo and discouraging entrepreneurship and adaptation to changing economic circumstances (May and Hollett 1994; McMahon 2000a; Wallace 2002: 179-83).

Many policy analysts have pointed to the National Policy as the historical root of Atlantic Canada's economic disadvantages, as it undermined the economic competitiveness of many of the region's industries and gradually contributed to the creation of a culture of economic dependence (Matthews 1983; McMahon 2000a). Although Nova Scotia, in particular, developed strong financial and manufacturing industries during the late nineteenth century, high transportation costs, relatively long distances to markets, and the effects of protectionist federal policies in shifting the focus of economic development westwards contributed to the region's relative economic decline (Savoie 2001: 16-21). Savoie notes that Maritime goods-production dropped from 14 per cent of the Canadian total in 1880 to 9 per cent in 1911 and 5 per cent in 1939 (Savoie 2001: 21). Although federal policies during World War II nurtured the war industries which became a significant element in the renewal of central Canada's postwar manufacturing sector, the economic development of Atlantic Canada lagged significantly until the 1960s (Savoie 2001: 21-28). Ottawa's emphasis on Keynesian demand management during the immediate postwar years did relatively little to promote regional economic development, although McMahon notes that employment and income gaps between the Atlantic region and the rest of Canada began to shrink noticeably during the 1960s (McMahon 2000a). However, the cumulative effect of these trends has been to create a deep suspicion of economic change in much of the political culture of Atlantic Canada and is likely to work to the region's disadvantage.

The significant growth of federal transfers since the 1960s has contributed to higher income levels and more extensive public services than might otherwise have been the case. However, it has also created a level of dependence on government subsidies and transfers which has done as much to undermine as to support economic initiative.

Total government spending in Atlantic Canada is about 50 per cent higher than the country as a whole, as noted in Table 7.7, while, as noted by Murrell and others, the ratio of federal and provincial business subsidies (including those to government business enterprises) to direct business taxes is more than 80 per cent above the national average, although this is still substantially less than in Quebec (Murrell 2001; Statistics Canada 2002f). The cumulative effect of these policies has been a highly politicized economy in which the distribution of economic opportunities is closely linked to the activities of governments in fostering growth or preserving existing industries and employment against the effects of external economic forces or technological change.

Table 7.7: Government Spending, Revenue In Atlantic Provinces, per cent of GDP, 2001

	Provincial Spending	Total Government Spending	Revenue	Net Surplus/ (Transfer) from ROC
Canada	19.1%	37.5%	39.3%	1.7%
NF	30.8%	57.8%	35.3%	- 22.4%
PEI	28.6%	61.2%	41.7%	- 19.5%
NS	22.9%	54.8%	37.7%	- 17.1%
NB	27.0%	53.3%	38.4%	- 14.9%
Atlantic	26.3%	55.3%	37.6%	- 17.7%

Source: Statistics Canada (2004c); author's calculations.

The fishing industry is an example of this challenge. Many communities in coastal Newfoundland, Nova Scotia, and New Brunswick have traditionally depended on fishing and fish processing for their livelihoods. Technological change, the use of widely scattered fish processing plants to support employment in small communities, and generous federal unemployment insurance subsidies contributed to overcapacity, over-fishing, and the gradual depletion of the resource. Although the industry has modernized somewhat in recent years, provincial governments in the region are reluctant to provoke a political backlash from the closure of smaller, less efficient processing plants.

The pursuit of economic diversification has often led to ill-judged economic ventures, initially subsidized by provincial governments, which have turned into costly sinkholes for taxpayers' money. Federal and provincial subsidies to the Cape Breton coal and steel industry preserved employment in the impoverished region for many years but without the managerial or technological changes necessary to make the industry competitive.

The Churchill Falls power project of the 1960s, built by offshore interests with the encouragement of the Newfoundland government, became a symbol of squandered economic opportunities when the province signed a long-term agreement selling much of the project's output to Hydro Québec, thus missing the windfall gains from rising energy prices during the 1970s. These and other failures heavily influenced Newfoundland's decision to link its approval of the huge Voisey's Bay nickel development in northern Labrador to a long-term commitment by Inco to process much of the ore at Argentia on the Avalon peninsula. The political passions aroused by the issue (and cultivated by successive governments) resulted in six years of negotiations before a politically and economically viable deal could be struck (Crowley 2000: A15; Macdonald 2002).

Other provinces have invested heavily in the diversification of their economies, often using Crown corporations or favoured industries as engines of growth. During the 1990s, New Brunswick successfully attracted new business investment by promoting its strong telecommunications system to promote telephone service centres and communications technology industries, reducing regulatory barriers to investment, and engaging in an aggressive program of domestic business promotion (Savoie 2001: 99-104; New Brunswick 2002).

The construction of the Confederation Bridge, an all-weather link to Prince Edward Island, during the 1990s was intended to encourage a more diverse provincial economy. However, PEI remains Canada's poorest province, heavily dependent on primary industries and tourism, with low labour productivity, and higher than average personal and corporate income taxes (Canada 2003).

Some policy analysts have suggested that increased cooperation among the Atlantic provinces in promoting region-wide economic development and the cultivation of new export markets will be a key factor in the region's future growth (Tomblin 2004; Savoie 2004). Others, noting the effect of aging populations and low immigration rates on a declining labour force in the foreseeable future, suggest that governments will need to encourage continued migration to the region's cities to take advantage of these opportunities and sustain existing levels of public services (Crowley 2003).

The North

Canada's northern territories have long existed at the margins of the market economy. The region north of latitude 60 accounts for more than one-third of the country's land mass but only 0.3 per cent of its population—about 93,000 in the 2001 census.

Gold strikes near Dawson City prompted the initial settlement of the Yukon Territory at the end of the nineteenth century, although after the end of the Gold Rush, its population did not regain 1901 levels until the 1990s (Statistics Canada 2002a: 7). The necessity of enforcing and maintaining Canadian sovereignty and occasional efforts to develop mineral resources of the Yukon and Northwest Territories have been the primary impetus for European settlement and business investment in the region.

Yukon's economy is heavily dependent on mining, construction, and government services. The public sector provided 37 per cent of territorial employment in 2000, compared with the national average of 23 per cent. Three-quarters of Yukon's population is located around its capital, Whitehorse (Yukon, Bureau of Statistics 2001).

The economic structure of the Northwest Territories (NWT) is even more heavily weighted towards government services, although the transportation, mining, and retail/wholesale trade sectors also add significantly to employment and economic activity. Diamond mining has replaced oil and gas production as the NWT's largest industry in recent years (Northwest Territories 2001). Agreements with the NWT government have led to the creation of a diamond cutting and polishing industry in Yellowknife (Burleton 2003: 8). Employers in the NWT pay among the highest wages in Canada to compensate for high costs of living and the harsh climate. However, there are significant differences in living standards between those working in the wage economy and many people in Aboriginal communities with a limited economic base.

The Aboriginal people who make up a small majority of the NWT population have largely taken control over its political life. The discovery of large oil reserves on Alaska's north shore in the late 1960s and offshore oil and gas exploration in the Beaufort Sea following the OPEC oil price shocks of the early 1970s prompted discussions of a possible Mackenzie Valley pipeline to carry energy resources to southern markets. These proposals were derailed by the 1977 report of the Berger Commission of Inquiry, which recommended a moratorium on pipeline construction until environmental concerns could be addressed and agreements reached with Aboriginal populations over land claims and economic benefits.

Ongoing negotiations of self-government and land claims agreements with the seven major First Nations groups in the NWT has created a second level of government in the region. These agreements provide for effective Aboriginal control over resource development on their territories. As a result, resource industries and pipeline companies must negotiate both rights of access and economic agreements providing for royalty payments, local employment, and other economic spin-off benefits to each First Nation community related to these developments (Anderson 2002; Burleton 2003: 6-7). In recent years, Aboriginal communities have invested some of the proceeds from these developments in new businesses as they seek not only to capture the economic benefits of resource development, but to create upstream and downstream economic opportunities from these resources. As a result, the Canadian Association of Petroleum Producers estimates that 22 separate federal, territorial, and Aboriginal regulatory agencies had jurisdiction over various aspects of the development of the proposed Mackenzie Valley natural gas pipeline in early 2004, prompting calls for a more streamlined regulatory process. These factors, which involve both significant issues of political and regulatory complexity and coordination, will significantly affect future energy mega-projects (Burleton 2003; Stringham 2004).[5] Federal, territorial, and Aboriginal governments are negotiating a framework agreement to develop responsibility for land and resource management in the NWT. This process involves a complex balancing act in coordinating government policies to achieve shared responsibility for policy development, to promote sustainable economic development, and to ensure that governments receive a net fiscal benefit from resource development sufficient to provide and maintain related infrastructure and other public services (Burleton 2003: 19-26).[6]

---

5 By May 2005, 14 of the 22 agencies had entered into a regulatory cooperation plan in efforts to address these concerns (Vollman 2005).

6 In early 2005, Aboriginal communities demanded that pipeline-related energy firms fund local social services. Business promptly warned that the project could collapse if other levels of government did not take direct responsibility for addressing these disputes, resulting in direct federal intervention.

Following extensive negotiations, the NWT were divided in 1999, with the Inuit majority region of Nunavut becoming a separate territory. Nunavut's population—28,000 in 2001—is widely dispersed across the eastern and northern Arctic. The territory's official economy, both private and public sector, revolves almost entirely around government, with total government spending accounting for 128.6 per cent of GDP in 2001, primarily financed by federal transfers. Even so, the informal (or land-based) economy contributes significantly to the livelihoods of many residents. Oil and gas drilling in the high Arctic has provided the largest source of private eco-nomic activity in recent years, with tourism and arts and crafts following at a dis-tance (Statistics Canada 2004a; Nunavut n.d.). The environmentally sensitive nature of much of the territory and high costs of business operations suggest that Nunavut will be slow to reach economic self-sufficiency and that most business activities will depend on close working relations with governments and Inuit communities.

Conclusion: Federalism, Regionalism, and the Environment for Business-Government Relations

The institutions of federalism have been created to recognize and accommodate regional differences and competing pressures for political accountability, while seek-ing to maintain both the economic and social dimensions of the Canadian union. Both levels of government attempt to maintain a degree of autonomy and flexibility in their respective areas of jurisdiction in order to carry out their commitments to voters. The organization of business interests—discussed further in Chapter 10—parallels the political and regulatory structures governing different industries. As a result, the decentralization of business and other economic interests is very much a by-product of the institutional structures and jurisdictional divisions created by the evolution of federalism.

Industries regulated primarily at the federal level—particularly banks, broadcast-ing and telecommunications industries, and interprovincial transportation sectors—have structured their representative associations at a national level and focus their lobbying activities on the federal government. Major shifts in federal policies—or prolonged policy problems primarily within federal jurisdiction—may also prompt the emergence and growth of new business associations and coalitions. For example, the Canadian Manufacturers' Association (CMA) emerged from late nineteenth-cen-tury efforts to coordinate industry support for protective tariffs and, subsequently, the development of new markets. During the 1990s, Ottawa's commitment to trade liberalization resulted in the CMA's merger with the Canadian Exporters Associa-tion (changing its acronym to CME in the process) and the evolution of other groups such as the Canadian-American Border-Trade Alliance. Similarly, the Canadian Fed-eration of Independent Business (CFIB) was formed in response to proposed federal tax reforms of the early 1970s. Both the CFIB and CME have subsequently set up regional divisions to deal with provincial issues.

These economic interests support strong federal leadership in national economic policies, along with reductions in regulatory and other barriers to interprovincial trade that undermine Canada's national economic union. Labour unions and other social interest groups champion a stronger federal role in social policy, both in establishing national standards for provincial social programs and in expanding federal-provincial transfers, as a counterweight to economic pressures to limit the growth of provincial spending and taxes.

Provincial responsibility for economic development policies and many areas of provincial regulations have spawned a wide range of business groups and other economic associations that monitor and seek to influence their activities. Examples of this form of business organization include chambers of commerce and industry associations representing real estate, trucking, construction, hospitals, doctors, and many other industry and professional groups.[7]

National and regional economic interests often coalesce to mobilize whichever level of government will best serve their purposes. This multiple crack theory of the policy process has numerous examples in recent Canadian history. The bitterness of federal-provincial (and interprovincial) debates over energy taxation during the 1970s and early 1980s was reinforced by industry-government coalitions in both energy-producing and energy-consuming provinces whose vital interests were often diametrically opposed (Simpson 1980; Doern and Toner 1985). A major challenge in Canada's management of the protracted softwood lumber dispute with the US has been to balance and accommodate the widely varying interests of the forest industries of at least six Canadian provinces, which often have different regulatory systems and policy orientations.

Debates over the reduction of interprovincial trade barriers, which prompted lengthy negotiations leading to the signing of the Agreement on Internal Trade in 1995, were complicated by the presence of cross-cutting interests within provincial governments, reflecting both their own institutional interests and competing pressures from sectoral interests within their own economies. The result was a patchwork quilt of agreements, based on principles in existing international trade agreements that preserved considerable provincial regulatory discretion in the accommodation of regional interests while making some reductions in trade barriers (Brown 2002; Hale 2005c).

The politics of federalism and regionalism also interact with structural changes in capital markets. Provincial and resulting federal policy changes during the 1980s triggered the opening of the securities industry to foreign investment and the entry of Canadian chartered banks into investment banking and the marketing of securities. The result has been calls for greater regulatory coordination among provinces from bank-owned securities dealers and even for the wholesale shift of regulatory responsibility to a single national regulator. Provincial governments have responded by increasingly coordinating their activities through interprovincial bodies such as the Canadian Securities Administrators and comparable bodies in the insurance

---

7 Coleman (1988) notes that these groups tend to be organized as federations rather than unitary groups.

and pension sectors. However, Quebec and other provinces have resisted the creation of a national securities regulator, based in Ottawa or Toronto, to ensure their capacity to maintain a regulatory environment supportive of regional industries, particularly Canada's highly regionalized market for smaller publicly traded companies (Carpentier and Suret 2003; Melchin 2004: FP19; Hale and Kukucha 2006).

Another frequent outcome of policy fragmentation is competitive rent-seeking, either through regulatory preferences or government subsidies by interest groups, to promote economic development or protect vulnerable sectors from competition. Rent-seeking has been facilitated in the past by organizing government bureaucracies on a sectoral basis to mirror the composition of major stakeholder groups, as noted in Chapter 6. Rent-seeking may also manifest itself at a provincial level when provinces compete to attract particular industries with targeted subsidies or tax reductions, which are then usually financed by less mobile businesses and taxpayers.

These challenges contribute to both the complexity and the dynamism of state-society relations as new political coalitions—both within and across provincial boundaries—emerge to contest the status quo or seek greater accommodation within the political system. Canada's growing integration within North America, and to a lesser extent within the global economic system, adds one more dimension to the balancing of regional, societal, and economic interests in government policy. This component of Canada's economic structure is the main focus of Chapter 8.

Key Terms and Concepts for Review (see Glossary)

Agreement on Internal Trade	federal spending power
Caisse de dépot et placement	Quiet Revolution
complementary federalism	regional ministers
economic union	regionalism
executive federalism	societal federalism
federalism	

Questions for Discussion and Review

1. What is the difference between federalism and regionalism? What major factors have helped to make Canada one of the most decentralized federations in the world? How have the constitutional and political structures of federalism shaped the context for business-government relations in Canada?

2. How do regionalism and the decentralization of fiscal and economic power within Canada affect the environment for business-government relations? To what extent do these effects vary by province or region?

3. What is the difference between regional differences and regional disparities? What are three different political strategies for promoting regional economic

interests through the political system? Which strategies have been prevalent in which provinces during the past 25 years?

4. BC and Alberta both evolved as resource-based economies whose development was financed largely by foreign capital. Explain the major differences in the political and economic environments of the two provinces. Does it still make sense to describe the prairie provinces as a cohesive economic region? Why or why not?

5. To what extent is central Canada an economic region or a collection of regions? What are the major similarities and differences between the economies of Ontario and Quebec? What implications have these differences had on their attitudes towards regionalism? Towards government?

6. What are major reasons for Atlantic Canada's relative economic underdevelopment and dependence? To what extent do they reflect a mixture of broader structural economic factors, national policy decisions, and regional responses?

Suggestions for Further Readings

Arbour, Pierre. 1994. *Quebec Inc. and the temptation of state capitalism*. Montreal: Robert Davies.

Bakvis, Herman, and Grace Skogstad (Eds.). 2001. *Canadian federalism: performance, effectiveness, and legitimacy*. Toronto: Oxford University Press.

Canada West Foundation. 2001. *Building the new west: a framework for regional economic prosperity*. Calgary: Canada West Foundation (October).

Courchene, Thomas J. with Colin Telmer. 1998. *From heartland to North American region state*. Toronto: Faculty of Management, University of Toronto.

McMahon, Fred. 2000. *Retreat from Growth*. Halifax: Atlantic Institute for Market Studies.

Ontario, Institute for Competitiveness and Prosperity. 2002. *A view of Ontario: Ontario's clusters of innovation*. Toronto: Ministry of Entrepreneurship, Opportunity and Innovation (April).

Savoie, Donald J. 2001. *Pulling against gravity: economic development in New Brunswick during the McKenna Years*. Montreal: IRPP.

Simeon, Richard, and Ian Robinson. 1990. *State, society and the development of Canadian federalism*. Royal Commission on the Economic Union and Development Prospects for Canada. Background Paper #71. Toronto: University of Toronto Press.

Stevenson, Garth. 1993. *Ex uno plures: federal-provincial relations in Canada: 1867-1896*. Montreal and Kingston: McGill-Queen's University Press.

Tomblin, Stephen G., and Charles S. Colgin (Eds.). 2004. *Regionalism in a global society: persistence and change in Atlantic Canada and New England*. Peterborough, ON: Broadview Press.

CHAPTER 8

Business, Government, and the North American and Global Economies

The politics of economic policy—or of business-government relations—in Canada have never taken place in a cocoon isolated from or unrelated to international economic forces or political events. The interrelationship of national, regional,[1] and international economic structures varies with the degree to which particular industry sectors depend on foreign markets for goods and services produced in Canada (or vice versa), for access to improved technologies, or for the investment capital necessary to finance the development of domestic industries.

But more and more in recent years, the environment for Canadian businesses—and their relations with governments—are being influenced by events beyond Canada's borders and by the skill, creativity, and adaptability with which Canadians in business, government, and other sectors anticipate and respond to these trends and events. A few examples may help to bring these realities into context.

1. On September 11, 2001, three airliners crash into targets in New York City and Washington, DC, killing more than 3,000 people. The next day—and for weeks to come—security clampdowns at the US border leave thousands of Canadians facing long lineups at airports and border crossings. Thousands of trucks carrying billions of dollars of Canadian exports idle on roads and highways in queues stretching for miles back from the border. Workers in auto plants are laid off in large numbers. Business groups, seeing ready access to their largest export market endangered, press federal and provincial governments insistently to consider a comprehensive review of their political, economic, and security relations with the US as a key element in Canada's economic security. Five years later, governments in Ottawa and Washington—and tens of thousands of Canadian businesses—are still adapting to the new realities.

2. Lower inflation rates in Canada and much of the industrial world result in sharply lower interest rates during the 1990s. This contributes to rapid business growth, leading millions of Canadians and Americans to shift their savings into other kinds of investments such as stocks and mutual funds, fostering a stock market boom through much of that decade. The boom prompts the development of many creative new financial techniques, some of them less than honest. When stock markets drop

---

1 To reduce confusion, the term "regional" in this chapter refers to domestic subnational regions within each country. "Continental" or "cross-border" will refer to regional economic zones crossing national boundaries, such as NAFTA, the European Community, Asia-Pacific Economic Cooperation (APEC), and Mercosur (Argentina, Brazil, Paraguay, Uruguay, and Venezuela).

sharply after 2000, regulators scramble to catch up, and large investors demand major changes in corporate governance. Having listed their shares on US and other foreign markets during the boom, 70 per cent of Canada's biggest corporations are directly affected by new US laws. But how should Canada's provincial securities regulators respond, especially as 80 per cent of companies listed on Canadian markets are too small to qualify for listings on US markets?

3. After years of relative political and economic isolation, China signs a series of economic agreements culminating in its admission to the **World Trade Organization** (WTO). International investment accelerates. Hundreds of millions of Chinese workers and consumers expand their participation in the market economy, hugely increasing inexpensive Chinese exports to the rest of the industrial world. This creates a huge competitive challenge for businesses around the world, while changing the buying patterns of millions of consumers across North America. Rapidly growing Chinese demand for raw materials (paralleled by India and other emerging economies) drives up global commodity prices, especially for oil and natural gas, triggering a boom in western Canadian resource industries. These trends, combined with growing political risks in many developing countries, also prompt Canadian firms to sell off many of their foreign resource holdings, often to state-owned firms from India and China, and to focus their activities on countries (like Canada) with more stable and transparent legal and political systems (Callaway 2002; Jones 2005; Cattaneo 2005). However, they also raise questions about how Canadian governments should respond to agents of foreign governments seeking to gain control over Canada's natural resources and the implications of their responses for Canadian firms doing business in those countries.

These events and trends—and many others reported daily by the financial media—underline Canada's deep economic interdependence with both the US and the larger global economic system. They speak not only to the dynamic responses of innumerable businesses and individuals through the processes of market economies, but also to the economic and social roles of government in sometimes guiding the forces that shape the international economic system, sometimes responding to these forces and assisting Canadians to adapt to seemingly endless waves of economic competition and change. They directly address the concepts of **sovereignty**—the capacity of governments to choose among potentially viable policy options to pursue economic, social, and political goals valued by their citizens—and of interdependence: the reality that the actions of governments, businesses, and other social groups in one country affect and are affected by those of other countries with which they have extensive economic and social relationships. The effects of interdependence are magnified by the pervasive role of international trade and investment in the Canadian economy not only for large corporations or financial institutions, but for the workers, consumers, savers, and investors whose economic opportunities and well-being are linked to these trends directly or indirectly by the effects of economic **globalization** and progressive North American integration.

This chapter examines the different approaches of Canadian governments to balancing domestic and international considerations in framing their economic policies. It reviews the growing interdependence of Canada's economy with those of the US and the wider international economy and considers both the interaction of these trends on Canadian federalism and varied regional interests and their effects on business-government relations. As part of this analysis, it also reviews debates over the options available to Canadian governments in managing market-driven trends towards increased North American economic integration, the evolving impact of foreign investment on Canada's economy and business-government relations, and the ways in which the challenges of promoting competitiveness shape government policies and interaction with business in different contexts.

Economic Interdependence and the Politics of Intermesticity: National Economic Structures and International Economic Networks

Canadian governments have always played a variety of roles in mediating relations between domestic economic and social interests and the international economic system, as noted in Chapter 4. However, several major factors have contributed to the growing interdependence with the economies of its North American neighbours, especially the US, and the broader international economic system.

During the 1980s, most Canadian governments and businesses came to recognize that relatively small countries like Canada could not stand aside from aspects of economic globalization such as global trends towards the liberalization of trade and investment flows, the effects of technological change on production systems and distribution networks, and the resulting pressures of international competition on domestic industries. They also recognized Canada's vulnerability both to the emergence of regional trading blocs in Europe and Asia and the periodic risks of protectionism in the US which then, as now, is the principal market for Canada's exports.

These trends have blurred the distinctions between domestic and international politics and policies in many areas (for example, see Doern, Pal, and Tomlin 1996; Watson 1998; and Rosenau 2003). They have helped to redefine the context for government policies, the ways that governments think about traditional political concepts such as sovereignty, and the mix of policies used to foster increased business competitiveness in a rapidly changing economic environment. Canadian governments have sought in many ways to adapt to the pressures of globalization while preserving their capacity for meaningful policy choices.

Balancing Globalization and the Maintenance of Policy Discretion

Globalization and continental economic integration have forced most governments of major industrial economies to pursue new economic strategies to promote more traditional objectives of economic development, economic stabilization, and social cohesion. Hoberg has noted that globalization may function in at least three different dimensions—economic, cultural, and political—with differing degrees of integration visible from country to country and one policy sector to another (Hoberg 2000; Hoberg 2002). This continuum of policy options and choices is summarized in Box 8.1.

Box 8.1: The Continuum for International Integration

National Policies Unrelated	Sphere	National Policies Fully Integrated
←——→		
No international exchanges (autarky) (closest example: North Korea).	**Economic**	Common currency; common market; economic transactions a function of size, distance (no border effects) (closest example: European Union).
←——→		
Distinctive National Values • limited influence of Western or other regional influences in national culture.	**Cultural**	Shared values resulting from assimilation or some other form of dominant external cultural influence.
←——→		
Autonomous nation states; distinctive policies reflecting domestic conditions with few, if any, international constraints.	**Political**	All relevant decision-making transferred to supranational authority, or, if there is a continued division of powers, nation-states get full political representation in supranational bodies; uniform policies imposed from without.

Source: adapted from Hoberg 2002: 9.

Canadian governments have consistently attempted to compartmentalize these debates by dealing with them in separate contexts. As noted in the 2002 report of the Commons Foreign Affairs Committee, "every international relation that is not hostile, subservient or purely unilateralist implies some sharing or pooling of sovereignty for mutually agreed purposes" (Canada, Standing Committee on Foreign Affairs and International Trade 2002: 18). The political challenge lies in coming to agreement on these purposes and the most effective ways of achieving them. The result is often a decentralized approach to policy-making in which functional or line government departments address the overlap between international and domestic—hence, "intermestic"—issues in specialized policy communities (Hale 2003; Higginbotham and Heynen 2005).

The efforts of Canadian governments to maintain their discretion in international political and economic relations have centred on two basic strategies. First, Canada has always attempted to balance its bilateral diplomatic, economic, and military dealings with the US with the pursuit of similar or complementary goals in multilateral organizations. In recent years, these have included the United Nations, the North Atlantic Treaty Organization (NATO), the WTO, and the multilateral environmental policy processes that led to the signing of the Kyoto Protocol.

A second major strategy, particularly in international trade and environmental negotiations, has been to emphasize the principle of non-discrimination in the application of national laws to citizens of participating countries: the **national treatment** principle. Although this approach rejects economic nationalism as a central principle of economic policy, it provides for extensive national discretion in the application of national (or provincial) government rules as long as these are not designed in ways that apply different legal standards to nationals and non-nationals. This approach, which Scharpf, MacDonald, and others describe as **negative integration**, stands in sharp contrast to **positive integration**: the harmonization of laws, policies, and regulatory regimes in different jurisdictions based on the imposition of a central set of rules across territorial boundaries, with limited exemptions and exceptions. Schwanen suggests that the concept of "interoperability" involves a wide range of options involving different combinations of "positive" and "negative" integration (Scharpf 1997a; MacDonald 2001: 139; Schwanen 2001: 46-49; Schwanen 2003: 12-19).

These techniques have been described as elements of a two-level game in which national governments attempt to combine the pursuit of shared interests and economic opportunities in dealings with other countries with the balancing of competing domestic interests and the preservation of some degree of political and policy discretion (Milner 1997; Cameron and Tomlin 2000).

In some cases, such games may involve a degree of mutual recognition and other practices related to negative integration that allow governments to pursue broadly shared objectives in different ways, subject to agreements not to discriminate against one another's nationals, or to accept the validity of one another's practices within agreed boundaries. For example, elements of **NAFTA** allow for broad variations of environmental rules between countries, as long as they are applied consistently to businesses from all NAFTA countries and are not used as instruments of trade protection.

In other cases, national governments may use international negotiations and treaties as ways of disciplining political or policy demands from particular economic or social interests so that they can pursue desired policy priorities while shifting some of the political blame to outside interests. Some of the implications of these policies have already been discussed in Chapter 5.

Such agreements usually provide for reductions in subsidies or limits on preferences for domestic producers in return for increased access for export-oriented industries. However, they may also provide for stronger legal safeguards for due process in the distribution of economic benefits by governments or require compensation if government policies arbitrarily impinge on existing contractual or property rights. For example, the power of the Canadian International Trade Tribunal has grown dramatically under FTA and NAFTA, forcing federal public servants to pay far closer attention to due process in awarding contracts or face greatly increased risks of litigation (and public exposure) from disappointed bidders (Allen 2005; see also *Attorney General of Canada v. George College of Applied Arts and Technology*, 2004 FCA 285).

These policy approaches, combined with the effects of geographic proximity and market forces, have contributed substantially to the growth of Canada's economic interdependence with other countries, particularly the US, and the growing complexity of the decentralized economic and administrative networks through which this interdependence is expressed.

Interdependence by the Numbers

Canada's growing economic interdependence with other countries in the international economic system is reflected in its large volume of trade with the rest of the world (and the distribution of that trade inside and outside North America), the international involvement of Canadian businesses and capital markets, and the many institutional linkages created to provide a stable but adaptable legal framework for business activity within this dynamic environment. As such, it involves not only involves markets for goods, services, and capital, but also the integration and interdependence of production facilities, transportation and distribution systems, and related public goods such as infrastructure and education systems.

Table 8.1: Indicators of Economic Openness (per cent of GDP)

	Exports of Goods and Services			Stock of Foreign Investment (Inbound)		
	1989	1997	2003	1989	1997	2003
Canada	25.4	39.2	37.7	18.6	22.0	29.3
Germany	26.0	24.9	36.0	6.2	9.1	22.8
France	21.4	26.8	29.2	6.7	13.9	24.7
United Kingdom	23.6	28.6	24.7	17.9	19.1	37.4
Italy	18.3	27.2	24.4	5.7	7.0	11.8
Japan	10.5	11.1	12.2	0.3	0.6	2.1
United States	8.9	11.2	9.3	6.8	8.3	14.1
G-7 Total	14.3	16.9	na	6.3	8.2	na

* maximum1989-2002 16.9 (1997)   14.9 (2002)
* minimum 1989-2001 14.7 (1999)   6.6 (1993)
Source: Canada 2005: Table 1B.

International trade accounts for a larger share of economic activity in Canada than in any other major industrial economy. In 2004, 38.1 per cent of Canada's domestic income was earned from exports, an increase of almost half from 1989, the year the FTA took effect, although it was below the peak year of 2001. Between

1998 and 2002, all Canadian provinces except Manitoba exported more to foreign countries, mainly the US, than to other Canadian provinces, although the degree of export dependence and diversification varied widely from one part of Canada to another (International Trade Canada 2005: 6; Byrd and Genereux 2004). Among other G-7 nations, only Germany approaches Canada in its relative dependence on trade (see Table 8.1).

More than 40 per cent of these exports are the product of intra-corporate trade: exchanges among divisions of multinational and transnational corporations based in Canada and elsewhere. As much as one-third of Canadian exports are composed of components imported from other countries (Cross 2002a). These patterns reflect dense networks of business relationships within North America and, to lesser degrees, with the rest of the world. They also cushion much of Canada's manufacturing sector against fluctuations in exchange rates and economic activity, such as the sharp rise in the value of the Canadian dollar since 2002.

As a result, the growth of trade has been accompanied by the substantial growth of foreign investment both by Canadian companies and investors in the US and elsewhere and by foreign companies in Canada. The value of **Canadian direct investment abroad**—controlling investments in foreign business operations by Canadian firms—has more than doubled from 15.9 per cent of GDP in 1992 to 34.0 per cent of GDP in 2004. During the same period, **foreign direct investment** in Canada has increased from 19.3 per cent to 28.3 per cent of GDP (International Trade Canada 2005). **Portfolio investment** abroad—the purchase of foreign stocks and bonds by individuals, mutual and pension funds, and other institutional investors—has also increased rapidly since the early 1990s.

These trends have three major sets of implications. First, growing economic integration, particularly within North America, has meant that trade and investment increasingly reinforce one another. Rugman and others have noted that there is a close relationship between Canadian direct investment abroad and the likelihood that Canadian companies and their workers will derive a major part of their earnings from export sales. Canadian investors now receive more in dividends from abroad than foreign investors receive from their investments in Canada (Rugman 2000; Cardillo 2002; Hejazi and Pauly 2002; Cross 2002b).

Secondly, the expansion of Canada's international economic interests means that Canadian policies towards international trade and investment are increasingly shaped by the interests of Canadian businesses and investors in receiving equitable treatment in foreign markets as much as by domestic political or economic considerations. For example, the federal government's handling of the long-running dispute with the US over the harassment of Canadian softwood lumber exports is shaped by three major factors: the need to maintain a common front among disparate regional interests *within* Canada, the avoidance of retaliatory measures that would hurt Canadian businesses and workers in other industries as much or more than their US counterparts, and the need to abide by WTO rules governing such disputes to avoid providing grounds for legal or political retaliation on other fronts.

Thirdly, as indicated by these examples, continuing trends towards **North American economic integration**—the growing interdependence of businesses, investors, workers, and consumers on flows of goods, services, capital, and technology within North America—has vastly increased the importance and complexity of managing relations between Canada and the US. The US accounted for 78.7 per cent of Canada's exports of goods and services and 66.9 per cent of total imports in 2004. Studies of corporate activity by Rugman and Moore indicate that most major multinational corporations (MNCs) are regional rather than global, with a sizeable majority of sales concentrated within one of three major regional trading blocs: North America, Europe, and the Asia-Pacific region. Of the 16 Canadian-based MNCs listed in the 2002 edition of the Fortune 500, only five—Alcan, Nortel, Bombardier, Onex, and Magna—could be said to be global firms by virtue of generating more than 30 per cent of their revenues outside North America (Rugman 2000; Moore and Rugman 2003: 45). (See Table 8.2.)

Political, economic, and technological shocks in the US—ranging from intense concerns over security issues in the aftermath of the 9/11 terrorist bombings, to US efforts to manage its dependence on foreign energy sources, to sweeping changes to rules governing capital markets following the corporate governance scandals in 2000-02, to cross-border spillovers of major power failures and gasoline shortages in recent years—can often have significant effects on Canadian businesses and the policy-making environments for Canadian governments (Whitaker 2005; Gattinger 2005). So do parallel trends in US-Mexico relations which, magnified by the growing influence of "Sun Belt" states in US politics and the political influence of 20 million Mexican-Americans, are playing an increasingly important role in the politics of North American integration (Andreas and Bierstecker 2003; Manley, Aspe, and Weld 2005). The cumulative effect of these trends has put a premium on the management of Canada's growing interdependence with other countries, particularly the US.

Table 8.2: Intraregional Trade as a Share of Total Two-Way Trade (per cent)

	European Union	North America	East Asia
1980	53.2	32.6	28.8
1990	60.6	42.8	35.0
1999	61.7	54.6	39.1

Source: Pastor 2001.

However, the day-to-day realities of interdependence take place within a broader framework of international political economy that both helps to shape the context for these issues and frames the complex networks of relationships through which domestic economic systems interact with broader continental and global economic systems.

Interdependence and the Politics of International Trade and Investment

The debate over globalization takes place on a number of **levels of analysis**: the relationship of individual national states to the international political and economic system, the role of trade and investment regimes and policies in fostering citizens' economic well-being, and the direct and indirect effects of these policies in shaping and limiting policy choices in particular policy fields. We will now look at the evolution of international governance and regulatory systems for trade and investment and the ways in which these processes have shaped the interaction among federal and provincial governments, business interests, and other societal interests.

A number of factors may contribute to **policy convergence**—the tendency of policies in different jurisdictions to display increased similarity—and the development of both formal and informal transnational structures for policy coordination. Governments may face parallel domestic political or economic pressures that lead them to seek policy coordination with neighbouring states. For example, rising inflation levels during the 1970s led to increased and ongoing consultation and cooperation among the central bankers and finance ministers of major industrial states. Even though capital markets are subject to widely varying national (and in Canada, provincial) regulations, regulators meet frequently to develop common technical standards in response to the growing mobility of capital and, sometimes, to coordinate enforcement activities.

Box 8.2: Factors Contributing to International Policy Convergence

- parallel domestic pressures
- international political agreements
- emulation
- international economic integration

Source: Hoberg, Banting, and Simeon 2002.

The political or economic effectiveness of policy innovations in one country may also lead to emulation by other countries. Policy parallelism may result from government initiatives, political initiatives by opposition parties campaigning for election, or interest group campaigns (including those led by business) to seek market opportunities or regulatory changes similar to those enjoyed by their competitors in other countries. For example, the **demonstration effects** of Britain's initiative in financial sector deregulation, trucking deregulation in the US, changes in telecommunications regulations and tax reform initiatives in several industrial countries all resulted in partial or general changes to Canadian government policies during the 1980s and 1990s. Policy emulation can also lead to the growth of regulation, as with Kyoto-inspired initiatives to limit CO_2 emissions and recent changes to corporate governance practices in response to the Sarbanes-Oxley (SOX) legislation in the US.

Growing international economic integration may lead governments to seek bilateral or multilateral economic agreements in order to preserve their capacity to pursue more effective economic policies and to regulate the negative externalities resulting from technological and other economic changes (Coleman and Perl 1999). Canada has signed many such agreements over the years. These include:

- sector-specific arrangements, such as the Canada-US Auto Pact of 1965, which responded to efforts by North American auto makers to rationalize their operations on both sides of the border and make them more efficient;
- policy-specific arrangements, such as Canada's bilateral or multilateral environmental agreements or its more than 90 bilateral tax treaties with other countries, designed to avoid the double taxation of business and personal income and thus facilitating trade, investment, and the movement of their citizens between countries;
- general economic agreements such as the FTA, NAFTA, or the Uruguay Round of the General Agreement on Trade and Tariffs (GATT) which led to the creation of the WTO.

Governments may also initiate international political agreements to deal with broader concerns that have significant economic impact, such as efforts to contain the spread and use of dangerous or addictive substances, to police international criminal activity, to encourage the conservation of species and other environmental initiatives, and to promote collective security among nations. For example, Canada's work at the United Nations to regulate the international trade in conflict diamonds directly affects the marketing efforts of the north's growing diamond industry. Initiatives such as the Ottawa Convention banning the production and distribution of land mines may also result from the efforts of transnational citizens' groups.

These agreements also include a wide range of less formal arrangements ranging from protocols interpreting existing agreements and Memoranda of Understanding (MOUs) to mutual recognition agreements by which two countries rely on each other's regulatory systems to some degree on issues ranging from the review of educational credentials to the administration of environmental or securities rules affecting some aspect of cross-border relations (Higginbotham and Heynen 2005: 132).

The institutional and regulatory systems that result from these agreements are known as **regimes.** Just as the political constitutions of individual countries define the extent and limits of governmental powers and establish broad frameworks of rules to govern and empower citizens and businesses in dealings with one another and with governments, cooperation among governments through international treaties and agreements increasingly shape the economic constitutions that guide and channel the actions of citizens, businesses, states, and international organizations. Regulatory regimes coexist at national, international, regional, and sectoral levels, with the latter affecting particular policy areas and industry sectors (Doern, Hill, Prince, and Schultz, eds. 1999: 3-26). Rather than forming a world government, international economic regimes are shaped by a series of special purpose bodies established by groups of states (sometimes by the United Nations) to address specific issues of policy coordination.

This process—sometimes described as multilevel governance or governance without government (Doern and Johnson 2006; Held et al. 1999: 52)—places a premium on shared norms and intellectual frameworks (or paradigms) for policy development among member countries. It also requires significant effort for national governments to build and maintain a consensus among policy elites and interest group stakeholders about the principles and policy objectives that should guide international cooperation through these organizations. Failure to do so, or a lack of transparency in the processes surrounding their activities, may breed popular discontent, political challenges, and, at the margin, the spread of conspiracy theories that feed on popular suspicion of elites.

Interdependence: Governmental and Societal Networks

The capacity of Canadian governments to design effective economic policies under such circumstances is also linked to their ability to work effectively within the specialized bilateral or international networks of policy-makers, usually organized on a sectoral basis. The involvement of senior and mid-ranking government officials with organizations such as the International Monetary Fund (IMF), the Organization for Economic Development (OECD), the International Organization of Securities Commissions (IOSCO), and a host of others provide opportunities for international cooperation and for the exchange of information and ideas within an international economic system characterized by a relatively high degree of decentralization.

Less formally, these networks often take the form of bilateral or multilateral working or advisory groups dealing with specific policy issues, personnel exchanges or secondments between governments, and joint planning or training exercises on issues or activities that may require greater cross-border or international cooperation in future (Kahler and Lake 2003; Hanson, Honahan, and Majnoni 2003; Higginbotham and Heynen 2005: 123-40). Such networks may also result in the development of international stakeholder advisory groups, composed of widely varying mixtures of business, professional, and non-governmental organizations (NGOs). International and cross-border effects on regional interests are also contributing to increased provincial engagement with such networks, particularly regular cross-border meetings of provincial premiers and state governors, provincial and state legislators, and varied private sector and other non-governmental interests (Tomblin and Colgan 2003; Sada and Hale 2003).

As noted in Chapters 8 and 10, the structures of intergovernmental or international institutions also affect the activities of business and societal groups including unions and social and environmental activists. The technological revolution of the 1990s, particularly the spread of the Internet, has encouraged a wide range of transnational coalitions to monitor and challenge the activities of both governments and businesses. In some cases, these pressures have prompted multinational firms to become more proactive in addressing social and environmental concerns under the umbrella of corporate social responsibility. In others, it has led to disinvestment in countries with poor human rights records or to the introduction of meliorative business practices in efforts to mitigate cultures of political corruption and foster increased opportunities for local networks of suppliers.

Economic liberalization and globalization have not resulted in a uniform global marketplace, as feared by some, but in the evolution of regional or continental economic systems whose effective operation depends on the cooperation of national states and, in Canada's case, of provincial governments as well. Borders still matter, both in structuring consumer and investment decisions and in shaping differences in cultural identities, legal systems, economic relationships, and political and policy choices (Watson 1998; Helliwell 2000; Hoberg 2000; Hoberg 2002).

North American Integration: Implications for Governments, Businesses, and Policy Development

The Canadian government's decision to institutionalize its commitment to free trade and economic integration in North America through FTA and NAFTA has made the jobs and businesses of its manufacturing and other goods-producing sectors overwhelmingly dependent on access to US markets, although Canada's export markets have diversified somewhat in recent years.

This reality heavily influences the political and lobbying priorities of major Canadian business associations. Extensive investments by Canadian firms in the US have often contributed to the development of coordinated lobbying strategies, which seek to harmonize technical rules and standards on both sides of the border and promote cooperative action by national governments in meeting common external threats. Sectoral examples include cross-border cooperation by steel producers in each country, the efforts of cattle producers and meat packers to develop common standards to allow the reopening of the US border to Canadian cattle and packaged beef exports after the discovery of isolated cases of BSE in Canadian herds in 2003, and the significant public relations efforts of Canadian energy producers in recent years. However, policy disputes between competing economic and social interests—for example, those between brand name and generic drug manufacturers in Canada over patent protection, supporters and opponents of licensing satellite television and radio stations, Aboriginal groups and public utilities over land claims and environmental practices, and a host of others—can also spill over into cross-border disputes, pitting competing coalitions of interests against one another.

As a result, in the absence of overarching political or policy challenges that force governments to take a more coordinated approach, these issues tend to be managed on a highly decentralized basis in each country (Clancy 2004; Hale 2003; Higginbotham and Heynen 2005). Cross-border trade conflicts are most visible in sectors, particularly agricultural and resource industries, with disproportionate numbers of small domestic producers, especially in the US.

Political shocks, such as the border slowdown prompted by the US reaction to the 9/11 terrorist bombings or the US government's disregard of repeated rulings by NAFTA dispute resolution panels on the protracted softwood lumber dispute, are more likely to promote a more coordinated approach, either prompted by business

pressures or initiated by governments. In the former case, four major Canadian business associations pulled together a coalition of more than 50 business groups to
develop a coordinated approach to managing border security issues over several
years. Their efforts contributed significantly to the development and implementation of the 30-point Smart Border Accord to facilitate the efficient passage of low-
risk goods and travelers across the Canada-US border and to similar arrangements
on the US-Mexico border. They also convinced senior federal officials of the need
for a more coordinated approach to managing Canada-US relations that has led to
significant organizational changes within the federal government in recent years
(Coalition for Secure and Trade-Efficient Borders 2001; Canada, Department of Foreign Affairs 2001; Andreas and Bierstecker 2003; Hale 2005b).

Although major business groups—particularly the Canadian Council of Chief
Executives—have sought to promote a "Grand Bargain" for the broadening and
deepening of North American institutions in response to these concerns and as part
of a broader strategy to foster the competitiveness of Canadian businesses (Dobson
2002; D'Aquino 2005), their strategic agenda has had far less appeal to Canadian governments than a more incremental agenda dealing with day-to-day business issues.
The Security and Prosperity Initiative of March 2005, which provided for the creation
of 23 sector committees to examine ways of rationalizing regulations and facilitating
the efficient passage of low-risk goods and travelers across North American borders,
is a joint effort by the US, Canada, and Mexico to institutionalize the management
of these issues through a series of cross-border working groups (Hale 2003; Hale
2005b; NAFTA Secretariat 2005).

Canada's international economic policies must also balance the importance of
US markets and economic influence with the need to diversify its own trade and
investments with other countries, particularly in the Western Hemisphere and
Pacific Rim. Its parallel at the political level is the federal government attempt to
balance multilateral trade negotiations to maintain an open international trading
system with the ongoing discussions with the US and Mexico noted above.

The development of continental and international trading systems—and cross-
cutting domestic pressures for governments to maintain some degree of domestic
political and policy discretion—increase the political importance of policies to assist
both citizens and businesses to adapt to ongoing economic changes. Such policies
often take the form of encouraging research and innovation, fostering increased
access to education, and reducing regulatory barriers to mobility and trade within
Canada. However, the traditional leadership roles of provincial governments in
many of these fields create new challenges for federal-provincial relations and for
the balancing of regional, national, and transnational interests in a growing number
of policy sectors (Hale 2004; Hale 2005a: 145-62).

However, economic integration often creates countervailing reactions, sometimes described as "fragmegration" (Rosenau 2003: 11)—the simultaneous processes
of social and market integration and fragmentation—as regional economic and
social interests seek to assert their particular identities and interests within (and

sometimes against) broader economic and political systems. In a Canadian context, the politics of fragmegration reflect both competition among economic sectors, based on variations in the nature and extent of their exposure to international competition, and the different ways in which the politics of federalism and regionalism overlap with the internationalization of Canadian economic policies. Simeon and others have noted the persistence of federalism as a key factor constraining the effects of globalization on Canadian public policies and institutions (Simeon 2003; for European parallels, see VanHouten 2003).

The decentralization of Canadian federalism since the mid-1980s, particularly in fiscal and economic policies, may have made it easier for provincial governments and interests to develop more specialized regional strategies when adapting to North American integration, thus helping to reduce regional tensions within Canada. Examples include New Brunswick's systematic cultivation of cross-border relationships with New England, Alberta and BC's efforts to foster broader public and private sector networks through a Pacific Northwest Economic Region, and the emergence of major regional variations in cross-border energy relations during the 1990s (Doern and Gattinger 2003; Hale 2005a).

However, the persistence of distinct regional interests, which are often expressed through strong provincial governments, has also limited the extent to which major federal or corporate interests can impose uniform national policies or use ongoing economic integration to accelerate regulatory harmonization. For example, although some provinces have reduced business taxes in recent years in efforts to compete for investment or to make their business sectors more competitive, provincial fiscal and tax policies tend to be far more reflective of local political conditions than external economic pressures (Hale 2001b; Hale 2006a; Mintz, et al. 2005). Efforts to achieve regulatory streamlining or harmonization within Canada, such as the Agreement on Internal Trade (AIT) and provincial efforts to negotiate mutual recognition agreements (the passport system) in securities regulation, reflect the principles and patterns of negative integration discussed earlier.

The AIT, which took effect in 1995, was intended to reduce internal barriers to trade and mobility between provinces; it has done so to a degree, particularly in the area of labour mobility. However, provinces have used language similar to that in other trade agreements to carve out significant exceptions in order to protect entrenched regional and governmental interests (Brown 2002: 162-72). Despite the globalization of capital markets and regulatory changes that allowed Canada's major banks to acquire control of much of its securities industry since the mid-1980s, provincial governments have effectively resisted efforts by both federal and major corporate interests to introduce a uniform national system of securities regulation by citing differences in regional capital markets as well as philosophical differences among regulators (Hale and Kukucha 2005). Canadian energy firms' heavy dependence on exports, particularly to US markets, has contributed significantly to considerable policy convergence between the two countries. However, the provincial ownership of natural resources, combined with the very different political and regulatory agendas of provincial governments, has largely precluded either large-scale regulatory har-monization or the development of a new national energy strategy as suggested by some major sectoral interest groups (Doern and Gattinger 2003; Hale 2005a).

These examples, and many more, demonstrate the challenges of policy coordina-tion in circumstances requiring the collaboration of different governments and levels of government. They also reflect the continued ability of social and economic interests to secure recognition and protection of their interests from governments in spite of continuing trends towards economic globalization and North American integration.

The Economics and Politics of Foreign Investment
and Canadian Direct Investment Abroad

Canada has always depended on foreign capital for the development of its economy, as previously discussed in Chapter 4. Foreign direct investment has been a major source of investment capital and management and technological expertise for the develop-ment of many sectors of the Canadian economy. Guillemette and Mintz (2004) note three major types of foreign direct investment: acquisitions of existing business assets in another country; reinvestments of earnings by foreign subsidiaries; and other capi-tal inflows, primarily loans from parent firms to their foreign subsidiaries.

Foreign investments in Canadian resource and manufacturing industries dur-ing the 1950s and 1960s helped to reinforce the country's orientation towards North American rather than British or European markets. As noted in Chapter 5, this spawned a backlash from economic nationalists, including some Canadian business leaders, culminating in the Trudeau government's limited restrictions on foreign investment during the 1970s and its more assertive efforts to regain Canadian con-trol over the energy sector that culminated in the National Energy Program of the early 1980s. However, the nature of the debate over foreign investments has changed substantially since the early 1980s, reflecting Canada's growing integration within the North American and global economies, the emergence of hundreds of Canadian-based MNCs, and the maturing of Canadian capital markets.

The integration of Canadian firms within continental and global supply networks means that issues of ownership have become secondary to the capacity to generate value-added production and contribute to the development of clusters of special-ized economic activity. The ongoing changes in management styles and the types of business activities conducted by MNCs are seen increasingly by economists and federal policy-makers as sources of networked technological and managerial exper-tise as well as a stimulus for increased productivity by their Canadian suppliers and competitors (for example, see Baldwin and Hamel 2000). Greater economic spe-cialization in the organization of individual businesses and their production facili-ties are considered to be a response to earlier critiques of the relative inefficiency of branch-plant firms created to produce broad product lines for limited Canadian markets (Baldwin, Caves, and Gu 2005).

Canadian governments have adapted both their policies and rhetoric to the new realities. Economic studies increasingly emphasize the contribution of foreign investment to increased productivity, the use and diffusion of new technologies, and competitiveness. These practices prompt both innovation and emulation by Canadian suppliers and competitors, particularly those in export-oriented industries (Eden 1994; Globerman and Shapiro 1998; Hejazi and Pauly 2002; Cross 2002a; Harris 2003). Rather than a threat, speeches by senior federal cabinet ministers and their officials emphasize the need to maintain Canada's attractiveness as a target market for foreign investment (Martin 2000; Lynch 2000; Manley 2002).

The second factor driving North American economic integration is that Canadian business investments in foreign subsidiaries have grown far more rapidly than foreign direct investment in Canada since the 1970s with the country becoming a net exporter of capital in 1997. Box 8.3 notes the respective levels of Canadian direct investment abroad and foreign direct investment in Canada as a percentage of total Canadian business assets between 1983 and 2003.

Box 8.3: Foreign Direct Investment Stocks as a Proportion of Canadian Business Assets*

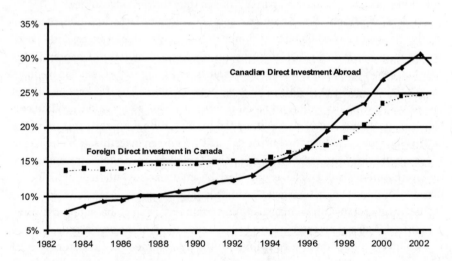

Note: *Business assets refer to total assets, corporations, and GBEs.
Source: Guillemette and Mintz 2004: 2: reproduced by permission.

Flows of foreign direct investment into Canada also increased sharply during the 1990s, from a mix of new investments, business mergers, and acquisitions (or takeovers). However, due to the parallel growth of Canadian firms, the degree of foreign control in the Canadian economy, as measured by the share of assets in all corporations owned by non-residents, has remained relatively stable at about 22 per cent (Statistics Canada 2004a: 2 November). Foreign direct investment in Canada continues to come primarily from the US, while more than half of Canadian direct investment abroad since 1997 has been in other countries.

At the end of 2004, the total value of Canadian direct investment abroad was $445.1 billion, about 22 per cent higher than foreign direct investment in Canada. Total Canadian equity investments abroad, including both direct investment and the book value of foreign stocks, totaled $633.6 billion, which was 34 per cent greater than the value of foreign equity investments in Canada that year. However, total foreign portfolio investment, including the debt of Canadian governments and corporations, still exceeds Canadian holdings of foreign debt by a wide margin.[2]

The rapid growth of investments by Canadian pension funds, mutual funds, and other institutional investors in US and other foreign markets has also reinforced the processes of North American economic integration while contributing to the innovation and dynamism of Canadian capital markets. As a result, support for trade promotion and enhancement measures increasingly outweighs political pressures for protectionist policies among business interests, even in traditionally protected sectors such as airlines, telecommunications, and financial services. Symbolic of this change was the 1996 merger of the Canadian Manufacturers Association, once the strongest business voice for protectionism, with the Canadian Exporters Association.

However, in addition to the usual critics of capitalism and market-oriented policies, the takeover boom of the late 1990s also led some analysts and Canadian business leaders, especially those in traditionally protected or strategic industries, to initiate the **hollowing out debate**. They stressed the vulnerability of Canadian businesses to foreign competition and control, suggesting that market forces were resulting in the departure from Canada of major decision-making functions even in Canadian-based businesses. They also noted that many large Canadian firms were interlisting their shares on both Canadian and US stock exchanges, reporting their financial statements in US dollars, and basing investment decisions on their companies' competitive positions outside Canada (Reguly 1999: B2; Estey 1999; Curren 2000; Rubin 2002: FP1; Packham 2002: FP15).

Some of these concerns proved to be short-lived, particularly after the collapse in 2000 of the technology boom in North American stock markets and the rapid rise of income trusts as a major financing vehicle for Canadian corporations due to particular anomalies in the Canadian tax system. Others are inherent in the decision of Canadian governments to reduce restrictions on foreign investment and the cross-border allocation of capital, which shifts some power from corporate executives to institutional investors seeking competitive returns on their clients' investments, affecting performance incentives for managers of widely held companies (Hale 2005d).[3]

---

2 This figure is based on book values of both direct and portfolio investments, a more stable figure than market values (Statistics Canada 2005a: 19).

3 The 2005 federal budget removed foreign capital property restrictions on investments outside Canada by pension funds and other tax-sheltered investment vehicles such as RRSPs. Previously, the federal government had introduced phased increases in the foreign investment limit from the historical 10 per cent to 30 per cent, in order to allow them greater diversification and potentially higher returns.

Empirical studies show that although subsidiaries of foreign firms remain major actors in the Canadian economy, the percentage of large Canadian firms with significant voting equity held by foreigners actually declined between 1997 and 2003, as demonstrated in Table 8.3. Statistics Canada research indicates that the overall numbers and employment levels of head offices in Canada actually increased between 1999 and 2002, the height of the hollowing-out scare. Employment in managerial, business professional, scientific, and engineering positions grew by three times the rate of other occupations between 1996 and 2002, suggesting that the threat to head office-type jobs may be overstated (Guillemette and Mintz 2004: 7; Baldwin, Beckstead, and Brown 2003; O'Neill 2002: 18).

Table 8.3: Percentage of Canada's Largest Firms with Voting Equity Held by Foreigners (per cent of firms)

	10 per cent or more		100 per cent	
	1997	2003	1997	2003
Largest 100 firms*	58.0	34.0	24.4	16.0
Largest 500 firms	49.6	37.0	26.8	27.4
Largest 800 firms	43.8	31.4	22.3	23.0

* by revenue.
Source: Financial Post FP500 (1998, 2004); Guillemette and Mintz 2004: 7.

Increasing international competition, economic integration, and the growing turnover in business ownership have had two major effects on government policies at both the federal level and in many provinces. Rather than traditional policies of direct government assistance to particular national champions or industry sectors—except perhaps for the aerospace sector—they have stimulated increasing attention to the creation of a macroeconomic policy framework of low inflation, low interest rates, sustainable public finance (balanced budgets and debt repayment), and, to a lesser extent, competitive tax rates on business and investment in order to make Canada an attractive and competitive market for export industries and foreign investment.[4] They have also created an increasing focus on microeconomic competitiveness creating conditions conducive to the efficient allocation of resources by business, increased managerial and technological entrepreneurship and innovation, and the nurturing of adaptable, skilled, and creative workers and managers. We will now look at the complementary government policies designed to balance their pursuit with the effective and efficient provision of public services and regulatory activities and their effects on government interaction with business.

---

4 The federal government reduced general corporate income tax rates from 28 to 21 per cent between 2001 and 2005 in response to the 1998 report of the Technical Committee on Business Taxation. However, economist Jack Mintz suggests that due, in particular, to high provincial business taxes, Canada still retains one of the highest tax rates on capital and investment income in the industrial world (Mintz 2005).

The Political Economy of Business Competitiveness

The OECD defines competitiveness as "the degree to which a country can, under free and fair market conditions, produce goods and services meeting the test of international markets, while maintaining and expanding the real incomes of its people over the long term" (Garelli 2001). There is no *one* successful model of competitiveness in the world today. Just as economic structures and the organization of capitalist systems vary widely around the world, so do the specific mixes of domestic economic and social policies that contribute to high levels of economic growth and dynamism.

Maintaining competitiveness in an open changing economy requires adaptation to changing circumstances—something that cannot be taken for granted. Businesses and governments may grow complacent from success or simply fail to recognize a changing environment. Countries that are highly successful in one period, such as Germany and Japan during the 1970s and 1980s, or the US in the 1960s and 1990s, may stagnate or face difficult transitions to a new era of greater prosperity.

The World Competitiveness Yearbook ranked the US and Canada as two of only four countries with more than 20 million people in its list of 20 most competitive economies since 2000. Britain and Germany are the other two. Table 8.4 outlines average competitiveness rankings for large and small countries based on a series of benchmarks developed by the Institute for Management Development in Switzerland.

Table 8.4: World Competitiveness Ranking

Large Economies	2005	2000-2005	Small Economies	2005	2000-2005
United States	1	1	Singapore	3	4
Canada	5	6	Luxembourg	10	4
Germany	23	18	Finland	6	5
Britain	22	19	Hong Kong	2	7
			Iceland	4	8
			Netherlands	12	9

Source: *World Competitiveness Yearbook* 2005.

Economists Michael Porter and Jeffrey Sachs, whose comparative economic research has heavily influenced the microeconomic policies of the federal and some provincial governments, have identified three major dimensions of competitiveness that can be found in most of these countries (see Box 8.4). The first, microeconomic (or current) competitiveness, deals with the conditions that determine a country's sustainable level of productivity: the output of goods and services resulting from a stated value of inputs, either labour, capital, or both (Porter, Sachs, and Warner 2000: 16). As noted in Chapter 2, increasing productivity is critical to higher living standards. Without it, increased international competition turns globalization into a zero-sum game, sometimes described as a race to the bottom, in which the ability of companies to adapt to growing international competition comes at the expense of lower real wages for workers, lower returns for investors, or higher government subsidies financed by present or future taxpayers.

Box 8.4: Competitiveness, A Three Dimensional Challenge

STRUCTURES **INTERNATIONAL ECONOMIC** POLICIES	STRUCTURES **DOMESTIC ECONOMIC** POLICIES	STRUCTURES **DOMESTIC, POLITICAL, and SOCIAL** POLICIES

• Multinational, transnational corporations
• International economic and trade agreements
  • multilateral
  • regional
  • bilateral
	Economic activities Framework legislation
	• business organization
	• financial markets and institutions
	• taxation
	• regulatory systems
	• competition
	• interprov. trade, mobility
	• workplace rules/ systems
		Government
		• Federalism and fed./prov. relations
		• Organization, financing of social policies
		  • health
		  • education
		  • pensions
		  • transfers
		• Social, cultural, political attitudes and expectations

Porter and other economists have identified a number of conditions, both political and economic, that contribute to increased productivity and competitiveness without undermining social stability or cohesion. Both Canadian and foreign-controlled firms with strong export orientations favour new technologies and more efficient production processes that result in higher productivity and rising incomes. A flexible, highly skilled, and educated workforce is more likely to have the capacity to adapt to these new technologies and market conditions. The resulting more widespread culture of innovation and of entrepreneurship fosters the creation of new businesses, products, processes, and approaches to customer service and facilitates greater social trust among employers and employees, businesses and governments, consumers, investors, and lenders. This encourages a climate of social stability and adaptability rather than the fear of change that contributes to political conflicts (Fukuyama 1995; Porter, Sachs, and Warner 2000; Courchene 2001c).

These ideas have heavily influenced Canadian social and economic policies in recent years. Virtually all new job creation in Canada during the 1990s came in positions requiring some form of post-secondary education. Both federal and provincial governments have responded by expanding support for post-secondary education, by providing additional financial support for students (directly and through the tax system), by investing in the physical expansion of colleges and universities, and by increasing the number of places for qualified students (Hale 2002).

Economic competitiveness is also influenced by the macroeconomic environment, particularly those factors contributing to high rates of per capita GDP growth. The competitiveness and efficiency of national tax systems, especially on mobile factors of production such as business and investment income, are directly under government control. So are investments in public infrastructure, such as transportation systems, abundant and competitively priced sources of energy, clean water, and other public health areas.

Business attitudes and decisions are as important as the political and regulatory environment. Managerial attitudes and relatively cooperative workplace relations facilitate economic growth and greater efficiency. Their absence is likely to undermine them. High levels of investment, contributing to continuous improvements in technology and equipment, are a key factor in achieving high levels of growth. Access to capital often depends on the flexibility and creativity of capital markets. These factors may be encouraged or constrained by regulatory factors, but they also depend on an economic culture that encourages and rewards creativity and entrepreneurship, reflecting another dimension of the **complex interdependence** of political and economic factors discussed earlier in this chapter (Porter, Sachs, and Warner 2000; Garelli 2001; Courchene 2001c).

A third dimension of competitiveness—one that has become central to the economic rhetoric of the federal government and several provinces—is economic creativity. Government support for the knowledge economy, including basic and applied research and development, technology transfer, skills training, educational accessibility, and performance—are central to economic competitiveness (Warner 2000; Courchene 2001c). The effectiveness of these policies in fostering the conditions for a competitive economy is largely dependent on their internal coherence—the ways that government policies and actions are mutually reinforcing rather than functioning at cross-purposes. However, it also depends on the degree to which these policies are supported by social and cultural attitudes that reflect the choices, interests, and values of their citizens and the businesses for which they work.

These elements of complex interdependence are evident in local, regional, and cross-border economic networks that link suppliers, customers, and investors in what are called the economic clusters that have become the subject of considerable research (Ontario, Institute for Competitiveness and Prosperity 2002; Munn-Venn and Voyer 2004). They also reflect the mix of public and private institutions, discussed in Chapter 6, which support innovation and the spread of new ideas, products, and technologies (Rugman and D'Cruz 1991; Martin and Porter 2000).

Conclusion: Business, Government, and the Politics of Competitiveness

The challenge of translating contemporary theories of competitiveness into practice faces three major hurdles. Competitive conditions vary widely by sector and within the diverse subsectors of particular industries, particularly when Canada's far-flung geography is thrown into the equation.

Governments can, and sometimes do, pursue broadly based horizontal policies designed to encourage greater competitiveness by moving towards economically neutral tax systems to avoid discriminating among different types of economic activity and away from industry-specific subsidies, as well as by investing in infrastructure and social services that enhance rather than undermine economic efficiency, productivity, and personal opportunities. But the realities of politics and bureaucratic organizations necessary to deal with such a diverse, decentralized economic system lend themselves to the politics of bureaucratic clientelism and rent-seeking by specialized economic interest groups, including those representing different fragments of the business community.

The approaches taken by individual corporations and business associations to governments and politics vary depending on the range and scope of their activities, the degrees to which they are subject to direct sectoral regulation as opposed to general rules governing business activity, and the degree to which they are located in growing or declining markets. Broadly based business organizations are more inclined to favour the strategic approaches discussed earlier in this chapter, whereas sectoral or industry associations rely on the extent and nature of their past and present relations with governments.

Business groups in rapidly growing economic sectors tend to seek facilitative policies such as flexible regulations, support for infrastructure, and skills training, that identify and address specific barriers to the expansion of their activities. Those whose competitors in other countries are heavily subsidized or subject to preferential regulatory treatment look for comparable treatment by Canadian governments. For example, the aerospace industry has been relatively successful in protecting subsidies delivered through the Technology Partnerships Program despite critiques by international trade bodies and Canada's auditor general.[5] The brand-name pharmaceutical industry has successfully lobbied the federal government first to secure, then to protect strong patent protection rules in the face of vigorous competition from generic drug manufacturers and provincial governments. Canada's automotive sector developed an extensive industry-union-government partnership to address problems of over-capacity and competitive subsidies from US state governments. Regionally concentrated industries can often extract this kind of preferential treatment from governments, particularly in areas in which investments and highly paid employment have become subject to politically driven competition from other jurisdictions.

Both governments and business executives frequently place a greater rhetorical emphasis on the politics of competitiveness than on taking specific actions to do something about it. Most economists suggest that high taxes on capital and investment income impose a disproportionate drag on economic activity and that a larger portion of revenues from business should be drawn from user fees and other benefit-

---

5 The federal government announced another makeover of the Technology Partnerships Program in September 2005. It remains to be seen how effective it is in avoiding the accusations of corporate welfare labeled at its predecessor (Aubry 2005).

related taxes related to their consumption of public services (Canada, Department of Finance 1998). However, practical politics dictates that cuts to business taxes be balanced by even larger cuts to taxes on individuals, particularly the lower- and middle-income earners who account for the vast majority of voters. As the visible tax bills of these voters are often relatively low, politicians see greater benefits in increasing public spending that directly benefits these groups, at least during periods of relative prosperity. Although a few provinces have cut corporate income taxes, such cuts are more likely to be targeted at locally based small businesses than at larger national or multinational corporations.

Internationally competitive firms are more likely to emerge in response to the pressures of competitive markets or as the by-product of their executives' entrepreneurial drive, vision, and skills. A relatively small minority of dynamic, innovative firms contribute disproportionately to increases in business productivity. Similarly, firms subject to aggressive international competition—or which regularly face such competition in their export markets—are more likely to adopt innovative processes and promote a culture of continuous improvement in their businesses than businesses focused on domestic markets, particularly if they enjoy regulatory protection from governments.

The structural realities of globalization and North American integration provide both opportunities and challenges for businesses and governments. To some extent, they constrain the normal tendencies of governments, businesses, and other interest groups towards clientelism and rent-seeking either through the limits imposed by international agreements or the risks that market forces and more creative, aggressive competitors will reshape the business environment in ways that force governments and other businesses to play catch-up. The physical and geographic diversity of Canada's economy noted in previous chapters literally makes it impossible for governments to be all things to all people.

The openness and dynamism of the North American economy and the rapid changes facing many business sectors make it relatively difficult for governments to micro-manage economic activity and for most business groups to coalesce and stick together long enough to recreate the kinds of cozy, clientelistic sector strategies that long characterized relations between Canadian governments and oligopolistic industries. To some degree, these forces impose competitive disciplines on both governments *and* businesses.

Canada's adaptation to the increasingly competitive global environment of the past 20 years has not been without challenges or difficulties. But its relative success in responding to these challenges can be seen in its adaptation to the politics of fiscal sustainability discussed in Chapter 5 and in its leading record of economic growth—at least among major industrial countries—since the mid-1990s. The relatively smooth adaptation of the Canadian economy to the appreciation of the Canadian dollar from $US 0.62 to $US 0.90 between 2002 and 2006 with modest effects on levels of economic growth or employment—whatever the effects on individual companies—suggests that Canadian businesses have been able to adjust successfully to the challenges of global dynamism and to the creative destruction of the contemporary market economy.[6] However, the day-to-day realities of relations between businesses and governments are sufficiently complex and diverse to create innumerable opportunities for effective policy advocacy and the marriage of private interests (on both sides of the fence) to the exercise of political power.

Key Terms and Concepts for Review (see Glossary)

Canadian Direct Investment Abroad
complex interdependence
demonstration effect
foreign direct investment
globalization
hollowing out debate
levels of analysis
NAFTA
national treatment

negative integration
North American economic integration
policy convergence
portfolio investment
positive integration
regimes
sovereignty
World Trade Organization

Questions for Discussion and Review

1. What is complex interdependence? How does this concept apply to the relationship among trade, investment, the organization of business operations, and government policies?

2. How have globalization and economic interdependence affected the ways in which governments seek to maintain or expand their discretion in making domestic economic, social, and other policies?

3. What are four major factors contributing to policy convergence among nations? To what extent is each one a reflection of domestic political and economic choices? External pressures?

4. What factors are contributing to the continuing economic integration of North America? What options do Canadian governments have in responding to these pressures? How would you respond to these pressures? Why?

5. Canada has historically depended on foreign capital for a significant share of its economic development. How has Canada's role in international capital markets

---

6 There is little consensus over the interaction of high global energy prices, exchange rates, macroeconomic policy variables, and the competitiveness of Canada's manufacturing sector, at least in the short term. The global energy price spike of recent years increases the difficulties faced by business executives and government policy-makers in adapting to resulting uncertainties in market conditions and the broader economic structure. For example, see Scoffield 2005: B6.

changed since the 1970s? What implications have these trends had for Canadian economic policies? For the operations of Canadian businesses?

6. What are the three main dimensions of economic competitiveness discussed in this chapter? What implications does each have for government policies? To what extent do national governments have political discretion in the ways that they approach each of these concepts?

Suggestions for Further Readings

Canada, Department of Foreign Affairs and International Trade. 2005. *Sixth annual report on Canada's state of trade—trade update.* Ottawa: DFAIT (April).

Canada, Standing Committee on Foreign Affairs and International Trade. 2002. *Partners in North America: advancing Canada's relations with the United States and Mexico.* Ottawa: House of Commons (December).

Doern, G. Bruce, Margaret M. Hill, Michael J. Prince, and Richard J. Schultz (Eds.). 1999. *Changing the rules: Canadian regulatory regimes and institutions.* Toronto: University of Toronto Press.

Doern, G. Bruce, and Brian Tomlin. 1991. *Faith and fear: the free trade story.* Toronto: Stoddart.

Hart, Michael. 2002. *Canada: a trading nation.* Vancouver: University of British Columbia Press.

Helliwell, John F. 2000. *Globalization: myths, facts and realities.* Toronto: C.D. Howe Institute (September).

Hoberg, George (Ed.). 2002. *Capacity for choice: Canada in a new North America.* Toronto: University of Toronto Press.

Rugman, Alan G. 2000. *The end of globalization: why global strategy is a myth and how to profit from the realities of regional markets.* New York: Amacom.

Watson, William. 1998. *Globalization and the meaning of Canadian life.* Toronto: University of Toronto Press.

CHAPTER 9

Government Business Enterprises: The State Sector in Transition

Governments' role in the economy is often complicated by their direct involvement in the marketplace as providers of goods and services through arm's length agencies or through private providers subject to contractual or regulatory controls (see Chapter 3). The role of **government business enterprises** (GBEs)—often known in Canada as Crown corporations, Crown agencies, or public enterprises—has changed significantly in recent years with the maturing of the Canadian economy and changes in the political and management philosophies of many Canadian governments. These changes, variously described as "the new governance" or "new public management" (Salamon 2002; Kernaghan, Marson, and Borins 2000), have blurred many traditional distinctions between business and government. In so doing, the range of policy tools or instruments available to governments for the delivery of public services and the delivery of public policy goals has been greatly expanded. These innovations have created both new opportunities for cooperation between business and government and new challenges in ensuring that the use of private means actually serves public ends as intended (Poschmann 2003; see also Salamon 2002: 600-10; Delacourt and Lenihan 1999).

GBEs are legal entities engaged in the sale of goods and/or services to citizens, businesses, or other parts of government. They are hybrid entities, enjoying varying degrees of operational autonomy from governments but frequently serving public policy goals of one kind or another. They usually have some degree of commercial orientation requiring greater attention to customers and operating efficiency than traditional government bureaucracies. They may also have legal or regulatory privileges not available to other businesses in the marketplace, often including exemptions from some taxes. The inherent tension between commercial and political mandates is a challenge for governments seeking to balance competing political goals, for businesses seeking either commercial advantage or level playing fields in competitive markets, for public sector unions, and for citizens and consumers, depending on their share of the costs and benefits of such arrangements. (For a discussion of these trade-offs in the context of the delivery of postal services, see Campbell 2003 and Campbell 2002).

The choice of policy instruments—including direct government ownership as opposed to regulating or subsidizing private business activity or organizing joint public-private ventures to provide particular goods or services—is an inherently political decision, which is a matter not only of the philosophical or ideological orientations of key government decision-makers, but also of public expectations, specific circumstances that require some form of political response, the relative influence of key stakeholders in the relevant policy processes, and increasingly, as noted in Chapter 8, the international environment affecting both government and business decision-making (Prichard and Trebilcock 1983; Foster 1997; Wiseman and Whorley 2002; Peters 2002).

Direct government engagement in business allows for the choice of a wide range of policy instruments and, arguably, has always done so. Governments may produce or distribute goods and services:

- as alternatives to private market provision, as in government monopolies over some telecommunications services, the distribution of alcoholic beverages, and the marketing of some agricultural products;
- in competition with private business, as in Canada Post's involvement in the courier business, the CBC's role as a general interest broadcaster dependent on both advertising revenues and government subsidies, and formerly the airline and aircraft manufacturing sectors;
- in cooperation or partnership with private sector businesses (e.g., in managing government-owned casinos) and independent non-profit organizations (in delivering many public services); or
- in the provision of specialized services that complement or supplement the workings of private businesses in the marketplace, as with many government-run financial institutions.

Governments may also form strategic alliances with major corporations as instruments of government policy—such as the Grand Trunk and Canadian Pacific railways in the nineteenth century, Dome Petroleum during the National Energy Program of the 1980s, or Bombardier as Canada's largest exporter of transportation equipment—creating what John Shepherd has described as **hidden Crown corporations** (Shepherd 1981: 40-42).

The impact of GBEs on the economic structure of a region, province, or specific industry depends on their relative position within the marketplace; the degree to which particular firms receive preferred regulatory treatment as instruments of government policy; and the degree to which Crown corporations as policy instruments are intended to complement, compete with, or contain the influence of private businesses in the marketplace.

This chapter outlines the wide variety of GBEs in the contemporary marketplace and their relative importance in particular regions and economic sectors. It examines traditional explanations for governments' use of GBEs and the factors that have influenced changes in their organization and objectives in recent years. Finally, it considers several major issues that are shaping debates over direct government involvement in business, including the increasing number of **public-private partnerships** (PPPs), the varied implications for business-government relations, and the relationship between the political and economic roles of GBEs.

GBEs in the Economy: Scope and Types

The size and scope of GBEs vary widely between provinces and industry sectors. Statistics Canada estimated revenues from GBEs at $123.4 billion in 2002. As noted in Table 9.1, provincial GBEs accounted for more than two-thirds of overall government revenues from business operations and almost two-thirds of net profits in 2002.

Table 9.1: Government Business Sector Revenues and Assets for the Fiscal Year ending nearest 31 December 2002 (in billions of dollars)

	Revenues	Net income*	Assets
Federal	23.1	5.9	176.5
Provincial	84.0	11.8	198.6
Local	16.3**	0.48	na
Total	123.4	18.2	

* after provision for income taxes.
** includes $ 1.7 billion in provincial subsidies, mainly for transit systems.
Source: Statistics Canada 2003b: 22 November, 20 December; Statistics Canada 2005e: 68-69.

GBEs play a major role in the energy sector, especially the large provincial utilities that generate electricity, which accounted for as much as 47 per cent of energy industry assets in the mid-1990s. Provincial lottery and casino corporations became a major source of government revenues in the 1990s, often in partnership with private firms in casino management and in providing retail distribution networks for lottery tickets. Hydro, liquor, and gambling sectors accounted for 99 per cent of provincial GBE profits in 2002. Municipal electric utilities and transit systems account for virtually all municipal GBE revenues. GBEs also play regionally significant roles in the fields of:

- property and casualty insurance, through government auto insurance firms in four provinces—BC, Saskatchewan, Manitoba, and Quebec—and provincial workers' compensation systems;
- financial services, particularly the investment banking activities of Quebec's **Caisse de dépôt et placement**, which has played a major role in that province's industrial strategy, and the retail banking services provided by the Alberta Treasury Branches (ATB Financial);
- rail transportation, particularly through BC Rail (freight), Via Rail (passenger services in Ontario and Quebec), and the Ontario Northland Railway.

Quebec has the largest state enterprise sector in absolute terms because of the size and financial power of the Caisse de dépôt, the investment arm of the Quebec Pension Plan. Provinces such as Manitoba and Saskatchewan with long histories of social democratic governments also have large state sectors relative to the overall sizes of their economies.

Table 9.2: Largest Crown Corporations by Revenue, Compared with All Corporations

Fiscal Year Ending 2003

	Owner	Type	Sector	Revenue (in millions)	Rank
Hydro Quebec	prov.	commercial	Electric utility	$13,002	22
Canada Post	fed.	hybrid[+]	Communications • mail, courier	$6,154	40
Ontario Lottery & Gaming Corp.	prov.	hybrid[+]	Gambling	$5,762	44
Ontario Power Generation*	prov.	commercial	Electric utility	$5,178	52
BC Hydro	prov.	commercial	Electric utility	$4,407	62
Hydro One*	fed.	commercial	Electric utility	$4,058	66
Caisse de dépôt et placement	prov.	hybrid	Financial services • investment bank	$3,662	71
Canadian Wheat Board	fed.	hybrid[+]	Agricultural	$3,340	84
Insurance Corp. of British Columbia	prov.	commercial[+]	Financial services • general insurance	$3,189	86
Alberta Gaming and Liquor Commission	prov.	commercial[+]	Gambling, liquor wholesaler	$3,152	87
Liquor Control Board of Ontario	prov.	commercial	Retail, wholesale	$3,119	88
Loto-Québec**	prov.	hybrid[+]	Gambling	$2,779	97

* Formerly parts of Ontario Hydro.
** Subsidiary of Caisse de dépôt et placement, Quebec.
[+] Legislated monopoly in core business area.
Source: *National Post Business* 2004.

Typology

GBEs may be categorized in several ways, depending on an observer's emphasis on their legal and organizational status within government, their principal mandates, or their relationship with commercial markets. One typology focuses on the degree of GBE's managerial independence in carrying out administrative, regulatory, and service delivery functions for governments. Another approach, used for several years by BC, distinguishes three broad types of public enterprises—**commercial Crown corporations, economic development Crown corporations,** and **social and government services corporations**—depending on their relative financial and commercial independence from governments and the degree to which they are subject to market disciplines in their provision of goods and services (British Columbia

2000: 107). Although these categories do not do complete justice to the complexity and diversity of GBE functions, mandates, and operations, they provide a useful starting point in defining the relationships among government departments, GBEs, and the business marketplace.

Commercial Crown Corporations

Commercial Crown corporations generate revenues by selling services at commercial rates as defined either by market competition or the need to cover their costs and generate market returns for their government shareholders. They pay their own operating expenses, including interest on their debts. Commercial GBEs which operate at arm's length from governments in designing and implementing their business strategies are also known as proprietary corporations. Examples include provincial and municipal electric utilities, automobile insurance companies in four provinces, SaskTel (Saskatchewan's main telephone company), and ATB Financial. In 2003, commercial and quasi-commercial GBEs accounted for 12 of Canada's 100 largest corporations measured by revenues, as noted in Table 9.2; 21 of the 25 largest public enterprises listed in the 2004 *Financial Post 500* list of companies are in four sectors: electric utilities (nine), financial services (six), liquor and gambling (six) (*National Post Business* 2004).

During the 1980s and early 1990s, the federal government responded to fiscal pressures by gradually withdrawing from most business activities whose purposes were primarily commercial rather than policy-oriented. Changes in regulatory and market environments for integrated oil companies (Petro-Canada), telecommunications (Teleglobe Canada), passenger air travel (Air Canada), rail transportation (Canadian National), and other areas—as well as political attitudes towards GBEs—led to the **commercialization** or **privatization** of several major federal Crown corporations (to be discussed later in this chapter).

Economic Development Crown Corporations

Economic development Crown Corporations generally sell goods or services to the public or undertake projects that provide economic benefits to citizens and communities as instruments of public policy. As such, they might also be described as quasi-commercial corporations. Some of these firms, which are also known as agency crown corporations, provide procurement, construction, and disposal operations (Treff and Perry 2003: 17:3). They frequently receive financial assistance or dedicated revenues from government, although in recent years, changes in their mandates have required some of these firms to cross-subsidize some of their operations from profits earned by commercial activities in other areas.

Examples at the federal level are Atomic Energy of Canada Limited, the CBC, the Canadian Dairy Commission, VIA Rail, and Marine Atlantic (which manages interprovincial ferry services in Atlantic Canada). Counterparts at other levels of government include corporations and agencies responsible for transportation, infrastructure, business financing, and tourism and tourism development (including several municipal convention centres). The major political and economic rationales for these ventures will be examined later in this chapter. Table 9.3 notes that four companies accounted for almost 76 per cent of the $4.8 billion in subsidies budgeted for federal GBEs in 2004-05.

Table 9.3: Federal Budgetary Funding for Crown Corporations, 2004-05

Canada Mortgage and Housing Corporation	$2,222.2	46.0%
Canadian Broadcasting Corporation	1,034.3	21.5%
Canada Post Corporation	197.2	4.1%
Via Rail Canada Inc.	191.3	4.0%
Canada Council for the Arts	151.0	3.1%
National Capital Commission	131.6	2.7%
Telefilm Canada	129.7	2.7%
Atomic Energy of Canada Limited	127.8	2.7%
International Development Research Centre	119.1	2.5%
Other (15 corporations)		10.7%
Total	$ 4,821.5	100%

Source: 2004-05 Main Estimates, Department of Finance; Treff and Perry 2005: 17:8.

Two vital subsets of this type of GBE are investment corporations, such as the Caisse de dépôt and the Canada Pension Plan Investment Board (CPPIB), which manage public investment funds such as public service and public pension funds on behalf of governments, and financial services corporations, which provide loans, loan guarantees, and direct investments in particular markets as instruments of public policy. Among the latter are Business Development Bank of Canada, Canada Deposit Insurance Corporation, Export Development Canada, Farm Credit Canada, and comparable development banks and agencies in most provinces. The relationship between the policy and competitive functions of these organizations are often contested, particularly when individual GBEs are expected to serve several competing political and economic objectives. The economic development roles of GBEs, and the ideas and policy goals that shape them, will be discussed in greater detail later in this chapter.

Some Crown corporations are hybrids that function as competitive commercial GBEs in one part of their operations while serving significant regulatory functions or benefiting from regulatory preferences, government subsidies, or both as instruments of government policy.

Canada Post is a good example of a hybrid GBE. It benefits from a statutory monopoly over first class mail that enables it to maintain a uniform set of postal rates for large cities and remote communities alike, but it also manages competitive parcel, courier, and electronic communications services. Provincial lottery and casino corporations, which typically promote and manage gambling ventures often in partnership with private developers and retail distribution networks, are another GBE hybrid.

Social and Government Services Corporations and Agencies

Social and government services corporations and agencies generally receive financial assistance from governments to deliver social programs and other government services, ranging from the management and disposal of government assets (e.g., Canada Lands Corporation, BC Buildings Corporation, and provincial counterparts); to tax collection (Canada Revenue Agency, BC Assessment Authority); to special purpose corporations and agencies established to manage museums and other cultural institutions, parks, and public housing; to inspection services and a wide range of other public services.

Several governments have set up Financing Authorities for the management of public debt and the financing of public infrastructure projects; they perform services traditionally carried out by civil servants but subject to different governance structures. However, governments may also reabsorb GBEs into traditional government departments, as Ontario converted its Superbuild Corporation in 2003 into a reorganized Ministry of Public Infrastructure Renewal. These agencies are good examples of the ongoing mutation of GBEs in a variety of organizational structures, often involving a mixture of mixed government private, non-profit, and even intergovernmental ownership.

The renewed emphasis in recent years on quasi-commercial, user-pay arrangements to finance and, sometimes, operate public capital projects such as airports, highways, bridges, water and waste-water systems, and even schools and hospitals has contributed to the spread of public-private partnerships of various kinds. The politics and economics of **mixed enterprises**, and their implications for business-government relations, will be discussed later in this chapter.

Table 9.4: Federal Crown Corporations: Organizational Structures

	2004	1997	1982
Parent Crown corporations	43	47	72
Wholly owned subsidiaries	21	25	114
Other subsidiaries*	36	23	89
Mixed enterprises	1		
Joint enterprises	3	3	17
International organizations	18	3	
Shared governance organizations	141		
Other entities		86	23

* Other subsidiaries, associates, and legal partnerships
Source: Treasury Board of Canada 2004; Treasury Board of Canada 1998; Kernaghan and Siegel 1999: 227.

As noted in Table 9.4, shared governance organizations, some of whose directors are appointed by the federal government, are now the most numerous type of federal enterprises.

These categories are fluid, accommodating a variety of different forms and legal arrangements—including procurement from or distribution through private businesses and non-profit organizations—along with shape-shifting to become more or less commercialized, depending on the political and economic environments in which they function. Canada Post was a heavily subsidized government department until transformed into a Crown corporation with a mandate to become financially self-sustaining in the early 1980s. Prairie steelmaker Ipsco Inc. was formed in 1958 as a mixed enterprise partly owned by the Saskatchewan (and later Alberta) governments before its privatization in the 1980s. Transport Canada managed both airports and air traffic control services before these were spun off as shared governance or non-profit organizations in the late 1980s and early 1990s. During the 1990s, public sector managers have introduced a variety of managerial and organizational innovations for the delivery of public services collectively known as alternative service delivery (Kernaghan, Marson, and Borins 2000; Zussman 2002).

These choices among organizational and service delivery options have implications for the management of government, where issues of efficiency and political accountability are major considerations, and to the study of business-government relations, particularly when determining whether governments should produce particular goods and services or purchase them from private or non-profit suppliers and, if so, under what conditions.

Major Objectives of Public Ownership

Despite the prevalence of private economic activity, Canada has a long history of public ownership of economic enterprises. The choice of government ownership, as opposed to other forms of economic intervention, is justified sometimes on the normative grounds of promoting economic development or protecting the public interest and at other times on the ideological grounds of promoting political or social transformation. It may also be justified on the pragmatic grounds that government ownership is necessary to deal with specific economic problems or that GBEs are a more flexible policy tool than traditional forms of government organization.

Critiques of government ownership have often focused on GBEs' relative inefficiency, particularly when subject to political interference with their operations, their use as instruments of political favouritism towards some social and political groups at the expense of others, and perceptions that business decisions should be left to the private sector. Guy Peters (2002: 552-53) suggests that the choice of policy instruments or tools depends on the interaction of five major factors, what he calls the "Five I's": institutions, ideas, interests, individuals, and the international environment. These objectives often overlap with one another, often changing with political and economic circumstances.

There are six major historic rationales for government ownership of commercial activities:

1. promoting economic development;
2. correcting market failures or filling "market gaps";
3. promoting a government's ideology;
4. exercising policy control over strategic industries;
5. protecting employment; and
6. commercializing an under-performing area of public sector activity.

We will look at each in turn, examining their application to specific government enterprises, and some of the practical limitations or conditions for their effective application.

1. Promoting Economic Development

Government promotion of economic development is central to Canada's political culture and transcends the ideologies of particular governments. The political decision to choose government ownership over the regulation or provision of economic incentives to private industry has been justified most frequently in cases of government construction or takeovers of major transportation and infrastructure projects that have opened up large parts of Canada for settlement or in the need to maintain the economic viability of existing communities. These decisions may be pragmatic ad hoc responses to particular situations or part of a broader industrial strategy linking a range of policy initiatives.

Chandler (1983a: 209-12) has identified three ways in which Crown corporations have been used as instruments of economic development and nation-building or province-building. Some GBEs have served all three roles from time to time. First, "Facilitative corporations ... supplement and support private sector economic development and are not viewed as an extension of state control" (Freeman 1995: 5). The purpose of government ownership in these cases is to create a supportive environment for private businesses in general or for specific business sectors which compete in international markets characterized by extensive government intervention and mercantilistic support.

The decision of successive Ontario Conservative governments between 1905 and 1930 to support the development of public power through Ontario Hydro, rather than providing concessions to private power corporations, as in Quebec, is one example of this strategy (Freeman 1995: Chapters 2-4). Most provinces used provincial hydro-electric utilities as instruments of economic development from the early twentieth century until the mid-1960s, sometimes complementing private firms, sometimes competing with them, and eventually replacing them.[1] Although electricity generation may be suited to a competitive market, its transmission and distribution were natural monopolies in which it was usually more efficient for a single firm to operate with

---

1 Most other Canadian provinces followed similar patterns between the 1920s and the 1960s—New Brunswick in 1920, Saskatchewan in 1950, Newfoundland and Labrador in 1954. Public and private utilities competed in Manitoba until 1953, in BC until 1962, and in Quebec until 1963.

economies of scale, particularly on mega-projects such as the huge generating facilities on the rivers of the BC interior, eastern and northern Quebec, and northern Manitoba. Rather than attempting to regulate the monopoly profits of private producers, most provinces eventually opted for public ownership, regardless of the ideological orientation of their governments. The cheap power generated by these projects created strong constituencies for public power development which cut across the political spectrum, at least until opposition from Aboriginal communities and environmental groups began to exert greater influence in the 1970s and 1980s. They also developed strong political linkages between Crown corporations and private engineering, construction, and other firms which benefited from their activity and growth.

A more contemporary example is the federal government's use of Export Development Canada to provide export financing and insurance to major export industries, particularly aerospace and transportation equipment manufacturers such as Bombardier that often compete with government-supported firms in other countries (Jack 2003: FP1, 4). This approach to public enterprise has been quite common among Liberal and PC governments in the absence of major conflicts with dominant private industry players.

A second approach to the use of public enterprises to promote economic development involves the use of "redistributive corporations (that) ... challenge the distribution of economic and political benefits and thus extend state control over the economy" (Freeman 1995: 5). Such an approach may combine an ideological agenda of social change and the pursuit of policy control over strategic industries as the means of promoting different approaches to economic development.

Government ownership as a tool of redistributive economic development was used most broadly by social democratic governments in Saskatchewan and Quebec, the former between the 1940s and the 1970s, the latter during the Quiet Revolution of the 1960s and 1970s (Chandler 1983b). Post-1960 Quebec governments used a wide range of GBEs as a way of fostering the development of a French-speaking business community and in reducing its dependence on English-Canadian and US capital for economic development. Although sometimes critical of the province's statist economic policies, most Quebec business groups have adapted to Quebec's corporatist networks of interlocking political and economic relationships between individual business, government, and GBE decision-makers.

A third approach to public enterprise entails the use of "nationalistic" corporations as "an amalgam of facilitative and redistributive corporations" (Freeman 1995: 5) competing for political and economic power not only with private corporations but with other political jurisdictions. Such corporations may be used to pursue federal or provincial policy goals in key sectors through the production and distribution of strategic goods and services or by becoming major players in the world of finance capitalism and investment banking.

During the 1970s, the Saskatchewan NDP government took over most of that province's potash companies after court decisions frustrated its attempts to shape industry development through complex tax and royalty schemes. The federal government's creation of Petro-Canada and Ontario's purchase of a controlling interest in Suncor during the same period were part of a larger political contest with energy-producing provinces and multinational oil companies for control over the economic benefits of fast-rising world oil prices (Doern and Toner 1985).

For many years, the Quebec government used the Caisse de dépôt as a central element of its industrial strategy. The Caisse has invested heavily in the expansion of major Quebec-based businesses, often combining commercial and political objectives in ways that provoked political controversy. Although the Caisse is formally independent of political direction in its investment strategies, the sovereigntist PQ government of Jacques Parizeau planned to use the Caisse's financial resources to back its strategy for negotiating independence had the referendum of 1995 resulted in a "Yes" vote (Yakabuski 1998: B1, 4).

However, GBEs whose functions are primarily redistributive may become counter-productive as instruments of economic development. Political favouritism or interference, conflict with other business and economic interests, questionable business plans, or simply poor management decisions may detract from economic development through the misallocation of resources and by fostering business uncertainty over the fairness or predictability of market rules. The use of public pension funds, in particular, to promote national or provincial champions, whether in the public or private sectors, is not without its risks. Pension plans have legal and moral obligations—fiduciary responsibility—to manage investments on behalf of future pensioners in ways that limit risks while pursuing competitive returns on investment. The politicization of investment funds mortgages the future income security of pensioners to governments' political objectives, which usually have a much shorter time horizon, or to undue exposure to market risk when favoured entrepreneurs make serious misjudgements in their corporate strategies.

In recent years, governments have sought to insulate themselves from such risks by subjecting public pension plans to commercial and regulatory disciplines similar, if not always identical, to other employer or employee-managed funds. Rising concerns over these issues have prompted Caisse management to move away from its traditional role as the financier of "Quebec Inc." towards a greater emphasis on maximizing investment returns and managing risks for future generations of Quebecers (Yakabuski 2003; Pouliot 2004). Since its creation in 1997, the Canada Pension Plan Investment Board (CPPIB) has actively sought to insulate itself against perceptions of political favouritism, poor risk management, or the indulgence of questionable corporate governance practices by firms in which its pensioners' funds are invested. However, the huge pools of capital managed by the Caisse ($174.7 billion in assets in 2004), the CPPIB ($87 billion in mid-2005), and other public sector investment funds are a constant temptation to politicians and interest groups who would like to influence their management to serve their political objectives.

A central challenge in using GBEs to promote economic development has always been to provide political guidance and accountability in defining their mandates while limiting the degree of political interference in day-to-day operations. The developmental function of GBEs, often linked to a nation-building or province-building vision of their executives, has sometimes clashed with the demands of financial accountability to governments whose resources, while substantial, are not unlimited. GBE decision-makers who are able to develop supportive economic constituencies among businesses, farmers, municipal leaders, or consumers can enjoy considerable political and managerial discretion. GBEs that report serious operating losses or that antagonize major constituencies of the governing party put themselves at risk of much closer political supervision or even court the spectre of privatization (Freeman 1995; Wiseman and Whorley 2002).

Governments may choose to recognize and correct such mistakes by changing a public corporation's mandate or its regulatory environment or by selling their interests in under-performing corporations when they no longer serve a vital policy mandate. BC's retreat from its venture into manufacturing fast ferries as a way of improving public ferry service while revitalizing the province's shipbuilding industry is one example of the risks of public entrepreneurship. Another was Ontario's ill-timed purchase of Sunoco's Canadian assets at the height of the oil price bubble, while Ontario Hydro sank billions of dollars into nuclear power reactors whose technical problems and cost overruns during a period of falling energy prices drove the provincial utility to the verge of bankruptcy by the mid-1990s (Daniels and Trebilcock 1996: 6).

These failings are anything but unique to public enterprises—as a number of spectacular failures in the private sector have shown. However, whether facilitative or redistributive, the success or failure of GBEs in balancing political goals and economic disciplines depends on both the relative ability or limitations of government and other public sector decision-makers in evaluating market opportunities and failures and the mix of policy instruments most likely to provide the one and avoid or correct the other.

2. Correcting Market Failures, Filling Market Gaps

GBEs may emerge or expand as political and economic instruments to correct market failures, to take advantage of unmet market opportunities, or to fill political demands for the provision of particular services that may not be economically viable in existing market (and technological) environments. In the first case, government ownership may be a *corrective* to negative externalities. In the second, it may be *catalytic*, generating positive externalities beneficial to society as a whole, including many businesses. In the third, rather than increasing the net economic well-being of society, government ownership is primarily *redistributive*: a means of transferring benefits (and costs) from one segment of society to another. In the last two examples, governments accept the risks inherent in business ventures and the political consequences of economic success or failure.

Regulating Negative Externalities

Public enterprise is one of several policy instruments, including various forms of economic regulation, for the delivery of particular goods or services that may lend themselves to negative externalities: the involuntary shifting of economic or social costs from business activity. As noted in Chapter 3, governments may set up GBEs to deliver quasi-public goods such as clean water, electric utilities, or public transit as an alternative to their provision by private monopolies.

Public ownership of liquor distribution networks, introduced in most provinces between the 1920s and the 1940s, was originally viewed as a political trade-off between the social problems associated with the widespread private distribution of alcohol—crime, public drunkenness, and domestic abuse—and the inability of governments to enforce prohibition in the absence of broad public support. As public attitudes changed, bodies such as the Liquor Control Board of Ontario (LCBO) and its counterparts in other provinces gradually shifted from a quasi-regulatory outlook to a more commercial one.

Governments face many of the same challenges in regulating public monopolies as in regulating private monopolies or dominant firms: clearly defining the public interest, developing the expertise necessary to evaluate the policy demands of monopoly interests, developing and enforcing checks and balances on monopolistic practices, and avoiding capture of regulators by special interests, which, in the case of GBEs, could be by their executives, unions, and/or associated private interests.

Capturing Positive Externalities

Government investment and ownership have frequently been justified for their potential value in filling market gaps: promoting economic innovation and generating positive externalities from ventures perceived to be too risky for private investors and entrepreneurs, either independently or without government support. Alternately, some forms of economic activity such as basic research may generate economic benefits, or positive externalities, which cannot be captured effectively by private firms and which may thus not benefit from optimal levels of investment. This risk-sharing approach to public enterprise is often linked to the facilitative strategies for economic development discussed earlier.

During the mid-twentieth century, many policy analysts viewed GBE investments as preferable to large-scale government subsidies to private businesses in support of public policy objectives. The principle of risk-sharing in such cases suggests that if governments assume a share of the risks that would otherwise be borne by private investors, they should also share in the economic returns (Poschmann 2003: 3).

Governments at all levels have created GBEs to manage the building and operation of public infrastructure—bridges, port authorities, municipal utilities, and airport authorities—on a more or less self-sustaining basis. GBEs have also been active in fostering mega-project development, the development and commercialization of new technologies, and the provision of financial support for key industries on commercial or quasi-commercial terms. Examples include the federal government's use of Atomic Energy of Canada Limited to promote the development of nuclear technologies and related industries in Canada, the creation of Canada Mortgage and Housing Corporation to stimulate private sector lending to promote individual home ownership, and the developmental role of large-scale provincial investments in BC Hydro and Alberta's Syncrude tar sands project in the 1960s and 1970s (Mitchell 1983: 284-332; Taylor, Warrack, and Baetz 1999: 114).

Both federal and provincial governments have sought to play a catalytic role as complementary or supplementary lenders or investors in private firms that might not otherwise be viewed as commercially viable by private lenders. The Industrial Development Bank (now Business Development Bank of Canada) was created during the 1940s to provide supplementary financing for private firms. Export Development Canada provided credit insurance for exporters, along with other financial services, when most Canadian banks lacked the resources or expertise to finance international business activity except for well-established clients in major centres. Most provincial governments have established economic development corporations targeted at particular sectors. As Canada's financial services industry has matured and become more entrepreneurial, governments have adjusted the mandates of its financial sector GBEs, sometimes shifting towards more commercial mandates and in some cases adopting them to new quasi-commercial developmental roles.

The activities of financial GBEs have been subjected to a variety of criticisms from charges of unfair competition from Canadian banks and foreign competitors to accusations of excessive caution and red tape from prospective clients, especially in the small business sector. Debates over the use of government funds to subsidize, share, or substitute for the risks of private business investment in the interests of economic development and, later, job creation, are as old as Canada. Indeed, they continue in current debates over the role of public-private partnerships in providing public services and the rules that should govern such investments to protect the public interest (Boase 2000; Poschmann 2003).

One risk of such approaches, whether delivered by GBEs, government regulations, or subsidies, is that they may simply become ill-disguised forms of political favouritism either to deserving groups in society for the purchase of votes or as rewards to friends and supporters of the current government. The Chrétien government was embroiled in a series of scandals arising from such accusations in recent years. Although there are still strong constituencies for this sort of distributive politics in many parts of Canada, economists and other policy-makers have become increasingly critical of both government regulation and GBEs as tools of political favouritism in the marketplace both on grounds of efficiency and fairness.

3. Promoting Government Ideology

The promotion of economic development and growth is usually a major priority for any government, regardless of its ideology. However, the relationship between government and business, and the role of GBEs as one element in that relationship, is often heavily influenced by the ideology of the party in power.

It has already been noted that most Canadian governments, regardless of their formal ideologies, have often resorted to GBEs as instruments of public policies. Wiseman and Whorley (2002) have noted that social democratic governments, particularly in Saskatchewan, Quebec, and Manitoba, have been more inclined to use Crown corporations as instruments for economic coordination and planning, while business-oriented governments are more likely to use public enterprise to deal with particular policy problems in ways that complement or supplement private business operations in the marketplace.

The creation of GBEs as tools for the redistribution of political and economic power from large private corporations to governments has often followed the replacement of a conservative, business-oriented government with a socialist or social democratic one, as in Saskatchewan during the 1940s, Quebec in the 1960s, or BC in the 1970s. However, a reverse swing of the political pendulum may result in the commercialization or privatization of such businesses, particularly if they have not yet established a strong public constituency. For example, the BC Resources Investment Corporation (BCRIC), created by a short-lived NDP government during the 1970s, was privatized by its Social Credit successors, which distributed shares in the corporation to all BC residents as an expression of conservative populism. During the late 1980s, Grant Devine's PC government in Saskatchewan reversed the previous NDP government's nationalization of the Potash Corporation of Saskatchewan (and several other firms) by turning it into a mixed enterprise with gradually expanding private ownership to facilitate the company's expansion and financial returns to the taxpayers of Saskatchewan over an extended period (Heggie 1998). Similar approaches were taken in the Mulroney government's conversion of Petro-Canada to a mixed enterprise after 1988 and its privatization of Air Canada in the early 1990s, as well as the Chrétien government's privatization of Canadian National Railways (CNR) in the mid-1990s.

These developments suggest that ideological divisions over the role of the state in the marketplace are not only based on conflicts between social democratic and free enterprise political outlooks, but also by the degree to which governments—of whatever ideological outlook—emphasize technocratic goals of economic efficiency and commercial viability as opposed to populist goals of protecting employment in state industries or subsidizing economic benefits to particular social and economic constituencies. These trade-offs are illustrated in Box 9.1.

Another ideological dimension to public enterprise in Canada has traditionally been the role of GBEs as instruments of economic nationalism, province-building, and sometimes both, as discussed earlier in this chapter. The idea of Crown corporations as instruments of nation- or province-building goes beyond promoting economic development to shifting the benefits from controlling particular industries from outsiders to Canadians or residents of a particular province through their governments. These ideas were implicit in the slogan of Quebec's Quiet Revolution, "*Maîtres chez nous*" (masters in our own house), and in the growth of federal and provincial Crown corporations during the 1970s to promote technological sovereignty and greater Canadian control over resource development. More recently, they have been visible in the participation of Aboriginal communities in major resource developments through the creation of their own GBEs, especially in Canada's north.

Box 9.1: Ideologies and GBEs: Cross-Cutting Pressures

	Technocratic	Efficiency-oriented Commercialization	Greater resort to PPPs, potential for privatization
Social Democratic			Business-oriented
Planning/ centralization			Facilitative/ad hoc decentralized
	Populist	Distributive Emphasis on employment protection, subsidizing key government constituencies	

4. Exercising Policy Control or Influence Over Strategic Industry

The use of GBEs as instruments of state-building and economic nationalism also illustrate a third major factor in the growth of public enterprise in Canada: the desire of federal, provincial, and sometimes municipal governments in Canada to exercise policy control or influence over strategic industries in competition with private interests or other governments. Such power may be exerted through the use of regulatory controls over market entry, production levels, or restrictions on levels of foreign ownership. However, the use of GBEs to shape the evolution and growth of particular industry sectors, or of industrial development on a broader scale, has been most visible in industries associated with the development of the transportation, energy, and communications sectors and those related to national defence.

Even staunch champions of private enterprise, such as C.D. Howe between the 1930s and 1950s or BC Premier W.A.C. Bennett (1952-72) favoured Crown corporations as a way of serving specific policy goals. Howe gave Trans-Canada Airways (later Air Canada) a privileged position in the Canadian air transportation market which persisted until the late 1970s (Clancy 2004: Chapter 4). Although many of the GBEs created to support Canada's effort during the Second World War were privatized after 1945, companies in strategic sectors such as nuclear energy, uranium mining (Eldorado Nuclear, now Cameco Corp.), aircraft manufacturing (Canadair), international telecommunications (Teleglobe), and synthetic rubber (Polysar) remained under government ownership for many years or are still part of Canada's public sector (Atomic Energy of Canada). After private sector projects failed to produce promised benefits, Bennett expanded BC Hydro to enforce the province's claims to control the hydroelectric potential of the Columbia and Peace River systems, successfully challenging the federal government's efforts to control development on the Columbia in its treaty negotiations with the US (Mitchell 1983). Peter Clancy notes the competing efforts of provincial governments including Saskatchewan (Ipsco), Quebec (Sidbec), and Nova Scotia (Sysco) to foster or preserve local steel companies between the 1950s and 1980s as instruments of provincial industrial strategies, sometimes in ways that resulted in politically and economically perverse outcomes (Clancy 2004: Chapter 3).

The global oil price shocks and threatened energy shortages of the 1970s and early 1980s gave both the federal and several provincial governments a strong political incentive to enter or expand their presence in the oil and gas sector as a counter-weight to the market dominance of the OPEC oil cartel and multinational oil companies. Petro-Canada was explicitly created in 1977 as one of several instruments of federal energy policy before falling world oil prices and the bitter political conflicts surrounding Canada's National Energy Program subsequently led successive federal governments to yield jurisdiction to the provinces, subject to international commitments under the FTA of 1988.

Provincial governments continue to use a mix of public ownership and regulation in asserting policy control over industries such as liquor distribution, gambling, and car insurance. These ventures may be used as instruments of social control, to manage the pricing of services in politically sensitive industries, or to generate windfall profits as an alternative to higher general tax rates.

5. Protecting Employment

Historically, a major factor in the extension of government ownership of business has been the preservation of employment, particularly in less developed parts of Canada. As noted in Chapter 4, government assistance to business in the development of major infrastructure or industrial development projects has often resulted in their financial overextension and vulnerability to external economic shocks (Bliss 1985). Rather than risk widespread economic damage from major business failures, governments have often stepped in to preserve key industries, often at the cost of facing years of subsidies to their uneconomic operations.

The nationalization during the First World War of the bankrupt Grand Trunk and Canadian Northern Railroads, which were later consolidated into the CNR, was seen at the time as a vital step in preserving the economic viability of hundreds of communities dependent on these railways for their main links to the outside world. The nationalization during the 1960s of Nova Scotia's Dominion Coal and Steel Co. (see Clancy 2004: Chapter 3) was seen as critical to the preservation of employment in several chronically depressed Cape Breton communities, although the nationalized firms never became commercially viable, swallowing more than $3 billion in federal and provincial subsidies over the next 30 years.

On occasion, governments that had invested in the expansion or revitalization of major local employers found themselves saddled with ownership of a white elephant when the private entrepreneurs they had supported ran out of money. During the 1960s and 1970s, Newfoundland inherited a series of money-losing private ventures co-sponsored by governments desperate for job-creating investment. Alberta lost at least $71 million from its investment in the Gainers meat packing plant in the mid-

1980s when industry restructuring, mismanagement, and a sharp downturn in the Alberta economy bankrupted the company (Koch 2003: 64).

These high profile failures have made governments more reluctant in recent years to take ownership of the problems of private companies. Governments—even social democratic ones—are more likely to design adjustment packages for employees of firms facing major job losses due to restructuring or to facilitate the reorganization of ailing firms under new ownership, often with financial assistance from government-owned financial institutions, than to resort to public ownership in such circumstances.

6. Commercializing an Under-Performing Area of Public Sector Activity

By contrast, the **commercialization** of public services involves the application of market disciplines—including full cost accounting, financial self-sufficiency (or its logical extension, full cost recovery), greater customer orientation, and, frequently, exposure to market competition—to the provision of services by and to public sector agencies and departments.

All governments have faced budgetary pressures for greater efficiency and fewer subsidies to their business operations during the past generation. In some cases, heavily subsidized operations were reorganized and separated from commercially viable ones. For example, the CNR's 1977 reorganization split Via Rail's heavily subsidized passenger services from its generally profitable rail freight operations. In 1981, the Post Office Department, notorious for its inefficient mail delivery and acrimonious labour relations, was converted into a Crown corporation and mandated to move towards financial self-sufficiency. The reorganization of the Alberta Treasury Branches—now called ATB Financial—into a profitable, increasingly competitive Crown corporation in 1996 is a comparable example of commercializing a troubled government agency at the provincial level (Koch 2003).

Commercialization has also been applied to internal government services such as:

- printing, with the conversion of the federal Queen's Printer, a division of Supply and Services Canada, to the Canada Communications Group in the 1990s;
- the management of government buildings and real estate (e.g., BC Buildings Corporation);
- the management of ports, airports, airport security, and air navigation services, often through their devolution to non-profit corporations or joint ventures with other levels of government;
- the reorganization of provincial property tax assessment services for municipal governments and other public registry services in Ontario, BC, Saskatchewan, and Alberta, often through temporary or ongoing joint ventures with private businesses;
- the devolution of responsibility for the management of some GBEs engaged in legislated monopoly enterprises, such as the Canadian Wheat Board,

within a shared governance organization of producer and government representatives; and

- the management of public pensions, through the creation of the arm's length Canada Pension Plan Investment Board and of public sector employment pensions, often by transferring their management to independent trustees rather than using them as an inexpensive source of government borrowing.

The multiple and varied forms of GBEs embodied in these arrangements reflect their changing face and the growing range of policy instruments or tools available to governments in the provision of public services, the promotion of economic development, and the organization of economic and social regulation.

The Changing Face of GBEs

The size, scope, and role of the government business sector has changed significantly since the mid-1980s. Just as Peters's Five I's—ideas, institutions, individuals, interests, and the international environment—have played a role in the expansion of public enterprises, they have also affected changes in their mandates, organizational structures, and relations with governments, businesses, and citizens.

These changes have led to a sharp decline in the role of GBEs in some sectors, particularly transportation, telecommunications, and resource development. In others, particularly financial services, public utilities, and infrastructure, GBEs continue to play a significant role, although one that often reflects varying political priorities and relationships between public and private sectors in different jurisdictions. The commercialization of traditional regulatory or public service functions has also resulted in the creation of new GBEs as governments look for ways to improve the delivery of public services or to increase public revenues.

Ideas

Neo-classical economists during the late 1970s and early 1980s persuaded many government decision-makers that government subsidies to business (including GBEs) were a major source of economic inefficiency and that removing regulatory barriers to competition would increase the efficiency, competitiveness, and output of both private and many public sector enterprises (Economic Council of Canada 1981). Fiscal pressures on governments from rising deficits and relatively slow economic growth won a supportive audience among many government decision-makers as well as other political and business leaders. Initially championed by neo-conservative political parties and some business liberals during the 1980s, these ideas were adopted in varying degrees by neo-liberal and moderate social democratic governments in the 1990s.

A parallel influence within government was the gradual spread of ideas generally described as the new public management (NPM). The reorganization of governments in most English-speaking countries was intended to promote greater political accountability, economic efficiency, and responsiveness to citizens through a mix of organizational restructuring, separation of some political and administrative functions, and the introduction of a variety of business management methods to the public sector. Aucoin, Kernaghan, and other scholars of public administration note that most Canadian governments have been fairly selective in their adoption of NPM methods, adopting a tool-kit approach to the introduction of new methods and structures suited to particular organizations and circumstances, rather than large-scale systemic change (Aucoin 1995a; Aucoin 2000; Kernaghan, Marson, and Borins 2000: 1-16).

Crown corporations and other GBEs have always been a partial exception to hierarchical, command-and-control approaches to the workings of government bureaucracies. However, the new governance paradigms emphasize a greater flexibility in organizational structures and policy tools that lends itself to the proliferation of GBEs, mixed enterprises, and other non-traditional forms of government or quasi-governmental organizations (Kernaghan, Marson, and Borins 2000; Salamon 2002: 1-48). The collective effect of these changes, summarized in Box 9.2, is often a blurring of traditional distinctions between public and private sectors, as well as greater emphasis on less hierarchical, more network-oriented or transactional approaches to management.

Box 9.2: The New Governance Paradigm

Classical Public Administration	New Governance
Program/agency	Tool
Hierarchy	Network
Public vs. private	Public + private
Command and control	Negotiation and persuasion
Management skills	Enablement skills

Source: Salamon 2002: 9.

Institutions

Institutions describe not only organizational structures but also stable systems of rules and the means for their enforcement in public, private, and non-profit sectors. As noted in Chapters 5 and 8, Canada's growing integration in the North American and global economic systems, reinforced by its obligations under FTA, NAFTA, and other international agreements, has reshaped both the domestic and international environment for its economic policies and the context in which many commercial and quasi-commercial GBEs must operate by reducing opportunities for regulatory discrimination in favour of domestic businesses, including public enterprises. The routine use of political influence to direct procurement contracts by governments or GBEs to favoured or troubled corporations now puts such firms at significant risk of legal penalties in export markets, imposing new disciplines on the use of direct and indirect government subsidies (see "The Algoma-Sysco Rail Dispute" in Clancy 2004; see also Jack 2003). Formal and informal fiscal rules, such as requirements for balanced budgets, reductions in public debt to GDP ratios, and other measures to promote greater fiscal sustainability of public services have also reinforced trends towards the commercialization of many public services and the financing of many capital works projects.

The partial economic deregulation of air and rail transportation, telecommunications, and financial services sectors have often followed sectoral changes introduced by other major industrial countries, creating a more competitive market environment. Major technological changes have transformed both the operations of many industries and the information collection and management processes of governments. The spread of microcomputer technologies has facilitated the growth of business and service networks that blur traditional boundaries between the public, private, and non-profit sectors. Technological change and increased private sector competition have also fostered a culture of consumer sovereignty which has greatly increased public expectations of quality, timeliness, and choice both in the workings of commercial GBEs and in the delivery of many public services as well.

Many of these ideas have been adopted by federal and provincial auditors general in their value-for-money critiques of government operations, although their demands for political accountability often work at cross-purposes with proposals for greater managerial autonomy for GBEs and other arm's-length agencies of government (Roberts 1996).

Individuals and Interests

Individual politicians, senior public sector managers, and GBE executives often play a significant role in the selection of particular policy tools and trade-offs, although this role is often veiled by the lack of transparency in many policy processes. The role of individuals is often interwoven with that of particular interests inside and outside governments—geographic or industry constituencies, individual government departments, public service unions, and other political actors. However, while business interests have frequently supported the commercialization and privatization of GBEs, the policy decisions made in specific cases, the balancing of political and policy trade-offs, and the selection of particular policy instruments or tools frequently come down to the exercise of personal discretion by senior public sector decision-makers.

Ontario NDP Premier Bob Rae's willingness to accept a public-private partnership to build Highway 407, a privately managed toll highway across the northern and western suburbs of Toronto, contrasted sharply with the ideological orientation of many of his party's strongest supporters during the early 1990s. However, it made political sense in the context of a slumping economy, high unemployment among unionized construction workers, and his government's own fiscal constraints. Published reports suggest that the highway's ultimate privatization owed less to ideology than to the short-term political and revenue needs of Rae's PC successors (Boase 2000: 85-86; Ibbitson 2000).

Similarly, the 2003 reorganization of Quebec's Caisse in response to significant market losses reportedly owed as much to Quebec PQ Premier Bernard Landry's readiness to replace CEO Jean-Claude Scraire, a veteran public sector executive committed to the corporatist Quebec Inc. model of economic development, with former Laurentian Bank President Henri-Paul Rousseau, who appears more oriented towards traditional concepts of pension fund management (Marotte 2002: B1; McNish, Marotte, and Seguin 2002: B1).

The Ontario government's restructuring, partial privatization, and subsequent re-regulation of Ontario Hydro and its successor companies between 1998 and 2003—while open to legitimate debate on both political and economic grounds—reflected as much, if not possibly more so, of the personalities, ambitions, and political judgements of senior political, bureaucratic, and Hydro decision-makers as it did any coherent ideological agenda or economic analysis (Grant 2002: 56-62; Ingram 2002).

Implications for GBEs and Business-Government Relations
In summary, changes in the organization and mandates of GBEs, and in their interaction with the private and non-profit sectors, have paralleled shifts both in the domestic and international economic environments and in the climate of ideas governing the role of governments, their relationship to the market economy, and their management philosophies. The effect of these changes on the GBE sector and on business-government relations in Canada can be summarized as follows: commercialization, privatization, hybridization, and innovation.

Commercialization
Most commercial and economic development Crown corporations have become increasingly commercialized, or subject to the competitive disciplines of the marketplace: they require greater (if not full) economic self-sufficiency, greater responsiveness to consumers and economic efficiency, and greater managerial accountability based on transparent business plans and performance criteria.

Most private sector business associations have supported the trend towards balanced budgets, lower government subsidies to business, and the removal of many regulatory preferences for GBEs. In general, the contracting-out of public sector functions that could be performed more efficiently by private sector suppliers has enjoyed broad business support, although this often guarantees conflicts with public sector unions.

In some cases, commercialization has meant shifting a larger share of costs to the consumers of public services through full cost recovery demands and the introduction of new, value-added services. For example, during the early 1990s, the ownership and management of most airports across Canada was shifted from Transport Canada to local airport authorities, many of which sought to transform them into instruments for local and regional economic development, usually with the active participation of local governments and businesses. The new authorities were also forced to find new sources of revenues to make up operating deficits, to find ways of reducing costs, or both. In other cases, governments have increased fees for non-discretionary services. The rapid growth of user-fees resulting from commercialization is more controversial when individual or business taxpayers have few substitutes or little choice in the use of particular services (Blair Consulting Group 1999; Canada, Standing Committee on Finance 2000).

Privatization

A logical extension of commercialization in some cases is privatization: the shift of a controlling ownership of a government enterprise to private ownership. The logic of commercialization might reduce the extent to which governments choose to use Crown corporations as instruments of public policy, particularly if policy decisions reduce their efficiency or add unduly to their operating costs.

The deregulation of energy, transportation, and telecommunications sectors during the late 1980s, often in response to regulatory changes in other countries, forced several commercial Crown corporations to compete with private firms in the open marketplace. Large deficits limited the capacity of governments to finance their expansion. Governments which emphasized competitiveness and efficiency, rather than other policy goals, became increasingly open to allowing private investment in GBEs, particularly if social or equity-related policy goals could be met through other forms of regulation. Managerial autonomy from political interference was a key requirement to obtain private investment. These factors were significant in the federal government's sale of part or all of its shares in Teleglobe Canada (1987), Petro-Canada (1988), Air Canada (1991), and the CNR (1995-96).

The level of privatization among provincial governments has varied widely, depending on the ideological orientation of individual governments and market conditions of particular industries. Generally speaking, the greater the levels of competition present in industries such as natural resources and telecommunications after the introduction of regulatory reforms in 1987, the greater the likelihood of full or partial privatization. Major provincial privatizations during this era included Alberta Energy Company (1975-93), Potash Company of Saskatchewan (1989-93), Alberta Government Telephones (now Telus Corp) (1990-91), and Manitoba Telephones (1997). Technological and regulatory changes have led to growing competition in electricity distribution. However, only Nova Scotia (NS Power, 1992) has privatized its electrical utility to date. Although Ontario's PC government created a central agency responsible for privatization after 1995, it had only a minimal impact on the province's broader public sector.

The trend towards privatization has been limited by a number of factors:

- *Poor commercial prospects.* Some government enterprises are inherently unprofitable or must spin off uneconomic elements before they become attractive to private investors. Governments unwilling to make such changes because of political commitments or competing policy goals—as in Ontario's 2003 decision to cap electricity rates below the costs of production—are likely to look for other policy alternatives.
- *Monopoly profits.* Some government enterprises, such as liquor distribution and gambling GBEs, are highly profitable and thus a valued source of

government revenues. Although the Ontario PC government of Mike Harris succeeded in improving the efficiency and profitability of the province's liquor control board by threatening to consider its privatization during the mid-1990s, the resulting financial windfall proved too lucrative for any provincial treasurer to abandon, particularly when seeking the fiscal flexibility necessary to reduce personal and corporate income taxes without reductions to core public services.

- *Natural monopoly.* Some services, such as the transmission of electricity, are natural monopolies at either the local or provincial level. Moving from a public to private monopoly is not a guarantee of greater efficiency, nor does it preclude the need for some form of arm's length regulation of monopoly services to protect the public interest. Consumers (including businesses) are likely to oppose privatization of public services or monopoly GBEs unless they have a choice of greater value or cost-effective alternatives to the services they provide. The Ontario government's retreat in 2003 from its proposal to privatize Hydro One, the province's electricity distribution utility, is a classic example of the political and economic challenges of shifting ownership of a natural monopoly from the public to the private sector.

- *Political resistance from public or influential constituencies.* Many GBEs have developed strong constituencies—public service unions, direct beneficiaries of public services or government subsidies, cultural elites—with the political and economic resources to challenge privatization. For example, the Alberta PC government has been reluctant to risk a political backlash from rural and small business constituents concerned over possible branch closures and reduced competition in many communities despite calls from some sources to privatize ATB Financial Corporation (Koch 2003).

A more controversial rationale for privatization is the generation of revenues from asset sales to finance the ongoing operating expenses of governments. Rather than carrying out an underlying policy rationale—such as access to capital necessary to finance service improvements, the internal logic of privatizing commercial GBEs in a competitive marketplace, or even debt reduction through the sale of assets marginal to government operations—such privatizations may result in no net benefits to citizens and taxpayers while contributing to ongoing increases in the costs of some public services.

Hybridization

New forms of GBEs have blurred the lines between government and business, creating a wide variety of public-private partnerships. Boase (2000) notes that these partnerships may take several forms, ranging from formalized consultative arrangements to different kinds of contributory or operational partnerships in which governments fund societal organizations to achieve shared goals.

At the federal level, these arrangements include more than 140 shared governance organizations, with both government and various forms of societal representation on their boards of directors. The Canadian Wheat Board is among the most prominent of these organizations. Boxes 9.3 and 9.4 illustrate the range of governing instruments and collaborative arrangements used by governments in the delivery of policies, programs, and services.

Box 9.3: Alternative Service Delivery: Multiple Policy Instruments

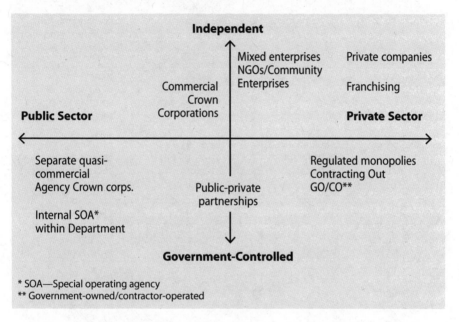

Poschmann argues that public-private partnerships are preferable to privatization when GBEs produce "goods or services that have no predominant *public good* component" in the economic sense that equitable cost-recovery from individual consumers is impossible or impractical (Poschman 2003: 3). However, the greater the risks or uncertainties associated with the delivery of public services, the greater the difficulties in structuring public-private partnerships to ensure the consistent delivery of services and a fair sharing of risks and rewards between public and private sector partners (DeBettignies and Ross 2004: 148-49).

Public-private partnerships are frequently used for the construction or maintenance of public infrastructure, such as toll highways, bridges, airports, municipal sewer and water treatment facilities, and sometimes school or hospital buildings, although, typically, the operations of the latter remain in the hands of public authorities. Examples include the Confederation Bridge linking New Brunswick and PEI, maintenance or management of provincially owned casinos, and a wide range of other services provided both to the general public and to individual government departments and agencies.

Box 9.4: Collaborative/Partnership Arrangements at Federal and Provincial Levels

Type	Example	Partners	Purpose
Contracting-Out and franchising	Canada Post retail outlets	Federal Crown corporation, private sector	Sell Canada Post products and services
PPPs with private sector	Teranet Land Registration*	Ontario government, private sector	Development, management of electronic land registry system
PPPs with third sector	Career Edge	Federal government, YMCA, private sector	To develop internships for youth in private sector
Devolution	Building Healthy Communities Strategy	Federal government, Aboriginal community	Facilitate community control of health resources
Privatization to regulated or third-sector industry	Nav Canada	Federal government, non-profit corporation	Allow user groups to manage Canada's air navigation
Simple privatization	Air Canada	Private sector	Deliver air transport services to Canadians

* Fully privatized 2003.
Source: Adapted from Zussman 2002: 67.

Governments enter into such arrangements for many reasons. The cost of financing rising public debts between the 1970s and 1990s sharply cut into public infrastructure spending, which yielded fewer political benefits than increasing transfer programs or spending on high profile services such as health care and education (Poschmann 2003: 3-4). Commercial ventures may allow for the financing of capital projects without drawing on limited public sector resources (or allow them to be financed off-budget). When replacing subsidized public ventures, there may be a means of improving service through the use of innovative technologies and management methods while using restructuring as a means of moving towards full-cost recovery. They may enable governments to obtain access to greater expertise and efficiency in project management and operations or to develop industries with the capacity to develop such expertise on a larger scale, creating potential export industries for the future.

The blending of public and private business raises a number of cautions and concerns about balancing business disciplines and protecting the public interest. Governments have purchased many different kinds of goods and services from private businesses for many years. Contracting procedures require transparency, impartiality, and accountability for performance of the contract, based on clear standards to avoid accusations of political favouritism, self-dealing by politicians or government officials, or legal challenges in export markets. Businesses that invest time and effort in competing for public contracts are usually as anxious as taxpayers (and often more so, due to their increased exposure) that the rules governing the process be transparent, impartial, and subject to some form of independent or legal review.

However, the structuring of Requests for Proposals (RFPs) for major projects is often complicated by processes that encourage private bidders to suggest new and innovative ways of meeting government objectives, thus externalizing more of the trade-offs inherent in designing public policies or delivering many public services. The long-running saga of the Defence Department's contracts for new search-and-rescue helicopters to replace its decrepit fleet of Sea-Kings suggests the degree to which the design of major projects can become politicized both inside and outside government (Robinson 2002; Conference of Defence Associations n.d.). The issue of transparency is often problematic in other areas, both for companies seeking to protect proprietary information such as intellectual property or internal cost-management practices and for governments seeking to strengthen their bargaining position when negotiating with several parties or to protect themselves against criticism by offended interest groups (especially public sector unions), the media, or the public (Poschmann 2003: 2).

Normal business ventures, whether carried out by GBEs or private firms in a competitive marketplace, are characterized by the confidentiality of private contracts. However, such arrangements make it difficult for the auditor general and others charged with monitoring the efficient and responsible use of public funds to do so effectively. Several governments have introduced checks and balances, such as the use of independent advisors to structure processes for the design and awarding of public-private partnerships, conflict of interest regulations, and external checks on the probity and transparency of such processes to protect the public interest. Both Boase (2000) and Poschmann (2003) argue that greater transparency is essential to preserve public confidence that PPPs are structured in ways that provide general public benefit.

Other major issues involve issues of risk-sharing and contract safeguards to ensure that contractual obligations are met on both sides. Box 9.5 outlines the range of potential risks faced in public-private infrastructure partnerships and the relative capacity of partners to assume particular risks. The underlying principle of risk assignment in such cases is that the party that has the greater capacity to control the matters at risk should assume the related financial liabilities in order to limit moral hazards from one partner arbitrarily offloading risks to another.

Citizens' and taxpayers' interests must be protected against the substandard or non-fulfillment of contracts; for instance, by preventing substandard construction, defining and maintaining public health or safety standards, or insuring against the financial instability of contractors. More controversial are arrangements that mandate the use of union workers and the transfer of previously unionized government employees. Taxpayers also want to be protected against the possibility of large cost increases, particularly if they have little or no choice in the use of particular services. On the other hand, contracting firms seek protection against changes in the terms of government contracts, political risks, and other unforeseen hazards. The Chrétien government's cancellation in 1994 of the multi-million dollar contract for the building of a new terminal at Toronto's Pearson International Airport ultimately resulted in legal action which cost taxpayers as much as $700 million.

Box 9.5: Typical Infrastructure Project Risks and Hypothetical Allocations

Risk Category	Examples	Partner Likely to Bear Risk*
Technical risk	Engineering or design failures	Private
Construction risk	Cost escalation owing to faulty technique or delays	Private
Operating risk	Costly operation and maintenance	Private
Revenue risk	Deficient revenue owing to low volume or price of delivered service	Public/private
Financial risk	Costs of inadequate revenue hedging, debt management	Private
Force majeure	Losses from war, acts of God	Public/private
Regulatory/political risk	Changes in law or policy that undermine project finances	Public
Environmental risks	Damage through adverse environmental impacts/liability	Private
Project default	Failure through any combination of the above or other factors	Public/private

* Private partner includes outside lenders or investors.
Source: Poschmann 2003: 7.

More difficult to negotiate is the sharing of unforeseen environmental and market risks and benefits. Neither governments nor businesses should be expected to enter into one-sided contracts that allocate all the economic risks to one party and all the benefits to another. However, examples such as the financial sinkhole of Alberta's Swan Hills Hazardous Waste Disposal plant suggest that the negotiations of such arrangements still have elements of trial and error for both governments and their private partners (Poschmann 2003: 6-12).

Innovation, the New Economy, and the Triple Helix

The shift towards network governance structures can also be seen in the growth of mixed enterprises and partnership arrangements in the promotion of research, innovation, and the New Economy. Governments at all levels are promoting the development of new technologies and economic innovation in complex networks that involve cooperation among governmental (or intergovernmental) agencies, independent non-profit organizations such as universities and hospitals, and private corporations. These arrangements involve complex issues of intellectual property, positive externalities such as the fostering of innovation and human capital, and academic freedom. They may span the full range of contributory, consultative, and cooperative partnerships or be limited to one or more of these.

Governments both support and contract directly for research, fund research indirectly through specialized granting councils and independent foundations, and provide tax incentives for research and development by private businesses. Businesses may sponsor research, finance the testing of new products and processes, and hire researchers (and graduates) of universities and medical research facilities. Universities and medical facilities seek new sources of funding to maintain and expand their operations while seeking to preserve their institutional integrity.

Although these arrangements are sometimes politically controversial, particularly to those ideologically opposed to the influence of capitalism and private corporations in society, they face the same challenge of creating checks and balances to ensure that they are providing benefits to all participants. Such measures should acknowledge and balance the legitimate interests and specialized functions of different participants, ranging from commercial concerns over the confidentiality of proprietary processes, to the continuing need for accountability for the use of public funds, to safeguards related to conflict of interest and professional ethics. As these objectives sometimes conflict, the ongoing viability of partnership arrangements will depend on the capacity of all parties to maintain transparent and effective standards capable of bridging their varied interests and obligations.

Conclusion

The contribution of GBEs to Canada's economic structures reflects the interaction between market and political decision-making at several levels: the broad ideological and policy preferences of governments; their place in shaping industry structures and patterns of political and economic competition in provincial, national, and international markets; and their impact on the investment and operating decisions of individual businesses. They also reflect the pragmatic responses of businesses and politicians to specific problems and challenges, often in ways that involve the pursuit of second- or third-best solutions to complex issues in response to competing political, bureaucratic, and economic priorities and related societal pressures.

The paradox of government involvement in business is that its effectiveness requires shared but distinct responsibilities. It is the government's responsibility to define a clear mandate for GBEs and to provide managers with the autonomy, resources, and incentives necessary for them to achieve these objectives. Governments are expected to hold GBE executives accountable for the financial outcomes of their business operations, which may otherwise become a drain on the public purse, while refraining from interference in their day-to-day business operations. Trends towards commercialization in recent years have led to a growing separation of the economic roles of GBEs from the policy and regulatory functions appropriate to governments, enabling the more even-handed application of regulatory authority and the selection of policy instruments best suited to particular roles and goals.

Canada's open economy, the effects of continuing technological and other economic changes, and the political trade-offs involved in these changes ensure that governments will continue to play an active role through various forms of public enterprise and that this activity will be subject to a wide range of cross-cutting political and economic pressures. The nature of these interactions—and the role of lobbying and government relations industries—will be addressed in greater detail in Part III.

Key Terms and Concepts for Review (see Glossary)

Caisse de dépôt et placement
commercial Crown corporations
commercialization
economic development Crown
   corporations
government business enterprises
   (GBEs)

"hidden Crown corporations"
mixed enterprise
privatization
public-private partnerships (PPPs)
social and government services
   corporations

Questions for Discussion and Review

1. What are three different types of Crown corporations or GBE's discussed in the chapter? Compare and contrast their mandates and degrees of autonomy from government. Give examples of each.

2. What are six major policy objectives used to justify both the creation of public enterprises or GBEs and the nationalization of private businesses? What are some of the policy trade-offs associated with each approach?

3. What are three different types of economic development strategy involving the use of Crown corporations? How does each affect relations among state actors, businesses, and other societal interests? Give examples.

4. How may GBEs be used to correct market failures or fill market gaps? What are the major differences between the two approaches? Give examples.

5. To what extent do ideological factors play a role in defining the objectives of GBEs and the degrees to which they are used as instruments of public policies? What are some of the limitations of using ideology as an explanation for the role of public enterprise?

6. How have governments used GBEs as policy instruments to apply market disciplines to the provision and delivery of public services since the 1970s? What are some of the trade-offs involved in this approach to public sector management?

7. What major factors have contributed to changes in the organization and scope of public enterprise in Canada since the 1970s? How have these changes affected the GBE sector and its relationship to the market economy?

8. What is the difference between the commercialization and privatization of GBEs or Crown corporations? What factors contribute to government decisions to select one approach or the other? Give examples.

9. What are major reasons for the use of public-private partnerships? What are some of the trade-offs of this type of mixed enterprise for governments? For private sector businesses? For non-profit organizations? Give examples.

Suggestions for Further Readings

Boase, Joan Price. 2000. Beyond government: the appeal of public-private partnerships. *Canadian Public Administration* 43(1): 75-92.

Canada, Treasury Board Secretariat. 2004. *2004 Annual Report to Parliament—Crown Corporations and other corporate interests of Canada*. Ottawa: Treasury Board Secretariat (December).

Clancy, Peter. 2004. *The micro-politics of Canadian business: paper, steel, and airlines*. Peterborough, ON: Broadview Press.

DeBettignies, Jean-Etienne, and Thomas W. Ross. 2004. The economics of public-private partnerships. *Canadian Public Policy* 30(2): 135-54.

Economic Council of Canada. 1981. *Reforming regulation*. Ottawa: Supply and Services Canada.

Foster, Kathryn A. 1997. *The political economy of special purpose government*. Washington, DC: Georgetown University Press.

Freeman, Neil B. 1996. *The politics of power: Ontario Hydro and its government.* Toronto: University of Toronto Press.

Kernaghan, Kenneth, Brian Marson, and Sandford Borins. 2000. *The new public organization.* Toronto: Institute for Public Administration of Canada.

Poschmann, Finn. 2003. Private means to public ends: the future of public-private partnerships. *Commentary* # 183. Toronto: C.D. Howe Institute.

Prichard, J.R.S. (Ed.). 1983. *Crown corporations in Canada: the calculus of instrument choice.* Toronto: Butterworth.

Wiseman, Nelson, and David Whorley. 2002. Lessons on the centrality of politics from the Canadian Crown enterprise. In *The handbook of Canadian public administration*, ed. Christopher Dunn. Toronto: Oxford University Press. 382-96.

PART 3

Political Competition, Interest Groups, and the Political Marketplace

Introduction

This third part of *Uneasy Partnership* looks at how business, interest groups, and government actors compete with each other to influence the policy process. In so doing, it considers the internal and external processes for designing and implementing public policies. Some observers have likened the workings of these processes to those of a "political marketplace" in which various groups compete for influence, power, and a larger share of the outputs of government.

The marketplace analogy is more effective in some contexts and less effective in others. The spread of government has created a market for political benefits that is driven partly by supply: the actions and promises of politicians in providing benefits to economic and social groups, including geographic constituencies. It is also driven by political demands: the expectations of citizens and businesses for various kinds of government action as articulated by or through interest groups, the news media, pollsters, and political parties, among others. Parts of this marketplace are relatively open to public inspection—directly and through the news media—allowing citizens, journalists, and interest groups to compare a range of political and policy options in various settings, though often with imperfect information. Others are anything but transparent as policy-makers seek to maintain control of their agendas through the techniques of news management and control over public access to information.

The nature of political and policy processes is directly affected by their relative openness to effective participation by citizens and organized interests, the degree of transparency that allows for public scrutiny and effective debate, and the extent to which power is concentrated or diffused within governments. The size and scope of modern governments are far too great for citizens, businesses, or even political leaders to deal with the State as a whole. As a result, governments, businesses, and other societal groups all organize themselves in ways that contribute to the specialization and compartmentalization of political and policy processes. The emergence of a government relations industry of professional lobbyists and public affairs consultants is a by-product of that specialization.

However, the successful political and lobbying activities of interest groups and public affairs professionals may well redistribute the costs and benefits of government to favour some groups at the expense of others. Citizens, businesses, and other groups who perceive themselves to be disadvantaged—or the public interest to be shortchanged—as a result are likely to be critical of the influence of special interests. They may also demand improvements in political and legal checks and balances to make the political process more open and responsive. These perceptions of undue interest, sometimes combined with the reality of actual corruption, have fostered a number of political and legal reforms in recent decades, ranging from new codes of ethics and measures to regulate lobbying and impose checks on potential conflicts of interest or abuses of power to the tightening of legislation regulating the financing of political parties.

One of the inherent dilemmas of democratic politics is how to balance the efforts of governments to set priorities and take actions that respond to the expectations of diverse social and economic interests with the capacity of societal groups to influence those priorities and actions and to modify them within the constraints of democratic and constitutional norms. In a democracy, citizens should be able to challenge governments that use their powers in ways that ignore or devalue important societal interests. The political values expressed through laws and public policies should be open to challenge, on principle, by political parties and socio-economic groups with different views of the public interest. Such challenges should be possible not only at election time but between elections as well.

At the same time, there are limits on the capacity of governments to accommodate every societal interest or flurry of public opinion before their policies become fragmented, incoherent, and ineffective in serving the broader society. Although competing societal demands may be reconciled through creative political leadership and effective public management, both these qualities require the willingness and capacity to set and enforce priorities, subject to democratic accountability. Governments whose policies or priorities offend large enough segments of the voting public may well be removed from office at a subsequent election. Politicians and civil servants who play fast and loose with legal and constitutional safeguards against the abuse of power may be disciplined by the courts or by quasi-judicial tribunals established to manage disputes among societal interests or between citizens and the state.

Part III addresses five different dimensions of the political marketplace, public policy processes, and the interaction of government, business, and other interest groups through different aspects of the political process. Chapter 10 examines the political organization of business, its relations with governments and other societal interests through a variety of policy communities and networks, and the role and regulation of the growing government relations industry. Chapter 11 considers the multiple contexts for policy formation in government, their implications for the interactions of elected officials, public servants, and societal groups (including those representing business), and the development of public policies at different stages of the policy cycle. It also outlines a number of principles and practices that can help citizens, businesses, and interest groups to engage the policy environment more effectively. Chapter 12 assesses the external policy processes through which governments, the mass media, and assorted interest groups, including those representing business, attempt to shape both public opinion and the environment for government decision-making. Chapter 13 considers the role of litigation and the administrative justice system on relations among business, governments, and other societal interests as well as the rules of competition through which political, business, and other interests attempt to influence these processes. Chapter 14 examines the relations between businesses and political parties, the evolving role of money in politics, and the implications of these issues for the competition of political parties and societal interests through the electoral process.

Several common themes emerge. Relations between government and business take place within a multidimensional, fragmented political and policy process involving many actors and levels of analysis. The workings of the political market-place involve the interaction of numerous institutions, ideas, and interests that shape both the internal and external policy processes of governments. The concept of "actor-centred institutionalism" advanced by Fritz Scharpf (1997b) and others emphasizes that the actions of individual decision-makers both shape and are shaped by the organizations and institutions through which they work. The result is often an uneasy partnership involving elements of cooperation and competition within and among governmental, business, and other societal interests—and sometimes an open contest for power and control in the political arena.

As in the economic marketplace, the political marketplace is often characterized by significant disparities in political and economic power or in the resources necessary to exploit them. Political and economic insiders, especially those whose interests have become institutionalized within particular policy communities or areas of political activity, have a substantial advantage over outsiders. However, the complexity and diversity of the political process rarely allow any set of political actors or interests to enjoy unchecked power. Those who may enjoy relative political dominance in some areas are often dependent in others on the cooperation or accommodation of other political and economic actors as part of the broader exchange processes of political life.

Outsiders and challengers can compensate for disadvantages in some areas through creative appeals to interests or values shared by other interests or the general public, particularly in responding to real or perceived abuses of power. The increasing activity of the judicial system and the networks of quasi-judicial agencies and tribunals that deal with many routine disputes between or among governments, citizens, businesses, and other societal groups is evidence of the many ways in which political competition, if frustrated at one level of the policy game, may surface at another.

The result is a policy process that oscillates between dynamic bursts of political activity and innovation and the slow, grinding processes of incremental adaptation to changing circumstances whose successful management usually requires substantial investments of time, effort, and awareness of the often hidden workings of political and policy processes.

CHAPTER 10

The Political Marketplace: Interest Groups, Policy Communities, and Lobbying

All governments face the challenge of balancing responsiveness to public opinion, the provision of coherent political leadership, and adaptability to the interests and concerns of particular economic and social interests. Although this balancing act is most visible at election time or during periods of minority government, it is a constant reality in the political marketplace.

In previous chapters, we have seen that Canada's economy and society are characterized by high degrees of diversity and complexity, openness and dynamism, reinforced by a relatively high degree of social and economic individualism. They limit the capacity of governments or politicians to plan or coordinate their activities so that all agencies of the State function as a cohesive whole. They also contribute to the fragmentation of political representation. In such circumstances, no single political actor or institution can consistently articulate the full range of public demands, suppress the agendas of competing interests, identify all the implications of policy issues, or deliver benefits effectively to citizens without the cooperation of other groups inside and outside government.

This chapter examines the role and function of **interest groups** and government relations professionals within the political and policy processes. It notes the different functions performed by industry, trade, and professional associations as they interact with other political and economic interests within the political marketplace. It explains the development of an independent government relations industry to advise clients, including businesses and other societal interests, on effective approaches for dealing with governments, the media, and public opinion and outlines different forms of business and interest group interaction with government through a variety of policy communities and networks. Finally, it considers the efforts of governments to regulate the process of lobbying in order to balance the accessibility of Canadians, including businesses and interest groups, to the political process with the need for greater transparency and accountability for both government decision-makers and those who seek to influence their actions.

Lobbying, Strategic Analysis, and the Political Marketplace

The idea of **lobbying** sometimes has a vaguely disreputable aura in which well-connected individuals seek special favours from governments for themselves and their clients. Although it would be naive to pretend that the systematic pursuit of self-interest by those inside and outside government is not a pervasive feature of modern political, economic, and social life in Canada, as elsewhere, the realities of lobbying or **government relations** are rather more complex.

Lobbying is an extension of the historic right of petition whereby individuals, communities, and other groups could approach their rulers in order to obtain the legal right to carry out certain activities (whether for private or public benefit) or to seek their assistance in correcting an injustice, responding to a calamity or natural disaster, or remedying a larger social problem. It may also involve efforts by individual firms to influence the design of government contracts and procurement processes or to balance the efforts of other interests seeking to do the same thing.

The spread of lobbying and the professionalization of government relations are logical responses to the rapid growth during the twentieth century of activist government and state intervention in almost all aspects of the economy and society. The politicization of ever larger areas of social and economic activity has created a market for the exercise of political influence and policy entrepreneurship by politicians and societal interests seeking to advance or defend their interests (for a broader discussion of this phenomenon, see Templeton 1979 and Cairns 1986). The greater the degree of government intervention, the greater the extent to which these relations tend to become institutionalized through interest groups that provide citizens with alternative forms of political representation and intermediation in dealing with governments.

As noted in Chapter 3, government organizations and decision-making processes are complex and not particularly transparent, particularly to the casual observer. Their increasing complexities are natural by-products of bureaucratic organization and specialization resulting from the growth of government. Under these circumstances, it is not surprising that the sizeable financial implications of many government policies and decisions for businesses and other societal interests have contributed to the growth of a government-relations industry to provide guidance and advocacy skills in presenting their clients' cases to appropriate decision-makers in a timely and effective manner.

Many citizens, business-owners, and managers are busy enough making a living and getting on with life that government policies, rules, and regulations often seem like a force of nature, much like the weather, about which they regularly complain but feel they can do nothing much to influence. However, the more such policies affect the ability of businesses to compete effectively, the more important it is for them to formalize their public affairs functions and to include strategic analysis of their political environments within their broader business planning processes.

Public affairs is the process of managing an organization's relationships with governments, the media, and other societal interests to facilitate or complement the pursuit of its main objectives. Large firms, including public sector organizations, frequently set up internal public affairs departments to organize and manage relationships with governments, shareholders, the media, and other organizations. In smaller companies and organizations, this function is usually carried out by the president or chief executive. Government relations is a subset of public affairs relating specifically to an organization's dealings with government. Lobbying is the activity of attempting to influence decisions by governments or other authoritative actors that have the power to confer benefits or disadvantages by their actions or inaction. Lobbying can be **direct**—involving direct contact with relevant decision-makers—or **indirect** as businesses, interest groups, and organizations attempt to influence the climate of elite and public opinion—sometimes called the market-place of ideas—which sways the choices and decisions of governments as well as other political and societal actors.

Such activities can be *defensive*—responding to actual or proposed changes initiated by others; *sustaining*—oriented to the management of day-to-day relationships necessary for the effective operation and development of existing policies; or *proactive*—actively seeking to initiate change within some aspect of the political system or policy network. Each of these functions can be carried out independently by individual businesses and interest groups or in cooperation or competition with other political and economic actors.

The public choice theorists discussed in Chapter 3 have noted similarities between the political marketplace and the economic marketplace, even though there are important differences as well. The political marketplace is often multi-dimensional, fragmented, competitive, and only partially transparent, with decision-makers often acting on the basis of incomplete information. Stanbury likens the political market-place to an **exchange process** in which participants seek to balance their assets and liabilities through cooperation and tacit bargaining with one another (Stanbury 1993: 138-42). Despite the centralization of political power fostered by the evolution of Canada's cabinet-parliamentary system of government, and the vast disparities of power and influence within that marketplace, all participants still require the cooperation and support of other players to some extent in order to achieve their main objectives. These trade-offs and their impact on the workings of government policy processes, will be discussed further in Chapter 11.

Just as well-run businesses need to understand the markets in which they operate if they are going to compete successfully, organizations and interests competing in the political marketplace (including businesses) that want to be effective need to acquire the tools necessary to make the best use of their limited resources in dealings with governments and other societal interests.

Strategic Analysis and the Political Marketplace

Influencing governments and the policy process begins with **strategic analysis**, an assessment of the opportunities and risks facing specific businesses and organizations (or their members) as a result of the actions or inactions of governments and other political actors, specific issues that may affect the organization's ability to pursue its main priorities (e.g., business expansion, increased market share, profitability, competitiveness), and the political actors inside and outside governments whose attitudes and actions can materially contribute to or detract from their success.

The increased use of strategic political analysis is a response to criticisms that noted the often self-absorbed, reactive, and defensive responses of businesses and business organizations to political challenges during the 1970s and 1980s (Gillies

1981; Grefe 1981). Public affairs consultant Edward Grefe has suggested four major steps in effective strategic analysis:

1. *Issues awareness and profile*: This typically involves monitoring of the news media, legislative developments, and policy literature for the emergence of issues with the potential to benefit or damage a company, industry, or other organization. Grefe divides politically relevant issues into three main categories. *Vital* issues are central to the firm or industry's viability or existence. *Lateral* issues shape or influence the broader environment for the company or organization's activities, but are not central to its survival or growth. *Tangential* issues may generate marginal benefits or costs for a company or organization, but not to the extent of requiring significant management attention or response (Grefe 1981: 25-32).

2. *Identifying elements of a potential political support system*: This element of strategic analysis searches out other businesses, organizations, groups of citizens, individual legislators, or constituencies within government that may share common or overlapping interests and may potentially be open to cooperation or support in dealing with them. It is vital to the development of issues networks and advocacy coalitions (Grefe 1981: 43-55).

3. *Identifying potentially competing and/or adversarial interests*: Paralleling the previous step, this process profiles other businesses, organizations, groups of citizens, individual legislators, or constituencies within government whose interests or outlooks may bring them into conflict with one's own business or organization over an issue.

4. *Identifying and cultivating sources of information* on relevant decision-makers, their priorities and attitudes towards key issues, the likely timing of and processes for policy development, and opportunities to influence policy-makers directly and indirectly is necessary to translate the previous steps into practical action. The earlier such information can be obtained and acted upon, the greater the organization's capacity to achieve a more satisfactory outcome than would otherwise have been possible.

Timely and well-focused strategic analysis of the political environment is vital to the effectiveness of interest groups and government relations professionals. However, for individual businesses, strategic analysis is only one dimension of a broader process of business planning whose importance varies with the degree to which government regulations and policies affect their competitive environment.

Relatively few businesses have either the resources or the incentive to carry out a comprehensive strategic analysis on political and economic factors affecting their business environment. As noted in Chapter 3, most invest their limited resources in monitoring and attempting to influence the activities of government agencies and the development of issues that are likely to have the greatest impact on their operations. Just as the business marketplace lends itself to a degree of specialization in order to increase economic efficiency and competitiveness, the political market-place also lends itself to specialization through the activities of interest groups and government relations professionals.

Interest Groups and the Political Marketplace

Interest groups may be defined as "formal organizations, sharing common goals and with some autonomy from government, which seek to influence public policy" (Stanbury 1993: 119; Berry 1997). It is common for politicians or journalists to describe such groups as "special interest groups," particularly when they represent socio-economic or policy orientations that are particularly self-centred or at odds with the observer's viewpoint. Because no interest or advocacy group can encompass the interests or values of an entire society, all interest groups may be seen as special interests to the extent that their claims on the political system are prejudicial to the interests or values of a significant segment of society. The political effectiveness and legitimacy of interest groups is directly related to their ability to demonstrate how their policy proposals will benefit the broader society and not just their own memberships (Stanbury 1993: 114-25).

Interest groups have a number of functions in common, although some play more highly specialized roles than others. Pross notes five key functions of interest groups in the political process. The core function of interest groups is to *mobilize* or *aggregate* social, economic, or ideological interests in support of shared objectives or values. This function requires *communication* with government, other interest groups, and the general public. Interest groups seek *legitimation*, both in the sense of validating the claims of particular social or economic groups to recognition or accommodation in government policies and in providing political validation to government policies. Selected groups with specialized expertise may also engage in *negotiation*—involving formal recognition and inclusion by governments in the internal processes of policy development—and *administration*, by serving as agents of government in the delivery of public services or the supervision of regulatory processes (Pross 1986: 87-96).

Interest Aggregation

Interest mobilization or aggregation is the most vital function of business and other interest groups. Groups that can credibly claim to represent a specific group of citizens or businesses, usually through the voluntary payment of membership dues or the capacity to demonstrate active membership support for their positions, have greater political legitimacy than those whose positions derive primarily from a self-appointed leadership. The greater the number of individuals or businesses that are members of a particular group, the greater the proportion of firms represented within a particular industry sector, or the larger the market share of its membership within an economic sector, the greater becomes its claim to consideration by governments in relevant policy fields. For this reason, business groups often seek to boost membership levels by offering tangible economic incentives to members such as participation in group buying or insurance programs, discounts on particular business services, and access to low-cost education or consulting services, among others.

Interest aggregation may also take the form of coalition-building or the development of interest networks among groups (Hula 1999). An increasingly important by-product of such coalition-building is the formation of special purpose organizations that enable them to coordinate their lobbying or public relations activities and to achieve economies of scale in research and the hiring of expert technical advice on specific policy issues. The role of special purpose coalitions will be addressed below.

Communications

Interest groups may perform multiple communications functions, depending on their structures, policy emphases, strategic objectives, and tactical choices. Historically, business groups have concentrated on seeking to communicate directly with key policy-makers, such as cabinet ministers responsible for overseeing relevant government departments or regulatory agencies; public servants responsible for designing and administering policies and programs; and, at the margins, individual MPs and members of provincial legislatures (Gillies 1981; Cairns Group 1998; Public Policy Forum 2002). Depending on the range of issues and interests at stake, individual corporations also engage in direct contact with political and bureaucratic decision-makers. Small businesses are more likely to contact their local elected representatives, who frequently devote much of their time to helping constituents in their dealings with government bureaucracies.

Communication with government is often a two-way street. Ministers and their parliamentary secretaries regularly speak to business audiences to communicate their political messages and obtain feedback. Senior public servants may attend conferences sponsored by interest groups, including **think tanks**, to exchange ideas and test the waters on potential policy initiatives. In some cases, governments will commission think tanks to sponsor research, conferences, or consultations related to particular policy topics or initiatives as part of a broader effort at consensus-building among **major stakeholders**. These projects may be commissioned directly by government departments, or through specialized bodies such as the federal government's Policy Research Initiative.

Stanbury suggests that interest groups engage in at least three major communications functions: signaling, providing, and relaying information (Stanbury 1993: 119-20). Signaling transmits voter or business interests by visibly monitoring government policy processes, communicating directly with governments, and engaging in indirect lobbying through the news media or other efforts to shape the broader political and policy environments. Advocacy advertising, discussed further in Chapter 12, is often used as a signaling mechanism to catch the attention of decision-makers and other stakeholders. The earlier a group can be involved in a particular policy process, the greater its likelihood of influencing the process or ensuring that its interests are recognized and accommodated.

A second function is the provision to governments or attentive publics of specialized information and research about industry conditions and the actual or prospective impact of government policies. This research may be commissioned internally or contracted to third parties with credible professional standing and reputation.

The communications function also involves the provision of relay points, as a way of networking inside and outside government. Interest groups engage in lateral communication with one another, direct communication with their members through newsletters and restricted access websites, and communication with the general public through various news media and the Internet. The role of communications strategies in mobilizing public opinion or influencing governments through the media will also be discussed further in Chapter 12.

Legitimation

A key objective of most interest groups is to validate their claim to consideration in the policy process. Their tactics often depend on whether their primary objective is to influence the decisions of specific policy-makers, to catch the attention of politicians or the news media, or to build support from particular social or economic interests. As such, they are closely related to the lobbying and communications strategies of particular groups.

Institutionalized interest groups that have secured recognition or established their place within the government policy process are more likely to base their efforts to legitimate policy proposals on established government policies or priorities whose formation they may have influenced in past years. Established **industry associations** such as the Canadian Council of Chief Executives (formerly the Business Council on National Issues), the Canadian Pulp and Paper Association, the Canadian Steel Producers Association, and the Canadian Association of Petroleum Producers have established close (if not always cordial) working relationships with senior officials responsible for their major policy interests. Many such associations reinforce these linkages by hiring former ministerial aides, senior civil servants, and even former cabinet ministers, although federal (and some provincial) conflict of interest rules usually preclude such individuals from lobbying former colleagues within 12 to 24 months of having responsibility for particular policy files (Clancy 2004; author's discussions with current and former association executives).

Many businesses and organizations in the broader public sector have pursued a similar strategy by forming interest associations (such as provincial associations of school boards, hospitals, and universities) to coordinate relationships with governments. Many public sector organizations have hired vice-presidents of public affairs or government relations to carry out strategic analysis, monitor and build working relationships with relevant government officials and political leaders, protect or expand existing revenue sources, and oversee the public relations and image-building activities of their organizations to promote positive public perceptions of their actions.

Outsider groups, both those representing business and other societal groups, are more likely to appeal to media and public opinion in an effort to obtain recognition or accommodation for their ideas or interests as part of a broader public interest. Some of these groups, such as the Canadian Federation of Independent Business (CFIB) or the Independent Contractors and Business Association of British Columbia (ICBA), become established players within the political process with the passage of time. Others take a more adversarial approach, challenging government from the margins of the political process and often attempting to influence positions taken by opposition political parties.

As with communication, governments may use interest groups as a vehicle for legitimizing policy decisions by demonstrating that key stakeholder groups either support or have been actively consulted in the development of particular policy initiatives. These approaches may involve consultations by parliamentary or legislative committees or the development of more elaborate round-table consultations intended at building consensus. The latter approach has been used by governments as ideologically diverse as the Harris PCs in Ontario and Glen Clark's NDPs in BC during the 1990s in efforts to build consensus among environmental, resource industry, Aboriginal and tourist groups, and local community leaders in reconciling competing political, economic, and environmental claims (Howlett et al. 2001; Ontario 1999). We will return to the use of formal consultation processes by both governments and interest groups to promote their policy agendas in Chapter 12.

Negotiation and Administration

Government intervention in social and economic relationships often creates, affects, or redistributes economic rights and interests within society. Interest groups whose members are seen to have the capacity to facilitate or block the effective implementation of particular government policies may be able to secure formal recognition within the policy process that enables them to negotiate the details of policy design or implementation.

Examples of this approach include the active involvement of provincial bar associations in the design of legal aid programs and rules providing for professional bodies or self-regulated industries to set and enforce the criteria, standards, and/or quotas for the training, admission, or expulsion of their members. They often include the development of technical or safety standards for products and services. Such negotiations may also take place informally, with government officials being instructed to identify policy choices that are acceptable to key stakeholder groups before recommending formal policy decisions. Major professions and industries characterized by extensive degrees of self-regulation and regulatory delegation include lawyers, accountants, a number of health professions, real estate and insurance brokers, and securities and mutual fund dealers and exchanges. These structures and powers—and the industries affected by them—vary significantly from one jurisdiction to another.

A major challenge of such arrangements is to structure them in ways that reduce real or apparent conflicts of interest between the advocacy and regulatory roles of organizations. Self-regulating professions and industry groups often represent the professional and other economic interests of their members in dealings with governments. At the same time, they carry out a variety of regulatory functions with power delegated by governments. This regulatory (or administrative) role often involves designing and enforcing legal standards for market entry and conduct and, where these are infringed upon, disciplining members. Rather than administering a particular policy or program directly, governments may establish an arm's-length organization involving private or non-profit sectors to administer a quasi-public program. Examples of this approach include the Canadian Standards Association, a non-profit association empowered to set technical and product standards for industry; professional disciplinary bodies established under legislative authority; and arm's-length foundations with mixed public sector-private sector boards of directors established by federal and provincial governments to oversee a variety of functions.

Most business associations perform the first three functions to one degree or another, with a limited number of specialized organizations performing the last two. However, the diversity of economic interests, combined with Canada's vast geography and the realities of federalism, have contributed to the emergence of large numbers of relatively specialized groups representing businesses on several different levels.

The Political Organization of Business and Canada's Government Relations Industry

"It is incorrect to speak of a single business community in Canada" (Coleman 1988: 219).

Business interests take a number of very different forms, from broadly based groups that seek to represent a broad cross-section of business interests to trade associations with highly specialized roles in promoting the interests of their members. Since the 1970s, the emergence of a number of specialized think tanks, or policy advocacy groups, has added an additional voice to the mix of interests that seek to influence government policies. Unlike some countries in which governments have encouraged corporatist forms of business organization, there is no **peak association** capable of speaking for the Canadian business community as a whole.

The absence of any overriding, authoritative organizational representative of business within the political process is sometimes frustrating for both scholars and ideologues who believe that this approach to social organization would enable governments to subordinate business interests to rational political management and control. However, it reflects the realities of Canada's firm-centred business culture described in Chapter 3 and what Clancy describes as the "business-industry dichotomy" in business-government relations (Clancy 2004: Chapter 2). Even industries with relatively high levels of corporate concentration experience high levels of competition for market share between individual firms. Policy competition may also result from the conflicting interests of different industry subsectors. Scotia Bank's active lobby against the proposed mergers of four of its rivals in 1998 and ongoing rivalries within the financial services sector over the design of future merger rules are clear examples of how business competition often spills over into politics and policy development (Whittington 1999; Kalawsky 2004: FP1,7; Hartt 2004: 61-65).

Government policies that fail to recognize and accommodate these differences are likely to face cross-cutting pressures not only from individual businesses and industry groups but also from their networks of suppliers, related labour organizations, provincial governments, and local communities whose interests may be adversely affected as a result. In some cases, such as state procurement decisions or choices among competing approaches to regulation, government policies may create a zero-sum game in which benefits conferred on one industry or economic group may come at the expense of others (for example, see Whittington 1999; Clancy 2004; McArthur 2004).

Scholars of the political organization of business, such as Stanbury and Coleman, outline three broad types of business organization (Stanbury 1986, 1993; Coleman 1988: 81-99). **Broadly based or comprehensive associations** represent businesses across a range of industry sectors. As a result, they tend to focus on horizontal issues that apply to different industries. Much of their political influence and effectiveness depends on their capacity to develop consensus positions on such issues within their memberships. The four largest and most influential business organizations of this kind are the Canadian Council of Chief Executives (CCCE, formerly the Business Council on National Issues), the Canadian Chamber of Commerce, the Canadian Federation of Independent Business (CFIB), and the Canadian Manufacturers and Exporters (CME). Broadly based provincial associations include provincial chambers of commerce, the Conseil du Patronat de Québec, and the Business Council of British Columbia (Coleman 1988).

Major **sectoral associations** represent a cross-section of business interests within major economic (including non-profit) sectors such as retailing, construction, agriculture, tourism, and health care. Just as broadly based business associations attempt to aggregate business interests from a number of sectors, sectoral associations seek to aggregate specialized interests within a particular economic sector. Major sectoral associations include the Retail Council of Canada, the Canadian Federation of Agriculture, the Canadian Tourist Industries Association, and the Canadian Construction Association. In recent years, the Canadian Advanced Technology Association has emerged as the leading voice of firms in the high technology sector.

Many industries are diverse enough that they have spawned a wide variety of specialized **trade (or industry) associations**, which may be organized on a provincial or national level, depending on the scale of industry operations and the level of government with the most direct impact on business operations. Industry segments may be differentiated in several ways, depending on such sectorally relevant factors as ownership, relative specialization, size of business, and geographic structure or location. For example, North American and non-North American auto makers are represented by the Canadian Vehicle Manufacturers Association and the Association of International Automobile Manufacturers (and the Japan Automobile Manufacturers Association of Canada), respectively. The Food Processors of Canada, Food and Consumer Products of Canada, the Canadian Council of Grocery Distributors, and several other associations represent different segments of the food processing and distribution industry. The Retail Council of Canada represents primarily large and medium-sized firms, while provincial retail merchants' associations typically represent smaller firms within the sector, many of whom are also members of local chambers of commerce.

Box 10.1: Broadly Based or Comprehensive Business Associations in Canada

	Date of Founding	Structural Type
Federal Groups		
Canadian Chamber of Commerce	1926	Mixed confederation*
Canadian Council of Chief Executives**	1976	Unitary
Canadian Federation of Independent Business	1971	Unitary with regional sub-units
Canadian Manufacturers and Exporters***	1996	Federation
Regional Groups		
Business Council of British Columbia****	1966	Mixed confederation
Chambre de commerce du Québec	1901	Mixed confederation*
Chambre de commerce du Montréal Métropolitain/Board of Trade of Metropolitan Montreal	1992	Unitary
Conseil du Patronat du Québec	1969	Confederation****

* Organization has confederal form but also accepts direct memberships.
** Formerly Business Council on National Issues, renamed December 2001.
*** Formed as Alliance of Manufacturers and Exporters Canada from the merger of the Canadian Manufacturers Association (1871) and the Canadian Exporters Association (1943).
**** Affiliated with Canadian Council of Chief Executives.
Source: Coleman and Mau 2002; Business Council of British Columbia 2002.

Both sectoral and trade associations often seek to attract members by providing industry-specific services to members, including shared promotional activities and educational, technical, and consulting services. Trade associations tend to focus their lobbying activities on specialized policy and technical issues. These activities may overlap, complement, or compete with the broader activities of sectoral and broadly based business associations. Smaller associations with limited budgets may contract with an association multi-manager with several clients to provide administrative support and lobbying guidance to their organizations.

Business organizations may be organized as unitary organizations (with or without regional divisions), or as federal and confederal organizations. Unitary organizations are centralized, with any regional divisions dependent on the central organization for policy, staff, and other resources. Federal associations include regional bodies with independent resources and decision-making powers and usually have a single set of business dues divided between the national and regional organizations. Confederal associations are composed of autonomous member groups, although some, like Canadian and provincial chambers of commerce, also make provisions for direct business membership (Coleman and Mau 2002). Box 10.1 outlines major horizontal associations operating at national and regional levels. Composite associations may include both individual members and associations representing related industries or trade groups.

Table 10.1: Interest Groups Registered Under *Lobbyist Registration Act,* March 2003

Business Organizations	142	48%*
• major broadly based and sectoral organizations	7	
• industry associations	47	
• trade associations	64	
• provincial and local associations	24	
Public sector organizations	31	11%
Professional associations	28	10%
Miscellaneous advocacy	25	9%
Agriculture	24	8%
Health + Advocacy	17	6%
Labour unions	14	5%
Cultural/religious organizations	12	4%
Total	**293**	

* Figures may not add to 100 per cent due to rounding.
Source: Public Registry, Lobbyist Registration; available at <http://www.strategis.ic.gc.ca>.

Many businesses may hold memberships in more than one organization; for example, a business may belong to its local Chamber of Commerce, provincial or national industry or trade association, and a broadly based group such as the CFIB. A 2002 survey of 800 large corporations conducted by the Public Policy Forum indicated that 62 per cent of respondents were members of two to five industry or trade associations, with 17 per cent belonging to six or more groups (Public Policy Forum 2002).

Group membership may be *direct* (participation by individual businesses), *organizational* (participation by organizations), or *federal* (national organizations or federations of provincial organizations). Large corporations may hold direct membership in the CCCE and/or their sector association, as well as national and provincial chambers of commerce and particular trade associations. These relationships contribute to interlocking networks of business interests that help to broker differences among particular corporations or industry groups (Coleman 1988; Carroll 1986).

Table 10.1 outlines the range of business associations and other interest groups engaged in lobbying government officials in 2003. The tremendous diversity of business interests is evident in the wide range of specialized industry and trade associations registered under the *Lobbyist Registration Act*. Business groups made up almost half of the interest groups registered under the act in 2003. Other interest groups actively engaged in lobbying activities, notably professional organizations, organizations representing a variety of public sector interests, agricultural groups, a handful of major unions, and a variety of other advocacy groups.

Special Purpose Organizations

Business and other economic interests may establish ad hoc or temporary interest coalitions to deal with a particular political or policy challenge. Temporary issue-specific coalitions of interest groups are not as common in Canada as in the US, but they may emerge when several groups recognize the potential benefits of pooling their resources to pursue a common policy goal or when political debate becomes polarized on particular issues. Such polarization may pit a consensus of major business interest groups against networks of other social and economic interests, as in the free trade debate of 1987-88 or in the periodic conflicts over major changes to provincial labour laws and environmental policies. It may also reflect major divisions *within* the business community as happened in the GST debate of 1989-90 and in the reactions to proposals for multiple bank mergers in the late 1990s.

Coalition-building may also result from the efforts of governments, business groups, and other societal organizations to build partnerships for common societal goals or to bridge societal differences. Box 10.2 outlines a typology of interest group coalitions, including those limited to the representation of businesses and business associations, and cross-cutting coalitions which link business with labour, consumer, and even governmental organizations.

The range of issues addressed by special purpose organizations and how long they remain in operation (their temporal character) also affect coalition-building. Special purpose organizations may be created to address specific issues, usually on a time-limited basis. For example, telecommunications firms promoting regulatory reform and an end to telephone monopolies created the Canadian Business Telecommunications Alliance as a broadly based network of business and consumer interests during the mid-1980s. This approach enabled them to demonstrate the existence of extensive business and public support for proposed regulatory changes intended to expand their market share and potential profitability as well as providing increased choices and, sometimes, lower costs for consumers.

Box 10.2: Coalition-Building

Actors	Breadth of Issues	Temporal
Business Coalition • single industry • limited cross-sectoral • horizontal	Single Issue • special purpose (project-oriented) • continuing	Event-specific Project-oriented (extended period)

Business-Labour Coalitions
• usually sector specific
	Issue Cluster
	(related sectoral
	  issues)
		Continuing
		• issue/project
		  oriented
		• institutionalized

Business-Government Coalition • sector-specific • multi-sector, policy-field specific Producer-Consumer Coalition • business-to-business • business-individual consumers (NGOs) Business-Other NGOs Multi-Sector (including business) • including government • advocacy to government		

Alternately, business groups may create ongoing coalitions to pool expertise and create economies of scale in research and lobbying on ongoing structural issues requiring the concertation of economic interests. Examples of such groups include the employer councils organized to coordinate business positions on labour and workplace issues in several provinces including Ontario, Manitoba, Saskatchewan, BC, and Newfoundland and Labrador.

After 9/11, several major business groups assembled the Coalition for Secure and Trade-Efficient Borders to coordinate lobbying on border administration and security related issues and to serve as a clearing house to provide both businesses and governments with relevant information on a wide range of cross-border administrative issues (Coalition for Secure and Trade Efficient Borders 2004); the group's March 2004 report list 55 different member organizations.

Even the largest national business associations have limited resources to deal with the full range of policy issues addressed by governments. However, many initiatives in advancing business interests at a societal level come from four broadly based national organizations: the CCCE, the Canadian Chamber of Commerce, the CFIB, and the CME.

1. *The Canadian Council of Chief Executives*: One of Canada's most influential business groups is the CCCE, formerly known as the Business Council on National Issues (BCNI). Unlike most broadly based business associations, the CCCE is composed of the chief executives of 150 major corporations with annual revenues of more than $500 billion who play an active role on the association's major policy committees. About 80 per cent of CCCE members run Canadian-based firms, with the balance representing the Canadian subsidiaries of transnational firms (<http://www.bcni.com>, March 2003).

   The CCCE has played a leading role in building consensus on major issues among its members across sectoral lines by commissioning policy research on major national, North American, and global issues and attempting to influence government policies through regular meetings with senior cabinet ministers and public servants. Unlike many business groups, which tend to react to government initiatives, the CCCE frequently takes a proactive approach to policy development, identifying major systemic issues of concern to its members and attempting to develop strategic approaches that can be marketed to governments, other business groups, and other opinion leaders (interview, CCCE 2001).

   Its standing committees focus primarily on "fiscal and monetary policy, regulatory, environmental, competitiveness and corporate governance issues" at the national level. Periodically, it forms special task forces on pressing national issues such as the National Energy Policy and Canada-US Free Trade during the 1980s, "fiscal responsibility" and international competitiveness during the 1990s, and North American Integration since 2002 (interview, CCCE 2001; D'Aquino and Stewart-Patterson 2001; D'Aquino 2003). Although the CCCE occasionally launches high profile challenges to federal policies, such tactics may well backfire—particularly if politicians or other interest groups respond by appealing to public opinion against what is often perceived as the self-interested exercise of corporate influence.

2. *Canadian Chamber of Commerce*: The Canadian Chamber of Commerce is a hybrid organization representing both provincial and local chambers throughout the country, along with a number of large corporations that purchase memberships directly in both the national and provincial bodies. The chamber's decentralized federal structure often makes decision-making difficult, as the association's senior staff must balance their own leadership role with input from a board of directors composed of provincial and directly elected representatives and the resolutions passed at the annual convention by delegates from more than 300 local chambers across the country. In recent years, the chamber has been actively engaged in building ad hoc coalitions on major issues with other major national business groups.

   Provincial chambers of commerce are the leading business umbrella groups in most provinces, combining large and small business representations through local chambers. The balance of power and influence between provincial and local chambers varies widely with big-city chambers or boards of trade in Toronto, Montreal, Calgary, Edmonton, Vancouver, Winnipeg, and other cities playing active and sometimes independent political roles in their respective provinces.

Municipal chambers of commerce play greater or lesser roles in promoting business development and influencing local and provincial government policies. Their focus and level of activism tends to depend on the character and inter-ests of local leaders and their capacity to recruit and renew their leadership from within their communities.

3. *The Canadian Federation of Independent Business*: The CFIB emerged during the tax reform debates of 1969-71 as the activist, sometimes strident, anti-big govern-ment voice of small business. It now has more than 100,000 members across the country, drawn primarily from owner-managed businesses and self-employed professionals. Members help to shape the CFIB's policies and priorities through monthly membership ballots circulated online, through the organization's news-letter, and through a variety of membership surveys conducted annually and in response to specific issues.

Unlike the Chamber's federal structure, the CFIB is a unitary organization with regional offices in most provinces. Its policy focus is heavily oriented towards tax, financing, and regulatory issues in both federal and provincial politics, with a strong emphasis on labour and workplace issues. In recent years, it has taken a more active role in municipal issues.

4. *The Canadian Manufacturers and Exporters*: The CME is the continuation of one of Canada's oldest business organizations. Formed as the Ontario (later Cana-dian) Manufacturers' Association (CMA) in 1871 to campaign for tariff increases and other protectionist policies, the CMA played a leading role in promoting the development of the National Policy and resisting reciprocity with the US. As part of its efforts to support growing trade links within the British Empire (later Com-monwealth), it sponsored the formation of the Trade Commissioner Service in the late 1890s (Forster 1986; Marchildon 1996; <http://www.cme-mec.org>). Its con-version to free trade in 1983, in recognition of its members' growing dependence on US export markets and the looming threat of American protectionism, was a key factor in shaping business support for the negotiation of the FTA in 1986-88.

The growing integration of Canadian manufacturers in North American and global markets was symbolized by the CMA's 1996 merger with the Canadian Exporters Association to become the CME. Like the CFIB, the CME is organized on a national basis, maintaining divisional offices in most Canadian provinces. In addition to its political activities, it placed a heavy emphasis on trade promo-tion. In recent years, it has sponsored a wide range of research and educational activities to promote its members' competitiveness and their adaptation to the emerging KBE. Like the chamber and CFIB, it has been willing to engage in coalition-building activity in recent years, playing a leading role in the Coalition for Secure and Trade-Efficient Borders and other inter-industry coalitions.

The Role of Professional Lobbyists and Public Affairs Professionals

The government relations industry plays a role distinct from that of industry and trade associations, even though the latter are frequently among its clients. Businesses have often had recourse to major law firms and public relations companies to guide them in their relations with governments, regulatory agencies, and the media. Many of these professionals have close personal and political relations with politicians and governments, creating a symbiotic relationship that contributed to the cozy and sometimes corrupt world of business-government relations since the nineteenth century.

The problems encountered by individual businesses and industry associations in navigating the increasingly complex world of politics and government discussed in Chapter 5 led to the growth of an independent industry of government relations professionals during the 1980s.

These actors now advise clients in the private, public, and non-profit sectors on their dealings with politicians, government officials, the news media, and others. They develop their own specialized clienteles ranging from politicians and government departments to interest groups, businesses, and public sector agencies seeking to understand and influence the policy processes that affect them most directly.

Some engage directly in lobbying on behalf of clients. This work is comparable to that done by the leaders and staff of interest groups or corporate public affairs departments, some of whom are their clients. Others provide strategic advice or technical information on the complex and often hidden processes of central agencies, government departments, and other public sector organizations. Government relations consultants may also take advantage of the complexities of government programs and processes to market their services to businesses, often by positioning themselves as "grant-getters" who can help clients access government subsidies, often for a generous contingency fee. The federal government has attempted to limit such practices by extending requirements for lobbyist registration and for ensuring that grant agreements and contracts prohibit the use of program funds for the payment of contingency fees (Treasury Board Secretariat 1997; Canada, Industry Canada 2005). Even so, the highly publicized problems of its Technology Partnership Program suggest that patterns of compliance and enforcement have been spotty, at best, leading to calls for more restrictive rules governing lobbyists and more stringent provisions for their enforcement (*The Lobby Monitor* 15(11) 2004: April 14; Doyle and Aubry 2005: A1).

Another major function of government relations firms is to provide clients with information on ongoing political and policy developments in their particular markets that goes beyond what they can readily find in the general or business media. Some organizations publish regular newsletters which provide a combination of political analysis and commentary, insights into federal or provincial legislative

326 | UNEASY PARTNERSHIP

and regulatory activities, and lists of major government appointments to agencies, boards, and tribunals. These firms also transmit information through seminars, which are often used as a business development tool, and customized research carried out on behalf of individual clients.

A 1998 survey of 74 major corporations and industry associations showed that 72 per cent of respondents used outside consultants in lobbying government, although the heavy weighting of the sample towards regulated industries suggests one reason for this response (Cairns Group 1998; Sallot 2005: A5). During the 1980s, the growth of the government relations industry and persistent rumours of political influence-peddling prompted the Mulroney government to introduce Canada's first *Lobbyist Registration Act* in 1989 in an effort to provide greater transparency to the system (Sawatzky 1987; Cameron 1995). Similar legislation has been passed subsequently in Ontario, Quebec, Nova Scotia, and BC.

The growth of the lobbying industry, as opposed to the activity of interest groups, is a reflection of the complexity of government activity; the recognition of many interest groups and corporations that they lack the technical expertise to deal effectively with governments; and the broad range of government activities that affect the interests of businesses, large non-profit organizations, and many other social groups. Businesses and industry associations may hire government relations professionals as one way of obtaining a competitive advantage over competitors in the political marketplace or of keeping rival groups from gaining an advantage over themselves.

Table 10.2: Registered Lobbyists, by Type of Organization, 1998–2004

	Firms/ Associations	Lobbyists	Firms/ Associations	Lobbyists	% Change (Firms/ Associations)
	1998		**2004**		
Consultants	279	584	571	980	104.7%
Corporate	192	367	164	298	-14.6%
Organizations	327	327	324	330	-0.9%
Total	798	1,278	1,059	1,608	32.7%

Source: Lobbyists Registration Act, *Annual Report*, year end 31 March 1998: 9; year end 31 March 2004.

The annual report of the federal Lobbyist Registration Branch indicated that 1,059 consulting firms, corporations, and organizations registered their lobbying activities in 2003-04. Table 10.2 notes that although the number of registered interest groups has ranged between 300 and 400 since 1998, the number of consulting firms, including lawyer/lobbyists, has grown rapidly in recent years (Office of the Ethics Councillor 1998-2003).

There has been little study of government relations industries at the provincial level. Although a few national and international firms maintain offices in the larger provinces, provincial government relations sectors tend to be localized, reflecting the very different political cultures and networks surrounding the governments of the ten provinces.

Like the world of business associations, the government relations industry has developed a certain degree of functional specialization, although it has not grown to anything like the extent of its counterpart in the US. Lawyer Sean Moore, a practitioner and regular commentator on the industry, identifies four categories of government relations practitioners:

1. *Contact specialists* make extensive use of personal connections with senior politicians and government officials. They are frequently former political or campaign organizers or ministerial advisors who have either been recruited for their personal connections and political skills, or who have gone into the government relations business on their own account.

2. *Process specialists* monitor and provide strategic advice on government policy processes, often in areas of specialized expertise. Such advice is particularly valuable for business people and interest group executives who do not interact regularly with governments and who are likely to lack the relationships and detailed understanding of policy processes needed for effective interaction with politicians and civil servants.

3. *Policy specialists* focus on particular areas of public policy; they are often former civil servants or industry executives.

4. *Communications specialists* are usually engaged to design or conduct public relations, polling, and issues management campaigns (Moore 2002c).

Some government relations firms such as GPC International, Global Public Affairs, and Hill & Knowlton Canada are full-service organizations, which provide a wide range of other public relations and market research services and which are sometimes connected with international public affairs organizations. Others are more specialized or boutique firms, often formed by former public servants, association executives, or corporate public affairs professionals.

Unlike the US, relatively few former politicians go into the government relations business, although some, like the CME's Perrin Beatty, have been recruited to manage major business associations, usually after a period outside of active politics to reduce memories of partisan affiliations.[1] A handful of others, like former Chrétien-era ministers Doug Young and David Dingwall, developed successful government relations practices, though not without some controversy. However, former ministe-

---

1 Beatty, a minister in the Mulroney government between 1984 and 1993, was named president of the CBC by Prime Minister Chrétien in 1994. He joined the CME after the expiry of his five-year term at the CBC. The CCCE's Thomas D'Aquino also worked in the office of Prime Minister Trudeau in the early 1970s.

rial assistants often find their ways into the ranks of government relations professionals. Conflict of interest rules and other regulations governing lobbying activities
are addressed later in this chapter.

Table 10.3: Think Tanks and Policy Advocacy Organizations

	Conference Board of Canada	Fraser Institute	Institute for Research in Public Policy	Canadian Centre for Policy Alternatives
Website	www.conferenceboard.ca	www.irpp.org	www.fraserinstitute.ca	www.policyalternatives.ca
Number of Staff	200	50	18	20
Expenditures (2003 annual report*)	$30.1 million	$5.3 million	$2.8 million	$2.7 million
Percent of revenues received from:				
a) Individuals	0	8		21
b) Business	63	29		1
c) Foundations	0	63		***
d) Governments	37	0	91**	***
e) Unions	0	0		19
f) Other	0	0	9	54***

	C.D. Howe Institute	Canada West Foundation	Canadian Policy Research Networks	Public Policy Forum
Website	www.cdhowe.org	www.cwf.ca	www.cprn.org	www.ppforum.ca
Number of Staff	18	13	17	21
Expenditures (2003 annual report*)	$2.3 million	$1.5 million	na	Approx. $3 million
Percent of revenues received from:				
a) Individuals		2		
b) Business		3		40
c) Foundations	na	40	na	—
d) Governments		40		60
e) Unions				
f) Other		15		

* or latest available in June 2004
** interest from original government-funded endowment from the 1970s
*** projects or joint projects, often funded by governments or foundations
Source: Milke 2004; Public Policy Forum.

Think Tanks and Policy Advocacy Groups

Business associations have two major weaknesses in contributing to the policy process. They frequently lack the specialized professional resources necessary to carry out timely and effective policy research, although groups such as the CCCE have invested heavily in policy research over the years (D'Aquino and Stewart-Patterson 2001). Perhaps more importantly, policy research directly sponsored by business groups, unions, and other interest groups is discounted by many policy-makers on the grounds of self-interest. For this reason, in recent years a number of policy advocacy organizations or think tanks have emerged as sponsors of active policy research and advocacy intended to inform debate among interest groups and other societal actors.

Research findings on the political and intellectual influence of particular think tanks vary. Some groups, such as the strongly libertarian Fraser Institute and the leftist Canadian Centre for Policy Alternatives, are strongly committed to ideological advocacy within the policy process. More influential are groups such as the C.D. Howe Institute, the Conference Board of Canada, the Institute for Research on Public Policy, and the Caledon Institute, which develop focused, topical studies that are intended to link empirical research with a broader range of policy views. However, some observers have suggested that politicians and government officials tend to be more responsive to think tanks that frame policy issues in terms with which they are already sympathetic (Abelson 2001; Carroll and Shaw 2001; Milke 2004b).

The role of think tanks parallels that of interest groups in some respects. The core function of most think tanks is to communicate ideas intended to promote a certain concept of the public good through the policy process. Policy communications may be directed directly to governments, to specialized publics or the news media, or through networking functions bringing together assorted stakeholder groups and policy elites, depending on the particular strategy of individual groups. Although think tanks may challenge the policy status quo, they also serve as "policy legitimators" by "provid(ing) intellectual or scientific justification" for the policy proposals of governments, parties, or individual politicians (Baier and Bakvis 2001: 109-10). Governments may also contract with think tanks to carry out arm's-length consultations on certain issues in the hope of giving them additional credibility in the eyes of stakeholder groups.

The closure of internal government think tanks such as the Economic Council of Canada, the Science Council of Canada, and the Ontario Economic Council during the 1980s increased the influence of private think tanks by reducing the capacity of governments to generate effective research and policy analysis not linked to their institutional interests. Since balancing its budget in the late 1990s, the federal government has attempted to repair this gap in policy capacity by investing in internal policy development, contracting with leading academics to carry out research on behalf of individual departments and agencies such as the Policy Research Institute, and contracting with insider groups such as the Public Policy Forum and the Canadian Policy Research Networks to carry out policy research and consultations.

Funding of think tanks varies widely according to their policy interests, policy focus, political or ideological orientations, and funding strategies. Table 10.3 lists a number of major Canadian think tanks, their annual budgets, and major sources of funding.

The overlapping, often competing activities of individual corporations, business organizations, government relations firms, think tanks, assorted interest groups, and governments themselves tend fragment the political marketplace and the challenges of policy analysis and advocacy even further. As a result, one of the starting points for strategic analysis and effective policy advocacy is to identify the actors responsible for managing or administering particular areas of public policy, along with the interest groups and other **attentive actors** whose interests may directly or potentially be affected by those policies and programs. One concept used in the mapping of these interests, inside and outside of government, is that of policy communities.

Policy Communities

The terms **policy communities** and **policy networks** are often used interchangeably to describe clusters of organizations and interests inside and outside governments that focus on a common set of policy interests. The concept of policy communities implies greater cohesiveness and stability among participants than policy networks, which are often more open to the engagement or departure of participants, especially among societal actors.

These concepts are of more than academic interest. As noted earlier, government policy processes tend to be specialized, fragmented, and quite limited in their transparency. Civil servants and interest group representatives who specialize in particular policy fields often have a significant advantage in influencing policy developments over outsiders. This should not be a surprise. After all, non-lawyers are rarely successful in representing themselves in court, and few people would want to trust non-specialists in most kinds of surgery. Policy processes have parallels with some aspects of diagnosis and surgery on the body politic or of effective advocacy on behalf of its members.

Types of policy communities or networks are distinguished by the number of participants, the degree of openness of the process to input from different interest groups and the general public, and the degree to which governments define the policy agenda rather than responding to the policy preferences and demands of citizens (VanWaarden 1992). The character of policy communities is directly affected by the number of participants, both inside and outside governments, and the degree of formal recognition extended to participants. Participants normally include representatives from one or more departments of government, one of whose branches typically serves as the **lead agency** responsible for steering and guiding the policy process. Other participants may include cabinet ministers and departments or agencies

whose activities are affected by proposed policy changes and parliamentary or legislative committees responsible for conducting policy reviews or examining legislative
changes. Other governmental actors that are formally or informally involved, either
through interdepartmental committees, cabinet committees, or intergovernmental
negotiations, are considered to be part of the **subgovernment** responsible for policy
development and implementation.

Table 10.3: Policy Communities

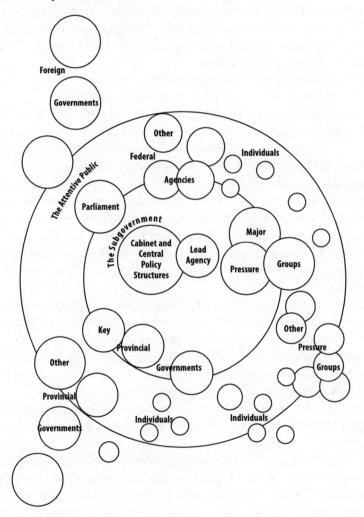

Source: Pross 1995: 267.

   Policy communities frequently include interest groups, individual businesses,
and others affected by the issues at stake; policy experts in academic and professional circles; and journalists and other members of the news media who monitor

or report on particular issues or policies. These individuals or groups may be seen as major stakeholders to the extent that their vital interests are engaged or their cooperation is seen as necessary for governments to take effective action. Alternatively, they may be attentive actors (or the attentive public) who may function at the margins of the policy process, but whose influence and support may become important in the event of major disputes within or among the subgovernment or major stakeholders (Pross 1986: 97-107). Attentive actors, particularly the news media and highly organized interest groups, may become important channels of communication to the general or specialized publics should disputes within the policy community become matters of significant political importance. Pross's amoeba-like diagram of a typical policy community, outlined in Box 10.3, indicates the concept's fluidity and adaptability as a tool of policy analysis.

Policy communities and networks perform several different functions within the policy process. Networks are channels of communication both within governments and among societal interests that are actively or potentially interested in the outcomes of a particular process. Both government decision-makers and interest groups may attempt to mobilize networks of interests to consult with other actors on perceptions of policy problems and proposed responses. Networks can be used to fine-tune policy proposals to make them more responsive to the needs of particular interests or to mobilize public opinion on a particular issue. In certain cases, they may serve as channels for formal or informal negotiation between governments or between governments and key societal interests, or they may be used for consensus-building among overlapping and competing interests. The broader the range of issues at play, the more complex the likely interactions among these groups (Van-Waarden 1992).

As noted earlier, participation in the policy process often takes place under conditions of partial uncertainty and imperfect information. Different players may have a limited understanding of one another's agendas, attitudes, or objectives. Reducing uncertainty depends in large measure on the degree of knowledge, understanding, and trust that different players can develop through multiple interactions with one another over time. This process privileges regular participants (institutional actors, policy insiders) and forces outsiders to go through an informal initiation until their position both as stakeholders and (usually subordinate) partners in the policy process is defined.

No group is compelled to participate in this institutionalized routine. Many prefer to remain outsiders in order to promote their interests without a sense of mutual obligation towards institutional stakeholders and the resulting constraints on their freedom of action or to protect their ideological purity in a contest of ideas. However, such **issue-oriented interest groups** are likely to remain outsiders whose influence will be dependent on their capacity both to mobilize media and public opinion in support of their positions and/or to develop alliances with other groups within their policy networks that are willing to play by the rules of the game to be recognized as professional stakeholders within the process.

Types of Policy Communities

The organization of policy communities—and their evolution over time—reflects different expressions of power relations between state and societal interests. Van-Waarden summarizes four generic expressions of these relations: the relative autonomy of state/public administration vis-à-vis an organization's interests; the capture or colonization of state agencies by business or other interests; the capture of private interests by the state; and a symbiotic balance between particular state and societal interests (VanWaarden 1992). Following typologies outlined by Coleman and Skogstad in Canada and VanWaarden in his analysis of European politics (Coleman and Skogstad 1990; VanWaarden 1992), we can identify seven different types of policy communities. Four represent pluralist policy networks characterized by very different structures of power relations between state and societal interests. The other three represent narrower, more closed forms of policy communities with differing capacities for policy coordination on the part of state and major organized societal interests.

Pressure Pluralism

The **pressure pluralist policy community** carries on many traditions of the Canadian governmental system. Government decision-makers weigh and balance the claims, demands, and suggestions of a number of interest groups, none of which exercises dominance or effective control over the policy process. As a result, governments are partly autonomous and able to make decisions independently of particular societal interests, although the known interests and views of stakeholder groups and citizens are considered.

Not all stakeholder groups or interests have equal weight in this policy process. Some have greater expertise and professional or organizational resources than others. Some may be marginal players, whether due to size or competing priorities (including those addressed in other policy communities). Others may devote most of their limited resources to attempting to affect one or two specific aspects of a specific policy debate, rather than attempting to influence its development as a whole.

Pressure pluralist policy communities include those relating to federal budgetary and tax policies and changes to labour or workplace legislation under liberal or small-c conservative governments. Under normal circumstances, one of the avowed objectives of policy-making in these areas is to balance competing societal expectations and internal policy processes so that major interest groups recognize that some of their priorities have been included within the government's policy package. Sector policies affecting industries in which producer interests are divided, as in market-driven segments of agriculture, or in which consumer interests are strongly organized, as in the balance between steel and auto industries (Clancy 2004), are likely to be characterized by the politics of pressure pluralism.

Clientele Pluralism

Clientele pluralist policy communities display a mutual identification of interests by one or more major stakeholder groups and policy-makers in the lead agency.

Ministers and departmental officials tend to perceive the public interest as broadly consistent with the interests of these key client groups. Although policy-makers may respond to the actions of particular interest groups, more often their decisions reflect an internalized set of bureaucratic priorities that are periodically reinforced by political action.

Clientele pluralism was long associated with departments and agencies responsible for the promotion, oversight, or regulation of oligopolistic industries. It may often be seen in the operations of industry sector branches in a ministry of economic development or in the creation of a sector ministry responsible for mines, forests, fisheries, natural resources, cultural industries, or the like. A labour ministry may identify the public interest with that of organized labour or related societal interests, or a regulatory agency may be captured by the interests it was originally intended to oversee due to changes in personnel or the convergence of philosophies between regulators and regulated.

Clientelist political relationships are common in political cultures that emphasize the distributive role of government as a source of benefits for many societal interests. In such cases, governments' organizational structures facilitate the segmentation of relationships to permit particular groups their voice within government. However, these privileged relationships may also hinder the capacity of governments to respond to changing social, economic, or fiscal conditions that require a broader concept of the public interest, as with regulatory reforms in the transportation and financial services sectors during the 1980s or in reducing chronic budget deficits during the 1990s (Hartle 1994). Other sectors that display some characteristics of clientelist policy communities include federal broadcasting and cultural policies and the regulation of resource and securities industries in some provinces (Coleman 1988: 172-92; Wilson 1990; Howlett et al. 2001; Harris n.d.).

Governments may restructure their operations in order to break up cozy clientelist relationships. One way of doing this is either to group related policy functions within a single department or agency in order to balance overlapping and competing interests or to pursue a significantly different policy framework. For example, the Trudeau government combined the functions of trade policy and promotion with foreign policy and representation in a new Department of External Affairs and International Trade (later DFAIT) in 1982. This move resulted in a bureaucratic culture shift that contributed to the negotiation of the FTA a few years later.

A large-scale government reorganization in 1993 reduced the number of federal departments from 40 to 23. It consolidated a number of special sector-oriented ministries and created several new super-ministries intended to organize horizontal policy development and coordination. For instance, the new Department of Human Resources Development (HRDC) brought together parts of three previous departments responsible for welfare, employment, and labour matters. However, government priorities change, as do the political circumstances that shape them. Prime Minister Martin's reorganization of government in 2003-04 broke up both DFAIT and HRDC into their component parts under the direction of a much larger cabinet.

After a minority Parliament rejected legislation splitting DFAIT in 2004, the Conservative government elected in January 2006 reversed Martin's reorganization.

Co-optive Pluralism

The emergence of **co-optive pluralist policy communities** in governments is often a temporary phenomenon whose durability depends on the relative political influence of government officials and the client groups that they create to provide societal validation for their policy initiatives. Such groups are usually perceived to be socially or politically disadvantaged and under-represented within the political process, for example, Aboriginal and women's groups during the 1970s and 1980s. The creation of the Court Challenges Program to finance constitutional challenges to laws that were seen to impede the equity agendas of certain government departments that saw themselves as representatives of particular social interests is another example.

Interest group participants in such policy communities are initially dependent on government funding for a significant share of their budgets. However, public funding can foster a culture of entitlement that undermines the group's sense of obligation towards or dependence on government so that any effort to reduce funding is met by determined political resistance. In some cases, the result has been the institutionalization of interest groups as part of a broader policy network. In others, confrontations have led to reductions in group funding as responsible politicians and their officials grow weary of subsidizing an adversarial culture.

The problem of interest group funding raises overlapping questions of group autonomy, intergroup equity, and financial accountability. The capacity to pursue one's interests within the political system is a significant aspect of democracy, but one that becomes potentially controversial when paid for by forced subsidies from other taxpayers who may not have access to similar advantages. These debates can raise questions of equity, particularly when interest group funding becomes a form of bureaucratic patronage favouring one group and its agenda over another. They also raise questions of accountability: both the ability of governments to hold groups effectively accountable for the use of taxpayers' money in the general interest and that of group members to set their priorities independently of government. These questions become increasingly relevant—and complicated—when governments engage in societal or public-private partnerships, as discussed in Chapter 9.

Parentela Pluralism

Parentela pluralism involves the politicization of the civil service and government agencies as particular interest groups allied with governing parties arrange to have their representatives appointed to positions within the government. This approach not only prevents the emergence of an independent civil service committed to serving the state or the public, it actively encourages political parties to infiltrate their supporters into the ranks of the civil service to ensure that their interests will be looked after and not sabotaged by either bureaucratic elites or their political opponents. There are similarities between parentela pluralism and the politics of the spoils system in which victorious political parties assign government jobs to their supporters and civil servants owe their primary loyalty to the political party or government faction that appointed them rather than to the government of the day or to the state as a whole.

The extension of civil service reforms and the development of a professional public service tradition on the Westminster model between 1910 and 1970 limited the spread of parentela pluralism in Canada. Political partisanship, while rare, is not unknown at senior civil service levels in some provinces. In the federal government, there is a tradition of former political assistants to ministers moving into the public service. Although many absorb the norms of non-partisanship which are central to Canadian traditions of public service professionalism, the head of the federal Public Service Commission has been highly critical of policies that permit the appointment of cabinet ministers' political staff to permanent civil services positions—often in their previous departments—without going through the competitions required of other applicants (Kernaghan and Siegel 1999: 417-18; Curry 2005: A7).

The veneer of non-partisan professionalism is often thinner in the appointments of the executives and members of many administrative and regulatory agencies that ostensibly function at arm's-length from federal and provincial governments. Governments of all political persuasions have been known to appoint their political friends and trusted professional advisors to chair or staff agencies, boards, and commissions, although terms of appointment may require a member's separation from potentially compromising outside interests. Agencies that are subject to high levels of politicization—such as labour-related agencies in provinces with ideologically polarized political systems or the federal Immigration and Refugee Board—have long been viewed as examples of parentela pluralism in action (Houle 2004: 51-55; Jiminez 2004: A1).

Liberal Corporatism

Canada has experimented on a number of occasions with corporatist policy structures. **Liberal corporatism** attempts to provide for the formal representation of major stakeholder groups within the relevant decision-making structures of governments in order to build, maintain, and enforce policy consensus in response to deep social divisions. Such groups may be formally representative. However, they are often partially autonomous from the societal interests they represent in order to be able to negotiate differences with other stakeholders and develop an elite consensus capable of pursuing a broader public interest. These policy structures are common in the segmented societies of Scandinavian and other European countries such as Germany, Austria, and the Netherlands (Streeck and Schmitter 1985; for recent discussions of corporatist policy-making processes in coordinating economic and social policies, see McMahon 2000b).

Corporatism in Canada has been attempted on a number of occasions, primarily by social-democratic provincial governments capable of exercising some leverage over both business and labour groups. The federal Anti-Inflation Board (1976-78) had both formal corporate and labour representation, and Canada's free trade negotiation process attempted to co-opt both business and labour into the development of industry sector consensus-building, although most unions refused to participate.

Corporatism in Quebec evolved from industry-worker parity committees in the 1930s into a wide range of participatory policy structures involving many different sectors of Quebec society during the 1970s and 1980s. Liberal and NDP governments in Ontario attempted to extend corporatist structures in several areas between 1985 and 1995, including the Premier's Council—a strategic advisory council on economic and related social policies—and a number of labour and employment-related organizations. However, these groups were rapidly dismantled after the 1995 election replaced Rae's NDP government with a PC government firmly committed to economic individualism. BC has used corporatist strategies to reconcile industry, union and environmental interests in the province's vital forest industries—with varying degrees of success (Howlett et al. 2001).

The success of corporatist policy strategies depends on sustained government commitment, preferably involving a measure of bipartisan consensus on the value of such initiatives; the willingness of stakeholder groups to recognize one another's vital interests and develop the trust necessary for effective collaboration in the policy process; and, at times, on the ability of corporatist structures to accommodate a variety of interests or to segment the policy process to reduce conflict among interests whose interests and policy preferences are deeply opposed to one another.

Canada's adversarial parliamentary political culture does not lend itself to corporatist policy-making. Neither does the fragmented, highly individualistic character of many Canadian business associations nor the challenge of policy-making within a highly decentralized federal system. These tendencies are reinforced by the relative influence of small business groups, the most individualistic element of Canada's business community.

As a result, corporatist policy communities tend to occur at a sectoral level where different interests are able to accommodate their differences and build a consensus with government officials on the policy measures most likely to promote the interests of their industries. Recent examples include the efforts of federal and Ontario governments to coordinate major corporate, union, and supplier interests in the promotion of automotive policies, and the persistence of labour-management coordination in a number of policy fields related to labour and workplace issues in larger provinces (McIntosh 2000; Canada, Industry Canada 2002).

Concertation Networks

Concertation networks are policy communities in which state actors deal on more or less equal terms with a dominant stakeholder organization or coalition representing societal interests to negotiate a policy representing the public interest. Concertation networks tend to be most feasible in oligopolistic industries with high levels of industry concentration, particularly in dealings with a highly professional, centralized government department or agency with the capacity to make authoritative policy decisions.

Coleman suggests that such concertation networks are more typical of highly structured societies such as Japan or France than of Canada, although the chartered banking sector, operating through the Canadian Bankers' Association, once served as a Canadian example of this kind of policy-making. In recent years, changes to the composition and regulation of the financial services sector and political disputes over the desirability of large bank mergers has disrupted traditional patterns of interest group accommodation, leading to a more open, highly contested approach to policy-making (Coleman 1988: 184-90; Whittington 1999; Harris 2004).

State-Directed Networks

State-directed policy networks function with a high degree of **state autonomy** from societal interests. They are characterized by authoritative state agencies with concentrated and often autonomous authority. This autonomy may be related to the highly technical or secretive character of their work. It may also result when agencies are extensively involved in state-to-state relationships which, by their very nature, tend to subordinate or marginalize societal interests to the government's view of the national interest.

State-directed policy networks at the national level include the development of monetary policy by the Bank of Canada and the work of the Canadian Security and Intelligence Service (CSIS) and its oversight body, the Security Intelligence Review Commission.

Challenges to Government Relations Practices and the Spread of Lobbying Regulations

The process of formally regulating lobbyists began in the late 1980s in response to abuses by some firms which were widely perceived to be engaged in securing preferential political treatment for their clients through their close political connections. The *Lobbyists' Registration Act*, which was amended in 1995 and 2003, attempts to balance the right of petition for all citizens and organized groups with efforts to bring greater transparency to the political process. Similar legislation has been passed in Ontario, Quebec, BC, and Nova Scotia.

Lobbyists who are retained by clients to engage in direct lobbying activities are required to register with the Lobbyists' Registration Branch, a division of Industry Canada, as are executives of interest groups (organization lobbyists) and officers of corporations "who devote a significant part of their duties to public affairs or government relations work." Regulations under the act define this as 20 per cent or more of an executive's time (Canada, Lobbyist Registration Branch 2000: 5). The preamble of the act notes that:

- free and open access to government is an important matter of public interest;
- lobbying public office holders is a legitimate activity;
- it is desirable that public office holders and the general public should be able to know who is attempting to influence government; and

- the system for the registration of paid lobbyists should not impede free and open access to government.

Lobbying is defined by the act as "(*a*) communicat(ing) with a public office holder in respect of (i) the development of any legislative proposal by the Government of Canada or by a member of the Senate or the House of Commons, (ii) the introduction of any Bill or resolution in either House of Parliament or the passage, defeat or amendment of any Bill or resolution that is before either House of Parliament, (iii) the making or amendment of any regulation as defined in subsection 2(1) of the *Statutory Instruments Act*, (iv) the development or amendment of any policy or program of the Government of Canada, (v) the awarding of any grant, contribution or other financial benefit by or on behalf of Her Majesty in right of Canada, or (vi) the awarding of any contract by or on behalf of Her Majesty in right of Canada; or (*b*) arrang(ing) a meeting between a public office holder and any other person." (Canada, *Lobbyists Registration Act*, RS, 1985, c. 44 4th Supp., s.5 (1)).

The *Lobbyist Registration Act* requires disclosure of a number of activities including:

- names of clients on whose behalf lobbying occurs;
- names of parent or subsidiary firms that might benefit from such activity;
- organizational members of coalition groups;
- names of federal departments or agencies contacted;
- source and amount of federal funding received by organizations lobbying the government;
- subject matter of contact;
- description of previous public offices, elective or appointive, held by the lobbyist;
- disclosure of contingency fee arrangements related to success of lobbying efforts; and
- the communications techniques used, such as grass roots lobbying. (Canada, *Lobbyists Registration Act*, RS, 1985, c. 44 4th Supp., s.5 (2))

This information is publicly available on a website maintained by the Lobbyists Registration Branch of Industry Canada.

Regulations governing particular programs may require disclosure of lobbyists' fees related to project applications or preclude the payment of program funds for contingency fees to lobbyists or other advisors. Treasury Board ethics guidelines also preclude former public service managers from:

making representations for, or on behalf of, persons to any department or organizations with which they personally, or through their subordinates, had significant official dealings during the period of one year immediately prior to the termination of their service; or giving advice to their clients using information that is not available to the public concerning the programs or policies of the departments or organizations with which they were employed or with which they had a direct or substantial relationship. (*The Lobby Monitor* 15(2) 2003: November 120)

However, a series of highly publicized government audits have led observers to suggest that enforcement of these rules, particularly those governing consultant lobbyists, has been sporadic, with very limited consequences for non-compliance (Doyle and Aubry 2005). A routine audit of the Technology Partnerships Program disclosed significant problems of this kind in 2005, resulting in legal action to secure the repayment of funds and several embarrassing disclosures of the lobbying efforts of a former federal cabinet minister (Sallot 2005: A5). Government relations professionals interviewed by the author have suggested that changes to the lobbyist registry, which are regularly reported by industry publications such as *The Lobby Monitor*, serve as a form of advertising by lobbyists and public affairs firms that can be used to promote their current activities and to attract clients (confidential interviews, government relations industry, July 2002).

The government relations business can be highly political, with senior political advisors to ministers (or opposition leaders) migrating to public affairs firms while maintaining close personal or political relationships with cabinet ministers and opposition parties. Lobbyists may be actively involved in the management of political parties' election campaigns or in the campaigns of candidates seeking the leadership of their political parties. The services of specialized public affairs consulting firms such as Earnscliffe Strategy Group or Capital Hill Group were integral parts of the political networks of Paul Martin, John Manley, and other Liberal leadership aspirants during the latter years of the Chrétien government.

Some observers have expressed concern over the potential for revolving door relationships between former government officials (or ministerial staff) and private sector clients, as members of both groups attempt to market their skills, contacts, and expertise after leaving government. The political conflicts and accusations of scandal surrounding the Chrétien government during its final years in office prompted both a review of federal ethics legislation governing the behaviour of cabinet ministers and MPs and amendments to the *Lobbyist Registration Act*. Most provincial legislation is similar to the federal act, although Quebec legislation also applies to the municipal government sector and to officers of all Crown corporations and government agencies.

The Conservative government elected in January 2006 promised to implement "accountability" legislation to extend to prohibit lobbying by "former ministers, ministerial staffers, and senior public services" for five years after they leave government, to "require ministers and senior government officials to record their contacts with lobbyists," and to ban "success or contingency fee arrangements." It also committed to make officials responsible for administering and enforcing the law independent of the executive (*The Lobby Monitor* 17:7, 2006, 2).

Conclusion

The lobbying activities of business organizations and individual corporations take place within a political marketplace in which governments use a wide variety of policy tools to organize and regulate economic activities, as well as redistributing economic benefits among individuals, businesses, societal interests, and regional communities.

The capacity of some groups to obtain benefits, or to control or redistribute the costs of government activities to other less favoured groups, fosters increased political competition to influence the policy process. This competition takes place on several levels: within and among governments, among business groups and individual corporations, and between business groups and competing societal interests. Citizens wishing to engage the policy process to make it more responsive to their interests—or to a vision of the public interest which reflects their well-being—need to develop a better understanding of the multi-dimensional policy processes of governments, how they interact with one another, and what efforts compete to shape public opinion.

Key Terms and Concepts for Review (see Glossary)

attentive actors

broadly based (or comprehensive)
  business associations

exchange process

government relations

industry associations

interest aggregation

interest groups
  • institutionalized interest groups
  • issue-oriented interest groups

lead agency

lobbying
  • direct lobbying
  • indirect lobbying

lobbyist

Lobbyist Registration Act

major stakeholders

peak association

policy communities
  • clientele pluralist
  • concertation networks
  • co-optive pluralist
  • liberal corporatist
  • parentela pluralist
  • pressure pluralist
  • state-directed networks

policy networks

public affairs

sectoral associations

state autonomy

strategic analysis

subgovernment

think tanks

trade (or industry) associations

Questions for Discussion and Review

1. Look up the websites of three broadly based business associations. Compare and contrast their organizational structures, policy priorities (from publications or summaries of government relations activities listed on websites for the past 12-24 months), and policy positions taken on similar issues, with attention to similarities and differences.

2. Look up the websites of four sectoral and trade associations and discuss their:
   - organizational profile (number, size, and market profile of membership; organizational structure; leadership)
   - principal services offered to members
   - government-relations priorities.

   Compare and contrast policy positions taken on major issues with those noted in your responses to Question 1.

3. Profile the policy community for a high profile business issue discussed in the national or regional media, or that is under parliamentary or legislative review. Clearly define the lead agency or agencies, major components of the subgovernment, major stakeholders, and attentive actors. What type of policy community is engaged with the issue? Explain your choice. (Hint: review the reports of parliamentary or legislative committees set up to examine a particular bill or policy initiative for major participants; do an Internet scan for media coverage and commentaries by major interest groups, government departments or agencies, and other observers.)

4. What principles should guide the government funding of interest groups, and why? How does public funding of interest groups contribute to conflicts among different ethical norms and concepts of equality and accountability?

Suggestions for Further Readings

Abelsen, Donald E. 2001. *Do think tanks matter?* Montreal and Kingston: McGill-Queen's University Press.

Berry, Jeffrey M. 1997. *The interest group society*, 3rd ed. New York: Longman.

Clancy, Peter. 2004. *Micropolitics of business: paper, steel, airlines.* Peterborough, ON: Broadview Press.

Coleman, William D. 1988. *Business and politics: a study in collective action.* Montreal and Kingston: McGill-Queen's University Press.

Coleman, William D., and Grace Skogstad (Eds.). 1990. *Policy communities and public policy in Canada: a structural approach.* Toronto: Copp Clark Pitman.

Pross, A. Paul. 1992. *Group politics and public policy.* Toronto: Oxford University Press.

Public Policy Forum. 2002. *Bridging two solitudes: a discussion paper on federal government-industry relations.* Ottawa: Public Policy Forum (October).

Streeck, Wolfgang, and Philippe Schmitter (Eds.). 1985. *Private interest government: beyond market and state.* London: Sage Publications.

Stanbury, W.T. 1994. *Business-government relations in Canada*, 2nd ed. Toronto: Nelson.

VanWaarden, Frans. 1992. Dimensions and types of policy networks. *European Journal of Political Research* 21.

CHAPTER 11

The Internal Policy Process: Balancing Different Views of the Public Interest

Early policy studies described the workings of government as a "black box" into which various societal interests pour their demands and preferences, from which emerge government decisions, policies, programs, and other "outputs" in response (Easton 1965). Opening the black box to some degree of public scrutiny contributes to better public understanding of the pressures and trade-offs facing policy-makers and the contexts in which citizens and interest groups must function when attempting to make these processes more responsive.

Earlier chapters of this book examined the role of political and economic ideas on relations between government and business and their implications for the policy process. They noted that both the extent and limitations of business influence are evident in the outcomes of government policy decisions and the ways in which business groups and other societal interests interact with the varied policy processes of governments.

This chapter looks at the internal policy processes of governments and the factors that help to shape the choices made by government decision-makers in defining their priorities, framing or extending policy goals, and balancing competing societal interests and demands, including those of businesses. It reviews the institutional context for policy-making: the impact of the organizational structures, rules, and commitments of governments on policy choices and decisions and the ways that they are implemented. It assesses both the roles played by different government decision-makers and their advisors and the implications of these roles in dealings between businesses (or their representatives) and governments. It addresses the major stages of the policy processes, along with ways that governments attempt to manage—and interest groups attempt to influence—these processes at each stage. It considers some of the implications of these processes and relationships for the strategies used by interest groups, lobbyists, and other government relations professionals in their efforts to influence the contents and implementation of public policies. Finally, it outlines a number of key principles that can affect the relative effectiveness of interest groups and citizens in their dealings with government policy-makers.

The Context for Public Policy

Public policies may be defined as the principles, rules, and decisions which govern the actions (or inaction) of governments and the ways in which they relate to citizens and other governments. Public policies may be expressed through a wide range of **policy instruments**: the means or "tools" that governments have at their

343

disposal for implementing policies (Howlett and Ramesh 2003: 87). The choice of instruments influences both the extent and nature of government intervention in the choices and decisions of individuals and businesses. This continuum ranges from conscious decisions not to seek governmental solutions to perceived problems or challenges to the management of some aspect of economic or social life under the complete ownership and direction of a government department or agency. However, there are often plenty of viable alternatives in between as Box 11.1 outlines.

Box 11.1: Policy Instruments: The Tool Box of Government

Information/ Persuasion ...	Taxation ...	Regulation ...	Partnerships/ Mixed Enterprises...	Government Enterprises ...	Direct Government Delivery/ Control
Information Exhortation Advertising Sponsored research Direct research	Tax expenditures Benefit-related taxes General consumption and licence taxes/ user fees Redistributive taxes Goods-specific taxes/tax penalties	Subsidies Guidelines Permissive regulations Command-and-control regulations	Public-private partnerships Partial private share ownership Multi-government partnerships	Commercial Semi-commercial/ business development Government-services corporation/ agency	Government department Regulatory agency
			.... contracting-out		

←――→

Less government control   More government control

The fragmentation of policy processes discussed in Chapter 10 is a necessary by-product of the development of specialized bureaucratic organizations, each with their own decision-makers, to manage the operations of governments' different components and their relationships with different segments of society. Governments are not "unitary actors" as much as collections of overlapping and competing interests with varying degrees of power and access to relevant information (Milner 1997: 10-12). Just as social and economic life tends to resist confinement within the tidy little boxes of government organization charts, public policy processes often overlap, challenging policy analysts and decision-makers to find coherent ways of describing and managing the ways in which they interact.

Policies are designed and implemented within the broader context of what political scientists call regimes and institutions: the overlapping fields of legal, political, economic, and administrative authority and competence that empower, shape, and constrain the behaviour of governments and citizens alike. Although institutions may shape the behaviour of individual actors, they are also shaped by them. Institutions affect not only the ways that governments define and carry out their functions but also the behaviour and expectations of businesses and of citizens in a wide variety of economic, social, and political settings. By establishing and reinforcing patterns of behaviour inside and outside government—and identifying the promotion of certain ideas and interests with the public interest—institutions increase the likelihood that certain policy choices and options will be considered, while others will be marginalized.

As a result, most policy-making is the product of incremental or step-by-step changes to existing rules and processes. Most major policy changes are more likely to emerge when senior decision-makers recognize and respond to the existence of a policy crisis or the failure of existing policy systems to meet important public expectations (Hall 1988: 378-79). Less frequently, major policy innovations can emerge from the efforts of political or bureaucratic entrepreneurs who identify an opportunity for creative political action and manage to obtain the political backing necessary to pursue it.

Institutions also help to define or structure the processes for determining which issues or problems will be given priority by political and bureaucratic authorities, which policy options will be considered, which experts or interests are likely to be consulted (and when), and how proposed policies are to be implemented. Familiarity with the often complex policy processes of governments and the people who make them work can make a significant difference to individuals and groups attempting to promote their interests and agendas in a competitive political marketplace.

The Public Policy Process: Levels of Analysis

"For every complex problem, there is a solution that is simple, easy, and wrong."
H.L. Mencken

Public policies are formed at several different levels. Government policy-making often involves the interaction of as many as five different sets of **policy regimes**, the systems of organizations, rules, and processes and the ideas and interests associated with them that shape the context for public policies (adapted from Doern, et al. 1999: 9). There are five different **levels of analysis** that may be used to analyze and interpret different aspects of the policy process: international, constitutional, macro- (or government-wide), framework, and sectoral.

Levels of analysis are more than a theoretical academic construct. They speak to the contexts that inform the attitudes, actions, and priorities of different actors within the policy process. For example, political advisors to a prime minister or premier may be largely indifferent to the technical details of particular policies. However, they should be keenly sensitive to how particular policies contribute to or detract from the government's broader political agenda and its prospects for re-election. Senior public servants have to balance the implications of particular policy changes for their own departments and agencies with the ways in which they may complement or conflict with other government priorities, and then they must find ways to reconcile or manage potential conflicts between the two. By contrast, the focus of mid-ranking and front-line civil servants is more likely to be on the detailed workings of specific policies and programs for which they are accountable, although they may also have to deal with the consequences of other government actions over which they have little or no control. As noted in Chapter 10, each of these processes engages the attentions of particular interest groups depending on the composition of their particular policy communities.

Each of these policy systems influences the workings of micro-policies that directly affect the day-to-day lives of citizens and businesses and their interactions with governments. The success of political actors inside and outside government usually depends on their capacity to approach particular policy issues in ways that are informed by and responsive to the policy contexts of the individual decision-makers and organizations with which they are dealing. Failure to take into account how these different levels of analysis fit together is often a major reason that policy proposals that seem attractive in theory may not work nearly as well in practice. It also increases the likelihood of political conflict among competing interests and agendas.

The Constitutional and Quasi-Constitutional Level

Government policies are usually subject to a constitutional framework, which defines the powers, responsibilities, and limitations of governments and those who exercise authority on their behalf. Political disputes over the constitutionality of public policies may be carried out through the courts, as discussed in Chapter 13. They may also evolve through various processes of intergovernmental negotiation and accommodation or through gradual adaptations to the basic rules of the political game. Examples include the growth of prime ministerial (and premiers') powers and the corresponding decline of parliaments and legislatures within Canada's cabinet-parliamentary system. Political logjams may result in unilateral actions which test both existing legal and constitutional boundaries and the degree to which political and legal systems will accommodate these actions.

International treaties signed by national governments and federal-provincial agreements may serve as quasi-constitutional arrangements which may expand or constrain **state capacity**—the ability of governments to mobilize the resources necessary to design and implement policies that will achieve their objectives in particular areas—depending on the mechanisms for their enforcement. These by-products of intergovernmental cooperation may increase the capacity of governments to manage their political agendas or to respond to international forces that prompt them to adjust their policies in order to protect other valued objectives (as discussed in Chapter 8).

Policy processes that involve dealings between governments—or between governments and societal groups whose activities straddle national or provincial boundaries—are often described as a **two-level game** in which political leaders pursue their goals in overlapping arenas while attempting to build political coalitions or alliances that will "maximize their own ability to satisfy domestic pressures while minimizing the adverse consequences of foreign developments" (Putnam 1988: 434; see also Milner 1997; Mayer 1998). In Canada, regional pressures sometimes add a third level to this game.

Changes to international policy commitments typically engage decision-makers at the higher levels of government. They may have sufficient implications for citizens and businesses to prompt the intensive engagement of interest groups throughout society. However, as the internationalization of public policy leads to increasingly specialized sectoral arrangements that cross national borders, the policy focus often shifts to line departments and those social and economic sectors most directly affected by related policy processes (Doern, Pal, and Tomlin 1996; see also Hale 2003).

Government-Wide Policies and Priorities

Macro-level policies, usually defined or applied at the highest levels of government, help to set the context for the workings of a government or political system as a whole. Such policies—such as institutional bilingualism and the decentralization of Canada's federal system during the Pearson and early Trudeau years, Ottawa's adaptation of North American free trade and neo-liberal economic policies during the Mulroney and Chrétien eras, and the constitutional agendas of successive Quebec governments since the 1940s—may dominate national or provincial political agendas and shape the context for a wide range of other policy initiatives. Other political programs, such as Trudeau's new National Policy (discussed in Chapter 5) or Mulroney's constitutional reform agendas, may so polarize political life and consume the energies of senior political leaders and civil servants that a crisis must be reached and passed before governments can focus on other policies and priorities.

During the 1990s, a number of political leaders used detailed campaign platforms, such as the Liberal Red Book of 1993 and the Ontario PCs' Common Sense Revolution of 1995, to define their macro-policy agendas and priorities for change. However, election-driven agendas for large-scale policy change have usually been the exception rather than the rule of Canadian politics in recent years, for example, Kim Campbell's ill-timed comment before her government's 1993 electoral destruction that elections are "not the time to get involved in a debate on ... serious issues" (McLaughlin 1994: 207-08).

Interest groups and line department officials who can align or package their policy ideas in ways that reinforce or complement the centre's priorities tend to have a significant political advantage over groups that cannot or will not do so.

Framework Legislation

Framework legislation embodies the major principles and structures that govern the operation of those areas of public policy that have a widespread impact on the economic and social system as a whole. Although individual laws and regulations may be the subject of periodic or incremental changes, the major principles and structures that govern these systems—such as national or provincial tax, social security, labour relations systems, and the organization of monetary policies or the financial services sector—are sufficiently durable that they have been described as elements of the "economic constitution" (Hale 2001b: 63-87).

The trade-offs embedded in these laws are usually important enough that proposals for major changes will usually trigger intense competition among competing business interests. This occurs most often in the case of competition laws or policies governing the financial services sector, or in proposals to amend tax, social security, and labour laws that affect business groups and other social and political interests.

Horizontal or broadly based business groups that can successfully balance competing membership interests can often exercise a substantial influence over proposed changes to framework policies and their enabling legislation. Sectoral associations may play an influential role if they can provide governments with information that demonstrates more effective ways of accommodating their distinctive realities while still promoting broad legislative goals. Examples of this approach include different treatments of large and small firms in some aspects of federal and provincial tax and labour law and different labour law regimes that recognize the reality of multi-employer contracts in many parts of the construction sector.

Sectoral Policies

Sectoral policies govern the operations of specific industry, economic, or social policy sectors. They usually have a disproportionate impact on a particular industry or cluster of industries. Most of the political activities of business, and the regulatory activities of governments, are more likely to relate to the activities of particular departments or industry sectors than to government or the economy as a whole. As a result, sectoral policies frequently reflect the organizational structures of governments and their decisions to assign responsibilities for particular sector policies to particular departments and agencies.

For example, to the frequent frustration of developers, building contractors, and owners, the design and enforcement of building and fire codes have traditionally been the responsibility of different government departments. Employment training policies take very different forms depending on whether they are administered by federal or provincial departments of education, human resources, labour, or economic development or are largely delegated to community, labour-management, or other private sector bodies by one or more of these departments. Similarly, the design and administration of border management may vary significantly depending on whether the emphasis is to generate revenue, facilitate (or regulate) trade, control migration, or protect national security—a reality familiar to Canadian exporters, importers, and business travelers.

Industry sectors which can organize themselves to present a single, cohesive voice to governments, particularly if they link business and labour, may exercise effective control over the development of major economic policies affecting their sectors. Alternately, sector policy debates may involve competition between producers and consumers, economic interests in different geographic regions, different market segments, or other societal interests.

Micro-Policies

Micro-policies affect the routine or technical activities of individual citizens, businesses, and particular government departments or agencies. The implications of these policies may be specific to an individual business in its dealings with government or may affect a wider group of firms as well as other societal interests. Changes to macro-, framework, or sectoral policies are likely to trigger a wide range of micro-political or economic effects that engage the attention of many businesses and other interests in ways that are well below the radar screens of politicians or civil servants introducing such policy changes. A great deal of the political activity of businesses is dedicated to fine-tuning or adapting rules and policies in order to enhance the benefits or limit the damage to their particular interests potentially caused by broader government policy shifts.

Of course, policy processes often take place on more than one level, involving any combination of negotiations between independent state actors, federal-provincial discussions, the adaptation of macro- or framework-level policies to national or international policy changes, specialized discussions involving specific industry sectors, and a myriad of related micro-policy issues. For example, Doern and Tomlin have described the 1986-88 negotiations leading to the signing of the FTA as a "three ring circus" involving separate processes of bi-national, federal-provincial, and domestic and international sector-level negotiations (Doern and Tomlin 1991; see also Mayer 1998). Multi-level policy games may occur in domestic politics as well, such as in debates over budgetary and tax policies or the coordination and balancing of environmental protection and economic development policies and in efforts to manage the differences between unionized and non-unionized sectors of the workplace while accommodating other societal interests (Kumar 1993; Campbell and Pal 1994; Hale 2001b; Clancy 2004).

Governments, business groups, and other societal players in the policy game frequently work under conditions of imperfect information. For this reason, both public and private sector actors may attempt to enhance their positions by assembling formal or informal coalitions through their policy networks and by retaining outside advisors, including independent experts and facilitators, pollsters, and public affairs or government relations consultants to assist them in developing strategies and managing policy processes. Central to these strategies is the need to understand the organizational contexts for policy development and the attitudes and backgrounds of senior policy-makers within those organizations.

Organizational and Interpersonal Contexts

The capacity to influence public policy largely depends on a participant's awareness, understanding, and capacity to manoeuvre within the highly specialized, often arcane policy processes of governments. If the policy process can be understood as a game played on several levels, people who want to play the game—or just to understand how it is played—need to understand both the organizational and interpersonal dynamics of the policy process as two distinct but related aspects of strategic policy analysis.

Public policies are made by specific governmental organizations and the people who work within them. Each organization has a legal mandate, a managerial structure that confers varying degrees of formal authority on individuals holding different positions within it, and an administrative culture that helps not only to define how members of the organization relate to one another and to various stakeholder groups but how they are likely to perceive the public interest. Although these factors help to define the terms under which political and bureaucratic decision-makers *may* conduct themselves under different circumstances, individual dynamics—including the personal background, ideological orientation, and political or managerial style of particular decision-makers— also play a significant role. Access to this kind of knowledge is usually limited to insiders or to those who have invested sufficient time to build effective relationships with them.

Turning a theoretical understanding of the policy process into a practical one is an exercise in discovery, particularly when it comes to identifying the specific roles of elected officials, senior public servants, and middle management or more junior officials on particular files. Political decisions may take place at several levels, whatever the formalities of official cabinet decision-making processes. These include:

- decisions subject to the political discretion of individual cabinet ministers, such as the content and balance of overall departmental priorities or the decision to accommodate or marginalize the views and input of particular interest groups in departmental decision-making; such decisions are often, but not always, made with the advice of a minister's senior officials;
- decisions to delegate extensive decision-making authority to departmental officials or specialized government agencies, enabling ministers to avoid direct involvement except when they (or cabinet as a whole) determine that major policy changes are required;
- dealings between the Prime Minister's or Premier's Office and individual ministers;
- the formal decision-making processes of cabinet or arm's-length government agencies.

Although political assistance may be helpful in resolving the problems of citizens, businesses, and interest groups in dealing with the everyday workings of bureaucracy, few cabinet ministers have either the time or the inclination to focus on more than a handful of issues at one time. As a result, their first response to the questions or challenges posed by their constituents is to refer inquiries to the responsible civil servants, through the bureaucratic chain of command, for their response. As a result, a business or interest group appealing for political support in its dealings with the bureaucracy may have its concerns recycled to their point of origin within that very bureaucracy.

Most policy development and implementation functions are carried out by civil servants at different levels of the bureaucratic hierarchy working within government departments and agencies with more or less specialized functions, and most lobbying is concerned with the mundane details of policy or program design that are the responsibilities of these civil servants. The need to translate political and policy decisions into administrative action requires the active support and involvement of deputy ministers or the chief executives of particular government agencies.

Deputy ministers are the principal policy advisors to cabinet ministers and are responsible to them for the management of their departments and the provision of advice on all issues requiring ministerial decisions or communications with cabinet. Strong and experienced ministers, particularly those enjoying close relations with their prime ministers, may exercise considerable political discretion. Weaker or less experienced ministers lean heavily on their deputies for advice and guidance. As these relationships are far from clear to outsiders, a key challenge facing businesses and other interest group stakeholders is to identify the priorities and preferences of senior decision-makers when monitoring relevant policy processes and attempting to develop effective strategies to influence their actions and decisions.

The broad scope of many government departments and the wide range of policy and administrative issues associated with their effective management often require deputy ministers to delegate considerable discretion to senior departmental executives, usually associate or assistant deputy ministers (ADMs) responsible for the major administrative divisions of a department. ADMs responsible for technical policy issues often have extensive experience in the administrative workings of their departments; their institutional memory may predispose them to support or challenge certain approaches to policy that reflect the bureaucratic traditions of their departments or their knowledge of past practices and decisions.

Although businesses or interest groups seeking to influence government policies may interact with senior departmental management, for more routine or technical issues, they are far more likely to deal with the middle or line managers—executive directors, directors general, directors, or chiefs—responsible for specific issues of policy, programming, or regulation. These managers may have greater or lesser degrees of experience, professional expertise, and influence. However, they frequently serve as gatekeepers and advisors for the day-to-day workings of the policy process. They prepare—or sign off on—the briefing notes provided to ministers and senior department executives with background and advice on everyday issues of government. As a result, they may be effective conduits for the advice, concerns, and inputs of individual businesses or particular interest groups. Alternately, if they view business or interest group representations as unduly self-interested or inimical to the best interests of their department or the broader public, they may serve as significant filters or obstacles.

Businesses and interest groups that develop effective working relations with responsible line managers in governments, getting to know them as people and understanding their motivations and the contexts in which they work, tend to be much more effective than those who simply show up to expound upon their problems or proposals for making the world more sensitive to their concerns. However, few businesses or interest groups possess the frequency of exposure, expertise, or inclination to develop these relationships effectively except, perhaps, on a very narrow range of issues of vital importance to their own or their members' interests. These omissions may be entirely understandable given the pressures of running a competitive business. However, they tend to reinforce the gaps in professional training, experience, temperament, and outlook between business people (or their interest group representatives) and civil servants, a gap described by a recent think tank report as the "two solitudes" of business and government (Public Policy Forum 2002).

These differences in culture and experience have several implications for state-society relations in general and business-government relations in particular. Influencing the policy process requires an understanding of the organization of government and the contexts in which government decision-makers function. Acquiring this understanding requires a willingness to ask questions. Who is responsible for what decisions? What factors or past decisions have defined the contexts in which these decisions are made? What constraints—legal, organizational, financial, or political—shape the choices available to particular decision-makers and their ability to respond to business or interest group concerns?

It is not necessary to agree with or support the past decisions or current constraints of policy-makers to recognize the conditions under which they function. Just as governments may be rightly criticized for intervening in the lives or operations of citizens or businesses without understanding the conditions under which they must survive and function from day-to-day, businesses or interest groups may reduce their political effectiveness by making demands upon government which ignore or disregard the context in which politicians or public servants must function. Developing this understanding is the first step towards the creation of a strategic approach to mobilizing the political and/or bureaucratic resources necessary to achieve desired changes in cooperation with—or despite the opposition of—other players within the policy process.

The Policy Cycle

Public policies emerge from the complex interactions of individuals and organizations in an often chaotic world subject to the unpredictable actions of government decision-makers and other political actors including interest groups, the news media, the courts, and voters. The formal study of public policy attempts to impose reason and order on this seeming chaos through the logic and techniques of the social sciences. However, the real world of policy-making is often a lot messier.

Kingdon outlines three broad approaches to the policy-making process. Advocates of the **rational policy-making** model suggest that in an ideal world, policymakers should clearly define their goals (and/or the problems proposed policies are intended to solve), formulate and compare policy alternatives or options to determine the likely costs and benefits of each one, and then choose the option most likely to achieve their objective at an acceptable cost (Kingdon 1984: 82). However, as comprehensive rationality often requires greater levels of time, information, resources, and political discretion than governments typically possess, many policy decisions are made on the basis of **incrementalism**. Existing policies, or the **status quo**, are used as the starting point for policy analysis, and policymakers "make small, marginal adjustments in their existing behaviour" (Kingdon 1984: 83). This approach to policy may indeed be rational when existing policies are more-or-less effective in reaching their goals and the disruptions (or transitional costs) from introducing large-scale policy changes would create as many problems as potential benefits.

However, many policy decisions are disruptive, costly, and not particularly effective in achieving declared goals—presuming that these goals were clearly articulated in the first place. The often erratic processes[1] that lead to such results have been described as the **garbage-can model** of organizational or policy choice (Cohen, March, and Olsen 1972; Kingdon 1984: 88-94). This approach to policy-making often functions by trial-and-error, pragmatic intervention in crises, and by invoking one-dimensional responses to multi-dimensional problems. The more senior the decision-makers in question, the more likely the costs of "putting out the garbage" will be externalized to the broader population or to those societal interests whose political support is considered dispensable.

In reality, policy processes can include elements of all three models. Formal approaches to policy analysis often attempt to link policy decisions to informed analysis through a process sometimes described as the **policy cycle**, although the workings of the cycle are rarely linear, seldom proceeding smoothly in a logical progression from one stage to the next. Five major elements of the policy cycle are **agenda-setting; policy formulation** and design; the multi-stage process of **policy approval**, which often involves significant changes to policy design; **policy implementation**; and, hopefully, **policy evaluation.**

In theory, citizens, interest groups, and elected officials may participate in each of these stages. However, the size and complexity of government and the huge range of policy issues under consideration at any one time limit the degree of public participation in any one issue to a handful of political actors, broadly defined, who participate in the particular policy communities or policy networks discussed in Chapter 10. In practice, government officials within the lead agencies of particular policy communities often serve as gatekeepers to manage competing public demands on the resources of their department or agency, including time, money, and people.

---

1 Irreverently described by one of the author's former employers as "BS baffles brains."

Agenda-Setting: Shaping Priorities, Defining Problems

Much as many politicians would like to be all things to all people, they face many constraints that force them to set priorities in what policy issues they choose to engage and how they engage them. The political agenda may be defined as "the list of subjects or problems to which governmental officials, and people outside of government closely associated with those officials, are paying some serious attention at any given time" (Kingdon 1984: 3-4).

Politicians, civil servants, and interest groups may be able to advance the ideas they wish to promote through existing policies, programs, and money. But getting political approval (or more resources) is usually a competitive process between and among ministers and departments—and often within departments—to insert their own policy priorities and those of their major stakeholder groups on to the government's broader policy agenda. Political scientists define agenda-setting as "the means by which issues and concerns are recognized as candidates for government action" (Howlett and Ramesh 2003: 120).

To influence either departmental or government-wide priorities, politicians, government officials, and interest groups must win the support of powerful sponsors within the political and bureaucratic hierarchies, especially cabinet ministers and their senior advisors. A significant part of the external policy process, discussed further in Chapter 12, is the competition, particularly for groups who feel their concerns have not received sufficient attention in a government's agenda, to catch the attention of governments, the news media, and opposition political parties.

Advancing one's issues on the public agenda depends on two separate, but related processes: problem recognition and problem definition. It is one thing for politicians or government officials to recognize that something is a problem either for themselves or for particular societal groups. It is something very different— and rather more critical for effective action—to identify the nature and sources of particular problems in ways that help policy-makers identify viable or effective responses to them.

Priority Setting

There is no shortage of people with creative ideas—or strongly-expressed concerns— to engage the agendas of governments and other political actors. Kingdon (1984) suggests three broad sources or streams of ideas that can influence the government agenda. The *problem stream*—debates within the media or policy communities over problems potentially requiring government action—is usually no farther away than the morning newspaper or the evening television news. Such debates may have multiple participants: politically active citizens, interest groups, journalists and their media outlets, academics, elected officials, and even periodic appearances by Mother Nature.

The *policy stream* is the detailed analysis of problems and suggestions for possible responses by experts inside and outside government and is closely related to the process of problem definition. This stream is dominated by civil servants, think tanks, and academics associated with one or both; however, while these groups often possess some technical expertise, the effectiveness of their participation in the agenda-setting process often depends on their skills as policy entrepreneurs or on the sponsorship of authoritative decision-makers willing to consider or promote their ideas. The ways that problems (or their primary causes) are defined can affect the priority given to them by these senior political actors. Problems that are conceptualized to allow political leaders to appear decisive or responsive to constituents are often given higher priority than those that suggest that governments may only be able to moderate the effects of **policy shocks** that are largely beyond government control—at least in the short term.

Box 11.2: Avenues for Priority Setting

	Throne Speech ⟷	Annual Budget ⟷ Cycle	Election Platform Commitments	Responses to Policy Shocks
Inputs from:	PM and cabinet Central agencies • in consultation with senior officials of line departments	Finance Minister and PM • cabinet consultations • input from line departments • public consultations (often parliamentary or legislative committee)	PM's political staff Party strategists and pollsters	Economic crisis • general • regional • industry specific Natural catastrophe National security crisis Foreign government action
	Department business plans		Electoral cycle	

The political stream includes events and processes related to the normal political and electoral calendars of government as noted in Box 11.2: regular agenda-setting exercises such as throne speeches and annual budget processes and the priority setting exercises that mark the approach of an election campaign. It is also affected by broader factors such as public moods towards various kinds and degrees of government action and the relationship of particular problems to the **political business cycle**: the interaction of political and economic factors in government decision-making (Howlett and Ramesh 2003: 125).

However, government priorities are often subject to the problem of contingency—unforeseen events central to the protective functions of government that demand some form of response—and to policy shocks which change the context for government action. Such policy shocks include market shocks, resulting from the workings of economic forces; natural disruptions resulting from environmental or public health risks; issues of national security, such as the need for improved border security and management systems following 9/11; and government shocks, ranging from the effects of ill-judged domestic policy changes to hostile policies of foreign governments (for example, see Iacobucci, Trebilcock, and Haider 2001).

In some cases, businesses and labour unions may pressure governments for prompt remedial actions to safeguard their economic well-being. In others, the restoration of public confidence may require intense cooperation between business and government to manage or screen out perceived risks to public safety or security.

Businesses that fail to respond to proven threats to public health, consumer or environmental safety risk significantly greater punitive actions from governments—in addition to increased burdens of regulatory compliance related to risk avoidance and management in the production, use and disposition of hazardous substances. Periodic scandals have also increased the sensitivity of governments, and many institutional investors, to regulatory and governance issues related to the workings of capital markets and the financial services sector.

Finally, the timing of issues within an electoral cycle will often affect the priority given to them by governments. Potentially controversial policies or major policy shifts whose implementation may require two or three years for benefits to be acknowledged by the general public are far more likely to be introduced early in a government's mandate than in the year or 18 months prior to an anticipated election. Governments tend to introduce measures requiring spending cuts or higher taxes early in their mandates, often finding revenue 'windfalls' to finance popular spending measures or tax cuts closer to an election (Kneebone and McKenzie 1999).

It is easier for interest groups, including business groups, to take advantage of this process if a particular policy theme has already been identified as a priority in the government's latest election platform, throne speech, or annual budget speech. Interest groups which have developed close and cooperative working relations with civil servants have an even greater advantage in such processes—particularly if specific priorities can be incorporated into the mandates and business plans of individual departments or agencies (Lindquist 2001).

Identifying the existence of a problem is only one part of the agenda-setting process, however much it may increase pressures on governments to do something about it. Figuring out what to do, and how to evaluate the relative benefits and risks of potential policy options, often depends on how policy-makers perceive and define the problem.

Problem Definition

"Toronto needs more jobs like I need another hole in the head."
Federal Industry Minister Ed Lumley, 1982.

Effective **problem definition** includes not only an explanation of the problem that some action by government is supposed to address, but also an assessment of its causes, context, and relative significance.

The importance of perspective in problem definition is often summarized by the phrase "where you stand depends on where you sit." The perception of a problem—for example, youth unemployment in Toronto—may be very different to a civil servant in Ottawa, a politician representing inner city Toronto, young people who can't find stable employment, small business owners who can't find qualified employees, or union leaders in other parts of Canada for whom Toronto is a traditional oasis of prosperity compared to the chronically high unemployment levels of their own regions.[2]

Box 11.3: What's the Problem?

When the author was a provincial civil servant in the late 1980s, he was told to develop options for presentation to his department's senior officials on the problem of cross-border shopping. This had become a major irritant for retailers in Ontario's dozen or so border communities when the value of the Canadian dollar approached US$0.90, and hundreds of thousands of Canadians flocked across the border every month in search of bargains. Not only were Ontario retailers losing money, the province was missing out on tax dollars from resulting purchases, many of which either went unreported or were below the threshold for customs declaration under the new FTA.

However, Canada Customs was a federal bureaucracy, and the Ontario Treasurer wasn't too keen on its condition for collecting retail sales taxes at the border: harmonizing Ontario's provincial sales tax (PST) with Ottawa's planned GST. Although increasing border bridge tolls might slow down traffic a bit, the province had little or no control over them, and tourist operators would complain if higher tolls discouraged cross-border tourism in the other direction. At any rate, prices on many products *were* lower in the US due to different distribution patterns and the faster growth of big box stores south of the border.

Finally, after extensive study, it was decided that the *biggest* cause of the problem was an overvalued Canadian dollar—something completely beyond provincial jurisdiction—and that a $0.05 drop in the exchange rate would do more to correct the problem than any amount of money that could be spent promoting "buy Canadian" programs in border communities. The provincial cabinet still decided to spend a little money on an ad campaign (after all, an election wasn't far away). However, by the time Ontario agreed, years later, to contract with Canada Customs for PST collection at the border, the value of the Canadian dollar had dropped to US$0.75, and the cross-border shopping issue was but a distant memory.

In practice, the decision of authoritative political or bureaucratic actors to accept a particular definition of a problem frequently determines the context for government action. The greater the complexity of an issue, and the more difficult it is to summarize in the 30- to 60-second clips that are the standard format for present-

---

2 Actually, at 7.7 per cent of the labour force, Toronto's unemployment rate ranked nineteenth among 25 major metropolitan areas across Canada in December 2003 and December 2004, slightly above the national average of 7.6 percent and 7.0 percent respectively. See <http://www.statcan.ca>.

ing television news, the more likely that civil servants within the **lead agency** in a particular policy field will be responsible for framing a definition of the problem and options for a government response. As a result, groups that can shape the ways in which politicians and civil servants perceive and define the problems they face thus have an advantage over those who merely clamour for governments to do something about a particular problem. This advantage becomes even greater when groups can link their concerns to the existing priorities of a particular department or the government as a whole.

However, like the proverbial iceberg, most of the public policy process takes place under the waterline of public scrutiny. Indeed, as discussed in Chapter 4, governments will often attempt to limit public discussion of particular issues in order to be able to control their own priorities and to shape policy formulation and design according to their own preferences.

Effective research—or access to proprietary information not available to politicians and civil servants—can give well-organized business groups an advantage in persuading governments to buy into their definition of policy problems related to specific industries or in modifying initial efforts at problem definition by civil servants to accommodate industry perspectives. Although interest groups may be able to use in-house information to influence a particular policy process, it is often less persuasive than arm's-length studies commissioned from appropriately credentialed experts. Government departments and agencies that have invested in policy capacity, either by developing in-house expertise or contracting with outside academic and technical experts, are in a better position to evaluate, and sometimes contest, such potentially self-interested policy advice than those lacking such resources. The publication of rapidly growing volumes of government-sponsored research on the Internet has helped to bridge the gap between the traditionally closed policy communities surrounding many government departments and their attentive publics.

Ultimately, senior government decision-makers must assess the credibility of competing sources of problem definition and decide whether there is either political or technical justification for particular government actions. When political justification is reinforced by technical policy analysis, governments may adopt the rational decision-making approach preferred by many academic policy-makers and public servants either in the incremental adaptation of existing policies or in the introduction of more wide-ranging changes. When politics trumps technical policy considerations, civil servants and/or affected interest groups may attempt to use the next stages of the policy process to limit the adverse effects of these decisions on their operations.

Policy Formulation and Design

Policy formulation involves either the development of specific policy options for consideration by senior government decision-makers in response to a particular problem or the development of detailed plans for government action. It may overlap with the process of agenda-setting or emerge from it, depending both on the degree to which new policy initiatives emerge from government bureaucracies as opposed to other influential political actors and on the extent to which the definitions of problems requiring government action are contested.

Key elements in the policy formulation process are the nature and extent of the political will driving particular policy changes, the resources available to governments in designing and implementing proposed policies, and their feasibility either in dealing with perceived problems or achieving other intended political and policy goals. Other factors include the number, diversity, and relative power of state and societal actors engaged in the process and the extent to which the process may be said to be relatively open or closed to external influences.

Political Will/Feasibility: Who Is Behind the Policy and By How Much?

Policy formulation may reflect the political will that drives public servants to design detailed policies to carry out the preordained objectives of senior politicians, the tacit negotiation between politicians and public servants over the feasibility of particular policy options in achieving shared goals, or a search for policy options capable of mobilizing a consensus among competing political or societal actors.

Canadian governments supported by parliamentary or legislative majorities can often force through major policy changes over strong public or interest group opposition if the prime minister or premier is prepared to invest the necessary personal attention and political capital to do so. Savoie describes the unbridled exercise of prime ministerial prerogative as "governing by bolts of electricity" (Savoie 1999: 313-36). Examples are not hard to find: the Mulroney government's introduction of the GST in 1989-90; sustained deficit-reduction programs introduced (in different ways) by federal and provincial governments during the 1990s; and Chrétien's decision to ratify the Kyoto Accord over widespread provincial and business opposition. Under such circumstances, the role of public servants is to carry out their instructions while warning their political superiors of legal or constitutional roadblocks that might derail their plans. Interest groups may be able to affect government plans at the margin, but only over issues of implementation—a subsequent stage of the process. Governments which seriously miscalculate the effects of their decisions—or the popular reaction to them—may suffer the political consequences at the next election.

Most policy changes are generally subject to the test of political feasibility: to what extent are the proposed policies politically acceptable? Proposed policies may be evaluated on the basis of their consistency with a recently elected government's election promises (although these are far from sacrosanct), their impact on societal or interest groups closely related to major elements of the governing party, their prospective impact on a government's chances of re-election, or simply the amount of effort required to implement them given competing political priorities. In some cases, the personal values, experience, and political commitments of senior cabinet ministers and public servants may also play a significant role.

However, on many framework and sectoral policy issues that are secondary government priorities, policy formulation is heavily influence by the composition and dynamics of the relevant policy communities.

Who Else is Involved?

Business-government relations during the process of policy formulation and design depend heavily on the nature of the relevant policy community and on the degree to which responsible civil servants and major interest group stakeholders share common views of policy objectives and the most effective means to achieve them. Box 11.4 notes two dimensions of relative openness and cohesion in policy communities, the number and types of participants, and the degrees of cohesion between state and societal actors composing a particular policy community.

Policy communities may be relatively closed, with senior officials selecting stakeholder groups for consultation, depending on their relative economic importance, perceived legitimacy, or relationship to the government of the day. In such cases, relevant officials may restrict effective participation in the policy process to persons or groups of their choosing. Conversely, they may be more open, with governments accommodating the participation of multiple, often competing interest groups. The greater the number of governmental participants in a particular policy community, the greater becomes the likelihood that societal interest groups with whom they have regular dealings will ultimately become engaged as well.

Box 11.4: Dynamics of Policy Communities

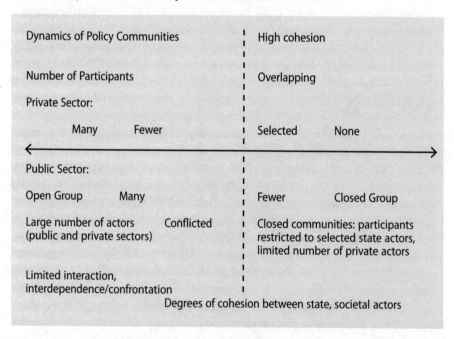

Dynamics of Policy Communities · High cohesion

Number of Participants · Overlapping

Private Sector:

Many · · · · Fewer · · · · Selected · · · · None

←──→

Public Sector:

Open Group · · · · Many · · · · Fewer · · · · Closed Group

Large number of actors · · · · Conflicted · · · · Closed communities: participants restricted to selected state actors, limited number of private actors
(public and private sectors)

Limited interaction, interdependence/confrontation

Degrees of cohesion between state, societal actors

Another major factor shaping patterns of engagement between government officials and outside stakeholders is their relative cohesion: the degree to which both groups share common or overlapping interests or perceptions of the public good. Policy communities characterized by high levels of interaction and trust between a relatively narrow group of government officials and major stakeholders are more likely to engage stakeholders in discussions of problem definition and policy options before decisions are made public (Montpetit 2003). Governments may also allow greater participation by outsider groups, but attempt to direct policy discourse (or the terms of debate) towards the interests and objectives of the lead agency and major stakeholders.

Governments may also take authoritative actions to impose their policy choices on stakeholder groups and citizens, allowing limited (if any) opportunities for participation in the decision-making process. Such decisions may or may not require formal legislative change or even cabinet approval for implementation. However, even if they do, the subject matter is often technical enough that it usually will not attract enough media or public attention to become politically controversial. Significant public debate generally occurs only when a major segment of the relevant policy elite defects from the consensus, appealing either to another part or level of government, the courts, or public opinion.

Box 11.5 Closed and Open Policy Systems

Closed Policy Systems
- Governments have the capacity to limit interest group access to the policy-making process and to set and enforce conditions of participation.
- Balancing of interests and policy objectives within and among political, economic, and administrative elites are emphasized, rather than the accountability of elites to a fragmented or divided society/electorate.
- Institutional stakeholders are accountable primarily to authoritative state decision-makers and one another.
- System maintenance, elite cohesion, and the cooperative pursuit of shared goals become dominant values.

Open Policy Systems
- Many participants are involved in the policy process; governments must strive to build consensus based on shared interests due to lack of control over participants and other governments.
- State autonomy is subject to limits imposed by public and stakeholder opinion and the availability of an alternative governing coalition.
- State capacity often depends on obtaining the trust and cooperation of relevant social and economic stakeholders.

Governments often create advisory councils as institutionalized vehicles for input on departmental or ministerial decision-making. Advisory councils bring together representatives of major stakeholders, policy experts, and friends or supporters of the government from a particular policy sector and may be given a mandate to examine and make recommendations on particular issues or to serve as an ongoing sounding board for a minister and/or departmental officials on issues related to a particular sector. They may be used as a vehicle for consensus-building in a particular area or for co-opting interest groups so that they have a greater interest in cooperating with governments rather than engaging in noisy public confrontations.

However, ongoing participation in an advisory council is usually conditional on playing by the rules of the institutional game, which discourages vocal dissent from government positions. This is understood by most institutional actors, whether business or other societal groups, who must be willing to accept both occasional policy losses and the inevitable compromises of the political game. However, groups whose interests are consistently ignored or marginalized are more likely to challenge the structure of the game through public dissent and the creation of opposing coalitions in the hope of changing either its rules or the people who make those rules.

Differences in interests and values within a policy subsystem can be accommodated through the decentralization of policy development and/or administration. For instance, policies and programs for employment training and labour market development may be decentralized, or decision-making powers may be delegated to local representative bodies for the implementation of national or provincial policy goals in ways consistent with local, regional, or sectoral interests.

Policy formulation in more open or pluralistic policy networks may take a number of different forms. Politicians and government officials wishing to maintain control over a potentially controversial policy agenda may minimize publicity and consultation until they have either obtained cabinet approval for regulatory or legislative action or have introduced legislation in Parliament or a provincial legislature. At this point, the principles of cabinet solidarity and party discipline in the case of a majority government make it difficult for interest groups or opposition parties with major concerns to obtain significant changes, let alone defeat the proposal.

Relatively open policy communities may also result when internal policy disputes arise among the different departments and agencies of a particular subgovernment. The decision to go public before introducing legislation in Parliament may be a symptom of internal government debates or a calculated strategy for the management of public opinion. The issues of timing and different approaches to public consultation as part of the policy formulation and legislative processes will be discussed further in Chapter 12.

Administrative Feasibility: What Resources Are Available to Address the Problem?

Governments may possess the political will or support to address particular policy problems. However, effective policy formulation also depends on taking the steps necessary to achieve administrative feasibility: the capacity of governments to mobilize the legal, fiscal, and personnel resources necessary to translate their objectives into desired outcomes.

Governments have the legal and constitutional authority to carry out their policy objectives by invoking existing legislative or regulatory powers or seeking parliamentary approval for legislative changes. The latter approach is usually more time-consuming and requires either greater political commitment or a minister's capacity to secure time on the parliamentary timetable. Business and other interest groups that have limited success in challenging the substance of some policy proposals directly may secure accommodation by drawing attention to significant legal constraints on government actions. Other issues of administrative feasibility may arise from the potential for overlap, duplication, and conflict between the mandates and activities of different government departments and agencies.

Issues of administrative feasibility heavily affect the choice and mix of policy instruments used in developing particular policies. Relative budgetary constraints, government-wide priorities, and financial management rules allow governments to shift or defer the costs of particular policies through the use of policy tools that enable them to draw on—or conscript—the resources of businesses, other interest groups, and individual citizens to achieve their objectives without cutting into existing government programs or staff resources. For example, governments often impose user fees or benefit-related taxes to recover much or all of the costs of providing particular services from citizens or businesses that receive a disproportionate benefit from such services. Gasoline taxes, toll highways or bridges, licence or inspection fees, workers' compensation premiums, and tipping fees for landfill sites are only a few of many such policy instruments.

Government officials must also decide whether to provide certain benefits or services directly, either by hiring more government employees or setting up specialized government agencies or business enterprises, or to provide a variety of incentives to businesses and citizens to act in ways that serve government policy priorities. These choices have both administrative and political implications. For example, many business groups prefer the use of tax preferences to direct government grants. So do some ministers and senior officials working in federal and provincial finance departments—not least because it allows them to maintain some control over the uses to which these resources are put rather than deferring to the priorities of other government departments. Officials in other government departments, and the major stakeholder groups with which they interact regularly, may have a very different view of the feasibility of such policy instruments. In other cases, the creation of Crown corporations or special-purpose agencies may provide a means of overcoming administrative obstacles within existing government structures and processes.

Interest groups that can point to the successful use of particular policy instruments in addressing comparable problems in other jurisdictions often use this information to shape political and administrative perceptions of the relative administrative feasibility of certain policy options that serve their interests over others. Effective policy research can also identify the conditions under which policy proposals are more or less effective in meeting their goals, enabling interest groups to demonstrate an awareness of governmental concerns that may contribute to mutual accommodation with government objectives. These issues often involve issues of technical feasibility or ways of influencing the broader policy environment to engage stakeholders and citizens in order to increase the likelihood of effective implementation.

Policy Approval

Federal and provincial cabinets possess formal authority to make policy and recommend legislative actions to Parliament or legislatures. Under the principle of cabinet government, this authority is exercised collectively as the Governor-in-Council, the name reflecting the constitutional convention that a cabinet enjoying the support of a parliamentary majority acts on behalf of the Crown-in-Parliament.

Formal cabinet decisions usually result from a process coordinated by the Privy Council Office (PCO) or provincial cabinet office. The PCO or cabinet office may accept a Memorandum to Cabinet (M/C) or cabinet submission, forwarding it to the ministers and staff of the relevant cabinet committee to review, recommend changes, or reject, although most ministers and their deputies will attempt to avoid rejections on major proposals either by seeking prime ministerial support or by pursuing compromises with colleagues in other departments. Any lobbying which may occur at this stage of the process may well be a by-product of ministers' or departments' efforts to mobilize stakeholder support for discreet discussions within the government. Proposals approved by cabinet committees will normally be approved by full cabinet, although some proposals may be referred to the government caucus for discussion before taking final form. In most governments, proposals for new spending that do not involve significant policy changes are typically managed through budgetary estimates authorized by Treasury Board within the general budgetary policies of the Department of Finance. Some governments combine the two functions in a single department.

The consistency and details of these processes vary from one government to another. They also indicate the decision-making styles of individual prime ministers or premiers, who determine the agendas of cabinet meetings and who typically have extensive discretionary power to make decisions independent of cabinet and to intervene in the decisions and priorities of individual departments (Savoie 1999; Simpson 2001; Stanbury 2002). Unless a policy proposal requires actual changes to legislation, cabinet approval is sufficient for implementation of a policy decision or regulation. Legislative review and approval, as the most public dimensions of the policy process, will be discussed in Chapter 12. However, even with cabinet and parliamentary approval, the key test of most policy decisions comes in the implementation stage.

Policy Implementation

Most politicians have long since given up on the magic wand syndrome of government decision-making: the idea that once a politician has made a decision, something will happen. Even good ideas don't simply materialize in actions by governments, businesses, and citizens. Someone has to implement them.

In theory, major issues of implementation—the process of translating decisions into action—should be addressed during the formulation or design stage of the policy cycle. However, effective policy implementation usually requires that the people who will be directly involved in its real-world application be consulted to some degree on the implications of proposed changes for policy delivery. The greater the level of confidentiality in policy formulation and design, as discussed above, the less likely this sort of consultation will have taken place. The less the degree of trust between senior decision-makers and front-line civil servants, or between government decision-makers and the citizens and businesses most likely to be affected by their decisions, the greater the likelihood that implementation will be characterized by serious delays at best and limited cooperation (if not obstruction) at worst.

Effective implementation of government decisions can take place in the absence of consensual decision-making if governments are willing to invest sufficient resources in enforcement and coercion and if they are supported in these actions by a large enough segment of the relevant public. However, governments have discovered that effective policy implementation is usually easier when both civil servants and members of relevant publics have both positive as well as negative incentives for cooperation. As a result, many businesses, professionals, and interest groups may have opportunities to influence the implementation of particular policies and programs, depending on the nature of policy communities and the relative openness of public servants to feedback from stakeholders. This process may take place among policy elites or through the organization of information sessions organized by business associations, government relations and other professionals, and other groups on behalf of clients.

Stanbury notes the distinction between "outputs" and "outcomes" in the implementation stage of the policy process (Stanbury 1993). Policy outputs are the things that governments do—or that they organize other groups such as broader public sector organizations, NGOs, and other intermediaries to do on their behalf. Such outputs may include the passage of regulations; the distribution of grants, subsidies, or other transfers; the hiring of public servants; the contracting-out of particular services; the spending of public funds; and a variety of other activities. The political effect of such activities is often related to the expectations created by governments among businesses or other societal interests.

Policy outcomes are the effects—or lack thereof—of policies and programs in meeting their intended objectives and in generating other results that may or may not have been intended. The organization of policy outputs often takes months, sometimes years. Policy outcomes, while often harder to measure, may take longer to generate and may be very different from those originally intended. To the extent that policy outcomes meet or exceed public expectations, including the expectations of businesses, they will often generate political support for the government or diffuse opposition over time. However, policies that generate adverse effects for large numbers of citizens or businesses are likely to trigger another policy cycle as one government's solution becomes the source of new problems for its successor.

A number of factors, some of which may be visible to active members of the policy community or influenced by their behaviour, can influence the effectiveness of policy implementation. These include:

Box 11.6: It Seemed Like a Good Idea at the Time

The 1981-82 recession resulted in record federal deficits. Although spending increased sharply, a significant source of revenue losses was delayed payments; in some cases income, payroll, and sales taxes owing were not paid at all. Employers are legally required to pay taxes deducted from employee incomes monthly or quarterly, depending on the size of their remittances. But in many cases, the complexity of both income and sales tax systems meant that the precise level of tax bills owing was often in technical and legal dispute. Under the *Income Tax Act* at the time, tax reassessments were payable upon receipt even if subject to legal disputes, placing the onus on taxpayers to prove their innocence before being able to secure repayment of artificially inflated tax assessments.

Revenue Canada decided to increase collections by hiring new tax auditors and creating an incentive program for collections, establishing essentially a quota system for reassessing and collecting taxes owed by businesses and individuals. In early 1983, opposition revenue critic Perrin Beatty began to receive disturbing information that officials in his riding's local Revenue Canada office were using arbitrary and sometimes abusive tactics in collecting taxes, sometimes jeopardizing the survival of his small business constituents.

Beatty raised questions in the House of Commons which were generally sloughed off or stonewalled by the revenue minister on the advice of his senior officials, who contended that most complaints simply reflected taxpayers' unwillingness to meet their obligations. However, the more questions Beatty asked, the more he began to receive tips from junior officials, along with a flood of taxpayer complaints about abusive practices. As more and more complaints surfaced, the issue became a daily event in Question Period. The stand-off continued until the PMO, facing an imminent election, decided to step in after eight months of bad publicity. The minister and deputy minister were replaced, and procedures were instituted to introduce new checks and balances to the tax collection process, including an independent review of tax disputes before collection procedures were initiated. The controversial tax collection quotas for auditors were discarded. These measures were confirmed and extended by Beatty when he became revenue minister following the 1984 federal election (Hale 1985).

During the 1990s, Revenue Canada and its successor agencies have encouraged computer filing of tax returns to facilitate collections and improve service to taxpayers. Tax enforcement practices are targeted at industries with the greatest risk of non-compliance, including businesses with large volumes of cash transactions or high levels of employee turnover. The balancing act between tax collection and even-handed tax administration has resulted in the appointment of a number of private sector tax professionals to the board of the Canada Revenue Agency as provincial representatives, among other measures.

- the degree to which the cooperation or compliance of other members of the policy subsystem is necessary or present during the implementation process;
- cooperation or conflicts between (or even within) government departments and agencies;

- available funding and the capacity of senior public sector managers to make effective or efficient use of it;
- the quality of policy formulation, particularly in the timeliness or effectiveness of problem definition and the selection of policy instruments used to implement a particular policy;
- changes in the external environment during the period between initial government engagement with a particular policy challenge and the implementation of proposed responses;
- the degree to which the legal instruments—particularly legislative statutes and related regulations—provide clear direction or guidance in the use of administrative discretion or the implementation of formal decisions or create opportunities for legal challenges;
- the degree of cooperation or compliance extended by these actors or, alternately, their effectiveness in delaying, avoiding, or obstructing the implementation of policy decisions.

Policy Evaluation

The degree of political and bureaucratic self-interest associated with the design and administration of public policies is often not conducive to effective or impartial policy evaluation. Policies and programs have often lacked clear objectives or been subject to multiple, competing political and administrative priorities that hamper effective public management. Every program or benefit creates a set of beneficiaries and stakeholders to defend the status quo and who are often ready to fend off other groups that might challenge or attempt to share in their benefits. As most governments lack the resources to carry out consistent external reviews of programs and services, the main responsibility for policy and program evaluation tends to be delegated to the civil servants responsible for their administration. However, federal and provincial auditors general also carry out periodic reviews of policies and programs. Their evaluation criteria usually emphasize financial accountability—adherence to internal procedures for financial control—and value for money.

Intense budgetary constraints during the 1990s increased pressures on governments at all levels to clarify their priorities and objectives and to seek improved performance through the use of business planning and performance measurement techniques. Such techniques, which attempt to define the main priorities of individual organizations and their component parts and to quantify key performance objectives for civil servants, may be helpful but are not panaceas (see Box 11.6). They put a premium on transparency, the use of performance measurements clearly connected to policy outcomes and not just outputs, and the creation of feedback loops for both staff and program clients to identify problems and suggest improvements. These criteria are not always associated with traditional bureaucratic culture in Canada, nor are they always welcomed by stakeholder groups who have established close clientele relationships with individual departments or agencies.

As with problem definition, policy formulation, and implementation, interest groups may play a significant role in program evaluation by identifying successes and failures in meeting known program objectives or by suggesting variations and improvements. However, given the different cultures and, often, different priorities of politicians, government officials, and business and other societal groups, the effective use of policy evaluation tools depends on the capacity of governments to build consensus on their major priorities and objectives and on the willingness of interest groups to frame their own interests in a context that recognizes and accommodates other stakeholders as part of a broader public interest.

Strategies for Outsiders to Influence the Policy Process

Interest groups whose primary focus is on direct lobbying—efforts to influence public policies through more-or-less systematic communication with government decision-makers—need to recognize the context of specific decision-making processes, the major government and societal decision-makers within relevant policy communities, and the stage of the policy cycle in which they are engaged.

However, relatively few businesses (or citizens) outside heavily regulated sectors of the economy devote a significant part of their working lives to dealing with the policy process even though they may spend a lot of time dealing with government. Just as relatively few government officials have a detailed understanding of business unless they have worked in or with private industry for an extended period, most business owners and executives find that the culture of government is often very different from that of business, small or large. As we have seen, studies of business and government have often described their relationship as one of "two solitudes" (Public Policy Forum 2002).

The Public Policy Forum report cited above suggests that neither most business executives nor government officials see themselves as well-served by the principal intermediaries in the government relations process: interest groups and government relations professionals (Public Policy Forum 2002). Government officials frequently perceive business people and their representatives as ill-informed about the context of government decision-making and dogmatic and unreasonable in their expectations of government. Business people frequently view government officials as poorly informed about the real world of business activity and sometimes indifferent to the actual or potential impacts of their policies on the taxpayers and businesses that pay their salaries. Although the level of ideological antagonism between business and government is much lower in the early twenty-first century than at most times during the 1970s and 1980s, these themes often resurface in discussions with business officials, interest group leaders, politicians, and government officials. A similar cultural divide is also visible in relations between governments and citizens engaged in other kinds of lobbying efforts.

Former federal cabinet minister Perrin Beatty, who spent 21 years as a member of the House of Commons and, a decade later, became president of the CME, suggests five major conditions necessary for businesses or interest groups in the development of effective government relations strategies.³ Understanding the whys and hows of each of these approaches is helpful to groups seeking to influence the policy processes of governments.⁴

1. *Take time to understand the process, to understand who makes decisions at what level. Don't ask ministers to take on problems that will only be referred to their mid-ranking and junior officials anyway.*

As discussed in Chapter 10, strategic analysis—taking the time to understand the policy environment—is critical to effective government relations. Among other things, this involves identifying both potential actions by government that may influence a particular business or sector and issues that may create pressures for government action. It also requires an understanding of the processes most relevant to policies that affect particular companies, industries, or policy sectors. Some of this information may be gleaned from the news media, trade journals, government publications (including those on the Internet), or government relations bulletins. However, much of it requires an investment in time, effort, and professional expertise to understand the internal policy context in which political and bureaucratic decision-makers typically act.

Part of the challenge of managing government relations is to identify the responsibilities and policy preferences of departmental officials and to provide them with timely information that can assist them in fulfilling their responsibilities. This information may be provided to ministers' offices, but unless of significant importance, it will usually be referred to responsible officials within their departments for comment and response unless the minister takes a hands-on approach to the process. The minister's political staff may play a more or less active role depending on their experience, relationship with the minister, the latter's management style, and the willingness of the deputy to tolerate policy input from this source. The cultivation of ministerial staff may be of value for interest groups that have the ability to develop close relationships at this level. However, as their loyalty is first and foremost to their ministers, such relationships are likely to gain results only to the extent that political staff view a particular interest group's support as politically valuable to their minister.

Institutionalized groups have an inherent advantage over single issue and most issue-oriented groups in that they already have established personal relationships and issue networks in government, particularly within the major policy communities of which they form a part. However, any interest group entering into a new policy field must go through the same steps, relying on its

---

3 These comments are drawn from a seminar led by Mr. Beatty in the author's Business-Government Relations class at the University of Western Ontario. They are supplemented by the author's observations and more recent examples of each strategy's practical application in business-government relations.

4 After several years on the other side of the business-government divide, Beatty suggests a sixth principle: "Your credibility is your most important asset. If you develop a reputation for sloppiness or dishonesty, the sound of doors slamming shut will deafen you" (correspondence with author, 12 August 2003).

established constituency and its reputation for honest, straight-forward dealing on the issues.

2. *Build personal relationships with policy-makers at each level of the policy process.*

Government policy-makers are subject to all sorts of internal and external pressures in carrying out their responsibilities. These responsibilities are usually circumscribed by their positions within the cabinet or bureaucratic hierarchy, the formal policy commitments of the government, and the need to manage policy proposals through a formal and often complex process. Interest group representations are likely to be viewed from the perspective of whether they will assist policy-makers in reaching their desired policy or political goals or will complicate or attempt to obstruct these goals.

The development of personal and professional relationships with policy-makers is a key part of the process of government relations. It enables both business and interest group representatives, on the one hand, and government decision-makers on the other to gain a greater insight into one another's attitudes towards shared policy interests and to develop the personal and professional trust needed to evaluate potentially disputed issues.

Politicians and civil servants are far less likely to take casual acquaintances into their confidence than people who have demonstrated their trustworthiness, professionalism, and willingness to respect the formal and informal rules of the lobbying process. As most of these are the product of experience and awareness of the norms of particular political and bureaucratic processes, interest group representatives who take the time to build relationships are more likely to develop mutual trust and goodwill in their relationships with cabinet ministers and their senior officials than are those who have only a peripheral relationship to the policy process.

3. *Don't take a self-centred approach or emphasize your problems. Propose solutions that will take into account the political needs of public sector decision-makers and accommodate their concepts of the public interest.*

Groups that are seen to represent a clear constituency have a significant potential advantage within the political process. However, translating this potential into a political asset largely depends on the attitudes projected by interest groups and their lobbyists. One critical factor is the ability to link the interests of one's group with those of political decision-makers and their perceptions of a broader public interest. Most decision-makers attempt to balance competing interests within a broader philosophical or intellectual approach to defining the public interest. Groups which take a blatantly self-interested approach run the risk of alienating decision-makers, particularly those who are not normally sympathetic to their agendas.

Stanbury lists a number of recommendations for building effective relationships, including basic principles of interpersonal relationships such as treating others as you would want to be treated and seeking to build points of common grounds so that your actions will be seen as a potential asset to a policy-maker or institution, rather than a liability (Stanbury 1993). One should identify one's policy proposals with the policy concepts already embraced by the government, rather than approaching it in the language or terminology of its political opponents. Business groups that attempt to work closely with unions in approaching NDP governments or that champion certain policies as likely to generate employment and opportunity for workers and socially vulnerable groups are more likely to be politically effective than those that vocally champion free enterprise and limited government. Similarly, business and other interest groups that approach conservative governments without recognizing the political or ideological trade-offs necessary to balance competing interests within brokerage political parties are less likely to be successful than those groups that pursue win-win approaches to policy.

4. *Be pro-active, not reactive: deal with problems before they become major issues, not afterwards.*

The earlier that organizations can engage the policy process, the greater their capacity to influence government decisions before senior policy-makers have invested significant political capital—and their own credibility—in the process. Decisions that are made in the relative confidence of bureaucratic processes can be adapted or amended before they become the subject of major partisan controversies. After a formal decision is taken, or legislation is introduced in Parliament or a provincial legislature, major policy initiatives may be amended at the margins, but the partisan dynamics of the legislative process tend to reduce the receptiveness of senior decision-makers to major changes.

5. *Don't surprise or blind-side your government contacts, especially when going public on an issue.*

Political and policy disagreements are normal in a democracy. However, groups that actively seek to embarrass senior decision-makers, or to take them by surprise, are likely to be treated on the same partisan basis as the government's legislative opponents—as an adversary to be overcome rather than constituents to be reasoned with. Perhaps the outstanding example of this truism was the political mistake of senior bankers who announced plans to merge two large chartered banks early in 1998, catching Finance Minister Paul Martin by surprise in the middle of a major review of federal financial sector policies. The review was allowed to take its course. However, the banks needlessly squandered political goodwill and made it politically attractive for Martin to veto the merger in December 1998 (Whittington 1999).

Although fairly straightforward in principle, these ideas are often more difficult to apply in practice, particularly as many businesses and other groups may lack the expertise or lead time necessary before faced with political events that require them to become more actively engaged in lobbying government. For this reason, many businesses, industry associations, and other interest groups make use of government relations professionals—lobbyists—to help them in organizing their government relations strategies, obtaining timely information on specialized policy processes and making contact with key decision-makers.

Conclusion

The internal policy processes of government are complex, fragmented, and far from transparent. Although understanding its formal rules and processes is important to groups wanting to influence the policy process, so are the political and administrative cultures of particular governments and departments and the broader policy networks with which they interact.

Most elements of the government policy process take place away from the public eye or the scrutiny of the news media. However, several major factors may force the relatively private world of bureaucratic politics into the public spotlight. Governments frequently need to explain and legitimize their policies to citizens and organized interests. Citizens, businesses, and interest groups may contest these rationales or the practical effects of the policies that stem from them. The legal decision-making processes of governments may bring policy issues into the legislative arena, increasing the potential for public scrutiny and debate. And the policy elites which normally dominate the internal policy processes of government may fall out with one another, encouraging them to take their cases to the news media and the court of public opinion in pursuit of greater political advantage and support. These four elements are central to the external or public policy processes of government, which will be subject of the next chapter.

Key Terms and Concepts for Review (see Glossary)

administrative feasibility
agenda-setting
framework legislation
garbage-can model
incrementalism
lead agency
levels of analysis
micro-policies
policy approval
policy cycle
policy evaluation
policy formulation
policy implementation
policy instruments

policy outcomes
policy outputs
policy regimes
policy shocks
political agenda
political business cycle
problem definition
public policy
rational policy-making
sectoral policies
state capacity
status quo
two-level game

Questions for Discussion and Review

1. How does the concept of the policy process as a two-level or multi-level game illustrate the relevance of approaching policy debates and processes from at least two different levels of analysis? Discuss these concepts in the context of a recent policy debate involving different governments and/or business sectors in the news media.

2. Using the front pages of the main news and business sections of a major national or regional newspaper for the past week, list the headlines that appear to relate to agenda-setting activities of governments and other political actors. How many (and which ones) appear to reflect Kingdon's categories of problem stream, political stream, and policy stream? Based on your analysis of a week's headlines, what are the major issues that appear to be driving the political agenda? Discuss your findings.

3. Based on your review of recent media discussions of major policy issues, identify an issue affecting relations between government and business in which the nature or definition of the problem to be resolved is seriously contested. What are the implications of these debates over problem definition for the ways in which governments could respond to this issue?

4. Compare and contrast the main features of the rational, incremental, and garbage-can models of policy-making discussed in this chapter. Which of these models appears to be most relevant to the policy processes discussed in each of the short case studies? Why?

5. Using a recent policy debate involving some aspect of business-government relations, discuss the relative importance of political, administrative, and technical feasibility in shaping the outcomes of the policy process.

6. Some policy analysts suggest that some of the limitations of the rational policy-making model can be traced to the separation between politics and administration. What factors increase the importance of making implementation-related considerations a significant part of the decision-making (or policy approval) process?

Suggestions for Further Reading

Brooks, Stephen, and Lydia Miljan. 2003. *Public policy in Canada: an introduction,* 4th ed. Toronto: Oxford University Press.

Campbell, Robert M., Leslie A. Pal, and Michael Howlett. (Eds.), 2004. *The real world of Canadian politics: cases in process and policy.* 4th ed., Peterborough, ON: Broadview Press.

Doern, G. Bruce, Margaret Hill, Michael Prince, and Richard Schultz (Eds.). 1999. *Changing the rules: Canada's changing regulatory regimes and institutions*. Toronto: University of Toronto Press.

Doern, G. Bruce, Leslie A. Pal, and Brian W. Tomlin (Eds.). 1996. *Border crossings: the internationalization of Canadian public policy*. Toronto: Oxford University Press.

Hale, Geoffrey. 2001. *The politics of taxation in Canada*. Peterborough, ON: Broadview Press.

Howlett, Michael, and M. Ramesh. 2003. *Studying public policy: policy cycles and policy subsystems*. 2nd ed. Toronto: Oxford University Press.

Iacobucci, Edward M., Michael J. Trebilcock, and Huma Haider. 2001. *Economic shocks: defining a role for government*. Toronto: C.D. Howe Institute.

Kingdon, John W. 1984. *Agendas, alternatives and public policies*. New York: Harper Collins.

Pal, Leslie A. 2001. *Beyond policy analysis: public issue management in turbulent times*. 2nd ed. Toronto: Nelson Thomson Learning.

Salamon, Lester M. (Ed.). 2002. *The tools of government: a guide to the new governance*. New York: Oxford University Press.

CHAPTER 12

The External Policy Process: Public Relations, Public Opinion, Political Advocacy, and Parliament

Most policy-making in Canada takes place below the waterline of public visibility. However, at some point, public policies must past one or more tests of political legitimacy, including those of legality, effectiveness or performance legitimacy, and acceptance by significant elements of public opinion. Much of the art of democratic politics involves the evaluation, cultivation, and leadership of public opinion, often in a highly competitive environment.

The fragmentation of policy processes and of public opinion itself—by geographic region; by socio-economic interest or sector; and by elite, specialized, and mass publics—ensures that the attempts of most political actors to engage public attention are similar to carrying on a conversation in a crowded room. This process has been further reinforced in recent years by the growing segmentation of news media into increasingly specialized channels of communication in which different parts of government or specialized publics may carry on a series of quasi-public conversations independently of one another (Mendelsohn and Nadeau 1996). The casual observer of government economic policies or of relations between governments and different business sectors can get a better picture of these dynamics by comparing the news makers, issues, and perspectives that get regular coverage in the news and business sections of national and regional newspapers and television newscasts. However, some political issues can galvanize public attention in a way that dominates a nation's consciousness while distracting media and public attention from the mundane details of everyday life—much like the shout of "Fire!" in a crowded room.

The competent management of **public relations**—the deliberate management of public image and information in the pursuit of organizational interests (Cottle 2003: 3)—is vital to governments and other political actors in their attempt to consult with citizens and organized interests, to engage and mobilize public opinion, or to seek the support of other opinion-makers in the public square. This chapter considers the role of governments, the news media, interest groups, and legislatures in **agenda-setting** and **indirect lobbying**: efforts to shape, mobilize, and enlist media or public opinion to influence the policies or priorities of governments and other authoritative political actors. It reviews the ways in which businesses and other interest groups may use the external policy process to influence government policies. It also examines the use of formal and informal consultation processes and other practices by governments both to assess, manage and engage public opinion and to structure the participation of interest groups and the news media in their policy-making and legislative processes. Finally, it considers the role of Parliament and provincial legislatures in influencing, legitimizing, and debating existing and proposed policies.

Agenda-Setting and Public Opinion

A major part of political leadership, and of the constant competition of political actors and interests to influence or challenge its use, involves engaging, mobilizing, and managing public opinion. Democratic governments generally attempt to manage public opinion as part of the broader environment within which they seek power and re-election; set priorities; design and administer policies, programs, and services; and appear responsive to citizens' concerns. So do many other political actors—business and interest groups, elements of the news media, and opposition political parties—all of whom operate with a wide range of motives.

Governments exercise considerable autonomy within the policy process, as noted in previous chapters. Sometimes this policy discretion involves taking actions that are deeply controversial or contrary to much of public opinion, while attempting to persuade citizens and organized interests that these policies are needed to achieve outcomes desired by many voters. Some of these approaches have already been discussed in Chapter 3. More often, government policies are designed in ways that consciously reflect general public expectations and work within the constraints of public opinion. Policies based on this "permissive consensus" (Mendelsohn, Wolfe, and Parkin 2002) may enjoy general public support. However, most citizens are content to let the experts, including major stakeholder groups, figure out how general principles should be translated into specific policies unless the results work to their significant disadvantage.

The ultimate legitimacy of government policies and governments' ability to win re-election depend on the ability of political leaders to persuade a plurality of voters that their goals and priorities are consistent with their broader interests and expectations—or at least more so than those of their major competitors—and that citizens are or will be better off economically and socially as a result of their policies.

Groups hoping to influence government policy must first catch the attention of the appropriate decision-makers. However, effective lobbying requires either enlisting their support within the existing context of a department's policies and programs or drawing sufficient public attention to the problem in ways that persuade decision-makers to change their priorities.

The roles, goals, and tactics of political actors in the external policy process—as with the internal policy processes discussed in Chapter 11—often depend on the degree to which their interests are institutionalized within particular policy communities or the political and economic systems as a whole. In the parlance of political sociology, "dominant interests" have advantages in their access to and ability to mobilize political, organizational, financial, and cultural resources to "manage and manipulate" political, public, and media agendas in their favour

(Cottle 2003: 21). Outsider groups and challengers need to compensate for these advantages through a combination of creativity, persistence, and appeals to interests or values shared by different elites, journalists, or broad segments of the general public.

However, interests that enjoy relative dominance in some institutions or policy communities are often peripheral in others, or they depend on the cooperation of other actors within their policy networks as part of the broader exchange processes of political life. These realities lead to varying degrees of political competition at each stage of the policy cycle, combining strategic action, ad hoc improvisation, and selective engagement with the political process.

Getting Public Attention—But Which Public?

The fragmentation of the political marketplace is reflected in the fragmentation of public opinion and the different degrees of importance (or **political salience**) that various issues have for assorted elements of the general public, particular business or societal interests, and elites whose attitudes and actions may shape the policy environment. The importance of public opinion increases with the political salience of various issues and the degree to which different groups of opinion leaders can maintain their visibility through the news media (for comparisons of agenda-setting through media, public, and policy agendas, see Soroka 2002). The narrower the salience of certain issues—that is, the more particular the public to which such issues are of vital importance—the more likely such issues are to be debated or discussed within the boundaries of its policy community and the communications media (or their sub-segments) associated with it.

Public opinion may be segmented according to demographic characteristics, such as region, age, ethnicity, family status, and education levels; economic characteristics, including income levels, occupation or industry sector, and relative dependence on government or market forces for economic opportunity and security; or social and cultural outlooks. As noted in Chapters 10 and 11, governments are typically organized along functional lines that allow them to segment public opinion into narrower, more manageable attentive publics to which particular departments or agencies normally relate.

Elly Alboim, whose Earnscliffe Strategy Group provided former Prime Minister Paul Martin with polling services and communications advice for many years, suggests that public opinion is further divided between an engaged minority of citizens and a relatively disengaged majority. The first group, estimated at about 30 per cent of the population, follows news and public affairs relatively closely and is engaged to varying degrees in the political process. The larger group accounts for as much as 70 per cent of the population, about half of whom may be marginally engaged. These findings are consistent with the evidence of government-commissioned polls, declining voter turnout levels in federal and most provincial elections, and numerous studies reflecting low levels of public trust for governments in general (Alboim 2000: 2-3; opinion polls released by Department of Finance 1995-

2001).[1] The size and composition of attentive publics are even smaller and more segmented for relatively specialized business issues, especially concerning issues which may not attract the attention of the national or major regional financial press.

These realities create a major communications challenge for participants in the political marketplace: how to provide both substantive information to a minority of politically engaged citizens and general information easily condensed into media sound-bites accessible to the majority of marginally or minimally engaged citizens. As a result, governments and societal interests (including business groups) wishing to influence public opinion are well advised to target the content and delivery of their messages using media or channels of communications best suited to both the message, media intermediaries, and the particular audience (including media intermediaries) whom they wish to address.

The application of these principles can often be seen in the delivery of information by governments and major interest groups through the Internet. News releases transmitted to the media (and reproduced online) usually transmit a simple, easy-to-understand message suitable to a general, diverse audience, while background pieces and technical reports may provide more detailed information. Written documents may be supplemented by audio or video messages, ranging from interviews and speeches to advertisements and multi-media presentations. Although good policy may or may not be good politics, effective communications need to pay attention to both.

General public opinion is most relevant to policy formation on issues on which elites, including major political actors and policy experts inside and outside of government, are divided. When policy communities are divided on major policy issues and priorities, politics becomes a contest for public support, based either on general principles, pragmatic considerations of what works, or distributive considerations of who gets (or loses) what. For example, the debate over the tax treatment of income trusts, discussed later in this chapter, shifted significantly as trusts became an increasingly popular form of business organization with corresponding implications for federal tax revenues.

Public opinion is least relevant on issues dominated by technical detail and specialized expertise. Governments or interest groups may choose to focus on the technical aspects of particular issues to manage the terms of debate. Such an approach makes it more difficult for most journalists and the general public to understand them, potentially reducing their public profile and increasing the relative autonomy of policy communities.

Both governments and interest groups may be able to shift different aspects or components of elite and public opinion over a period of time as new information becomes available, new ideas gain more general circulation and acceptance among

---

1 A 2003 Ekos study shows that only 24 per cent of Canadians surveyed indicated high levels of media consumption related to news and public affairs and that these respondents are drawn disproportionately from among upper income and university-educated voters. (Ekos Research 2003: 35).

relevant elites and publics, and the social environment adapts to political and economic change. Many of these debates take place among the elites and major stakeholders within specific policy communities and are accessible to the news media and citizens who wish to monitor them, but off the radar screen of broad public awareness.

Alternatively, political actors (including journalists) may attempt to influence or control the public agenda by engaging public opinion through the use of simplistic but effective publicity techniques that increase the political risks of challenging public perceptions, whatever their substance or superficiality. In such cases, public discourse may be framed as expressions of general principles, as slogans which attempt to boil down complex issues to bumper-sticker length, or as appeals to widely held symbolic values open to varied interpretations. The costs of future adjustments may be shifted to other citizens or social groups or simply may be deferred until after the next election. Box 12.1 provides several different examples of these approaches from the author's research into the politics of taxation and tax reform.

Box 12.1: Framing Issues for Public Debate on Taxation and Tax Reform

General Principles	Slogans	Symbolic Values
"Tax reductions should be sustainable, distribute benefits fairly throughout the population, enhance Canada's business competitiveness, and *not* be financed with borrowed money" (Martin 2000).	"Broader base, lower taxes." "Make the rich pay." "A Buck is a Buck." "Don't steal: the government doesn't like competition."	"Protecting universality of social benefits." "Targeting assistance to where it's needed most." "Help for small businesses, family farms." "Exploiting stealth taxes."

Shaping and Responding to Public Opinion: The Multiple Faces of Government

Canadian governments use a variety of news and information management techniques to expand both their autonomy and influence over the policy process. Thus, the approaches taken by governmental actors are a good place to start in examining the political competition inherent to external policy processes and policy debates.

Governments both respond to public opinion and attempt to manage (and, sometimes, lead) it in order to pursue their own agendas, secure re-election, and influence or define the terms of debate. The creative tension between leadership and responsiveness is evident in the efforts of political leaders, their advisors, and officials to balance different agendas in ways that speak to public preoccupations with economic, social, environmental, and other dimensions of public policy.

Formalized events are often used to structure and communicate governments' broader political agendas. Less visible are the structures and internal processes used to develop systematic news and information management strategies or to adapt these strategies to the circumstances of particular policy communities and issues. The techniques of agenda management and public relations can also be seen in the varied approaches used to engage in crisis management and problem deflection on occasions when unplanned or previously unpublicized events intrude into the public agenda, the different processes used for public consultation at various stages of the policy cycle, and the partisan political contexts of legislative processes and election campaigns.

Governments face a variety of institutionalized and societal constraints in managing and responding to public opinion, some of which work at cross-purposes. Access to information laws give journalists and researchers, including opposition parties, the tools to force government officials to disclose information they might prefer to remain accessible only to a select group of insiders. Protection of privacy laws limit the ability of governments to use or disclose private data provided by individual citizens or businesses for purposes unrelated to the terms under which they were collected. Although there is still a certain deference to expert authority within Canada's political culture, it is often contested by egalitarian and populist elements that react strongly against perceptions of the manipulative or self-serving use of authority by governmental, business, and other elites. All of these factors help to shape the environments in which governments attempt to define and manage their political agendas.

The Political Agenda

The public dimension of this balancing act is most visible in the political agenda discussed in Chapter 11: the regular or periodic occasions in which a government defines its priorities and the specific policies to be used in pursuing them. On such occasions—throne speeches, annual budget speeches, the announcement of campaign platforms, or other important events for publicizing government policies—the cultivation of images may be as important as the substance of particular policies. For example, the Chrétien government's mantra of balance between economic and social objectives—symbolized by its commitment to reinvest 50 per cent of future budget surpluses in new spending initiatives while devoting the rest to a mix of debt reduction and tax cuts—provided a central, easily understood framework for defining its public agenda and constraining competing public demands in the aftermath of its deficit reduction campaign of the mid-1990s (Hale 2001a; Hale 2001b; for an updated version, see Hale 2003). Most Canadian governments, whatever their ideological orientation or commitment to brokerage politics, look for similar ways to package the different elements of their agendas.

Molotch and Lester have noted that well-established patterns of packaging the news give "event promoters ... habitual access" to the news media (Molotch and Lester 1981; Cottle 2003: 11-12). This control of what is considered newsworthy is strengthened by the limited resources available for information gathering by most media outlets, cultural norms of what is considered "newsworthy," and the tendency of journalists to give some degree of deference to authoritative sources and experts who have developed some degree of **political capital**: credibility and trust based on a mixture of political skill, relevant expertise, and past performance.

Although governments may have a built-in advantage in communicating certain parts of their message within the political marketplace, most attempt to strengthen their competitive position in dealings with the media, opposition political parties, and assorted interest groups by engaging in more or less systematic efforts at news and information management.

News and Information Management

> For high profile public figures and public institutions, access (to the media) does not have to be acquired. Public relations is all about managing routine access or, perhaps more importantly, restricting media access. (Davis 2003: 39)

All governments engage in some degree of news and information management to define and promote their agendas, shape public perceptions, and appear responsive to varied societal interests.

News management is a contemporary label for the systematic public relations activities of public authorities, including elected officials and government departments and agencies, intended to guide, manipulate, or control the timing and emphasis of media coverage of their actions. The type of news and information management varies according to the content, timing, and distribution of information; the organization and packaging of events; and the interaction between the internal policy processes of government, which are often confidential or only partially transparent, and external policy processes involving particular interests, elements of the news media, and, sometimes, the general public.

News management can be *strategic*, in the sense of systematically promoting the reputations, actions, and policy agendas of an organization and its leaders. It may be *reactive*, responding to events such as political and administrative challenges or other external shocks. Much of it is *routine*: the day-to-day dissemination of information about the organization's activities and priorities and those of its leading officials. Occasionally, it becomes *diversionary*, deflecting media and public attention away from areas of actual or potential vulnerability to other issues which give governments or their component parts greater latitude in managing their primary agendas. These processes can be seen in the centralization of news management functions in both federal and provincial governments; the development of *messaging strategies* intended to manage public expectations and link specific policy initiatives with broader themes of government policy; and the explosion of information provided by governments, politicians, political parties, interest groups, and other political actors over the Internet, 24-hour news channels, and other sources of public information.

Information management involves the packaging and dissemination of information generated from within the organization or collected under its auspices. In addition to the routine news management activities noted above, it also includes publicity on the products and services provided or sold by the organization, relevant information on its activities or policies, and the research and advocacy activity it has commissioned as part of the policy process. While this information may be helpful to citizens in dealing with different public sector organizations, it can be vital for policy experts and interest groups in monitoring the activities of governments (and competing societal groups), evaluating their intentions, and shaping their responses to engage the policy information thus made publicly available.

Box 12.2: The Information—Propaganda Continuum

$\longleftarrow$ $\longrightarrow$

Information Distribution	News Management	Propaganda
• large quantities • multi-dimensional • limited "message control" • potential contestability (may be limited by volume, technical complexity of information, audience fragmentation)	• may be strategic or reactive • purposive—linked to organizational priorities, responses to external problems or challenges • often linked to agenda-setting, service of major priorities of political/organizational actors • building, protecting credibility of organization key priorities • may be diversionary, using timing or volume of information to deflect unwanted media or public attention • checks and balances: freedom of information, contestability	• strategic—designed to dominate political discourse, silence or discredit challengers • manipulative—highly selective use of facts or assertions to define, control public perceptions of reality • requires media collaboration or tight control of access to, distribution of information

The Internet has contributed to a tremendous increase in the volume and kinds of information provided by governments to Canadians, along with the demands and challenges of effective communications in both directions (Alexander 2000). Other large organizations in both the public and private sectors, including businesses and interest groups, must also balance the demands of news and information management in an era of information overload. The very volume of information released by governments in the name of openness increases the challenge faced by government relations professionals—and, even more so, by non-specialists—both in separating the important from the routine and in identifying politically significant signals or trends buried within the seemingly endless avalanche of data.

The concept and practices of news management can be controversial in a society that prides itself on its relative openness and commitment to democratic values. To the extent that news management practices contribute to the suppression or distortion of information in the pursuit of partisan political agendas, they can be likened to a form of propaganda (see Box 12.2). However, in a political environment characterized by relatively high levels of political openness, competition (among interest groups, political parties, and competing concepts of the public good), and a mix of political and legal checks and balances, some degree of news management is both an inevitable and necessary tool of effective government, even if it is one subject to potential abuses.

Factors Shaping Government Communications Strategies

"It's now a very good day to get out anything we want to bury."
Jo Moore, communications advisor to British Prime Minister Tony Blair, 11 September 2001. (*The Daily Telegraph*, 10 October 2001: 2; cited in Franklin 2003: 45)

The balance between managing and responding to public opinion can also be seen in the ways that governments manage the problem agendas that emerge from economic or social trends, media or interest group campaigns, or unforeseen events which catch public attention and the policy agendas that come from the workings of different policy communities. Montpetit suggests that the number of participants, relative openness of policy processes, and relative interdependence of major actors play central roles in shaping government communications strategies.[2]

Governments' management of public issue agendas often reflects the degree of openness of particular policy communities, the degree of consensus between major governmental and societal stakeholders on broad policy objectives and the general means necessary to achieve them, and the degree to which outsider groups are successful in challenging these institutionalized policies and relationships. As noted in Chapters 10 and 11, government agencies functioning within relatively closed policy communities are less likely to engage in the public discussion of issues than to develop a policy consensus behind close doors, possibly in quiet consultation with major stakeholders, and then to announce their decisions in ways that leave limited room for public response. Open policy processes may involve considerable levels of discussion among major stakeholders, the timely publication of research and policy documents for public review and discussion, and active media coverage

---

2 This analysis is based on Montpetit's study of consultation processes, but it is equally applicable to the broader field of government communications (Montpetit 2003: 100-02).

before definitive decisions are taken. Depending on the steps taken by governments or societal groups to manage the process, the structuring of open policy processes may be a means by which dominant interests within particular policy communities legitimize their policy preferences or in which the competing agendas and interests of different governmental and societal actors may lead to intense public debate.

Governments often engage in information management strategies that provide for selective openness in the way they release information on government intentions or processes, to whom they release it, and when they do so. However, such strategies are open to manipulation and potential sabotage. Participants may release unauthorized information to the news media in ways that trigger controversy (leaks or whistle-blowing), alert stakeholders and the broader public to internal government conflicts, or prompt the disavowal of alleged government intentions. These incidents encourage "risk avoidance" (Alboim 2000: 1) and news management in government as both politicians and civil servants attempt to maintain control of their agendas at some cost to openness and public dialogue.

Alternately, highly placed officials may use informal disclosures of information to the media to test public or interest group responses to proposed policies (that is, sending up trial balloons) or to shape public expectations against which eventual policy decisions will be measured. In recent years, despite a nominal policy of pre-budget secrecy, the flood of leaks emanating from informed sources has ensured that the media and public are broadly informed about most major elements in federal budget speeches before they are officially released.

Interdependence Between Governmental and Societal Interests
Interdependence between government and societal actors may take a number of forms, depending on the structure of the policy community, the number of actors involved, and the degree to which some actors have the capacity to act independently of others, as discussed in Chapter 11. In policy communities characterized by relatively high levels of interdependence among major stakeholders, policy discussion and debates may be conducted primarily through the internal policy processes of governments, with limited and specialized media coverage. Some scholars of media politics suggest that such specialists often come to share the assumptions and policy outlooks of their major sources, so that they become vehicles for the transmission or reinforcement of an elite consensus favoured by dominant interests to attentive publics (Franklin 2003: 58-60).

Pressure pluralist policy communities, characterized by more intense competition among societal groups and a more distant relationship between these groups and government decision-makers, are more likely to be governed by what David Good has described as "the politics of anticipation" (Good 1980). Both governments and interest groups act on the basis of incomplete information, calculating their actions partly in terms of their capacity to deal effectively with perceived problems and partly in terms of possible responses by other governmental and societal actors. In such cases, public discussion of the issues is heavily influenced by the degree to which government officials or interest groups are willing to go public, the news management techniques used to send signals to other players, and the intensity or variety of media responses.

Linkage and interdependence may affect public discourse and the feasibility or timeliness of policy options in other ways. Highly publicized problems involving corporate irresponsibility, environmental damage, or product safety can often provide political impetus for increased government regulation of business activities or undermine initiatives for deregulation or market-oriented regulatory reforms. For example, the spillover effects of corporate scandals in the US (e.g., the Enron effect) between 2000 and 2003 led Canadian regulators to copy or parallel several aspects of the resulting Sarbanes-Oxley legislation, while also taking a more aggressive approach to the enforcement of existing regulations.

Highly publicized government failures—prominent abuses of political or regulatory power, huge cost overruns, or the performance problems of government business enterprises—may have the opposite effect, as it did with the troubles of Ontario Hydro, BC Ferries, or Ottawa's dysfunctional ethics regime in recent years. The political salience of these issues is determined by their timing within the **electoral cycle**.

Distribution of Resources and Policy Capacities Within Networks

Issues of political, financial, or technical interdependence are often linked to the distribution of resources and policy capacities within policy networks. Technical capacity may be related to relative policy expertise, a clear understanding of pertinent issues and the ability to communicate them effectively to the relevant public, or the ability to draw on these resources from well-disposed stakeholders in other sectors.

Governments usually act unilaterally in defining policy problems or spelling out their policy intentions when they are confident that they possess sufficient analytical and financial resources to act independently of societal actors (and, if necessary, to buy their support). They may also do so when the likelihood of external political challenges turns policy debates into an exercise in raw political power, however camouflaged in the language of political persuasion. The greater the degree of uncertainty within government over the nature of the problems to be addressed by proposed policies, the potential impact on particular constituencies of various policy options, or the relative political costs and benefits of pursuing particular policies, the more likely governments are to engage major stakeholders and the general public in formal or informal consultation processes at various stages of the policy cycle.

Policy capacity is closely linked to another important factor in government communications strategies: the management of public expectations. Politicians who promise results they cannot deliver run the risk of diminished credibility, both for themselves and for their policy proposals.

Consensus versus Conflict Within the Policy Community

Policy-makers confident of broad public support for their major policy objectives often have considerable latitude in designing their technical details as long as their communications strategy consistently links these measures to clearly stated principles enjoying broad popular or stakeholder support. However, policy-makers can run into difficulty when they are unable to translate technical concepts on which proposed policies are based into terms that are accessible and understandable to the general public or which involve major changes to policies to which the public or major stakeholders attach great political, economic, or symbolic importance.

Schlesinger notes several ways in which conflicting interests inside and outside governments can influence public debates and media coverage of contested issues: contention between official sources, the behind-the-scenes manoeuvrings of sources, the competitive and shifting nature of key sources *within* privileged elites, the longer term shifts in the structure of access, and the ability of media outlets to define issues independently of power centres (Schlesinger 1990: 66-67; Cottle 2003: 13).

Stakeholders inside or outside government that have an independent policy capacity but whose views may have been discounted by policy insiders may choose to release studies challenging the dominant policy outlook. This approach is often taken by think tanks such as the Fraser Institute, the Canadian Centre for Policy Alternatives, and other ideologically driven organizations.

Public debates may be carried out in the media or in public conferences organized to draw public attention to their agendas by surrogate groups with linkages to major stakeholders inside and outside government. Public servants and insider groups may work on parallel, but less publicized, tracks to advance similar arguments or alternatives. The likelihood of public confrontation increases with the ability and willingness of other government departments, other levels of government, and major societal actors, including business groups and major think tanks, to challenge the credibility of a lead agency's preferred definition of a policy problem or the feasibility of its proposed policy responses. Unlike the 1970s and 1980s, when highly publicized confrontations between governments and the broader business community were fairly common, most public disputes between industry and government in the early twenty-first century tend to involve fairly narrow groups of interests or conflicts among competing groups of business and other societal interests.

These factors also shape the timing and choice of consultation processes. Governments may choose to work around interest groups whom they believe will be strongly opposed to their policy proposals by limiting public discussions of their plans before they are formally announced. Lawyer and columnist Sean Moore calls this approach "D...A...D...": decide, announce, defend (Moore 2002b). The greater the degree of partisan political conflict on particular issues, the more likely the government is to circle the wagons and use its control over the policy-making and legislative processes to limit its vulnerability to attacks by opposition parties and associated interest groups.

Governments' approaches to public disclosure, discussion, and debate on issues are also influenced by the timing of proposals within the electoral cycle, the degree to which proposed policies are consistent with the public mood, and the relative importance of particular initiatives either in furthering or threatening to derail the government's broader agenda. As noted in Chapter 11, governments prefer to pursue politically unpopular projects earlier in their mandates, while tailoring their approaches to controversial issues more closely to public moods with the approach of an election year.

Another major factor in governments' efforts to assess and manage public opinion is the independent role of the news media as transmitters, creators, and interpreters of information. Both governments and interest groups seeking to engage or shape public opinion must take the media into account if they are to do so with any prospect of success.

Shaping Elite and Public Opinion: The Mass Media

> Canadian Parliamentary Press Gallery: Unofficial Rules
> 1. We ask the questions. You provide the answers.
> 2. You propose the message. We decide the presentation.
> 3. Ignore rules 1 or 2, and the consequences can be deadly.
> Don Martin (*Calgary Herald*, 10 June 2001)

The news media—newspapers, television and radio stations, magazines, and other specialized publications—perform multiple roles within the political and policy processes. They provide the public with basic information on political and economic events and processes; interpret and analyze these events to give their audience some degree of context; and serve as forums for public debate involving policy elites, organized interests, and ordinary citizens. At times, they promote certain causes or agendas by initiating public discussion or amplifying and even championing the voices of particular groups. They interpret a society, or different aspects of society, to itself by providing basic information not only on political events but also on the environment in which political, social, and economic activities take place.

The media can function as referees in public debates among competing political actors, active participants in these debates, or both. Sometimes individual media executives, producers, editors, and journalists are clearly objective observers and commentators, while, at other times, they display obvious political or ideological partisanship. More frequently, casual or even engaged observers find it difficult to determine the relative weight of partisan involvement to media coverage of issues and events.[3]

Agenda-Setting

Three major political functions of the news media are **agenda-setting, gatekeeping,** and the **framing** of public issues. Major media executives, senior journalists, and reporters often attempt to shape the political agenda (agenda-setting) by defining

---

3 For assessments of media bias in the 2005-06 federal election, see Soroka and Maioni 2006 and Observatory on Media and Public Policy 2006.

what is newsworthy and interpreting the public interest according to their own values, interests, and judgement of the relative importance of the issue in a particular context. They engage in agenda-setting by determining what stories or issues are worthy of news coverage or by the prominence or frequency of coverage given to political actors and issues (Nesbitt-Larking 2001: 335-67).

Authoritative political figures, such as prime ministers, provincial premiers, and senior cabinet ministers, often make news by virtue of their positions, although this prominence is no guarantee of favourable or accurate coverage. Media outlets may or may not tell their audiences what to think. Research suggests that many people filter out stories that are of little interest or that are strongly at odds with their existing beliefs and values, but to the extent that major national and regional media converge in providing extended coverage of particular issues, there is some truth to the adage that they are likely to influence what citizens think about.

Media outlets typically function in a commercial marketplace in which profitability (or, for public and non-profit organizations, economic viability) is linked to market share and advertising revenues. As a result, agenda-setting techniques are used to compete both for market share and public influence. This is the subject of considerable academic controversy. Liberal pluralists argue that, while imperfect, competition in the marketplace forces media corporations to remain open to multiple social interests and points of view, if only in their own self-interest. Critical theorists, often arguing from a neo-Marxist perspective, contend that corporate-owned media institutions reinforce existing patterns of social and economic dominance, either by active partisanship, by failing to challenge dominant social or cultural assumptions, or by failing to give what they consider an adequate hearing to outsider groups that challenge the social order (Nesbitt-Larking 2001: 113-26; Cottle 2003: 9-14). Conservative and libertarian social critics offer a mirror image of these criticisms aimed at what they perceive to be excessive liberal or leftist media biases (Miljan and Cooper 2003; *On Balance*, Fraser Institute, monthly), although the emergence of a range of articulate conservative voices in some media outlets has qualified these critiques in recent years.

In some cases, journalists and media outlets actively lend their support to the promotion of the agendas of selected governments, business groups, or other political actors with little attempt at balance. In others, agenda-setting degenerates into an adversarial approach sometimes described as "gotcha journalism" in which journalists actively seek to discredit politicians or other political actors whom they perceive as vulnerable or ideologically suspect (Bain 1994). Alboim suggests that many Canadian journalists are "suspicious of power and its exercise," particularly in consumer-sensitive media or on issues in which the interests of "ordinary people" appear to be at odds with those of the rich, powerful, or well-connected (Alboim 2000: 1). While far from universally applicable, this observation appears to apply to journalists scattered across the political spectrum.

These environmental factors influence the ability of business groups—and those challenging business interests—to compete for media attention and favourable coverage. Groups that can couch their positions in ways that take advantage of prevailing social and cultural outlooks or a broader community of interest shared by editors and journalists frequently have an advantage in this competition.

Gatekeeping

Media outlets serve as gatekeepers, or active filters, that determine which political actors, stakeholders, or experts should be sought out, accommodated, or marginalized in news coverage as interpreters of particular events, trends, and processes. Journalism often promotes generalists with limited specialized knowledge, although major newspapers may assign reporters to cover certain topics long enough to develop substantial expertise. As a result, reporters are often relatively open to the expertise of others, particularly when it comes with authoritative credentials or strong self-marketing skills. Thus, government officials, academic or scientific experts and popularizers, and articulate interest group representatives are given privileged positions as voices for public opinion. A growing volume of literature in the field of media studies examines the selection of sources for news stories and the relationships between sources and journalists.

Framing

"There is a word for a government's comments when they are not vetted for positioning: gaffe."
Timothy Lewis (2003: 19)

The ways in which issues are recognized by major elements of the news media often help to determine how they will ultimately be addressed by policy-makers. The **framing** of issues—the interpretation of issues and the context in which they are presented to the public—speaks to both the problem recognition and problem definition stages of the policy process discussed in Chapter 11 (Howlett and Ramesh 2003: 120-22).

Journalists and their editors exercise considerable discretion in framing issues or events in the news. News stories or events are framed as contests of personalities, interests, ideas, or ideologies; as part of an agenda-setting process; or to attract, engage, or entertain an audience. These contests may take place at two levels. News makers—governments and interest groups—compete for media coverage that enables them to present their message. At the same time, they have varying degrees of ability to influence the presentation, context, or meaning attributed to their positions by elements of the news media (Wolfsfeld 2003). As noted in the unofficial rules of the Parliamentary Press Gallery quoted above, journalists jealously guard their prerogative to control the latter, whatever the efforts of other political actors to promote their messages.

Politicians and interest group leaders who have developed positive relationships with individual journalists or the media as a whole are able to transmit their positions and ideas more clearly than political actors who either lack credibility or fail to appeal to journalists' values, instincts, or self-esteem. The actions or comments of political actors and activists that may be seen as signs of authenticity, originality, or thoughtfulness in some circumstances can be portrayed as personal failings or gaffes in others.

Globe and Mail, 21 June 2002: A1

The framing of news stories is also influenced by the technological capacities and formats of journalistic and broadcast media. This encourages public relations professionals and activists to position or promote their stories by providing journalists visually interesting backdrops suited to preferred story lines. However, more complex issues that do not lend themselves to such creative packaging are much more vulnerable to reinterpretation by journalists or to political challenges by competing interests.

Case Study: A Question of Trust(s)

The rapid growth of the income trust sector and the federal government's responses to it became the single most heavily covered story within Canada's business and financial media in 2004-05. Income trusts are forms of business organization that hold income-producing assets and make payments directly to unit holders. Distributions of trust income are only taxed once they are in the hands of investors, in contrast to corporate dividends that, historically, have been paid from after-tax income.

Income trusts emerged during the mid-1980s as a tool of financial entrepreneurship rather than as an expression of government policy (Brethour and Chase 2005: B6). However, it was not until the stock market implosion of 2000-03 that the market for income trusts took off, driven by a mixture of investor demand and business recognition that trust structures provided many firms with lower costs of capital and sharply lower business taxes.

While their market value totaled only a modest $18 billion in 2000, trusts soon became the fastest growing investment product in Canada's equity markets. The Finance Department's laissez-faire approach to income trusts was reinforced by a sharp backlash from pension funds and other institutional investors against provisions in its 2004 budget, later withdrawn, that would have restricted their ability to invest in trusts. Larger provinces accommodated the sector's growth with legislative changes extending to their unit-holders the same privileges of limited liability enjoyed by shareholders of corporations. By the end of 2004, the market value of trusts had increased to $118 billion. It jumped by 44 per cent to more than $170 billion by August 2005, accounting for 10 per cent of the total value of shares on the TSX and raising serious concerns among Finance officials about potential revenue losses and other economic effects and a formal review of related tax policies by the department (Canada, Department of Finance 2005; Hale 2005d).

Framing the Issues I

Agenda-setting on the income trust issue emerged from the combination of media recognition of major shifts in market and business activity with policy inaction by the federal government and widespread uncertainty over the implications of the market trends for both businesses and ordinary investors. Financial media coverage was further stimulated by the disproportionate share of investments in income trusts held by individual investors and debates over whether income trusts were a legitimate market development resulting from excessive taxes on business and investment income, or a form of aggressive tax avoidance that should be curbed by the government.

Reporters framed the issue around two major themes. First, the "bull market trend" in income trusts could be construed as the financial equivalent of "horserace journalism," centred on the question of "who's getting into trusts this month?" The second theme, which we can call "business as usual," often involved coverage of individual business decisions and reports solicited from investment analysts on underlying business strategies and their implications for investors and financial markets. Editorialists, columnists, and other commentators expressed concern alternately over the effects of tax distortions on business and economic activity and over Ottawa's uncertain response. Some emphasized the issue of revenue losses, but this perspective was muted by consistent federal surpluses despite sharp increases in spending.

A Finance Department discussion paper released in September 2005 described the issues and options available to the government in a dispassionate, technical style, without sending clear policy signals, thus supporting the business-as-usual theme. That week, four major corporations announced proposed income trust conversions valued at $17 billion. A senior bank official mused publicly that if the trend continued, major banks might be forced to take similar actions (Canada, Department of Finance 2005; deCloet, Chase, and Kennedy 2005: B1).

Framing the Issues II

Finance Minister Ralph Goodale's reaction was to announce a freeze on advance tax rulings for proposed conversions to income trusts, significantly increasing the potential risk for investors. Unnamed sources expressed increased concerns over revenue losses and the failure of major businesses to interpret the government's signals (deCloet, Chase, and Stewart 2005: B6). Extensive media coverage, almost exclusively in the business and financial press, explored the issues from several angles while noting the difficulty of introducing significant tax changes that would not create further distortions in the tax system. The opposition Conservatives stirred the pot by circulating petitions to financial advisors and main street investors urging a hands-off approach to income trusts.

Box 12.2: Eight Levels of Citizen Participation in Consultation

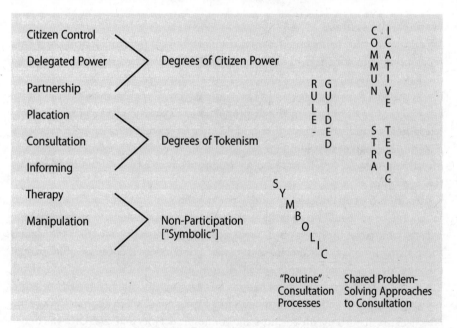

Source: Arnstein, "A Ladder of Public Participation," cited in de la Mothe 2003: 181; Montpetit 2003: 98.

In November 2005, with the government facing imminent defeat in Parliament over other tax measures contained in its fiscal update, Finance Minister Ralph Goodale announced that he would resolve the income trust debate by reducing the double taxation of corporate dividends to create a more level playing field between different classes of investments (Canada, Department of Finance, 2005).

Under normal circumstances, Goodale's response to his critics might have avoided an inconvenient debate on the issue during the ensuing election campaign. However, a suspiciously sharp increase in stock market activity just hours before his announcement sparked allegations that certain well-placed investors had benefited from leaked information—prompting opposition calls for a police investigation. The RCMP's announcement, a month later, that it had launched an investigation coincided with a sharp drop in public support for the government, contributing to its subsequent electoral defeat.

Many Choices, Many Voices

Like governments and interest groups, the media is not a unitary actor. Mass media organizations often separate editorial functions from news gathering and reporting. General news coverage often takes place at arms length from that relating to coverage of business or financial markets. Most major Canadian cities now have a degree of competition among mass media outlets, including daily newspapers and television stations, with varying degrees of differentiation among target audiences and ideological orientations, although newspapers in smaller centres often enjoy a virtual monopoly in the coverage of local issues. Some media outlets actively foster competing points of view through their editorial, commentary and news reporting functions, while others are more monolithic in tone and content.

Specialized media organizations, including industry and "special interest" publications have always existed. However, technological change has greatly expanded the diversity of media outlets, ranging from dozens of specialty cable challenges to the creative anarchy of the Internet. However, although growing competition may lead to more voices, however specialized, it can also cut into the resources available for general news coverage by mass media outlets, whose owners often place a stronger emphasis on market share and profitability than on the substance of news content. (Nesbitt-Larking 2001: 127-31; Franklin 2003: 60.)

These trends tend to enhance the advantages already available to government officials responsible for news management and to increase the competition for favourable media attention by most other interests. Schlesinger suggests that the "success of interventions (by aspiring sources of news) in their 'tug of war' with the news media will depend on their incentives, power, ability to supply suitable information, and geographic and social proximity to journalists" (Gans 1979: 117; Cottle 2003: 12).

Conventional wisdom has suggested that corporate ownership imposes implicit restrictions on news coverage, tending to bias it in favour of business and corporate elites. This may be true of some newspapers and other media outlets, although there are often significant differences in the tone and content of business coverage in major outlets such as *The Globe and Mail, Financial Post,* and *Toronto Star.*

These concerns are reinforced by trends towards the convergence of media ownership *and* operations between newspaper chains and broadcast networks, although these trends are offset to a degree by the ongoing ownership turnover of particular media outlets. However, some professional observers of the news media believe the concept of an embedded corporate agenda to be a myth propagated by self-serving media elites to promote their own professional and political autonomy. (For discussions of this issue, see Hayes 1992; Davis 1998; Taras 2001; and Miljan and Cooper 2003.) A more relevant constraint on journalistic resources may be the management styles and finances of media corporations whose pursuit of increased market share through the acquisition of new outlets may have resulted in excessive debt, weak profits or financial losses, and fewer journalists to cover a wider range of stories (Franklin 2003: 59-60).[4]

A growing body of literature suggests that technological innovation and the proliferation of media outlets has contributed to the increased fragmentation of media markets, an increased reliance on narrow-casting to specialized audiences, and a greater emphasis on "soft" news and entertainment—sometimes described as "tabloid journalism" (Mendelsohn and Nadeau 1996; Langer 2003: 135-51). Although other innovations such as 24-hour news channels and dedicated public affairs stations have created new markets for political actors to communicate their messages, they also reinforce the competitive nature of the external policy process, increasing the challenges for interest groups—and politicians—trying to communicate their messages to a broad public audience.

"Going Public": Interest Groups, the Media, and Government

One of the major tasks of business associations, interest groups, and their public relations advisors is to develop a communications strategy that can identify the interests of their clients with the general interests of society as a whole or of other groups in society which may be recruited to their political coalition in an effort to sway the decisions of politicians and government officials.

The choice of a business or other interest group to "go public" on a particular issue, rather than lobbying quietly behind the scenes, and its selection of tactics used to advance its interests or outlook often reflect its relative standing within the policy community and the degree to which it depends on the goodwill of senior politicians and government officials for its competitive position.

Interest group tactics in seeking media attention often depend on whether the group in question has an established constituency within government or is trying to obtain government recognition of its interests by attracting public attention, sympa-

---

4 In recent years, financial newspapers have provided extensive coverage of financial problems and layoffs at major media conglomerates such as CanWest Global, Quebecor World (including Sun Media), and Bell Globemedia, the owners of most major regional newspapers and television stations across Canada. The CBC's chronic financial and management problems are another story.

thy, or support. Outsider groups are more likely to pursue media and political attention by creating public controversy than those that have already achieved a degree of influence in relevant policy communities. Protest groups, usually made up of political outsiders seeking media attention for their grievances, will often "take a ride" on public events sponsored by others, ranging from parliamentary hearings to meetings of governmental organizations. Many media outlets will provide a welcome forum for such controversy, at least for a time. Community groups seek to draw attention to their concerns or grievances by using public petitions, open letters to senior politicians, or even catchy billboards, which may trigger additional media attention.

Some business groups such as the Canadian Federation of Independent Business (CFIB) and the Independent Business and Contractors' Association of British Columbia (ICBA) began as "issue-oriented" outsider groups organized to challenge the political status quo of the 1970s. Eventually, most such groups either evolve into institutionalized groups (as with the CFIB), become marginalized, or fade away.

"Institutionalized" interest groups with consistent access to government officials as the recognized voice of a particular industry or societal interest, such as organized labour or environmental groups, may choose to go public if their interests are seriously threatened or if they face a public challenge from other actors within the policy community. However, the informal norms of government relations usually encourage a more "professional" approach usually characterized by political restraint, the avoidance of overt political partisanship, or tactics that would embarrass politicians or civil servants with whom they have developed working relationships.

These approaches may be likened to a parent's expectation that children who have reached a certain stage of maturity will learn to distinguish between "inside" and "outside" voices, rather than yelling for (or at) a parent or sibling when they fail to get their way. They also reflect the institutional division of labour between elected politicians and civil servants. Whatever their personal views, public servants working within Canada's traditional bureaucratic cultures usually consider their mandate is to provide advice to cabinet ministers on policy priorities and technical options for their implementation, not to serve as referees in ideological combat among competing societal groups. Interest groups that fail to make the distinction between the internal and external policy processes, or between their own interests and ideological priorities and the broader context of political decision-making, risk their own marginalization in the policy process. (For example, see Stairs 2001: 161-76.)

Governments may often apply sanctions against groups that ignore these rules, deferring meetings with ministers or quietly ignoring their policy recommendations with a polite brush-off. They may also seek out other groups representing the same segment of society that are viewed as more likely to meet the government "part way" on disputed issues. The capacity of governments or senior officials to "freeze out" interest groups is even stronger in political systems in which one party is consistently dominant, as in federal politics between 1993 and 2003 and Alberta politics under the 35-year reign of successive Conservative premiers. Business groups that challenge social democratic governments on primarily ideological grounds have

acknowledged similar handling. Groups heavily dependent on government contracts or funding for the delivery of public services, particularly in the non-profit
sector, are often reluctant to bite the hand that feeds them, particularly if there are
other groups that could easily take their place at the public trough.

Getting the Message Out: Playing the Angles

The communications strategies used by interest and advocacy groups in dealing
with governments and the media may reflect existing public values and patterns of
public policy or seek to mould public opinion to accept policy ideas more consistent
with their interests and outlooks either by appeals to shared values, shared interests,
or "expert" research findings.

There is a growing tendency to segment communications functions among interest groups working within broader policy networks. Individual interest groups are
more likely to address specific issues of current concern through traditional forms of
communications such as news conferences or "media events," open letters to cabinet ministers or government leaders, the sponsoring of or participation in policy
conferences on current issues, or the writing of *op-ed* pieces in major national or
regional newspapers.

Broader proposals for policy change—particularly those requiring significant
shifts in public or elite opinion—are more likely to be initiated by special purpose
coalitions of interest groups created for that purpose (see Chapter 10), think tanks,
or academic researchers (Abelson 2000). The release of policy studies by think tanks,
other interest groups, and well-resourced businesses such as the economics departments of major banks is a tactic used frequently to highlight major problems requiring government action or to challenge the analysis of other groups, including governments. In addition to publishing detailed research studies, staff and sponsored
researchers for most of these groups will also summarize their findings in op-ed
articles published by major national and regional newspapers to give their ideas
broader circulation.

Established interest groups with strong finances may be able to "create" news
events that generate publicity by commissioning and publishing research studies
or the results of opinion polls or even by publicizing their leaders' speeches on slow
news days, particularly if comments contribute to public debate or controversy on
a significant issue. For example, when rapidly rising oil and gas prices in 2004-05
began to raise the spectre of major conflicts among competing regional and government interests over the division of resulting revenue windfalls, a well-publicized
study released by the Canadian Energy Research Institute (CERI) suggested that the
federal government stood to be the greatest fiscal beneficiary of oil sands development, after all sources of government revenues are taken into account (Laghi 2005:
A1; Ebner 2005: B1).[5] However, most groups find it a more efficient use of limited
resources to "take a ride" on current issues or official forums such as pre-budget

---

5 CERI research is jointly funded by industry and federal and provincial government sources.

consultations, parliamentary or legislative hearings, or meetings with senior cabinet ministers (Gold 1975: 80-104).

Newer technologies such as the Internet provide both governments and interest groups, large and small, with a useful tool to get their messages out "unfiltered" by the media. Many activist groups may also be successful in "narrow-casting" their messages to supporters or members of policy networks through the mass circulation of e-mail and comparatively inexpensive software that has made such communications tools broadly accessible.

Stanbury notes that, rather than attempting to challenge public opinion in their dealings with governments, many major business organizations have learned to align their public statements with the general direction of public opinion on matters of general principle while suggesting different ways that governments might be able to achieve desired goals to accommodate business interests (Stanbury 1988: 326-27).

This approach often requires business groups to take the **political business cycle**—the interaction of general political and economic trends in agenda-setting— into account in attempting to influence government priorities. Periods of relative prosperity tend to be accompanied by increased public support for activist government and increased public spending and limited public responsiveness to business concerns over the effects of "excessive" or misplaced public spending (and taxes) on their competitiveness. Periods of general economic downturn tend to result in greater public resistance to increases in public spending, especially those from which particular groups are less likely to benefit, and greater responsiveness to business advocacy on economic issues (Mendelsohn 2002).[6] However, perceived business indifference to issues of consumer, public, or environmental safety or abuses of market power at the expense of ordinary citizens are likely to provoke some degree of public resentment at any time. Such resentments can be fanned into a political backlash, often leading to new legislative or regulatory initiatives, if championed by a creative policy entrepreneur inside or outside government.

Combining Style with Substance

The style and substance of public relations initiatives depends largely on a government or interest group's intended audience and the effect sought. A politician or interest group intending primarily to disrupt or discredit the efforts of opponents can often get away with outrageous oversimplifications that force a government or industry group on the defensive. Publicity stunts or "public theatre" designed to discredit airline security, expose environmental or product safety problems with a particular company or product, or expose a current or proposed government policy to public ridicule may often be effective in capturing media and public attention, particularly if carried out by political "outsiders" or "underdogs."

---

6 These generalizations are also supported by more specific surveys conducted on behalf of major economic policy ministries (Ekos Research 2002, 2003; Earnscliffe Strategy Group 2000, 2001).

Lawyer and author Sean Moore suggests that to be effective, business and advocacy groups should structure their presentations to governments and public forums to be *succinct*—including well-written executive summaries to focus problem definition and prescriptions; *coherent*—logically linking research with problem definition and proposed remedies; *imaginative*—going beyond "a fairly firm grasp of the obvious"; *pragmatic*—practically workable in the existing political context; and *understandable*—written in plain clear language (Moore 2002).

Stanbury notes that effective public relations utilizes many of the same tools as effective lobbying: building relationships with key reporters who cover political affairs or policy fields; being pro-active, rather than reactive; preparing carefully for key events; and taking advantage of "local angles" or other potential areas of common ground with journalists or members of the targeted public. So do major business errors in judgement in dealing with the media: being unprepared or inarticulate, providing inaccurate or deceptive information, or taking an adversarial approach to journalists (Stanbury 1988: 524-42).

Public relations professionals describe media coverage generated by the use of such strategies as "earned media." Another way for governments and interest groups to get their messages to a broader public is with the use of "bought media"—paid advertising for the communication of information, image-building, and political advocacy.

Advocacy and Image-Oriented Advertising

Groups may also engage in **advocacy advertising**—"advertising which presents information or a point-of-view on a publicly recognized controversial issue" (Advertising Standards Canada, n.d.)—to promote their positions. Advocacy advertising may be used to signal the concerns of interest groups or aspiring opinion leaders to the media and government, to draw public attention to a group's more detailed policy positions, to mobilize public opposition to a government or a particular policy initiative, or to recruit support for an interest group's ongoing political activities.

Governments also use advocacy advertising to promote major elements of their policy agendas, to challenge the actions of other governments (particularly in federal-provincial relations), and to respond to the publicity campaigns of major interest groups or competing political parties.

Many government relations advisors view advocacy advertising as a relatively poor investment for business groups attempting to influence governments, since it has little short-term effect on public opinion and far less effect than effective policy analysis or advocacy targeted directly at relevant public-sector decision-makers. A full-page advertisement in a single major newspaper typically costs between $20,000 and $50,000, with multiple and repeated advertisements necessary to reach regionally segmented media markets. Political debates over the use of advocacy advertising during election campaigns will be addressed in Chapter 14.

Individual businesses or industry associations are more likely to use image-building advertisements or "advertorials" to communicate their activities on issues of social concern, such as resource and environmental management practices, the "human dimension" of their business activities, or their contributions to the community. For example, steel-maker Dofasco broadcast such image-making advertisements for years in southern Ontario, based on the slogan "Our Product is Steel—Our Strength is People." Brewers and distillers frequently purchase "responsible drinking" ads, especially around Christmas. Such approaches may have their place as part of a broader business communications strategy, particularly if backed up by actions that give substance to claims of corporate responsibility. However, they have only limited and indirect relevance to most policy debates, complementing ongoing dealings on specific issues with government policy-makers.

Governments are typically the largest purchasers of image-based advertising. Self-promotion may take the form of providing information on public programs and services, promoting new policy initiatives, and sometimes issuing fuzzy "feel-good" advertisements that often provide a barely hidden subsidy for politically favoured community organizations, advertising agencies, and local media outlets. The federal government alone spent an average of $159 million annually between 1998 and 2003 on all kinds of advertising (Canada, Office of the Auditor General 2003: Chapter 4) from "feel-good" ads supporting Canada Day celebrations, to anti-tobacco campaigns, to the Canada Revenue Agency's advertisements to promote timely filing of income tax returns. The use of government advertising and sponsorship programs as instruments of political patronage and cronyism came to a head in the so-called "Groupaction" or "Adscam" scandals of 2001-03 in which large sums of money were funneled to firms headed by political associates of the federal public works minister for services of questionable value.

However, the fastest growing public forum for the interaction of interest groups, businesses, and governments in recent years has been the expansion of the formal and informal consultation processes of governments. The widespread loss of public trust in politics and government during the 1980s and 1990s led most governments to resort to far more extensive consultations with policy stakeholders and the general public in order to rebuild their political capital and regain the political discretion necessary to manage their policy agendas effectively.

Consultation Processes as Agenda Management

"Democracy means government by discussion, but it is only effective if you can stop people talking."
Former British Prime Minister Clement Attlee (Moore 2004)

"The insolence of office comes into play whenever commissars encounter citizens."
George Jonas (Jonas 2004)

Consultation has become a major element of the external policy process. Consultation may help governments to manage public expectations, build political capital, and earn sufficient trust to exercise greater policy autonomy on a wide range of issues. However, poorly managed consultations may also create inflated or unrealistic public expectations, squander political capital, and risk turning debates over specific policies into lightning rods for generalized public discontent.

Several factors have contributed to the growing use of formal consultation by governments as part of the public policy process. As noted in Chapter 5, the growth of government intervention in economy and society since the 1960s prompted the proliferation of pressure groups demanding to be heard on issues relating to their interests. These groups often challenged the relatively closed political cultures of many federal and provincial departments and agencies, forcing governments to find ways of appearing more responsive while attempting to maintain control of policy processes.

Politicians and civil servants discovered that their policy initiatives often affected citizens and businesses in very different ways than they had anticipated or that the policies of different departments and agencies sometimes worked at cross-purposes to one another. In some cases, adverse public and business reaction often made it difficult to implement proposed policies as planned initially. These factors increasingly challenged the legitimacy of government policies, particularly if organized groups affected by those policies felt their interests had not been consulted.

One objective of consultation is to provide a greater degree of legitimacy to government policies either by creating a forum to demonstrate or enhance the prospective benefits of proposed policies and programs to major stakeholders, the news media, and, where relevant, the general public or to provide relevant interest groups with the opportunity to participate to some degree in the process of policy formation. Montpetit describes the first process as "output-oriented" legitimacy, and the second as "input-oriented legitimacy" (Montpetit 2003).

Consultation processes in governments take a number of forms, depending on the nature of the policy communities in question, the political cultures of particular departments or jurisdictions, the number of significant policy stakeholders inside and outside government, the degree of policy consensus among governmental actors and major stakeholders, and the potential degree of controversy associated with particular policy initiatives (Montpetit 2003). Consultation processes are also organized to provide different levels of participation by citizens and interest groups, as noted in Box 12.2, ranging from the primarily symbolic to extending substantive influence over the formulation and implementation of government policies.

Symbolic Consultation

Public consultations by relatively closed policy communities are characterized as exercises in **symbolic legitimacy**. These processes use consultation as a public relations technique to extend nominal recognition of their right to contribute to discussions of government actions and public policies or to confer symbolic public recognition of particular groups.

Governments often make policy decisions while using public consultation with interest groups and designated experts as a formality to convey the appearance of listening to the concerns or positions of stakeholders or citizens. In some cases, consultations follow cabinet decisions and the introduction of legislation in Parliament or legislatures, often giving the appearance of being little more than ritual exercises expressed through the formalities of parliamentary hearings. A few technical amendments may be made to the policy or legislation, but neither interest groups nor the parliamentary opposition is likely to have a significant impact unless the government has blundered seriously, and the process can be stretched out long enough to bring significant public opposition to bear.

Governments may also appoint ministerial or departmental advisory committees including representatives of major stakeholder groups in order to build relationships, give symbolic recognition to certain groups (or party supporters representing particular constituencies), provide early warning systems of political or administrative problems that might otherwise be overlooked, and to provide a symbolic sense of inclusion in government policy processes. Other forms of symbolic consultation include "town-hall meetings" on particular issues held by local members of parliament and surveys conducted by governments to solicit feedback on specific initiatives or to assess levels of customer satisfaction with the administration of particular government programs or services.

Such activities provide the appearance of public input, but usually in structured forms intended to assist governments or political parties in promoting their own agendas rather than engaging in substantive discussions capable of influencing public policies. As such, they may provide a degree of therapy for citizens and interest groups that might otherwise feel ignored or slighted by governments. They may have some value in informing citizens of the context in which governments are addressing particular problems. However, in many cases, they are often little more than political window-dressing.

Consultation: Framing Issues and Seeking Procedural Legitimacy

Consultation may also encourage a sense of **procedural legitimacy** by providing a broad cross-section of citizens and interest groups with the opportunity to be heard in the development of particular policies or in the review of proposed legislation. Governments often use this approach to consultation as a way of legitimizing their policy initiatives by framing issues for discussion by stakeholders, the news media, and the broader public while attempting to maintain control of their broader agendas.

Procedural and symbolic consultation are distinguished by the degree of time and effort made by governments to engage attentive publics; the degree to which participants engage in dialogue, rather than simply speaking to or past one another; and the relative likelihood that participants can persuade those engaged in consultation to modify their policy proposals at the margin or to accommodate particular interest group concerns at the implementation stage of the policy cycle.

As noted in Chapter 10, government departments or agencies may release a discussion paper—sometimes called a Green Paper or Coloured Paper—on a particular issue as a way of soliciting public input on problem definition and policy design or of fieldtesting particular policy initiatives before they have come to a firm decision on proposed policies. In such cases, politicians and government officials obtain information that helps them to frame their policy priorities or proposals in ways that are likely to accommodate public opinion or stakeholder interests while still pursuing their key priorities.

Cabinet may decide to refer a **White Paper** outlining government policy intentions to a parliamentary or legislative committee to carry out publicly advertised nation-wide or province-wide hearings that provide a broad cross-section of interests with opportunities to provide their views to the government. In recent years, the federal government and most provinces have conducted extensive pre-budget hearings as a way of communicating government financial priorities and soliciting expert and interest group feedback on more detailed aspects of policy.

Provisions for extended public hearings may also be made for controversial legislation when governments wish to ensure that both supporters and opponents have an opportunity to present their case to legislators. Such consultations may have a symbolic element to them. However, they reflect a political decision that the policies, issues, or interests at stake are significant enough to require extensive public discussion and debate before policy decisions are finalized or legislation is passed and implemented. Governments may choose to make either substantive or marginal changes to proposed policies or legislation as a result of consultations, but such decisions are usually made at the discretion of the government if officials can be convinced that they increase the policy's potential effectiveness or fairness.

Procedural legitimacy may have legal as well as political aspects, such as consistent adherence to established legal or regulatory procedures for governments to take administrative action, introduce new regulations, or enforce existing laws. Failure to observe these norms may prompt litigation and the possibility that policy or legislative changes may be reversed or modified as a result of judicial review.

Substantive Consultation

Consultations may be said to be substantive—or to confer **substantive legitimacy**—when a government actively uses them to seek support from major stakeholders or to visibly address their major concerns in changes to proposed policies or legislation. Such legitimacy may be achieved on political grounds, by securing widespread public acceptance for proposed policies or actions; on ethical grounds, as the "right thing to do"; or on ideological grounds, based on their consistency with the political goals and standards of a particular group.

The use of consultation as a vehicle for consensus-building reflects the input-oriented legitimacy referred to above. The use of sectoral corporatism is an explicit effort to encourage political buy-in and consensus-building from interest group leaders engaged in the process. It may also create ongoing political incentives for

cooperation with governments and other stakeholders by making such cooperation a condition of privileged access to the policy process. The earlier that legislative
consultations take place during the policy process—for example, through the use
of pre-study by legislative committees or hearings after First Reading, before a bill
has received parliamentary approval in principle—the more likely they are to be
substantive in nature than procedural or symbolic.

Such approaches may be bilateral or trilateral, as in efforts to bring together major
corporate and union leaders on issues of labour market development and training or
the development of a sectoral consensus on government assistance to the automotive sector. Others are multilateral, as in the business-environmental round tables
involving different resource industries (logging, pulp and paper, mining, oil and gas),
their respective unions, tourist operators, environmental groups, and local community leaders, including those from major Aboriginal communities, which have been
created by governments of different political stripes in Ontario, BC, and Quebec.

Governments are more likely to engage in this sort of consultation when interest
groups have the capacity to obstruct the implementation of policies which threaten
their core interests or when the risks of political polarization on controversial issues
threaten to divide a government from its core constituencies if policies favoured by
one group of supporters are chosen at the expense of another. Groups with high levels of technical expertise, particularly professional groups such as lawyers, doctors,
and teachers, may be able to take advantage of their central positions within the
legal, medical, and educational systems to negotiate the details of policy changes
affecting their sectors, although this is no guarantee that governments will not challenge their privileged positions in pursuit of fiscal savings or policy changes desired
by a wider public. Similar negotiations may take place with dominant sectoral interest groups on policy changes which affect the vital interests of a major regional or
provincial industry unless governments actively encourage the mobilization and
engagement of countervailing societal interests.

Alternately, governments may attempt to engage in the politics of *triangulation*:
identifying major policy principles or goals pursued by major stakeholders in a particular policy field and attempting to demonstrate how their policies respond to
inputs from these groups, while giving cabinet ministers and their officials considerable discretion in the precise mix of policies chosen. Political leaders such as Paul
Martin and Alberta's Ralph Klein have used this technique with considerable success in framing their deficit reduction and tax reform policies in recent years. Similar approaches can be seen in the reports of major House of Commons committees,
which frequently dress up their recommendations with quotes and statistics from
the testimony of expert witnesses and interest group leaders.

Even when governments keep firm political control over consultations, their
political legitimacy and effectiveness are frequently related to their capacity to manage public expectations in framing issues and designing outcomes. Governments
that take pains to emphasize the need to balance specific goals and outcomes and
that establish clear but modest benchmarks for measuring the success of particu-

lar policies or programs can enhance their credibility—and political capital—by exceeding these objectives (Moore 2002a). Governments whose rhetoric creates inflated expectations among supporters or major stakeholder groups and who fail to deliver on their commitments make themselves vulnerable both to attacks by political opponents and the news media and to strategic behaviour by interest groups that calculate that they may be able to hold out for more favourable treatment from opposition parties or a subsequent government.

Parliaments and Legislators in the External Policy Process

Any discussion of the external policy process would be incomplete without a discussion of parliaments and legislatures. The progressive decline of parliamentary democracy as a forum for debating and shaping public policies has become a standard element in Canadian discussions of democratic reform. (For only a few of many examples, see Savoie 1999; Simpson 2001; Gibson 2002; Rempel 2003.) The causes of parliamentary decline are well-known: the predominance of leader-centred politics and party discipline over deliberative democracy, the institutionalized adversarialism of party politics, and the shift of moral and legal authority to the courts, among others.

However, parliamentary institutions and forms still serve a number of practical functions within the policy process. Legal formalities for parliamentary approval of legislation enforce a degree of constraint on governments, especially when they are faced with a congested legislative agenda. The conventions of parliamentary accountability, while often flouted, provide an opportunity for reviewing both proposed legislation and the effectiveness of its implementation, particularly given the appointment of parliamentary officers such as auditors general and independent commissioners responsible for monitoring the ethical conduct of elected members and government officials in some jurisdictions.

Parliamentary and issue-specific caucuses provide focus groups for party leaders and forums for the assertion and balancing of regional, sectoral, and other interests. Parliamentary and legislative committees often serve as useful instruments to mobilize, engage, and evaluate public and interest group opinion. The gradual relaxation of the rules governing **private members' bills** has allowed individual MPs greater freedom to champion personal causes, or those of political outsiders, for possible legislative implementation or adoption as government policy. For purposes of simplicity, this section will refer to Parliament and MPs, although similar practices often exist in provincial legislatures and affect their MLAs (members of the Legislative Assembly), MPPs (members of the Provincial Parliament), MNAs (members of the National Assembly), or MHAs (members of the House of Assembly), depending on the formal designation of provincial parliaments.

Legal and Procedural Formalities

Formal parliamentary approval is often necessary for governments to initiate or implement major policy initiatives, including significant changes to the organization of governments, rates and objects of taxation, and the administrative and enforcement powers of government departments and agencies. Despite the extensive powers of majority governments, citizens, businesses, and interest groups can use the principle of judicial review to appeal to the courts or to quasi-judicial tribunals to ensure that governments follow established legal rules of conduct, a subject discussed more extensively in Chapter 13.

Government bills are often subject to the *confidence principle*, according to which MPs from the governing party are expected to support the bill as an expression of the government's capacity to maintain the confidence of Parliament: the capacity of governments to maintain the support of a majority of elected members for their legislation. Although there have been widespread calls for parliamentary reform in recent years to provide MPs with greater discretion in initiating and reviewing legislation, the culture of partisanship, reinforced by tight party discipline, remains a major barrier to substantial changes.

The parliamentary process also provides a number of opportunities to challenge government policies or amend government bills. The longer a particular piece of legislation is delayed in Parliament, the greater the potential capacity of interest groups to arouse public opinion or lobby governments to make significant changes to accommodate their interests through the internal policy processes discussed in Chapter 10. Issues of timing may cut at least two ways. A government may run out of parliamentary time for the consideration and passage of proposed legislation, particularly when the parliamentary calendar is congested with several major or politically sensitive pieces of legislation at the end of a session. However, governments may also introduce several pieces of legislation near the end of a session, using closure to limit debate and force their passage without adequate public consideration or debate. The management of legislative agendas is often subordinated to the broader political priorities of prime ministers, premiers, and their senior advisors—priorities that are not always apparent to observers without access to the highest levels of government.

Parliamentary Accountability and Review: Committees and Officers of Parliament

Public perceptions of parliamentary accountability are often limited to the political theatre of Question Period, with its built-in adversarialism, point-scoring, and self-justification. More substantive forums for political accountability are found in the work of parliamentary committees and independent officers of Parliament (and provincial legislatures).

The composition and mandates of parliamentary committees are defined by the standing orders of Parliament. Parties with parliamentary majorities usually dominate the membership and agendas of committees, although some details may be negotiated with members of minority parties depending on the degree to which the dominant culture of partisanship is tempered with civility, mutual respect, and accommodation. Although periodic reports have recommended broader mandates for legislative committees with reduced applications of party discipline, the degree of genuine debate and deliberation that takes place is usually governed by the government's political requirements and sensibilities.

Such sensibilities may be called into play when governments possess overwhelming parliamentary majorities, as they did in New Brunswick, PEI, Alberta and BC at different times during the 1990s and early 2000s. Governments with lopsided majorities tend to relax party discipline or to delegate greater responsibility to parliamentary committees in an effort to create internal checks and balances on ill-judged government actions. For example, in recent years Alberta Premier Ralph Klein has required most legislative proposals to be approved by standing policy committees of the government caucus and sometimes by full caucus prior to final cabinet review, although this process has effectively marginalized opposition parties in the legislature. The role of legislative committees in reviewing legislation will be discussed below.

Individual legislators often lack the political motivation, expertise, and resources to monitor the day-to-day activities, policies, and programs of government for their effectiveness or compliance with rules and standards intended to promote financial and administrative accountability, along with good management. These functions are increasingly performed by independent officers of Parliament whose accountability is to Parliament (or legislature) as a whole rather than the government of the day. These officers include:

- federal and provincial auditors general, who are responsible for reviewing the compliance of government departments, agencies, and corporations with government-wide rules on financial management and accountability, as well as performing value-for-money audits to assess the efficiency and effectiveness of government policies and programs;
- commissioners responsible for monitoring and/or advising on ethics, privacy, access to information, conflict of interest, and sometimes environmental legislation or guidelines.

The structures, mandates, and reporting responsibilities of these offices vary from one jurisdiction to another.

The roles of officers of Parliament straddle internal and external policy processes. On one hand, they are sources of expert, usually non-partisan review of government actions and procedures whose recommendations generally lack the force of law. The mandates of some provincial ethics and conflict-of-interest commissioners may involve enforcement as well as advisory functions. However, in all cases, officers of Parliament are expected to be politically disinterested. On the other hand, their recommendations are often widely publicized and may provide opposition parties and interest groups with a basis for challenging government actions (Roberts 1996; Johnson 2002: 319-26).

Parliamentary and Issue-Specific Caucuses

Backbench MPs and their counterparts in provincial legislatures often play a marginal role in the public policy process, a reality often reflected in the lobbying priorities of interest groups and business lobbyists (Public Policy Forum 2002). Their effective role frequently depends on the leadership styles of individual prime ministers, premiers, and opposition leaders, and the degree to which individual cabinet ministers cultivate caucus opinion and feedback as part of their political styles. It also depends on the political skills of individual MPs or MLAs and their ability to exploit the opportunities available to them within the internal processes of party caucuses or the public forums of parliament.

First ministers and their cabinets tend to dominate the internal policy processes of governments. However, just as conflicts among policy elites and major stakeholders increase the relevance of public opinion to the policy process, they also create opportunities for individual MPs to exercise influence, either by building coalitions within government caucuses or by challenging government actions in Parliament. The ways in which this influence is used depend on several factors:

- the stage in the electoral cycle; that is, the proximity of an election or leadership change and the related jockeying for influence among parties and politicians;
- the political salience of an issue; that is, its relative capacity to generate media coverage and a wide public audience as opposed to issues mainly of concern to specific social or economic constituencies whose support is valued or desired by particular parties;
- the political skills of individual MPs in building intra-party (and sometimes cross-party) coalitions and their gifts for political or policy entrepreneurship.

In addition to their roles on Parliamentary committees, MPs may exercise collective influence through the provincial or regional caucuses of their respective parties and through special-purpose caucuses that bring them together according to the social or economic interests of their constituents or shared personal interests. Clancy (2004) notes that the automotive caucus was composed of 70 Liberal MPs with significant auto industry interests in their constituencies during the late 1990s, while the 35 members of the steel caucus were drawn from across party lines. MPs also organized informal caucuses focused on agricultural issues, insurance and financial services industries, family issues, child poverty, and environmental and economic development issues. Such groups can become politically significant when regional interests square off over government policies or when issues become the subject of intensive political scrutiny, as happened during the highly politicized debate over bank mergers in 1998 (Curtis 1999; Whittington 1999). The *Lobby Monitor* claims that some special interest caucuses are "built, informed and maintained" by major lobby groups and their government relations consultants (*Lobby Monitor* 15:8, 18 February

2004). However, unlike some groups in the US, most have been sufficiently discreet in their tactics to avoid provoking either scandals or public backlash.

MPs must balance the constraints of party discipline—and being seen to be a team player by colleagues and more senior politicians—with the need to assure constituents and friendly interest groups of their efforts to promote their interests within the political system or to cultivate media and public support for their positions. However, the centralization of political power and the cultural norms of Canadian political life generally restrict the autonomy of MPs and their willingness to challenge party hierarchies in favour of discreet internal advocacy on behalf of constituents' economic and social interests.

Interest groups may attempt to identify and cultivate potential champions of their concerns among MPs who will serve as advocates for their interests and provide guidance on the most appropriate ways of framing issues or dealing with parliamentary colleagues (*Lobby Monitor* 15:7, 4 February 2004). Lobbying of MPs may include periodic meetings with lawmakers and staff, sometimes as part of a formal Lobby Day when associations bring large numbers of their members to visit their local legislators to build or reinforce relationships and to provide analysis or information on particular issues (*Lobby Monitor* 14:20, 15 December 2003).

Interest groups often attempt to increase their profile or promote their agendas by testifying before a parliamentary committee. On rare occasions, assiduous lobbying by insider groups may influence potential changes to a government or committee report. However, most lobbyists and interest groups devote a much larger part of their time to dealing with ministers and public servants. It remains to be seen how current proposals for parliamentary reform will affect these processes.

Committees: Mobilizing Consent, Balancing Interests

Although parliamentary committees occasionally initiate the study of policy issues, their primary role is to provide a forum for public consultations initiated by governments and to review legislation, usually after Second Reading in Parliament. Legislative committees in some provinces may also initiate review of order-in-council appointments and government regulations within certain limits.

Legislative hearings may provide opportunities for substantive input by interest groups and expert witnesses, enabling them to draw attention to the shortcomings or opportunities for improvements in current or proposed policies and legislation. They are also an opportunity to educate MPs, the media, and the general public on the factors influencing significant areas of public policy and to propose adaptations (and occasionally major changes) to government policies. At the federal level, Standing Committees on Finance, Industry, and Foreign Affairs and International Trade have conducted a number of major studies, often of considerable quality, on important policy issues in recent years.

Committees may provide a somewhat more collaborative environment for the review of legislation, although their capacity to transcend partisanship depends heavily on the personality and political skills of the committee chair and the willingness of both governments and opposition parties to relax their reflexive partisanship enough to accommodate independent action by individual MPs. The relative effectiveness of committees is also influenced by their ability and willingness to draw on independent sources of research and to accommodate a variety of regional and sectoral interests in public hearings.

The rules governing legislative hearings vary from one jurisdiction to another. Typically, the extent and terms of public hearings will be negotiated by party house leaders, usually in consultation with committee chairs and senior opposition critics. Party discipline and government majorities usually limit the degree to which opposition parties can force the government to accept amendments to legislation, although governments may have to negotiate such changes in minority government settings. The combination of stakeholder views expressed in committees, adverse media attention, and behind-the-scenes lobbying may persuade ministers and their departmental officials to table amendments either during the committee stage or before legislation comes up for Third Reading.

However, as with most aspects of the parliamentary process, government members control most committee processes and outcomes, except during fairly rare periods of minority government. The exercise of this power is almost always subject to party discipline and the overriding authority of cabinet. The greater the degree of partisanship and confrontation displayed in committee hearings, the greater the likelihood that legislative processes will revert to reflex displays of partisanship, modified only to the extent dictated by ministerial judgement and political prudence. Government members may be able to persuade a cabinet minister that his or her legislation requires certain amendments. However, most interest groups seriously interested in influencing the policy processes will carry on complementary public and private lobbying efforts.

Conclusion

The public or external policy processes of governments are as dynamic, complex, and diverse as the political marketplace within which they take place. Institutionalized interests, particularly governments and established stakeholders in major policy communities, enjoy certain advantages in obtaining access to media coverage and in possessing the professional and financial resources to engage in both the news management and image-building aspects of public relations within their selective areas of influence. However, their visibility may also make them vulnerable to challenges by outsider groups, especially when they fail to live up to public expectations they may have cultivated. Changes in government—whether of parties, personnel, or priorities—may also disrupt traditional relationships between governments and stakeholder groups and bring changes to policy discourse: the terms on which issues are discussed or debated.

As with the internal policy processes discussed in the previous chapter, the effectiveness of business and other interest groups in influencing external policy processes requires an ongoing awareness of the markets they are attempting to influence inside and outside government, effective planning and networking with other interests (including the news media), persistence, sound judgement, and a certain amount of luck.

Outsiders who cultivate these qualities can be successful in influencing public debates, although it is difficult for most outsider groups to maintain their motivation and engagement with the political process over an extended period. Those political actors who are most successful are those that invest in the game for the long run by building lasting relationships and taking the time to build the resources, networks, and credibility necessary for effective involvement in the political process. While relatively few outsiders—or even institutionalized actors—succeed in making major changes to the political system, persistent engagement can contribute to significant changes at the margin or to the steady accumulation of incremental changes that add up to a significant legacy for those with the courage, vision, and skill to pursue it.

Key Terms and Concepts for Review (see Glossary)

advocacy advertising
agenda-setting
electoral cycle
framing
gatekeeping
government bill
indirect lobbying
news management
political business cycle

political capital
political salience
private member's bill
procedural legitimacy
public relations
substantive legitimacy
symbolic legitimacy
White Paper

Questions for Discussion and Review

1. Review the last week's editions of a major national or regional newspaper. Using the front pages of the main news and business sections for each day, count the number of stories relating to agenda-setting proposals for policy change. Indicate what percentage of agenda-setting activities are initiated by:
   • elected government officials (federal, provincial, municipal)
   • other government officials
   • MPs or MLAs representing opposition political parties
   • business interest groups
   • other interest groups
   • journalists (by drawing attention to problems)
   • individual business executives
   • individual citizens
   Discuss your findings.

2. What is the difference between public relations and news management? Between news management and propaganda? Give examples of news management as a) a means of promoting a government's agenda; b) a response to structural demands of news coverage; c) a defensive tool for risk avoidance or conflict management; d) a means of diverting public attention from potentially controversial or embarrassing issues.

3. What major roles do the news media play in the policy process? How do these roles reflect the concept of politics as an exchange process, as discussed in earlier chapters?

4. What are three approaches to government consultation processes discussed in this chapter? What opportunities does each approach offer for stakeholders or members of the general public to influence the public policy process?

5. To what extent would you describe the role of Parliament in the policy process as formalized or effective? What factors contribute to or undermine the effectiveness of MPs and legislators in contributing to the policy process? What implications do these processes have for interest groups attempting to lobby governments?

Suggestions for Further Readings

Adams, Michael. 1998. *Sex in the snow: Canadian social values at the end of the millennium*. Toronto: Penguin Canada.

Bricker, Darryl, and Edward Greenspon. 2002. *Searching for certainty: inside the new Canadian mindset*. Toronto: Anchor Canada.

McInnes, David. 1999. *Taking it to the hill: the complete guide to appearing before and surviving parliamentary committees*. Ottawa: University of Ottawa Press.

Mendelsohn, Matthew. 2002. *Canada's social contract: evidence from public opinion*. Discussion Paper P-01. Public Involvement Network. Ottawa: Canadian Policy Research Networks (November).

Mendelsohn, Matthew, and Richard Nadeau. 1996. The magnification and minimization of social cleavages by the broadcast and narrowcast news media. *International Journal of Public Opinion Research* 8(4).

Miljan, Lydia, and Barry Cooper. 2003. *Hidden agendas: how journalists influence the news*. Vancouver: University of British Columbia Press.

Montpetit, Eric. 2003. Public consultations in policy network environments: the case of assisted reproductive technology policy in Canada. *Canadian Public Policy* 29(1): 95-110

Nesbitt-Larking, Paul. 2001. *Politics, the media and society*. Peterborough, ON: Broadview Press.

Rose, Jonathan. 2000. *Making pictures in our heads: government advertising in Canada*. Toronto: University of Toronto Press.

CHAPTER 13

Litigation and the Judicial System: Lobbying by Other Means?

The political system contains a variety of checks and balances on the use and abuse of power. These checks include the federal division of powers and competition among interest groups for the recognition and accommodation of their rights and interests as part of a broader public interest or of the agendas of specific government agencies. Competition among political parties for the support of societal interests, the news media, and public opinion is often significant, particularly when an election approaches.

Another set of checks and balances involves different aspects of the legal system. Constitutional rules and conventions, interpreted, applied, and sometimes invented by the courts, govern the organization of the political system. Laws and legal systems are both expressions of power and systems for constraining and regulating the exercise of power. They prescribe the nature and legal limits of state power and establish protected spheres for the rights of individuals and groups within society.

Canada's Constitution incorporates the conventions of cabinet-parliamentary government, the federal division of powers, and other powers defined in the *Constitution Act, 1867* (formerly the *British North America Act*) and its formal amendments. It also includes assorted laws that serve as provincial constitutions, the *Charter of Rights and Freedoms* (hereafter referred to as the Charter) adopted in 1982, and treaties between the Crown and Canada's Aboriginal peoples. Constitutional interpretation by the courts is heavily influenced by the traditions of British common law, judicial philosophies borrowed from other countries, and the ongoing rulings of the Supreme Court. As a result, the principle of **judicial review**—the power of the courts to determine the constitutional validity of legislation and thus to interpret the meaning and application of constitutional law—is deeply entrenched in Canadian constitutional history. However, the principles that should govern the use of this power are subject to ongoing political, philosophical, and legal disputes (Manfredi 1993; Mellon and Westmacott 1999; McCormick 2000; Morton and Knopff 2001; Weiler 2002). These concepts are closely related to the concept of the **rule of law**: the principles that governments require legal authority for their actions and that citizens, businesses, and governments have both rights and obligations under law.

The proliferation of laws, and the inevitable disputes that arise among citizens or between citizens and governments over the details and principles governing their application to specific circumstances, require the courts to engage in **statutory interpretation**. A principal function of the courts in Anglo-American legal systems has always been to explain, apply, and balance laws that may be interpreted in different ways, although Parliament has usually retained the right to correct these interpretations through the passage of specific legislation. As a result, although judges usually attempt to remain at arm's-length from the political process, particularly its more partisan aspects, citizens, businesses, and political actors have appealed their disputes to the courts from the earliest days of Canadian history (Smith 1983; Strayer 1988; Stevenson: 278-300).

On a more mundane level, citizens, businesses, and interest groups regularly resort to the courts as forums for **dispute resolution**, either in conflicts between governments and private interests, or between private interests over the enforcement of laws and contracts, or to prompt specific actions by governments. However, there remains an inherent tension between the legal function of the courts to interpret laws and the political functions of elected Parliaments and legislatures to define the public interest within their respective areas of jurisdiction. This tension—and the latitude with which judges interpret their powers—may contribute to the **judicialization of politics**: active judicial involvement in the policy-making processes of government.

The interrelationship between law and politics is also visible in the structures and processes of **administrative law** and related disputes which sometimes spill over into the courts. These processes, which allow policy-makers to assign, manage, redistribute, and offload the costs and benefits of regulatory actions, can be used and sometimes abused by politicians, interest groups, businesses, and government officials.

Both **litigation**—the assertion of legal rights and pursuit of legal remedies through the courts and other quasi-judicial bodies—and the efforts of governments and interest groups to define the legal and institutional context in which these disputes are addressed, may be considered a form of lobbying by other means. Traditional lobbying involves the mobilization of political influence or power to promote or protect the interests of particular groups through the political process. Resort to the legal system provides an alternate means for businesses and citizens to assert their rights and interests by enlisting the courts to define the obligations of governments or of private parties in disputes touching on the public interest. It may also serve as a means for societal interests, governments, or businesses to promote alternative policy agendas, especially if the courts can be persuaded that significant constitutional issues are at stake.

This chapter examines the role of the legal system, including the courts and quasi-judicial agencies and tribunals, in managing disputes among societal interests, including businesses, and between societal interests and governments. It examines different forms of litigation to which businesses and interest groups may resort, either by initiating legal action or in self-defence, and considers the implications of these strategies for businesses, governments, and the political process.

Box 13.1: The Law

The Rule of Law: The application of known, predictable, and impartial rules of conduct to rulers and ruled alike. Citizens may be punished by the state only for actions that violate known laws. Governments may exercise authority only under powers and within limits prescribed by such laws.

Administrative Law: Regulations, guidelines, and processes established under enabling legislation to enable and facilitate design, implementation, and enforcement of government policies, often by specialized agencies and tribunals. It usually involves provisions for dispute resolution by specialized tribunals.

Litigation: The assertion of legal rights and pursuit of legal remedies through the courts and other quasi-judicial bodies.

Judicial Review: Courts have the power
- to declare legislation unconstitutional (*ultra vires*)—constitutional interpretation—and
- to review the application of legislation to determine whether governments have proper legal authority to take certain actions—statutory interpretation—or
- whether they have complied with the legal conditions for the exercise of that authority.

The Legal System: Lobbying by Other Means

Litigation involves a wide range of legal actions that can be taken by individuals, businesses, governments, and interest groups. Litigation may be *offensive* in nature, as businesses or other interests use the legal process to challenge an existing government policy. It may be *defensive*, resisting government policies or the actions of other economic or societal actors that may infringe legal obligations in ways that harm the interests of particular businesses, industries, or other societal interests. Litigation may also be an instrument of interest group conflict, as particular groups may use legal action as a way of recruiting the direct or indirect support of particular government agencies or of changing the balance of power between particular societal interests.

Litigation may affect both political processes and economic activity at several levels. Disputes over the interpretation of *private law*, such as legally binding contracts between two or more parties, may set precedents in a wide range of cases under principles of *common law*. They may also prompt varying degrees of government intervention, using a variety of legal tools, in ways that help to structure the environment for the conduct and resolution of legal disputes. Box 13.2 outlines several different types of law which shape the conduct of individuals, businesses, and governments.

Government actions routinely shape and sometimes extend the playing field for private litigation by the ways in which they define the mandates of government departments or quasi-judicial agencies. They may also expand or constrain grounds for private actions. Legal innovations in recent years have broadened the grounds for class-action lawsuits, enabled lawyers to cover the costs of lawsuits by charging contingency fees to their clients, and expanded rights of private legal action to enforce competition and environmental laws, along with the definitions and enforcement of shareholder rights under corporation laws. They also restrict rights of legal action by limiting claims for personal injury under "no fault" insurance or divorce laws, by legislating **privative clauses**, and by restricting the grounds of legal actions against governments, although these measures may be subject to challenges in the courts.

Box 13.2: Types of Law

Private Law
- Legal forms and processes established by agreement among two or more persons.
- Includes private contracts and articles of association (e.g., partnerships, corporate or organizational charters).
- Legal context may be established under *common law, statute law,* related *administrative laws,* or private bills of Parliament or a legislature.
- Disputes may be resolved through appeals to the courts, designated administrative tribunals, or private mediation and arbitration, depending on circumstances and prior arrangements.

Common Law
- Legal principles, practices, and processes that have evolved over many years of judicial rulings on specific legal cases involving both public and private litigants.
- May be modified by amendments to statute law which limit or extend the jurisdictions of the courts or transfer some jurisdiction to administrative law bodies.
- May be used to interpret the wording or application of specific legislative statutes (statutory interpretation) or to modify them to conform to common law principles that have achieved constitutional or quasi-constitutional status.

Statute (or Public) Law
- Laws (or statutes) passed under the authority of Parliament or provincial legislatures within their constitutional jurisdictions.
- May delegate law-making or regulatory authority to other public or private bodies.

Administrative Law
- Specialized forms of law derived by regulatory agencies and quasi-judicial tribunals in particular areas of legal jurisdiction conferred and modified by legislative authority.
- Usually based on regulations and guidelines developed by civil servants or regulatory agencies under delegated legislative authority and the administrative rulings of specialized tribunals on specific cases brought before them.
- Legal processes may be heavily influenced by principles and practices of common law, or by specialized practices and precedents particular to specific areas of legal practice (e.g., labour law, trade law, municipal and related land use laws, environmental law, human rights law, etc.).
- Legal changes may be introduced by changes to enabling statutes, changes in regulatory standards, changes in internal administrative practices, rulings of specialized tribunals, or judicial rulings in response to litigation.

Constitutional Law
- Legal interpretations of formal constitutional instruments, common law principles that have attained constitutional status, and the interaction between them.
- Carried out by the courts, subject to judicial review.
- Subject to formal amendment processes, modification through the ratification of international treaties, and through judicial reinterpretation.

Canada's growing integration within the North American and global economies offers opportunities for litigation over alleged business or government infringement of international treaties governing trade and investment rules and practices, as well as compliance with existing labour and environmental laws in countries that are signatories to such agreements.

Hein notes that societal groups, businesses, and citizens can initiate a variety of legal actions to secure favourable government intervention under existing laws, to limit or discipline the exercise of government power, or to expand the size and scope of governments through judicial action (Hein 2000: 12-13). Such legal actions range from litigation against private (or non-governmental parties), to contesting hostile legal and regulatory actions by governments or other societal actors, to challenging the legal or constitutional validity of statute laws and regulations (Hein 2000: 7).

Governments may also initiate legal action, either to enforce their interpretations of particular laws or to seek favourable rulings from the courts on legal issues that are subject to disputes over the interpretation of specific laws and regulations and their application in particular situations. These actions have political implications to the extent that their outcomes influence the future behaviour of political and economic actors.

More indirectly, government officials and advocacy groups may seek to influence the direction of the courts by sponsoring legal research and publications in areas in which legal innovations may contribute to political and social changes. Monahan and Finkelstein (1993: 46) note that the growing political influence of the courts since the introduction of the Charter has created "a tremendous incentive to try to shape perceptions of the Charter's meaning so as to advance one's political goals."

British common law traditions inherited by Canada's courts have tended to limit legal **standing** in court cases to individuals or groups that are direct parties to a lawsuit, either by initiating legal action or responding to it. In recent years, however, the Supreme Court has become more receptive to written briefs from interest groups that are not parties to a specific legal action on legal issues of public interest. Brodie notes that the most frequent applicants for **intervenor status** are federal and provincial attorneys general, civil liberties and feminist groups, and professional associations representing lawyers (Brodie 2002b: 295-97; Brodie 2002a: 38, 45). Box 13.3 outlines the tactics and targets of litigation by business and other societal groups in ascending order of their potential strategic and political importance.

Hein notes that interest groups seek to redirect government intervention by persuading courts and other legal authorities to interpret existing rules in ways that favour their interests. They may also enlist the power of legal authorities to require governments to exercise their unused statutory powers, often in dealing with disputes between two private parties. Examples of this strategy include appeals to the courts or administrative law tribunals to interpret or apply existing labour legislation and a wide variety of administrative laws and regulations. It may also include legal action to enforce intellectual, contractual, and other property rights under existing laws. Such cases usually involve the application of existing laws rather than efforts to use the courts as instruments in rewriting the law (Hein 2000: 12).

Box 13.3: Tactics and Targets
(in ascending order of strategic importance)

Litigation against private parties
- lawsuits between businesses or between businesses and other private interests (individuals, unions, other societal groups)
- may set precedents for civil actions in unrelated cases

Responses to hostile litigation from other parties
- defence on grounds of fact, competing view of relevant laws
- alternately, may choose to settle out-of-court

Litigation against bureaucratic officials or cabinet ministers
- inappropriate exercise of statutory powers or failure to observe statutory requirements
- may be launched by businesses, other societal groups, or other levels of government in response to perceived breach of contract, failure to abide by existing legal standards; usually does not challenge basic principle of legislation

Constitutional challenges to overturn statutes and regulations
- effort to change law or policy, not just the way it is implemented
- effort to use constitutional rules and principles to restrict or direct government action

Attempts to shape judicial interpretations
- third-party interventions, **amicus curiae** briefs on legal issues
- financing legal actions by other citizens or groups

Interest groups, usually of social activists and labour unions, also seek to use litigation as a means of extending state intervention into new areas to support their interests. This approach lends itself to the pursuit of **strategic litigation**: the *systematic* use of legal action to encourage judicial policy-making on behalf of a particular political or social agenda (Rabkin 1983: 42; cited in Morton 2002: 301). This may involve asking the courts to indicate that a benefit provided to one group of people must be provided to a wider clientele under the equality rights section of the Charter (Section 15), leaving the government to decide how to divide available resources. In *Schachter*, the Supreme Court required the federal government to make Unemployment Insurance maternity benefits available to both parents, while leaving the specific details of legislative adjustment to the discretion of Parliament (*Schachter v. Canada* [1992], 93 DLR 4th: 1).

In recent years, some advocacy groups have persuaded the courts to mandate the provision of particular services to disadvantaged groups, although in *Gosselin* [2002], a Supreme Court majority narrowly rejected the notion that social assistance to able-bodied citizens could be turned into a constitutional entitlement (Simpson 2002: A25). In other cases, litigation may challenge established government monopolies over major public services. In 2005, the Supreme Court ruled that Quebec's prohibition of private health insurance for procedures covered by the public health insurance system were unconstitutional as delays in treatment imposed by long waiting lists within the public system constituted an infringement of the Quebec Charter's guarantees of security of the person (*Chaoulli v. Quebec* [2005], 1 SCR 791, 2005 SCC 35).

Government support for interest groups to use legal action as a way of promoting policy change is controversial. Advocates of government support suggest that the courts have traditionally been dominated by the forces of political, economic, and social privilege, including but not necessarily restricted to business interests. As a result, financing legal challenges to laws or regulations on grounds of legal equity or the promotion of ideological change may enable members of underprivileged or outsider groups to have their day in court. The *political disadvantage theory* suggests that governments are just leveling the playing field among competing societal interests by giving groups with limited political or economic influence the capacity to influencing the political agenda in ways not normally open to them (for a summary of this view, from different sides of the issue, see Hein 2000 and Brodie 2002a: 99-102). Hein describes advocates for such groups and their ideological sponsors as "judicial democrats," implicitly suggesting that critics of their agendas or subsidies are somehow undemocratic (Hein 2000).

Another view of this process has been advanced by former MP John Bryden and by political scientists Ted Morton and Rainer Knopff, who contend that government sponsorship typically enables members of a "counter-elite" or "court party" to seek political and legal power to impose its agenda through the legal process. Rather than overcoming privilege, such influence depends on the sponsorship or favouritism of bureaucratic elites seeking to expand their own power at the expense of other groups inside and outside government (Bryden 1994; Morton and Knopff 2001; Brodie 2002a: 102-22). Ironically, similar concerns are often voiced by left-wing critics of business or interest group appeals to dispute resolution panels set up under international trade treaties. These competing views reflect very different views of democracy and the role of legal systems in governing relations between state and society.

The Role of the Courts and Quasi-Judicial Bodies

Like Canada's political system, its legal system is organized along hierarchical and specialized lines, whose specific details are defined by parliamentary or legislative statutes. The *Constitution Act, 1867* gives Parliament the right to regulate the organization of the federal court system. Legislation governing the composition and powers of the Supreme Court of Canada, the Federal Court of Appeal, the Tax Court of Canada, and federal superior courts fall within parliamentary jurisdiction, although the courts have been quick to strike down any legal or administrative measures they perceive to threaten the independence of the judiciary (*Valente v. the Queen* [1985]; *Reference re: Remuneration of Judges of the Provincial Court* [1997]; excerpted in Morton 2002: 212-37).

Provincial governments may seek legislative authorization to reorganize superior courts, provincial courts, and specialized bodies such as Family or Small Claims Courts, although such proposals are always closely scrutinized by lawyers' associations, legal scholars, and senior judges.

Box 13.4: Canada's Judicial and Administrative Law System

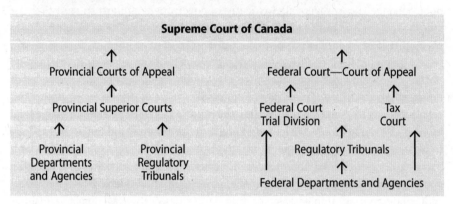

Source: adapted from Johnson 2002: 490.

Both federal and provincial governments have established a series of specialized **quasi-judicial tribunals** and agencies to adjudicate disputes arising from the administration of particular statutes. At the federal level, these tribunals include the Canadian Industrial Relations Board, which hears disputes under the *Canada Labour Code*; human rights tribunals, established under the authority of the *Canadian Human Rights Code*; and the Canadian International Trade Tribunal, the Competition Tribunal, and the Canadian Transportation Agency. Provincial governments have established a wide range of administrative law tribunals to deal with issues ranging from the application of provincial labour and workplace laws to municipal and environmental regulations, securities laws, property tax appeals, and appeals for the removal of professional or business licences, to name only a few (Ontario 1989; Ontario, Agency Review Commission 1997).

How governments structure the enabling legislation governing these institutions makes a substantial difference in the level of political and administrative discretion enjoyed by agency executives and members. It can also help to shape the context in which these agencies attempt to balance competing policy goals or societal interests through their activities or in which their powers are used to advance particular societal interests or ideological perspectives.

For purposes of this discussion, the courts and related agencies may be said to perform three broad functions: **boundary maintenance**: determining whether governments possess the jurisdiction and legal authority to carry out particular functions; **statutory interpretation**: the interpretation and application of specific laws to determine their meaning in particular situations; and **dispute resolution**: applying the law to the specific facts of individual cases brought before them by litigants.

Boundary Maintenance and Constitutional Issues

A central function of judicial review is to adjudicate jurisdictional disputes between governments or between governments and societal interests, including business. They may also address basic questions of property and civil rights central to the economic freedoms and democratic rights of citizens and businesses alike.

Historically, boundary maintenance by the courts has involved the interpretation and enforcement of statutory, administrative, or contractual rules so that "no man is punishable or can be lawfully made to suffer in body or goods except for a distinct breach of law established in the ordinary legal manner before the ordinary courts of the land" (Dicey 1959: 188). This principle is central to the traditional Anglo-American concept of the *rule of law*: the consistent application of known, predictable, and impartial rules of conduct to governments and citizens alike (Dicey 1959: 188-96). As a result, both governments and businesses are liable to legal action if they withdraw unilaterally from the terms of contracts they have signed, although governments sometimes seek legislation to release themselves from their contractual obligations: an action that usually triggers appeals to the courts from aggrieved employees, unions, businesses, or other levels of government.

Prior to the passage of the Charter in 1982, much of the work of the Supreme Court of Canada was taken up with what Brodie describes as "routine commercial appeals" (Brodie 2002a: 26). Many of the major exceptions to this rule were disputes, often referred by business litigants, involving the federal-provincial balance of powers. In some cases, private interests challenged the constitutional jurisdiction of federal or provincial governments to enforce particular legislation. Mallory has suggested that these tactics exploited the federal division of powers by business as an opportunistic strategy for resisting the exercise of state power (cited in Brooks and Stritch 1991: 171). Although there is some truth to this interpretation, many of these actions also enjoyed the active support of other governments actively seeking to extend their own jurisdictions or promote the economic interests of their citizens. Between the 1880s and the 1920s, the Judicial Committee of the Privy Council ruled repeatedly in favour of provincial governments, establishing broad provincial jurisdiction over property and civil rights, the regulation of particular industries, and the provincial regulation of labour relations and other workplace issues (Stevenson 1994; Jackson 2001: 179-80). Broad provincial jurisdictions over economic policies and capital markets are an enduring legacy of these judicial contests; this is in sharp contrast to the relative centralization of powers over economic policies in the US and most other federal states.

However, the jurisdictional tug-of-war can work both ways. During the late 1930s, the Supreme Court of Canada ruled that Alberta's efforts to regulate banks were **ultra vires**, or beyond the legal authority of provincial governments. During the 1970s, resource industries successfully challenged Saskatchewan's efforts to extend its resource taxes to capture windfall profits as an indirect tax that effectively interfered with interprovincial and international trade (Chandler 1983: 58). More recently, the Supreme Court has cautiously expanded federal jurisdiction over some areas of environmental policy as a result of its ruling in *Crown Zellerbach* (*R. v. Crown Zellerbach* [1988] 49 DLR 4th; Baier 2002: 26-27).

Brodie claims that a key factor in shifting the balance of issues considered by the Supreme Court was the 1974 act of Parliament that abolished litigants' right of appeal in commercial cases involving more than $10,000. As a result, the Court enjoyed greater latitude in focusing on a narrower number of cases with broader policy implications. Public law cases accounted for 76 per cent of cases heard by the Supreme Court by 1983, and there have been more in subsequent years (Brodie 2002a: 25-26). Hein notes that although corporations accounted for almost half the legal actions brought in federal courts between 1988 and 1998, most of these actions involved specific legal issues of individual businesses, rather than broad constitutional or policy issues. Interest groups and legal advocacy groups played a much more active role in these areas (Hein 2000).

The introduction of the Charter has expanded the scope of boundary maintenance by the courts in a number of areas. Corporations are viewed as legal persons under the law, generally enjoying the same legal rights as individual citizens. This principle, while challenged on ideological grounds by advocates of more stringent government regulation of business (Mandel 1988: 167-72, 217-38), is consistent with traditional common law rights. The right of businesses to constitutional rights under the Charter was affirmed in *R. v. Big M Drug* (*R. v. Big M Drug Ltd.* [1985] 1 SCR: 295). Some advocacy groups have argued for a formal entrenchment of property rights in the Constitution. Despite strong business support for the principle, it has failed to win general support from smaller provinces who are fearful that it might impair their traditional powers to regulate land use, natural resources, and other forms of property (Sheppard and Valpy 1982: 151; Mandel 1988: 217-18).

Although corporations use the Charter to challenge legislation far less frequently than do interest groups (Hein 2000: 9-13), they have benefited both directly and indirectly from constitutional protections of due process, mobility rights, and free speech arising from Court decisions. They have also been directly affected by Court decisions arising from the equality provisions of the Constitution and the implications of a number of decisions relating to its interpretations of Aboriginal treaty rights.

The most sweeping effect of the Charter on business-government relations has been its implications for the due process rights of citizens and businesses in their dealings with governments. Prior to the enactment of the Charter, government departments and agencies might set up arm's-length appeal processes of bureaucratic decisions, but they were under no obligation to do so. So, civil servants might serve as investigators, prosecutors, and judges in the same case, with limited opportunities for appeal to the courts. To limit court challenges to this inherent conflict of interest, and to reduce the volume of routine court cases, both senior levels of government set up a series of quasi-judicial (or administrative) tribunals to hear appeals of administrative decisions. As a result, businesses or individuals threatened with economic or administrative penalties could receive an independent hearing on disputed issues of fact or law. Although governments have sought to limit further appeals through the frequent use of privative clauses, the courts have often asserted a prior right of judicial review on major legal issues.

The Charter has also imposed greater restrictions on **reverse onus** legislation that forces citizens or businesses to establish that they have *not* broken the law. These tests, which also apply to the *reasonable limits* clause of Section 1 of the Charter, were summarized in *R. v. Oakes* [1986]. First, the restriction on Charter rights, including the right to the presumption of innocence (s. 11), must be a "pressing and substantial objective" for society. Should this test be fulfilled, the means chosen to achieve the objective must be "reasonable and demonstrably justified" according to the following tests:

- a "rational connection" between the government objective and the means used to reach that objective;
- the right that is limited "should be impaired as little as necessary" to achieve the objective; and
- "proportionality" should be achieved between the potentially negative effects of the restriction and the benefits obtained from imposing it. (*R. v. Oakes* [1986], 1 SCR: 103)

Decisions of this kind depend on evidence presented to the courts by parties to legal action, the fact-finding procedures used by the courts to guard against biased or false evidence, and the tension that exists in any judicial process between the consequences of a court's interpretation of evidence for parties to specific cases and their broader implications for public policy. The degree of **judicial deference** used by the courts in evaluating policy evidence presented by governments or quasi-judicial agencies whose decisions are challenged reflects the degree to which judges believe they possess the capacity to "make informed and effective policy choices" (Morton 2002: 363-64). Morton notes that, since the passage of the Charter, judges have demonstrated a greater willingness to engage in judicial policy-making, although the degree of deference that they show to more specialized legal bodies varies widely (Morton 2002: 387-95; see also Johnson 2002: 520-23).

Businesses have also benefited from Charter rights limiting the arbitrary search and seizure of private property, thereby restraining the ability of government regulators to go on intrusive fishing expeditions through corporate records without being able to demonstrate reasonable cause to believe that a law has been broken (*Hunter v. Southam Inc.* [1984], 2 SCR 145; Mandel 1989: 169; McCormick 2000: 121-22). However, while the Supreme Court has acknowledged the right to commercial speech as a form of free speech, it has acknowledged narrower limits to commercial speech that does not bear on "the pursuit of truth, participation in the community, or individual self-fulfillment and human flourishing" (*Irwin Toy Ltd. v. Quebec Attorney Gen-*

eral [1989], 1 SCR 927 at 931-32). Subsequent court rulings have applied similar limits to political speech by corporations and interest groups during election campaigns.

Another aspect of boundary maintenance that has received increased attention in recent years is the role of Canadian courts and international dispute resolution tribunals in defining and limiting the application of state powers through the interpretation of NAFTA and other international agreements administered by the WTO. As noted in Chapter 8, both NAFTA and WTO provisions require foreign firms to receive national treatment, imposing due process requirements on Canadian governments in their application of domestic laws. Parallel challenges to federal legislation were brought forward in 1997; the first, under NAFTA, attempted to ban the gasoline additive MMT made by Ethyl Corporation, and the second was by four resource-producing provinces under the Agreement on Internal Trade. Both demonstrated that legal disputes may often involve cross-cutting alliances among business, governmental, and other societal interests to enforce legal boundaries valued by several parties (Curtis 1999: 62-72).

Litigation and Statutory Interpretation

The meaning and application of laws and regulations are often open to dispute. Unlike the US, where members of Congress and state legislatures exercise active detailed oversight over legislation, the role of elected MPs and MLAs in the review and passage of legislation has been severely diluted in recent decades by executive dominance and the constraints of party discipline.

The legislative drafting process is usually dominated, at both federal and provincial levels, by Justice Department officials who are not always technical experts in the policy or regulatory issues that they are attempting to distil into precise legal language. Moreover, legal language may paper over internal policy disputes or ambiguities that are not resolved during the legislative process. On issues of technical business or tax law, some Senate committees have often been able to draw on high levels of technical expertise, either from prominent senators with extensive legal backgrounds or from corporate lawyers retained to provide expert review of legislation (Hale 2001b: 125; interviews, legal counsel to Senate Banking Committee), leading some observers to suggest that its members have sometimes served as a "corporate lobby from within" (Campbell 1978).

However, whatever the expertise or policy intent of legislative drafters, the complex and dynamic nature of the Canadian economy and of state-society relations frequently leads to disputes over the interpretation and application of laws and regulations. Morton notes that:

> try as they might, legislators will never be able to draft statutes that encompass all future situations. This is due in part to the inherent tension between the generality of words and the specificity of reality, and in part to human ignorance about the future. As new situations inevitably arise, the applicability of the original wording of statutes becomes increasingly questionable. (Morton 2002: 391)

Such circumstances inevitably give judges and courts considerable discretion when interpreting laws and applying them to novel circumstances. To avoid the arbitrary use of discretion, which may bring the law into disrepute, judges frequently rely on the principle of **stare decisis**: the use of existing precedents in order to make similar rulings in similar cases.[1] The outcome of many legal actions depends on the determination of the relevant facts in specific cases. However, disputes over which legal precedents should apply in particular cases often result in appeals to a higher court, and ultimately the Supreme Court of Canada.

Judicial decision-making involves a balancing act between traditional common law processes for determining judicial precedents, which are based on the logical analogy that is nearest in the point of similarity, and fundamental principles of justice, which subordinate existing legal practices to higher principles of equity. Traditional arguments for precedent are rooted in the principle that the law should be predictable, although subject to the capacity to adapt to changing circumstances. Arguments for judicial innovation suggest that political processes are slow and unpredictable and that judges should have the freedom to correct anomalies and injustices in the law if the benefits of such actions would outweigh the potential disruption to existing rights and interests (Post 2002: 397-98; Weiler 1974: 57-65).

Similar processes take place, in more specialized circumstances, in specialized quasi-judicial tribunals such as provincial labour relations boards or the dispute resolution tribunals established under the FTA and NAFTA. These processes will be discussed below.

Implications for Business, Societal Interests, and Public Policy

Litigation may be an effective tool for interest groups and businesses seeking to increase the public and political visibility of an issue, particularly if they can frame the issues in terms capable of mobilizing public opinion. For this reason, interest groups such as the conservative National Citizens Coalition or the feminist Legal Education and Action Fund may use legal test cases as a fundraising tool to complement their other activities. However, such strategies usually have limited appeal to most businesses and business groups, which must deal with the government of the day whatever the outcome of a legal action.

Legal action may be an effective way of undercutting the effectiveness of another interest group by forcing it to devote its limited resources to fending off legal action or of delaying government action until public officials decide that their objectives are more likely to be served by seeking a compromise or out-of-court settlement than in protracted political and legal conflict. However, only businesses or groups with substantial financial, legal, and political resources are likely to pursue such strategies and then only when their other political options are severely limited. Liti-

---

1 A judicial precedent may be defined as "a judicial decision, a form of proceeding, or a course of actions that serves as a rule for future determinations in similar or analogous cases" (Post 2002: 395).

gation requires the financial capacity for a long battle. Civil cases may take three or four years to reach court to obtain an initial ruling. If lower court rulings are appealed and significant legal issues are involved, the entire process may take as long as ten years to get to the Supreme Court, should the latter choose to hear such appeals. Although relatively few groups other than governments and large corporations have the deep pockets necessary for such protracted warfare, the risks of suing the government are increased by the latter's capacity to change the law, even if its initial defence is unsuccessful (Stanbury 1993: 401).

More problematic are legal cases in which companies suffer serious losses, even being driven into bankruptcy by the deceptive or abusive behaviour of public servants, who are sometimes implementing other government policies and sometimes attempting to protect their own reputations or institutional interests by using their legal or regulatory powers to shift political and economic burdens of adjustment on to specific businesses. Such cases may be resolved fairly promptly or drag on for years, depending on the willingness of senior politicians or their officials to take remedial action or to provide political cover for such behaviour. (For example, see Beatty 1999, discussing *Carrier Lumber v. HMQ*, BC; McIntosh 2003b, discussing *Amertek v. Canadian Commercial Corporation*; and McIntosh 2003a: A1.) On the other side, private interests with substantial legal and financial resources (or political connections) can often negotiate settlements of tax or regulatory disputes with government officials, while individuals or businesses with few such resources may be driven to the wall (CBC News 2001: May 2003).

As noted earlier, federal and provincial governments provide funding for some interest groups, such as feminist organizations and anti-poverty or Aboriginal groups. Brodie has demonstrated that most advocacy groups intervening in constitutional cases benefited from continuing financial support from the federal government (Brodie 1997: 90; see also Morton and Knopff 2001: 87-105). However, such grants are rarely available for middle-class taxpayers whose interests may not be served by members of social movements. In some cases, these funds are advanced against the anticipated benefits to be received from potential settlements, for example, in land claims against the government. A protracted case may either deplete the value of any settlement or provide litigants with an incentive to expand their claims further. Although businesses are rarely direct participants in such cases, the political and economic activity resulting from this litigation may affect levels of investment in certain regions, notably BC, where more than 90 per cent of the province is subject to unresolved Aboriginal land claims.

Litigation is a two-edged sword for most businesses. On the one hand, major commercial litigation involving governments can often result in damages of millions—and in some cases, hundreds of millions[2]—of dollars, particularly in major

---

2 Prominent damage settlements in recent years include more than $500 million for the Chrétien government's arbitrary 1993 cancellation of the construction contract for Toronto Airport's Terminal III; $350 million for the *Carrier Lumber* case in BC in 1999, and $170 million in *Amertek v. Canadian Commercial Corporation* in 2003.

public works projects in which litigation drags on for an extended period. On the other hand, legal costs for a major action may well exceed $1 million. In civil cases, the unsuccessful party may be required to pay the winning party's costs. However, the courts usually take the parties' relative ability to pay into account when awarding costs. Businesses that are successful in challenging government agencies in court may still face an adversarial, and even vindictive regulatory environment, thus limiting the potential value of litigation as a tool to achieve significant policy change. As a result, business challenges to public policies often take the form of one-shot efforts to resolve specific legal problems that cannot be remedied by political means or through mutual accommodation within the regulatory process.

The capacity of governments to introduce remedial legislation to reduce or eliminate the benefits of a legal victory makes it necessary for businesses or interest groups to combine political and public relations strategies with their legal strategies as an essential element in risk management. A good example of this process is reflected in government responses to the Supreme Court ruling in *Eurig* (*Re: Eurig Estate* [1998], 2 SCR 565). The Court ruled that the probate fees which provinces used as a de facto inheritance tax on deceased taxpayers' estates before they could be distributed to their heirs—a sizeable sum for many business and farm owners— were illegal because they had not been specifically authorized by legislative action. Most provinces, with the exception of Alberta, simply introduced remedial legislation authorizing the collection of a long list of fees for specific government services. Similarly, the former head of the federal Competition Bureau responded to a 2003 Federal Court of Appeal ruling expanding the use of the efficiency defence in *Superior Propane* by taking steps to overturn the Court's ruling by amending the federal *Competition Act* (Rubin 2003: FP10).

As a result, many observers view litigation as largely a negative weapon, especially for interest groups, that is rarely capable of generating, let alone implementing a new government policy—unless the courts can be persuaded that a significant constitutional issue is at stake.

Administrative Law: The Nuts and Bolts of Business Regulation

Litigation involving citizens, businesses, governments, and other societal interests extends well beyond Canada's court system. During the past 50 years, a parallel system of administrative agencies and tribunals has emerged to deal with specialized areas of policy-making, regulation, dispute resolution, and the enforcement of laws and regulations addressing specialized areas of legal, economic, and social activity. Indeed, the number of legal disputes addressed by administrative agencies and tribunals significantly exceeds those addressed by the courts. These disputes range from routine appeals of property tax assessments or of the rulings of Workers' Compensation Boards on individual eligibility for benefits to complex arbitration and other legal proceedings with the potential to shape the legal environment for thousands of businesses and millions of workers and consumers.

The law, politics, and economics of administrative tribunals and agencies mirrors other aspects of relations between governments and businesses in several ways. Like the policy communities of which they are a part, they are characterized by varying degrees of fragmentation and specialization. The federal government and most larger provinces each have as many as 40 agencies and tribunals with independent regulatory and/or quasi-judicial functions.[3] Major specialized fields of administrative law of relevance to businesses and associated societal interests include those of:

- competition law
- energy and natural resources
- the environment
- human rights
- international trade
- labour relations
- other employment laws
- municipal law and land use regulation
- occupational health and safety
- regulation of securities and financial services
- residential tenancies
- telecommunications.

Agencies and tribunals range from bodies that combine policy-making and administrative and quasi-judicial functions to specialized dispute resolution tribunals which "adjudicate disputes about ... statutory rights and benefits" (Ellis 2003: 1). Many of these policy subsystems are more competitive and open to politically driven change than others, depending in large measure on the relative stability of political and economic relationships and their vulnerability to external political, economic, or technological shocks. Most evolve incrementally as a by-product of the interaction of political, economic, and social forces and of legal trends in one policy field that may spill over into others.

Purposes of Administrative Law

Governments may create specialized administrative agencies and tribunals for several reasons. The core purpose of the structures, principles, and practices of administrative law is to *structure the exercise of discretion* in the balancing of political interests, policy objectives, legal principles, and administrative consistency in the application of technical administrative functions and the adjudication of related dis-

---

3 A review of the federal government's central website identifies at least 41 administrative and quasi-judicial agencies in 2004. The 1996 report of Ontario's Task Force on Agencies, Boards, and Commissions identified 79 quasi-judicial agencies within provincial jurisdiction (Hale 1998a). A 2001 review in BC noted the existence of 67 administrative tribunals before their consolidation in 2001-03 (British Columbia, Administrative Justice Project 2002b: 3). Quebec's 1998 consolidation of tribunals dealing with appeals of rulings relating to administration of social benefits, immigration, land use, business and professional licences, and several other regulatory areas is a notable exception to this general pattern.

putes (Johnson 2002: 523-29). Johnson notes that administrative law both provides governments with a framework for the exercise of their legal power in implementing public policies while clarifying the "legal entitlements, protections and obligations ... of individuals, groups, and corporations" when dealing with public bureaucracies (Johnson 2002: 487).

At one level, independent regulatory agencies were intended to facilitate the creation of independent organizations run by technical experts with the capacity to determine and apply public benefit tests to the regulation of economic activity or management of particular social problems. Such agencies might be created to serve the interests of particular economic interests at arm's-length from the normal workings of government or to institutionalize certain policy trade-offs in the administration of government regulations (Woll 1977: 43-51). Although nominally disinterested, the leaders of these agencies—such as Adam Beck of the Ontario Hydro-Electric Commission during the early twentieth century—have often been policy entrepreneurs with a strong sense of mission and the political skills necessary to challenge established economic interests and build supportive political coalitions to sustain their initiatives (Freeman 1996: 10-58).[4]

Administrative agencies may have explicitly political functions, or they may be used to *depoliticize* the distribution of social or economic benefits or the resolution of disputes between competing interests. In practice, depoliticizing issues usually means extending extensive discretion to self-perpetuating elites of experts to define the concepts and methods that will be used to define and apply the public interest, the administration of justice, or the enforcement of rights as a complement or substitute for democratic or private authority. (For a discussion of the trade-offs of balancing legal, expert, public, and private authority within the political system, see Skogstad 2003.)

These approaches involve competing conceptions of the role of law and regulation: one emphasizes the use of state power to *champion* certain social and economic interests over others as an expression of countervailing power or an instrument of social change; the other is an instrument for the *balancing* of social and economic interests and the *impartial* application of rules within legal boundaries established by legislation. The first approach is often advocated by social democratic and some liberal interests in the hope of curbing the power of large corporations or promoting desired changes in social structures and attitudes. The second is often advocated by centrist politicians, in whatever context, in attempting to balance competing views of the public good or competing social and economic interests whose support they wish to cultivate (Weiler 1968; Galbraith 1975; Wilson 1980). In both cases, businesses and other economic interests are likely to advance their policy arguments at whatever level and in whatever form is likely to serve their individual or collective

---

4 The classic US study of this phenomenon is Caro 1975. These philosophies are inherently political and elitist in that they assume both the technical capacity and moral responsibility of governments to manage these questions in ways conducive to a discernible public interest (Dorreboom 1981: 83-123).

interests. (For recent discussions of the micropolitics of regulation, see Clancy 2004; Goldstein, Cohen, Weiss, and Warrick 2004.)

Delegating legal and regulatory power to administrative agencies fulfills a number of other purposes associated with the criteria of administrative and technical feasibility discussed in Chapter 12. Delegating extensive authority to regulators functioning at arm's-length from government provides them with the potential flexibility to deal with evolving circumstances in the market or social setting that they are attempting to regulate in the public interest without having to return to cabinet, Parliament, or legislature for formal grants of legislative authority. In essence, it is an expression of public trust akin to saying "you're the experts; get on with it." The delegation of so-called rule-making authority to provincial securities commissions, Workers' Compensation Boards, Labour Relations Boards, and other bodies with extensive discretion is a major example of this approach to combining legal, policy, and administrative functions in one body.

The diversion of routine administrative disputes from the courts to specialized bodies with responsibility for dispute resolution may also enable citizens, businesses, and other stakeholders the opportunity to obtain timely, relatively cost-effective dispute resolution or access to justice in individual cases. In practice, giving ordinary citizens efficient access to administrative justice requires a strong philosophical and managerial commitment by agency executives and the systematic organization of legal and administrative processes to ensure their timely provision to litigants.

However, the pursuit of such objectives can easily work at cross-purposes. For example, the *average* time required to resolve complaints to the Canadian Human Rights Commission was 25.2 months before recent administrative reforms cut the average turnaround time roughly in half (Galloway 2004: A4). Indeed, Moreau notes that frequent delays of up to three years in resolving citizens' complaints to administrative tribunals were a major factor in the introduction of reforms to Quebec's tribunal system between 1998 and 2001 (Moreau 2003: 2).

Delegated powers can also be applied to purposes not contemplated by the governments that originally granted them or which emphasize the independence of administrative agencies at the expense of their accountability to governments, citizens, or generally applied common law principles. Regulatory bodies created to serve one perspective of the public interest may come to take a very different view, either as the result of political appointments that reorient their regulatory thrust or prolonged interaction with advocates of particular economic or social interests with whom they come to share a common view of the public interest. These processes are described by Marver Bernstein's theory of regulatory life-cycles: regulatory processes of incremental adaptation and mutual accommodation often lead, over time, to the "regulatory capture" of particular agencies by the economic interests they were originally intended to control (Bernstein 1955; see also Lowi 1985 and Olsen 1986 for the broader application of these ideas to theories of interest group liberalism).

Perhaps the greatest challenge of administrative law is to balance the competing conceptual demands and objectives of quasi-legislative, administrative, and judicial processes. The rule-making processes of regulatory agencies involve competing concepts of democratic accountability and responsiveness that are inherently political to some degree. Rule-making must have some degree of transparency, openness to the participation of relevant publics, and ultimate accountability to elected governments in setting priorities and implementing electoral commitments.

At the same time, effective administration requires that governments delegate sufficient power and discretion to expert authorities to enable them to carry out their responsibilities and to deal with unforeseen circumstances in an often dynamic policy environment (Skogstad 2003). In some cases, policy effectiveness may require the capacity for regulatory agencies to "exercise legislative and judicial power on an independent basis" (Woll 1977: 45; Anisman 2004; also see British Columbia, Administrative Justice Project 2002a and 2002b). However, combining such powers not only raises issues of political accountability, especially following a change of government. It also places administrative and regulatory agencies in an inherent conflict of interest between their partisan role of enforcing a particular view of the public interest and their judicial role of applying the law in ways consistent with the impartial adjudication of disputes.

The political character of these trade-offs exposes them to political competition and legal challenges at a number of different levels.

The Politics of Administrative Law: Contesting Priorities, Processes, and Outcomes

The politics and processes of administrative law involve competition, conflicts, and efforts at consensus-building at several different levels, with the proviso that losers in political or bureaucratic contests that involve significant legal issues of principle or process (or significant transfers of economic power and resources) may attempt to shift the conflict into the general courts.

Administrative law disputes focus on:

- · questions of policy: the purposes or public good to be served by a particular agency and the policy instruments and priorities chosen to serve those objectives;
- · questions of process: have government departments or agencies followed established processes in reaching their decisions, or can innovations or changes in these processes help some or all of the political actors achieve their main objectives more effectively?
- · issues of power: which set of actors should control the priorities and processes of the agency, and in cases of disputed authority, who should have the last word, and why?

By their very nature, political contests to shape and control the exercise of administrative and legal power take place outside the public eye, often within the realm of bureaucratic politics and fairly specialized policy processes. They take place on at least four separate levels: direct political action; appeals to the courts or intermediate tribunals created to resolve administrative law disputes; bureaucratic politics and incremental changes to regulations, administrative guidelines, and processes; and changes to agency or tribunal personnel.

Direct Political Action

Most government regulations are subject to periodic reviews. Sometimes, these reviews are triggered by statutory requirements. At others, they are initiated either by cabinet, senior departmental officials, or regulatory authorities themselves in response to stakeholder pressures, changes in the political or economic environment, or perceived problems limiting an agency's effectiveness.

Regulatory reviews are often the subject of formal consultation processes, such as those discussed in Chapter 12. The extent to which they are symbolic or substantive largely depends on whether they are initiated in response to external political pressures (including those created by a new minister or newly elected government) or the agency's internal requirements and the degree to which agency management is supported or challenged by major stakeholder groups. During the 1980s and 1990s, some governments introduced government-wide policies requiring new regulations to be published for public review and comment, a process mainly of interest to core stakeholder groups and their legal advisors. Others have imposed selective requirements for regulatory impact statements on key constituencies such as small business, women, or the environment.

Legislative and policy reviews are influenced by developments in other Canadian, and sometimes foreign jurisdictions. Political staff, government or agency officials, or interest groups may point to legislative or regulatory developments in other provinces (or at the federal level) as examples either to be emulated or avoided, depending on their political implications and administrative outcomes. As a result, the existence of parallel regulatory processes in Canadian provinces—sometimes at both federal and provincial levels—can serve as a laboratory for policy innovation.

Regulatory structures that are based on the balancing of interests tend to be more diverse between jurisdictions, which at times leads to countervailing demands by business or other interests for greater harmonization of regulations. (For ongoing debates over proposed reforms of securities regulations, see Carpentier and Suret 2003; Committee to Review 2003.) Regulatory institutions whose policy orientation emphasizes the protection and extension of rights may engage in copycat behaviour, with innovations in one province often leading to imitation in other jurisdictions.

The highly technical nature of regulatory activities and quasi-judicial agencies often makes governments reluctant to reopen their enabling legislation except as necessary to implement housekeeping changes initiated by departmental or agency officials. However, extended pressure from major stakeholder groups may lead a government to introduce corrective legislation.

Governments may also attempt to reorganize agencies that are seen to be sources of political or administrative underperformance. This process, while usually requiring legislative authorization, is designed to refocus an agency's mandate to achieve greater administrative efficiencies, to encourage greater responsiveness to the concerns of major constituencies of the governing party, or to resolve territorial conflicts between senior departmental and agency executives. For example, the Ontario government merged the functions of a number of agencies and tribunals during the mid-1990s, partly to achieve greater administrative efficiencies and partly to make them more responsive to the priorities of a newly elected government. More recently, Quebec introduced wide-ranging reforms through the *Tribunal administratif du Québec*, which was created in 1998 to combine the activities of a number of unrelated administrative tribunals, comparable to administrative changes introduced in Australia during the 1970s (Moreau 2003; *Tribunal administratif du Québec* 2006; External Advisory Committee 2003). BC's Administrative Justice Project of 2001-03 combined the consolidation of a number of smaller tribunals with provisions for the standardization of agencies' statutory processes, reforms to appointments processes, and the creation of an ongoing framework for management and governance reforms across the agency sector (British Columbia, Administrative Justice Project 2002a and 2002b; *Administrative Tribunal Act* 2004, Bill 56, 37th Parliament, 5th Session, passed 19 May).

Legal Action

Most enabling statutes creating administrative law agencies make provisions for appeals of agency decisions, including the terms under which they can appeal to the courts. Such actions may involve a dispute between private parties; for example, the dispute may be between an employer and employee, citizens and businesses (or unions), or any of the above and a particular government department or agency. Disputes may be based on issues of fact, issues of administrative or legal process, or substantive issues of legality.

As noted above, the Charter caused both federal and provincial governments to review the structures and mandates of major administrative and quasi-judicial agencies to reduce the likelihood of Charter challenges. In many cases, governments have separated the policy-making and enforcement functions of agencies from those involving dispute resolution and quasi-judicial functions to reduce the likelihood of conflicts of interest. However, Court rulings on these issues tend to vary depending on whether disputes involve "purely economic issues" or broader questions of constitutional rights (Lamer 2001: 41; see also *Newfoundland Telephone Co. v. Newfoundland Board of Commissioners of Public Utilities* [1992] 1 SCR: 623; 2747-3174 *Québec Inc. v. Québec Régie des permis d'alcool* [1996] 3 SCR: 919). In some cases, as noted above, governments have also introduced privative clauses in efforts to limit or narrow the grounds of appeal to the courts.

Historically, the courts have evolved standards that govern the application of **judicial deference** to the decisions of specialized agencies or tribunals on issues of policy within their expertise and jurisdiction. Box 13.5 outlines a number of the tests that the general courts have come to apply when considering whether to allow appeals of tribunal decisions and, if so, whether to uphold or overturn these decisions in whole or in part. Key factors include:

- the relative expertise of tribunal members on the legal and technical issues at stake;
- its members' degree of independence from government;
- the terms under which their enabling statute allows appeals to the courts (and their consistency with existing precedents of constitutional and common law);
- the presence of substantive legal issues that might call the correctness of the decision into account;
- an agency or tribunal's failure to observe its established procedures; and
- the consistency of those procedures with basic constitutional standards of due process.

The greater the degree of expertise and independence possessed by tribunal members, and the greater the extent to which they have developed an extensive jurisprudence (or body of legal doctrines) to balance different aspects of the public interest in carrying out their functions, the more the courts are likely to extend deference to their decisions.

Box 13.5: The Continuum of Judicial Deference to Administrative Tribunals

Correctness	Reasonableness *Simpliciter*	Patent Reasonableness
No deference	Some deference	Deference
Jurisdictional issue	Pragmatic and Functional Factors	Intra-jurisdictional issue (jurisdiction not contested)
Appeal		Full Privative Clause
No Expertise		Expertise/Specialized
Adjudicative Role		Polycentric/Policy
Issue of Law		Issue of Fact
(General		Specific/Narrow)

Source: Carver 2003.

Bureaucratic Politics

The incremental processes of bureaucratic politics are the least transparent and the most likely to be dominated by institutional stakeholders within the system, particularly departmental or agency officials, consultants and lawyers representing key stakeholders, and the chairs of major appellate tribunals.

Initially, policy disputes may be addressed through the creative interpretation of existing regulations. Officials or litigants often seek to introduce creative interpretations of regulations in order to give them greater flexibility or capacity to pursue desired goals through the regulatory process or at the hearings of specific cases by relevant tribunals.

Should such tactics be unsuccessful, departmental or agency officials (or interest groups enjoying support within relevant bureaucracies) may pursue technical regulatory changes under existing statutory authority. Such changes may be given routine approval by cabinet, unless they are subject to external review or effective scrutiny; requirements for prior public notice of changes to regulations have expanded the opportunities available to major stakeholders to review and challenge them. However, regulatory changes may be subject to legal challenge, particularly if it can be established that the regulation exceeds the authority delegated by its enabling legislation. For example, the Ontario government's plans to privatize Hydro One, its electricity transmission utility, were derailed in 2001 when a judge ruled that it lacked the authority to dispose of the utility's assets under the latter's enabling legislation (McFarland 2002: B1).

Regulatory changes, once introduced, may or may not be reversed. However, this process becomes more difficult if government officials can persuade cabinet officials to incorporate the regulations into their enabling legislation either to confirm disputed authority or to codify existing practices and give them formal legislative and cabinet sanction, making them more difficult to challenge or reverse in future except through a major investment of political will.

More controversial are unilateral assertions of regulatory authority, often by quasi-judicial tribunals that wish to redefine or extend their mandates in disputes over the balancing of interests or legal principles at stake in particular cases. Such actions are usually vulnerable to legal appeals and judicial review by the courts, either at the initiative of governments or other aggrieved parties to the case. Claims of constitutional rights to social benefits, or the unilateral extension of Workers' Compensation benefits on terms not previously authorized by boards under enabling statutes are examples of tribunal decisions that have found their ways to the courts.

Agency and Tribunal Appointments

Appointments to government agencies and tribunals are among the last bastions of patronage by governments of all political stripes. Although some governments have created nominal processes for screening potential applicants to ensure their qualifications, most appointments are also screened for political acceptability.

Some appointments, made on the prerogative of the prime minister or provincial premiers, are implicitly political. Others may involve nominations submitted or screened by cabinet ministers (or their staffs) or government MPs or MLAs and may include civil servants with relevant legal or administrative expertise. Senior government officials and agency chairs who have developed working relationships of mutual respect with the government of the day may also play a significant role in the process. Newly elected governments may often attempt to fill vacancies on agencies, boards, and commissions (ABC) with known supporters, if only to limit the capacity for obstruction of their policy initiatives by appointees of the previous government. Most ABC appointees are appointed for limited terms, often three years, but unless they are found to have engaged in illegal or unprofessional conduct, they are generally protected from wholesale removal by an incoming government.

This process has a number of implications for the administrative law process. Governments may choose to correct the behaviour of agencies or tribunals whose actions have generated controversy among key stakeholder groups through personnel changes rather than formal legislative or regulatory changes. This may contribute to tensions within the agency or increase the number of split decisions open to appeal to the courts. Some agencies may become overtly politicized, leading either to legal confrontations, growing political conflicts among stakeholder groups, or the reorganization of particular agencies to limit their capacity to challenge the government of the day. This phenomenon has been particularly apparent in provinces such as BC, Ontario, and Saskatchewan with histories of bitter political and ideological partisanship. BC has recently introduced government-wide guidelines in an effort to professionalize tribunal appointments and apply broader corporate governance principles to the leadership of administrative tribunals and Crown corporations (Watson 2003; British Columbia 2003; Administrative Justice Office, Ministry of the Attorney General, 26 October).

However, there are ways in which governments can contribute to the professionalism and effectiveness of administrative agencies and related legal processes while balancing accountability on issues of policy with independence, accessibility, and even-handedness in the resolution of disputes.

Balancing Accountability, Effectiveness, Responsiveness, and Independence

The low political profiles, technical complexity, and entrenched stakeholder interests characteristic of most policy communities associated with administrative agencies and tribunals create few political incentives for generalized agency and administrative law reforms. However, growing concerns within the administrative law community over the need to encourage higher managerial and administrative standards have contributed to a number of proposals for reform, some of which have been introduced selectively in some Canadian jurisdictions.

These reforms have focused on four broad areas: organizational structures and the structuring of administrative discretion through agency mandates, the standardization of general procedural rules, professional standards for ABC appointees, and the spread of performance standards to improve the delivery of services to the general public.

Structural Reforms

Structural reforms may be designed to increase or reorganize the exercise of regulatory discretion by particular agencies or clusters of agencies, either in response to administrative (including budgetary) concerns or the perceived capture of particular agencies by bureaucratic or societal interests whose ideological outlook or perception of the public interest may vary significantly from those held by the government of the day. Although such changes may be carried out by administrative means, they usually require the passage of enabling legislation to redefine the mandate and accountability relationships of each agency affected.

Other factors that influence agency reorganizations include the desire of governments to streamline regulatory processes, to rebalance the mix of generalists and specialists appointed to particular agencies or commissions, or to coordinate the policy-making activities of lead agencies in related policy communities. For example, in recent years, Quebec and Saskatchewan have consolidated specific agencies responsible for the regulation of insurance, securities, and other financial services industries under the authority of a single organization. Similar initiatives have been attempted in several provinces in the regulation and adjudication of labour and employment-related disputes, although agency consolidation does not necessarily mean the creation of a single agency to serve every aspect of a particular policy field or economic sector.

Structural reforms may also be organized to clarify mandates and accountability. The general trend towards the separation of policy-making and enforcement responsibility from dispute resolution and quasi-judicial functions through the creation of separate policy-making agencies and appeals tribunals has already been noted. Governments may grant considerable latitude to appellate tribunals in reviewing the policy decisions of administrative agencies, often through the loose or ambiguous drafting of enabling legislation or regulations, or strictly limit their discretion by redefining their legislative mandates. However, the more narrowly such mandates are defined, the greater the likelihood that aggrieved stakeholders, especially businesses, will appeal rulings or policy decisions they consider arbitrary to the general courts.

Stakeholder groups who believe that their interests might be or have been sidelined or disregarded by such reforms may also lobby either for the restoration of sector-specific agencies and tribunals or for the creation of specialized divisions within such agencies with the capacity to recognize and accommodate their particular interests. Trends towards consolidation during one period—for example, the deficit reduction campaigns of the 1990s—are often followed by a subsequent decentralization of agency responsibilities, as governments respond to renewed pressures from bureaucratic or societal stakeholders to accommodate their interests and policy agendas.

Failing specific constitutional challenges to enabling legislation, the Supreme Court of Canada affirmed this right of legislative oversight and direction in *Ocean Port Hotel v. British Columbia*:

> Administrative tribunals ... are, in fact, created precisely for the purpose of implementing government policy. Implementation of that policy may require them to make quasi-judicial decisions. They thus may be seen as spanning the constitutional divide between the executive and judicial branches of government. However,

given their primary policy-making function, it is properly the role and responsibility of Parliament and the legislatures to determine the composition and structure required by a tribunal to discharge the responsibilities bestowed upon it. (*Ocean Port Hotel Ltd. v. British Columbia* [2001]: 24)

Government-Wide Procedural Standards

A key dimension of the rule of law is the transparency and predictability of legal processes to define both the rights and responsibilities of government officials, individuals, or businesses, and their legal representatives within administrative law. The vulnerability of agency processes to legal appeals on constitutional grounds of due process, has led some governments to introduce core procedural requirements for their agency sectors such as those outlined in Ontario's *Statutory Powers Procedure Act* and British Columbia's *Administrative Tribunals Act*.[5]

Johnson notes several elements which have become core requirements of "natural justice" in quasi-judicial proceedings, although they may not apply to the operations of all administrative agencies:

- a government hearing on a matter prior to a decision being made;
- notification of such a hearing;
- legal representation at a hearing;
- examination and cross-examination of any and all evidence and argument to be introduced at the hearing;
- direct access to the decision-makers regarding the merits of the case;
- reasonable adjournments;
- conduct of hearings by a fair and impartial adjudicator; and
- written reasons explaining the adjudicator's final decision (Johnson 2002: 492; Johns and DeVillars 1999: Chapter 8).

Government-wide procedural standards are intended to balance basic standards of legal principles and processes governing quasi-judicial agencies and tribunals while enabling each institution some discretion in designing rules and processes best suited to its clientele, mandates, and administrative culture. Other government-wide initiatives may also address such issues as qualification and training of appointees, rules governing ethical standards (including conflicts of interest), and grounds for the termination of tribunal members.

Recent legal innovations in some jurisdictions have also facilitated the adoption of **alternative dispute resolution** (ADR) and case management systems by agency executives to streamline and expedite their administrative processes. ADR includes the creation of specialized or multi-disciplinary teams to address particu-

---

5 *Statutory Powers Procedure Act*, RSO 1990: Chapter S.22. A few other provinces have similar measures, including Alberta's *Administrative Procedures Act*, RSA 2000: c. A-3; Quebec's *Code of Civil Procedure*, RSQ C-25; and BC's *Administrative Tribunals Act*, Bill 56, passed 19 May 2004.

lar or recurring types of appeals or complaints, requirements for pre-hearings to clarify the key facts and legal issues in dispute, and provisions in some cases for third-party arbitration or mediation of disputes. Effective management, a transparent commitment to fairness and impartiality, and ongoing investments in training of both agency members and staff are key factors in the successful implementation of such innovations (Finkel 2003).

These provisions may also facilitate the adoption of performance and service standards for agencies in dealing with the public, sometimes by establishing guidelines and suggested timelines for the processing of complaints, the scheduling of hearings, and the preparation of written rulings. These reforms have been facilitated by the spread of computer and communications technologies that allow for electronic exchange of information and the electronic publication of previous rulings.

However, the effectiveness of such approaches depends heavily on strong leadership by agency executives, especially their willingness and capacity to de-emphasize the entrenched adversarialism that often contributes to time-consuming and highly legalistic approaches to dispute adjudication, in favour of a greater emphasis on timely, fair, and efficient dispute resolution (Hale 1998; Galloway 2004). It may also depend on their capacity or willingness to apply and enforce sanctions such as awards of costs or even the dismissal of cases against both government agencies and private legal counsel who abuse or unreasonably delay agency or tribunal processes.

Such reforms can win the support of business and other societal interests by providing citizens and stakeholder groups with timely, efficient, and cost-effective access to dispute resolution. The greater their transparency, and the greater the commitment of those who conduct them to the fair and impartial application of administrative laws, the more likely that both governments and other societal interests are to resort to such processes in preference to costly and time-consuming litigation through the courts.

Conclusion: Litigation, Policy Advocacy, and the Judicialization of Politics

Overall, the Charter's importance for business and business-related groups has been that the courts have interpreted it with an intermittently individualist slant. They have typically required governments to bear the burden of proof that proposed regulatory restrictions related to Charter issues deal with legitimate public concerns in ways that do not infringe disproportionately on the rights of businesses or other citizens. These restrictions may be objectionable in principle to advocates such as Mandel (1988) who view corporations, large and small, as a privileged class undeserving of the legal protections available to ordinary citizens. However, they have been structured in ways that both allow governments to design regulatory restrictions on business that meet the test of demonstrable public benefit and allow businesses and other societal interests to challenge the reasoning and evidence underlying proposed government actions.

This process shifts considerable discretion to the courts and to the philosophical and policy-making judgements of jurists who may or may not possess the wisdom necessary to serve as latter-day Platonic guardians. However, the judicialization of politics reflects not only the willingness of judges to exercise a much broader policy-making function than in the past, but also the steady decline of checks and balances provided by the parliamentary process. As a result, interest groups are more likely to challenge disputed legislative and regulatory actions in the courts, and politicians are more likely to defer to judges, particularly on highly contested issues, rather than relying on parliamentary review or internal policy processes to strike a reasonable balance among competing interests.

Larger businesses may possess the legal financial resources to protect their interests in such settings, especially when their core interests are at stake. However, doing so on a broader range of issues requires a capacity to address issues of societal legitimacy and to identify particular business interests with more generalized ideas of the public good, not just narrow technical details of law. Although these ideas are likely to be contested at the best of times, current research suggests that those groups most likely to do so are those with strong, clearly defined—if sometimes sharply contrasted—visions of the public interest (Hein 2000; Brodie 2002a).

The Charter has changed the playing field for the use of litigation as an instrument of interest group or business-government conflict. It has contributed to a great degree of constitutional litigation on major policy issues, although, to date, it has done as much to extend as to challenge the legal and economic rights of business within the political process. It has certainly contributed to a shift towards a **rights-based discourse** in the discussion of legal issues and a reduced emphasis on contests over the federal-provincial distribution of powers. Some researchers—notably Morton and Knopff—suggest that litigation by a "Court Party" of Charter-based advocacy groups has lent itself to the creation of a hierarchy of rights, in which some Canadians are "more equal" than others (Morton and Knopff 2001).[6] However, this process has been offset to a degree by the tendency of the courts to favour the rights of individuals over those of institutions.

There are clear parallels between the advantages enjoyed by institutionalized groups and professional advocates in lobbying through litigation and the pursuit of political advantage through the internal and external policy processes discussed in Chapters 11 and 12. Most researchers agree that the advantage in both Charter and non-Charter cases is held by professional litigants: those groups inside and outside governments with the legal, intellectual, and financial resources to familiarize themselves with current legal debates and contest them to best advantage. Typically, governments, ideologically driven advocacy groups—particularly those enjoying the moral and financial support of governments—and major corporations are

---

6 See also Ellis 2003, which uses rights-based discourse as an expression of the author's ongoing attempt to promote his perspective of administrative tribunals as qualitatively indistinguishable from courts, and *The Attorney General of Quebec v. Barreau de Montreal* [2001], JQ #3882, and *Ocean Park Hotel v. British Columbia* [2001].

most likely to possess these resources. They are also likely to focus their efforts in areas likely to provide the greater return on their investment, either in offensive or defensive litigation (Hein 2000; Brodie 2002a: 99-122).

These factors place a heavy responsibility both on governments and on the judicial system to balance a commitment to the rule of law with principles of justice that transcend the interests of any particular social and economic group. It also increases the challenge of balancing interests within the political system and ensuring its openness and responsiveness to Canadians from all regions and walks of life. It is this perceived lack of responsiveness—and the willingness of politicians, civil servants, interest groups, and other policy advocates to cut corners in their exercise or pursuit of power—that makes the legal system a vital safety valve for citizens. Short of significant changes in Canada's political culture, this reality is unlikely to change soon.

Key Terms and Concepts for Review (see Glossary)

administrative law
alternative dispute resolution
amicus curiae
boundary maintenance
dispute resolution
intervenor status
judicial deference
judicial review
judicialization of politics
litigation

privative clauses
quasi-judicial tribunals
reverse onus
rights-based discourse
rule of law
standing (legal)
stare decisis
statutory interpretation
strategic litigation
ultra vires

Questions for Discussion and Review

1. What is litigation? In what ways may it be used for offensive and defensive purposes as an alternative or complement to more traditional forms of lobbying?

2. What are major differences between private law, common law, statute law, administrative law, and constitutional law?

3. What major effects has the introduction of the Charter of Rights and Freedoms had on relations between businesses and governments? On the ways in which governments organize and manage their regulatory processes affecting citizens and businesses?

4. What are three major functions of the courts discussed in the chapter? What implications does each one have for relations between and among governments, businesses, and citizens?

5. How does the political system impose practical constraints on the use of litigation as an alternative to lobbying in political and legal disputes between businesses and governments?

6. What are five major ways in which the structures and processes of administrative law help to structure the exercise of discretion in the design, implementation, and enforcement of many laws and government policies?

7. How does the combination of policy-making and judicial functions associated with administrative law expand opportunities for litigation as a form of lobbying? What measures can governments take to structure their exercise of discretion to reduce both opportunities and incentives for litigation as an expression of political and economic competition and conflict?

8. What factors contribute to expressions of judicial deference towards administrative agencies and tribunals? What factors increase the likelihood of successful appeals of tribunal decisions to the courts?

Suggestions for Further Readings

British Columbia, Administrative Justice Project. 2002. White Paper: On balance: guiding principles for administrative justice reform in British Columbia. Victoria, BC: Ministry of the Attorney General (July).

Brodie, Ian. 2002. *Friends of the court: the privileging of interest group litigants in Canada*. Albany, NY: SUNY Press.

Hein, Gregory. 2000. Interest group litigation and Canadian democracy. *Choices* 6:2. Montreal: Institute for Research in Public Policy (March).

Johnson, David. 2002. Canadian administrative law. In *Thinking government: public sector management in Canada*. Peterborough, ON: Broadview Press. 487-523.

Manfredi, Christopher. 2000. *Judicial power and the Charter: Canada and the paradox of liberal constitutionalism*, 2nd ed. Toronto: Oxford University Press.

McCormick, Peter. 1994. *Canada's courts*. Toronto: James Lorimer.

Morton, F.L. (Ed.). 2002. *Law, politics and the judicial process in Canada*, 3rd ed. Calgary: University of Calgary Press.

Mullan, David (Ed.). 2003. *Administrative law: cases, text and materials*, 5th ed. Toronto: Emond Montgomery Publications.

Ontario (1989). Macauley Report: *Directions: review of Ontario's regulatory agencies*. Toronto: Management Board of Cabinet (September).

CHAPTER 14

Business, Political Parties, and the Electoral Process

The relationship between business and political parties is a perennial source of controversy in Canadian politics. These controversies are caused partly by the ideological debates over the exercise of business influence and power discussed in Chapter 3, especially the link between large-scale financial contributions to political parties (or the ability to mobilize such contributions) and the visible pursuit of political influence by business and professional interests allied to the governing party. At another level, they relate to the fine line between patronage and corruption, particularly in the distribution of economic benefits by governments to individual businesses and professionals, and their potential impact on the integrity and efficiency of government operations.

There is a broader issue: are political parties instruments of representation in the political life of the nation or vehicles for political and social elites (and aspiring counter-elites) to mobilize voters through processes of political persuasion, manipulation, and control? The shift of power within party organizations from elected officials to clusters of unelected strategists and personal networks clustered around party leaders, which has paralleled the steadily declining influence of Parliament and legislatures within the Canadian political process, has arguably changed the nature of relationships between businesses, interest groups, and political parties, even as it has changed the nature of parties themselves (Whitaker 2001).

This chapter explores the evolving relationship among businesses, interest groups, and political parties as a reflection of the different structures and changing functions of political parties, interest group competition, and the recruitment of political elites. It examines the relationship between money and politics and the different approaches taken by government to the regulation of party and campaign financing and the involvement of non-party organizations in election campaigns.

Political Parties: Representation, Mobilization, and Competition among Interests

Political parties are formal associations organized to contest elections and elect candidates to public office. Like interest groups, they serve as what some political scientists have described as "intermediaries between societies and the state" (Carty, Cross, and Young 2001: 16). Although parties are often described as instruments of political representation, largely through the candidates they nominate and succeed in electing, they are also instruments for the mobilization of financial resources, campaign workers, and popular support to serve the interests of party leaders, elites, and candidates between and especially during election campaigns.

The relationships among businesses, business groups, and political parties have evolved during the past 30 years in tandem with the proliferation of interest groups, the professionalization of interest advocacy, and changes to the regulation of financial contributions to political parties. Just as differences in government organization and the legal and constitutional powers exercised by governments, noted in previous chapters, affect the ways in which businesses organize to influence public policies, the interaction between businesses (and other interests) and political parties reflects varying and evolving patterns of party structure, organization, and competition.

The changing forms of business engagement with political parties—as with involvement by union and other societal activists of different kinds—are shaped in part by what Carty and Eagles describe as the "franchise structures" of local party organizations (Carty and Eagles 2005). Individuals and groups whose interests are localized tend to participate in party organizations as volunteers, mobilizing volunteer and financial support for candidate nominations and local election campaigns; however, relatively few corporate executives are attracted to political careers. A smaller group of businesses (and, more rarely, business organizations), including major law, government relations, and advertising firms, provide employment opportunities for party organizers and strategists, usually as part of ongoing investments in the political process. Although changes to federal campaign finance laws passed in 2003 place strict limits on donations to federal political parties by businesses, unions, and other organizations, business contributions remain a significant source of financial support for political parties in most provinces.

Business Influence and Political Parties: An Exploration

The notion of business influence reflects the elite or class-based concepts of political competition and power described in Chapter 3 that distinguish between the actions of individuals who happen to own or manage businesses and the capacity of a cohesive group of business leaders or interests to shape the priorities of other political actors to accommodate or conform to their priorities and preferences. Questions of business influence appear over politically contentious issues in which the interests of most businesses are seen to conflict with those of governments or of a broader public or in which political decision-makers are seen to be beholden to particular economic interests in ways that conflict with widely held views of the public interest.

Functional specialization within the political marketplace has reduced the role of political parties—at least in their nominal roles as representative political organizations—in government policy processes. Political parties, whether on a national, provincial, or local scale, serve as vehicles for the selection and development of political leaders and candidates, the organization and financing of party and leadership campaigns, and the framing of broad priorities by parliamentary parties— particularly when in opposition—which may either accommodate or marginalize business interests in their pursuit of power. Contests between and within political parties often help to shape the context for the external policy processes of governments (discussed in Chapter 12), largely as contests for positioning as part of the adversarial game of parliamentary politics. However, a more important function may be that of selecting and recruiting political leaders capable of winning public office and shaping party priorities and policies on major issues.

Leadership Selection

The centralized authority of political party leaders, particularly in governing parties or parties considered effective competitors for power at an upcoming election, makes their selection one of the most significant functions of modern Canadian political parties. Strong leaders effectively define their party's tone and public image and determine its priorities in defining campaign themes and appeals for public support. They decide which of their colleagues will play leading public roles by appointing them to senior cabinet and critics' positions, and they sometimes go beyond party ranks to recruit prominent candidates.

In recent decades, business influence in the selection of party leadership candidates has usually been indirect, at least in parties that actively solicit their political and financial support. The extent of business influence depends partly on the rules governing leadership conventions or elections and the funding required to compete effectively for party leaderships. The move from leadership conventions, which involved the mobilization of local party leaders to support individual candidates at a national or provincial convention, to various forms of one-member, one-vote elections during the 1990s, appears to have significantly increased the costs of contesting effective leadership elections. Some observers have suggested that it has also shifted power within parties from local and regional party organizations to groups of professional campaign strategists and party activists capable of mobilizing the organizational and technical resources necessary to mount effective leadership campaigns (Whitaker 2001; Bateman 2001).

One advantage that large corporations, major law firms, and, more rarely, industry associations may offer to prospective leadership candidates and their senior advisors is the prospect of a well-paid sabbatical from electoral politics that enables them to recharge their intellectual and financial batteries, cultivate their personal networks, and prepare for an eventual return to the political fold. This pattern can be seen by the temporary retirements of former Prime Ministers Turner and Chrétien into major Toronto law firms before returning to contest the leadership of their parties, former Prime Minister Brian Mulroney's tenure as president of Iron Ore of Canada between his party leadership races of 1976 and 1983, and a few prominent cases in Ontario and Alberta politics.

Leadership candidates whose personal campaign networks can mobilize significant financial resources, as Paul Martin's organization did in 2002-03, or who are wealthy enough to finance much of their own campaigns, as Belinda Stronach was reported to have done in contesting the 2004 Conservative leadership race, can both attract professional campaign talent and effectively marginalize or pre-empt capable but less well-heeled candidates. Conversely, the PC Party's substantial dependence on Toronto business interests to fund its campaigns after its fall from power in 1993 made it vulnerable to the threat of a potential boycott from its principal fundraisers, who ultimately pressured its leader Peter MacKay to accede to a merger with the Canadian Alliance after publicly promising that he would never do so in order to secure his party's leadership in 2002.[1]

Although Paul Martin raised more than $10 million in his campaign to replace Jean Chrétien as federal Liberal Party leader, Chrétien got revenge by introducing changes to federal campaign finance legislation that sharply limited business financial contributions to political parties, local candidates, and leadership campaigns and that replaced parties' largely voluntary and unenforceable codes of disclosure with public disclosure of contributions through Elections Canada. Regulations governing limits on or the disclosure of donations to provincial leadership candidates vary widely.

Setting Party Priorities

The capacity of business interests to influence the broad priorities and election platforms of political parties depends on several factors, not least the extent that individual parties identify themselves with pro-business or pro-market economic policies. Social democratic parties such as the NDP or the PQ, which are not traditionally sympathetic to corporate interests, may still seek to accommodate business as a way of projecting a commitment to competent fiscal and economic management. Other parties, particularly in provincial two-party systems characterized by historically business-oriented and social democratic parties, may actually discount business support on many issues in order to appeal to swing voters capable of influencing election results in marginal constituencies. These observations are consistent with Anthony Downs's marginal voter model of political competition first articulated in the 1950s (Downs 1957).

Patterns of party competition also influence leadership selection processes, how leaders of governing parties engage particular economic interests, and the degree to which business interests are perceived within society to contribute to or detract from politically significant aspects of public well-being in comparison to governments or competing societal interests. Leaders of well-entrenched governments are more likely to set the terms for their engagement with business and other economic interests, whatever their ideological perspective, thus requiring businesses to conform to prevailing political or policy norms within particular jurisdictions. The capacity of business and other economic interests to exercise political leverage largely depends on the nature of party competition and the existence of strong opposition parties willing to ask for business support in developing alternative appeals for public support.

---

1 Well-placed sources within the Canadian Alliance have told the author that Toronto business interests attempted to use similar tactics against Stockwell Day during the 2000 federal election. However, Day's ultimate ouster from the party leadership was largely the result of internal party divisions and a decline in the large number of personal contributions on which both the Reform and Alliance parties historically depended.

Structures of Party Competition

The capacity of business interests to influence the context of party competition depends on how many political parties have the capacity to compete for political power, either by winning the parliamentary majorities that often emerge from Canada's single-member plurality (SMP), or first-past-the-post electoral system, or by holding the balance of power in a minority government. Structures of party competition reflect prevailing party systems in two ways: how parties are organized and how leaders and party elites mobilize the resources necessary to win and hold power.

Political scientist Kenneth Carty has identified four broad party systems that have shaped Canada's political system. The first, extending roughly from Confederation to the end of the First World War, was made up of loose coalitions of partisans and their economic associates or clients, whose loyalty often depended on the promise or provision of patronage in the forms of jobs, government contracts, and public works. Business and professional people frequently sought to promote the economic interests of their communities and regions, which were often hard to distinguish from their own, through networks of political factions that eventually coalesced into two relatively stable political parties—the Liberals and the Conservatives—albeit with differing patterns of regional support (Carty 1992; Carty 2000; Stewart 1986; Noel 1992). Political fundraising usually took the form of soliciting contributions from the business and professional networks surrounding party leaders or of extracting contributions from party supporters who had received government jobs and contracts.

The second party system, from the 1920s to the end of the 1950s, resulted from fragmentation of political parties along regional and class lines following the economic disruptions caused by the First World War and the Great Depression. Its major innovation in federal politics was the emergence of extra-parliamentary parties, which served to distance party leaders (and public works ministers) from the necessity of personal engagement in party fundraising and organization with the accompanying risks of scandal (Whitaker 1977). A key function of extra-parliamentary parties was to separate policy development from party building, although the persistence of close personal ties between some cabinet ministers and leading business figures somewhat blurred these distinctions.

The regionalization of the federal party system was paralleled by the emergence of provincially and regionally distinct patterns of party competition, several of which have persisted to the present day. BC and Saskatchewan have been characterized by ideologically polarized patterns of two-party competition between socialist or social democratic parties and business-friendly coalitions with varying degrees of populist coloration. Alberta has been managed by a series of single-party dominant governments based initially on agrarian interests (United Farmers of Alberta, 1921-35); then on farmer and small business support (Social Credit, 1935-71); and subsequently on a coalition of corporate, small business, and agrarian interests under PC governments that have held office since 1971. Manitoba has had a relatively stable two-party system since the 1940s, although the NDP replaced the Liberals as the primary centre-left party during the late 1960s. Similarly, while Ontario's current three-party system emerged during the late 1930s, the PCs' capacity to build evolving coalitions of urban, rural, and later suburban interests under successive leaders enabled them to retain power for 42 years between 1943 and 1985. Quebec's party system has been polarized between broadly federalist and nationalist parties since the mid-1930s, with the sovereigntist PQ replacing the Union Nationale as the main party of Quebec nationalism in the early 1970s. Party politics in Atlantic Canada were generally characterized by single-party dominant Liberal regimes between the 1930s and the 1950s, followed by two-party brokerage politics characterized by strong leaders and patronage-driven politics.[2]

The regionalization of provincial party systems effectively privileges local economic interests, including those of particular businesses and industries, over external business interests. The growing separation of federal and provincial party systems since the 1970s contributes to the development of separate networks of influence around federal and provincial parties and governments, although some party organizers, many of whom populate the ranks of the government relations industry, may gravitate back and forth between Ottawa and their provincial capitals depending on the political fortunes of political leaders with whom they are connected. The capacity of outside business interests to obtain access to such networks of influence may be a significant factor in their competition with established local interests in dealings with provincial governments.

The third federal party system, prevailing between the early 1960s and the early 1990s, encouraged more widespread participation in political parties, particularly at the local level and in leadership politics, in the hope of creating pan-Canadian parties that could transcend both the regionalism of earlier party systems and the cozy, sometimes corrupt backroom networks that often insulated party organizations from public opinion and popular influence. In practice, the hopes and promises of these reforms were fulfilled primarily in the *franchise bargain* (Carty and Eagles, 2005) of party organizations. With some exceptions, party elites allowed local activists to control the selection of local parliamentary and legislative candidates and to play an active role in periodic leadership elections. However, control over party policies, priorities, and the packaging of election campaigns remained primarily in the hands of party leaders and, to varying degrees, cabinet ministers (for governing parties) and parliamentary caucuses (for opposition parties), with periodic party conventions serving an advisory role, at best. Many of these characteristics have been carried over into the current party system, which emerged from the break-up of the Mulroney government coalition into its regional components, with much greater regional fragmentation in party support.

Business influence is most likely to be significant in single-party and two- or three-party systems dominated by **brokerage parties**, as in Ontario, Atlantic Canada, and

---

2 The primary exceptions were Newfoundland, characterized by Liberal dominance under its founding Premier Joey Smallwood until 1972, and Nova Scotia, with a closely balanced three-party system since the early 1990s.

federal politics during much of the twentieth century. Brokerage parties attempt to assemble broad cross-sections of social and economic interests, including elements of business, geared to winning a majority of electoral districts. Business usually has significant representation in at least one of the two major parties, which compete to demonstrate their competence in economic management, encouraging business investment and economic diversification, along with other issues. Business influence is usually least significant in minority government settings, particularly when a social democratic party holds the balance of power and is able to extract significant policy concessions from the governing party in order to retain its support.

Persistent single-party dominant systems, such as those prevalent in federal politics during the 1990s and Alberta politics since the 1940s, incorporate a range of business interests into broader strategies of economic and social development mediated by party leaders and the government bureaucracy. Business interests are usually well represented in setting government priorities, but only to the extent that they are consistent with the government's retention of political dominance, as dominant party leaders usually have sufficient political security and autonomy to determine who will be consulted on which issues and when.

The main exceptions to the dominance of brokerage parties in Canadian politics are found in provincial politics, particularly in provinces characterized by strong social democratic parties committed to extensive state regulation of business and economic activity. The polarization of Quebec politics around the sovereignty issue since the early 1970s has typically resulted in the alignment of much of the private corporate sector with the Quebec Liberal Party, much of the state-based corporate sector (and most public and private sector unions) with the PQ, and competition between both parties for the support of small business interests. Party competition in Manitoba, Saskatchewan, and BC—all of which have elected NDP governments in recent years—reflects varying degrees of ideological polarization mitigated by the persistence of populism, especially in party appeals to swing voters and the extensive rural hinterlands of each province.

A serious side effect of the regional fragmentation of federal political parties under the fourth federal party system has been that no political party has been able to secure consistent electoral support from all parts of the country. The Liberal Party's domination of the largest region—Ontario—allowed it to form majority governments during the decade after 1993. However, their organizational weakness in Quebec, combined with the near loss of the 1995 sovereignty referendum, created political conditions for the systematic diversion of millions of dollars of public funds by government departments and Crown corporations to government-friendly advertising agencies and party organizers during the late 1990s that subsequently became notorious as the Quebec sponsorship scandal. The immediate result of this scandal, discussed later in this chapter, was the introduction of federal campaign finance legislation substantially limiting corporate contributions to political parties. However, the scandal—and the revelations of the Gomery Commission of Inquiry appointed to determine its extent and causes—also points to the hollowing-out of party organizations, particularly those of federalist parties in Quebec, and the relative weakness of Canadian political parties as broadly based instruments of popular representation.

Proposals for electoral reform now circulating in several provinces[3] could change the nature of the relationship between voters, political activists, and parties, depending on how candidates are selected or traditional patterns of geographical representation replaced by some degree of proportional representation reflecting province-wide distributions of votes. However, as with existing variations among federal and provincial party systems, businesses and other societal interests are likely to adapt their engagement with the political system to these changes.

Changing Structures, Functions, and Patterns of Influence

The evolution of party systems discussed above reflects both the broader dynamics of political contests and the effects of technological and legal changes affecting the competition of political parties for the support of voters and organized interests. Even as party organizations were being opened to varying degrees of popular influence during the 1960s and 1970s, several other factors combined to shift the overall emphasis of political parties towards political mobilization in the service of party elites and aspiring leadership candidates.

Television became an increasingly important tool for party strategists and advertising and marketing specialists to reach a mass audience and contributed to the centralization of power around party leaders, along with the progressive depersonalization of parties' representative functions. The technologies and organizational apparatus of modern fundraising and campaign organization require large sums of money, together with the professional expertise to use it effectively. As a result, the professionalization of politics in the era of mass communications has encouraged the centralization of power within political parties.

At the same time, the progressive bureaucratization of the policy process has marginalized political parties as agencies for policy debate and advocacy. Established governments look to their credentialed advisors in the public service as the main conduits for policy ideas, for guidance on effective policy implementation, and for dealing with interest groups and public consultations (as discussed in Chapters 11 and 12). Opposition parties are more likely to borrow policy ideas from think tanks, business groups, and other economic interests, particularly when these groups are shut out of official consultation processes. However, the packaging of election priorities, platforms, and messages still usually remains the tightly guarded privilege of advertising executives, pollsters, and campaign strategists clustered around party leaders and focused on appeals to carefully targeted groups of swing voters.

Since the early 1990s, the spread of leadership election rules providing for the emergence of a mass selectorate, based on some version of one member-one vote, appears to have transformed political parties into personal vehicles for political entrepreneurs

---

3 At time of writing, five provinces—BC, Ontario, Quebec, New Brunswick, and PEI—are considering reforms to their electoral systems.

who can mobilize significant professional resources, and the funds to pay for them, to use as platforms for the pursuit of office. Whitaker (2001) notes that these **virtual parties** of professional organizers and communications experts have come to play central roles in organizing the resources necessary to take control of party organizations, mobilizing different elements of the voting public to support their bids for power and, if successful, in colonizing the upper reaches of governments.

Business executives and partners in major professional firms may provide employment to the key organizers of favoured leadership candidates, chair fundraising events, and provide other services, thus influencing the potential viability of competing campaigns even before candidacies are formally declared (Winsor 2001: A7). Although some political and campaign staff later become candidates for public office, many others gravitate into positions in government relations firms, large corporations, interest groups, and the public service which may enable them to develop independent careers while continuing to participate in party politics.

This cross-pollination of personal, professional, and political networks often provides a fertile source of strategic, organizational, and financial support for party leadership candidates. All major candidates in the 2002-03 federal Liberal leadership race drew heavily on the support, expertise, and networks of government relations professionals with previous government experience, several of whom were reported to have received significant retainers to lobby the departments headed by their preferred candidates (Clark 2002: A4; Delacourt 2003). These relationships prompted widespread expressions of concern over the ethical implications of revolving doors between party backrooms, government relations firms, and senior appointments in the PMO. Similar trends have been observed within the governing parties of most larger provinces.

These concerns have been reinforced by the traditionally unregulated and often opaque nature of fundraising for leadership campaigns. Some candidates systematically exploited their government positions to raise funds from business clients of their departments, while others established large trust funds of unregulated and largely unreported corporate and other private donations (Leblanc 2003: A4). These controversies probably contributed to legislative changes in 2003, which sharply limited corporate donations and made all donations over $200 to party leadership and local candidate nomination campaigns subject to public disclosure through Elections Canada. Provincial leadership contests are subject to varying degrees of regulation and transparency.

Politics, Bureaucracy, and the PAL Syndrome

The emergence of virtual parties of pollsters, advertising executives, and lobbyists, combined with continued bureaucratic dominance of the policy process, has increased the challenges of designing and marketing government policies in ways that contribute to their legitimacy by addressing or responding to public sentiments and priorities while maintaining traditional distinctions between the activities of public servants and political professionals. As a result, the **PAL syndrome**—the close relationships of political strategists (many of them former political staff of or campaign advisors to elected officials), consultants, advertising executives, and lobbyists with bureaucratic policy-makers—has become increasingly visible. These relationships are often associated with the application of more relaxed rules on government contracting for polling, advertising, and legal services often provided by people and businesses that just happen to have close personal and professional ties to the party in power. Thus patronage in these functions persists, often in sharp contrast to other areas of government purchasing, along with efforts to maintain it within politically acceptable limits by attempting to limit perceptions of improper influence and the appearance of outright corruption.

At one level, the system reflects the specialization of functions within the political marketplace. Public servants often have limited expertise in the marketing of public policies, particularly when it comes to identifying current public perceptions or patterns of public opinion, and in presenting policies in ways that engage such perceptions or priorities effectively. These skills are part of the stock-in-trade of market research professionals who work for polling, advertising, and government relations firms whose personnel tend to overlap with governing party networks (for example, see McGregor 2005: A1; Clark 2005: A6; Canadian Press 2005: A14). Since politicians prefer to work with people they know and have come to trust, the balancing of policy goals with political objectives is often carried out through the cooperation of senior public servants with professional consultants whose talents can be applied with equal facility to the marketing of policy ideas and political campaigns.

The management of these relationships requires considerable political and ethical judgment on the part of all participants in order to minimize real or perceived conflicts of interest or the misuse of public funds for largely partisan political purposes, such as those revealed by the Gomery Inquiry of 2004-06 into the Quebec sponsorship scandal. These perceptions are likely to be more damaging when cabinet ministers or senior political staff become involved in allocating public funds or when former political associates resurface as lobbyists (registered or otherwise) for economic interests seeking favourable policy consideration or government contracts.

Another dimension to these relationships is how market research or government relations firms that are part of the PAL system, other economic interests, and major media outlets serve to mobilize networks of interest or generate publicity that appear to be unconnected to influence from political parties. For example, it is not uncommon for certain market research firms with close professional ties to governments, political parties, and well-known political figures—or all of the above—to publish the results of proprietary polls that suggest clear links with the agenda-setting strategies of different clients nominally at arm's-length from one another.

Changes to federal lobbyist registration legislation passed in 2005 (paralleling similar measures in Quebec) require disclosure by former public office-holders of their former positions of trust when filing disclosures of intent to lobby governments, along with the names of their clients and the subject of their activities. Other changes proposed following the release of the Gomery Report include longer cooling-off periods before former politicians, political staff, and public servants can lobby former colleagues; more extensive provisions for lobbyist disclosures; and the elimination of all corporate and union financial contributions to political parties (Conservative Party of Canada 2005).

As noted in Chapter 10, the federal Conservative government elected in 2006 was pledged to the introduction of "accountability legislation" that would preclude lobbying by "former ministers, ministerial staffers, and senior public servants" (*Lobby Monitor*, 2006: 2) for five years after leaving government along with other reforms to increase transparency and accountability in government. Provincial standards continue to vary widely from minimalist approaches in Alberta and parts of Atlantic Canada to more extensive regulations in Quebec, Ontario, and BC.

For some observers, these issues simply mirror the traditional interaction of party elites and businesses, with each trying to structure the relationship to serve their respective interests. For others, they are part of a larger debate over the proper identities of political parties—as voluntary private associations or formalized (public) institutions for structuring political representation—that raises basic questions of the measures needed to bring greater openness, accountability, and integrity to public life (Institute for Research on Public Policy 2002: 20-21, 46).

Historically, these issues have focused on the politics of party finance and the ways in which its regulation by the state may enforce greater transparency and accountability on political parties.

The Politics of Party Finance

The relationship between money and politics is a perennial source of controversy in Canadian politics. Political parties need money to contest elections and finance ongoing operations such as party organization, candidate recruitment, polling, and periodic leadership elections. In recent years, national party budgets between elections have ranged from $3 million to $8 million annually.[4] Historically, much of that money has come from businesses, particularly for Canada's two traditional parties, the Liberals and Conservatives; in fact, the federal Liberals received 75 per cent of corporate contributions to major national parties between 2001 and 2003 (Stanbury 1991: 291-93; Stanbury 2001: 182-85). Local party campaigns frequently depend on large numbers of contributions from small businesses and local professionals, although local spending patterns vary heavily with party strength in different parts of Canada (Carty and Erickson 1991; Sayers 1999: 89-100).

Academic discussions of the political power of business have focused on the position of large corporations as the major source of campaign funds for Canadian political parties. A significant portion of major business contributions have often come from companies that are beholden to governments for contracts and public works spending or that are members of regulated industries. Over the years, the size

---

4 2003 Liberal Party spending totaled more than $20 million, including the costs of the party's leadership convention (Elections Canada).

of their contributions have raised concerns over the potential for corruption or the exercise of undue influence. These issues become increasingly controversial during periods of intense class conflict or during economic downturns, when the role of governments in allocating economic opportunities became more visible.

Since the mid-1970s, federal and provincial election laws have sought to democratize the process of political fundraising through a combination of tax subsidies for smaller private donations and increasing levels of public funding. They have also attempted to make political contributions and party spending more transparent through increased public and media scrutiny in order to enhance political accountability and limit opportunities for the improper exercise of influence by large donors. A series of political scandals arising from the use of public funds for partisan political purposes by the Chrétien government between 1997 and 2003 has led to a series of changes in campaign finance legislation intended to close previous loopholes, limit political contributions from businesses and other socio-economic interests, and expand public funding of political parties.

Money, Political Parties, and Business: An Historical Overview

The politicization of economic policies and opportunities has drawn businesses into political involvement since the earliest days of colonial government (see Chapter 4). Parties extracted political contributions from businesses in return for access to government contracts, while major companies often invested large sums of money in political campaigns in the expectation that their investment projects would receive favourable treatment from government. The abusive fundraising practices noted by political observers included practices such as **tollgating**—the payment of fees in return for consideration for government contracts—and **kickbacks**: the payment of a percentage (or sliding scale) of contracts to the governing party as a type of insurance policy. While these tactics gradually became illegal as forms of extortion or bribery, subtler variations have evolved with the passage of time.

Outright bribery was comparatively rare and was usually considered politically and socially unacceptable when it was found to occur. However, large corporate contributions to a government's campaign funds were a well-recognized way of securing favourable consideration for the donor's interests. The Macdonald government was thrown out of office as a result of the Pacific Scandal of 1873, after it was discovered that its recent election victory had been largely financed from the deep pockets of Sir Hugh Allan, Macdonald's preferred choice to oversee the building of the CPR. Interests associated with the Beauharnois Power Company contributed $750,000 (worth at least 10 times that amount in 2000) to Prime Minister Mackenzie King's unsuccessful re-election campaign of 1930 in order to have preferred access for contracts to build a hydroelectric dam on the St. Lawrence River near Montreal.

Between the 1930s and 1960s, both major political parties were heavily dependent on the corporate and financial interests of Montreal, Toronto, and Vancouver to finance their campaigns. During that period Stanbury (1991: 316) has noted that

90 per cent of both the Liberal and Conservative parties' funds came from Canada's largest corporations.

The Election Expenses Act of 1974

The rules of the fundraising game were changed dramatically by the federal **Election Expenses Act** of 1974. The act required full disclosure of all campaign contributions of $100 or more and gave tax credits on a sliding scale to contributors. It also imposed spending limits on election campaigns and provided partial refunds on campaign spending from tax revenues as long as parties complied with federal regulations. Other federal laws regulated party access to television advertising during elections.

Election expenses reform had several purposes, some complementary, others expressing different political philosophies that have subsequently come into conflict. On the one hand, the three leading parties of the time sought to prevent large-scale spending in local constituency races in order to limit the capacity of wealthy candidates to buy their election, even though contemporary evidence suggested that such lavish displays of political extravagance could prompt as much voter resentment as support. In theory, spending limits created the potential for more competitive riding contests; in practice, the regionalized support of most political parties limited the number of genuinely competitive races in most elections. On the other hand, the relatively loose spending limits imposed on national parties and the broad loopholes in defining these limits imposed relatively few restrictions on national political parties. Parties with the capacity to raise and spend large amounts of money through corporate, direct mail, and other fundraising techniques would receive generous subsidies from the Canadian taxpayer.

The provision of tax credits for individual contributions—75 per cent on the first $100 ($200 after 2000) up to $550 on a total contribution of $ 1,075—helped parties to broaden their fundraising base. The federal PCs and NDP rapidly developed broad fundraising networks to complement their traditional reliance on corporate and union funds, respectively. The federal Liberals gradually followed suit.

It was hoped that the application of full disclosure rules for corporate contributions to parties and individual candidates would limit the potential for undue influence and corrupt practices, although the 1990s witnessed the exploitation of a series of loopholes in the act, including anonymous donations to local constituency funds or MPs' private trust funds, although such donors would not be eligible for tax credits (Stanbury 2001: 196-97).

Provincial governments have passed similar legislation, although the details on contribution or spending limits and what should be reported, vary widely from province to province. All provinces impose rules on spending and donations. Newfoundland is the least restrictive, as it only limits the amount of anonymous donations. Quebec and Manitoba are the most restrictive, permitting only individual voters to make contributions to parties and/or candidates (Mowrey and Pelletier 2002: 2-8). Table 14.1 notes that five provinces limit the total contributions allowed by individuals or businesses in a calendar year. Changes to the federal *Election Expenses Act* in the late 1990s raised the ceiling on tax credits payable to donors while expanding the reporting requirements for expenditures. In practice, these rules are to the advantage of incumbent MPs in most constituencies.

Stanbury has noted that only a "tiny fraction" of business corporations, and fewer than 40 per cent of Canada's largest corporations, made political contributions during the 1980s, a pattern that has continued in recent years. However, large contributions—those of $10,000 or more—have accounted for more than 20 per cent of Liberal and PC revenues in recent years (Stanbury 1996: 77). Although the federal PCs retained much of their business support following their huge losses in the 1993 election, the Liberals gradually become the major beneficiary of business contributions, especially after 1997.

Table 14.1: Regulations on Election Spending

Jurisdiction	Limits on election expenses	Limits on contributions during a year or election period	Regulation of third-party advertising in an election year	Blackout period	Restrictions on opinion polls
Canada	X	X**	X	X	X
Newfoundland/ Labrador	X			X	
PEI	X				
Nova Scotia	X				
New Brunswick	X	X		X	
Quebec	X	X	X	X	
Ontario	X	X		X	
Manitoba	X	X			
Saskatchewan	X				
Alberta		X			
BC	X		X	X	X
Yukon Territory					
Northwest Territories*	X	X		X	
Nunavut*	X	X		X	

Notes *Political parties do not exist in Northwest Territories or in Nunavut.
** Added by Bill C-24, 2003.
Source: Mowrey and Pelletier 2002: 2-8.

The federal NDP has relied on a wide range of small donations from supporters, significant contributions from union locals, and from its provincial wings, which historically had broader fundraising capacity due to their status as the governments or official oppositions in three of the four western provinces. The Reform Party and its successor, the Canadian Alliance, were largely dependent on large numbers of individual donors, especially between elections, although the Alliance was able to access the support of the Ontario PCs' successful fundraising apparatus during the 2000 campaign.

The extent and importance of businesses' financial support for provincial parties varies widely depending on local campaign finance rules and patterns of political competition. As noted above, Quebec and Manitoba ban contributions by businesses, unions, and non-residents. A review of election expense disclosures in recent provincial elections notes sizeable variations in both contribution and spending levels in other large provinces. Table 14.2 summarizes major party contributions in the most recent elections in Ontario, BC, and Alberta.

Table 14.2: Party Finances in Recent Provincial Elections

	Contributions Received	Per cent from Individuals	Corporations	Unions	Others	Government Subsidies
Ontario (2003)*						
Liberal	$10.1 mm.	37.8%	38.5%	6.1%	6.2%	17.5%
PC	$9.3 mm.	40.2%	42.0%	0.2%	–	17.6%
NDP	$2.9 mm.	60.9%	4.9%	15.0%	–	19.2%
BC (2004)						
Liberal	$11.3 mm.	20.2%	70.0%	0.0%	9.8%	–
NDP	$6.0 mm.	65.0%	3.3%	31.2%	0.4%	–
Alberta (2004)*						
PC	$3.4 mm.	43.2%	56.8%	–	–	–
Liberal	$0.3 mm.	65.6%	33.8%	–	–	–
NDP	$0.4 mm.	97.2%	1.2%	1.5%	–	–
Alberta Alliance	n/a					

Notes: * Includes contributions to constituency associations; bold: winning party; italic: incumbent government.
Source: Provincial Electoral Commissions.

The rules of party competition—how party leaders and local candidates are selected, parties are organized, elections are contested, and campaigns and party organizations are financed—are usually defined by party elites to facilitate their pursuit of power, subject only to the need to preserve a façade of legitimacy in the eyes of party supporters and the more attentive elements of the general public.

Reforming Federal and Provincial Election Finance Laws

Campaign finance laws were subject to relatively minor changes during the 1990s. Critics noted that these changes contained numerous loopholes that protected the interests of political party elites, including:

- the lack of regulations governing contributions to leadership campaigns;
- no requirements for disclosure of contributions to trust funds or local constituency associations;
- minimal restrictions on spending outside the formal election or writ period, allowing parties or candidates to engage in substantial pre-election spending off the books;
- the creation of revolving funds, including the so-called in-and-out method by which party supporters made donations to campaigns, were reimbursed for their volunteer service, and then donated the money back to the party, thus attracting larger tax credits for the donor and greater public subsidies for the local campaign;
- the lack of restrictions or requirements for disclosure of staff time donated to campaigns by professional lobbyists, unions, businesses, and other organizations. (Stanbury 2001: 196-202)

Several of these issues were addressed in **Bill C-24**, election finance legislation introduced by Prime Minister Chrétien prior to his retirement in 2003 in response to the sponsorship scandal noted earlier. The legislation imposed strict contribution limits on individuals, corporations, and trade unions. Individual donations were limited to an annual maximum of $5,000 to each registered party and its electoral district associations, candidates, constituency associations, and nomination contestants. A separate $5,000 contribution limit was imposed for contributions to leadership campaigns.

Corporations, unions, and other organizations were precluded from contributing to national party or leadership campaigns, although total donations of up to a maximum of $1,000 to a party's candidates, nomination contestants, and electoral district associations were still allowed to accommodate existing patterns of fundraising, particularly from local small businesses.

National party spending limits were increased and public subsidies to parties increased sharply to an annual maximum of $1.75 for each vote received during the previous federal election to compensate for the loss of business and union donations. Direct subsidies to local candidates were also increased from 50 per cent to 60 per cent of election spending for candidates receiving at least 10 per cent of the popular vote. Spending limits were also imposed on nomination campaigns. The tax subsidy for individual donations to political parties was also increased to 75 per cent of the first $400 donated annually to a maximum of $650 for total donations of $1,275 or more (Robertson 2003). Table 14.3 outlines patterns of public subsidies to political parties in federal and provincial legislation.

Arguably, Bill C-24 has substantially reduced the financial influence that businesses can exert over parties in federal politics. However, it has also increased the autonomy of party elites from citizens and voters, reinforcing broader trends of recent years. It is too early to determine whether these changes will inspire emula-

tion from the provinces or what implications, if any, they will have for public participation in the political process.

Table 14.3: Provisions on Public Funding

Jurisdiction	Tax credit on contributions	Annual allowances to political parties	Reimbursement of election expenses to political parties	Reimbursement of candidates' election expenses
Canada	X	X**	X	X
Newfoundland/ Labrador	X			X
PEI	X	X		X
Nova Scotia	X			X
New Brunswick	X	X		X
Quebec	X		X	X
Ontario	X		X	X
Manitoba	X		X	X
Saskatchewan	X		X	X
Alberta	X			
BC	X			
Yukon Territory	X			
Northwest Territories*	X			
Nunavut*	X			

Notes: *Northwest Territories and Nunavut do not have political parties.
** Added by Bill C-24, 2003.
Source: Mowrey and Pelletier 2002.

Political Competition: "Third" Party Campaigns and Contending Views of Democracy

The regulation of party and campaign finance has long raised questions over the
relationship between political parties and interest groups as well as over the rights
of individuals or groups other than political parties to promote their interests and
agendas during election campaigns. The 1991 report of the Royal Commission on
Electoral Reform and Party Finance recommended that the right of interest groups
to engage in advertising during election campaigns be strictly curtailed.

Changes to federal election laws introduced in 1993 and 1996, but subsequently
overturned by the courts, sought to outlaw non-party advertising campaigns during
election campaigns or to impose strict limits on non-party spending, respectively.
This legislation was successfully challenged in the courts for infringing on constitu-

tional guarantees of freedom of expression. Bill C-2, passed before the 2000 federal election, allowed for a $1,000 maximum limit for individual or group contributions, with limits on the pooling of contributions by associated groups.

The debate over non-party advertising during election campaigns involves contending views of democracy, freedom of political speech, and the relationship between political parties and other societal interests—including those representing business and organized labour—in the electoral process. Different Canadian jurisdictions have dealt with these issues in different ways, depending in part on the balance of political forces, the self-interest of political elites, and prevailing cultural attitudes towards the political system.

In some cases, non-party campaigns involve efforts by interest groups or citizens to promote their views on issues in order to inject them into the public debate with or without the support of political parties. In others, the role of parallel non-party advocacy campaigns has become a major public issue. For instance, during the 1988 federal election, federal political parties placed different levels of emphasis on the issue of free trade and the proposed FTA, but business groups supporting the agreement and union and other activist groups opposing it ensured that free trade became the dominant issue of the campaign. Business groups are estimated to have spent at least $6 million in support of the FTA. Organized labour and other groups opposed to it, including some business interests, spent at least $1 million, although many observers believe that they received comparable public relations value for their investment.

In the absence of credible evidence to determine the relative impact of non-party advocacy campaigns during elections on voter choices, political and legal debates on the issue have tended to polarize on three different levels:

- the appropriate means to provide equality of political speech and opportunities for participation in the political process;
- the relative merits of political parties and interest groups as instruments of representation within the political process; and
- more recently, the capacity of governments to restrict political contributions and expenditures to ensure a level regulatory playing field.

Egalitarianism versus Freedom of Speech

The classic argument in favour of limiting non-party advertising during election campaigns is that it tends to privilege large, well-organized, well-funded interest groups at the expense of ordinary citizens. Although it is sometimes phrased in terms of hostility to political activism by business groups, the argument could be made with equal force against the electoral activities of organized labour and related groups, which have organized major campaigns to defeat small-c conservative governments in recent years. The egalitarian argument emphasizes the right of all citizens to equal participation in the political process. As only a relatively small minority of citizens possesses the disposable income necessary to engage in expensive advertising campaigns, the logic of this argument suggests that all citizens should be so restricted.

This position is strongly disputed by some social groups as a fundamental affront to the principles of freedom of speech and freedom of association. They note that contemporary political parties are rigidly centralized, leader-dominated organizations dedicated primarily to the pursuit of power. Major party election campaigns focus on the techniques of news management (discussed in Chapter 12), the cultivation of a favourable image, the repetition of a few key messages selected by party strategists and pollsters, and the systematic disparagement of their opponents. As a result, the only way for citizens or interest groups who believe their interests to be marginalized in this game of mutual manipulation is to seek alternative ways of bringing their messages to the attention of the general public.

A side effect of regulating and restraining electoral speech by unauthorized actors may well be to discourage independent citizen participation in elections, as suggested by political scientist Bradley Smith (2001: 8), without enhancing participation in or commitment to political parties as the dominant vehicles for political participation.

Evidence of the effectiveness of non-party campaigns is mixed. For example, organized labour and other opponents of the Harris government made systematic efforts to promote strategic voting in the 1999 Ontario election, but with limited success. However, this campaign may also have facilitated that government's efforts to polarize the campaign by portraying its opponents as tools of special interests and to win an additional term in office. However, Stanbury notes that the regulation of campaign financing has been accompanied by declining levels of participation by both citizens and businesses, while Cross indicates that individual membership in political parties is increasingly sporadic and linked to the mobilizing efforts of leadership or local candidates (Stanbury 1996; Cross 2004).

Parties versus Special Interests

The role played by political parties as instruments of representation through the electoral process is the second subject of debate. In Canada's parliamentary system, elections are intended to select a government rather than to debate particular issues. Candidates and political parties should be judged on their relative fitness for office or on their capacity to organize a leader, team, and platform capable of governing the country in the broader public interest. Interest groups, by definition, represent a particular view rather than the good of the country or community as a whole. As they are not seeking election, their participation independently of political parties and candidates is seen either as irresponsible, in the sense of pursuing power without accepting political responsibility to voters as a whole, or as providing an unfair advantage to parties or candidates whose interests they may champion.

This position may be challenged either on pluralist or populist grounds. Interest groups can bring alternative perspectives to the discussion of public issues that might otherwise be ignored by political parties or candidates attempting to avoid inconvenient or controversial issues. Alternately, non-party campaigns may be seen as a way for citizens to challenge the systematic manipulation of public opinion by political elites.

Leveling the Regulatory Playing Field

The introduction of strict limits on campaign contributions by individuals and businesses has added a third dimension to the debate: the need for regulation of campaign spending to be comprehensive in order to be effective. The prevailing regulatory regime between 1974 and 2003 emphasized very high overall national spending limits for political parties and relatively modest limits in local constituencies. The campaign finance reforms introduced in 2002-03 added limits on individual contributions to all "emanations" of political parties. Failing to regulate spending by individuals could be seen as creating an *unlevel* playing field for candidates and parties. The rebuttal emphasizes that spending restrictions are so restrictive—an average of $3,000 for associated groups in individual constituencies, $160,000 across the country—that groups other than political parties are effectively excluded from participation in electoral debates.

Judicial responses to such arguments vary with the cultural context in which litigation is carried out. Courts in Quebec are much more sympathetic to collectivist approaches to the regulation of electoral speech, as indicated in the Quebec Court of Appeal's ruling in *Libman v. Quebec* [1997] 3 SCR 569. The Ontario Superior Court accepted both the necessity of a common registration requirement and the notion that existing spending limits of $1,000 per constituency for individuals and $3,000 for groups acting in concert tended to preclude rather than merely regulate electoral speech (*Commissioner of Canada Elections v. National Citizens Coalition*, Ontario Court of Justice [2003]).

However, in a ruling released during the 2004 general election, the Supreme Court of Canada strongly sided with the restrictionist outlook, indicating that Parliament was within its rights to impose a regulatory regime on both individual contributions to political parties and to independent non-party spending (*Harper v. Canada, Attorney General* [2004] 1 SCR 827). It remains to be seen whether this ruling resolves the issue of non-party campaign spending or whether a future government will be willing to accept broader spending limits that expose it to the prospect of organized non-party challenges during future elections.

Conclusion

Recent trends in the organization and regulation of political parties and the financing of election campaigns may well be related as much to the perceived needs of political elites to address appearances of corruption as to actual corruption, as suggested by moral authorities as different as former Prime Minister Jean Chrétien and the US Supreme Court (*Buckley vs. Valeo* [1971], cited in Smith 2001: 6). Although the changes to campaign finance laws discussed above are too recent to provide any evidence of their impact on Canadian politics, the historic effects of campaign finance reforms have been to redirect, rather than to limit, the role of money in politics, whatever its origins.

Some corporate executives and business owners will welcome the respite from the fundraising activities of political parties. Others will seek opportunities to exercise influence over them, perhaps in ways far less transparent than the remaining requirements of provincial campaign finance laws for public disclosure of campaign contributions.

Issues of campaign financing may address, at the margins, questions of the capacity of political parties to provide effective representation to societal interests. However, the general irrelevance of Canadian political parties, as organized electoral machines, to policy formation ensures that such debates are likely to be carried out in response to the calculations of political elites and the evolving bureaucratic processes of government with greater or lesser degrees of public consultation. To the extent that the domination of political processes by political, economic, and cultural elites discourages the engagement of ordinary citizens and business people, Canada's democratic processes will continue to be impoverished and greater scope will be given to opportunists of all political complexions to exploit the resulting spread of public cynicism.

The main constraints on such outcomes are likely to be the diffusion of political and economic power, the exposure of self-interested behaviour by measures calculated to increase the transparency of the political process, and the willingness of citizens to hold governments accountable for their actions between and during elections. To the extent that citizens—including business people—can gain an informed understanding of how the system works and can link this understanding to a vision that both includes and transcends their own interests, they may give added substance to their citizenship and enhance the incentives of other political actors to do the same.

Key Terms and Concepts for Review (see Glossary)

Bill C-24 (2003)	PAL syndrome
brokerage party	tollgating
Election Expenses Act (1974)	virtual parties
kickbacks	

Questions for Discussion and Review

1. What are three major functions of political parties? How do the factors necessary for electoral success both create opportunities for and limits on business influence within political parties?

2. What implications has the professionalization of political entrepreneurship had for the representative functions of political parties and their relationships with business and other societal interests?

3. What were the major features of the *Election Expenses Act* of 1974? What impact did the act have on fundraising by political parties?

4. What major changes to federal party finance laws were introduced by Bill C-24 in 2003? What are some of the implications for political parties? For relations among party elites, party members, and contributors?

Suggestions for Further Readings

Cross, William. (Ed.). 2001. *Political parties, representation and electoral democracy in Canada*. Toronto: Oxford University Press.

Sayers, Anthony. 1999. *Parties, candidates, and constituency campaigns in Canadian elections*. Vancouver: University of British Columbia Press.

Stanbury, W.T. 1991. *Money in politics: financing federal parties and candidates in Canada*. Toronto: Dundurn Press.

Stanbury, W.T. 2001. Regulating federal party and candidate finances in a dynamic environment. In *Party Politics in Canada*, 8th ed., ed. Hugh Thorburn and Alan Whitehorn. Toronto: Prentice Hall. 179-205.

Whitaker, Reg. 1977. *The government party: organizing and financing the Liberal Party of Canada: 1930-58*. Toronto: University of Toronto Press.

Young, Lisa, and Keith Archer (Eds.). 2002. Regionalism and party politics in Canada. Toronto: Oxford University Press.

administrative feasibility: The capacity of governments to mobilize the legal, fiscal, and personnel resources necessary to translate their objectives into desired outcomes.

administrative law: Regulations, guidelines, and processes established under enabling legislation to enable and facilitate design, implementation, and enforcement of government policies; often involves provisions for dispute resolution by specialized agencies and tribunals.

advocacy advertising: Advertising that presents information intended to advance the sponsor's point of view on a particular issue.

agenda-setting: 1) The means by which issues and concerns are recognized as candidates for government action; 2) the selection of issues for intensive or extensive media coverage, reinforcing or challenging political, economic, and cultural assumptions that shape perceptions of the public interest.

aggregate demand: The overall consumption of goods and services within a particular time period and jurisdiction.

Agreement on Internal Trade (1995): The agreement between federal and provincial governments to reduce barriers to the movement of goods, services, people, and capital among provinces.

alternative dispute resolution (ADR): Non-traditional approaches to the resolution of legal disputes that provide for the diversion of all or part of certain legal actions from the courts or quasi-judicial tribunals, either at the discretion of the parties to the dispute or as means of expediting the judicial process.

amicus curiae: Literally, friend of the court; a brief submitted on legal or constitutional issues associated with a particular legal action by an individual or organization that is neither the plaintiff or defendant in the case.

attentive actors: Individuals and organizations that function at the margins of a particular policy community or process, but whose influence and support may become important in the event of major disputes within or among the subgovernment or major stakeholders.

automatic stabilizers: Policies that have the effect of automatically contributing to the growth of overall purchasing power (see **aggregate demand**) by increasing the income available to individuals or the cash flow available to businesses during economic downturns without discretionary actions by governments. Conversely, policies may increase taxes or reduce income transfers on individuals and businesses, thus constraining levels of economic activity during periods of above-average growth.

Auto Pact (1965): The agreement between Canada and the US providing for tariff-free trade for automotive products between the two countries. It resulted in the rapid growth of the Canadian industry within an integrated North American automotive sector.

Bill C-24 (2003): Federal legislation which sharply restricted contributions to political parties by businesses and unions, and expanded disclosure requirements for political contributions and spending to include constituency nomination and party leadership campaigns.

boundary maintenance: The role played by courts and quasi-judicial bodies in determining whether governments possess the jurisdiction and legal authority to carry out particular functions in response to legal challenges initiated by governments or private parties.

bounded rationality: The concept that individuals or groups invest in various activities (including the pursuit of political information, expertise, and influence) to the degree they stand to benefit from these activities, but no further.

broadly based (or "comprehensive") business association: Organization representing a broad cross-section of businesses from a wide range of industry sectors.

brokerage party: Political party which seeks to assemble broad cross-sections of social and economic interests in the pursuit of power rather than emphasizing ideological consistency.

brokerage politics: An approach to politics that attempts to balance a broad variety of interests within a political party in order to secure power rather than emphasizing ideological considerations or the interests of particular regions, social, or ethnic groups.

business liberalism: A political outlook committed to the fostering of private enterprise and a favourable business climate while accommodating competing interests in government policies to promote political and social stability.

Caisse de dépôt et placement: Crown corporation that serves as the investment arm of the Quebec Pension Plan; a major participant in Quebec's "province-building" strategies since the 1960s.

Canada-US Free Trade Agreement (FTA) (1988): Comprehensive trade agreement negotiated between the US and Canada in an attempt to secure Canadian access to US markets, and to limit the effects of US protectionism. Later expanded to include Mexico under the North American Free Trade Agreement (see **NAFTA**), it reinforced the growing economic integration of Canada and the US.

Canadian direct investment abroad (CDIA): Investments by Canadian companies in subsidiaries located outside Canada.

capital gains/losses: Profits or losses made from the sale of business assets or shares of corporate ownership.

capital markets: Processes for organizing and mobilizing savings and investments from varied sources to meet the financial needs of individuals, businesses, governments, and other economic actors.

cartel: Economic agreement among businesses or governments to manage markets and limit competition.

C.D. Howe: Leading federal cabinet minister (1935-57) responsible for economic reconstruction after the Second World War, he was the champion of business-oriented policies and strategic government intervention in key industries; he also supported large-scale foreign investment to promote economic development, a policy which was later challenged by **Walter Gordon.**

central agencies: Government agencies or organizations for the coordination of government-wide policies and priorities.

class-based theories: Emphasize the role of economic and class interests in shaping political and economic institutions and choices. Some theories emphasize class conflict as a primary element in defining political debate (see **Marxism**).

clientelism: A clientele relationship exists when an interest group succeeds in becoming, in the eyes of a given administrative agency, the natural expression and representative of a particular social sector which, in turn, constitutes the natural target or reference point for the activity of the administrative agency.

closed policy communities: Policy-making systems in which governments have the capacity to limit interest group access to the policy-making process, and to set and enforce conditions of participation.

closely held companies: Ownership and control of a corporation is held by a small group of shareholders; effective control may be held by shareholders with as little as 10 per cent of voting shares.

commercial Crown corporations: Government business enterprises (**GBEs**) that generate revenues by selling services at commercial rates, defined either by market competition or the need to cover their costs and generate market returns for their government shareholders. They pay their own operating expenses, including interest on their debts.

commercialization: The application of business practices to the delivery of government services up to and including full privatization. It may include the competitive provision of goods and services under normal commercial conditions, the contracting-out of the production or delivery of goods and services by government departments and agencies, the creation of internal markets to encourage competitiveness and greater efficiencies in the provision of public services by public sector employees and contractors, and the introduction of other market conditions in the management and delivery of public services.

complementary federalism: An approach to federal-provincial relations in which federal and provincial governments carry out related but operationally independent functions that recognize areas of common and discrete jurisdiction.

complex interdependence: The effect of multiple relationships among nations and their citizens that prevent national governments from taking independent action in one area without creating political, economic, and social consequences for themselves and their citizens in other areas.

corporate concentration: The degree to which particular industries are controlled by a relatively small number of corporations; usually associated with **oligopolistic** industries.

corporate governance: The legal and managerial processes for setting priorities and providing internal accountability within corporations, accommodating shareholder preferences, and ensuring compliance with external legal requirements.

corporatism: A **regime** characterized by direct participation in the policy-making process by central (or "peak") organizations representing major economic stakeholders (e.g., business, organized labour). In return for preferential access to the policy process, stakeholder groups tend to lose a degree of their policy-making autonomy. (See also **sectoral corporatism** and **societal [or liberal] corporatism**.)

countervailing power: The ability to mobilize political or economic power to offset or limit the influence of competing groups.

deadweight loss: The net economic gain or surplus that could be generated by achieving a more efficient distribution of resources.

defensive economic nationalism: Theory of government-led policies of economic development and national self-assertion initiated as a defensive reaction to US political and economic expansionism and British indifference to Canadian interests; linked to neo-mercantilist policies such as the **National Policy**, extensive use of Crown corporations as instruments of economic development, restrictions on foreign investment, and the **National Energy Program**.

demonstration effect: Examples of policy innovations in other jurisdictions which prompt governments to take comparable action, either on their own initiative or in response to interest group pressures.

developmental clientelism: The development of relations of mutual dependence between political leaders and major economic interests to further government economic development policies. Investors and entrepreneurs look to governments for political, financial, and regulatory support and protection for their activities, providing access to private capital, employment, tax revenues, and political contributions in return.

developmental state: Outlook on the state that emphasizes its role in fostering economic development, growth, and diversification, both through direct action and the creation of institutions and structures to mobilize the resources of other economic actors, including private businesses and capital markets.

dispute resolution: The adjudication or arbitration of disputes over the application of laws or contracts to individual cases by an independent third party; may be carried out by the courts, quasi-judicial agencies or tribunals, or private forms of arbitration and mediation.

economic development (or "quasi-commercial") Crown corporations: Government business enterprises (**GBEs**) that sell goods or services to the public or undertake projects that provide economic benefits to citizens and communities as instruments of public policy.

economic dynamism: The relative openness of an economic system to adaptability and change as a result of competitive market forces, and economic, political, and technological innovations.

economic efficiency: The relative measure of value obtained from the investment of a particular set of economic inputs or resources given existing economic (including tax and regulatory) conditions.

economic geography: The special and sectoral distribution of economic activity.

economic neutrality: The principle that government policies should attempt to minimize efficiency-reducing distortions in the allocation of economic resources so that workers, managers, investors and consumers will make the most of the resources available to them.

economic openness: The degree to which citizens, businesses, and other organizations are free to enter, adapt, or withdraw from particular forms of economic activity—both within particular political jurisdictions and across political boundaries—without extensive and intrusive government regulation and control.

economic scarcity: The principle that human needs and wants are usually greater than the resources available to fulfil them.

economic structure: The basic characteristics and divisions of economic activity within a particular geographic area or overall economic network.

economic union: Constitutional and administrative provisions for the free movement of goods, services, capital, and labour within a shared economic space; provided for in Section 121 of Canada's *Constitution Act* (1867) and Section 6 of the *Charter of Rights and Freedoms.*

Election Expenses Act (1974): Federal legislation which inaugurated the modern era of campaign finance regulation by imposing limits on campaign spending, requiring disclosure of contributions to political parties, providing tax incentives for individual donations, and introducing subsidies for political parties and candidates meeting certain requirements.

electoral cycle: The timing of an event in relation to the normal scheduling of elections.

elite pluralism: Theory suggesting that real power in a democracy is controlled by shifting coalitions of elites which represent (directly or indirectly) major political, economic, and social interests. Membership in these elites may be achieved by virtue of control over political, bureaucratic, judicial, or economic power; leadership of major interest groups; or senior positions in information and cultural elites.

elite theory: Theory suggesting that real power in a democracy is controlled not by the mass of voters but by a single cohesive elite representing major segments of society that defines the national interest and legitimates its control of society through control of political parties and the choices offered to voters through the political process.

embedded liberalism: The institutionalization of prevailing liberal assumptions in legislation, government, economic, and social structures in ways that both reflect and shape public attitudes, expectations, and behaviour.

exchange process: A concept of political and policy processes as a marketplace based on informal or implicit transactions among individual actors and groups in which participants seek to balance their "assets" and "liabilities" through cooperation and tacit bargaining with one another.

executive federalism: Formal and informal processes of intergovernmental relations conducted between senior elected officials and civil servants of different orders of government.

external policy shocks: Major changes to the political or economic context for government policies that threaten to destabilize major elements of a political or economic system.

federalism: A system of government characterized by the constitutional division of governmental authority between two or more orders or levels of government.

federal spending power: The policy-making authority derived by the federal government from its power to allocate funds to areas of provincial jurisdiction; may be expressed either through the negotiation of conditional transfer or "shared cost" programs with the provinces or by the unilateral dictation of terms governing the allocation of federal funds.

financial intermediation: The process carried out by financial institutions—including banks, investment dealers, trust and insurance companies, and other organizations—of matching sources and uses of funds by individuals and organizations through a wide range of financial instruments and transactions.

fiscal policies: Major **policy instruments** that shape the overall level and distribution of government revenues and spending, and the budget balances (surpluses or deficits) that result.

foreign direct investment (FDA): Investments in companies whose ownership is controlled by residents or citizens of other countries.

Foreign Investment Review Agency: Federal agency established in 1973 to screen foreign direct investment and foreign takeovers of firms in Canada to ensure that they would provide net benefit to Canada. Its replacement in 1985 by Investment Canada signaled a policy shift away from nationalist economic policies towards the renewed encouragement of foreign investment.

framework legislation: Laws that shape the design of major policy systems affecting the economy or society as a whole.

framing: The process by which journalists create a context for the presentation or interpretation of events, trends, and processes.

garbage-can model: An approach to the design of public policies characterized by trial-and-error, "seat of the pants" responses to real or perceived crises, or one-dimensional responses to multi-dimensional policy problems.

gatekeeping: The process by which journalists provide selective or privileged access to news sources or commentators in making or interpreting the news.

generational equity: The relative status or economic well-being of individuals in different generations, usually assessed in terms of the impact of decisions made by members of one generation on the living standards and opportunities of succeeding generations.

globalization (economic): The progressive integration of national economies in regional and international markets for goods, capital, and technologies, with a resulting erosion of the capacity of individual governments to manage national and local economies independently of one another.

government bills: Draft legislation presented to Parliament or provincial legislature for debate and approval with formal cabinet and government support. Support of government bills is mandatory for members of cabinet, and usually for MPs of the governing party.

government business enterprise (GBE): Organization created and owned by one or more levels of government to sell goods and/or services to citizens, businesses, or other parts of government; includes Crown corporations.

government failure: Unintended consequences of government actions that impose serious costs on the economy, society, or the workings of the political system.

government relations: A subset of public affairs relating specifically to an organization's dealings with government.

Great Depression: The prolonged economic and social disruption during the 1930s that reinforced public support for a greater government role in managing economic activity and extending social security.

"hidden Crown corporations": Major private corporations that serve as instruments of government policy, often benefiting from preferential regulatory treatment, receipt of large-scale public subsidies, and other preferential treatment in the marketplace.

hollowing out debate: Debate over effects of economic globalization, international trade agreements on autonomy, and independent decision-making capacity of major Canadian corporations.

horizontal equity: Concept of fairness emphasizing the desirability of comparable treatment of individuals or groups in comparable circumstances.

horizontal integration: The acquisition or consolidation of firms with complementary lines of products and/or services within a single company or corporate group.

imperial preference: The lower tariffs (or free access) provided to colonial exports to other markets within an empire, compared with imports from other countries. Imperial preferences may be extended on a bilateral basis between the "mother country" and its colonies or within all jurisdictions within an imperial trading network.

income trusts: A form of business organization that holds income-producing assets and makes payments directly to unit holders. Distributions of trust income are only taxed once they are in the hands of investors, in contrast to corporate dividends paid from after-tax income (until tax changes announced in November 2005).

incrementalism: A step-by-step approach to policy change, based on marginal adjustments to existing policies or organizational structures.

industry associations: Synonym for **trade associations**.

information asymmetries: Differences in information available to buyers and sellers of goods and services which provide one with a material advantage over the other in determining their value relative to related products or services available in the marketplace.

institutional investors: Professional investment managers responsible for directing the investments of pension funds, mutual funds, and other large pools of capital on behalf of (usually) large numbers of individual investors.

intellectual power: The ability to shape underlying policy assumptions, enabling groups to define the terms of debate to serve their interests or to exclude policy options contrary to their interests from active consideration.

interest aggregation: The process of organizing or mobilizing citizens, businesses, or organizations for purposes of advocacy or representation; may also take the form of coalition-building or the development of interest networks among groups.

interest group: Organized body of individuals or organizations sharing common goals that seeks to influence public policy.

- **institutionalized interest groups:** Interest groups that are recognized stakeholders in particular policy communities. They tend to be characterized by relative permanence, a stable membership base, professional leadership, and relatively stable financial resources.
- **issue-oriented interest groups:** Interest groups that tend to focus on related issues of particular interest to its leadership and/or a particular segment of society. Their activities are often ideologically motivated, oriented towards the promotion of social or policy changes, and directed towards mobilizing or transforming public opinion as much as to the direct lobbying of government.

internal policy failures: The inability of existing ideas or institutions to respond effectively to changing political, economic, or social conditions.

intervenor status: A legal term indicating that an individual or organization is allowed by a judicial or regulatory authority to comment on legal issues of public interest associated with a particular legal action, even though not a direct party to the case.

interventionist nationalism: Policies intended to promote national economic development under direct government ownership or regulatory control.

judicial deference: The practice of judges or courts in giving legal priority to the expertise and legal judgements of specialized tribunals or quasi-judicial agencies within their fields of specialization.

judicial review: The power of the courts to:
1. review the application of laws and regulations to determine whether government officials have proper legal authority to take certain actions or have abided by existing legal requirements for the exercise of that authority;
2. determine the constitutional validity of legislation, thereby interpreting the meaning and application of constitutional law.

judicialization of politics: The active involvement of judges and courts in the policy-making priorities and processes of government.

Keynesian economic policies: Economic policies based on theories of economist John Maynard Keynes that provided the rationale for an expanded role for government in the economy. Keynesian theories heavily influenced economic policy-making in Canada, the US, Britain, and other industrial countries between the 1940s and 1970s.

Keynesian stabilization policies: The use of discretionary government policies (fiscal and/or monetary) and *automatic stabilizers* to stimulate or reduce the growth of aggregate demand to reduce the "peaks and troughs" of the business cycle to encourage sustainable levels of economic growth.

kickbacks: Payment of a percentage (or sliding scale) of contracts to the governing party in return for the receipt of government contracts.

knowledge-based economy (also "New Economy"): Economic sectors, activities, and occupations characterized by the development and/or widespread use of new and emerging technologies that have the effect of transforming traditional production and distribution processes in existing industries or creating new products or services for use by businesses and consumers; includes but is not limited to innovations in information and communications technologies, biotechnology and life sciences, other forms of scientific research, and a wide range of related industries and processes.

lead agency: Government organization responsible for providing policy leadership within a particular policy community.

levels of analysis: Different contexts that shape the attitudes, actions, and priorities of political actors and analysts in the policy process.

liberal continentalism: Policy of encouraging increased economic growth and employment through encouragement of foreign investment, increased integration of the Canadian and US economies, and increased emphasis on competition and market forces to increase the efficiency and competitiveness of Canadian businesses.

liberal corporatism: See **corporatism**.

liberal nationalism: Policy of encouraging economic development through fostering Canadian industry, particularly in sectors of strategic importance such as transportation, financial services, energy, and cultural industries; supports cooperation of governments with Canadian (or regional) business interests.

liquidity: The ability of businesses or investors to obtain sufficient cash or equivalents in a timely manner to meet their commitments and obtain greater flexibility in the use of their assets through access to credit.

litigation: The assertion of legal rights and the pursuit of legal remedies through the courts and other quasi-judicial bodies.

lobbying: Efforts to influence decisions by governments or other authoritative actors that have the power to confer benefits or impose disadvantages by their actions or inaction.

- **direct lobbying:** Lobbying that involves direct contact between societal interests or their representatives and relevant decision-makers.
- **indirect lobbying:** Efforts to shape, mobilize, and enlist media or public opinion to influence the policies or priorities of governments and other authoritative political actors.

lobbyist: A person engaged in representation or advocacy intended to influence the design or administration of public policies and programs on behalf of particular organizations or clients.

Lobbyist Registration Act: Legislation which regulates lobbying of officials of the federal government; comparable legislation exists in several provinces.

Macdonald Commission (1982-85): Royal commission chaired by former Trudeau-era minister Donald Macdonald. Its report recommended negotiation of a comprehensive free trade agreement with the US, the introduction of more market-oriented economic policies, and increased coordination between economic and social policies. It provided much of the intellectual influence behind the Mulroney and Chrétien governments' restructuring of economic and social policies in the late 1980s and 1990s.

macroeconomic policies: Government decisions relating to the overall levels of **aggregate demand** or economic activity; major elements include fiscal and monetary policies.

major stakeholders: Participants in a policy community whose vital interests it engages or whose cooperation is seen as necessary in order for governments to take effective action in a particular policy field.

market failure: Events resulting from the inability of economic actors to maximize the efficient use of resources and/or to maximize social welfare in the normal course of economic activity.

market liberalism: System of economic and political ideas that emphasizes individual liberty, the private ownership of property, the rule of law, and the diffusion of political and economic power to maximize the social and economic well-being of individuals and society.

market power: The capacity of a producer or consumer of goods and services to dictate prices or the terms of market competition to other market participants over an extended period; may be subject to the countervailing exercise of regulatory power by governments.

Marxism: Theoretical tendencies that provide an ideological challenge to the theory and practice of capitalism by advocating worker or state control over the means of production. Two major variants of Marxist political economy are:

1. **instrumentalist theories of the state**, which perceive the state and its agencies as active instruments of the capitalist domination of society.

2. **structuralist theories of the state**, which acknowledge the partial autonomy of the "capitalist" state, consistent with the accommodation of the needs of capitalist organization and the preservation of the broader social and economic system.

Mechanisms of Interaction School: Theory of business-government relations in the 1970s and 1980s that attributed friction between business and government to inadequate consultation processes capable of providing for effective interest group input to appropriate government decision-makers that could provide each group with an adequate understanding of the objectives and concerns of the other to enable mutual accommodation through the policy process.

mercantilism: The organization and regulation of economic and trade policies to promote a positive balance of exports over imports, economic self-sufficiency, and a surplus in the precious metals needed to finance the growing military and administrative power of the state; frequently associated with the growth of colonial trading empires, state-conferred monopolies, and extensive regulation of commerce; dominant economic policy of most major European states between the sixteenth and eighteenth centuries.

methodological individualism: An approach to the social sciences which assumes that social trends and the actions of institutions can be interpreted as the products of individuals' decisions and actions.

micro-(economic) policies: Government policies that directly or indirectly influence the economic decisions of individuals and groups, including industry sectors and government actors.

mixed enterprise: Corporation combining majority private ownership with significant direct government shareholdings; sometimes used as instruments of public policy, or as transitional stage in gradual privatization of **government business enterprises**.

monetary policies: Policies affecting the value and supply of money within the economic marketplace, including interest rate and exchange rate policies.

monopolistic competition: Competitive market characterized both by high degrees of specialization and consumer capacity to obtain substitute products or services that limit the market power of individual producers.

monopoly: Market condition in which there is only one seller of a particular product or service in a particular market

monopoly rent: The economic benefit that may be obtained by monopolies or dominant firms, and often their workers, in the forms of higher profits and wages compared with those in more economically competitive sectors. Monopoly rents may also be exercised as a result of legally protected innovations (e.g., patents), specialized expertise, or locational advantages.

monopsony: Market condition in which there is only one buyer of a particular product or service in a particular market.

NAFTA (North American Free Trade Agreement): Comprehensive trade agreement negotiated among Canada, the US, and Mexico (1992-94); it extended the principles and mechanisms of the 1988 **Canada-US Free Trade Agreement** and created tri-national commissions to monitor enforcement of national environmental and labour laws and standards.

National Energy Program (NEP): Federal policy (1980-86) intended to expand Canadian ownership of energy industries, along with increasing federal control over and revenues from oil and gas development in Canada; prompted serious conflict with energy-producing provinces and organized business interests; major cause of later business and provincial support for the **Canada-US Free Trade Agreement**.

National Policy (late nineteenth-early twentieth century): National economic development policy centred on high protective tariffs, the building of a transcontinental railroad system, and the opening of the Canadian prairies (and later, other frontier regions) to European settlement and agricultural development to create an integrated national market for Canadian products and services.

national treatment: Recognition of a non-resident individual or business as a resident of a host country for purposes of regulation; intended to provide basis for non-discrimination under international economic agreements.

negative externalities: Direct or indirect effects of economic activities that harm other people.

negative integration: Approaches to economic integration that provide for considerable discretion, within agreed limits, in the application of national (or provincial) government rules as long as these are not designed in ways that apply different legal standards to "nationals" and "non-nationals" in violation of the **national treatment** principle.

neo-conservatism: Ideological tendency committed to limiting the size and scope of government on both normative and empirical grounds; usually reflects a commitment to principles of personal responsibility, limited government, a market-oriented capitalist economy based on widespread private ownership of property, and internationally competitive tax levels.

neo-liberalism: The technocratic use of economic analysis and market forces to discipline the operations of government in achieving public policy goals; tends to emphasize fiscal discipline, balanced budgets, the accommodation of market forces, and the integration of economic and social policy objectives through a selective use of state intervention.

neo-mercantilism: Policies of economic nationalism intended to promote the development and growth of domestic industries through protective and supportive government policies including protective tariff and non-tariff barriers, requirements for domestic ownership, regulations to limit or structure competition to support favoured businesses or industry sectors, and extensive government subsidies.

neo-pluralism: Concept of interest group politics that shares with pluralism the assumption that political power is decentralized and interest groups are competitive; also suggests that the fragmentation of policy-making has contributed to increasing the autonomy of various parts of government at the expense of the common good.

news management: The systematic public relations activities of public authorities intended to guide, manipulate, or control the timing, content, and emphasis of media coverage of their activities.

normative: Related to norms, or standards of right and wrong, applied to moral, ethical, or ideological standards of conduct for individuals and societies.

North American (economic) integration: The growing economic interdependence of individuals, businesses, and governments across North America as a result of rising levels of trade, investment, and the integration of business operations across national borders.

oligopoly: An industry dominated by a few firms, each of which has a significant market share; usually characterized by high barriers to entry and considerable price or product competition among participants to maintain and/or enhance market share.

outcome manifestations (of power): Evidence of the ability of an individual or group to impose its policy preferences on an otherwise unwilling political system or to prevent policy outcomes conflicting with its interests.

Pacific Scandal: Political scandal over linkage between contracts for the building of the Canadian Pacific Railway and huge campaign contributions in the 1872 federal election which brought down the government of Sir John A. Macdonald in 1873.

PAL syndrome: The interpenetration of partisan political strategists, consultants, advertising executives, and lobbyists with bureaucratic policy-makers.

Pareto efficiency: The allocation of resources so that it is impossible to make anyone better off without making someone else worse off. A Pareto improvement results if "winners" from an economic transaction are able to compensate the "losers" and still be better off.

participation rate: The percentage of people of working age (usually 15-64) engaged in the labour force.

path dependence: A process by which the logic of successive policy changes and the resources committed to implement them influences and constrains future policy decisions.

peak association: type of business organization, typical of corporatist political systems, that is widely recognized to speak for the business community as a whole in advising governments on matters of public policy.

perfect competition: Market condition that can be said to exist when an economic sector is characterized by large numbers of willing buyers and sellers of similar products or services, relatively easy market entry and exit, and sufficient information available to both producers and consumers to make informed decisions in setting prices for goods or services.

performance benchmarks: Formal, documented comparisons of levels of activity or achievement either with a particular standard, competing products, or other political jurisdictions in order to evaluate policy or system outcomes.

pluralist theory: Theory emphasizing the division of political and economic power among multiple and competing interests so that no single group in society can achieve dominance on more than a temporary basis; suggests that all major interests in society have the opportunity to organize themselves to protect and advance their interests within the political system.

policy approval: Formal authorization of public policies by a legally recognized authority.

policy community: Clusters of organizations and interests inside and outside governments that focus on a common set of policy interests; often called **policy networks**.

- **clientele pluralist:** Policy community in which the public interest is identified by policy-makers to coincide with the core interests of its major organized stakeholders.

- **concertation network:** A policy community in which state actors deal on more or less equal terms with a dominant stakeholder organization or coalition representing societal interests to negotiate a policy representing the "public interest."

- **co-optive pluralist:** Policy community in which government policy-makers attempt to define the public interest and seek to co-opt groups whose interests are affected by these policies in order to legitimize their actions and provide feedback on the effectiveness of current and proposed policies.

- **liberal corporatist:** Policy community characterized by direct participation in the policy-making process by organizations representing major economic stakeholders (e.g., business, organized labour). In return for preferential access to the policy process, stakeholder groups tend to lose a degree of their policy-making autonomy.

- **parentela pluralist**: Policy community characterized by the infiltration of policy-making bodies within the government bureaucracy by individuals or organized interests closely allied with the political party(ies) in power.
- **pressure pluralist**: Policy community characterized by multiple participants, none of whom are capable of dominating the policy process, and a measure of state autonomy in balancing the interests of competing groups along with broader government objectives.
- **state-directed network**: Policy community in which authoritative state actors establish public policy without direct reference to the actions or policy preferences of societal actors.

policy convergence: Growing similarities between policies of different jurisdictions; may result from responses to domestic political pressures, **demonstration effect**, or emulation of policy changes in other jurisdictions; international treaties; or international economic pressures.

policy cycle: The processes by which public issues and concerns are recognized as candidates for government action, leading to the development of potentially viable policy responses capable of securing authoritative political approval; their implementation by government departments, agencies, or related societal groups; and subsequent evaluation for their effectiveness.

policy evaluation: Process for measuring or assessing relative success of policy or program design and implementation in achieving intended objectives, complying with government administrative standards, correcting previously identified problems, and/or providing value for taxpayers' money.

policy formulation: The development of specific action plans or policy options for consideration by governments.

policy implementation: The process of translating policy decisions into action.

policy instruments: The means or "tools" that governments have at their disposal from which they choose to formulate policy.

policy networks: Clusters of organizations and interests inside and outside governments that focus on a common set of policy interests; sometimes called **policy communities**. Policy networks are "channels of communication" both within governments and among societal interests that are actively or potentially interested in the outcomes of a particular process. They tend to be characterized by a greater degree of openness to the entry or departure of participants, especially among societal actors.

policy outcomes: The results or effects of a policy decision or action, intended or otherwise.

policy outputs: Actions taken or organized by governments.

policy regimes: The systems of organizations, rules, and processes and the ideas and interests associated with them that shape the context for public policies.

policy shocks: Events that disrupt government priorities and the normal workings of government policies; may result from political, economic, social, or environmental (including technological) events beyond the immediate control of individual governments.

political agenda: The subjects or problems to which governmental officials and **attentive actors** are paying some serious attention at any particular time.

political business cycle: The interaction of political and economic factors in agenda-setting and government decision-making, sometimes linked with the **electoral cycle**; also reflected in linkages between public attitudes towards the extent of government intervention in economy and current levels of economic prosperity.

political capital: Credibility and trust within a relevant political constituency or policy community based on a mixture of political skill, relevant expertise, and past performance.

political salience: The relative importance of issues or events within a particular political context.

political shocks: Threats to the political **status quo** that force governments to rethink established policies or political values

portfolio investment: Non-controlling ownership of a company's equity (shares) or debt.

positive externalities: Benefits to society from a particular activity or service which may be greater than related economic benefits captured by its producers and consumers.

positive integration: The harmonization of laws, policies, and regulatory regimes in different jurisdictions based on the imposition of a central set of rules across territorial boundaries, with limited exemptions and exceptions.

private corporation: Corporation whose shares are held by individuals or a small group of shareholders; no legal provision for public trading of shares.

private member's bill: Draft legislation presented to Parliament or legislature at the personal initiative of individual MPs or MLAs. Legislative rules governing the procedures for reviewing and debating private members' bills vary widely.

privative clauses: Legislative provisions limiting or precluding the right of appeal to the courts; generally subject to judicial review at the discretion of the courts.

privatization: The full or partial transfer of ownership of a government or public service to private ownership. Degrees of privatization may range from contracting-out or the development of **public-private partnerships** through the partial or full sale of share ownership to private businesses or investors.

problem definition: The assessment of the nature, causes, extent, and relative importance of issues claiming the attention of government policy-makers.

procedural legitimacy (or legitimization): Processes related to the observation of customary or legally required procedural formalities to secure approval for a particular policy or legislative initiative; may include extensive public consultations on the formulation or implementation of public policies.

process manifestations (of power): Examples of the effective use of the political process to advance the interests of particular individuals or groups.

productivity: The relative output of goods and services generated by a fixed input of labour and capital (including technology).

public affairs: The process of managing an organization's relationships with governments, the media, and other societal interests to facilitate or complement the pursuit of its main objectives.

public corporation: Corporation whose shares may be offered to and traded by members of the public, subject to compliance with legal requirements.

public goods: Include two kinds of goods:

- **pure public goods**: Goods or services that all or most individuals in a particular market can obtain without having to pay for them directly ("non-excludable") and without diminishing the supply available to other persons ("non-rival").
- **quasi-public goods**: Goods and services that provide significant public benefits above and beyond those obtained by their providers and consumers under normal market conditions.

public policy: Principles, rules, and decisions which govern the actions (or inaction) of governments and the ways in which they relate to citizens and other governments.

public-private partnerships (PPPs): Variety of business and legal arrangements involving formal cooperation between governments and individual corporations in the provision and/or delivery of public services. Concept may also be expanded to include partnerships with non-profit and community organizations in cooperative policy development.

public relations: The deliberate management of public image and information to serve the interests of an organization or individual client.

quasi-judicial tribunals: Specialized agencies with some court-like powers established under specific legislative mandates to adjudicate disputes arising from the administration of particular government laws, regulations, and related policies.

Quiet Revolution: Modernization of Quebec's economy and society under the leadership of the Quebec state between 1960 and 1980. Characterized by the secularization of Quebec's traditional society, the growth of a strong Quebec state as the main political representative of French-speaking Québécois, and extensive state involvement in economic development.

rational ignorance: The decision not to invest time and effort in obtaining detailed information or expertise in certain areas, based on the assumption that the benefits to be obtained from such knowledge are either smaller than those available from pursuing other activities or not worth the related costs.

rational policy-making: An approach to the policy process inspired by the social sciences, based on the pursuit of rational choices among policy options to achieve specific goals or the discovery of effective responses to clearly defined problems in order to maximize the net benefits to society.

recession: Two consecutive quarters of decline in *aggregate demand*.

Reciprocity Treaty of 1854: Limited free trade agreement between Britain's North American colonies and the US which provided tariff-free access to 90 per cent of existing two-way trade; cancelled by the US in 1866.

regimes: Systems of organizations, rules, and processes that shape the context for public policies; may involve varying degrees of overlap among international, national, regional, and sectoral policy systems.

regionalism: The shared identification of citizens with a region as a distinct political or social community based on conscious differences in political, economic, and social interests and structures; also an emphasis on the distinctive regional (or provincial) characteristics or differences that make issues of regional (or provincial) equity and influence over public policy major considerations in Canada's political processes.

regional ministers: Federal cabinet ministers with political and administrative responsibilities for promoting the interests of their provinces or regions within the federal government.

rent-seeking: The pursuit of economic self-interest beyond market rates of return through the political process; usually reflected in the provision or pursuit of fiscal or regulatory advantages by particular individuals or groups which have the effect of shifting costs on to other economic actors.

reverse onus: A legal provision shifting the normal burden of proof from the prosecution (in an administrative law or criminal case) or to the accused person.

rights-based discourse: An approach to the discussion of public issues that emphasizes the personal or collective rights of individual persons or groups as a dominant principle for the guidance of political and judicial action.

rule of law: The consistent application of known, predictable, and impartial rules of conduct to governments and citizens alike.

satisficing: To accept a choice or judgement as one that is satisfactory, even if not the best possible or available.

Second Industrial Revolution: Era of rapid industrial growth (1890-1930) in North America and Europe characterized by the applications of new technologies (e.g., electricity, internal combustion engine, new chemical processes) and the development of large capital-intensive industrial organizations.

Second National Policy: Name given to series of federal economic and social policies after the Second World War. These policies included the adoption of Keynesian macro-economic policies, the expansion of income transfer programs to stabilize the economy and promote social cohesion, Canada's growing integration into the international and North American economic systems, the promotion of collective bargaining in industry, and strategic government intervention in key industries, often through the use of Crown corporations.

sectoral associations: Associations that represent a cross-section of businesses (or non-profit organizations) within a particular industrial or economic sector, e.g., agriculture, health care, manufacturing, construction, retailing, mining.

sectoral corporatism: A form of liberal corporatism applied to major representative organizations (usually including both business and labour or a broad cross-section of producer groups), within a particular sector (e.g., agriculture, cultural industries).

sectoral policies: Major laws and policies governing operations of specific industry, economic, or social policy sectors.

social and government services corporations: Government business enterprises (**GBEs**) that receive financial assistance from governments to deliver social programs and other government services.

social or **welfare liberalism**: Ideology or set of political principles that emphasizes the regulatory and redistributive role of the state rather than the creation of wealth or the promotion of economic growth as the principal focus of state activity.

societal (or "liberal") corporatism: See **corporatism**.

societal federalism: The interaction of federalism with underlying economic and societal differences to create different political cultures and social and economic environments for the conduct of politics in Canada's provinces and regions. See also **regionalism**.

sovereignty: The final authority or power of decision within a political system.

stagflation: Simultaneous trends toward higher levels of inflation and unemployment, combined with slow economic growth. Experience of stagflation during the 1970s undermined consensus supporting **Keynesian economic policies** and increased social and political conflicts in Canada and other industrial nations.

standing (legal): The legal right to participate in a judicial or quasi-judicial process, either as a direct party to the dispute (e.g., plaintiff or respondent) or as an **intervenor** allowed to make submissions to the court on legal and other implications of the case.

staples theory: Theory of economic development which emphasizes dependence on the export of a dominant agricultural or resource staple to provide the basis for economic development and to finance the costs of imported capital.

stare decisis: Literally, "let the decision stand"; the use of existing precedents in order to make similar rulings in similar cases.

state autonomy: The capacity of governments and the organizations that compose them to define, pursue, and achieve their own policy objectives independently of societal actors and sometimes in substantial opposition to them.

state capacity: The ability of governments to mobilize the resources necessary to design and implement policies that will achieve their objectives.

state corporatism: The systematic exercise of state power to organize and incorporate representatives of all major societal interests into the formation and implementation of policy and the distribution of benefits as instruments for the promotion of state ideology and the exercise of state control.

statism: Theories and practices that identify the well-being of a nation (or other political community) with strong state institutions that have the capacity to define the national interest and to mobilize their own resources and those of the broader society in support of policies intended to achieve its goals. See also **state capacity**. Also used to describe attitudes or methods for enforcing the preferences of state decision-makers when they conflict with those of major societal interests or the general public.

status quo: Existing patterns of organization or behaviour.

statutory interpretation: The processes by which courts or judges interpret the meaning of laws and regulations and the principles governing their application to specific circumstances.

strategic analysis: The process of assessing opportunities and risks facing specific businesses and organizations (or their members) as a result of the actions or inactions of governments and other political actors, as well as economic, competitive, or societal trends.

strategic litigation: The systematic use of legal action to encourage judicial policy-making on behalf of a particular political or social agenda.

structural adjustment policies: Policies intended to address sources of economic rigidity and to increase the adaptability of businesses, governments, and individuals to changing economic circumstances; often include measures to increase the flexibility of labour markets, facilitate the adaptation of workers and employers to changing economic circumstances, and eliminate subsidies or regulations that cushion businesses against the effects of increased competition or technological change.

structural power: The capacity of a group to make its interests and values part of the "normal" environment guiding the political, economic, and social systems, implicitly reinforcing certain ideas of the public interest and marginalizing others.

subgovernment: Organizations that are directly involved in policy formation and/or implementation within a particular policy community; usually drawn from government departments or agencies whose activities are directly affected by its decisions.

substantive legitimacy (or legitimization): Processes for securing the acceptance of relevant publics for particular proposals or actions, whether on political, ethical, or ideological grounds.

sustainability: The capacity to balance the current consumption of goods and services with investments that will increase future economic opportunities; also refers to the ability of governments to combine improvements in citizens' material living standards with environmental preservation and related quality-of-life issues.

symbolic legitimacy (or legitimization): The use of public relations techniques to confer symbolic public recognition on particular groups or to extend nominal recognition of their right to contribute to discussions of government actions and public policies, but usually without any intention of allowing such participation to result in significant legal or policy changes.

think tanks: Organizations created for purposes of policy research and/or advocacy, but with varying degrees of independence from members or sponsors in their research activities.

Third National Policy: Name given to the Trudeau government's program of increased economic nationalism, federal assertiveness, and constitutional reform following its return to power in the 1980 election. Specific policies including the **National Energy Program**, proposed tax reforms, the expansion of federal social programs, and proposals for an industrial strategy; resulted in bitter conflicts between the federal government, organized business interests, and most provinces.

tollgating: Payment of political contributions to secure consideration for government contracts.

trade (or industry) associations: 1) Generic name for business associations; 2) associations that represent trade or industry groups, often within a broader economic sector.

triple helix: Term used to describe interactions and partnerships among government, business, and academic researchers and institutions, both in basic research extending the frontiers of knowledge and in the commercialization of these technologies.

two-level game: Description of policy processes in which political leaders and policymakers attempt to balance the pursuit of political or policy goals in dealings with other governments with the building or maintenance of a domestic political coalition supportive of their policies.

ultra vires: Unconstitutional, beyond the legal power of the authority attempting to exercise it.

vertical equity: Principles of fairness that emphasize the redistribution of income and opportunities from people with higher incomes or social status to those with lower incomes or social status.

vertical integration: A form of economic organization that provides common ownership or organizational control of businesses at different stages of the production and distribution chains from the extraction or initial processing of raw materials to the production and distribution of finished goods, and their sale to consumers or "end users."

virtual parties: Networks of professional political organizers and communications experts formed to support party leaders and aspiring leadership candidates.

Walter Gordon: Champion of Canadian economic nationalism during the late 1950s and 1960s; chair of the Royal Commission on Canada's Economic Prospects (1955-56) that recommended limits on foreign investments in Canadian industry; finance minister in Liberal government of Lester Pearson (1963-65).

welfare state: An approach to the organization of the state intended to guarantee widespread economic and social security and opportunity for individuals and social groups through the provision of a broad range of programs and services financed by varying combinations of social insurance and redistributive taxation.

White Paper: A formal statement of government policy intentions published for public consultation following cabinet approval but before initiating legislative action.

widely held companies: Corporations whose ownership is widely diffused; no controlling shareholder exists, either as a result of market arrangements or legislative requirements, resulting in exercise of effective control by senior management.

World Trade Organization (WTO): Organization formed in 1995 to implement international economic agreements among participating states governing international trade in goods and services and established standards for regulatory measures affecting the mobility and security of investment capital and intellectual property.

zero-sum game: Economic or political contest in which the gains of some players can only be achieved by imposing a loss on other players so that players as a whole are no better off after the game than before.

Abelson, Donald E. 2002. *Do think tanks matter?* Montreal and Kingston: McGill-Queen's University Press.

Abelson, Donald E., and Christine M. Carberry. 1998. Following suit or falling behind? A comparative analysis of think tanks in Canada and the United States. *Canadian Journal of Political Science* 21(3): 525-55.

Adams, Michael. 1998. *Sex in the snow: Canadian social values at the end of the millennium.* Toronto: Penguin Canada.

Aitken, H.G.A. 1967. Defensive economic expansion: the state and economic growth in Canada. In *Approaches to Canadian economic history*, ed. W.T. Easterbrook and M.H. Watkins. Toronto: McClelland and Stewart. 183-221

——. 1990. Government and business in Canada: an interpretation. In *The development of Canadian capitalism: essays in business history*, ed. Douglas McCalla. Toronto: Copp Clark Pitman. 109-23.

Alberta, Alberta Business Tax Review. 2000. *Report and recommendations.* Edmonton: Alberta Treasury (13 September).

Alberta, Ministry of Economic Development. 2002. *Highlights of the Alberta economy.* Edmonton: Ministry of Economic Development (January).

Alberta Finance. 2005. Record energy revenues boost province's surplus. Edmonton: Alberta Finance (16 November).

Alboim, Elly. 2000. Public policy and communication. Notes for discussion. Ottawa: Canadian Centre for Management Development (May).

Alexander, Cynthia. 2000. Cents and sensibility: the emergence of e-government in Canada. In *How Ottawa Spends: 2000-01*, ed. Leslie A. Pal. Toronto: Oxford University Press. 185-209.

Allen, Barbara Ann. 2005. Procurement policy in Canada: evolution and impacts—domestic policy, trade, and information technology. PhD Dissertation. Ottawa, School of Public Policy and Administration, Carleton University.

Allen, Richard. 1992. The social gospel as the religion of agrarian revolt. In *The prairie west*, ed. R. Douglas Francis and Howard Palmer. Edmonton: University of Alberta Press. 561-72.

Anderson, Mark. 2002. Brinksmanship and betrayal. *National Post Business* (January).

Andreas, Peter, and Thomas J. Bierstecker. (Eds.). 2003. *The rebordering of North America.* New York: Routledge.

Anisman, Philip. 2004. Securities reform: First, do no harm to investors. *Globe and Mail* (27 August).

Arbour, Pierre. 1994. *Quebec Inc. and the temptation of state capitalism.* Montreal: Robert Davies.

Association of Canadian Pension Management. 2000. Independence or self-reliance: which way for Canada's retirement income system? Toronto: ACPM (January).

Atkinson, Michael M. (Ed.). 1993. *Governing Canada: institutions and public policy.* Toronto: Harcourt, Brace, Jovanovich.

Atkinson, Michael, and M.A. Chandler. 1983. *The politics of Canadian public policy.* Toronto: University of Toronto Press.

Atkinson, Michael M., and William D. Coleman. 1989. *The state, business and industrial change in Canada*. Toronto: University of Toronto Press.

Aubry, Jack. 2005. Despite rules, lobbyists cash in on tech fund. *The Ottawa Citizen* (23 September).

Aucoin, Peter. 1995. *The new public management. Canada in comparative perspective*. Montreal: Institute for Research in Public Policy.

———. 2000. The public service as a learning organization. Paper prepared for Governance Research Project, Canadian Centre for Management Development, 15 April.

Axworthy, Thomas A., and Pierre E. Trudeau. 1990. *Towards a Just Society: the Trudeau years*. Markham, ON: Penguin Canada.

Baier, Gerald. 2002. Judicial review and Canadian federalism. In *Canadian federalism: performance, effectiveness and legitimacy*, ed. Herman Bakvis and Grace Skogstad. Toronto: Oxford University Press.

Baier, Gerald, and Herman Bakvis. 2001. Think tanks and political parties: competitors or collaborators. *ISUMA: Canadian Journal of Policy Research* 2(1): 107-13.

Bain, George. 1994. *Gotcha! how the media distorts the news*. Toronto: Key Porter.

Bakvis, Herman. 1991. *Regional ministers: power and influence in the Canadian cabinet*. Toronto: University of Toronto Press.

Baldwin, John R., Desmond Beckstead, and Mark Brown. 2003. *Hollowing-out, trimming down, or scaling-up? An analysis of head offices in Canada, 1999-2002*. Research Paper #019. Cat. #11F0027MIE2003019. Ottawa: Statistics Canada (December).

Baldwin, John R., Richard Caves, and Wulong Gu. 2005. *Responses to trade liberalization: changes in product diversification in foreign- and domestic-controlled plants*. Research Paper #31. Cat. #11F0027MIE200503. Ottawa: Statistics Canada (24 March).

Baldwin, John R., and Naginder Dhaliwal. 2001. Heterogeneity in labour productivity growth in manufacturing: differences between domestic and foreign-controlled establishments. In *Productivity Growth in Canada*, Cat. #15-204, ed. John R. Baldwin et al. Ottawa: Statistics Canada (February). 61-75.

Baldwin, John R., René Durand, and Judy Hosein. 2001. Restructuring and productivity growth in the Canadian business sector. In *Productivity Growth in Canada*, Cat. #15-204, ed. John R. Baldwin et al. Ottawa: Statistics Canada (February). 30-32.

Baldwin, John R., and Peter Hamel. 2000. *Multinationals and the Canadian innovation process*. Research Paper #151. Cat. #11F0019MIE2000151. Ottawa: Statistics Canada (27 June).

Banting, Keith, Andrew Sharpe, and France St. Hilaire. 2001. *The review of economic performance and social progress*. Montreal: Institute for Research in Public Policy.

Barman, Jean 1991. *The west beyond the west: a history of British Columbia*. Toronto: University of Toronto Press.

Barr, John J. 1974. *The dynasty: the rise and fall of Social Credit in Alberta*. Toronto: McClelland and Stewart.

Bateman, Thomas M.J. 2001. Party democracy increases the leader's power. *Policy Options* (September).

BC Stats. 2003. A profile of small business in British Columbia. Vancouver: Western Economic Development Canada and BC Ministry of Competition, Science and Enterprise. Available at <http://www.wd.gc.ca/rpts/research/profile 2003/sbp03_e.pdf>.

Beatty, Jim. 1999. Lumber case a tale of abuse, arrogance and deceit. *Vancouver Sun* (12 August).

Beckman, Christopher C. 1984. *The Foreign Investment Review Agency: perceptions and realities*. Ottawa: Conference Board of Canada.

Bell, Jeffrey. 1992. *Populism and elitism*. Washington, DC: Regnery Gateway.

Bell, Joel. 1990. Canadian industrial strategy in a changing world. In *Towards a Just Society: The Trudeau years*, ed. Thomas A. Axworthy and Pierre E. Trudeau. Markham, ON: Penguin Canada. 78-105.

Bellamy, Richard. 1999. *Liberalism and pluralism: towards a politics of compromise*. London: Routledge.

Bercuson, David, J.L. Granatstein, and W.R. Young. 1986. *Sacred trust? Brian Mulroney and the Conservative Party in power*. Toronto, Doubleday Canada.

Berger, Peter L., and Richard J. Neuhaus. 1977. *To empower people: the role of mediating structures in public policy*. Washington, DC: American Enterprise Institute.

Berman, David. 2005. Income trusts are new kings. *Financial Post* (13 July).

Bernstein, Marver H. 1955. *Regulating business by independent commission*. Princeton, NJ: Princeton University Press.

Berry, Jeffrey M. 1997. *The interest group society*. 3rd ed. New York: Longman.

Bertram, G.W. 1967. Economic growth in Canadian industry, 1870-1915: The staple model. In *Approaches to Canadian economic history*, ed. W.T. Easterbrook and M.H. Watkins. Toronto: McClelland and Stewart. 74-98.

Bérubé, G., and D. Côté. 2000. Long-term determinants of the personal savings rate: literature review and some empirical results for Canada. Working Paper 2000-3. Ottawa: Bank of Canada (February).

Bird, Richard M. 1970. The tax kaleidoscope: perspectives on tax reform in Canada. *Canadian Tax Journal* (September-October): 444-73.

Blackwell, Richard. 2000. Share ownership on the rise. *Globe and Mail* (27 May).

Blair Consulting Group. 1999. *User fees: where does the buck stop?* Ottawa: Alliance of Manufacturers and Exporters Canada (January).

Blanchard, James J. 1998. *Behind the embassy door*. Toronto: McClelland and Stewart.

Bliss, Michael. 1985. Forcing the pace: a reappraisal of business-government relations in Canadian history. In *Theories of business-government relations*, ed. V.V. Murray. Toronto, Trans-Canada Press. 106-17.

——. 1987. *Northern enterprise: five centuries of Canadian business*. Toronto: McClelland and Stewart.

Boadway, Robin, and Harry M. Kitchen. 1999. *Canadian tax policy*, 3rd ed. Canadian Tax Paper #103. Toronto: Canadian Tax Foundation.

Boase, Joan Price. 2000. Beyond government: the appeal of public-private partnerships. *Canadian Public Administration* 43(1): 75-92.

Bollman, Ray D. 2000. Rural and small town Canada: an overview. Ottawa: Statistics Canada (8 June).

Bothwell, Robert. 1998. Trudeau and the Americans. In *Trudeau's Shadow: The Life and Legacy of Pierre Elliott Trudeau*, ed. Andrew Cohen and J.L. Granatstein. Toronto: Vintage Canada. 209-21.

Bothwell, Robert, and William Kilbourn. 1979. *C.D. Howe: a biography*. Toronto: McClelland and Stewart.

Bottomore, T.B. 1964. *Elites and society*. New York: Basic Books.

——. 1985. *Theories of modern capitalism*. London: George Allen and Unwin.

Bradford, Neil. 1998. *Commissioning ideas*. Toronto, Oxford University Press.

Brady, Brigid, and Farid Navin. 2001. Factors affecting regional economic performance in Canada. *Bank of Canada Review* (Autumn).

Brander, James M. 1995. *Government policy towards business*, 3rd ed. Toronto: John Wiley.

Brennan, Geoffrey, and James M. Buchanan. 1980. *The power to tax: analytical foundations of a fiscal constitution*. Cambridge: Cambridge University Press.

Brethour, Patrick, and Steven Chase. 2005. The little trust that grew. *Globe and Mail* (13 October).

Breton, Raymond. 1985. Supplementary report. In *Report of the Royal Commission on the Economic Union and Development Prospects for Canada*. Vol. 3. Ottawa: Supply and Services Canada. 486-526.

Bricker, Darryl, and Edward Greenspon. 2002. *Searching for certainty: inside the new Canadian mindset*. Toronto: Anchor Canada.

British Columbia. 2000. Crown corporations and agencies. *Financial and Economic Review*. Victoria: Ministry of Finance and Corporate Relations (March).

——. 2003. Appointment guidelines: Administrative Tribunals. Victoria, BC: Board Resourcing and Development Office, Office of the Premier.

British Columbia, Administrative Justice Project. 2002a. Restructuring administrative justice agencies: core services review—Phase I report and results. Victoria, BC: Ministry of the Attorney General (5 February).

——. 2002b. White Paper: On balance: guiding principles for administrative justice reform in British Columbia. Victoria, BC: Ministry of the Attorney General (July).

Broadbent, Edward. 1999. Social democracy or liberalism in the new millennium. In *The future of social democracy*, ed. Peter Russell. Toronto: University of Toronto Press. 73-93.

Brodie, Ian. 1997. *Interest groups and the Supreme Court*. PhD Thesis, University of Calgary.

——. 2002a. *Friends of the court: the privileging of interest group litigants in Canada*. Albany, NY: SUNY Press.

——. 2002b. Intervenors and the Charter. In *Law, politics and the judicial process in Canada*, 3rd ed., ed. F.L. Morton. Calgary: University of Calgary Press.

Brodie, Janine. 1990. *The political economy of Canadian regionalism*. Toronto: Harcourt, Brace, Jovanovich.

Brooks, Stephen, and Lydia Miljan. 2003. *Public policy in Canada: an introduction*, 4th ed. Toronto: Oxford University Press.

Brooks, Stephen, and Andrew Stritch. 1991. *Business and government in Canada*. Toronto: Prentice Hall.

Brooks, W. Neil. (Ed.). 1988. *The quest for tax reform: The Royal Commission on Taxation twenty years later*. Toronto: Carswell.

Brown, Douglas M. 2002. *Market rules: economic union reform and intergovernmental policy-making in Australia and Canada*. Montreal and Kingston: McGill-Queen's University Press.

Bruce, Christopher J., Ronald Kneebone, and Kenneth McKenzie. (Eds.). 1997. *A government reinvented*. Toronto: Oxford University Press.

Bruce, Doug, and Andrea Dulipovici. 2001. Help wanted: results of CFIB surveys on the shortage of qualified labour. Toronto: Canadian Federation of Independent Business (February).

Bryden, John. 1994. Special interest group funding. Mimeo (November).

Buchanan, James M. 1999a. The constitution of economic policy, 1986 Nobel lecture. In *The Logical Foundations of Constitutional Theory*. Indianapolis: Liberty Press. 455-68.

——. 1999b. Politics without romance. In *The Logical Foundations of Constitutional Theory*. Indianapolis: Liberty Press. 45-59.

Buchanan, James, M., Robert Tollison, and Gordon Tullock. 1980. *Towards a theory of a rent seeking society*. College Station, TX: Texas A&M University Press.

Burleton, Derek. 2003. Canada's Northwest Territories: can gas and gems bring sustained growth to the north? Toronto: TD Economics (3 December).

——. 2004. Regional economic outlook. Toronto: TD Economics (22 July).

Burleton, Derek, and Don Drummond. 2001. Canada's talent deficit. Toronto: TD Economics (6 September).

Business Council of British Columbia. 2001. Submission to the standing committee on finance and government services in advance of the 2002 provincial budget. Vancouver: BCBC (9 October).

Byrd, Craig, and Pierre Genereux. 2004. The performance of interprovincial and international exports by province and territory since 1992. Cat. # 11-621-MIE2004011. Ottawa: Statistics Canada (May).

Cairns, Alan. 1986. The embedded state: state-society relations in Canada. In *State and society: Canada in comparative perspective*. Vol. 31, Background Papers, Royal Commission on the Economic Union and Development Prospects for Canada. Coord. Keith Banting. Toronto: University of Toronto Press. 53-86.

Cairns Group and McDonald and Co. 1998. Getting to government: 1998 national communications survey. Toronto: Cairns Group.

Callaway, Tim. 2002. Talisman unloads controversial Sudan assets. *Christian Week*, 26 November.

Cameron, Maxwell, and Brian Tomlin. 2000. *NAFTA: the making of a deal*. Ithaca, NY: Cornell University Press.

Cameron, Stevie. 1995. *On the take: crime, corruption and greed in the Mulroney years*. Vancouver: Macfarlane, Walter and Ross.

Campbell, C. 1978. *The Senate: a lobby from within*. Toronto: Macmillan of Canada.

Campbell, Colin, and George J. Szablowski. 1979. *The superbureaucrats: structure and behaviour in central agencies*. Toronto: Macmillan Canada.

Campbell, John L. 2001. Institutional analysis and the role of ideas in political economy. In *The rise of neoliberalism and institutional analysis*, ed. John L. Campbell and Ove Pederson. Princeton, NJ: Princeton University Press.

Campbell, John L., and Ove Pederson. (Eds.). 2001. *The rise of neoliberalism and institutional analysis*. Princeton, NJ: Princeton University Press.

Campbell, Robert M. 1987. *Grand illusions: the politics of the Keynesian experience in Canada 1945-1975*. Peterborough, ON, Broadview Press.

——. 2002. The post modern: it's time for serious postal reform. *Policy Options* (July-August): 33-38.

——. 2003. *The politics of postal transformation: modernizing postal systems in a technological and global world*. Montreal and Kingston: McGill-Queen's University Press.

Campbell, Robert M., and Leslie A. Pal. 1994. *The real world of Canadian politics*. Peterborough, ON: Broadview Press.

Campbell, Robert M., Leslie A. Pal, and Michael Howlett. (Eds.). 2004. *The real world of Canadian politics: cases in process and policy*, 4th ed. Peterborough, ON: Broadview Press.

Canada West Foundation. 2001. *Building the new west: a framework for regional economic prosperity*. Calgary: Canada West Foundation (October).

Canada. 1972. *Foreign Direct Investment in Canada*. Gray Report. Ottawa: Information Canada.

——. 2001. *Second annual report on the state of trade*. Ottawa: Department of Foreign Affairs and International Trade (June).

——. 2001a. *Speech from the Throne to open the first session of the 37th Parliament of Canada*. Ottawa: House of Commons (30 January).

——. 2002. *Knowledge matters: skills and learning for Canadians*. Ottawa: Human Resources Development Canada (February).

——. 2005. *State of trade: 2005–statistical index*. Rev. Ottawa: International Trade Canada.

Canada, Agriculture Canada. 2001. *Cooperatives in Canada*. Ottawa: Cooperatives Secretariat.

Canada, Department of Finance. 1992-1996. *Economic reference tables*. Ottawa: Department of Finance.

——. 1994. *Agenda: jobs and growth—a new economic strategy for Canada*. Ottawa: Department of Finance (October).

——. 1998. *Report of the Technical Committee on Business Taxation*. Ottawa: Department of Finance.

——. 2000-2003. *Fiscal reference tables*. Ottawa: Department of Finance (October).

——. 2005. Tax and other issues related to publicly listed flow-through entities. Ottawa: Department of Finance (8 September).

Canada, Department of Foreign Affairs. 2001. *Smart border declaration*. Ottawa: Foreign Affairs Canada (11 December). Available at <http://www.dfait-maeci.gc.ca/can-am/main/border/smart_border_declaration-en.aspwww>.

Canada, Industry Canada. 2002. *Achieving excellence: investing in people, knowledge and opportunity*. Ottawa: Industry Canada (February).

——. 2002. The Canadian Automotive Partnership Council. Ottawa: Aerospace and Automotive Branch, Industry Canada (18 December). Available at <http://strategis.ic.gc.ca/SSG/am01454e.html>.

——. 2005. Status report regarding identified compliance issues related to Technology Partnerships Canada Contribution Agreements. Available at <http://tpc-ptc.ic.gc.ca/epic/internet/intpc-ptc.nsf/en/hb00478e.html>.

Canada, Lobbyist Registration Branch. 2000. *Annual report, 1999-2000*. Ottawa: Industry Canada.

Canada, Royal Commission on Corporate Concentration. 1977. *Report*. Ottawa: Supply and Services Canada.

Canada, Royal Commission on Dominion-Provincial Relations. 1940. *Report*. Book 1. Ottawa: Supply and Services Canada.

Canada, Royal Commission on the Economic Union and Development Prospects for Canada. 1985. *Report*. Vol. 1, 2. Ottawa: Supply and Services Canada.

Canada, Standing Committee on Finance. 1999a. *Budget 2000: new era ... new plan*. Ottawa: House of Commons (December).

——. 1999b. Productivity with a purpose: improving the standard of living of Canadians. Report #20. Ottawa: House of Commons (10 June).

——. 2000. Challenge for change: a study of cost recovery. Ottawa: House of Commons.

Canada, Standing Committee on Foreign Affairs and International Trade. 2002. *Partners in North America: advancing Canada's relations with the United States and Mexico.* Ottawa: House of Commons (December).

Canada, Standing Committee on Industry. 2000. *Interim report on the Competition Act.* Ottawa: House of Commons.

Canada, Standing Committee on Industry, Science, and Technology. 2002. *A plan to modernize Canada's competition regime.* Report #8. Ottawa: House of Commons (April).

Canada, Standing Senate Committee on Social Affairs, Science, and Technology. 2002. *The health of Canadians: the federal role: recommendations for reform.* Vol. 6. Ottawa: House of Commons (October).

Canada, Task Force on the Future of the Canadian Financial Services Sector. 1998. *Report of the Task Force.* Ottawa: Department of Finance (September).

Canada, Task Force on the Structure of Canadian Industry (Watkins Task Force). 1968. *Foreign ownership and Canadian industry.* Ottawa: Queen's Printer.

Canada, Voluntary Sector Task Force. 1999. *Working together, a government of Canada/voluntary sector joint initiative: report of the joint tables.* Ottawa: Privy Council Office (August).

Canadian Federation of Independent Business. 1999. Small is big: national poll results on Canadians' attitudes about small business. Toronto: Goldfarb Consultants (October).

——. 2001. Building a better community (April). Available at <http://www.cfib.ca / research/surveys/community_e.pdf>.

Canadian Manufacturers and Exporters. 2001a. *Canada's excellence gap: benchmarking the performance of Canadian industry against the G7.* Toronto: CME (August).

——. 2001b. *The business case for innovation.* Ottawa: CME (16 August).

Canadian Press. 2005. Ad firm contracts called political reward. *Globe and Mail* (17 November).

Canadian Tax Foundation. 1982. On opening up the budget process. *Canadian Tax Journal* 30 (2): 161-69.

Caranci, Beata. 2004. Canadian exports duck blow from higher-valued loonie. Toronto: TD Economics (12 July).

Cardillo, C. 2002. Foreign affiliate trade statistics: how goods and services are delivered in the international market. *Canadian Economic Observer* (May 3): 1-6.

Caro, Robert A. 1975. *The power broker: Robert Moses and the fall of New York.* New York: Vintage.

Carpentier, Cecile, and Jean-Marc Suret. 2003. The Canadian and American financial systems: competition and regulation. *Canadian Public Policy* 24(4): 431-47.

Carroll, William K. 1986. *Corporate power and Canadian capitalism.* Vancouver: University of British Columbia Press.

Carroll, William K., and Murray Shaw. 2001. Consolidating a neoliberal policy bloc in Canada. *Canadian Public Policy* 27(2): 195-216.

Carty, R.K. 1992. *Canadian political party systems.* Peterborough, ON: Broadview Press.

——. 2000. *Rebuilding Canadian party politics.* Vancouver: University of British Columbia Press.

Carty, R.K., and Lynda Erickson. 1991. Candidate nomination in Canada's political parties. In *Canadian political parties: leaders, candidates and organization,* ed. Herman Bakvis. Vol. 13: Research Studies, Royal Commission on Electoral Reform and Party Financing. Toronto: Dundurn Press.

Carty, R. Kenneth, William Cross, and Lisa Young. 2001. A new Canadian party system, in William Cross, ed., *Political Parties, Representation and Electoral Democracy in Canada.* Toronto: Oxford University Press. 16.

Carty, R. Kenneth, and Munroe Eagles. 2005. *Politics is local: national politics at the grassroots.* Toronto: Oxford University Press.

Carver, Peter. 2003. Administrative law: error of law 2: the contemporary approach to standards of review. Edmonton: Faculty of Law, University of Alberta. Available at <http://www.law.ualberta.ca/courses/carver/admin/slide_12_review_error_2.htm>.

Cashore, Benjamin, George Hoberg, Michael Howlett, Jeremy Rayner, and Jeremy Wilson. 2001. *In search of sustainability: British Columbia forest policy in the 1990s.* Vancouver: University of British Columbia Press.

Castells, Michel. 1996. *The information age: economy, society and culture.* Oxford: Blackwell.

Castles, Francis, G. Rolf Gerritsen, and Jack Vowles. (Eds.). 1996. *The great experiment: labour parties and public policy transformation in Australia and New Zealand.* St. Leonards, Australia: Allen and Unwin.

Cattaneo, Claudia. 2005. Oil majors retreat from foreign assets. *Financial Post,* 19 September: B2.

Caves, R.E., and R.H. Hobson. 1980. An outline of the economic history of British Columbia: 1881-1951. In *Historical essays on British Columbia,* ed. J. Friesen and H.K. Ralston. Toronto: Gage Publishing. 152-65.

CBC News. 2001. Bronfman tax case back in federal court, 28 June. Available at <http://cbc.ca/cgi-bin/view?/news/2001/06/28/bronfman010628>.

Chandler, M.A. 1983a. The politics of public enterprise. In *Crown Corporations in Canada: the calculus of instrument choice,* ed. J.R.S. Prichard. Toronto: Butterworth.

———. 1983b. Provincial resource policy. In *The politics of Canadian public policy,* ed. M. Atkinson and M.A. Chandler. Toronto: University of Toronto Press.

Chaykowski, Richard P. 2001. Collective bargaining: structure, process and innovation. In *Union management relations in Canada,* 4th ed., ed. Morley Gunderson, Allan Ponak, and Daphne Gottlieb Taras. Toronto: Addison, Wesley, Longman. 234-71.

Christian, William, and Colin Campbell. 1990. *Political parties and ideologies in Canada,* 3rd ed. Toronto, McGraw Hill Ryerson.

Clancy, Peter. 2004. *Micropolitics of business: paper, steel, airlines.* Peterborough, ON: Broadview Press.

Clark, Campbell. 2002. Minister's key adviser a private lobbyist. *Globe and Mail* (31 January).

———. 2005. Untendered deal went to campaign manager. *Globe and Mail* (17 November).

Clarke, Harold D., et al. 1991. *Absent mandate,* 2nd ed. Toronto: Gage.

———. 2000. *A polity on the edge.* Peterborough, ON: Broadview.

Clement, Wallace. 1975. *The Canadian corporate elite.* Toronto: McClelland and Stewart.

———. 1983. *Class, power and property.* Toronto: Methuen.

Clement, Wallace, and John Myles. 1994. *Relations of ruling: class and gender in postindustrial societies.* Montreal and Kingston: McGill-Queen's University Press.

Coalition for Secure and Trade-Efficient Borders. 2001. Rethinking our borders: statement of principles. Ottawa: Coalition for Secure and Trade-Efficient Borders (1 November).

——. 2004. Rethinking Our Borders: Beyond the Plan. Ottawa Coalition for Secure and Trade-Efficient Borders (March). Available at <http://www.cme-mec.ca/coalition/english/home.html>.

Cohen, Michael, James March, and Johan Olsen. 1972. A garbage can model of organizational choice. *Administrative Science Quarterly* 17: 1-25.

Coleman, William D. 1988. *Business and politics: a study in collective action.* Montreal and Kingston: McGill-Queen's University Press.

Coleman, William D., and Tim A. Mau. 2002. French-English relations in business interest associations. *Canadian Public Administration* 454: 490-511.

Coleman, William D., and Anthony Perl. 1999. Globalization, regionalism and the analysis of domestic public policy. In *Regionalism, multilateralism and the politics of global trade*, ed. Donald Barry and Ronald C. Keith. Vancouver: University of British Columbia Press. 71-91.

Coleman, William D., and Grace Skogstad. (Eds.). 1990. *Policy communities and public policy in Canada: a structural approach.* Toronto: Copp Clark Pitman.

Commission for Labour Cooperation. 2003. Recent trends in union density in North America. Washington, DC: The Commission.

Committee to Review the Structure of Securities Regulation in Canada. (Wise Persons' Committee). 2003. Final Report: *It's time.* Ottawa: Department of Finance (December).

Conference Board of Canada. 2001. *Performance and Potential 2001-2002.* Ottawa: CBC (October).

Conference of Defence Associations n.d. Political parrying and parsimony: the Sea King helicopter and the evolution of the maritime helicopter project. Available at: <http://www.cda-cdai.ca/pdf/plamondon>.

Conservative Party of Canada. 2005. The Federal Accountability Act: Stephen Harper's commitment to Canadians to clean-up government. Ottawa: Conservative Party of Canada (4 November).

Corak, Miles. (Ed.). 1998. *Government finances and generational equity.* Ottawa: Industry Canada (February).

Cottle, Simon. (Ed.). 2003. *News, public relations and power.* London: Sage Publications.

Courchene, Thomas J. 1991. Towards a reintegration of social and economic policy. In *Canada at Risk?* ed. G. Bruce Doern and Bryne B. Purchase. Toronto: C.D. Howe Institute. 125-48.

——. 1994. *Social Canada in the millennium.* Toronto: C.D. Howe Institute.

——. (Ed.). 1997. *The nation-state in the global-information era: policy challenges*, Kingston: John Deutsch Institute, Queen's University.

——. 2001a. A Canadian perspective on North American monetary union. Paper presented to the annual meeting of the American Economics Association, January.

——. 2001b. Social dimensions of the new global order. In *Globalization and the Canadian economy*, ed. Richard P. Chaykowski. Kingston, ON: School of Policy Studies, Queen's University. 61-103.

——. 2001c. *State of minds: towards a human capital strategy for Canada.* Montreal: Institute for Research in Public Policy.

Courchene, Thomas J., with Colin Telmer. 1998. *From heartland to North American region state.* Toronto: Faculty of Management, University of Toronto.

Creighton, Donald. 1937. The economic background of the rebellions of 1837. *Canadian Journal of Economics and Political Science* 3(3): 322-34.

——. 1955. *Sir John A. Macdonald: the old chieftain*. Toronto: Macmillan.

——. 1976. *The forked road: Canada 1939-1957*. Toronto: McClelland and Stewart.

Cross, P. 2002a. Cyclical implications of the rising import content in exports. *Canadian Economic Observer*. Ottawa: Statistics Canada (December).

——. 2002b. The effect of dividend flows on Canadian incomes. *Canadian Economic Observer* Cat. # 11-010 (October).

Cross, William. (Ed.). 2001. *Political parties, representation and electoral democracy in Canada*. Toronto: Oxford University Press.

——. 2004. *Political parties*. Vancouver: University of British Columbia Press.

Crowley, Brian Lee. 2000. Silent partner in Voisey's Bay. *Globe and Mail* (18 January).

——. 2003. The future of work in Nova Scotia. Halifax: Atlantic Institute for Market Studies (30 April).

Crowley, Brian Lee, and Michel Kelly-Gagnon. 2001. The economic jig is up, Mr. Landry. *Globe and Mail* (March 19).

Crozier, Michel, et al. 1975. *The crisis of democracy: report on the governability of democracies to the Trilateral Commission*. New York: New York University Press.

CSIS Commission on Global Aging. 2001. *Global aging: the challenge of the new millennium*. Washington, DC: Center for Strategic and International Studies (August).

Curren, Reg. 2000. Lougheed fears for Canadian sovereignty as US corporations invade economy. *Ottawa Citizen* (28 January).

Curry, Bill. 2005. Fears raised for impartial public service. *Globe and Mail* (7 October).

Curtis, Jenefer. 1999. Big oil vs. big auto. *Report on Business Magazine* (March): 62-72.

Dahl, Robert A. 1982. *Dilemmas of pluralist democracy: autonomy vs. control*. New Haven, CT: Yale University Press.

Daniels, Ronald J., and Michael J. Trebilcock. 1996. The future of Ontario Hydro: a review of structural and regulatory options. In *Ontario Hydro at the millennium*, ed. Ronald J. Daniels. Toronto: University of Toronto Press.

D'Aquino, Thomas J. 2003. Security and prosperity: the dynamics of a new Canada-United States partnership in North America. Ottawa: Canadian Council of Chief Executives (14 January).

——. 2005. Beyond free trade: a Canada-United States partnership for security and prosperity. Notes for remarks in Dallas, Tucson, Phoenix, Cleveland and Buffalo. Ottawa: Canadian Council of Chief Executives (24 February-3 March).

D'Aquino, Thomas J., and David Stewart-Patterson. 2001. *Northern edge: how Canadians can triumph in the global economy*. Toronto: Stoddart.

Davis, Aeron. 2003. Public relations and news sources. In *News, public relations and power*, ed. Simon Cottle. London: Sage Publications.

Davis, Richard. (Ed.). 1998. *Politics and the media*. Englewood Cliffs, NJ: Prentice-Hall.

De Boer, Stephen. 2002. Canadian provinces, US states and North American integration: bench warmers or key players. *Choices* 8(4). Montreal: Institute for Research in Public Policy.

de la Mothe, John. 2003. Ottawa's imaginary innovation strategy. In *How Ottawa Spends 2003-04*, ed. G. Bruce Doern. Toronto: Oxford University Press.

DeBettignies, Jean-Etienne, and Thomas W. Ross. 2004. The economics of public-private partnerships. *Canadian Public Policy* 30(2): 135-54.

deCloet, Derek, Steven Chase, and Peter Kennedy. 2005. Ottawa flags lose tax revenue as income trust party grows. *Globe and Mail* (9 September).

deCloet, Derek, Steven Chase, and Sinclair Stewart. 2005. All eyes on Ottawa's next move. *Globe and Mail* (11 October).

Delacourt, Susan. 2003. *Juggernaut: Paul Martin's campaign for Chrétien's crown.* Toronto: McClelland and Stewart.

Delacourt, Susan, and Donald G. Lenihan. (Eds.). 1999. *Collaborative government: is there a Canadian way?* Toronto: Institute for Public Administration of Canada.

DeSoto, Hernando. 2000. *The mystery of capital.* New York: Free Press.

Dib, Kamal. 2002. Trends in federally regulated industrial sectors. *The workplace gazette.* Ottawa: Human Resources and Social Development Canada. Available at <http://www.hrsdc.gc.ca/asp/gateway.asp?hr=en/lp/wid/gaze/winter2002/Winter2002_industrial.shtml@hs-wzp>.

Dicey, A.C. 1959. *Introduction to the study of the law of the Constitution,* 10th ed. London, Macmillan. 188.

Diewert, Erwin. 2002. Productivity trends and determinants in Canada. In *Productivity Issues in Canada,* ed. Someshwar Rao and Andrew Sharpe. Industry Canada Research Series. Calgary: University of Calgary Press. 37-38.

Dobson, Wendy. 2002. Shaping the future of the North American economic space. *Commentary* #132. Toronto: C.D. Howe Institute.

Dodge, David. 1998. Reflections on the role of fiscal policy. *Canadian Public Policy* 24(3): 275-89.

——. 2002. The interaction between monetary and fiscal policies. *Canadian Public Policy* 28(2): 187-201.

Doern, G. Bruce. 1982. Liberal priorities: the limits of scheming virtuously. In *How Ottawa spends: national policy and economic development 1982,* ed. G. Bruce Doern. Toronto: Lorimer.

Doern, G. Bruce, and Monica Gattinger. 2003. *Power switch: energy regulatory governance in the twenty-first century.* Toronto: University of Toronto Press.

Doern, G. Bruce, Margaret M. Hill, Michael J. Prince, and Richard J. Shultz. 1999. Canadian regulatory institutions: converging and colliding regimes. In *Changing the rules: Canadian regulatory regimes and institutions,* ed. G. Bruce Doern et al. Toronto: University of Toronto Press.

Doern, G. Bruce, Margaret M. Hill, Michael J. Prince, and Richard J. Schultz. (Eds.). 1999. *Changing the rules: Canadian regulatory regimes and institutions.* Toronto: University of Toronto Press.

Doern, G. Bruce, and Robert Johnson. 2006. *Rules ... rules ... rules ... rules: multilevel regulatory governance in Canada.* Toronto: University of Toronto Press.

Doern, G. Bruce, and Mark MacDonald. 1999. *Free trade federalism: negotiating the Canadian agreement on internal Trade.* Toronto: University of Toronto Press.

Doern, G. Bruce, Leslie A. Pal, and Brian W. Tomlin. (Eds.). 1996. *Border crossings: the internationalization of Canadian public policies.* Toronto: Oxford University Press.

Doern, G. Bruce, and Richard W. Phidd. 1983. Canadian public policy: ideas, structure, process. Toronto: Methuen.

Doern, G. Bruce, and Ted Reed. (Eds.). 2000. *Risky business: Canada's changing science-based policy and regulatory regime.* Toronto: University of Toronto Press.

Doern, G. Bruce, and Markus Sharaput. 2000. *Canadian intellectual property: the politics of innovating institutions and interests.* Toronto: University of Toronto Press.

Doern, G. Bruce, and Brian Tomlin. 1991. *Faith and fear: the free trade story.* Toronto: Stoddart.

Doern, G. Bruce, and Glen Toner. 1985. *The politics of energy: the development and implementation of the National Energy Program.* Toronto: Methuen.

Dorreboom, Iris. 1981. *The challenge of our time: Woodrow Wilson, Herbert Croly, Randolph Bourne and the making of modern America.* Amsterdam: Editions Rodopi.

Downs, Anthony. 1957. *An economic theory of democracy.* New York: Harper and Row.

Doyle, Simon, and Jack Aubry. 2005. Minister backs tougher rules for lobbyists. *Ottawa Citizen* (11 October).

Drucker, Peter F. 1994. The age of social transformation. *Atlantic Monthly* (November).

Drummond, Don. 2001. The penny drops. Toronto: TD Economics (24 April).

Dunn, Christopher. (Ed.). 2002. *The handbook of Canadian public administration.* Toronto: Oxford University Press.

Earnscliffe Research and Communications. 2001a. Main findings of a national survey. Presentation to Department of Finance. Ottawa: Department of Finance (March).

———. 2001b. Main findings of a national survey. Presentation to Department of Finance. Ottawa: Department of Finance (September).

———. 2001c. Results of quantitative research, budget survey. Presentation to Department of Finance. Ottawa: Department of Finance (November).

Easton, David. 1965. *A systems analysis of political life.* New York: Wiley.

Ebner, Dave. 2005. Oil sands worth $ 1.4-trillion, study finds. *Globe and Mail* (30 September).

Economic Council of Canada. 1979. *Responsible regulation: an interim report.* Ottawa: Supply and Services Canada.

———. 1981. *Reforming regulation.* Ottawa: Supply and Services Canada.

Economist. 2003. Competition is all (December 6).

Eden, Lorraine. 1994. *Multinationals as agents of change: setting a new Canadian policy on foreign direct investment.* Discussion Paper #1. Ottawa: Micro-Economic Policy Analysis Branch, Industry Canada (November).

Edgar, Tim. 2004. The trouble with income trusts. *Canadian Tax Journal* 52.

Ekos Research Associates. 2000a. Rethinking citizen engagement. July.

———. 2000b. *Rethinking government: Canadian view of emerging issues.* Ottawa: Ekos, 30 August.

———. 2000c. Rethinking government: presentation to IPAC. 30 August.

———. 2003. Canadian attitudes towards international trade. Ottawa: Foreign Affairs and International Trade Canada (6 May).

Ellis, Ron. 2003. A smoking-gun reform strategy for Rights Tribunals. Notes for presentation to conference of Canadian Council of Administrative Tribunals, Ottawa, June.

Ellul, Jacques. 1979. Politicization and political solutions. In *The politicization of society,* ed. Kenneth S. Templeton, Jr. Indianapolis, IN: Liberty Press. 211-47.

England, Robert Stowe. 2001. Hard landings: white paper on the financial markets impact of population aging. Washington, DC: Center for Strategic and International Studies (16 January).

Eppler, Erhard. 1999. A program beyond Utopia. In *The future of social democracy,* ed. Peter C. Russell. Toronto: University of Toronto Press. 165-94.

Estey, Willard Z. 1999. The quiet hijacking of corporate Canada. *Globe and Mail* (16 December).

Etzioni-Halevy, Eva. 1993. *The elite connection: problems and potential of Western democracy*. Cambridge: Polity Press.

———. 1997. Introduction. In *Classes and elites in democracy and democratization*, ed. Eva Etzioni-Halevy. New York: Garland.

Etzkowitz, Henry. 2002. The triple helix of university-industry-government: implications for policy and evaluation. Working Paper 2002-11. Stockholm: Institutet for studier av utbildning och forskning.

Etzkowitz, Henry, and Loet Leydesdorff. (Eds.). 1997. *Universities in the global knowledge economy*. London: Cassell.

External Advisory Committee on Smart Regulation. 2003. Regulatory management assessment: Australia. Ottawa (22 October). Available at <http://www.smartregulation.gc.ca/en/03/01/bk-05.asp>.

Fallows, James. 1993. How the world works. *The Atlantic Monthly* (December).

Finkel, Allan. 2003. Building the competency base of your tribunal: from selection to training. Paper presented to conference of Canadian Council of Administrative Tribunals Ottawa (1-3 June).

Finlayson, Jock. 2001. Provincial perspectives on the role of immigration in meeting future labour shortages. Vancouver: Business Council of British Columbia (16 October).

Flanagan, Tom. 1995. *Waiting for the wave*. Toronto: Stoddart.

Flanagan, Tom, and Stephen Harper. 1998. Conservative politics in Canada: past, present and future. In *After Liberalism: essays in search of freedom, virtue and order*, ed. William G. Gairdner. Toronto, Stoddart.

Forster, Ben. 1986. *A conjunction of interests: business, politics and the tariff*. Toronto: University of Toronto Press.

———. 1990. The coming of the National Policy: business, government and the tariff: 1876-1879. In *The Development of Canadian Capitalism: Essays in Business History*, ed. Douglas McCalla. Toronto, Copp Clark Pitman. 124-40.

Fortin, Pierre. 1999. *The Canadian standard of living: is there a way up?* Toronto: C.D. Howe Institute (19 October).

Forum of Labour Market Ministers. 2001. *Report on implementation of the labour mobility chapter of the agreement on internal trade*. Winnipeg: Manitoba Education, Labour and Youth (July).

Foster, Kathryn A. 1997. *The political economy of special purpose government*. Washington, DC: Georgetown University Press.

Foster, Peter. 1982. *The sorcerers' apprentices*. Toronto: Totem.

Fougère, Maxime, and Marcel Merette. 1999. An econometric examination of the impact of population ageing on personal savings in Canada. Working Paper 99-03. Ottawa: Department of Finance (February).

Fowke, Vernon. 1952. The National Policy: old and new. *Canadian Journal of Economics and Political Science* 18(3): 271-86.

Franklin, Bob. 2003. "A good day to bury bad news": journalists, sources and the packaging of politics. In *News, public relations and power*, ed. Simon Cottle. London: Sage Publications.

Freedman, Charles. 2002. Monetary policy anchors. In *Canadian conundrums: views from the Clifford Clark Visiting Economists*, ed. Robert D. Brown. Toronto: C.D. Howe Institute. 10-22.

Freeman, Neil B. 1996. *The politics of power: Ontario Hydro and its government, 1906-1995*. Toronto: University of Toronto Press.

Friedman, Milton, and Rose Friedman. 1980. *Free to choose*. New York: Harcourt, Brace, Jovanovich.

——. 1983. *The tyranny of the status quo*. New York: Harcourt, Brace, Jovanovitch.

Fukuyama, Francis. 1995. *Trust: the social virtues and the creation of prosperity*. New York: Free Press.

Galbraith, J.K. 1975. *Economic and the public purpose*. New York: New American Library.

Galloway, Gloria. 2004. Rights board on road to recovery. *Globe and Mail* (9 August).

Gans, H.J. 1979. *Deciding what's news: a study of CBS Evening News, NBC Nightly News, Newsweek and Time*. New York: Pantheon.

Garelli, Stephane. 2001. *Competitiveness of nations: the fundamentals*. Lausanne: IMD.

Garelli, Stephane, and Jonathan Rauch. 2001. The new old economy: oil, computers and the reinvention of the earth. *Atlantic Monthly* (January).

Gattinger, Monica. 2005. Canada-US electricity relations: policy coordination and multi-level associative governance. In *How Ottawa spends: 2005-2006*, ed. G. Bruce Doern. Montreal and Kingston: McGill-Queen's University Press. 143-62.

Gellner, Andrew B. 1986. The effects of business-government relations on industrial policy. In *Industrial policy*. Vol. 44: Background Papers, Royal Commission on the Economic Union, coord. André Blais. Toronto: University of Toronto Press.

Gerlach, Michael L. 1992. *Alliance capitalism: the social organization of Japanese business*. Berkeley, CA: University of California Press.

Gerth, H.H., and C. Wright Mills. (Eds.). 1958. *From Max Weber: essays in sociology*. New York: Oxford University Press.

Gibson, Gordon. 2002. *Reforming Canadian democracy*. Vancouver: Fraser Institute.

Giddens, Anthony. 2000. *The third way: the renewal of social democracy*. London: Blackwell.

Gilder, George. 1981. *Wealth and poverty*. New York: Basic Books.

Gillespie, Irwin 1991. *Tax, borrow and spend*. Ottawa: Carleton University Press.

Gillies, James G. 1981. *Where business fails*. Montreal: Institute for Research in Public Policy.

Globe and Mail. 1998. Canada's small business hotbed: Yukon? (December 3).

Globerman, Steven, and Daniel Shapiro. 1998. Canadian government policies towards inward foreign investment. Working Paper #24. Ottawa: Micro-Economic Policy Analysis Branch, Industry Canada (September).

Goar, Carol. 2003. The delicate matter of paying. *Toronto Star* (24 January).

Gold, Vic. 1975. *I don't need you when I'm right: confessions of a Washington PR man*. New York: William Morrow.

Goldstein, Amy, Sarah Cohen, Rick Weiss, and Joby Warrick. 2004. The fine print: an agency takes a turn. *The Washington Post* (15-17 August).

Good, David A. 1980. *The politics of anticipation*. Ottawa: School of Public Administration, Carleton University.

Grant, John. 1983. Foreign investment: turning off and turning on. *Canadian Public Policy* 9(1).

——. 2002. Ontario's new electricity market. *Policy Options* (May-June): 56-62.

Green, Christopher, et al. 1994. *Unemployment insurance: how to make it work*. Toronto: C.D. Howe Institute.

Greenspon, Edward, and Anthony Wilson-Smith. 1996. *Double vision: the inside story of the Liberals in power.* Toronto: Doubleday.

Grefe, Edward A. 1981. *Fighting to win: business political power.* New York: Harcourt, Brace Jovanovich.

Grubel, Herbert G. 1999. *The case for the Amero: the economics and politics of a North American monetary union.* Vancouver: Fraser Institute.

Guillemette, Yvon, and Jack M. Mintz. 2004. A capital story: exploding the myths around foreign investment in Canada. *Commentary* #201. Toronto: C.D. Howe Institute (August).

Gunderson, Morley, and Andrew Sharpe. (Eds.). 1998. *Forging business-labour partnerships: the emergence of sector councils in Canada.* Toronto: University of Toronto Press.

Hale, Geoffrey E. 1985. Reforming Revenue Canada. *Policy Options* (April).

——. 1996. *The politics of Canadian tax policy 1978-88: tax reform as constitutional change.* PhD dissertation. University of Western Ontario.

——. 1997. Changing patterns of party support in Ontario. In *Revolution at Queen's Park: Essays on governing Ontario,* ed. S. Noel. Toronto: Lorimer. 107-24.

——. 1998a. Administrative justice reform in Ontario. Paper presented to conference of Canadian Council of Administrative Tribunals, Ottawa (1 June).

——. 1998b. Reforming employment insurance. *Canadian Public Policy* 24(4): 429-51.

——. 2000. The tax on income and the growing decentralization of Canada's personal income tax system. In *State of the federation: 2000-01—Towards a new mandate for fiscal federalism,* ed. Harvey Lazar. Montreal and Kingston: McGill-Queen's University Press. 225-62.

——. 2001a. Managing the fiscal dividend: the politics of selective activism. In *How Ottawa Spends: 2000-2001,* ed. Leslie A. Pal. Toronto: Oxford University Press. 74-84.

——. 2001b. *The politics of taxation in Canada.* Peterborough, ON: Broadview Press.

——. 2001c. Priming the electoral pump: framing budgets for a renewed mandate. In *How Ottawa spends: 2001-02,* ed. Leslie A. Pal. Toronto, Oxford University Press. 29-60.

——. 2001d. Reintegrating federal economic and social policies in the 1990s: implementing Macdonald's ideas by trial and error. Paper presented to Annual Meeting of Canadian Political Science Association, May.

——. 2001e. Responding to the emerging global economy: challenges and options for a changing Canada. Remarks to forum on "Fostering economic competitiveness in a global economy." Vancouver, BC, 7 September.

——. 2002. Innovation and inclusion: budgetary policy, the skills agenda and the politics of the new economy. In *How Ottawa Spends: 2002-2003,* ed. G. Bruce Doern. Toronto: Oxford University Press. 20-47.

——. 2003. The unfinished legacy: Liberal policy on North America. In *How Ottawa Spends: 2003-2004,* ed. G. Bruce Doern. Toronto: Oxford University Press. 25-43.

——. 2004. Complementary federalism and the challenge of North American integration. *Canadian Public Administration* 47(4): 497-524.

——. 2005a. Big bang or slow drip: energy interdependence and North American integration. Paper presented to annual meeting, Canadian Political Science Association, May.

——. 2005b. Cross-border relations: moving beyond the politics of uncertainty? In *How Ottawa Spends: 2005-2006*, ed. G. Bruce Doern. Montreal and Kingston: McGill-Queen's University Press. 121-42.

——. 2005c. Federalism and the Canadian economic union: the past twenty years. In *The Macdonald Commission twenty years on*, ed. David Laidler and William B.P. Robson. Toronto: C.D. Howe Institute. 145-62.

——. 2005d. Income trusts: what will Ottawa do? Lethbridge, AB: <http://www.policy.ca/reports/geofferyhale/Income%20Trust%20Paper%200905.pdf>.

——. 2006a. Balancing diversity and competition: comparing provincial fiscal and tax regimes. In *Provinces: Canadian Provincial Politics*, 2nd ed., ed. Christopher Dunn. Peterborough, ON: Broadview Press.

——. 2006b. Trading up or treading water? Federal fiscal and budgetary policies in search of a new mandate. In *How Ottawa Spends: 2006-2007*, ed. G. Bruce Doern. Montreal and Kingston: McGill-Queen's University Press.

Hale, Geoffrey E., and Christopher Kukucha. 2006. Investment, trade and growth: multilevel regulatory regimes in Canada. In *Rules ... rules ... rules ... rules: multilevel regulatory governance in Canada*, ed. G. Bruce Doern and Robert Johnson. Toronto: University of Toronto Press.

Hall, Peter A. (Ed.). 1989. *The political power of economic ideas*. Princeton, NJ: Princeton University Press.

Hanson, James A., Patrick Honahan, and Giovanni Majnoni. (Eds.). 2003. *Globalization and national financial systems*. New York: World Bank and Oxford University Press.

Harris, Richard G. (Ed.). 2003. *North American linkages: opportunities and challenges for Canada*. Industry Canada Research Series. Calgary: University of Calgary Press.

Harris, Stephen L. 2004. Financial sector reform in Canada: interests and the policy process. *Canadian Journal of Political Science* 37(1): 161-84.

Hart, Michael M. 1985. *Canadian economic development and the international trading system*. Toronto: University of Toronto Press.

Hartle, Douglas. 1988. *The expenditure budget process of the government of Canada: a public choice-rent seeking approach*. Toronto: Canadian Tax Foundation.

——. 1993. *The federal deficit*. Government and Competitiveness Series. Kingston: School of Policy Studies, Queen's University.

Hartt, Stanley. 2004. Good policy is good politics: Why Canada needs bank mergers now. *Policy Options* (May): 61-65.

Hartt, Stanley H., and Patrick J. Monahan. 2002. The Charter and health care: guaranteeing timely access to health care for all Canadians. *Commentary* #164. Toronto: C.D. Howe Institute (May).

Hayek, Friedrich A. 1944. *The road to serfdom*. London: Routledge and Kegan Paul.

——. 1960. *The constitution of liberty*. Chicago: University of Chicago Press.

——. 1973. *Law, legislation and liberty*. Vol. 1. Chicago, IL: University of Chicago Press.

Hayes, David. 1992. *Power and influence: The Globe and Mail and the news revolution*. Toronto: Key Porter.

Heggie, B.A. 1998. Remarks to meeting, Pinehurst, NC. Mimeo. Potash Corporation of Saskatchewan (31 August).

Hein, Gregory. 2000. Interest group litigation and Canadian democracy. *Choices* 6:2. Montreal: Institute for Research in Public Policy (March).

Hejazi, Walid, and Peter Pauly. 2002. *Foreign direct investment and domestic capital formation*. Working Paper # 36. Ottawa: Industry Canada (April).

Held, David, Anthony G. McGrew, David Goldblatt, and Jonathan Perraton. 1999. *Global transformations: politics, economics and culture*. Palo Alto, CA: Stanford University Press.

Higginbotham, John, and Jeff Heynen. 2005. Managing through networks: the state of Canada-US relations. In *Canada among nations 2004: setting priorities straight*, ed. David Carment, et al. Montreal and Kingston: McGill-Queen's University Press. 121-40.

Hill Times. 2001. Top 100 contributors to Liberals in 2001. (8 July).

Hoberg, George. 2000. Canada and North American integration. *Canadian Public Policy* 25(12): S35-48.

———. (Ed.). 2002. *Capacity for choice: Canada in a new North America*. Toronto: University of Toronto Press.

Hoberg, George, Keith Banting, and Richard Simeon. 2002. The scope for domestic policy choice: policy autonomy in a globalizing world. In *Capacity for choice: Canada in North America*, ed. George Hoberg. Toronto: University of Toronto Press. 252-98.

Hou, Feng. 2005. *The initial destinations and distribution of Canada's major immigrant groups: changes over the past two decades*. Cat. #11F0019MIE. Ottawa: Statistics Canada (June).

Houle, France. 2004. Comment mettre fin au patronage à la Commission de l'Immigration et du Statut du Refugié? *Policy Options* (May): 51-55.

Howe, Paul, and David Northrup. 2000. Strengthening Canadian democracy: the views of Canadians. *Policy Matters* 1(5). Montreal: Institute for Research in Public Policy.

Howes, Carol. 2001. United-Agricore merger the end of Western co-ops. *Financial Post* (31 July).

Howlett, Michael. (Ed.). 2001. *Canadian forest policy*. Toronto: University of Toronto Press.

Howlett, Michael, Alex Netherton, and M. Ramesh. 1999. *The political economy of Canada: an introduction*. Toronto: Oxford University Press.

Howlett, Michael, and M. Ramesh. 2003. *Studying public policy: policy cycles and policy subsystems*, 2nd ed. Toronto: Oxford University Press.

Hufbauer, Gary C. and Jeffrey J. Schott. 1993. *NAFTA: an assessment*. Washington, DC: Institute for International Economics (October).

Hughes, Jonathan R.T. 1991. *The governmental habit redux: economic controls from colonial times to the present*. Princeton, NJ: Princeton University Press.

Hula, Kevin. 1999. *Lobbying together: interest group coalitions in legislative politics*. Washington, DC: Georgetown University Press.

Human Resources Development Canada. 2001. Outlook for EI premium rates for 2002. Ottawa: HRDC (September).

Hutchinson, Bruce. 1953. *The incredible Canadian*. Toronto: Longmans.

Iacobucci, Edward M., Michael J. Trebilcock, and Huma Haider. 2001. *Economic shocks: defining a role for government*. Policy Study #35. Toronto, C.D. Howe Institute.

Ibbitson, John. 1997. *Promised land*. Toronto: Prentice Hall.

———. 2000. Cash grab prompted Tories' sale of Hwy. 407. *Globe and Mail* (21 February).

Ingram, Matthew. 2002. Hydro One now a game of pass the blame. *Globe and Mail* (6 June).

Innis, Harold A. 1930. *The fur trade in Canada: an introduction to Canadian economic history* (New Haven: Yale University Press).

——. 1956. *Essays in Canadian economic history*, ed. Mary Q. Innis. Toronto: University of Toronto Press.

Institute for Research on Public Policy. 2002. Transparency, disclosure and democracy: assessing the Chief Electoral Officer's recommendations. Montreal: Institute for Research on Public Policy (February).

International Trade Canada. 2005a. *Pocket facts: Canada—economic indicators.* Ottawa: ITC (June).

——. 2005b. *Sixth annual report on the state of trade.* Ottawa: ITC (April).

Investment Funds Institute of Canada. Available at <http://www.ific.ca>.

Jack, Ian. 2003. Bombardier nets $ 1.2B in fed backing. *Financial Post* (24 July).

Jackson, Richard. 2001. Collective bargaining legislation in Canada. In *Union-Management Relations in Canada*, 4th ed., ed. Morley Gunderson, Allan Ponak, and Daphne Gottlieb Taras. Toronto: Addison Wesley Longman. 179-80.

Jiminez, Marina. 2004. Refugee approval rates vary widely. *Globe and Mail* (24 July).

Jog, Vijay, and Liping Wang. 2004. The growth of income trusts in Canada and the economic consequences. *Canadian Tax Journal* 52(3): 853-80.

Johns, David, and Anne S. DeVillars. 1999. *Principles of administrative law.* 3rd ed. Toronto: Carswell Thompson Canada.

Johnson, David. 2002. *Thinking government: public sector management in Canada.* Peterborough, ON: Broadview Press.

Johnston, Donald. 1986. *Up the hill.* Montreal: Optimum.

——. 1999. Taxation and social progress. *OECD Observer* 215 (January).

Jonas, George. 2004. Officialdom's arrogance: two case studies. *National Post* (16 August).

Jones, Jeffrey. 2005. EnCana sells Ecuador oil assets to Chinese group. *Globe and Mail*, 14 September.

Jones, Laura, and Stephen Graf. 2001. Canada's regulatory burden. *Fraser Forum.* Vancouver: Fraser Institute (August).

Kahler, Miles, and David A. Lake. (Eds.). 2003. *Governance in a global economy.* Princeton, NJ: Princeton University Press.

Kalawsky, Keith. 2004. To kill a bank merger. *Financial Post* (24 January).

Kendle, John 1979. *John Bracken.* Toronto, University of Toronto Press.

Kennedy, Paul. 1989. *The rise and fall of the great powers.* New York, Fontana Press.

Kennedy, Suzanne, and Janine Robbins. 2001. The role of fiscal rules in determining fiscal performance. Working Paper #2001-16. Ottawa: Department of Finance.

Kernaghan, Kenneth, Brian Marson, and Sandford Borins. 2000. *The new public organization.* Toronto: Institute for Public Administration in Canada.

Kernaghan, Kenneth, and David Siegel. 1999. *Public administration in Canada,* 4th ed. Toronto: ITP Nelson.

Khoury, George, Janet Rostami, and Peri Lynn Turnbull. 1999. *Corporate social responsibility: turning words into action.* Ottawa: Conference Board of Canada (February).

Kingdon, John W. 1984. *Agendas, alternatives and public policies.* New York: Harper Collins.

Kirk, Russell. 1993. *The politics of prudence.* Bryn Mawr, PA: Intercollegiate Studies Institute.

Kneebone, Ronald D., and Kenneth J. McKenzie. 1999. Fiscal policy in Canada. *Canadian Public Policy* 25(4): 483-501.

Koch, George. 2003. Will this little piggy bank go to market? *National Post Business* (September).

KPMG. 2002. *Competitive alternatives: comparing business costs in North America, Europe and Japan.* Available at <http://www.competitivealternatives.com>.

Kukucha, Chris. 2005. The federal-provincial trade system on international trade: CTRADE—an extension of executive federalism? In *The administration of foreign affairs: a renewed challenge*, ed. Luc Bernier and Nelson Michaud. Toronto: University of Toronto Press.

Kumar, Pradeep. 1993. *From uniformity to divergence*. Kingston, ON: IRC Press.

Kwan, Carolyn C. 2000. Restructuring in the Canadian economy: a survey of firms. *Bank of Canada Review* (Summer): 15-26.

Laghi, Brian. 2005. "Conflict" looms over Alberta's oil wealth. *Globe and Mail* (16 September).

Laidler, David. (Ed.). 1985. *Approaches to economic well-being*. Toronto: University of Toronto Press.

——. (Ed.). 1997. *Where we go from here: inflation targets in Canada's Monetary Policy Regime*. Toronto: C.D. Howe Institute.

Laidler, David, and Finn Poschmann. 2000. Leaving well enough alone. *Commentary* #142. Toronto: C.D. Howe Institute (May).

Lamer, Chief Justice Antonio. 2001. *Ocean Port Hotel v. British Columbia General Manager, Liquor Control and Licensing Branch.* 2001 SCC 52: 41. Available at <http://www.lexum.umontreal.ca/csc-scc/en/pub/2001/vol2/html/2001scr2>.

Landes, David S. 1998. *The wealth and poverty of nations*. New York, W.W. Norton.

Langer, John. 2003. Tabloid television and news culture: access and representation. In *News, public relations and power*, ed. Simon Cottle. London: Sage Publications. 135-51.

Lasswell, Harold. 1950. *Politics: who gets what ... when ... how*. New York: P. Smith.

Leblanc, Daniel. 2003. Rookies zero in on funds amassed by MPs. *Globe and Mail* (28 January).

Levitt, Kari. (Ed.). 1970. *Silent surrender: the multinational corporation in Canada*. Toronto: Macmillan.

Lewis, David. 1972. *Louder voices: the corporate welfare bums*. Toronto: Lorimer.

Lewis, Timothy. 2003. *In the long run we're all dead*. Vancouver: University of British Columbia Press.

Lindquist, Evert A. 2001. How Ottawa plans: the evolution of strategic planning. In *How Ottawa Spends: 2001-2001*, ed. Leslie A. Pal. Toronto: Oxford University Press. 61-94.

Lipsey, Richard G. 1996. *Economic growth, technological change and Canadian economic policy*. Toronto: C.D. Howe Institute (November 6).

Lobby Monitor. 2006. As the GR world turns. (27 January): 2-3.

Lowi, Theodore. 1985. *The end of liberalism*. New York: Norton.

Lynch, Kevin G. 2000. *Building a global, knowledge-based economy for the 21st century*. Ottawa: Industry Canada (February).

MacDonald, Mark R. 2001. The agreement on internal trade; trade-offs for economic union and federalism. In *Canadian federalism: performance, effectiveness and legitimacy*, ed. Herman Bakvis and Grace Skogstad. Toronto: Oxford University Press.

Macdonald, Michael. 2002. Inco makes century-long commitment to Newfoundland with $2.9 billion deal. *Ottawa Citizen* (11 June).

MacEachen, Hon. Allan J. 1982. *The budget process, a paper on budget secrecy and proposals for broader consultation*. Ottawa: Department of Finance (30 April).

MacLachlin, Ian. 2001. *Kill and chill: restructuring Canada's beef commodity chain*. Toronto: University of Toronto Press.

Makin, Kirk. 2004. Require timely health care, Supreme Court is urged. *Globe and Mail* (9 June).

Mandel, Michael. 1988. *The Charter of Rights and the legalization of politics in Canada*. Toronto: Wall and Thompson.

Mandell-Campbell, Andrea. 2002. Protection or costly fairy-tale. *Financial Post* (23 May).

Manfredi, Christopher. 2000. *Judicial power and the Charter: Canada and the paradox of liberal constitutionalism*, 2nd ed. Toronto: Oxford University Press.

Manitoba. 2002. Budget paper A: the economy. *2002 Budget*. Winnipeg: Ministry of Finance (22 April).

Manley, John. 2002. My vision for the Canada-US relationship. Speech. Halifax: Atlantic Institute for Market Studies (15 May).

Manley, John P., Pedro Aspe, and William Weld. 2005. *Building a North American community: report of the task force on the future of North America*. New York: Council on Foreign Relations Press (17 May).

Manning, Preston. 1992. *The new Canada*. Toronto: Macmillan Canada.

Marchildon, Gregory P. 1996. *Profits and politics: Beaverbrook and the gilded age of Canadian finance*. Toronto, University of Toronto Press.

Marotte, Bertrand. 2002. Caisse undertakes dramatic shakeup. *Globe and Mail* (3 December).

Martin, Paul. 2000. Speech to the Toronto Board of Trade. Release #2000-067. Ottawa: Department of Finance (16 September).

Martin, Roger L., and Michael E. Porter. 2000. *Canadian competitiveness: nine years after the crossroads*. Toronto: Rotman School of Management, University of Toronto (January).

Matthews, Ralph. 1983. *The creation of regional dependency*. Toronto: University of Toronto Press. 14-16.

May, Doug, and Alton Hollett. 1994. *The rock in a hard place*. Toronto: C.D. Howe Institute.

May, Kathryn. 2003. Top PS bosses face big shakeup. *Ottawa Citizen* (24 October).

Mayer, Frederick. 1998. *Interpreting NAFTA: the science and art of political analysis*. New York: Columbia University Press.

McArthur, John W., and Jeffrey D. Sachs. 2001. The growth competitiveness index: measuring technological advancement and the stages of development. In *Global competitiveness report: 2001-2002*, ed. Jeffrey Sachs and Michael Porter. New York: Oxford University Press.

McArthur, Keith. 2004. *Air monopoly*. Toronto: McClelland and Stewart.

McBride, Stephen, and John Shields. 1997. *Dismantling a nation: the transition to corporate rule in Canada*, 2nd ed. Halifax: Fernwood.

McCall, Christina, and Stephen Clarkson. 1996. *Trudeau and our times*. Vol. 2: *The heroic delusion*. Toronto: McClelland and Stewart.

McCall-Newman, Christina. 1980. *Grits: An intimate history of the Liberal Party*. Toronto: Macmillan.

McCallum, John. 1999. Towards a medium-term fiscal anchor for Canada. Toronto: Royal Bank Economics (August).

McCormick, Peter. 1994. *Canada's courts*. Toronto: James Lorimer.

———. 2000. *Supreme at last: the evolution of the Supreme Court of Canada*. Toronto: Lorimer.

McDonald, Forrest. 1985. *Novus ordo seclorum: the intellectual origins of the constitution*. Lawrence, KS: University Press of Kansas.

McDougall, John. 1993. *The politics and economics of Eric Kierans*. Montreal and Kingston: McGill-Queen's University Press.

McFarland, Janet. 2002. Power failure: Ontario's aborted plan. *Globe and Mail* (16 November).

McGregor, Glen. 2005. Liberals hire lobbyist to run election war room. *Ottawa Citizen* (16 November).

McInnes, David. 1999. *Taking it to the hill: the complete guide to appearing before and surviving parliamentary committees*. Ottawa: University of Ottawa Press.

McIntosh, Andrew. 2003a. Bias alleged in $1B federal deal. *National Post* (5 September).

———. 2003b. Judge orders Ottawa to pay $70M for government bureaucrats' actions. *National Post* (13 August).

McIntosh, Tom. (Ed.). 2000. *Federalism, democracy and labour market policy in Canada*. Kingston: School of Policy Studies, Queen's University.

McLaughlin, David. 1994. *Poisoned chalice: the last campaign of the Progressive Conservative Party?* Toronto: Dundurn Press.

McMahon, Fred. 1997. *Looking the gift horse in the mouth: the impact of federal transfers on Atlantic Canada*. Halifax: Atlantic Institute for Market Studies.

———. 2000a. *Retreat from growth: Atlantic Canada and the negative sum economy*. Halifax: Atlantic Institute for Market Studies.

———. 2000b. *The road to growth*. Halifax: Atlantic Institute for Market Studies.

McMillan, Charles J., and Victor V. Murray. 1985. Strategically managing public affairs: lessons from the analysis of business-government relations. In *Government and enterprise in Canada*, ed. K. Rea and Nelson Wiseman. Toronto: Methuen. 297-302.

McNish, Jacquie, Bernard Marotte, and Rheal Seguin. 2002. New CEO Rousseau pledges to recast the Caisse. *Globe and Mail* (30 May).

McQuaig, Linda. 1987. *Behind closed doors: how the rich won control of Canada's tax system and ended up richer*. Toronto: Viking/Penguin.

———. 1993. *The wealthy banker's wife: the assault on equality in Canada*. Toronto: Penguin.

———. 1996. *Shooting the hippo: death by deficit and other Canadian Myths*. Toronto: Penguin.

Meisel, James H. 1962. *The myth of the ruling class*. Ann Arbor, MI: University of Michigan Press.

———. (Ed.). 1965. *Pareto and Mosca*. Englewood Cliffs, NJ: Prentice-Hall.

Meisel, John. 1991. Decline of party in Canada. In *Party Politics in Canada*, 6th ed., ed. Hugh Thorburn. Toronto: Prentice Hall. 178-201.

Melchin, Greg. 2004. Passport to reform. *Financial Post* (6 October).

Mellon, Hugh, and Martin Westmacott. (Eds.). 1999. *Political dispute and judicial review*. Toronto: Nelson Thomson Learning.

Mendelsohn, Joshua, and Alister Smith. 1999. The new economy: measuring the impact of technological change. *The Economic and Technology Development Journal of Canada*.

Mendelsohn, Matthew. 2002. *Canada's social contract: evidence from public opinion.* Discussion Paper P-01. Public Involvement Network. Ottawa: Canadian Policy Research Networks (November).

Mendelsohn, Matthew, and Richard Nadeau. 1996. The magnification and minimization of social cleavages by the broadcast and narrowcast news media. *International Journal of Public Opinion Research* 8(4). Available at: <http://qsilver.queensu.ca/%7Emattmen/papers/index.html>.

Mendelsohn, Matthew, Robert Wolfe, and Andrew Parkin. 2002. Globalization, trade policy and the permissive consensus in Canada. *Canadian Public Policy* 28(3): 351-71.

Michel, Robert. 1997. The oligarchical tendency of working class organizations. In *Classes and elites in democracy and democratization*, ed. Eva Etzioni-Halevy. New York: Garland. 243-50.

Migué, Jean-Luc. 1998. The quiet revolution and the decline of Quebec. *National Post* (21 November).

Miljan, Lydia, and Barry Cooper. 2003. *Hidden agendas: how journalists influence the news.* Vancouver: University of British Columbia Press.

Milke, Mark. 2004a. Canada's top 10 think tanks. *Calgary Herald* (13 June).

——. 2004b. The idea whisperers. *Calgary Herald* (13 June).

Mills, C. Wright. 1956. *The power elite.* New York: Oxford University Press.

Milne, David. 1986. *Tug of war: Trudeau, Mulroney and the provinces.* Toronto: James Lorimer.

Milner, Helen V. 1997. *Interests, institutions, and information: domestic politics and international relations.* Princeton, NJ: Princeton University Press.

Mintz, Jack M. 2001. *Most favoured nation: building a framework for smart economic policy.* Toronto: C.D. Howe Institute.

Mintz, Jack M., Duanjie Chen, Yvan Guillemette, and Finn Poschmann. 2005. *The 2005 tax competitiveness report: unleashing the Canadian tiger.* Commentary #216. Toronto: C.D. Howe Institute (September).

Mitchell, David C. 1983. *W.A.C. Bennett and the rise of British Columbia.* Vancouver: Douglas and McIntyre.

Molotch, Harvey, and Marilyn Lester. 1981. News as purposive behavior: on the strategic use of routine events, accidents, and scandals. *American Political Science Review* 39: 101-12.

Monahan, Patrick, and Marie Finkelstein. 1993. The Charter of Rights and public policy in Canada. In *The impact of the Charter on the public policy process*, ed. Patrick Monahan and Marie Finkelstein. Toronto: Centre for Public Law and Public Policy, York University.

Montpetit, Eric. 2003. Public consultations in policy network environments: the case of assisted reproductive technology policy in Canada. *Canadian Public Policy* 29(1): 95-110.

Moore, Christopher. 1997. *1867: How the fathers made a deal.* Toronto: McClelland and Stewart.

Moore, Karl, and Alan Rugman. 2003. Canadian multinationals are regional, not global. *Policy Options* 24(7).

Moore, Sean 2002a. From the Flip Wilson School of Communications Theory. *The Hill Times* (14 January).

——. 2002b. How to talk so that citizens will listen and listen so that citizens will talk. *The Hill Times* (7 January).

——. 2002c. A matter of substance. *The Hill Times* (8 April).

——. 2004. The wisdom of the wise ... *The Hill Times* (18 March).

Moreau, Anne. 2003. Measuring change following major reforms to Quebec's administrative tribunals: anatomy of a "practical" mistake? Paper presented to conference of Canadian Council of Administrative Tribunals, Ottawa (1-3 June).

Morton, F.L. (Ed.). 2002. *Law, politics and the judicial process in Canada*, 3rd ed. Calgary: University of Calgary Press.

Morton, F.L., and Rainer Knopff. 2001. *The Charter revolution and the court party*. Peterborough, ON: Broadview Press.

Mosca, Gaetano. 1939. *The ruling class*, ed. Arthur Livingston, trans. Hannah D. Kahn. New York: McGraw Hill.

Mowrey, Tim, and Alain Pelletier. 2002. Election financing in Canada. *Electoral Insight* 4(1). Ottawa: Elections Canada (May): 2-8.

Mueller, Dennis. 1989. *Public choice II*. Cambridge: Cambridge University Press.

Mullan, David. (Ed.). 2003. *Administrative law: cases, text and materials*, 5th ed. Toronto: Emond Montgomery Publications.

Muller, Jerzy Z. 1993. *Adam Smith in his time and ours*. Princeton, NJ: Princeton University Press.

Munn-Venn, Trefor, and Roger Voyer. 2004. *Clusters of opportunity, clusters of risk*. Ottawa: Conference Board of Canada.

Murrell, David. 2001. Following the money trail. Halifax: Atlantic Institute for Market Studies.

Myers, Gustavus. 1968 (1914). *History of Canadian wealth*. New York: Argosy Antiquarian.

Myles, John, and Paul Pierson. 1997. *Friedman's revenge: the reform of "liberal" welfare states in Canada and the United States*. Ottawa: Caledon Institute.

Nadeau, Serge, and Someshwar Rao. 2002. The role of industrial structure in Canada's productivity performance. In *Productivity issues in Canada*, ed. Someshwar Rao and Andrew Sharpe. Industry Canada Research Series. Calgary: University of Calgary Press.

NAFTA Secretariat. 2005. *Security and prosperity partnership of North America: report to leaders*. Ottawa: NAFTA Secretariat (June).

National Post Business. 2002. Financial Post 500 (May).

——. 2004. FP 500. Toronto (June).

Nesbitt-Larking, Paul. 2001. *Politics, the media and society*. Peterborough, ON: Broadview Press.

Nevitte, Neil, André Blais, Elisabeth Gidengil, and Richard Nadeau. 2000. *Unsteady state*. Toronto: Oxford University Press.

New Brunswick. 2002. *Greater opportunity: New Brunswick's prosperity plan*. Fredericton: Government of New Brunswick (2 February).

Newfoundland and Labrador. 2002. Statistical indicators: Newfoundland and Labrador. St. John's: Newfoundland and Labrador Ministry of Finance.

Newman, Peter C. 1968. *The distemper of our times*. Toronto: McClelland and Stewart.

——. 1999. *Titans: how the new Canadian establishment seized power*. Toronto: Penguin.

Nisbet, Robert. 1975. *The twilight of authority*. New York: Oxford University Press.

Noel, S.J.R. 1971. *The politics of Newfoundland*. Toronto: University of Toronto Press.

——. 1990. *Patrons, clients, brokers: Ontario society and politics 1791-1896*. Toronto: University of Toronto Press.

Nordlinger, Eric. 1981. *On the autonomy of the democratic state.* Cambridge, MA: Harvard University Press.

Norrie, Kenneth, and Douglas Owram. 1996. *A history of the Canadian economy,* 2nd ed. Toronto: Harcourt, Brace and Co.

Northwest Territories. 2001. *2001 Socio-economic scan.* Yellowknife: Ministry of Finance, Northwest Territories. (May).

Novak, Michael. 1982. *The spirit of democratic capitalism.* New York: Touchstone Books.

Nunavut. n.d. *Nunavut at a glance.* Iqaluit: Government of Nunavut.

O'Connor, James. 1973. *The fiscal crisis of the state.* New York: St. Martin's Press.

O'Neill, Tim. 2002. North American economic integration ... and its application to Canadian banks. Toronto: BMO Financial Group Economics Department (October).

Oakeshott, Michael. 1991. *Rationalism in Politics and Other Essays.* Indianapolis, IN: Liberty Press.

Observatory on Media and Public Policy. 2006. 2006 Canadian federal election newspaper analysis. Montreal: McGill University (January). Available at: <http://www.ompp.mcgill.ca/pages/2006election.htm#desc>.

OECD. 1999. The size and role of automatic fiscal stabilizers. *OECD Economic Outlook 66* (December 1999): 137-49.

——. 2001. Encouraging environmentally sustainable growth: experience in OECD countries. *OECD Economic Outlook* 69 (June): 187-207.

——. 2002. Fiscal sustainability: the contribution of fiscal rules. *OECD Economic Outlook* 72 (December 2002): 49-73.

——. 2003. *The sources of economic growth in OECD countries.* Paris: OECD.

Offe, Claus. 1984. *Contradictions of the welfare state,* ed. John Keane. Cambridge, MA: MIT Press.

Office of the Auditor General. 2002. Report to the Minister of Public Works and Government Services on three contracts awarded to Groupaction. Ottawa: Office of the Auditor General (May).

——. 2003. Advertising activities. *Report of the Auditor General.* Ottawa: Office of the Auditor General (November). Available at: <http://www.oag-bvg.gc.ca/domino/reports.nsf/html/20031104ce.html>.

Office of the Ethics Councillor. 1998-2003. *Lobbyist Registration Act: annual report.* Ottawa: Industry Canada. Available at <http://www.strategis.ic.gc.ca/SSG/lr01066e.html>.

Oliver, Peter. 1977. *G. Howard Ferguson: Ontario Tory.* Toronto: University of Toronto Press.

Olson, Mancur. 1965. *The logic of collective action: public goods and the theory of groups.* Cambridge, MA: Harvard University Press.

——. 1982. *The rise and decline of nations: economic growth, stagflation and social rigidities.* New Haven, CT: Yale University Press.

Ontario. 1989. Macauley Report: *Directions: review of Ontario's regulatory agencies.* Toronto: Management Board of Cabinet (September).

——. 1999. *Ontario's living legacy.* Toronto: Ministry of Natural Resources.

Ontario, Agency Review Commission. 1997. *Report.* Toronto: Management Board of Cabinet.

Ontario, Institute for Competitiveness and Prosperity. 2002. *A view of Ontario: Ontario's clusters of innovation.* Toronto: Ministry of Entrepreneurship, Opportunity and Innovation (April).

Ontario, Premier's Council. 1988. *Competing in the new global economy.* 3 vols. Toronto: Queen's Printer for Ontario.

Ornstein, Michael. 1998. Three decades of elite research in Canada: John Porter's unfulfilled legacy. In *The vertical mosaic revisited*, ed. R. Helmes Hayes and J. Curtis. Toronto: University of Toronto Press. 157-63.

Osberg, Lars. 1985. The measurement of economic well-being. In *Approaches to economic well-being*, ed. David Laidler. Toronto: University of Toronto Press. 49-87.

———. 2001. Needs and wants: what is social progress and how should it be measured. In *The review of economic performance and social progress*, ed. Keith Banting, Andrew Sharpe, and France St. Hilaire. Montreal: Institute for Research in Public Policy. 23-41.

Packham, William D. 2002. A threat to capital markets. *Financial Post* (23 May).

Pal, Leslie A. 2001. *Beyond policy analysis: public issue management in turbulent times,* 2nd ed. Toronto: Nelson Thomson Learning.

Pareto, Vilfredo. 1902-03. *Les systèmes socialistes,* 2 vol. Paris: V. Giard and E. Brière.

Parker, Richard. 1972. *The myth of the middle class.* New York: LiveRight.

Pastor, Robert A. 2001. *Toward a North American community.* Washington, DC: Institute for International Economics.

Peters, B. Guy. 1984. *The politics of bureaucracy,* 2nd ed. New York: Longman.

———. 2002. The politics of tool choice. In *The tools of government: a guide to the new governance*, ed. Lester M. Salamon. New York: Oxford University Press. 552-64.

Pierson, Paul. 1994. *Dismantling the welfare state? Reagan, Thatcher, and the politics of retrenchment.* Cambridge: Cambridge University Press.

Piva, Michael J. 1992. Government finance and the development of the Canadian state. In *Colonial leviathan: state formation in mid-nineteenth century Canada*, ed. Allan Greer and Ian Radforth. Toronto: University of Toronto Press.

Polsby, Nelson W. 1985. Prospects for pluralism. *Society* 22: 30-34.

Porter, John. 1965. *The vertical mosaic.* Toronto: University of Toronto Press.

Porter, Michael E., Jeffrey D. Sachs, and John W. McArthur. 2001. Competitiveness and stages of economic development. In *Global Competitiveness Report: 2000*. New York: Oxford University Press. 16-25.

Porter, Michael, E. Jeffrey D. Sachs, and Andrew Warner. 2000. Executive summary: current competitiveness and growth competitiveness. In *Global Competitiveness Report: 2000*. Geneva, World Economic Forum.

Porter, Michael. 1991. *Canada at the crossroads: the reality of a new competitive environment.* Ottawa: Supply and Services Canada.

Poschmann, Finn. 2003. Private means to public ends: the future of public-private partnerships. *Commentary* # 183. Toronto: C.D. Howe Institute.

Post, Gordon. 2002. *Stare decisis: the use of precedents.* In *Law, politics and the judicial process in Canada*, 3rd ed., ed. F.L. Morton. Calgary: University of Calgary Press.

Pouliot, Robert. 2004. Caisse de dépôt et placement du Québec: surveillant ou gérant? *Le Devoir* (31 January).

Prichard, J. Robert S., and Michael J. Trebilcock. 1983. Crown corporations in Canada: the choice of instrument. In *The politics of Canadian public policy*, ed. Michael M. Atkinson and Marsha A. Chandler. Toronto: University of Toronto Press. 199-222.

Pross, A. Paul. 1992. *Group politics and public policy,* 2nd ed. Toronto: Oxford University Press.

——. 1995. Pressure groups: talking chameleons. In *Canadian Politics in the 1990s*, 4th ed., ed. M.S. Whittington and G. Williams. Toronto: Nelson.

Public Policy Forum. 2002. *Bridging two solitudes: a discussion paper on federal government-industry relations*. Ottawa: Public Policy Forum (October).

Putnam, Robert D. 1988. Diplomacy and domestic politics. *International Organization* 42.

——. 2000. *Bowling alone: the collapse and revival of American community*. New York: Simon and Schuster.

Quebec. 1999. *The economy and public finances of Quebec*. Quebec: Ministère des Finances (October).

Quebec, *Tribunal administratif du Québec*. 2006. Available at <http://www.taq.gouv.qc.ca>.

Rabkin, Jeremy. 1983. The charismatic constitution. *The Public Interest* 73.

Rae, Bob. 1998. *The three questions: prosperity and the public good*. Toronto, Penguin Books.

Reguly, Eric. 1999. TSE, Corporate Canada goes American. *Globe and Mail* (23 November).

Reich, Robert B. 1992. *The work of nations: preparing ourselves for 21st century capitalism*. New York: Random House.

Reich, Robert. 2005. Divided they'll stand—maybe even taller. *The Washington Post* (31 July).

Reid, Frank, and Noah M. Meltz. 2001. Social, political and economic environments. In *Union management relations in Canada*, 4th ed., ed. Morley Gunderson, Allan Ponak, and Daphne Gottlieb Taras. Toronto: Addison, Wesley, Longman. 142-74.

Rempel, Roy. 2003. *The chatter box*. Toronto: Dundurn Press.

Rice, James J., and Michael J. Prince. 2000. *Changing politics of Canadian social policy*. Toronto: University of Toronto Press.

Richards, John. 1997. *Retooling the welfare state*. Toronto, C.D. Howe Institute.

Roach, Robert, and Loleen Berdahl. 2001. *State of the west: western Canadian demographic and economic trends*. Calgary: Canada West Foundation (April).

Roberts, Alasdair. 1996. Worrying about misconduct: the control lobby and the PS 2000 reforms. *Canadian Public Administration* 39(4): 489-518.

Robertson, James R. 2003. *Bill C-24: An Act to Amend the Canada Elections Act and the Income Tax Act Political Financing*. LS-448-E. Ottawa: Library of Parliament (11 June).

Robinson, Walter. 2002. Dithering in the skies. *Ottawa Sun* (9 March).

Robson, William B.P. 2001. Will the baby-boomers bust the health budget? *Commentary 148*. Toronto, C.D. Howe Institute (February).

Rocher, François, and Christian Rouillard. 2002. Redefining the locus of power. In *Capacity for Choice: Canada in a New North America*, ed. George Hoberg. Toronto: University of Toronto Press. 224-51.

Romney, Paul. 1999. *Getting it wrong: how Canadians forgot their past and imperiled Confederation*. Toronto: University of Toronto Press.

Rose, Jonathan. 2000. *Making pictures in our heads: government advertising in Canada*. Toronto: University of Toronto Press.

Rosenau, James N. 1992. Governance, order and change in world politics. In *Governance without government: order and change in world politics*, ed. James N. Rosenau and Ernst-Otto Czempiel. Cambridge: Cambridge University Press.

——. 2003. *Distant proximities: dynamics beyond globalization*. Princeton, NJ: Princeton University Press.

Ross, Thomas W. 1998. Introduction: the evolution of competition law in Canada. *Review of Industrial Organization* 13: 1-2, 3-8.

Rothenberg, Randall. 1984. *The neoliberals: creating a new American politics*. New York: Simon and Schuster.

Rotstein, Abraham. 1966. The 20th century prospect: nationalism in a technological society. In *Nationalism in Canada*, ed. P. Russell. Toronto: McGraw Hill.

Rubin, Sandra. 2002. Bay Street worries as takeovers accelerate. *Financial Post* (22 May).

——. 2003. Merger victory fleeting. *Financial Post* (2 April).

Ruggie, J.G. 1995. At home abroad, abroad at home: international liberalization and domestic stability in the new world economy. *Journal of International Studies* 24(3): 507-26.

Rugman, Alan G. 2000. *The end of globalization: why global strategy is a myth and how to profit from the realities of regional markets*. New York: Amacom.

Rugman, Alan G., and Joseph R. D'Cruz. 1991. *Fast forward: improving Canada's international competitiveness*. Toronto: Kodak Canada.

Russell, Peter H. 1993. *Constitutional odyssey*. 2nd ed. Toronto: University of Toronto Press.

Sachs, Jeffrey D., and Andrew M. Warner. 2000. Globalization and international competitiveness: some broad lessons of the past decade. *Global Competitiveness Report 2000*, 18-27. Geneva: World Economic Forum.

Sada, Carlos M., and Geoffrey Hale. 2003. A tale of two systems: contrasting federal and cross-border relations of sub-national governments in Mexico and Canada. Paper presented to conference, Relating to the Powerful One: How Canada and Mexico View Their Relationship with the United States. Harvard University (5-6 May).

Salamon, Lester M. (Ed.). 2002. *The tools of government: a guide to the new governance*. New York: Oxford University Press.

Sallot, Jeff. 2005. Forensic audits to tell the tale of TPC program. *Globe and Mail* (30 September).

Sartori, Giovanni. 1987. *The theory of democracy revisited*. Chatham, NJ: Chatham House.

Saskatchewan. 1999. *Report of the Personal Income Tax Review Committee*. Regina: Ministry of Finance (November).

——. 2002. *Economic review 2001*. Regina: Ministry of Finance.

Saunders, S.A. 1984. *The economic history of the Maritime provinces*. Fredericton: Acadiensis Press.

Savoie, Donald J. 1990. *The politics of public spending in Canada*. Toronto: University of Toronto Press.

——. 1999. *Governing from the centre*. Toronto: University of Toronto Press.

——. 2001. *Pulling against gravity: economic development in New Brunswick during the McKenna years*. Montreal: Institute for Research in Public Policy.

——. 2004. Regional economic development in Atlantic Canada: the next step. In *Regionalism in a global society*, ed. Stephen G. Tomblin and Charles S. Colgin. Peterborough, ON: Broadview Press. 107-26.

Sawatzky, John. 1987. *The insiders: government, business and the lobbyists*. Toronto: McClelland and Stewart.

Sawyer, Malcolm C. 1979. *Theories of the firm*. New York: St. Martin's Press.

Sayers, Anthony M. 1999. *Parties, candidates and constituency campaigns in Canadian elections.* Vancouver: University of British Columbia Press.

Saywell, John T. 1991. *Just call me Mitch: The life of Mitchell F. Hepburn.* Toronto: University of Toronto Press.

Scharpf, Fritz W. 1997a. Balancing positive and negative integration: the regulatory options for Europe. MPIfG Working Paper 97/8. Köln: Max Planck Institute.

——. 1997b. *Games real actors play: actor-centered institutionalism in policy research.* Boulder, CO: Westview Press.

Schembri, Lawrence. 2002. Foreign takeovers and the Canadian dollar: evidence and implications. *Bank of Canada Review* (Spring): 45-50.

Schlesinger, Philip. 1990. Rethinking the sociology of journalism: source strategies and the limits of media-centrism. In *Public communication: the new imperative*, ed. M. Ferguson. London: Sage.

Schumpeter, Joseph. 1942. *Capitalism, socialism and democracy.* New York: Harper and Row.

Schwab, Klaus, Michael E. Porter, and Jeffery D. Sachs. 2001. *The global competitiveness report: 2001-2002.* New York: Oxford University Press.

Schwanen, Daniel. 1997. *Trading up: the impact of increased continental integration on trade, investment, and jobs in Canada.* Toronto: C.D. Howe Institute (March).

——. 2001. After Sept. 11: interoperability with the US, not convergence. *Policy Options* (November): 46-49.

——. 2003. Let's not cut corners: unbundling the Canada-US relationship. *Policy Options* (April): 12-19.

Schwartz, Mildred. 1974. *Politics and territory; the sociology of regional persistence in Canada.* Montreal and Kingston: McGill-Queen's University Press.

Science Council of Canada. 1978. *The weakest link: a technological perspective on Canadian industrial underdevelopment.* Ottawa: Supply and Services Canada.

——. 1984. *Canadian industrial development: some policy directions.* Ottawa: Supply and Services Canada.

Scoffield, Heather. 2005. High oil, high dollar, and Dutch disease. *Globe and Mail* (26 September).

Scotton, Geoffrey. 2001. What makes Calgary tick? *Calgary Herald* (27 October).

Sharpe, Andrew. 1998. Productivity: the key to economic success. Ottawa: Centre for Study of Living Standards (March).

Shepherd, John J. 1981. Hidden Crown corporations. *Policy Options* 2(2): 40-42.

Sheppard, Robert, and Michael Valpy. 1982. *The national deal: the fight for a Canadian Constitution.* Toronto: Fleet Books.

Siegfried, André. 1992. Party politics in Canada. In *Canadian political party systems*, ed. R.K. Carty. Peterborough, ON: Broadview Press.

Simeon, Richard. 2003. Important? Yes. Transformative? No. North American integration and Canadian federalism. In *The Impact of Global and Regional Integration on Federal Systems*, ed. Harvey Lazar, Hamish Telford, and Ronald L. Watts. Kingston: Institute of Intergovernmental Relations, School of Policy Studies, Queen's University. 125-71.

Simeon, Richard, and Ian Robinson. 1990. *State, society and the development of Canadian federalism.* Royal Commission on the Economic Union and Development Prospects for Canada. Background Paper #71. Toronto: University of Toronto Press.

Simon, William. 1978. *A time for truth.* New York: McGraw Hill.

Simpson, Jeffrey. 1980. *The discipline of power*. Toronto: Personal Library.

——. 2001. *The friendly dictatorship*. Toronto: Stoddart.

——. 2002. Talk about a near thing. *Globe and Mail* (20 December).

Skelton, O.D. 1966. *Life and Times of Sir Alexander Tilloch Galt*, ed. Guy Maclean. Toronto: McClelland and Stewart.

Skidelsky, Robert. (Ed.). 1977. *The end of the Keynesian era*. London: Macmillan.

Skogstad, Grace. 2001. International trade policy and Canadian federalism: a constructive tension. In *Canadian federalism: performance, effectiveness and legitimacy*, ed. Herman Bakvis and Grace Skogstad. Toronto: Oxford University Press. 159-77.

——. 2003. Who governs? Who should govern?: political authority and legitimacy in Canada in the twenty-first century. *Canadian Journal of Political Science* 36(5): 955-73.

Smiley, Donald V. 1987. *The federal condition in Canada*. Toronto, McGraw-Hill Ryerson.

Smith, Bradley A. 2001. *Unfree speech: the folly of campaign finance reform*. Princeton, NJ: Princeton University Press.

Smith, David E. 1975. *Prairie liberalism: The Liberal Party in Saskatchewan 1905-71*. Toronto: University of Toronto Press.

——. 1996. Party struggles to win the prairies. In *Party politics in Canada*, 7th ed., ed. Hugh G. Thorburn. Toronto: Prentice Hall. 449-59.

Smith, Jennifer. 1983. The origins of judicial review in Canada. *Canadian Journal of Political Science* 16(1): 115-34.

Soroka, Stuart N. 2002. *Agenda-setting dynamics in Canada*. Vancouver: University of British Columbia Press.

Soroka, Stuart, and Antonia Maioni. 2006. Little sign of bias in news coverage. *Toronto Star* (1 February).

Spector, Norman. 2002. Lawrence of ACOA. *Globe and Mail* (23 October): A23.

Stairs, Denis. 2002. Transnational pluralism and the "democratization" of Canadian foreign policy at the turn of the millennium. In *Political Parties, Representation and Electoral Democracy in Canada*, ed. William Cross. Toronto: Oxford University Press. 161-76.

Stanbury, W.T. 1977. *Business interests and the reform of Canadian competition policy, 1971-1975*. Toronto: Methuen.

——. 1988. Corporate power and political influence. In *Mergers, Corporate Concentration, and Power in Canada*, ed. R.S. Khemani, D.M. Shapiro and W.T. Stanbury. Halifax: Institute for Research in Public Policy.

——. 1991. *Money in politics: financing federal parties and candidates in Canada*. Toronto: Dundurn Press.

——. 1994. *Business-government relations in Canada*, 2nd ed. Toronto: Nelson.

——. 1996. Getting and spending: the effect of federal regulations on financing political parties and candidates in Canada. In *Party politics in Canada*, 7th ed., ed. Hugh Thorburn. Toronto: Prentice Hall.

——. 2001. Regulating federal party and candidate finances in a dynamic environment. In *Party Politics in Canada* , 8th ed., ed. Hugh Thorburn and Alan Whitehorn. Toronto: Prentice Hall. 179-205.

——. 2002. PM runs an exclusive enterprise. *The Hill Times* (23 September).

Statistics Canada. 1999. *Historical Statistics of Canada*, 2nd ed. Cat. #11-516-XIE. Ottawa: Statistics Canada.

——. 2002a. *2001 Census analysis series: a profile of Canada's population, where we live.* Ottawa: Statistics Canada (12 March).

——. 2002b. *Canadian economic observer: historical statistical supplement.* Cat. #11-210-XPB. Ottawa: Statistics Canada. Cat. 11-010, 3,12,13.

——. 2002c. *The daily.* Ottawa: Statistics Canada.

——. 2002d. *Intercorporate ownership.* Cat. # 61-517. Ottawa: Statistics Canada (15 March).

——. 2002e. A profile of the Canadian population. Cat. #96F0030XIE010012001. Ottawa: Statistics Canada (12 March).

——. 2002f. *Provincial economic accounts: 2001.* Cat. #13-213. Ottawa: Statistics Canada.

——. 2003a. CANSIM II. Ottawa: Statistics Canada (22 January).

——. 2003b. *The daily.* Ottawa: Statistics Canada.

——. 2004a. *The daily.* Ottawa: Statistics Canada.

——. 2004b. *Provincial economic accounts,* Cat. #13-213. Ottawa: Statistics Canada.

——. 2005a. *Canada's international investment position.* Cat. #67-202. Ottawa: Statistics Canada (September).

——. 2005b. CANSIM. Ottawa: Statistics Canada (21 July).

——. 2005c. *National income and expenditure accounts.* Cat. #13-001. Ottawa: Statistics Canada (June).

——. 2005d. Provincial income disparities through an urban-rural lens: evidence from the 2001 census. Cat. #11-624-MIE 2005012. Ottawa: Statistics Canada (21 July).

——. 2005e. *Public sector statistics.* Cat. #213 Ottawa: Statistics Canada (July 2005).

——. 2005f. Employee pension plans (Trusteed pension funds). *The Daily* (22 September).

——. 2005g. *Gross Domestic Product by industry.* Cat. #15-001-XWE (October).

——. 2005h. Community profiles. *2001 Census of Canada.* Ottawa: Statistics Canada (December).

——. 2006a. *Labour force statistics.* Ottawa: Statistics Canada (25 January).

——. 2006b. Manufacturing shipments by province and industry. CANSIM Tables 304-0014, 304-0015. Ottawa: Statistics Canada (18 January).

Stevenson, Garth. 1994. *Ex uno plures: federal provincial relations in Canada.* Montreal and Kingston: McGill-Queen's University Press.

Stewart, Gordon T. 1980. Political patronage under Macdonald and Laurier: 1878-1911. *American Review of Canadian Studies* 10.

——. 1986. *The origins of Canadian politics, a comparative approach.* Vancouver: University of British Columbia Press.

Stinson, Marian. 2004. Surge in imports spurs hopes for gains in productivity. *The Globe and Mail* (14 July): B1, 6.

Strayer, Barry L. 1988. *The Canadian Constitution and the Courts: the function and scope of judicial review,* 3rd ed. Toronto: Butterworths.

Streeck, Wolfgang, and Philippe Schmitter (Eds.). 1985. *Private interest government: beyond market and* state. London: Sage Publications.

Strick, John C. 1999. *The public sector in Canada: programs, finance and policy.* Toronto: Thompson Educational Publishing.

Stringham, Greg. 2004. Canadian natural gas and crude oil. Presentation to Woodrow Wilson Forum on Energy Infrastructure, Washington, DC. Calgary: Canadian Association of Petroleum Producers (27 September).

Taras, David. 2001. *Power and betrayal in the Canadian media.* Peterborough, ON: Broadview Press.

Tarchys, Daniel. 1983. The scissors crisis in public finance. *Policy Sciences* 15: 205-24.

Taylor, D. Wayne. 1991. *Business and government relations: partners in the 1990s.* Toronto, Gage Educational Publishing.

Taylor, D. Wayne, Allan A. Warrack, and Mark C. Baetz. 2000. *Business and government in Canada: partners for the future.* Toronto: Prentice-Hall.

Technical Committee on Business Taxation. 1997. *Report.* Ottawa: Department of Finance.

Templeton, Kenneth S. (Ed.). 1979. *The politicization of society.* Indianapolis, IN: Liberty Press.

Therborn, Goran. 1977. The rule of capital and the rise of democracy. *New Left Review* 103: 3-41.

Thurow, Lester C. 1981. *The zero-sum society.* New York/Markham, ON: Penguin.

——. 1999. *Building wealth: the new rules for individuals, companies and nations.* New York: Harper.

Toboso, Fernando. 1995. Explaining the process of change taking place in legal rules and social norms. *European Journal of Law and Economics* 2(1): 63-84.

Tomblin, Stephen G. 2004. Conceptualizing and exploring the struggle over regional integration. In *Regionalism in a global society: persistence and change in Atlantic Canada and New England,* ed. Stephen G. Tomblin and Charles S. Colgin. Peterborough, ON: Broadview Press. 79-105.

Tomblin, Stephen G., and Charles S. Colgin. (Eds.). 2004. *Regionalism in a global society.* Peterborough, ON: Broadview Press.

Torys LLP. 2004. Budget impact on income trusts. #2004-13T. Available at <http://www.torys.com/publications/pdf/CM04-13T.pdf>.

Travers, Jim. 2002. Rot begins near top and runs deep. *Toronto Star* (7 May).

Treasury Board of Canada. 1998. *Crown corporations and other corporate interests of Canada: 1998 Annual Report to Parliament.* Ottawa: Treasury Board.

——. 2004. *2004 Annual report to Parliament: Crown corporations and other corporate interests of Canada.* Ottawa: Treasury Board (December). Available at: <http://www.tbs-sct.gc.ca/report/CROWN/04/cc-se-04_e.asp>.

Treasury Board Secretariat. 1997. Contracting policy: appendix M—lobbyists and contracting. Ottawa: Treasury Board (8 September). Available at <http://www.tbs-sct.gc.ca/pubs_pol/dcgpubs/Contracting/contractingpol_m_e.asp>.

Trebilcock, Michael, et al. 2000. *The law and economics of competition policy.* Mimeo. Toronto: University of Toronto.

Treff, Karin, and David B. Perry. 2002, 2003, 2005. *Finances of the nation.* Toronto: Canadian Tax Foundation.

Tulloch, Gordon. 1989. *The economics of special privilege and rent seeking.* Boston, MA: Kluwer Academic Publishers.

United States, Bureau of Economic Analysis. 2005. Gross domestic product by industry data. Washington (15 December). Available at: <http://www.bea.gov/bea/pn/GDPby-Ind_VA_NAICS.xls>.

United States, Bureau of Labor Statistics. 2005. Union members summary. Release # USDL 05-112. Washington, DC: Department of Labor (27 January).

——. 2006. *Employment situation.* Washington, DC: Department of Labor (6 January).

Urquhart, M.C. 1988. *Canadian economic growth 1870-1930.* Discussion Paper # 734. Kingston: ON: Department of Economics, Queen's University.

VanHouten, Pieter. 2003. Globalization and demands for regional autonomy in Europe. In *Governance in a Global Economy: Political authority in transition*, ed. Miles Kahler and David A. Lake. Princeton, NJ: Princeton University Press. 110-35.

VanWaarden, Frans. 1992. Dimensions and types of policy networks. *European Journal of Political Research* 21.

Vipond, Robert. 1991. *Liberty and community: Canadian federalism and the failure of the Constitution*. Albany: SUNY Press.

Vollman, Ken. 2005. Implementing smart regulation: how are we doing? Speech to CAMPUT Conference, Quebec City. Calgary: National Energy Board (2 May).

Walkom, Thomas. 1994. *Rae days: the rise and fall of the NDP*. Toronto: Key Porter.

Wallace, Iain. 2002. *A geography of the Canadian economy*. Toronto: Oxford University Press.

Warner, Andrew M. 2000. Economic creativity. *Global Competitiveness Review, 2000*.

Watkins, Melville H. 1963. A staple theory of economic growth. *Canadian Journal of Economics and Political Science* 29: 141-58.

Watson, Elizabeth. 2003. Appointments to public sector boards: the BC initiative. Victoria: Board Resourcing and Development Office, Office of the Premier (25 August).

Watson, William. 1998. *Globalization and the meaning of Canadian life*. Toronto: University of Toronto Press.

Watts, Ronald L. 1999. *The spending power in federal systems: a comparative study*. Kingston: Institute for Intergovernmental Relations, Queen's University.

Weiler, Paul. 1974. *In the last resort: a critical study of the Supreme Court of Canada*. Toronto: Carswell-Methuen.

——. 2002. Two models of judicial decision-making. In *Law, politics and the judicial process in Canada*, 3rd ed., ed. F.L. Morton. Calgary: University of Calgary Press. 38-45.

Wesson, Tom. 1998. The structure of Canada's economy. In *Canada and the New World Economic Order*, ed. T. Wesson. North York, ON: Captus Press. 73-81.

Whitaker, Reg. 1977. *The government party: organizing and financing the Liberal Party of Canada 1930-58*. Toronto: University of Toronto Press.

——. 2001. Virtual political parties and the decline of democracy. *Policy Options* (June): 16-22.

——. 2005. Made in Canada? The new public safety paradigm. In *How Ottawa spends: 2005-2006*, ed. G. Bruce Doern. Montreal and Kingston: McGill-Queen's University Press. 77-95.

Whitson, Dave, and Roger Epp. 2001. *Writing off the rural west: globalization, governments and the transformation of rural life*. Edmonton: University of Alberta Press.

Whittington, Les. 1999. *The banks*. Toronto: Stoddart.

Williams, Glen. 1994. *Not for export*, 3rd ed. Toronto: McClelland and Stewart.

Wilson, James Q. (Ed.). 1980. *The politics of regulation*. New York: Basic Books.

Wilson, Jeremy. 1990. Wilderness politics in BC: The business-dominated state and the containment of environmentalism. In *Policy communities and public policy in Canada: a structural approach*, ed. William D. Coleman and Grace Skogstad. Toronto: Copp Clark Pitman. 141-69.

Wilson, Michael. 1984. *A new direction for Canada: an agenda for economic renewal*. Ottawa: Department of Finance (November).

Winsor, Hugh. 2001. BC proves key to "non-existent" Liberal race. *Globe and Mail* (3 December).

Wiseman, Nelson. 2001. The pattern of prairie politics. In *Party politics in Canada*, 8th ed., ed. Hugh G. Thorburn and Alan Whitehorn. Toronto, Prentice-Hall. 351-63.

Wiseman, Nelson, and David Whorley. 2002. Lessons on the centrality of politics from the Canadian Crown enterprise. In *The handbook of Canadian public administration*, ed. Christopher Dunn. Toronto: Oxford University Press. 382-96.

Wolfsfeld, Gadi. 2003. The political contest model. In *News, public relations and power*, ed. Simon Cottle. London: Sage Publications. 81-95.

Woll, Peter. 1977. *American bureaucracy*, 2nd ed. New York: W.W. Norton.

World Competitiveness Yearbook. 2005. Lausanne, Switzerland: IMD (April).

Yakabuski, Konrad. 1998. Is it a caisse of politics? *Globe and Mail* (19 December).

——. 2003. One nest-egg, scrambled. *Canadian Business* (May).

Young, Lisa, and Keith Archer. (Eds.). 2002. Regionalism and party politics in Canada. Toronto: Oxford University Press.

Yukon, Bureau of Statistics. 2001. *Annual statistical review: 2000*. Whitehorse: Executive Council.

Zussman, David. 2002. Alternative service delivery. In *The handbook of Canadian public administration*, ed. Christopher Dunn. Toronto: Oxford University Press. 53-76.